THE PAPERS OF

# WOODROW WILSON

VOLUME 50

THE COMPLETE

PRESS CONFERENCES,

1913–1919

SPONSORED BY THE WOODROW WILSON
FOUNDATION
AND PRINCETON UNIVERSITY

Wilson and the White House Correspondents

# THE PAPERS OF

# WOODROW WILSON

THE COMPLETE PRESS CONFERENCES,
1913–1919

EDITED BY
ROBERT C. HILDERBRAND

## Volume 50

PRINCETON, NEW JERSEY
PRINCETON UNIVERSITY PRESS
1985

Copyright © 1985 by Princeton University Press
All Rights Reserved
L.C. Card 66-10880
ISBN-0-691-04710-3

*Note to scholars:* Princeton University Press sub-
scribes to the Resolution on Permissions of the Association of American University Presses, defining what
we regard as "fair use" of copyrighted works. This
Resolution, intended to encourage scholarly use of
university press publications and to avoid unnecessary
applications for permission, is obtainable from the Press
or from the A.A.U.P. central office. Note, however, that
the scholarly apparatus, transcripts of shorthand, and
the texts of Wilson documents as they appear in this
volume are copyrighted, and the usual rules about the
use of copyrighted materials apply.

Publication of this book has been aided by a grant
from the National Historical Publications and Records
Commission.

Printed in the United States of America
by Princeton University Press
Princeton, New Jersey

# FOREWORD

WHEN we began to edit the presidential volumes of *The Papers of Woodrow Wilson*, we decided to include only those portions of Wilson's press conferences which related to subjects of major importance in domestic and foreign affairs. We also decided at that time to commission an edition of all of Wilson's press conferences.

We think that this decision and our choice of an editor were wise ones. Herein, for the first time, are all of the transcripts of Wilson's press conferences during about two and one half years of his presidency. In these pages, we see the broad and varied range of Wilson's day-to-day concerns, the trivial and ephemeral and what might be called the medium-sized concerns, along with those of more obvious historical significance. Moreover, we see Wilson in the bright light cast upon him by the constant pressure of questioning by a group of intelligent people. We see Wilson in intellectual combat. We see him jousting and sparring with reporters, scolding them, joking with them, "grazing the truth" in order not to disclose secrets of state, and, more often, engaging in frank and open dialogue. By reading these press conferences in sequence, we get a picture of Wilson which could not be obtained in any other way.

Dr. Hilderbrand's research for his book, *Power and the People: Executive Management of Public Opinion in Foreign Affairs, 1897-1921*, had already deeply involved him with the transcripts of the press conferences before he undertook to edit Volume 50. His work on this volume can only be described as prodigious and his achievement superb. Since we have wrestled for many years with Charles Lee Swem's shorthand, we well know how difficult it is to transcribe it. To be sure, Dr. Hilderbrand had available Swem's own transcripts of about half of the press conferences and Jack Romagna's transcripts of the rest. However, both sets of transcripts are far from perfect, and Dr. Hilderbrand had to learn the Gregg shorthand style which Swem himself used before he could edit Swem's and Romagna's drafts. This he did with consummate ingenuity and skill. We thank Dr. Hilderbrand for his hard work and congratulate him upon his achievement. His annotation well illuminates the transcripts and adds much by way of detail to our knowledge of Woodrow Wilson as President of the United States.

This volume has gone through the same review procedures to which we subject the other volumes in *The Papers of Woodrow Wilson*.

ARTHUR S. LINK

*Princeton, New Jersey*
*January 3, 1985*

# INTRODUCTION

ON MARCH 15, 1913, Woodrow Wilson began a new era in presidential relations with the press. At 12:45 p.m., Secretary Joseph Patrick Tumulty ushered more than 100 Washington correspondents into the President's office in the White House for the first of Wilson's regular press conferences. Although no transcript of this conference exists, the proceedings were remembered thus by the reporter, Edward George Lowry: "There was a pause, a cool silence, and presently some one ventured a tentative question. It was answered crisply, politely, and in the fewest possible words. A pleasant time was not had by all."[1] Wilson, too, found this first conference awkward—perhaps an inevitable consequence of innovation. At their next meeting on March 22, he told reporters that he wished to eliminate the "degree of formality" which had permeated the first session and attributed his stiffness then to "the fatigue of the morning."[2]

Although previous Presidents had maintained contact with reporters, Wilson was the first to conduct regular press conferences. Theodore Roosevelt met frequently with the "fair-haired" members of his "newspaper cabinet" and regaled those whom he could trust with his plans and purposes. And William Howard Taft conducted periodic question-and-answer sessions with reporters. But neither President made these meetings regular occurrences at predictable intervals, or even at predictable times. Taft always scheduled his conferences for late in the afternoon—often on short notice—and frequently postponed them until after six in the evening, which forced reporters to wait until he could find time for them. Unlike his predecessors, Wilson promised to meet the press on a regular basis. He made the conferences a normal part of White House routine, scheduled them during business hours, and treated them as official appointments.

From the first meeting, there was evidence that reporters appreciated regular press conferences. On March 16, the *New York Times'* Charles Willis Thompson described Wilson's performance in glowing terms: "As he went on talking, the big hit he was making with the crowd became evident. There was something so unaffected and honest about his way of talking, that it won everybody, despite the fact that many of the men there had come prejudiced against him."[3]

[1] Edward G. Lowry, *Washington Close-ups: Intimate Views of Some Public Figures* (Boston, 1921), p. 19.
[2] See below, March 22, 1913.
[3] Typescript of story for the *New York Times*, March 16, 1913, Charles Willis Thompson Papers, NjP.

On November 1, L. Ames Brown of *Harper's Weekly* repeated this judgment in a story, "President Wilson and Publicity," which made clear what the meetings meant to reporters. For the first time, correspondents had the opportunity to question the President on a predictable and regular basis and to provide themselves with the type of information which they had previously acquired only by hit or miss.[4]

In later years, however, it became a journalistic convention to criticize the press conferences, much as it did to criticize Wilson himself. A spate of reporters' memoirs, published mostly in the 1920s, recalled the meetings with disdain. David Sheldon Barry concluded that Wilson's gatherings "were not in fact conferences at all." "The newspaper men would," Barry added, "when they screwed up courage enough to do so, ask questions bearing upon various phases of the news of the day, and the President would answer or sidestep them as he chose."[5] A similar position was taken by Thompson, whose opinion of the press conferences had been laudatory in 1913. This criticism may reflect reporters' later disenchantment with the conferences, but it probably reflects their later disenchantment with Wilson himself, especially following the Paris Peace Conference. In light of Wilson's failures in public relations there, journalists found it difficult to admit that Wilson had ever been adept at handling the press, or even that his innovations had really been novel.

Nevertheless, the conferences were new, and it was up to the President to make them work. An essential precondition was the establishment of the rule that Wilson's remarks were never to be quoted directly because, as he put it, he wanted an opportunity to open some part of his mind to the reporters, so that they might know his point of view a little better than perhaps they had had an opportunity to know it so far.[6] Wilson wanted reporters to utilize the conferences as a source of background information, the ideas of which, but not the actual wording, could be used without attribution in composing their stories. Direct attribution could not be permitted because Wilson did not want the press to quote off-the-cuff remarks that might be incorrect as well as ungrammatical. And, of course, indirect quotations were easier to deny.

The importance of this rule became apparent in July 1913, when

    [4] L. Ames Brown, "President Wilson and Publicity," *Harper's Weekly*, LVIII (Nov. 1, 1913), 19-20.
    [5] David S. Barry, *Forty Years in Washington* (Boston, 1924), p. 309. See also Charles W. Thompson, *Presidents I've Known and Two Near Presidents* (Indianapolis, Ind., 1929), pp. 273-74; and Arthur W. Dunn, *From Harrison to Harding: A Personal Narrative, Covering a Third of a Century, 1888-1921* (New York, 1922), pp. 235-36.
    [6] See below, March 22, 1913.

its violation nearly resulted in the termination of the conferences. When several newspapers published Wilson's comments on Mexico, an angry President threatened to discontinue the meetings altogether, saying that reporters could not be trusted with his confidences. The New York *Sun's* Elting Alexander Fowler responded by apologizing to Tumulty for his newspaper's violation of the no-quotation rule.[7] A more general reply came from Richard Victor Oulahan of the *New York Times*, who, as chairman of the Standing Committee of Correspondents, requested that the conferences be continued and that the regulations governing press conferences be stated more explicitly. Hereafter, Oulahan suggested, reporters should participate "with the distinct understanding . . . that there shall be no further quotation of the President direct or indirect without his express consent or the consent of his official representative."[8] After some hesitation, Wilson adopted the proposed regulations and agreed to continue the press conferences.

That Wilson tolerated such indiscretions is a good measure of the value which he placed on the press conferences. Although the idea for regular meetings had been Tumulty's, not his own, he quickly grasped their potential for positive public relations. For Wilson, press conferences supplied a valuable vehicle to alert reporters to important developments, to publicize his own policies, and to defend his position on controversial issues. Most important, they gave the President a degree of consistent influence over the news which was far greater than that which any previous Chief Executive had ever enjoyed. The press conferences soon became an integral part of Wilson's strategy in dealing with the press.[9]

In many ways, the regular press conference was ideally suited to Wilson's particular talents. To be sure, reporters would later dwell on the President's stiffness and inflexibility, but this—like so many other criticisms of Wilson—seemed to issue from the unhappy experiences of 1919 and afterward. The Wilson that emerges from the press conferences is not the cold stereotype of journalists' memoirs; he is filled with wit and often vibrant in his use of language. Take, for example, this exchange from the press conference of December 22, 1914.

> *Question*: Mr. President, it is understood in the House that the ship-purchase bill is ready to be put on the track and slipped through when the proper moment comes. Do you know anything about that?

---

[7] E. A. Fowler to J. P. Tumulty, July 22, 1913, WP, DLC.
[8] R. V. Oulahan to Tumulty, July 22, 1913, *ibid.*
[9] See Robert C. Hilderbrand, *Power and the People: Executive Management of Public Opinion in Foreign Affairs, 1897-1921* (Chapel Hill, N. C., 1981), pp. 93-104.

> *The President*: Perhaps it would be more appropriate to say "put on the ways." No, I don't know, speaking seriously, just what are the details of the plan of handling the bill in the House, but I am glad to hear that it is ready to be launched.

Or this from November 20, 1913.

> *Question*: The afternoon paper said Mr. O'Shaughnessy was there, they played the "Star-Spangled Banner," and Mr. Huerta embraced Mr. O'Shaughnessy.
>
> *The President*: I wish he had embraced his opinions.

Wilson's press conferences also benefited from his talent for impromptu speaking. Because he never liked to speak from a prepared text, Wilson felt reasonably comfortable while thinking "on his feet" as he answered reporters' questions. The results can be seen both in the usual clarity of the President's statements and in the quality of his grammar—especially taken in contrast to that of the journalists.

To grasp the full extent of Wilson's achievement, it must be remembered that he spoke without the assistance of briefing books or notes. This does not mean that Wilson did not prepare; he later told George Creel that he studied for the conferences as diligently as a professor did for a lecture. But preparation in Wilson's time meant individual effort, not the staff productions of later presidential performances. Any help that Wilson received came only from Tumulty, who attended most of the press conferences and occasionally reminded the President of items which he forgot or neglected to mention.[10]

This lack of assistance makes Wilson's ability to answer the reporters' wide-ranging questions seem all the more remarkable. On a typical day, the President fielded questions dealing with two or three major foreign-policy issues—Japan, Mexico, the Panama Canal tolls, the war in Europe—and several key domestic issues; he also had to be ready to discuss matters of only local or regional importance. Sixty years later, it is difficult for the historian to keep up with all of these concerns; that Wilson could address each of them intelligently on a twice-weekly basis is clear testimony to his keen powers of memory and concentration. The questions themselves are indicative also of the "killing load," as Wilson once described it, which all modern Presidents must carry.[11]

The conferences added to this "killing load": Wilson increasingly saw them as an intrusion on his already busy schedule. In time, other problems also arose and threatened the continuation of regular meetings. One difficulty was the reporters' habit of asking the

[10] See, for example, below, Dec. 1 and 8, 1914.
[11] WW to the Rev. John Fox, April 12, 1916, printed in *PWW*, Vol. 36, p. 465.

wrong kind of questions, such as when they tried to make Wilson speculate about what he might do in hypothetical situations. On other occasions, the newspapermen failed to address themselves to the President's special knowledge; on April 21, 1913, for example, a reporter asked a question about Congress. "You have been here much longer than I have," Wilson responded, "and you can make a better guess than I can." This sort of thing reflected the most fundamental difficulty of the conferences: the different goals which Wilson and the reporters had for the meetings. For Wilson, there was little to be gained from answering the journalists' questions about issues of interest to *them*; his goal was always to guide their thinking on topics which *he* considered ready for public education. But reporters had their own criteria for determining topics of public interest, and their apparent unwillingness to cooperate made the press conferences something of a disappointment for Wilson.[12]

All of these difficulties made Wilson question the value of press conferences, but what finally brought about their demise was the outbreak of the European war. After August 1914, Wilson worried that a reportorial slip might complicate his already difficult relations with England and Germany. He had never fully trusted reporters; now the stakes—war and peace—were too high for him to take reporters very far into his confidence. In July 1915, he canceled the sessions abruptly, citing increased pressure of foreign affairs for his action, and refused to set a day for their renewal. This announcement angered some newspapermen, one of whom charged that the President had "abandoned his press conferences as soon as he could find a suitable pretext" for doing so.[13] This was unfair to Wilson, but the reporters' disappointment is understandable. They had come to count on the press meetings as a source of information and would now find it difficult to do without them.

Accordingly, reporters put pressure on Tumulty to have Wilson resume the regular conferences. The campaign of 1916 seemed an ideal time for a new round of press conferences, and Wilson agreed to meet the press again late in September. The *Washington Post* reported that this conference marked the reinstatement of weekly sessions,[14] but this did not prove to be the case because Wilson refused to repeat the performance. Following Wilson's reelection in November, Tumulty again requested the President to fix a time for renewed press conferences. Wilson replied positively and informed his secretary: "I *can* make them a fixture for Mondays and

[12] See Hilderbrand, *Power and the People*, pp. 103-104.
[13] Jesse Frederick Essary, *Covering Washington: Government Reflected to the Public in the Press, 1822-1926* (Boston, 1927), p. 99.
[14] *Washington Post*, Sept. 30, 1916.

Thursdays at 12:30, but I would very much prefer 2:30 in the afternoon as the hour."[15] Tumulty canvassed leading correspondents and found that they considered one meeting a week to be sufficient, but that they preferred the earlier time on account of deadline pressures. Tumulty suggested to Wilson that he set the conferences for 12:30 p.m. on Mondays, and, when the President affixed his characteristic "Okeh," the meetings went back on his calendar.

They did not remain there long, however, because an immediate heightening of crises in foreign affairs persuaded Wilson to discontinue them once again. This time their eclipse was permanent; the entry of the United States into the World War in April 1917 presented problems of security which seemed insurmountable to Wilson. As the President explained a year later, press meetings made him dependent "upon the discretion and good will of the least discreet and friendly members of the conference." This made it "very difficult" for Wilson to talk as frankly as he should have liked to talk with the general body of correspondents, but he said that it was not a matter on which he had finally closed his mind "by any means."[16] This last remark does not quite ring true; Wilson had decided firmly to rule out future press conferences, at least until the end of the war. But he was truthful about his reasons for their cancellation. Press meetings had been difficult enough in peacetime; they seemed impossible in time of war. Wilson could not run the risk of breached security, and he held no regular conferences after January 1917.

What follows are transcripts of all the press conferences of Woodrow Wilson of which we have any evidence. They were taken down in shorthand by Wilson's private stenographer, Charles Lee Swem, who later won the title of "world's fastest shorthand writer" in international competition. Swem transcribed some of his notes immediately, and the transcripts were mimeographed and distributed to reporters and marked "for information only, not for publication." This task was obviously very time-consuming for the busy Swem, and in many cases he made no transcripts or only partial transcripts; this became increasingly true as the novelty of the conferences wore off later in 1913. Swem later gave his shorthand notebooks and other materials to the Firestone Library of Princeton University, where they were discovered by Arthur S. Link. Professor Link found an experienced White House stenographer, Jack Romagna, press correspondent for Presidents F. D. Roosevelt, Truman, Eisenhower,

---

[15] Tumulty to WW, with Wilson's replies, Dec. 6, 1916, WP, DLC. Emphasis Wilson's.
[16] WW to S. R. Bertron, April 18, 1918, *ibid.*

and Kennedy. In what can only be described as a Herculean effort, Mr. Romagna transcribed the remaining conferences from Swem's notebooks and made this edition possible.

Mr. Romagna's task (and the editor's) was complicated by serious difficulties in the shorthand notes. The most troublesome of these was the presence of gaps marked only with an "X" in Swem's notes, which sometimes leave the reader with no hint of what was being discussed. A number of factors caused these gaps: sometimes Swem could not hear, sometimes he could not follow the thread of the conversation, and sometimes he could not keep up with the discussion. Wherever possible, the editor has attempted to fill in these gaps, in brackets, either by extrapolation or from newspaper accounts of the press conference itself. Where this did not prove possible, the gap has been marked "blank."[17]

Swem's shorthand style caused other difficulties. Like most stenographers, he took frequent shortcuts in his outlines and thus wrote words and phrases which can be read in variant ways. It was usually possible to resolve such difficulties with the help of the context and contemporary sources. Swem also wrote proper nouns in shorthand, a practice that he always warned his students against. The names can be sounded out phonetically and, again with the help of context and contemporary sources, most names can be easily identified. On only a few occasions was it necessary to leave names indefinite in the text and unidentified in the notes.

The following transcripts are based upon transcripts originally prepared by Swem and Romagna, the originals of which are in WP, DLC, or WC, NjP. Both the Swem and Romagna transcripts are imperfect. I have, therefore, carefully reviewed all transcripts against Swem's notes. I have worked on the assumption that when literate men, particularly Wilson, talked, they usually made sense, even if they did not speak elegantly and grammatically at all times. Thus I have always given the benefit of doubtful readings to the original interlocutors. I have also modernized the somewhat archaic English of Swem's transcripts. Moreover, I have followed common sense in transcribing Swem's very abbreviated outlines for such words as "they," "it," "what," "where," "when," and so on. The results may occasionally be paraphrases, but I hope that they are accurate paraphrases. If the reader has any doubt about the accuracy of these transcripts, he can always compare them to the notes in the Swem Collection in the Firestone Library. Finally, Swem rarely used punctuation marks in his notes. In any event, all punctuation is mine,

[17] See the Editorial Notes by Arthur S. Link, "The Correction of Corrupt Transcripts of Extemporaneous Speeches" and "Swem and His Shorthand," in *PWW*, Vols. 24 and 25, pp. viii-xiii and xi-xiii.

and I have tried to use punctuation as one would use it in punctuating spoken English.

The Table of Contents indicates which transcripts were based upon Swem's transcripts and which upon Romagna's. I would be remiss if I did not add that I benefited greatly from the transcripts or partial transcripts already printed in *The Papers of Woodrow Wilson*. The Table of Contents also indicates whether my transcripts were based in whole or in part upon the transcripts printed in *The Papers*.

Finally, I thank the Editor, Professor Link, for his help in the preparation of this book. He read the manuscript three times and parts of it more times than this. He led me to restudy the outlines of every dubious reading, edited my notes with care, and suggested the addition of many new ones. Finally, he also read the page proof and reviewed the index. I am also grateful to Dr. David W. Hirst, Senior Associate Editor of *The Papers*, for reading my manuscript, the page proof, and index with great care and for suggested changes, which greatly improved the transcripts, and to Susannah H. Jones for her careful reading of the galley and page proofs. I can only hope that this volume meets the high scholarly and literary standards of *The Papers of Woodrow Wilson*.

ROBERT C. HILDERBRAND

*Vermillion, South Dakota*
*October 2, 1984*

# CONTENTS

## The Press Conferences, 1913-1919

### 1913

# ILLUSTRATIONS

Frontispiece: *Wilson and the White House Correspondents*

# ABBREVIATIONS

| | |
|---|---|
| CLS | Charles Lee Swem |
| DLC | Library of Congress |
| DNA | National Archives |
| FR | *Papers Relating to the Foreign Relations of the United States* |
| FR, 1914-WWS | *Papers Relating to the Foreign Relations of the United States, 1914, Supplement, The World War* |
| FR, 1915-WWS | *Papers Relating to the Foreign Relations of the United States, 1915, Supplement, The World War* |
| FR, 1916-WWS | *Papers Relating to the Foreign Relations of the United States, 1916, Supplement, The World War* |
| FR, 1917-WWSI | *Papers Relating to the Foreign Relations of the United States, 1917, Supplement, The World War, Volume I* |
| JR | Jack Romagna |
| NjP | Princeton University Library |
| PWW | *The Papers of Woodrow Wilson* |
| RG | Record Group |
| SDR | State Department Records |
| WJB | William Jennings Bryan |
| WC, NjP | Woodrow Wilson Collection, Princeton University Library |
| WP, DLC | Papers of Woodrow Wilson, Library of Congress |
| WW | Woodrow Wilson |

THE PAPERS OF

# WOODROW WILSON

VOLUME 50
THE COMPLETE
PRESS CONFERENCES,
1913–1919

# THE PAPERS OF
# WOODROW WILSON

## 1913

March 22, 1913

I feel that this gathering has a degree of formality which I wish
it might not have. If there were any other room[1] in which we could
have met, it would have been more pleasing to me. I asked Mr.
Tumulty to ask you gentlemen to come together this afternoon,
because the other day[2] when I saw you, just after the fatigue of
the morning,[3] I did not feel that I had anything to say; and, if it is
agreeable to you, I would be obliged if you would regard what I say
this afternoon as just between ourselves, because I want an opportunity to open some part of my mind to you, so that you may
know my point of view a little better than perhaps you have had
an opportunity to know it so far.

I feel that a large part of the success of public affairs depends
on the newspapermen—not so much on the editorial writers, because we can live down what they say, as upon the news writers,
because the news is the atmosphere of public affairs. Unless you
get the right setting to affairs—disperse the right impression—
things go wrong. The United States is just now at a very critical
turning point in respect to public opinion; not in respect of parties,
for that is not the part that is most interesting. They may go to
pieces or they may hold together. So far as the United States is
concerned, it does not make much difference whether they do or
not, because a party has no vitality whatever unless it is an em-
bodiment of something real in the way of public opinion and public
purpose. I am not interested in a party that is not an embodied
program based upon a set of principles; and our present job is to
get the people who believe in principles to stand shoulder to shoulder to do things from one side of this continent to the other.

Now, that being the case, I can illustrate one of the bad things
that the newspapers may do in order to speak of the good things
they may do. If you play up, every morning, differences of opinion
and predict difficulties and say there are going to be so many objections to this and so many complaints about that, and things will
pull at such and such cross purposes, you are not so much doing
an injury to an individual or to any one of the groups of individuals

you are talking about as impeding the public business. Our present business is to get together, not to get divided, and to draw a line and say, "Now, you fellows who do not believe that genuine public government will work, please stand on that side (I choose the left because it is scriptural); and you fellows who do believe that it will work, get on that side. And all the fellows who get on this side, then get together and just put these fellows to rout in such fashion that they will not stop until Doomsday."

In order to do that, you have a lot of fellows who in the news try to interpret the times and try to get the momentum in things without which they will not go. I do not mean in the least to imply that any of you gentlemen are interested in making trouble. That is not the point. I would be a mighty proud man if I could get it into your imaginations that you can oblige people, almost, to get together by the atmosphere with which you surround them in the daily news. And the atmosphere has got to come, not from Washington, but from the country. You have got to write from the country in and not from Washington out. The only way I can succeed is by not having my mind live in Washington. My body has got to live there, but my mind has got to live in the United States, or else I will fail. Now, you fellows can help me and help everybody else by just swathing my mind and other people's minds in the atmosphere of the thought of the United States. The great advantage that you enjoy is that you represent papers all over the country, and therefore you can import the opinion and the impulse of the country into Washington, and import it after a fashion that nobody else can employ. A Congressman has to import opinion according to the repairing of his fences—or, at least, he thinks he has. I do not think so. You have not got any fences to repair or to keep in order. Your interest is simply to see that the thinking of the people comes pressing in all the time on Washington. It would help me immensely, and it would help every man in public life immensely, should you do that.

So the thought I have in dealing with you fellows is this, that you, more than any other persons, can lubricate—quicken—the processes by which you are going to do, what? Serve the people of the United States. If we do not serve them (the "we" now applies to politicians) then we will go out of business; and we ought to go out of business. We will go out of business with the applause of the world; because if we do not serve the people of the United States, there is going to be so radical a change of venue—and it will be a new kind of trial for public men. So that I do not feel that I am engaged in a partisan enterprise or a party enterprise, or in anything except interpreting what you men ought to make it your business to bring the country. I have got to understand the country, or I will not understand my job. Therefore, I have brought you here to say to you this very simple thing: "Please do not tell the country what Washington is thinking, for that does not make any difference. Tell Washington what the country is thinking." And then we will get things with a move on, we will get them so refreshed, so shot through with airs from every wholesome part of the country, that they cannot go stale, they cannot go rotten, and men will stand up and take notice and know that they have got to vote according to the purposes of the country and the needs of the country and the interpreted interests of the country, and in no other way.

I sent for you, therefore, to ask that you go into partnership with me, that you lend me your assistance as nobody else can, and, then, after you have brought this precious freight of opinion into Washington, let us try and make true gold here that will go out from Washington. Because nothing better will go out than comes in. It is the old law of compensation, the law of equivalence. In proportion that Washington is enriched, so will the fruition in Washington itself be rich. Now, all this is obvious enough to you gentlemen. I am not telling you anything that you did not know before, but I did want you to feel that I was depending upon you, and, from what I can learn of you, I think I have reason to depend with confidence on you to do this thing, not for me, but for the United States, for the people of the United States, and so bring about a day which will be a little better than the days that have gone before us. I think we can cooperate with enthusiasm along that line, and if you agree with me, I shall be very happy.[4]

[1] This conference was held in the East Room of the White House.
[2] March 15, 1913. The first meeting, conducted in the President's office, had seemed excessively formal to Wilson and others. No transcript exists, but for a discussion of the conference see the *New York Times*, March 16, 1913.
[3] 12:45 p.m.
[4] A question-and-answer session undoubtedly followed, although there is no record of it.

April 7, 1913

Did anything come out of the conference with members of the Senate this morning about which you might speak?[1]

No. We were just discussing the matter of handling the bill.[2] We were not discussing the schedules or the contents of the bill at all.

Mr. President, did you get any idea as to what the chances are for the bill in the Senate, or did that come up?

That came up informally, and I got the impression that the chances are very excellent.[3]

Would it be the same bill in the Senate, Mr. President?

Oh, has that been—that, I believe, has to be finally determined. That is one of the things we were discussing.

Doesn't that have to begin in the House?

Oh, yes.

The introduction of the bill has to be in the House?

Oh, yes, it could not be done in the Senate.[4]

The Senate is practically a unit on the tariff?

Well, I think that only eight of the ten members—ten Democratic members—of the committee were present when we discussed it, and those eight were in favor of it. That's the way I remember it.

Mr. President, we are all very much interested in your going up to the Capitol tomorrow.[5]

Yes.

We thought perhaps you could tell us something about it. We think we understand why—what the precedents are and all that. Perhaps you could throw some light on it. There might be some line I don't know about it.

The reasons are very, very simply put. I think that that is the only dignified way for the President to address the houses on the opening of a session, instead of sending the thing up by messenger and letting the clerk read it perfunctorily in the clerk's familiar tone of voice. I thought that the dignified and natural thing was to return to a precedent which, it is true, has been dormant a long time but which is a very respectable precedent.[6]

Mr. President, in this morning's papers there was an intimation that there might be expected answers from Congress to the address.

Oh, no, I think they were saying that because they were looking for any answer except the legislative answer, that is all. I expect to do it just as simply as possible.

Do you expect a request from Congress to come there? There was an intimation also that they might send you a request that you come to address them.

I simply asked Senator Kern[7] and Mr. Underwood if it would be agreeable for me to come, and they both said that it would be entirely agreeable, and I don't expect any request. They felt sure they must speak to their colleagues in the Senate [and House] and that it would be entirely agreeable, that's all.

Mr. President, are you willing that we should quote you directly? That explanation of yours is exceedingly interesting. We further understand that we are not to quote you directly, but in that particular I think everybody would be glad.

Certainly.

Would you follow that system, Mr. President, with regard to Annual Messages hereafter?

An arrangement I would love to work with. To tell you the truth, I thought that that was the natural way to begin.

Mr. President, this tariff goes into effect on the night on which it is signed?

That would depend on the terms of the bill, of course. If it says, "This act shall take effect immediately," it does.[8]

Is that considered time enough for business to readjust its affairs?

I hadn't discussed that, no. I don't know that that matter has been determined by the committee.

In leather and textiles, that is six months I think.

Yes, it is.

In the sugar industry, too. I believe this bill abolishes the treaty with Cuba.

Oh, no. No abolition of a treaty.

The treaty provides specifically that the rates on sugar shall not be lowered by the United States during the time the treaty is in force.[9]

Does it?

Mr. President, about that arrangement with Cuba being in a treaty form and in bill form. They wanted to make it a treaty that would affect the revenues, and the extra session was coming, so they passed it in bill form, which makes it a mere matter of legislation, I understand, and not of treaty.[10]

I must say, I hadn't looked it up.

It was acted on by both houses, I know.

Affecting the revenues, it would necessarily.

The Cuban treaty could not be terminated on free sugar within six months,[11] and even today, on sugar, the Cuban treaty is not terminated.

Oh, no.

What is the status, Mr. President, of the United States Army and aviation, with regards to the commission on the general subject?

Whether it is going to be continued or not, do you mean?

Yes, sir.

Dr. Clifton[12] came with the other gentlemen to visit me the other day and simply tried to make me acquainted, as far as time would permit, with the work that the commission had done and with what would be necessary if its work should be continued, but I didn't express any opinion about it one way or the other.

Mr. President, do you expect to have the members of your cabinet accompany you to the Capitol tomorrow?

Oh, no.

In reading the precedents, it appears that President Adams had taken the members of his cabinet with him.

But there were only three members of the cabinet then.

They also received a call from the Speaker of the House and also from the members of the House in response.

That would be a large order.

Mr. President, could you give us any possible idea what you were discussing?[13] I wasn't quite sure as to what you said, whether that speech was constituting a question as to how the bill is to be handled. It was a question of procedure; that is, procedure in the Senate.

Yes, but of course procedure in the Senate involves procedure in the House, the form in which the bill is cast.

And they also determine—

They also determine it.

Has free wool been discussed? Is the number of votes in any doubt?[14]

Not so far as I am informed.

The only two that are in doubt are the Louisiana votes?

I don't think it would be proper for me to discuss how many or which Senators take any particular—

Mr. President, are we right in inferring that you prefer one bill, speaking of the tariff bill?[15]

The arguments for one or two bills, I must say, are so evenly balanced, that that is one thing I have jumped at, since two or three times I have been on both sides of the question. I could defend either, if you wish to have a debate. The question naturally comes to mind just which side I am on now. Well, I might be on a different side tomorrow, so perhaps I had better not say.

Have the developments of the last two or three days had any bearing on that situation?

No material bearing, with the argument standing just where it was.

Will it be determined by the caucus?[16]

Yes.

Do you expect to say anything about that in your address?

Oh, no.

Mr. President, may we look for some appointments today?

Oh, no, not today.

Mr. President, there was a statement today about the Mexican embassy, to the effect that whatever action might be taken in the name of the Ambassador would not be taken now because of its implied recognition of the Huerta government.[17] Do you care to say anything about that?

I saw that statement and it was, so far as I know, entirely unauthorized, because no statement had been authorized on that subject.

You wouldn't care to discuss that, I suppose?

No, I think not.

Mr. President, do you anticipate going to New Jersey before the first of May?[18]

Yes, sir.

Is the date fixed?

No, the date has not been fixed.

Have you any idea as to how long you will stay?

It depends on the condition of the caucus.

Will you visit only one portion of the state?

That is part of the question involved. I don't know. It depends.

Mr. President, with reference to China, have you taken any note of, or do you regard at all serious the question of the Mongolian independence of the Chinese republic?[19] Is that—

That has not been involved in our discussion.

It has not changed your position in any way?

No, it has not been brought in.

Are we at liberty to ask whether it was overlooked?

Oh, no, it was not overlooked but simply—

There was an effort to make it appear that the State Department had forgotten that matter.

Forgotten the matter of Mongolian independence?

But that Russia was led to recognize the independence of Mongolia.[20]

I think that is incorrect.

I am not aware of the facts.

I think that is incorrect. At any rate, we have had no intimation of it.

Has Representative Palmer[21] discussed with you the plan of possibly holding an open caucus?

He mentioned it to me this morning. I have always been in favor of an open caucus.

Would you think tomorrow is possible?

No.

He didn't say whether it had been taken up seriously?

No, he didn't say.

And you favor it? You always favored it?

Yes.[22]

Mr. President, were the members from Wisconsin here when the Senate Finance Committee was here?

No, none of them was here, and I am not quite sure that Mr. Palmer wouldn't know they were here yesterday. Only members of the Ways and Means Committee have been here this morning.

Did you canvass the income-tax section on credits? Would that mean, with your approval, it would be written into the bill?

Yes sir, we did, from the first, but we didn't discuss it any further.

Mr. President, have the other governments signified their intention with regard to China's independence? Have the charges against Mr. Henry Lane Wilson been received?[23]

Only in the newspapers. So far as I am concerned, I haven't seen them. They may be in the State Department, for all I know, but they have not been brought to my attention.[24]

Mr. President, with regard to China, would you care to say whether any action is to be taken as soon as you have word of the election of the constitutional President?[25]

That is a matter of such delicacy that I think I had better not say anything about it.

Mr. President, I should ask you about our acting district attorney. I am being prodded from my office, as to whether you have another name in shape to tell us about?

No, nothing at all.

There are some suggestions to the effect that there are some scouts around the District to make reports to you.

Oh, no.

Do you take this supposition of the papers as meaning you are ready to act?

Well, I may or may not.

Well of course I know, but assuming there's nobody out [there] representing you, looking over the file, I thought it would be necessary for you to take on the papers and talk with these people.

You see, I don't depend on how the papers feel about me. I always make my own inquiries. I wanted to remove the impression that I had anybody as a scout, in any proper sense of that word. I am simply asking the opinion of various people.[26]

Nobody was commenting against it, other than to say that you had taken it up in this form.

I am not ready to take it up in any form.

[1] A meeting with Democratic members of the Senate Finance Committee about tariff legislation.

[2] The Underwood bill. This measure was to put into effect the first phase of Wilson's reform program—downward revision of the tariff. On December 31, 1912, the President-elect called Representative Oscar Wilder Underwood, Democrat of Alabama, chairman of the House Ways and Means Committee, to Trenton to discuss the writing of a tariff bill. After his inauguration, Wilson continued to work with Underwood on what came to be known as the Underwood bill, which Wilson signed into law on October 3, 1913. See Arthur S. Link, *Wilson: The New Freedom* (Princeton, N. J., 1956), pp. 177-97, and Frank William Taussig, *The Tariff History of the United States*, 8th edn. (New York, 1939), pp. 409-46.

[3] The newspapers reported the opposite—that the bill was in danger unless the wool and sugar schedules were separated from it. See Link, *The New Freedom*, pp. 180, 184, and the *New York Times*, April 8, 1913.

⁴ According to the Constitution, all financial legislation has to originate in the House of Representatives.

⁵ To address Congress on the subject of tariff reform.

⁶ John Adams was the last President to address Congress in person. Jefferson abandoned the practice as monarchical. See Link, *The New Freedom*, p. 152.

⁷ John Worth Kern of Indiana, Democratic majority leader in the Senate.

⁸ It did.

⁹ Under the terms of the Reciprocity Treaty with Cuba of 1903, the tariff rate for Cuban sugar could be no less than 80 per cent of the schedule in the Dingley Tariff (1897). See the *New York Times*, April 10, 1913, and *United States Tariff, Customs Administration, and Income Tax Law* (New York, 1913), p. 112.

¹⁰ The Reciprocity Treaty of 1903 had been passed by the House as well as the Senate because it was "revenue effecting." The questioner is suggesting here that perhaps that made it a matter of municipal law rather than treaty law. He was wrong; the treaty had to be amended.

¹¹ Six months' notice was required to terminate the treaty.

¹² Alfred T. Clifton, pioneer aviator.

¹³ That is, with regard to Cuban sugar.

¹⁴ This is a reference to a report that the Louisiana Senators might combine with Senators from western states to vote against a tariff bill which included free wool and free sugar. See Link, *The New Freedom*, p. 184.

¹⁵ The question here was whether there should be one tariff bill or two, with the sugar and wool schedules in a separate measure.

¹⁶ That is, the House Democratic caucus.

¹⁷ Wilson had inherited a difficult problem in Mexico. Taft had taken no steps to recognize the new government of Victoriano Huerta, which was responsible for the death of ex-President Francisco Iglesias Madero. See Link, *The New Freedom*, pp. 347-50.

¹⁸ To speak in Newark, Elizabeth, and Jersey City on the subject of jury reform. He made the trip on May 1 and 2. See Link, *The New Freedom*, pp. 38-48.

¹⁹ Outer Mongolia had declared itself independent of the new Chinese government. See the *Washington Post*, April 7, 8, 1913.

²⁰ Russia had pointed out in a note to the United States that it was reserving its rights and special privileges in Mongolia. There was certainly reason to fear that it might support Mongolian independence. See Tien-yi Li, *Woodrow Wilson's China Policy* (New York, 1952), p. 62.

²¹ Representative Alexander Mitchell Palmer, Democrat of Pennsylvania.

²² An open caucus was rejected by House Democrats on April 8 because it would "advise the 'enemy' of the line of battle." See the *New York Times*, April 9, 1913.

²³ Luis Manuel Rojas, Second Vice-President of the Mexican House of Deputies, had just charged that Ambassador Henry Lane Wilson was "responsible morally" for the death of President Madero and Vice-President Piño Suárez. See *ibid.*, April 7, 1913.

²⁴ *Ibid.*, April 8, 1913, reported that the charges were received by Secretary of State William Jennings Bryan on April 7.

²⁵ That is, on the recognition of the new Chinese government. See Li, *Wilson's China Policy*, pp. 57-89.

²⁶ Wilson was considering appointment of the commissioners of the District of Columbia and had asked the opinions of a number of governmental officials. See the *Washington Post*, April 8, 1913.


April 11, 1913

Mr. President, have you taken up this question of continuing the Commerce Court¹ with any definite idea?

I haven't. I am uninstructed really on the merits of the case.

Of course, you have been foregathering from citizens who have very distinct ideas on the subject—

Yes, I have had some intimations that there were such ideas, but I don't feel that I know enough about the merits of the thing to have a right to an opinion. I hope I haven't done anything else unprecedented lately, have I? (Laughter)

Have you any plans to break any precedents?

No, I haven't at any time had any plans. I was just saying to a friend today that I have a queer impression of what must have been done usually in the District of Columbia, because every time I do something perfectly natural, it turns out to be unprecedented.

Speaking of plans, Mr. President, have you decided yet when you are going to New Jersey?

No, I am waiting on the New Jersey people to make their arrangements and I will go up and help.[2]

What is this eight o'clock business, Mr. President?[3]

My only information about that was from the morning papers.

What does that mean?

At the cabinet meeting today not a word was said about any plan of the kind. I think it was a misunderstanding. At any rate, I have not heard a word about it.

Mr. President, what is the status of the Chinese situation?

Why simply this: for reasons which, speaking for myself, I don't understand, the Constituent Assembly met on Tuesday and then adjourned for ten days, I think.[4] Why they adjourned, I am not informed, but they adjourned without a full constitution—I mean without electing officers, as I understand it—and therefore, I suppose, to get acquainted and form their plans; because, of course, China isn't a homogeneous unit.

Or waiting for a few more assassinations!

Oh, there has been only one, hasn't there?[5]

That is all.

That is enough, but I didn't know but that you had heard later news.

No, sir.

Mr. President, has there been any decision reached as to what you are going to do about fourth-class postmasters?[6]

No, sir, that is still under discussion.

Mr. President, have you had any opportunity to give Alaska attention lately?

Not any particular attention. Of course, I gave it a good deal of attention before I was inaugurated so as to inform myself just what was possible. The first thing I have to do is to find a Governor, and the Governor has to be chosen from the residents of Alaska under the law; so I am trying to inform myself about the candidates.

Is that a new law?

I don't know.

The present Governor was not a resident of Alaska—Walter Clark. He was the White House reporter for the New York *Sun*.

The candidates are before me then! (Laughter) To tell you the truth, I didn't look the law up myself. I was taking it from Secretary Lane,[7] who stated it to me. So that it must be a new law.

The new legislature may just have expressed that wish.

They did express that wish, but it was certainly the Secretary of the Interior's impression that that was the law.[8]

The Democratic national platform declared for that.[9]

Yes, I know it did.[10]

Mr. President, did Colonel Ewing[11] cause you to change any views you may have had with regard to sugar. I understand the Colonel was here this morning.

No, he didn't try. He came in and the first thing he said was, "I haven't come to talk about sugar."

Mr. President, our understanding of the changes in the customhouse in Philadelphia is that it is the beginning of changes in customhouses, or the important ones throughout the country, with an idea of having men there who were perhaps more in sympathy with the objects of the new tariff law—the forthcoming tariff law. Could you tell us anything about that?[12]

No, that is too large a conclusion to draw. It really was only an action with regard to that particular office.

I so understand.

I mean it wasn't a part of the general policy.

Mr. President, I would like to ask something regarding this California alien land law. I have been looking into it a little; I find that the present treaty stipulates that the citizens of each country, while in the other country, shall have a right to own houses and factories and shops, and to lease land. It doesn't say anything about owning land. I also find that in Japan the old laws against foreign ownership of land were abrogated, and laws permitting foreigners to own lands were passed, but the necessary edict to put them in force has not been issued, so that citizens of the United States cannot now own land in Japan; and it seems to me that if that was the case that the Japanese objections against the United States are possibly not well grounded.[13]

You see, the trouble about all those treaties is a trouble peculiar to ourselves because of our system.[14] Nobody can for a moment challenge the constitutional right of California to pass such land laws as she pleases. Now, insofar as the federal government has gone beyond its powers—its domestic authority—in making a treaty, just so far is it liable to damages, but it is helpless in the premises. You see, that is the complication always in those treaties. The facts as you have stated them are the facts as I understand them.

Do the Japanese really make representations regarding this matter? Are they still denying the same rights?

I want to say that the Japanese Ambassador[15] has acted in a most proper and delightful way about it. He didn't so much make representations to Mr. Bryan and me as a government but as treating us as friends of Japan who would wish to see the best relations prevail, and asked us to look into this legislation out there and see if anything could be done to take the sting out of it, or to make it acceptable to Japanese sensibilities; and we have been trying to act in that spirit. That is really the whole situation.

Is the treaty construed as giving the right to own land?

No, it isn't construed as giving the right to own land. As a matter of fact, it guarantees that they shall be treated on the same basis with the most favored nations.[16] It is the famous most-favored-nation clause that is in so many of the treaties.

Mr. President, are they not supposed to take note of the fact that the Constitution of the United States would not permit such a treaty to be made—are they on notice?

Of course they know, because the Japanese Ambassador said that he understood our domestic constitutional arrangements, but we couldn't as a treaty-making power take it for granted that they had what one might call judicial notice of that.

That whole matter came up in the Hennessey case in New Orleans.[17]

Yes, it did, and the federal government simply had to reimburse—

Mr. President, have you expressed yourself on including the sundry civil bill that caused the trouble in the legislation?[18]

No, I haven't.

Any development in the tariff situation today, Mr. President?

None that I have heard of.

Does it seem necessary to make some change in that provision which gives a reduction of 5 per cent for goods brought in in American bottoms.

I haven't heard of any suggestion that that change is necessary.

As violating existing treaties with other countries?

No, I haven't heard that objection.

Republicans up there seem to be rejoicing over the inclusion of the anti-dumping clause of the bill,[19] which they say they could never get into their bills on account of Democratic opposition!

Well, since we are running the government, we know what is safe. (Laughter)

Mr. President, with the new tariff in the form in which it is proposed, with the reciprocity provision, will there be any disposition to do away with the most-favored-nation clause?[20]

I don't see why we should.

Is reciprocity recognized as a justifiable exception to the most-favored-nation treaty?[21]

Yes, I think so; because the most-favored-nation clause doesn't exclude us from making special arrangements with particular nations.

There has been some difference between American construction and European construction. Are you liable to exclude this agreement between some states—Portugal, Italy, etc.?

Of course, that is so far in the future I hadn't taken that up in my mind. "Sufficient unto the day is the evil thereof."

When do you expect to come to New England,[22] Mr. President?

As soon as I can get back from Panama.[23]

What about the recognition of Mexico?

Well, I don't know. We don't decide that—that is decided between brawls! (Laughter)

Is it dependent upon the constitution?

I oughtn't to jest upon such a serious subject. Of course, what we are waiting for—what all the governments are waiting for—is the regular process by which they are expecting soon to constitute a constitutional government.

[1] The Commerce Court was created by the Mann-Elkins Act of 1910 to review decisions of the Interstate Commerce Commission. By 1913, it had made itself unpopular with both reformers and railroad men and was under attack in Congress. It was abolished late in 1913 despite support from Attorney General James Clark McReynolds. See Gabriel Kolko, *Railroads and Regulation, 1877-1916* (Princeton, N. J., 1965), pp. 103, 193, 198-202, and U.S. House of Representatives, Committee on the Judiciary, *Jurisdiction of Commerce Court—Its Enlargement, Hearings*, 63d Cong., 1st sess., June 21, 1913 (Washington, 1913).

[2] See above, April 7, 1913.

[3] Newspapers had reported that governmental employees would be required to begin work at eight o'clock in the morning.

[4] The Chinese Constituent Assembly convened on April 8, but it was not yet organized for business. Organization was completed on May 1. See Li, *Wilson's China Policy*, pp. 74-76.

[5] Sung Chiao-jen, political opponent of the Chinese President, Yüan Shih-k'ai.

[6] On May 7, Wilson overruled Taft's order of October 5, 1912, which placed all fourth-class postmasters on the classified list. Taft's order would have denied positions to Democrats; Wilson's order, which threw the offices open to competition, required all candidates to take a civil-service merit exam. Wilson described this as a genuine application of the merit system. See the *New York Times*, May 8, 1913.

[7] Secretary of the Interior Franklin Knight Lane.

[8] Lane was wrong. The law, signed by President Taft on August 24, 1912, required only that members of the new territorial legislature be residents for two years prior to their election. See *U.S. Statutes at Large*, XXXVII, 512-18.

[9] The Baltimore platform said that officials appointed to administer the government of territories "should be qualified by previous bona-fide residence."

[10] On April 17, Wilson nominated Maj. John F. A. Strong, editor and publisher of the *Alaska Daily Empire* of Juneau, to be Governor of Alaska. See the *New York Times*, April 18, 1913.

[11] Robert Ewing, New Orleans newspaper publisher and Democratic national committee-man for Louisiana.

[12] A reference to the announcement of the appointment of William H. Berry as the new Collector of the Port of Philadelphia.

[13] The reporter here was essentially correct. Under the Japanese-American Commercial Treaty of 1911, American and Japanese citizens were not permitted to own land in the opposite country. In March 1910, the Japanese Diet had passed a law allowing land ownership by aliens on a reciprocal basis, but this law had not been promulgated by April 1913. This meant that the Japanese case for protesting against the California land bill was very weak; Wilson did not exploit its weakness here because he was less concerned with the legalities of the matter than with what Japanese jingoes might make of it.

Wilson explained his strategy in an exclusive interview with a *New York Times* reporter, probably Charles Willis Thompson, on January 27, 1914. At that time, the President said, the State Department possessed documents relating to the negotiation of the Japanese-American treaty which, if made public, "would at once establish the American contention in the California dispute." "The explanation offered as to why the State Department does not now produce that correspondence to shut off Japanese protests against the California law," the report continued, "is that, while such a course would be a final answer to the present Japanese Government, it would fan the fury of the jingo element in Japan and probably cause the overthrow of the Government after a bitter parliamentary onslaught. That would simply result in putting the jingoes at the head of the Japanese policy, and with them the United States would find it more difficult than ever to deal." This report is printed in *PWW*, Vol. 29, pp. 180-84. See also the *New York Times*, Jan. 28, 1914, and *PWW*, Vol. 27, p. 287, n. 5.

[14] That is, under the Constitution, the federal government did not have a right to make a treaty which interfered with the right of a state to make local laws. Thus California could not be prevented from passing an alien land law; the federal government could only pay claims for damages resulting from the state's violation of the treaty. Wilson's interpretation here is very dubious because treaties, like the Constitution, are the supreme law of the land. See U.S. Senate, *The Constitution of the United States of America: Analysis and Interpretation* (Washington, 1953), pp. 415-17, and Arthur K. Kuhn, "The Treaty-making Power and the Reserved Sovereignty of the States," in Douglas B. Maggs, ed., *Selected Essays on Constitutional Law*, 3 vols. (Chicago, 1938), III, 397-409.

[15] Viscount Sutemi Chinda.

[16] Wilson was wrong here.

[17] On October 15, 1890, the popular New Orleans police superintendent, David C. Hennessey, was murdered. The local Mafia was blamed because Hennessey was investigating their activities, but a jury failed to convict its members. Angry over this decision, a mob stormed the prison on March 14, 1891, and killed eleven of the accused. The Italian Minister in Washington, Baron Francesco Saverio Fava, protested and asked the federal government to prosecute the lynchers and to pay an indemnity to the families of the victims. Secretary of State James Gillespie Blaine replied that the federal government could not intervene in the case, but he did agree to compensate the victims' families. See Alexander De Conde, *Half Bitter, Half Sweet: An Excursion into Italian-American History* (New York, 1971), pp. 121-25, 412.

[18] A reference to the Hughes-Hamill amendment to the sundry civil appropriation bill. See below, April 14, 1913.

[19] That is, to prevent foreign countries from selling in the United States at below the cost of production. This was to be done by adding to the tariff collected on an item an amount equal to any export bounty paid by a foreign government.

[20] The Underwood tariff bill authorized the President to negotiate trade agreements to create freer trade and enhance commercial expansion on a reciprocal basis. Such agreements would have to be ratified by Congress.

[21] That is, could rates be lowered in a reciprocity treaty with one nation without necessitating a similar lowering of rates to all nations enjoying "most-favored-nation" status?

[22] As a summer residence, the Wilsons had rented Harlakenden, the home of the American novelist, Winston Churchill, in Cornish, New Hampshire.

[23] Wilson was planning an inspection tour of the Panama Canal.

## April 14, 1913

Mr. President, if we may be permitted to ask one or two questions that we trust are proper, the first being the tariff which has now been before the country for just one week.[1] Have you reason to believe that in general it meets with the approval of the public?

I think it does, that is to say, of the general public. Of course, there are people whose interests will be affected by it who disapprove of it, and I daresay they are somewhat numerous. But the impression I get is that it is regarded as a fair bill. I have heard a good many men say, for example, they didn't expect us to work out a good bill, that it was a very much better bill than was to be expected—and that from not very friendly sources. So that I am encouraged to believe that its reception has been very much better than might have been anticipated.

Do you see any reason, Mr. President, why there should be any business depression following the passage of this bill?

None whatever.

Do you think that all healthy business should be able to continue without interruption?

Oh, I am sure it should. I don't see where healthy business is cut to the bone anywhere in the bill.

Mr. President, have you had a good deal in the way of a direct response to yourself? I mean, from people—Tom, Dick and Harry, generally—writing to you?

No, not much, unless in letters I haven't seen. There has been very little.

Nothing that especially impresses you in the way of a response?

No. I have received several letters wanting to be heard, ultimately, on the subject.

Mr. President, do you feel that the income tax[2] is also as popular as the tariff bill?

I have seen very little comment on that, but I am sorry to say I don't have time to read many of the papers. I have to get my impressions more or less indirectly.

What is your main reason for deciding on free sugar, Mr. President?

My main reason is that it is fair to the consumer.

Do you think he will get it?

Yes, I do.

That he will get the benefit of it?

Oh, I am sure he will. You see, as I have said all along, that is one of the articles from which I am confident he will get the benefit at once. That will not be true as a rule. I was careful to say what I, of course, believed in the campaign, that I don't expect the tariff to effect an immediate reduction of the cost of living. But what I do expect, and confidently expect, is this—that it will bring about a competitive situation which will make it impossible by arrangements of price to keep up the present artificial levels of cost. So that, by a process more or less rapid, it will break down those combinations which now keep prices at so high a level and will redound to the general benefit before long, and that to a very great extent. But, you see, what we are fighting just now is an artificial situation in which the prices are kept up by arrangements with which you are all more or less familiar. Now, those arrangements will become practically impossible when a truly competitive situation is created, and then the people will begin to get the benefit. But I think they will get it very promptly in sugar, because the competitive elements are there ready to contest with one another.

Mr. President, when you say there is criticism from interests that are affected, do you mean interests that are legitimately affected?

Yes.

Are there any legitimate interests involved in that?

Oh, yes, many of these are interests which I should call perfectly legitimate interests, but they feel that the cut in their cases is more than they can at present stand. That is all. I don't mean that they are illegitimate interests that are affected.

And you, yourself, don't look for any ruinous cut?

Oh, no, I don't see any cut that is ruinous at all. Because, you see, these gentlemen on the Ways and Means Committee have been studying this tariff now for over two years, and they have heard every person in interest, every party in interest, again and again; and their votes are the results of these hearings and their judgments based upon them.

Nine out of ten of the Ohio Democrats feel that free wool will be ruinous to the woolen industry.

Well, now, that is one of the subjects upon which I have been trying to inform myself, and I have read as much as I could lay my hands on, and I don't feel that that fear is justified by the facts. For one thing, just the other day I learned that the price of wool was the same on both sides of the water; and one Senator, who has been very much opposed to free wool—a Republican Senator— said, "We hope that it would not be put on the free list just now, because our predictions wouldn't be verified." Because they certainly would not, with the price of wool the same on both sides of the water.

That has always been fixed in London.

I know, but these competitive conditions would of course be affected by the whole thing.

Mr. President, it has been stated that you favor the reenactment of a sundry civil bill, with the labor exemption clause—it is printed in some of the papers.[3]

That is a matter upon which I have not expressed any opinion. Of course the bill itself will be put through.

You have expressed no opinion with reference to the exemption [clause of the] bill?

I talked it over with Senator Martin and Mr. Fitzgerald[4] the other day, and they asked my opinion about that, and I told them what my opinion of the clause was, but I didn't tell them for publication.

[It] more or less has been published—it is a very important matter.

Yes, of course it is. Where I stand will be found out eventually.

Mr. President, this bill[5] authorizes you to start arrangements for reciprocity with various countries. Will you take steps to that end as soon as the bill is passed?

I should certainly hope to.

That would not mean that the United States would have to give still lower rates to obtain anything from any other country?

Yes, very likely, or make arrangements for countervailing duties, and so forth.

Mr. President, has it been decided whether the Commerce Court appropriation will be restored, or whether the jurisdiction of the court will be provided for?[6]

So far as I am informed on that subject, no; but I haven't discussed it with anybody, except that I got a letter from one member of Congress, asking my opinion on it, and I told him that my mind was "to let."[7]

Mr. President, in connection with the tariff, does your confidence extend to the sugar factories, both beet and cane sugar—do you think they can all operate under free sugar?

Yes, certainly I do. They may shut down for effect for a little while, but they will open for business later on.

Mr. President, we are all very much interested in the situation created in California by the interesting fact that certain laws wholly within their own constitutional rights can create an international situation. I hoped that you might be willing to say something about your own position toward that. It has been rather vaguely hinted at. Could you give us anything to clarify our own minds?

I have felt this way about it: as President I had no right to intervene in the business against the undoubted constitutional powers of the State of California; but that, as an individual, and also as President, in view of my relations to foreign countries in that office, I was at liberty to seek counsel out there and to ask what was going on and to give intimations of what I thought would be just in the case, and I have been trying to do that in as tactful and proper a way as I could discover. I am not without hope that their legislation may be affected by the advices I make.

The impression that I had was that the best you could do was to get them to do what they did in a gentle rather than a rough way,[8] that you wouldn't hope to affect the real essence of the thing very much.

Well, I am afraid it won't be possible to affect it materially.

The bill now provides that no alien shall own land for more than one year without taking out his first citizenship papers.

Making his first declaration.

And that, as I understand it now, gives offense to other nations that say that they have treaty rights with the United States, under which Americans shall hold land without citizenship in their country, and that this would compel foreigners to take out their citizenship papers here if they wanted to own lands.[9]

In one state only. Of course they all realize that it affects only a particularly small part of our territory; and, as I think I was saying to you the other day, the awkwardness about all such treaty relations is that the federal government cannot promise more than it can deliver. If it does, then I don't see any remedy for it except payment of damages, as in the Louisiana case many years ago.[10]

Do you get the impression, Mr. President, that Japan pretty well understands the peculiarities of the situation?

Oh, I am sure she does.

So that that government itself couldn't take any offense on the basis of a misunderstanding?

I think that the only fear is that there will be a very strong national feeling in Japan against this action; but I haven't heard any intimation that the government itself feels that this government is at fault.

Will we make an endeavor in treating with that government not to include something we can't enforce?

I haven't really got to that. My desire would be not to promise anything we could not deliver.

Mr. President, does Japan complain of the discrimination against Japan and China, particularly because their citizens could not become naturalized, and therefore are excluded from this?

When I saw the Japanese Ambassador some weeks ago, the legislation was in another form. It was then directed explicitly against those who could not become citizens. And since then I haven't seen him, and just how he feels about the new form of it I cannot say.

Has there been any progress on that Russian treaty?[11]

No, not since this administration began. You see we haven't any Ambassador there yet. We shall have to wait until we have appointed a representative.

Mr. President, there seems to be some interest in the question as to how far the recommendations of Senators and Representatives will control in the appointment of men to office—with respect to postmasters particularly.

Yes, I understand it is particularly with those! (Laughter) I have nothing to say on that subject.

Do you contemplate a visit to the Capitol this week?

I don't know of anything that will take me there.

[1] The provisions of the Underwood bill were published in the *New York Times* and elsewhere on April 8.

[2] The Underwood bill included a provision for imposing a federal income tax. See Link, *The New Freedom*, pp. 182, 192-93; Davis Rich Dewey, *Financial History of the United States*, 12th edn. (New York, London, Toronto, 1939), pp. 488-491; and Sidney Ratner, *Taxation and Democracy in America* (New York, 1967), pp. 321-38.

[3] The Hughes-Hamill amendment to the sundry civil appropriation bill forbade Justice Department funds to be used to prosecute labor unions and farm organizations under the Sherman Antitrust Act. Wilson supported the amendment at this time but was not happy to see his support reported in the newspapers on April 13. See the *New York Times*, April 13, 1913, and Link, *The New Freedom*, pp. 265-68.

[4] Senator Thomas Staples Martin, Democrat of Virginia, and Representative John Joseph Fitzgerald, Democrat of New York.

[5] That is, the Underwood bill.

[6] See above, April 11, 1913.

[7] Wilson to William Charles Adamson, Democrat of Georgia, April 8, 1913, WP, DLC.

[8] On April 7, Wilson had suggested a gentler manner of handling the problem to Representative William Kent, a California Progressive. This was to exclude from land ownership those persons who had not made application for American citizenship. In the case of the Japanese, the exclusion would be absolute, because their application for citizenship would not be accepted. This was, as Arthur S. Link has put it, a "transparent ruse," but it would have satisfied the Japanese government. See Link, *The New Freedom*, pp. 289-91; Roger Daniels, *The Politics of Prejudice* (Berkeley, Calif., 1962), pp. 58-63; and Kent to WJB, April 7, 1913, printed in *PWW*, Vol. 27, pp. 265-66.

[9] This was correct, of course, but Wilson was more concerned about the Japanese situation than about potential complaints from other nations.

[10] The Hennessey case. See above, April 11, 1913.

[11] A reference to a new Russian-American commercial treaty to replace the Treaty of 1832, which had been abrogated by the Taft administration because of Russian discrimination against American Jews. See William Appleman Williams, *American-Russian Relations, 1781-1947* (New York, 1952), pp. 75-79.

April 18, 1913

Mr. President, have you taken a stand on the question whether there should be further hearings by the Senate concerning this tariff bill?

Oh, no; that is none of my business.

I thought some of the Senators had asked—

I attend to my own business. (Laughter)

Mr. President, is Mr. Janes to be recalled from Ecuador?[1]

No, sir. He has been. But I want it to be distinctly understood that that is no reflection on Mr. Janes in any way. We have nothing against Mr. Janes; we just thought the existing arrangement was not satisfactory.

Would you care to go into any more detail, Mr. President, about the reasons for which he has been recalled?

No, I do not think I had better go into that. It involves sensitive feelings on the part of some people. I do not think I had better go into that.

Mr. President, it has been stated that you understood he has financial interest in the railroad.

Oh, no, that is not true. I haven't even heard that intimated.[2]

Mr. President, how far does that principle[3] apply in a case of this sort?

It is hard really to say. Two cases are not alike. That is the trouble about generalization, but our general principle is this: we want to be sure, whenever we try to assist in straightening out any piece of business in another country at the request of the government of that country, that the hearings and the whole process should be as detached from the parties in interest as possible. That is the general principle; we want to be absolutely disinterested mediators when we mediate at all.

I did not quite understand, sir, how we weren't detached in this case, since Mr. Janes represented the United States. He was appointed by the United States, although he did represent the railroad as an arbitrator.[4]

Well, that was the trouble. It was difficult to determine which he represented.

Yes, sir.

Of course, we did not want any doubt in anybody's mind as to which he represented.

Mr. President, isn't the railroad paying him? Isn't he in their service?

No, not properly speaking; they were paying the expenses of the American arbitrator.

Mr. President, are there any further developments in the California situation?

I got a memorandum this morning, but I haven't had time to look at it, sir. I do not know the details. It apparently was about the contents of the bill that was pending; and apparently there are two bills that are meeting half way, one coming up from the Assembly and another going down from the Senate.

Mr. President, have you looked into that matter of the analogy between the pending bills and statutes of states and the United States as applied to the District of Columbia?

Well, it would have involved, in order to do it accurately, a great deal of work that there hasn't been time yet to do. But I had a digest before me yesterday of the laws of the several states[5]—not up to date quite, about four years old—that showed similar laws in several of the states; for example, one in New York, and one in Texas. And there is one in the District of Columbia. Of course, that latter would hardly be analogous, because the extent of the District is so small that there might be special reasons for not wishing the particular district of the national government to be owned by anybody but American citizens.

Doesn't that apply to all the territories over which we have jurisdiction—that is federal jurisdiction?

The foreign territories?

I am not sure about it at all.

I do not know.[6]

Well, Mr. President, are you thinking of sending any member of the cabinet or any other representative to California in order to—

No, sir, though we are in constant touch with them as to what they are doing.

Have there been any communications from any European nation except Italy concerning that land law?

I saw in the morning's paper that there had been a communication from Italy, but it is the first I have heard of it. Mr. Bryan has not spoken to me about it.[7]

He spoke to us about it!

It hadn't come to me in any form, except by the morning's newspapers. I do not know what the joke is. Do you mean that he spoke with some emphasis about it?

No, but it is the first time he has given us anything.[8] Mr. President, in these state laws that you looked at, do they prevent aliens from leasing lands.

This, as I said, was a mere synopsis, and I cannot give you the details of it at all.[9]

Mr. President, what is the situation in Japan? It is stated that the Imperial edict has never been issued whereby Americans and other aliens were allowed to own lands.

That is true.

Mr. President, there is some interest about the federal judges. Do you intend to appoint them very soon?

We are appointing them one by one, slowly.

I had in mind especially the situation in New England, where there is a vacancy caused by the election of Judge Colt.[10]

The Attorney General and I have conferred once or twice, briefly, about that, but we have not come to any conclusion.

Mr. President, is there any feeling because the British government has recognized the provisional government of Mexico?[11]

Oh, no.

It is being stated in the papers that there was.

Oh, well, that is quite untrue. There is no feeling at all.

You had practically recognized this existing government, hadn't you, by the transaction of diplomatic business with it?

Oh, no, no more than one would recognize a *de facto* government. But, of course, we haven't broken off diplomatic relations with Mexico and are dealing with the *de facto* government just as any other government would deal with it.[12]

That is practically recognition, isn't it?

I do not understand that it is by international precedent.[13]

I thought, when you carry on diplomatic relations, it was a recognition of the *de facto* government.

Well, we haven't carried on diplomatic relations except to this extent, that we have corresponded with Mr. Henry Lane Wilson about conditions there, and he has given us information, and we have made suggestions to him.

He is transacting business with the government, is he not—with the Mexican government?

Not of any sort that I have been directly connected with.

I see.

I cannot say what he has been doing; all that I know is that we haven't conveyed any messages yet to the existing government.[14]

Mr. President, have you taken up the controversy over the Panama Canal tolls?[15]

No.

Has there been any decision with regard to the Commerce Court,[16] Mr. President?

By whom?

By the gentlemen upon whom the responsibility would fall of continuing or discontinuing that court.

You mean Congress. I cannot continue it or discontinue it. I do not know; you will have to ask that at the other end of the avenue.

Mr. President, I met a Senator this morning, a brand new Senator with a fine set of whiskers,[17] and he seemed to think he knew whom you were going to appoint as Comptroller of the Currency. Can you say anything about that at all?

I should be very much interested to know, because I do not know myself.

Mr. President, have you fixed the date of your trip to New Jersey, or the length of the trip yet?

No, I daresay Tumulty has; I haven't.

Mr. President, what is your attitude toward Senator Ashurst's[18] plan for a direct primary for federal judgeships in Arizona?

Why, you fellows must think I am an "attitudinarian." I haven't any attitude toward it at all.

Mr. President, it is reported today in some of the papers that this administration finds a number of men in the diplomatic service whose presence is not desirable because of some business connections they are supposed to have.[19]

I daresay that is a generalization from one or two cases. We haven't been finding anything startling.

Mr. President, has there been anything in the tariff legislation that you could comment on?

Oh, it is going along all right, so far as I am informed. I see nothing to complain of.

Any District[20] appointments?

I am kept so busy with things, even just my own business, that I haven't had time.

---

[1] Henry L. Janes, American arbitrator in a controversy between the government of Ecuador and the Guayaquil & Quito Railroad Company, which had been constructed with American capital. The government of Ecuador objected to Janes' conduct, and he resigned on April 18. Wilson appointed Judge A. L. Miller to take his place. See Ray Stannard Baker, *Woodrow Wilson: Life and Letters*, 8 vols. (Garden City, N. Y., 1927-39), IV, 431.

[2] It was being "intimated" in the press. See the *New York Times*, April 18, 1913.

[3] That is, the principle that American officials in foreign countries should not be financially interested in those countries. This is a reference to Wilson's repudiation of Dollar Diplomacy as practiced by the Taft administration. See Baker, *Life and Letters*, IV, 61-69, and the *New York Times*, April 18, 1913.

[4] President Taft had appointed Janes under an agreement which stipulated that the railroad's arbitrator should be an American.

[5] Wilson probably referred to John Bassett Moore, *A Digest of International Law*, 8 vols. (Washington, D. C., 1906), IV, 32-50.

[6] The Alien Ownership Act of 1887 prohibited land ownership by foreigners in the District of Columbia and in the territories. See the *New York Times*, April 18, 1913, and Moore, *Digest of International Law*, IV, 37.

[7] The Italian government protested against the bill on April 18. See the *New York Times*, April 19, 1913.

[8] In the early days of the Wilson administration, Bryan was having a difficult time defining his relationship with the press. The result was that he usually followed excessive secrecy about the business of the State Department. See Hilderbrand, *Power and the People*, pp. 109-11.

9 The laws did not specifically discuss leasing. See Moore, *Digest of International Law*, IV, 33-34.

10 LeBaron Bradford Colt of Rhode Island, presiding judge of the Court of Appeals for the first circuit, had recently been elected to the United States Senate.

11 The British, on March 31, 1913, had announced their intention to recognize Huerta as "interim President." See Peter Calvert, *The Mexican Revolution: The Diplomacy of Anglo-American Conflict* (Cambridge, Eng., 1968), p. 165.

12 The United States had not recognized the Huerta government, and Wilson had put off recalling Ambassador Wilson, in whom he had lost confidence, because he could not replace him without recognizing the new government. See Link, *The New Freedom*, pp. 348-53.

13 This question of "practical recognition" was a new one raised by Wilson's decision to make legitimacy a prerequisite for recognition. The United States had normally recognized *de facto* governments; Wilson had changed that practice by dealing with the Huerta government on a *de facto* basis while withholding formal recognition. See Cline, *United States and Mexico*, pp. 141-42.

14 Wilson was here attempting to understate the extent of American relations with the Huerta government. Notice, for example, his reference to the Ambassador as *Mr.* Henry Lane Wilson.

15 In 1912, Congress had exempted American ships in the coastwise trade from paying tolls for use of the Panama Canal. This elicited an angry response from Great Britain, which regarded the exemption as a violation of the Hay-Pauncefote Treaty of 1901, in which the United States had promised that the canal would be open on "terms of entire equality" to vessels of "all nations." See Link, *The New Freedom*, pp. 304-305, and the Secretary of State for Foreign Affairs of Great Britain to the British Ambassador, Nov. 14, 1912, *FR, 1912*, pp. 481-89.

16 See above, April 11, 1913.

17 Senator James Hamilton Lewis, Democrat of Illinois.

18 Senator Henry Fountain Ashurst, Democrat of Arizona, later chairman of the Senate Judiciary Committee.

19 Another reference to the application of the rule which resulted in Janes' resignation. See the *New York Times*, April 18, 1913.

20 That is, the District of Columbia.

April 21, 1913

Mr. President, did you notice that Senator Chamberlain said that he was going to introduce into the Senate a resolution to abrogate the Hay-Pauncefote Treaty?[1]

No, I noticed that a newspaper published a dispatch from Washington saying that he did. That is all I know.

That hadn't been called to your attention before?

No, sir. It is so roundabout that I think it is not worth discussing. No, it had not been called to my attention at all.

Mr. President, I have seen some comment in connection with the appointment of the Director of the Census, upon the possibility of treating various so-called scientific bureaus as material for political appointments. I wondered whether you would say anything—draw any sort of line for us as to the extent to which you think what is proper to do, or intend to do?

Oh, I think it is very proper and necessary to treat scientific bureaus on perfectly nonpolitical lines. The Census Bureau seems to me to stand on a footing of its own, because so much judgment is involved in it with regard to the various business developments and connections of the country; so that it is perfectly proper in my mind that a man should preside over it who has something besides the scientific statistical training that is so necessary in the general conduct of the bureau.[2]

Mr. Willis Moore, I think, took the stand that he was not bound by the custom of handing in his resignation, because that was a scientific bureau—he seemed to think so.[3] And it did raise a very interesting question as to just where the line is drawn.

Well, the line there has nothing to do with that. (Laughter) We have seen the line as far as that is concerned! (Laughter)

Mr. President, is there anything you can discuss with us with regard to the Japanese situation today—in regard to California?

I haven't any information about it. I judged from what appeared in yesterday's newspapers that they are getting rather thoughtful about it out there—as to the possible improprieties of it—but I haven't heard anything more than the rest of you know about it.

The morning papers said that your memorandum to the Governor[4] was very well received in Japan—that it had a very soothing effect.

I saw that, too. I hope it was.

Mr. President, have you received any advices as to whether the Senate bill[5] would be unobjectionable to Japan?

No, I haven't discussed any particular bill with them; it has just been the problem I have discussed with the Japanese Ambassador here.

But you thought that the Senate bill would be less objectionable than the House bill?[6]

Well, my whole thought is, there ought not to be discriminations in the bill.[7]

Mr. President, are you at liberty to speak of the collectorship at Philadelphia— Mr. Berry's appointment?[8]

No, I really have nothing to say about that, because there, again, I have got it only through what is being said, and haven't handled it officially at all.

The same applies to the collectorship at New York?[9]

Yes.

The appointment of the New York Collector is not going to the Senate today, I judge?

We really are not ready with any appointments today.

Not Philadelphia?

No.

How about the working hours of the Washington employees,[10] Mr. President— any change of hours or anything of that sort?

No. All that, as far as I am concerned, has been in the newspapers only. It hasn't been brought to me directly.

Has any cabinet member spoken to you about it? Mr. Burleson[11] seemed to have some plan.

No, I think you are mistaken about anything Mr. Burleson told me. He had no plan about that. He said that you gentlemen met him outside one day, and he told you what he thought, but that he didn't have any plan.

I did not mean to call it a plan, because he had not mapped it out, but there was the nucleus of a plan then.
Mr. President, is there anything you can say on the progress of tariff legislation?

Why, it is making very satisfactory progress, if that is what you mean.

I thought possibly there was some development in it.

No, none whatever.

What time do you think the session[12] will adjourn, Mr. President? Have you received any intimations?

You have been here much longer than I have, and you can make a better guess than I can.

Everybody is venturing a guess!
Mr. President, are you hearing any reports concerning the business and commercial status of the country in view of the present pending tariff legislation?

No, I can't say that I have heard anything that could be called reports—I mean, definite—from responsible sources, but I have got the impression from letters that I have got from editors, for example, ordinarily on the other side of the fence, that this is regarded as a most reasonable bill, a well-thought-out bill, and a bill from which nothing is feared that will be embarrassing to the country.

During its pendency there apparently is in certain financial centers somewhat of a contraction of credits and deposits, also reports of the reduction of rates,[13] and I am wondering whether you have any observations to make on that.

Well, from the observations I have seen in the financial papers, they do not attribute those circumstances to the tariff at all.[14]

To what do they?

To general market conditions and trade conditions.

Mr. President, have you been hearing from outside—I mean from business interests—regarding a tariff commission, whether they would care to have that—[15]

No, I haven't heard anything along that line.

Some of the Congressmen have; I didn't know whether you had.

You see, as a matter of fact, the duties of the Tariff Commission were handed over by legislation to the Department of Commerce, but, of course, they are sleeping, because they have made no appropriation.[16]

Mr. President, you regard the reciprocity provision[17] of the tariff bill as workable?

Why, yes, I do not see why not.

Well, simply on this theory, where a tariff is made high to be traded down, reciprocity is safe; where it is calculated with respect to the American consumer, how are you going to trade it down?

Well, that raises the question, which do you want?—the advantages of the American consumer, or do you want the tactical advantages in negotiating treaties of reciprocity? Of course, we are legislating first of all for our own people, for their relief and advantage, and it is a very secondary consideration whether we have the cards to play in a reciprocity negotiation. I say that is a secondary question.

It is except with regard, perhaps, to sugar.[18]

I don't understand.

I mean that sugar is the key to reciprocity with the tropical countries.

How do you make that out? We don't get any sugar except from Cuba and Porto Rico and Hawaii.

Well, all these countries are—I know that conditions, of course, have changed since Porto Rico and Hawaii came in; it is emphatically true—

I mean you can't find in statistics of sugar imports any other countries with which we have important dealings. In that matter, practically all of the so-called raw sugar comes in, except from our own possessions, from Cuba, and we have a reciprocal relationship with her under a treaty now. So that I don't see that that is a card of any consequence.

Mr. President, have there been any developments in China which would seem to make it necessary to postpone the day of recognition?

Oh, no; they are, of course, delaying their final work—their Constituent Assembly—for various reasons which I don't fully understand. There is no delay on our part at all.[19]

Nothing has happened that would affect the policy of this government?

Nothing at all.

Mr. President, have you seen any reason to encourage or change your present attitude with reference to the introduction of currency legislation?[20]

No.

Would you be willing to say whether you really expect that to be negotiated at this session?[21]

Oh, that still depends on circumstances.

It stands about where it was before?

Just exactly.

I have talked with some Congressmen today on that subject, and they say you can introduce it, but if you are engaged any length of time on the tariff, you can never get it through, because they do not want to stay too long, and you would simply be putting up your hand to let the other fellows know how to play at the other end of the table.

I never play with my hands under the table.

Well, it doesn't always do to show your hand.

I am perfectly willing to play with the cards face up.

Mr. President, have you any observations to make with regard to the suggestion that the fleet will make a trip around the world?[22]

No, they are not flying kites at present.

---

[1] On April 21, 1913, Senator George Earle Chamberlain, Democrat of Oregon, introduced a joint resolution which declared the United States to be "free and exonerated" from all provisions of the Hay-Pauncefote and Clayton-Bulwer Treaties. This would have permitted the United States to charge discriminatory rates for ships passing through the Panama Canal. See the *New York Times*, April 22, 1913.

[2] Wilson was defending his right to make a political appointment to fill the position of Director of the Census. He nominated William Julius Harris of Georgia, and Senate Republicans promptly announced that they hoped to block the appointment. See *ibid.*, April 23, 1913.

[3] Willis Luther Moore, chief of the Weather Bureau since 1895, was removed by Wilson on April 16 for "misuse of power over employees" of the bureau in his campaign for nomination as Secretary of Agriculture. At this time, the Justice Department was considering criminal charges against Moore. See *ibid.*, April 17 and 20, 1913.

[4] On April 18, Wilson had Bryan send a telegram to California Governor Hiram Warren Johnson advising "earnestly" against the use of the words "ineligible to citizenship" in the alien land-tenure bill. Wilson said that a bill which limited ownership to citizens and to those who had declared an intention to become citizens would be "preferred." Such a bill would not discriminate especially against the Japanese. The telegram is printed in *PWW*, Vol. 27, p. 326. See also Link, *The New Freedom*, pp. 253-94. For the Japanese reaction to Bryan's telegram, see the *New York Times*, April 21, 1913.

[5] The Thompson-Birdsall bill, which limited land ownership to citizens and to aliens who had declared their intention to become citizens.

[6] The House bill, which had been adopted on April 15, denied persons "ineligible to citizenship" the right to own land.

[7] Wilson had Bryan state his preference for the Senate bill in the telegram to Johnson of April 18. See *PWW*, Vol. 27, p. 326.

[8] See above, April 11, 1913.

[9] The newspapers reported that Wilson would appoint Frank Lyon Polk to the position. See the *New York Times*, April 22, 1913. Polk's appointment was overruled by Senator James Aloysius O'Gorman, Democrat of New York, See *ibid.*, April 30, 1913.

[10] See above, April 11, 1913.

[11] Postmaster General Albert Sidney Burleson.

[12] The special session of Congress, called by Wilson for April 7, 1913.

[13] That is, reduction of commercial discount rates, indicating uncertainty in financial circles.

[14] This was true, for example, of the *New York Times*, April 21, 1913.

[15] The Chamber of Commerce of the United States of America and Republican members of Congress were supporting the creation of a commission to investigate questions relating to the tariff. Congress had created a Tariff Commission in the Payne-Aldrich Act of 1909, but the Underwood bill eliminated it. See Joshua Bernhardt, *The Tariff Commission: Its History, Activities and Organization* (New York, 1922), pp. 10-15, and the *New York Times*, April 30, 1913.

[16] The functions of the commission had been handed over to the Department of Commerce in May 1912. Congress appropriated $50,000 for this purpose in October 1913. See Bernhardt, *Tariff Commission*, pp. 13-14.

[17] See above, April 11, 1913.

[18] Sugar was to be placed on the free list.

[19] See above, April 11, 1913.

[20] That is, currency and banking legislation, the second item on Wilson's reform agenda.

[21] There was considerable debate at this time about whether currency reform could be accomplished during the special session. See the *New York Times*, April 29, 1913.

[22] Secretary of the Navy Josephus Daniels announced on April 20 that the navy would tour the Mediterranean during the winter. See *ibid.*, April 21, 1913.


April 24, 1913

Mr. President, as regards the Secretary of State's expression of policy in the Senate yesterday, could you elucidate or amplify that—his proposition for world peace?[1]

Well, he gave you the terms of it, didn't he?

Well, I don't know that he did.

Of course, it lies in our mind at present only in the most general form. Negotiation would have to bring it down to details and particulars. But the general proposal is this, that the contracting parties should never go to war before there had been an investigation of the facts involved and a report, with no further engagements on either side, that is to say, not binding the parties to abide by any decision, if a decision was involved, as to the merits of the controversy, but merely agreeing to wait until impartial persons had looked into the circumstances and made a report.

It is a question you have given, I presume, considerable study?

Yes; it seems to me an admirable suggestion.

Has there been any suggestion as to which country should be consulted first, or whether it should be done through a commission of all nations?

I understand that Mr. Bryan—perhaps you gentlemen will know—sent for the representatives of all of the countries and laid it before them in a body so as to avoid discrimination.[2]

Mr. President, there was struck out in the draft which was handed to the diplomatic representatives one sentence which was included when presented to the Senate Foreign Relations Committee, and it bore upon the matter of suspending warlike preparations during the period of investigation.[3]

It was stricken out, as I understand it, not because the Senate committee took exception to it at all, but because they thought that that was one of the details which had better be arranged by negotiation with each particular nation. You see, this was what lay in their minds: suppose that we were in danger of a collision with some other country. While that other country and we might agree not to increase our armaments as towards each other, the very fact that there was danger of war might lead some third party to increase her armaments so as to get ready to pounce on the one or the other of us when we got into trouble. That was the difficulty they suggested, so they said they feared it would be difficult to bring about such an arrangement, unless there could be a somewhat general international agreement to that effect, so that a third party would not take advantage of the difficulties that someone had gotten into that didn't affect them directly.

That apprehension is wholly ours, it didn't come from any foreign nation?

It is purely theoretical.[4]

---

[1] On April 23, Bryan discussed his new "peace plan" with the Senate Foreign Relations Committee. What he suggested was a modification of the limited arbitration treaties negotiated by Secretaries of State Elihu Root and Philander Chase Knox, which had run into difficulties with the Senate. Under Bryan's plan, signatory nations would submit all disputes to permanent investigating commissions and agree to accept a "cooling-off" period of six months to one year, during which time neither party would resort to war or increase its armaments. The commission's findings would not be binding; the cause of peace was to be served by allowing the disputing nations a time to "cool off." See Link, *The New Freedom*, pp. 281-82, and Paolo E. Coletta, *William Jennings Bryan*, 3 vols. (Lincoln, Neb., 1964-69), II, 239-49.

[2] April 24, 1913.

[3] "and neither party shall utilize the period of investigation to improve its military or naval status." See E. David Cronon, ed., *The Cabinet Diaries of Josephus Daniels, 1913-1921* (Lincoln, Neb., 1963), p. 26.

[4] On August 7, 1913, Bryan signed the first conciliation treaty with El Salvador; he eventually negotiated twenty-nine such treaties with nations including Great Britain and France. Twenty of these were ratified and promulgated. See Link, *The New Freedom*, p. 282, and Merle Eugene Curti, "Bryan and World Peace," *Smith College Studies in History*, XVI (April-July 1931), 143-64.

April 28, 1913

Mr. President, in your conference with members of Congress, has a guarantee of bank deposits been discussed at all?[1]

Not at all.

It hasn't?

It never has been so far as I know.

Is that because all the details of the banking and currency law have not been discussed or because that one thing has not been mentioned?

I think it is because that asks a question left necessarily for the future.

Mr. President, are you willing to give us any idea of your own views on that subject?

Well, I don't think that I am, simply because it is a subject that I have never thoroughly studied and I don't feel that I am entitled to an opinion about it yet.

Then statements of any kind that that represented a policy of yours would be grossly exaggerated.

Grossly exaggerated.[2]

Mr. President, there has been considerable discussion—probably you have seen it here in the last week—about the Democratic party and tolls.[3] Is there anything that you can say on that, that you feel that you can say?

There is nothing new on that at all. There is no pending action.

There is no pending action?

No, I haven't taken it up within the last two or three weeks at all.

There is a general impression, Mr. President, that your view agrees with Senator Root's. Are you willing to say what your own idea is?[4]

I must say that I think it is a very debatable subject. I thought at one time it had only one side, but I have come to believe it has two sides.[5]

You are still considering the matter, Mr. President?

Not actively, because it isn't pending.

Do you mind telling us, Mr. President, which side you thought it was?

Well, perhaps I had better not tell you where I began or you might guess where I am going to land.

Mr. President, are we warranted, then, in assuming that your mind isn't made up?

I want to say to you men very frankly that I will try until the moment of action to keep my mind absolutely open on this subject and not make it up, because I don't think that is the way for public men to do when action isn't necessary. When action is necessary, I will have an opinion.

Is it a fair question, Mr. President—I mean it to be—do you regard limitation of armaments in the proposed peace treaties of Mr. Bryan as essential?[6]

You mean the limitation of armaments as an essential feature?

An essential feature, yes, sir.

I think it is an essential feature. It may be embarrassing and difficult to get it embodied unless a very considerable number of nations combine in those agreements because of the difficulty I was explaining last week of a third party going forward with exceptional preparations while the others were standing still, and so taking advantage of a situation unfairly. But I think everybody would admit that it was a very natural part of such an agreement as Mr. Bryan had in mind.

My notion is that it would be very difficult to get done.

I don't know. You never can tell until you try. I think that the whole temper of the opinion of the world now is so in favor of doing the reasonable thing for the promotion of peace that we needn't despair of accomplishing a great deal. Mr. Bryan's suggestion to the representatives of the other nations was very kindly received, and the one or two of them who made comment upon it—they made very favorable comment.

That was with reference to that idea—

With reference to that proposal on an agreement to have everything looked into before hostilities started.

Have you heard anything, Mr. President, from Secretary Bryan this morning or from the California end of it? There has been nothing on the Japanese question?[7]

Nothing at all, no. Nothing since we last spoke, or I mean since the interviews with the Japanese Ambassador that you all know about.[8]

Last week?

Yes.

Is there anything new in the matter of the 5-per-cent clause in the tariff bill that affects the treaties?[9]

No, there is nothing new.

You anticipate going to the Capitol this week, Mr. President?

I don't know. I never know until a few hours beforehand whether it is convenient or not.

Mr. President, referring again to the California-Japanese situation, it appears from the dispatches that the California legislature is determined to utilize the phrase "eligible to citizenship" in some form in the bill. Would the use of that phrase, "eligible to citizenship," be still considered by the administration here and perhaps by the Japanese government as a discrimination?[10]

Well, I feel this way about it. I don't think we need discuss it on the basis of the speculations that come from Sacramento, because I don't think any of us knows the real state of mind out there, and I am waiting until Mr. Bryan gets there, and then I will feel that I really know what is going on.

[1] A guarantee of bank deposits had been recommended by the House Banking and Currency subcommittee in 1912 and was part of the proposed banking reform bill presented to Wilson by Representative Carter Glass, Democrat of Virginia, chairman of the subcommittee, on December 26, 1912. The measure was ultimately included in the Senate version of the federal reserve bill, but was eliminated by the conference committee. See Henry Parker Willis, *The Federal Reserve System, Legislation, Organization, and Operation* (New York, 1923), pp. 134, 145, 147, 515-18.

[2] In his meeting with the President-elect on December 26, Glass had received the impression that Wilson favored a guarantee of deposits. See Willis, *Federal Reserve System*, p. 147, n.

[3] That is, regarding what the Democratic administration would do about the discriminatory Panama Canal tolls. See above, April 18, 1913.

[4] Senator Elihu Root of New York had recently offered an amendment to repeal the provision which exempted American coastwise trade from the payment of tolls. See the *New York Times*, April 29, 1913.

[5] Wilson had approved the tolls exemption during the campaign of 1912, but he had been convinced by January 1913 that it should be repealed. He was being less than candid here

in order to avoid disrupting the Democratic party while the new tariff law was being debated. See Link, *The New Freedom*, pp. 306-307, and Daniels, *Cabinet Diaries*, pp. 36-37.

⁶ See above, April 24, 1913.

⁷ On April 24, Bryan had begun a four-day train trip to California to present the President's position on the alien land-tenure bill. During that time the news from the West Coast had grown worse because the California legislature was moving toward approval of a bill which would clearly discriminate against the Japanese. See Link, *The New Freedom*, pp. 294-95; Daniels, *Politics of Prejudice*, p. 61; and Spencer C. Olin, Jr., *California's Prodigal Sons: Hiram Johnson and the Progressives, 1911-1917* (Berkeley, Calif., 1968), pp. 80-90.

⁸ Meetings between Secretary Bryan and Ambassador Chinda.

⁹ The Underwood bill included a 5-per-cent tariff discount for all goods "imported in vessels admitted to registration under the laws of the United States." The bill also stipulated that this would not "abrogate or in any manner impair" provisions of treaties then in force. See *United States Tariff, 1913*, p. 104.

¹⁰ While Bryan was traveling to California, Governor Johnson and the state Attorney General, Ulysses S. Webb, drafted a new bill which altered the wording of the offensive House measure without affecting its intent. The stipulation, which specifically denied land ownership to "aliens ineligible to citizenship," was deleted only to be replaced by a clause allowing "all aliens eligible to citizenship" to own land. From the Japanese—and the President's—perspective, this was no improvement at all. See Daniels, *Politics of Prejudice*, pp. 61-62.

May 5, 1913

The Japanese situation?

No, nothing at all. I haven't heard anything that is not in the papers. I haven't heard all that is in the papers.

The morning papers say that Mr. Bryan declared out on the coast that Governor Johnson would probably hear from you, or rather that he would withhold his signature until he heard from you.¹ Have you intimated that you would send him some form of communication?

I think you misunderstood. We asked Governor Johnson not to sign the bill until he had given us time to see the act in its final shape.

They said they expected some form of communication from you.

I wouldn't give them any intimation that—

Has the bill been reported to you by telegraph?

Not yet. Unless it has come in. It is coming in now.

Do you expect to wait until you see Mr. Bryan before advising Governor Johnson?

I don't know how long Governor Johnson can wait before signing it, under his constitution.

Ten days, until the thirteenth of May.[2]

Then he would naturally wait until Mr. Bryan came back.

Mr. President, is there anything that you could say about the currency message, about the currency legislation?

I have no currency legislation. No telling what—

The morning papers had a good deal about it, about your having a message
coming on this week.[3]

That is a most interesting invention.

It is in the morning papers now.

Well, that is news to me, that is all I have to say. I learn a great
deal about myself in the newspapers that I haven't [known] heretofore.

Mr. President, could you give us any idea as to when the—what might be
the—views of the administration about the currency legislation which can be
stated or authoritatively given?

I tried to make that plain in answer to a previous question—I
mean, some days ago. I am trying to see just how far the views of
all the members can be worked together, or rather how far they
can be brought to work in harmony with regard to this matter, so
that we may know what momentum we may have for it. It is on
that rather slow and vague process—I mean that incalculable process of common counsel—that the whole thing is resting.

May I ask this: would you say up to this time that there is a considerable
degree of agreement on essentials?

I think there is. I think there is a growing agreement—a very
considerable agreement now. I mean, very general agreement.[4]

I imagine you won't want to answer this question. Is that agreement substantially in accord with your own views?

Yes.

Would you feel at liberty, can you give us any idea—

You know that is not fair. Don't you see, gentlemen, I so honestly believe in common counsel to settle these things that I don't like to say whether or not these are my views. I want to see as many fellows as possible come into it.

I was not going quite as far as that. I am wondering if you would feel it opportune to give us any notion of the general line of your thought rather than that of others.

I would rather wait until there is a correlated, formulated consensus, what the details are and the scheme that constitutes them, and whether it is workable or not workable according to the details.

I wasn't really honest in my question!
Mr. President, shall we look to the chairmen of the respective currency committees[5] for the formulated bills which will represent your views?

Naturally. Yes, sir.

Mr. President, is it your idea to have currency legislation before Congress adjourns?

Well, it is my hope that that may be, and I would know whether that—

These conferences are for the purpose of deciding that?

Yes.

That would give the House something to do while the Senate was wrestling with the tariff bill.

That would be very interesting.

Do you expect any slight change in the income-tax provisions such as was demanded by the insurance companies?[6]

Well, I understood that it inadvertently would be necessary [to remove a passage] with regard to insurance that was not in the original bill and which had been put there in committee. Am I not right about that?

One feature of it, yes. I don't think it's more than one.

Well, I haven't heard anything further about it since the committee did make the change that was made.

Mr. President, it is suggested that there may be a change in the Senate with regard to the raw wool schedule.[7] Do you expect a necessary change?

A change in which direction?

Upward.

Do you mean to increase it?

To take it off the free list and put a duty on raw wool.

Everybody has heard rumors to that effect, but I don't credit them. Nobody has said so to me.

I see the statement repeated, Mr. President, that you expect to go to Panama. Of course, that implies a comparatively early adjournment of Congress. You would not go there in August, would you?

I was told, unless my memory betrays me, I understood Colonel Goethals,[8] when I talked with him, to say that July and August were good months to go, that September was a bad month,[9] but that July and August were among the best months to go.

It is very difficult for anybody who lives in Washington to believe that.

I had expected, if Congress had given me a chance, to go there either in July or August.

There is a story in the morning paper that it is the policy of the administration to limit the service of federal judges to seventy years,[10] after that, implied retirement, and stating that it was your policy and, giving some specific instance, Judge Peelle's[11] retirement request—that is one reason—and there has been promised quite some attention to that story in the morning papers.

I know, but the public must have something new to interest them. The public is much interested in the truth.

Mr. President, as Mr. Krock[12] stresses, he didn't mean to imply that they aren't. I believe they would be more interested in the truth.
Mr. President, I want to ask something further about Japan. There is a statement about—that Mr. Chinda, the Japanese Ambassador, has been instructed by his government to protest.[13] Has that come to you in any way? Would it mean simply awaiting Mr. Bryan's return?[14]

So far as I am concerned. We don't think we can handle it without full information until Mr. Bryan returns.

So there will not be any other news until he gets back?

So far as I know now, no.

Have you got any assurances from Governor Johnson as to how long he will wait on the bill?

He said he would hold it, so far as I know, as long as they were constitutionally at liberty to hold it, so as to give us the full length of time to consider it.

Mr. President, is there any news concerning the appointment of the Comptroller of the Currency?

No, we haven't settled on that yet. It is a very difficult choice to make.

You haven't decided on that question of whether there should be an extra district judge instead of appointing a circuit judge in the vacancy that exists there?

You know there is a bill pending in Congress to create another judicial district.[15] It waits on the action of Congress with regard to that.

That wouldn't interfere with the appointment of a circuit judge.

I have already nominated a circuit judge.

There is the Illinois district, and the same issue was pending there, with an extra judicial vacancy on the circuit bench.

We haven't anything new on that.

You haven't determined whether you wanted to wait until Congress decided whether to act on that?

No, I have not.

Are you ready yet, Mr. President, to send a nomination for the Port of New York—that is not really New York—in New York?

No, that won't go in yet. There has been a perfectly unnecessary impression that there was an imbroglio there. There hasn't been anything of the kind. We have been trying to get a common agreement about it. We are all perfectly determined to have a common agreement on it.[16]

Is it fair to assume that it won't go in for several days?

That was just a necessary change. It won't go today.[17]

The Ohio members here inform us of their suspicion that they are not getting all the information they should have with regard to the qualifications of Dr. Gentsch for commissioner.[18]

Yes, sir.

Are they justified, do you think?

I am impressed that it is more than a suspicion.

Do you think they have all the information necessary?

Well, I don't know. We haven't any scales in here by which to measure the relative weight of the recommendations we have for the various candidates. I wish there were some psychological testing instrument.

Suppose you were to make a speech, Mr. President, wouldn't that assist?

Do you mean the nominations?

Yes.

Well, it might and it might not. It is astonishing how many men endorse others that don't need it.

Wouldn't that show up in the recommendations and affect that sort of thing?

It might "sickly it o'er with the pale cast of thought."[19]

Can you say anything relative to the proposed plan of development—for the proper development [of the department of Commerce]?

I understand Mr. Redfield[20] proposes to broaden the functions of the Department of Commerce, with much more direct use of business and bringing in more direct connections.

That would simply be to increase its activities. I thought you meant by legislative change?

Oh, no. Mr. Redfield has a great many interesting ideas as to how it can be rendered most useful and directly helpful to commerce, particularly to the development of commerce. I am a good deal interested in the advancement of commerce and its working with the government.

[1] The alien land-tenure bill passed the California legislature on May 3. See Olin, *California's Prodigal Sons*, p. 87.

[2] Under the California constitution, the Governor had ten days to sign a bill if the legislature was in session, thirty days if it had adjourned.

[3] On May 5, the *Washington Post* reported that Wilson would make an address on currency reform before the tariff bill was passed.

[4] There was, in fact, a great deal of disagreement. The original Glass bill, completed May 1, had placed primary control of the new Federal Reserve System in the hands of private bankers; progressives within the administration, and especially Bryan, favored governmental control. See Link, *The New Freedom*, pp. 202-13.

[5] Representative Carter Glass, Democrat of Virginia, chairman of the House Banking and Currency subcommittee, and Senator Robert Latham Owen, Democrat of Oklahoma, chairman of the Senate Banking and Currency Committee.

[6] The life-insurance companies were complaining about taxation of dividends from life-insurance policies as income. See the *New York Times*, May 4 and 5, 1913.

[7] Free wool passed the House on May 3, by a vote of 193 to seventy-four.

[8] Col. George Washington Goethals, Chief of the Canal Zone Commission.

[9] The worst part of the rainy season begins in September in Panama.

[10] About this, see WW to Charles A. Woods, April 19, 1913, in *PWW*, Vol. 27, pp. 335-36.

[11] Chief Justice Stanton Judkins Peelle of the Court of Claims of the United States had announced his retirement effective on his seventieth birthday.

[12] Arthur Bernard Krock of the Louisville *Courier-Journal*.

[13] That is, to protest against the passage of the California antialien land-tenure bill.

[14] Bryan was expected to return to Washington on May 8.

[15] S. 577, a bill to appoint an additional judge in the fourth circuit. See *Cong. Record*, 63d Cong., 1st sess., pp. 617-20.

[16] There was indeed a misunderstanding. See WW to J. A. O'Gorman, May 5, 1913, in *PWW*, Vol. 27, pp. 399-401.

[17] On May 7, Wilson nominated John Purroy Mitchel as Collector of the Port of New York.

[18] Dr. D. C. Gentsch of New Philadelphia, Ohio, was a candidate for Commissioner of Pensions. He was not appointed. See the *Washington Post*, May 8, 1913.

[19] "And then the native hue of resolution is sicklied o'er with the pale cast of thought." *Hamlet*, III, i.

[20] William Cox Redfield, Secretary of Commerce.

May 8, 1913

Can you tell us anything about currency legislation, Mr. President?

That's a large order. I would have to hire a hall. Just which part of it do you want, a simple—

The bill in Congress—your views as to whether something should be taken up?

I have always been expecting that we could take it up in this session.

Are you more hopeful now?

I think the prospects are very good.

Could you tell us other things you have agreed upon with the House leadership? Mr. Underwood informed us as he left this morning he would probably begin consideration of the currency bill on June first.

He could have told you that. I understand Congress is going to be organized by the first of June.[1]

The currency committee will be organized?

The currency committee,[2] I daresay it will. We didn't come to any agreement. I was discussing with them just how long it would take them to organize the House and just when they could expect the House as a whole to be back and get down to business—the big-business issues—from the organization of it to the committees. That is all that we discussed this morning.

He seemed to think that you expected an actual agreement as to the form of the bill at that time.

I expect to have satisfied myself as to the bill and to have conferred with as many people as I can get. That doesn't mean an agreement on any definite part of the process or on any one of the proposals.

How long will the House go on in recess, Mr. President?

Mr. Underwood seemed to expect that they would be in recess, that is to say, meaning going through the summer, meaning if they did that, for about three weeks, or until about the first of June.

The prospect is good for taking it up this session. Do you think the prospect is good for final action at this session?

Of course, final action would depend upon how rapidly progress was made on the tariff bill in the Senate, to get that out of the way for the Senate to act on the currency bill. I don't suppose anybody in the House would have such "cruelty to animals" as to sit all summer.

You are used to that, Mr. President.

I can stand it.

They have done it for several summers now.

I know. That is what made them sick of it.

Do you hope for final action [on the tariff bill] at this session, Mr. President?

Yes, I do.

Wouldn't you hope for final action [on the currency bill] if the Senate should pass the tariff bill by the first of August?

I don't know. I haven't gone into that. It depends upon whether we can all keep our momentum. We have got to have elasticity left in order to give elasticity to the currency bill.

Did Mr. Glass leave with you the measure he worked up?

He left a preliminary draft with me. It is just a provisional [bill].

You haven't had time to look over it?

Yes, sir, I have looked over it.

Is there anything you would care to say about it?

No.

As to the sundry civil service bill,³ Mr. President, have you signed that as it stands?

It hasn't reached me yet. Did it pass the Senate yesterday?

Passed the Senate yesterday.

I hadn't heard that.

Mr. President, is there much doubt somewhere, or anywhere in your mind— there is in mine—as to how you regard that particular rider exempting any use of that money for prosecution or investigation of farmers' alliances and associations and labor organizations?

Well, until the bill gets to me, I don't care to make any definite statement as to that.

You wouldn't say anything now?

Not now.

Have you seen Secretary Bryan, Mr. President, since——[4]

No, I am going to see him at four o'clock. I have been so busy all day, I haven't been able—

Will there be an announcement made, after you see him?

About what?

About the Japanese and California situations?

I don't think, no, that there will be anything to announce.

You might change your views after talking to him.

Well, I haven't heard that as for a fact.

Can you enlighten us, or tell us anything, Mr. President, as to what is the next step in that matter, what you consider—

No, there is no rule for that.

Mr. President, is the plan adopted and announced by you yesterday[5] substantially in line with the recommendations of the report of the Civil Service Commission?

The Civil Service Commission first recommended it and then withdrew its recommendation, so you can take your choice.

Has there been any report to you, Mr. President, on the investigation of the Weather Bureau by the Department of Justice?[6]

Nothing further.

Nothing from the Attorney General?

No.

It is understood that some of the Republican Senators are going to get vengeance for the ethics meeting on Mr. Cortelyou[7] when he left the Department of Commerce and Labor to become chairman of the [Republican] National Committee by holding up the appointment of Mr. Davies, on the grounds of his connection as secretary of the [Democratic] National Committee.[8] Have you discussed that subject with him? Anything to say on that matter of holding on to the two jobs?

Have you endorsed Governor Sulzer's plan to reconvene the New York legislature to reconsider the primary law.9

Oh, that is none of my business.

I know you have been credited with taking considerable interest in New York
State politics.10

Well, not trying to run them. I feel that I am excused in butting
in in New Jersey, but I am not working for the State of New York.

Could you tell me, Mr. President, when we can expect the District11 appointments?

No, I wish I could. I am expecting to [get to them] as soon as I
can get the time. I hoped to do that this week, and I haven't abandoned all hope for this week but am not ready yet.

Anything doing with reference to the use of the existing commission12 on
general work of that character?

No, I have been trying to do a hundred things today and haven't
acted. It is only ten forty-five.

This Mexican situation, is there any recent action with regard to the recognition of the *de facto* government?

No.

That investigation that is being made, is that independent of the embassy
there?

What investigation?

I understood that there was an investigation being made by the Department
of State looking into conditions down there?

Not that I know of.

Mr. President, could you define for us our Mexican policy, if we have one at
the present time, or the one that you think should be followed during the next
few months in matters such as conversations—

Of course, for the present, we are simply standing off, to see
whether the program of this provisional government is to be carried
out or not.

There has been no recognition of their faction?

No. Of course we have been dealing in recent time with the *de facto* government.

Necessarily so.

Necessarily so.

Isn't that so with the so-called *Constitutionalistas*?[13]

Where they have control.

Just the same, for instance, where the *Constitutionalistas* in certain parts of the northern states have absolute control.

Yes, but we have no official dealings with them.

You have no relations at all?

No, nor will [we] establish any. You see, our Ambassador—our only representative—is in Mexico City.[14]

To revert back to Congress, can you expect general work to be taken up after June first in the House?

I have heard no suggestion of a general program. Certainly I have none.

Will you probably communicate with the Governor today regarding the alien-land bill?

I have no idea.

---

[1] After passing the Underwood tariff bill on May 8, the House decided to take a series of three-day recesses until June 1.

[2] That is, the House Banking and Currency Committee.

[3] See above, April 14, 1913.

[4] Bryan returned to Washington from Sacramento on May 8.

[5] On May 7, Wilson ordered that all fourth-class postmasterships, except those which paid less than $180 a year, be filled by competitive examination. See the *Washington Post*, May 8, 1913.

[6] See above, April 21, 1913.

[7] George Bruce Cortelyou, who had left the cabinet to lead Theodore Roosevelt's campaign in 1904.

[8] Wilson had appointed Joseph Edward Davies of Wisconsin, secretary of the Democratic National Committee, to be Commissioner of Corporations. See the *Washington Post*, May 9, 1913.

[9] Governor William Sulzer, Democrat of New York, called the legislature into special session on June 18 to consider a statewide primary law.

[10] A reference to the misunderstanding over who would be appointed to the collectorship of the Port of New York. See above, May 5, 1913.

[11] That is, District of Columbia.

[12] A reference to the President's Commission on Economy and Efficiency, Frederick Albert Cleveland, chairman.

[13] Led by Venustiano Carranza, who on March 30, 1913, had proclaimed himself Provisional President of Mexico, this group actively opposed the Huerta government. See Link, *The New Freedom*, pp. 350-51, and Friedrich Katz, *The Secret War in Mexico: Europe, the United States, and the Mexican Revolution* (Chicago, 1981), pp. 128-36.

[14] Henry Lane Wilson.

May 12, 1913

Mr. President, there is a very interesting dispatch in the papers this morning in which Mr. Bryan, in a telegram, refers to the action of the Japanese Ambassador as a very earnest protest. Can we know whether that is the description of the Japanese Ambassador's action by the Secretary of State, or whether it is the Japanese Ambassador's own description?[1]

It is the Secretary of State's description.

The reason I ask is that the language of diplomacy is rather an exact science, and if the Japanese Ambassador himself described his action as a very earnest protest, it seems to me that a much greater degree of seriousness might attach.

No, that is the Secretary's own description.

It would not be possible, would it, Mr. President, to get a copy of the protest— or excerpts?

You see, we could not do that without the authority of the Tokyo government, and I do not understand that they desire it. The protest is not serious in the sense in which it was intimated just now.

Mr. President, then you would feel that Mr. Bryan's phrase, "very earnest," was colloquial rather than—

It was just to represent the character of it.

In the ordinary sense?

In the ordinary sense.

It seems to me, in a situation like this, that the fullest publicity that is consistent with all the interests concerned is very much to be desired, that we ought not be left to guess or hear rumors about that.

I think so, too. I quite agree with you there. Of course, as you know, I am a novice in international intercourse of this kind, and

I do not know the exact science that has been referred to. The whole thing—if I may say this just among ourselves—is being managed in a very friendly way but in a very frank way, setting forth opinions, and so forth. And, of course, there are certain kinds of frankness, which if published might give the thing a serious aspect which it is not meant to wear. And, therefore, it is best in the interests of all concerned to permit the greatest frankness, and that precludes publicity in some instances. But that is the present situation.

Is not the situation, Mr. President, such that we can eliminate the word "serious"?

Oh, yes. The word serious was not used—it was the word "earnest." No, nobody is using the word "serious" that I know of.

Mr. President, what remedy can Japan ask that is possible or—

I would rather you ask Mr. John Bassett Moore[2] that.

What remedy does she ask?

She has not asked any remedy.

Mr. President, the morning papers—one or two of them in New York—seem to indicate that Governor Johnson is practically certain to approve the bill today; that is, before noon, which is, I believe, the hour of the limit.

I thought it was tomorrow.[3]

But, anyway, in the event of his approving the measure, would it be appropriate to state what would be the probable next step?

No, I do not think "Ifs" are appropriate in a business of this kind. I do not think we ought to conjecture what we will do.

Mr. President, can we discuss certain things that are not conjectural then, but which seem to be facts. As, for instance, the real question at issue—as it has reached the stage where it is a question at issue—is that of the denial by the Americans of the right of naturalization to the Japanese?

No, that has not been raised at all.

But, isn't that the underlying, the fundamental, thing?

In one sense that underlies the definition of the law as it is framed in California, undoubtedly, but the law is scrupulous in observing the treaty obligations of the United States. It is founded on the treaty obligations.[4]

If Japanese were eligible to citizenship, there would be no protest against the California law.

I don't know about that!

It would lose its strength; it would remove the discrimination against them; so that the real question between Japan and the United States is with the federal government rather than with the California government.

No, I cannot say that, because there has been no intimation that that question has been raised. As you know, that is not explicit in the law. It is a matter of definition and interpretation.

That is a matter, as I understand it, of federal statute, is it not?

The eligibility to citizenship? Yes. The naturalization.

Is it plain, Mr. President, that that bill is really not a violation of the treaty?

It can't be; because it is based on the treaty. It explicitly grants to present residents, but who are not eligible to citizenship, the rights that are granted to them by treaty.

Upon what then is the Japanese protest founded?

Why, I think just upon the feeling that there is an effort to discriminate against their people, on the ground of their alleged ineligibility to citizenship.

Has there been an intimation from Japan that they prefer not to go to court over the question of their eligibility to citizenship?

No, there hasn't been any intimation of any sort; just a very respectful calling our attention to this discrimination.

Mr. President, is any mention made of a treaty in Japan's formal protest?

I don't think that I ought in the circumstances to discuss the protest, but there would naturally be a reference to our treaty relations. I feel uncomfortable in seeming to try to conceal what is in the protest. There is nothing in it that need be concealed; only I just feel that, if they want to confer with us in a way which will leave them free to say what they please, without offending any sensibilities, I should not discuss it. Therefore, I am acting as one gentleman would act with another.[5]

Someone spoke to the Japanese Ambassador, also with the Secretary of State, regarding making public this protest. The Japanese Ambassador said then he expected the White House to do it, and the Secretary of State said that that matter probably would be considered.

Well, that has not reached me at all.

Mr. President, would it be possible—would you regard it as proper—to get the permission of the Japanese embassy to make it public?

Do you mean for me to seek it?

I do not mean in any formal way—to ascertain whether it would be in any way offensive to them?

I would rather you ask that of Mr. Bryan than of me because the whole thing is in his hands.

Mr. President, in view of the fact that you say the treaty in the opinion of the Department of State is not violated, doesn't the situation resolve itself where the government is called upon to defend the action of the California legislature? Isn't that what it amounts to?

I think you can answer that question as well as I can. That is a matter of opinion, a matter of judgment.

[1] For this very strong formal protest against the Webb bill, see the Japanese Ambassador to the Secretary of State, May 9, 1913, *FR, 1913*, pp. 629-31.

[2] Counselor of the Department of State.

[3] On the question of the time limit, see above, May 5, 1913. Johnson signed the bill on May 19.

[4] The California law made a basic distinction between aliens "eligible to citizenship," who could own land, and other aliens who could hold land "in the manner and to the extent" prescribed by treaties between the United States and other countries. Thus the basis for discrimination against the Japanese was their ineligibility to naturalization. See the *New York Times*, April 30, 1913, and *FR, 1913*, pp. 627-28.

[5] The Japanese protest of May 9 argued that the law was "inconsistent" with the Japanese-American Commercial Treaty of 1911. See the Japanese Ambassador to the Secretary of State, May 9, 1913, *ibid.*, p. 629.

May 15, 1913

Could you tell us what headway has been made with currency in the past week, Mr. President?

Well, none has been made, because the bill is still in process of being put together.

Hasn't a conference been arranged for some time next week, or rather this week?

Not by me.

I understood that you were going to see Mr. Underwood and Representative Glass.

No. I may see them, but I mean there is no conference arranged.

Do you expect the bill to be ready by the first of June?

I hope so, but I really cannot tell yet.

Mr. President, your idea is to have the House take action on the currency bill now, isn't it?

My hope is, yes. My strong hope is that it will.

That is a strong possibility, isn't it?

I should say that it was, though I am not authorized to say that from any conferences with the leaders of the House.

Mr. President, is any particular bill being drawn with your knowledge, I mean a bill that would embody your ideas, and also the ideas of Mr. Underwood and Mr. Glass?

There are several tentative bills being drawn, and they are all of them more or less in consultation with me, and I suppose they all run along substantially the same lines.

You haven't brought in the chairmen of the two banking committees for that purpose?

Oh, no, sir.

Are these several bills you refer to one in the House and one in the Senate?

No. At least those that I know of are bills that are being drawn, one by a member of the House and one by outside parties, who are simply drafting it so that I can see what their idea is in detail, because, after all, the detail of the thing is the essential part.

Is the central idea the same, Mr. President, in the two?

I do not know whether it will be, because I haven't seen them.

Can you give us any idea of what your ideas are of what lines ought to be followed?

I could, but I don't think I will just now, because I think it is only fair to match my ideas with other men's before forming them finally.

Mr. President, is it fair to assume that they are all working along the same main line?

Yes, so far as I know they are. There is no conflict that has yet disclosed itself on essential points.

Mr. President, did I understand you to say that someone outside the House is drawing up a bill?

Well, to be plain, a friend of mine, a professor of political economy.[1]

Would you tell us who that is, Mr. President? I thought that perhaps it might be Mr. Untermyer[2]—someone associated with that committee?

No.

Mr. President, speaking with reference to Mr. Untermyer suggested a question, and that is whether the bill will go so far as the matters of clearinghouses and stock exchanges?

Well, that has nothing to do with currency reform.

I know it wouldn't; it might with banking.

This will be a strict currency reform bill. If that was taken up, it would be for other statutes.

Mr. President, not to dwell on the point, will you tell us who the gentleman is?

No, because I do not want him swamped by receiving all the correspondence I have received. This office can handle it, but his can't.

Mr. President, this bill will provide for the revision of the National banking laws, will it not?

Necessarily, you can't revise the currency without doing that.

Mr. President, we are all interested in the Japanese situation. There has been another turn given to it now.[3] I think we would all like to know what the next step is.

Well, the next step is to reply, of course, to the representations made by the Japanese government.

Has the Japanese Ambassador been furnished with a copy of the message of Governor Johnson?[4]

Oh, yes.

Can you say anything about what the tenor of that reply will be?

No, I can't say.

It will be delivered, I suppose, immediately, Mr. President.

I don't even know that. It will depend upon circumstances. Of course, we want to reserve all the deliberation that goes with courtesy.

Mr. President, is it your purpose to communicate any further with Governor Johnson?

Not my present purpose.

Mr. President, how soon would that answer be sent?

I couldn't tell you that; it would depend on circumstances.

It will probably be after the bill is signed. You will wait until the bill is signed?

Again, I will just have to say I don't know.[5]

Will the matter be one for cabinet deliberation tomorrow?

Oh, well, we generally compare notes and opinions on all important subjects, but I don't know whether I shall formally bring it up or not.

Mr. President, when Mr. John Purroy Mitchel[6] was here yesterday, it was said that he discussed with you the matter of economy and efficiency. Would you say along what lines—whether that was economy and efficiency of the federal government or of municipalities or making Washington a model city?

Well, you know Mr. Mitchel and several other gentlemen came down some weeks ago on a double errand; one had to do with making Washington a model city, and the other had to do with a systematic study of economy and coordination in the departments of the government which would enable us to have a scientific budget; and it was only the latter question that he brought up yesterday.

Mr. President, have you expressed yourself with reference to public hearings on the tariff by the Senate Finance Committee?[7]

No.

Would you care to say whether you favor public hearings or not?

Well, I feel that is the Senate's business. You know what Artemus Ward said. He said, "When I see a snake's hole, I walk around it, because I say to myself, 'That is a snake's hole.' "

Mr. President, a great deal of interest has been aroused by, first, Mr. Underwood's announcement in the House that the government would investigate any reductions of wages which seem to have been reduced for the purpose of politics, and then Mr. Redfield's very forceful speech last night; and I wanted to ask, sir, if you had any substantial or well-founded information that there was any purpose on the part of the manufacturers to reduce wages.[8]

No, nothing, except just the vague rumors that are always in the air at this stage of a tariff bill.

Mr. President, coming back to that matter of Mr. Mitchel, what I really had in mind was whether you were going to carry out some ideas that had been attributed to you to make Washington a model city, a model for the municipalities of the country.

Well, I feel that all depends upon whether I show real good sense in the commissioners I choose. That is a starting point; and until I find my men I really do not feel that I have laid the basis for any plan. If I can find men that are right material for such purposes, I certainly would use all the influence I have to bring that about.

Have you considered changing the form of government for the District; giving self-government to the District?

You mean, proposed it to Congress?

Yes.

No, sir, I haven't.

Do you plan, Mr. President, to have your own economy and efficiency commission for the government, such as President Taft had?

Do you mean appoint a new set of men? Well, you know there is no money for it at present, and no money in any of the pending bills.

Perhaps you could get it by asking for it.

Perhaps so, but so many other people are asking for money, and I am modest!

Is there anything in prospect with regard to your civil-service commissioners—changing the personnel of that commission?

I haven't taken that up yet.

Their resignations are in your hands, Mr. President?

Yes.

As a matter of formality?

I think that always is the case, because their relations with the President are necessarily so direct.[9]

Has there been any decision, Mr. President, as to whether the Consuls Generals who were promoted from the consular ranks are to be regarded as under the civil service, or whether they are to be regarded as diplomatic officers?

That has not been discussed.

Would you be willing to say what, Mr. President, your own thoughts are?

My own sympathy and purpose is entirely in accord with what has been done to put the consular services under the civil-service umbrella.

Would you include the Consuls General in that?

I suppose so; that is one of the subjects I haven't studied, and I am not entitled to a formal conclusion yet.

Mr. President, are you likely to make any move soon with regard to the Philippines in carrying out the plank in the Democratic platform about giving independence to the Philippines?[10]

I don't know whether I can say soon or not. That depends altogether upon the way public business shapes itself.

I meant in the appointment of the Philippine commissioners.

I hope to get to that as soon as possible. I haven't lost sight of it; I have simply not found the men I am looking for.[11]

You haven't found a Comptroller of the Currency yet?

No. There is one question which, if I am properly informed, I would ask me, if I were you! Am I correctly informed that any number of newspapers have been carrying the rumor that I was looking for some satisfactory compromise on the woolen schedule? Is that true? Somebody told me that this morning. I haven't seen it.

Wool and sugar both are mentioned, I think.

Was it said that I was considering compromising?

I have seen that.
That has been stated in a small number of papers; it isn't a general statement.

Well, when you get a chance, just say that I am not the kind that considers compromises when I once take my position. Just note that down, so that there will be nothing more of that sort transmitted in the press.

Does that apply to both sugar and wool, Mr. President?

Well, sir, I have taken my stand with the House leaders for the present bill. Enough said!

Would you say what you would do with a bill that came to you that materially changed those features?

No, I won't say what I would do. I will simply say that I am not looking for or accepting compromises.

Mr. President, if it be within the province and the power of the Bureau of Foreign and Domestic Commerce, after investigation, to say that certain rates of wages are unjust or certain proposed rates are unjust, and shall not go into effect, would it not be just as proper to say that certain present wages are unjust and ought to be raised?

Well, perhaps you did not mean to say what you did say. The bureau has no right to say that the wages shall be raised. All they have a right to do is to report on the facts as they find them.

That is very important, because the impression is abroad that what the Bureau of Domestic and Foreign Commerce says will go; and in fact it has been intimated that there will be criminal prosecutions if it didn't.

Do you find that in the law?

I don't; I will be frank; but just for the purpose of clearing the atmosphere, I merely asked you that question.

What will clear the atmosphere will be the facts which they find.

That would certainly be the present impression, that, if upon their finding as a fact that certain rates of wages or proposed rates of wages are unjust and should be changed, the government will take steps to follow it.

Well, probably, if you can find any support for that in the law, it will.

I can't; that is why I wanted you to say—

Well, you can read the law just as clearly as I can.

I think Mr. President, that that proposition was based on the possibility of some conspiracy to reduce wages, to keep them down. That might be in restraint of trade and commerce.

That would be another matter; but, of course, I need not say that this administration will not go beyond the law.

Mr. President, with regard to items in the tariff bill that are not subject to compromise, is the 10 per cent duty on wheat to be included in that?

Mr. Lincoln once told this story. He had spent a whole evening with a gentleman whom he was sending on a confidential mission, and, when the evening was over, the gentleman said, "Well, Mr. President, is there anything we have overlooked; have you any general instructions that you can give me?" And Mr. Lincoln said, "I will say what my little neighbor in Springfield said." "What do you refer to?" Mr. Lincoln said, "I had a little neighbor who, on her sixth birthday, received some alphabet blocks which she was very much charmed with and was allowed to take them to bed with her. She played with them until she got so sleepy that she could hardly see the blocks. She remembered that she had not said her prayers, and so she got on her knees again and said, "Oh, Lord, I am too sleepy to pray; there are the letters, spell it out for yourself."

I think your first opportunity for telling that story was when Henry Hall[12] interrogated you.

That is a story of large application.

Could you tell us how far, Mr. President, you have got in the selection of District commissioners?

Well, it is a journey that is hard to measure the stages of. I haven't got much farther than your last asking.

[1] Royal Meeker of Princeton University.

[2] Samuel Untermyer, New York lawyer and counsel for the so-called Pujo Committee, a subcommittee of the House Banking and Currency Committee, which had investigated the concentration of credit resources in the United States in late 1912 and early 1913. Untermyer was actively involved in consultations over the currency reform bill.

[3] On May 14, Governor Johnson defended the Webb bill and declared that he would sign it.

[4] H. W. Johnson to Bryan, May 14, 1913, published in the New York Times, May 15, 1913.

[5] The formal reply was made May 19, the same day on which Johnson signed the alien land-tenure bill.

[6] Nominated by Wilson on May 7 to be Collector of the Port of New York.

[7] On May 9, Republicans in the Senate had proposed public hearings on the Underwood tariff bill; the Democrats opposed the idea, and it was defeated on May 16. See the Washington Post, May 10 and 17, 1913.

[8] Because some manufacturers had argued that reducing the tariff would compel them to pay lower wages, it was feared that they might cut wages to win higher rates in the Underwood bill. See the Washington Post, May 15, 1913.

[9] On May 22, 1913, Wilson dismissed two of the three members of the Civil Service Commission, Gen. John Charles Black of Illinois and William Sherman Washburn of New York. See the New York Times, May 23, 1913.

[10] The Democratic platform for 1912 called for "an immediate declaration of the nation's purpose" to give independence to the Philippines as soon as a stable government could be established. See Garel A. Grunder and William E. Livezey, The Philippines and the United States (Norman, Okla., 1951), p. 147, and Arthur M. Schlesinger, Jr., and Fred L. Israel, eds., History of American Presidential Elections, 1789-1968, 4 vols. (New York, 1971), III, 2176.

[11] In October 1913, Wilson appointed a majority of Filipinos to the Philippine Commission. See Grunder and Livezey, The Philippines and the United States, pp. 149-51.

[12] Henry Noble Hall, then of the Pittsburgh Chronicle-Telegraph.

May 19, 1913

Mr. President, is there anything new in the Japanese situation?

Absolutely nothing new; nothing at all.

Mr. President, I would like to ask about that, whether you have any reliable information as to the state of public sentiment in Japan. What seems to be the troublesome thing?[1]

No, I haven't. Of course, we have the dispatches, and we have reports of public meetings—very unsettling reports. We don't know whom these public meetings represent. Altogether, we feel that it is a matter of conjecture still—what the real opinion over there is.

It seems to me that that is the real trouble spot over there.

Yes, I think it is, and yet, so far as I can gather from recent dispatches, the later meetings are rather more reassuring, rather more moderate in tone. We got a message from the Chargé d'Affaires over there, who said that the meetings seemed very reasonable.[2]

Mr. President, what is your impression about the sentiment in California in case a referendum is attached to the bill?[3]

Really, there again, I don't know. Apparently, the sentiment in the northern and southern parts of the state is different. I mean in the North there is a distinct and very much stronger support for this legislation than in the South. There again, you see I am conjecturing from what I hear and don't know.

Mr. President, can you determine when our reply will go to Japan?

No; that is in the hands of the Secretary of State, who is in communication with Baron Chinda.

Is he going to communicate further with Governor Johnson?

No, not so far as I know.

Are we right, Mr. President, in the impression that that reply to Japan will not go in any event until the Governor has acted on the bill?

I have assumed that it would not until the Governor has signed the bill, and I have not learned yet that he has.

Mr. President, is there anything in that report from Sacramento that the administration has asked the Governor of California to take the full thirty days to act on it?

No. Has the legislature adjourned?

I think so.
Yes, sir, it has.

I had not learned that it adjourned.

A dispatch this morning spoke of it as a thirty-day affair, and that, out of thirty, nine have passed.[4]
Mr. President, is it fair to inquire whether the American reply is completed?

Well, it is provisionally completed.

You couldn't give us any notion of its general tenor?

No, simply for the reasons that I very frankly explained to you men before. We want to have the freest kind of interchange of views between the governments, and anything that is published, of course, becomes a formal thing, even the language of which would assume a new significance because it was published.

Is it considered, Mr. President, that the Ambassador has been pressing for a reply?

No; he has simply been anxious about the situation. That explains his frequent visits to the State Department.[5] Baron Chinda is acting in an admirable spirit in the matter.

Mr. President, we have had nothing yet that is authoritative as to the nature of the Japanese Ambassador's protest; that is to any, as to the point of his protest. Is it possible to give us—

Well, I was saying to several of the men who asked me about that the other day, there is nothing in it that has not been again and again discussed. There is no new matter. It is all the familiar matter that we went over from the time Mr. Bryan went out to California until now.

I confess an inability to see what he can protest about in this situation.

Perhaps it would not be polite for me to agree with you.

The thing that puzzles me, Mr. President, all the time, is the suggestion that Japan, in taking any attitude in favor of giving the Japanese rights of naturalization here, would be the idea that they wanted to depopulate their own empire by making them all American citizens. That has puzzled me right along.

Of course, this is a thing I could not in any circumstances discuss out loud, but I am perfectly willing to tell you men the way it lies in my mind. I do not think that the real trouble arises out of any particular legislation. It arises out of the implication in it all that we do not want to have intimate association in our life with the Japanese, which is but an implication—a suggestion—of feeling on our part that they are not on the same plane with us. That, of course, is something that diplomacy itself cannot handle. It is a fundamental, subtle, delicate and yet radical thing. It touches a man's pride; he cannot tell you just where you touched it, but you have touched the sorest spot in him. That is at the bottom of it all, and you see in even the meager reports we get from the meetings in Japan that that is where their feelings go back to. Of course, it is a difficult thing to handle. I think that America feels a genuine respect and friendship for the Japanese, and I am sorry to have any question raised which would seem to embarrass them.

Mr. President, our naval officers say, privately, and have said it for years, that, ever since the Russo-Japanese War, the Japanese naval officers into whom they run have shown a sort of resentment against American naval officers which they have not shown against the officers of any other nation. It seems to resolve itself in the Japanese mind of not liking us or our not liking the Japanese. It all rests on that basis. There has been some feeling there for years, because army officers say the same thing.

I do not think you can say of Americans and the Japanese in America that they do not like each other, because I think there has been a great deal of admiration for the Japanese and for Japan.

That is for the individual Japanese.

No, I think for their extraordinary achievements and their sagacity. They do some things, for example, so much better than we do them, that they have commanded our respect. Any nation that can go through a war, for example, and lose only 2 per cent from disease has a scientific superiority over any other modern nation, which has to be admitted, and it impresses the imagination. And their practical capacity is extraordinary, and their adaptability, their genius for taking up things that were unfamiliar to them in their earlier civilization, and then doing them at once almost as well as anybody else can do them.

They are peculiarly imitative.

Yes, but they are more than that, because they can adapt what they take to their own uses so perfectly. There is this that lies back of it: for some reason that I cannot fathom (of course I am saying this to you gentlemen *entre nous*—these are things I ought not to discuss out loud), I get the information that they feel that we are in some way responsible for their not reaping a larger benefit from their war with Russia, because Mr. Roosevelt brought about the Portsmouth conference, and the Portsmouth conference awarded them something less than they had been led to expect and hope for. And this act of generosity and peacemaking on our part is what they regard as the origin of their not having gotten an indemnity, for example, out of Russia.[6]

I think Russia feels the same way, Mr. President.

It is just another illustration of [the rule that] when your neighbors quarrel, let it alone.

If they had given them an indemnity, they might be using it now for another purpose.

It is like a friend of mine who saw a man brutally beating his wife and intervened; and then the wife joined the husband and beat him. He then determined to let domestic quarrels alone. It is the irony of fate in the circumstances that that sort of feeling should arise out of an wholly disinterested act.

Mr. President, aren't the Japanese themselves to blame for that? They started the Portsmouth conference; they asked Mr. Roosevelt—

So I am told; I have no official knowledge of that, but I am told so.

Mr. President, is there any indication of sympathy with the Japanese government on the part of any other government? Has there been inquiry from Great Britain or China?

Oh, no. No. Of course, that would be an extraordinary thing for another government to do. There has been nothing done of that sort.

Mr. President, do you feel that the results of the tariff vote in the Senate last Friday indicated anything you did not know before? Do you feel any encouragement about the bill?[7]

Oh, no, I haven't felt anything about that.

Are you going to stay on the ground this summer if necessary?

I am.

Will you feel glad when you get away for vacation?

I don't know. I intend to fight it out on this line if it takes all summer.

How about currency, Mr. President?

Perhaps as the weather gets hotter, it will be unnecessary!

When do you expect to send your message?

I don't know. I haven't thought of that yet.

Is there no likelihood it will cause more difficulty?

You say the House—

You answered that before.
Which will then go into specific methods as to currency reform and not the guarantee of bank deposits?

Well, yes, the idea of bank deposits is another matter entirely apart from the currency.

Will you go into any specific matters in the message? Will it be a specific message?

Oh, I won't fire my arrows in the air, I will shoot at some mark.

Mr. President, it is reported in some quarters that an alternative measure to the Glass measure is being prepared outside of Congress with the administration's knowledge.

No, that is not true. The last part is not true.

But you previously acknowledged that that was true.

No, no, I said that I had been consulting with a friend of mine,
not with a view to an alternative measure at all, just as a sidelight.[8]

---

[1] The newspapers had reported numerous public meetings in Japan protesting against the
Webb bill.

[2] Arthur Bailly-Blanchard to the Secretary of State, May 17, 1913, WP, DLC. Press reports
were also "reassuring." See, for example, the *Washington Post*, May 18-19, 1913.

[3] There was discussion of a referendum by those who thought that the land-tenure bill was
too weak or too strong. The Asiatic Exclusion League of California wanted a referendum to
stiffen the bill; California Democrats wanted to alter the bill because they viewed it as an
embarrassment to the Wilson administration. The difficulty was that 20,000 signatures were
required on a petition to submit a bill to the voters. See *ibid.*, May 19-20, 1913.

[4] See above, May 5, 1913.

[5] See, for example, Bryan to WW, May 18, 1913, in *PWW*, Vol. 27, pp. 448-49.

[6] In August 1905, President Theodore Roosevelt brought the Russians and Japanese together
at Portsmouth, New Hampshire, to negotiate an end to their war in the Far East. Although
Japan had emerged victorious from the war, the treaty signed on August 23, 1905, reestablished
a near balance of power between the two nations in East Asia. Russia recognized Japan's
predominant interests in Korea, but many Japanese were dissatisfied because the Russians
had not been forced to pay an indemnity. For this they blamed the interference of the United
States. See Eugene P. Trani, *The Treaty of Portsmouth: An Adventure in American Diplomacy*
(Lexington, Ky., 1969). The treaty is printed, pp. 161-70.

[7] This was the defeat, on May 16, of the resolution by Senator Boies Penrose, Republican
of Pennsylvania, to conduct public hearings on the Underwood bill. For comment on the
meaning of this victory, see "The Tariff in the Senate," New York *Nation*, XCVI (May 22,
1913), 514.

[8] See above, May 15, 1913.

May 22, 1913

Well, what's the news? The President knows it.

I wish I did. I don't know of half as many things as you fellows
do.

Has it been brought to your attention, Mr. President, that changes will be
made in the tariff bill in the committee that is handling the agricultural schedule?[1]

No. I saw that in the paper this morning, but if you will permit
me to say so, I don't believe everything I see.

Neither do the rest of us. Would your statement that there will be no compromise apply to such changes as that?

Of course. I don't even know what changes were under discussion.

Did you refer to only radical changes, Mr. President, last time?

Well, I will wait until I see the changes before I say what it is I
refer to.

Well, according to Mr. John Sharp Williams,[2] you proposed to equalize certain duties either by putting raw materials on the free list or a duty on all. It was announced upon his authority that it was with your knowledge and consent. I suppose that was the point that we were driving at.

Well, are you sure that I said that?

Well, I only know what I saw in the paper. I don't believe everything I see in the paper. I heard him say it—with your knowledge and consent. Then I heard him say he would probably do that.

Oh, there, of course, it hasn't reached me.

This is the decision to equalize these schedules. It also was reported it had been reached with the knowledge of the President and not without his approval.

You see, that is very circuitously stated. As a matter of fact, I don't know anything about it.

Mr. President, do you expect to go over a completed draft of the Senate bill before it is submitted to the caucus?

Oh, I don't know. That depends entirely on the courtesy of the Senate committee.

Can you tell us anything about the currency bill—any progress that is being made with it?

No, I can't, because we are carefully going through the program that I laid out myself of comparing views and slowly getting down to a common basis.

The bill has not been completed yet?

No.

Mr. President, isn't the disposition of assets considered the vital question in the preparation of the currency bill—altogether twenty-one bills?

No, that is not the most difficult question at all. That would be easily enough handled if it came in with the rest of the scheme.

Do you know of any bill being prepared by Professor Scott[3] of the University of Wisconsin?

No, I hadn't heard of any. What Scott was that? Charles Scott?[4]

I thought he might be a friend of yours.

Well, I daresay I would recognize him [only] by his front name. There are so many Scotts.

Mr. President, have you been approached by any Republican Senators with the request that they be brought into your conferences on the currency bill?

No, not by intimation even.

Not yet?

Do you think that is coming?

I do, yes.

Well, it will be very interesting.

Is there a phase of the Japanese situation that can properly be discussed now?

Well, there isn't any new phase at all that has been brought to my attention since I saw you gentlemen last.

Unless there should be some information from Japan direct.

Unless there should be, but there hasn't been that I know of.

Mr. President, in your last confidential statement to the newspapermen you referred to a statement from the Chargé d'Affaires with reference to the feelings of Japan. Has there been any answer?[5]

I daresay we have continued to get them. I don't know that we have since that interview. All we get from him is reassurance as to the attitude of the government on the question based on the views of thoughtful people, people who will ultimately, I daresay, control the situation. I just remember, I had a talk with Mr. John Mott[6] this forenoon who has just returned from Japan. He gave me very reassuring accounts of their entire comprehension of the situation.

Is that the government, Mr. President, or the—

He made it a point to see so many sorts of missionaries and university men, not members of the official class. He didn't see any member of the government. I don't know whether he saw anybody in an official position or not.

Dispatches from Tokyo in the past three or four days have invariably started off with the assurance that the conservative class, and newspapers generally, would brake any high feelings, but the dispatches have also nearly always insisted there is very strong feeling, a fundamental resentment against the discrimination.

Yes, that is just what I was saying the other day. That is fundamentally the difficulty, although you can't blame the feeling of the Japanese.

Is there not at present some discretion with regard to immigration?

I sometimes wonder.

Well, there is what is generally known as a gentlemen's agreement under which they restrict emigration.[7]

Still, that is a mere friendly understanding.

I know it is, yes, sir. Is that the reason it could be abandoned by them without consultation with us?

Oh, I daresay.

But they are not anxious to have their people come to the United States?

I wonder, I wonder.

I wonder whether the public sentiment there, if it was strong against discrimination, might not manifest itself against the arrangement, which is entirely in Japanese control?

Of course that is possible, but I have never heard anybody intimate that is true.

Of course, they have a similar arrangement with Canada. It seems to be based on their understanding that their people could not live in close—

With ours, without any risks of disorders.

Then there is no official communication of any kind asking for acknowledgment of and reply to the protest which has been received?[8]

Not unless it has come within the last hour or two.

Mr. President, I would like to ask about the Mexican situation generally. There is a report today on the proposed loan agreement of one hundred million dollars.[9] They expect to get this money in France and England. The revolutionary government there[10] has given notice it won't recognize any obligation that grants any rights to the European creditors, and the markets discussed might be involved. Would that affect our consideration?

I am not rich enough to move forward in Mexican politics at all.

Mr. President, I understand, too, that that loan is to be guaranteed by 35 per cent of the customs. Is there any movement by this government looking to some such security of our claims against Mexico?[11]

No, there is no movement at all.

Would it be expected that our claims would be paid out of that loan made to Mexico; that is, if the present government gets the hundred million. Now, will that affect the payment of our claims?

I haven't the least idea. I know absolutely nothing except what was in the papers about it, and that is not well-founded in detail, at any rate.

Has there been any new effort, Mr. President, to collect the claims of United States citizens against Mexico which grew out of the previous revolution?

No, sir.

What is the status in Mexico and what is our relationship to the present government in Mexico?

Why, simply that we are treating them as a *de facto* government. Therefore, that the present government has been a *de facto* government and has been recognized by several foreign countries.

Does that hasten the process of recognition here?

Not necessarily.

Is this recognition being talked over at the present time with the Mexican government?

Every time you think of Mexico you think of—

Are you thinking any faster?
Mr. President, what is the most obvious obstacle to recognition of Mexico?

Why, I should say the absolute uncertainty of affairs there.

Wouldn't the making of the seventy-five-million-dollar loan to run the *de facto* government strengthen it in the eyes of this government?[12]

That remains to be seen. You see, we have to have all these rumors corroborated and the details made known to us.

Did you see the article by the editor of the [Mexico City] *Mexican Herald* the other day, urging the United States to recognize the present administration?[13]

Yes, I saw that.

It sounded very logical.

It was a very strongly written article.

Has it ever been stated categorically to the *de facto* government of Mexico that this government would not recognize it until the government had proved itself?

No, sir.

To be stable, which we did not have confidence it had so far?

No, sir.

Well, there is nothing in any way hampering you if you decide that it is a matter of expediency to recognize them?

No. We are absolutely free in any way we wish to act.

Mr. President, I am particularly asking a question about the appointment to them of an Ambassador, which more or less is very closely allied to that of recognition. Is there any new development in that situation?

You see, there necessarily could not be. To send a new Ambassador would be to recognize the government, so that the two are inseparably connected.

In other words, you can't appoint a new Ambassador until you have satisfied yourself that the importance of having a new Ambassador there would outweigh the granting of recognition?

Well, it might or might not. I mean—that is to say, you can't separate the two. You can't send a new man without giving him credentials to somebody, and to give him credentials to anybody would be to recognize the persons to whom you gave the credentials.

There hasn't been any selection [of an Ambassador to Russia]? We have no treaty with Russia. Is there any progress in the selection of an Ambassador?

No, there hasn't been. There has been no conclusion. It is in progress.

Has Mr. Mott definitely declined the Chinese position?

Yes, because of duties that he had undertaken which he thinks he ought not to lay down—I mean, with regard to the worldwide movement of cooperation in the general field of missions.

Did you take that matter up again with him this morning?

No, except to go over the ground. He wanted me to understand exactly why he felt bound to decide as he did. We didn't open it again, if that is what you mean.

Has anything been done with reference to the position at Paris?

No.

The governorship of Hawaii, is that coming to a decision pretty soon?

It is, yes, sir.

Mr. President, has any progress at all been made towards giving a reply to Sir Edward Grey to his protest?[14]

No, we haven't been able to take that up.

That seems strange to a good many of us, because Ambassador Bryce,[15] in his last communication to the government, said that Sir Edward Grey desired a prompt answer.

Yes, sir.

Would you mind explaining what the difficulty is, Mr. President?

Those are matters—there is no difficulty. I don't want to leave the impression in anybody's mind there is any difficulty. I just don't want to discuss it.

Is there any progress on the British arbitration treaty,[16] Mr. President?

Any progress?

Towards the renewal of the British general arbitration treaty?

We will seek to renew this treaty along the line.

I think you gave us that answer two weeks ago.

About a week ago I asked at the State Department, and they said nothing had been done. I expect my answer still remains.

Secretary Bryan told us not more than three days ago that good progress had been made. He said he thought it would probably be consummated without any change.

I hope so sincerely.

That was day before yesterday. Is there any announcement to be expected, necessarily, Mr. President, on the Public Printer?

On what?

The Public Printer.

Well, of course, I hope so. All these appointments are matters of perplexity, of course, because I have to take all the nominations and look over the credentials and see who supports this, that, and the other man, and then make up my mind.

In order to bring it alive, I might ask about the District commissioner too.

Well, you brought it up.

Mr. President, when may we look for your message on currency?

I don't know, sir. As soon as we get ready—must be in person.

Can you say anything about the commissioner?[17]

No, I am sorry I can't.

Two weeks ago, Mr. President, you brought up a very interesting question to us.[18] Is there anything on that?

What do you refer to?

You brought up the tariff proposition—no compromise.

There has been absolutely no change in the situation.

Do you mean there isn't anything of the kind to—any other lines you might—

No such further changes have been made.

[1] On May 22, the *Washington Post* reported that tariff duties on agricultural products and raw materials were to be "equalized" by the subcommittee on agricultural schedules of the Senate Finance Committee.

[2] Democratic Senator from Mississippi, chairman of the subcommittee.

[3] William Amasa Scott, Professor of Political Economy and Director of the School of Commerce.

[4] Charles Payson Gurley Scott, editor of *Century Dictionary*.

[5] See above, May 19, 1913.

[6] John R. Mott, a leader in the international Y.M.C.A. movement, whom Wilson had asked to serve as Minister to China. See Jerry Israel, *Progressivism and the Open Door: America and China, 1905-1921* (Pittsburgh, Pa., 1971), pp. 114-17, and WW to Mott, Feb. 24, 1913, in *PWW*, Vol. 27, p. 131.

[7] In 1907, during a previous crisis over Japanese immigration to California, President Roosevelt had negotiated the "gentlemen's agreement," under which the United States would not forbid Japanese immigration to the mainland of the United States if the government of Japan would curtail it.

[8] Secretary of State Bryan replied to the Japanese protest on May 19, 1913.

[9] See the *Washington Post*, May 19, 1913, and the *New York Times*, June 2, 1913.

[10] The Carranza government, then exercising authority in northern Mexico. See above, May 8, 1913.

[11] Huerta had previously stated that he would not pay American claims against Mexico until his government was recognized. See the *Washington Post*, May 9, 1913.

[12] A reference to a proposed loan totaling $77,000,000 being arranged by American financiers. See the *New York Times*, June 2, 1913.

[13] The editor argued that the Huerta government was the strongest to be had in Mexico, and that delay in recognition would bring chaos to Mexico and might result in deeper American involvement. The editorial was reprinted in the *Washington Post*, May 20, 1913.

[14] The British Foreign Secretary had protested against the exemption of American coastwise shipping from the payment of Panama Canal tolls. See above, April 18, 1913.

[15] James Bryce, the British Ambassador.

[16] Because of American unwillingness to accept arbitration of the issue of Panama Canal tolls, there was some doubt whether the British would approve a renewal of the Anglo-American arbitration treaty of 1908. The London government approved the renewal on March 11, 1914. See Link, *The New Freedom*, p. 314.

[17] That is, for the District of Columbia.

[18] See above, May 15, 1913.

## May 26, 1913

Mr. President, do you plan to appoint the industrial commission soon?[1]

Yes, sir. Very soon. This week some time. I am just waiting to get the last advices about one man I have in mind.

Is the Civil Service Commission coming this week, Mr. President?

I don't know. That is quite undetermined.

Do we have some intimation concerning the industrial commission?

Some intimation? Well, I have several alternative lists and there-fore it would be impossible to make up a list yet. There is really a wealth of good material that is pouring in on me.

Have you determined your attitude, Mr. President, on the Consuls General and the question of civil service?[2]

Well, I have been trying. I haven't gotten very clear information yet as to what has been the practice of the department about Con-suls General, whether they have been regarded as being semidip-lomatic agents in some parts or not, but we haven't taken any action yet at all about them.

Have we approached any nearer to recognition of Mexico in the last three or four days?

Not so far as I can see.

Have you fully made up your mind not to recognize Mexico until the elections?

Oh well, I don't permit myself fully to make my mind up about the changing scene.

I know you have intimated in one of the previous talks that that was the thinking and that stood in the way—that the government was not organized or could not be organized until the elections occurred.

Well, the government is, in a sense, organized now as a provi-sional government. The regular machinery of government is in large part in operation, but their plans seem to shift from time to time. That is what is puzzling me.

In your mind, is there any hazard for this country in recognizing the provisional government?

You mean any natural hazard?

They may not come back.

No, I suppose not.

I was thinking of the possibility of the government's being overturned—the provisional government's being overturned—in the election, and an entirely new set of men coming in, and their feeling toward this country?

I suppose in that case the present recognition would be passé immediately.

What is the principal obstacle now, Mr. President, to the recognition of Mexico?

Well, what do you think?

Well, the economic situation, probably.

Did you ever know a situation that had more question marks around it? Whenever I look at it, I see nothing but exclamation points. It is just a kaleidoscopic changing scene. Nobody in the world has any certain information about the situation that I have yet found. Their information is about a month old, or it is so new it isn't verified.

If it is verified, they deliberately leak it to the press.

I know only what I have seen in the dispatches. I don't know anything about it through any other channel.

Mr. President, is there anything new concerning the Japanese situation?

Nothing whatever.

Is there any news this morning, by the way, from the Emperor? He received several state officials yesterday.

So he seems to be improving.[3]

Have you got any intimation, Mr. President, as to whether—when any form of communication might be received from Japan?

No, sir, no intimation of any kind.

Is the Emperor himself responsible for the delay?[4]

I don't know, I am sure.

Has there been any further—has there been anything further from our representatives over there concerning public feeling?

Nothing since our last review.

How about currency, Mr. President, are you nearer to anything that you can tell us?

I am hoping that this week will produce some definite formulations so that we can get down to conferences on details, but I haven't seen the formulations yet.

Would you have us judge from that that you would be making a speech to Congress within this week?

Oh, I won't make any speech until I have made up my mind that I have got a bill that will hold water.

Then you will make the speech through a message?[5]

Probably, or in connection with a message.

Well, it is definitely determined, is it, Mr. President, that a bill will go in at this session?

No. Even that is not sure.

Do you regard it as extremely likely?

I most sincerely hope it will be possible, and I don't see why it should not be.

Might I ask, Mr. President, will you read your currency message in person?

Well, I don't know whether that has become a habit yet or not.

One of the papers reports, Mr. President, that Henry Parker Willis[6] is the gentleman who is advising you in this matter—the currency matter—in regard to the formulation of the bill. Is that correct?

No. The fact is, as I thought everybody knew, Mr. Parker Willis has been advising Mr. Glass for some months past, during the last session of Congress.

But he is not the one you referred to in the office the other day?[7]

No.

Is there anything in the tariff situation, Mr. President, that you can comment on?

No. So far as I know, things stand where they were.

Has the reported defection of Mr. Walsh and possibly Mr. Newlands[8] been reported to you in such a connection as to give you concern?

No, sir.

You are still calling on the Senate to accept the Underwood bill?

Yes, certainly.

Has there been anything concerning the income-tax feature?

No, no conference by members of either house. A number of outsiders have been to see me about it.

But they haven't asked you to express an opinion—

The chief things they have been seeing me about were the apparent ambiguity of the language in regard to certain insurance policies. I believe there is a hearing on about that.[9]

Do you think, Mr. President, that free sugar will be as ruinous to Porto Rico as the tariff witnesses suggested it would be the other day—

No, I don't. I don't think it will be ruinous at all if they improve their business methods. The great curse of the tariff is that it lets everybody drift and rest on their oars, never improving their prowess.

Do you think, then, if that applies to Porto Rico, it will apply to the beet-sugar industry in this country?

That is constantly improving. No, sir—you see, the whole question of the study of soils has had a recent development. I mean, we know a great deal more about it than we did. The fertility of the soil is more a matter of minute subdivisions with slight additions of certain chemical elements which are necessary. In proportion as they go on with this cultivation of the beet, the beet contains more saccharin matter, so that they are constantly improving their product in the mere process of cultivation. The claim is made, however, that in putting beets into new soil, the fertilization is very expensive, and that is true with regard to new soil. But, you see, there is a considerable acreage now devoted to that, and the yield, so far as the proportion of saccharin matter is concerned, is constantly improved.

Except in Colorado.

Except?

There hasn't been any improvement there.

Has there not? I haven't noticed that. That must be due to a failure to adopt the best methods.

It probably is. They don't seem to be very much up to date. You think, then, that the application of scientific methods of agriculture will enable Porto Rico to compete on an even basis with Cuba?

I think, so far as I understand it, it is not so much with Porto Rico a question of scientific methods of cultivation as business methods of handling this whole thing. Nothing has been so backward throughout the jurisdiction of the island as the organization of agriculture as a business, rather than as an art.

That does not apply to Louisiana, does it, Mr. President?

Yes, it applies to Louisiana, because there they have been very backward in their methods of cultivation. They haven't made an improvement, as I have heard of it, for thirty years.

It can be a matter of marketing conditions. This is a rapid industry.

Acting in large part—

They have a short season down there.

They have a short season, and the cane never really ripens as fully as it does in Cuba but, nevertheless, they can handle it.

More as a cash product for a big industry, is that what you mean?

I sometimes wonder.

Well, for use as a cash product, manufactured by themselves in the community or in the state for exportation in large quantities outside the borders of the state as a big industry?

Well, they couldn't make much out of it unless they exported it outside of the state.

Well, I understood they will have to cut down their production and improve their buying and selling.

You can understand anything you choose in this town, if you will only keep your ears open. I should think you fellows were missing a lot of stories about the extraordinary lobbying in this town at this time.

There is a good deal written about it, Mr. President.

Somehow you haven't gotten hold of it so that the country could notice it. This town is swarming with lobbies, so you can't throw bricks in any direction without hitting one, much inclined as you are to throw bricks. This is the most concerted and as concentrated an effort, I daresay, as has ever been made to influence governmental legislation by the pressure of private interests.

Do you refer especially to sugar?

Sugar, wool—those in particular. Those have the biggest lobbies. Of course, there are men, perfectly legitimate businessmen, who have come to town for some reason to represent their interests. I don't know about that, but there is a great deal besides that going on.

I think the country knows pretty well that lobbies are here.

I know, but you think just the usual scenery is in view. There is a good deal more than the usual scenery in view.

They have been pursuing you, Mr. President.

No, sir, I am immune.

Can you give us some names, pictures, in connection with that? Then we will start using—

Well, if I could collect this lobby around myself, I shouldn't like to be photographed with them. We can get the names out of our daily mail.

You mean, Mr. President, there is a corrupt lobby here.

I don't know that they could approach Congress in that way, but just a systematic misrepresentation of the facts and one of these organized processes by which people, just out of weakness, to please their friends, will write letters galore about things that they know nothing about. It is similar to the process of trying to get men appointed to office. I generally estimate a man in inverse proportion to the number of recommendations, because when the number passes a certain point I know there is machinery at work of the most elaborate sort, and that sort of thing is going on. But the men on the Hill know that and particularly understand that. I think they do.

It would be regarded as extremely—

It doesn't make me in the least nervous, although I would like to see these fellows made a bit ridiculous. That is what I would enjoy.

Mr. President, you said just a moment ago that you didn't think we were getting that fact out to the country. Wouldn't the most effective way to get it out be for you to authorize us to quote you on what you have just said?

Well, I'll tell you what I'll do. I don't know what I have just said, because I am not on guard in talking to you fellows this way. Before you get away from the office wire, I will try to dictate a few lines.[10]

That will get to the country.

All right.

Mr. President, are you informed or convinced that the Underwood tariff bill can pass the Senate without the vote of the binding Democratic caucus?

Well, to tell you the truth, I haven't bothered or inquired yet about the positions to reach a decision inside the party. I think the opinion of the country is going to take care of the thing.

Well, the opinion of the country would take care of most of it but not in the case of where the sentiment is strong and takes a different reaction.

Well, perhaps. I am not sure of that.

That is the case in Louisiana. I should say a great part of it is state sentiment rather than national sentiment.[11]

Still that is not true of all of Louisiana. You are thinking of only half of Louisiana.

If it is narrowed down, it is even a smaller area.

Yes, I daresay even smaller.

Mr. President, can you say anything concerning the sundry civil services exemption clause?

Well, if you fellows would tell me—is it expected I should sign the sundry—

It is in conference.
Mr. President, in saying something about the lobbies, could you remember to say something about the office seekers and how they can add to the situation?

[1] That is, the United States Commission on Industrial Relations, created by Congress on August 23, 1912, with wide powers to investigate the relationship between capital and labor in the United States. Taft's appointments to this nine-member commission had been held up by Democrats in the Senate, leaving Wilson the authority to make new nominations. See Graham Adams, Jr., *Age of Industrial Violence, 1910-1915: The Activities and Findings of the United States Commission on Industrial Relations* (New York and London, 1966), pp. 25-49.
[2] At this time, Secretary Bryan was attempting to remove the consular service from Civil Service. Wilson resisted this. See Link, *The New Freedom*, p. 107.
[3] Emperor Yoshihito had been suffering from lung inflammation. See the *Washington Post*, May 23, 1913.
[4] The Japanese had not yet responded to Bryan's note of May 19.
[5] That is, a message to Congress proposing currency reform legislation.
[6] Former Professor of Economics at Washington and Lee University, who was soon to serve as the House banking committee's expert adviser.
[7] See above, May 15, 1913.
[8] Senators Thomas James Walsh, Democrat of Montana, and Francis Griffith Newlands, Democrat of Nevada, who had stated their opposition to the tariff bill.
[9] Insurance companies were attempting to have dividends exempted from income taxation. See above, May 5, 1913.
[10] Wilson released the following statement: "I think that the public ought to know the extraordinary exertions being made by the lobby in Washington to gain recognition for certain alterations of the tariff bill. Washington has seldom seen so numerous, so industrious, or so insidious a lobby. The newspapers are being filled with paid advertisements calculated to mislead the judgment of public men not only, but also the public opinion of the country itself. There is every evidence that money without limit is being spent to sustain this lobby, and to create an appearance of a pressure of public opinion antagonistic to some of the chief items of the tariff bill.

"It is of serious interest to the country that the people at large should have no lobby and be voiceless in these matters, while great bodies of astute men seek to create an artificial opinion and to overcome the interests of the public for their private profit. It is thoroughly worth the while of the people of this country to take knowledge of this matter. Only public opinion can check and destroy it.

"The Government in all its branches ought to be relieved from this intolerable burden and this constant interruption to the calm progress of debate. I know that in this I am speaking for the members of the two houses, who would rejoice as much as I would, to be released from this unbearable situation."

Printed in *PWW*, Vol. 27, p. 473; see also, e.g., the *New York Times* and the *Washington Post*, May 27, 1913. For the impact of the statement, see Link, *The New Freedom*, pp. 187-90.

[11] Because of its provision for free sugar, Louisiana's Democratic Senators were voicing opposition to the Underwood bill.

May 29, 1913

Mr. President, there are reported statements that Doctor William Bayard Hale is in the City of Mexico on some mission for you, getting information or something of that sort. Could you say anything about that?

I saw that, but, like you, I disbelieved it. It is getting to be my habit now.

You knew he was there?

He came to see me just before Easter and told me he was going there.

Of course you will take advantage of any information?

Oh, very greatly, yes.[1]

Mr. President, are you in sympathy with the general purpose of the Cummins resolution?[2]

Oh, yes.

Is there any further information along that line that you could give us?

I would tell you if there was anything that I could give you fellows. I think you probably know more about it than I do.

I mean the—the information along the line that is called for in the resolution. Of course, I don't know whether you care to answer that.

In the action of Congress as soon as—I don't know that there is. Congress can do that. Evidently they—lobbyists—don't know that there was a vote last November, so they are continuing their old practices under the impression that the Congress of the United States was created to legislate for special interests.

A bill was introduced today by Mr. Weeks of Massachusetts[3] for the registration of lobbyists, I think along the lines of the Massachusetts law.

Yes. Well, that will do some good.

Mr. President, are you in a position to supply the names of these lobbyists if this resolution should be passed?

Oh, if public necessity arose, I could easily do so.

Mr. President, would you be willing to break precedent to the extent of going before that committee?

I don't know.

Well, in another way, have you been asked to?

No, indeed. You mean the committee to which the resolution was—

Yes, sir.

No, I haven't.

Mr. President, you will remember [speaking to] Congressmen the other day giving your express and cordial approval of a popular primary for the election of Presidents.

I have already, yes, sir, said that in the campaign.

Nomination?

Yes.[4]

Mr. President, that brings up the question of Japanese affairs. Have you had any word from Japan?

No. There hasn't been. Not a word.

Mr. President, is there anything new in a telegram to Governor Johnson in which he was asked to delay the [operation] of that bill? Reference was made to the fact that delay might offer an opportunity to remove the necessity for direct diplomacy. Is there any hope of doing that, despite the enactment of the bill?

Well, I don't see that there is anything to do in that direction. The intimation there was that we needed the consultation with the Japanese government to find some way to settle it with the legislature of California with regard to what is existing now. Now, you see, there is nothing new to take up, so far as that is concerned.

I notice the Tokyo government has given out some statement that lets it be known that the California affair hasn't been adjusted to their complete satisfaction at all.[5] I thought possibly you still had some hope of reaching an agreement?

Of course, we are always open to any suggestion that the Japanese government has to make, but it hasn't made any yet.

Would the reports from there indicate a varying public opinion?

I don't know. If we have had any, none has come to me from the State Department.

You know, it was said before that the government was rather strained. Mr. President, you had, I think, some talks in the last day or two with members of Congress who were engaged in preparing currency legislation?

Only with Mr. Glass and Senator Owen.

Now, is there a bill—could you say whether a bill is ready to be presented?

No, there is not. I have three bills[6] lying before me, as a matter of fact, and I am generously invited to make one bill out of the three.

I thought that the professor of political economy was going to do that.

He didn't, after all, make a draft. There were certain points I wanted his opinion on.

I have been told that the effort might be to make that a nonpartisan bill, so that Republicans might support it as well as Democrats, and that the caucus might not be invoked in the House.

Well, of course, that suggestion hasn't come to me. I hope it will be nonpartisan in this sense, that it is fair all 'round.

Is one of the bills before you Mr. Henry's bill?[7]

No, sir, I didn't know he had one.

Well, he made a suggestion of drawing one.

No, sir, that is not one of the three; I would be very interested to see his.

You talked with Mr. Howe[8] the other day, was that on—

Only incidentally; we principally gossiped about affairs in Princeton.

He is a member of the American Bankers' Association?

Yes, he is.

Have any Republican members of the House offered their assistance or cooperation in the matter of currency legislation?

No, sir; not to me.

Mr. President, could you tell us whose bills you have before you?

Why, I have a draft of a bill by Senator Owen, a draft by Mr. Glass, and a draft by the Secretary of the Treasury; and they are all along the same line. There is no essential difference that I have yet discovered.

You mean that the central idea is the same, Mr. President?

Yes, sir, in all three.

Mr. President, is there any disposition on your part to believe that the Senate committee is sending out questions to bankers in the apparent purpose to hear from bankers—isn't that unnecessary?

No, sir; I think, of course, it is a perfectly natural and proper thing to do.

I think there is some feeling on the House's side—

Of course, the gentlemen of the subcommittee of the last Committee on Banking and Currency do feel that they covered the ground pretty thoroughly in their own hearings; and they also sent out questionnaires such as the Senators sent out, and got very voluminous answers, I dare say more voluminous than any prudent person would ever care to read. It greatly increases the sale of paper.

Mr. President, does one of the bills before you provide for the regulation of stock exchanges?

No, sir.

That is to be one of the fundamentals of Mr. Henry's bill.

Oh!

Mr. President, that reminded me of one of the other questions asked: a Republican Senator said that there are a number of Republican Senators who would like to vote for a sound currency bill, and they thought they would make some effort, if it was possible, to see the bill or know what was going into it before it has the stamp of approval of the administration, and I wondered if any advances like that have been made.

No, sir; not yet.

I know one man, probably the same as Mr. Matthews,[9] who is I think a little anxious to support the bill, but he feels that, before he supports the bill, he ought to have an opportunity to offer objections and criticisms.

Well, he would naturally have that through the committee to which it would be referred. Of course, it ought to undergo the freest criticism after it is submitted.

Mr. President, you say you have before you the drafts of three bills with the suggestion that you make one bill out of them. Have you determined what course you are going to pursue in getting up a bill?

No, I have not, because, frankly, I do not feel competent, myself, to draft the details of it. I will have to make up my mind which of the details are best to retain and then put it in somebody else's hand to draft it.

That would naturally be the Secretary of the Treasury?

Very naturally, yes, sir.

[1] Wilson had, in fact, asked Hale to go to Mexico City to investigate and report. See Link, *The New Freedom*, p. 354, and Larry D. Hill, *Emissaries to a Revolution: Woodrow Wilson's Executive Agents in Mexico* (Baton Rouge, La., 1973), pp. 21-39.

[2] Following Wilson's statement about lobbyists, Senator Albert Baird Cummins, Republican of Iowa, offered a resolution to establish a select committee to investigate the lobby and to take testimony from Senators and the President. The attempt to embarrass Wilson failed, and an investigation was conducted. See Link, *The New Freedom*, pp. 189-90.

[3] Senator John Wingate Weeks, Republican of Massachusetts. On May 29, 1913, Weeks

introduced a resolution calling for the registration of all lobbyists and requiring them to list the industries in which they were interested. See the *Washington Post*, May 30, 1913.

[4] Wilson favored a measure proposed by Senator Lawrence Yates Sherman, Republican of Illinois, to create a national preferential primary for President. For comment, see *ibid.*, May 24, 1913.

[5] The executive committee of the Japanese opposition party attacked the government because it was not settling the California controversy properly. See the *Washington Post*, May 29, 1913.

[6] The Glass bill and bills prepared by Owen and Secretary of the Treasury William Gibbs McAdoo. For a discussion of their differences, see Link, *The New Freedom*, pp. 206-10.

[7] On June 13, Representative Robert Lee Henry, Democrat of Texas, introduced a bill which postponed action on the Federal Reserve bill and called for a renewed investigation of the so-called Money Trust. See *ibid.*, pp. 218-19.

[8] Edward Leavitt Howe, president of the Princeton Bank and Trust Company.

[9] An unidentified journalist.

June 2, 1913

Mr. President, could you tell us something about the interview you have just had with Senator Overman?[1]

Why, Senator Overman and Senator Reed[2] were on the committee to investigate the lobby and came up to see if I had any suggestions to make, and I made a few.

Would you mind telling us what those suggestions are?

Well, I daresay they will come out in the investigation.

Are you going before the committee, Mr. President?

Oh, no. I don't expect to. They haven't asked me to, at least.

Did they indicate that you would be?

No, they didn't.

Has it been brought to your attention, Mr. President, that there is, in addition to the protection lobby, a free-trade lobby in Washington?

I have heard that intimated, yes. I haven't seen any very great indications of it.

Is it your desire that they should be investigated as well as the protection lobby?

Well, that might extend to me because I am trying to have a reduction of duties.

What I particularly refer to is the wholesale clothiers' association and their lobby that is down here, as I understand it, to bring about free linens, and there are several such—

Well, so far as I am concerned, I want the whole thing investigated, no matter what it brings out.

Would you care to say, Mr. President, whether you have given or suggested any names?

Well, perhaps they will appear. I can't say anything further than that.

What about the progress on the currency bill, Mr. President?

Why, I am ashamed to say last week I took a vacation for ten days and I haven't heard anything about it.

There is nothing to be expected in the next few days?

It will depend on how many evenings I have the determination to work on it.

With reference to the lobbying act, Mr. President, do you also feel that this might cause some delay in the tariff settlement?

I assume not. I wouldn't expect it to.

Is there anything this morning on the California situation?

No. I see by the papers that it is reported that a note from the Japanese government is ready. We haven't received it.[3]

Have you received any intimation?

No, I haven't. It is possible, since I have communicated with the State Department, that they may have.

Mr. President, this question may have been asked of you the last time. I haven't heard the answer to it. Is it true that William Bayard Hale is in Mexico with some communication from you?

It is true that William Bayard Hale is in Mexico, and I know only that these are the facts as I know them. Before he left, I told him I would be glad to know anything he knew, but I said to you later that—[4]

Then there is a similar statement made with reference to Professor Ford earlier, at Princeton.[5]

Mrs. Ford[6] was in Washington on Saturday and came to see me and she said she had been questioned about things of that sort. As a matter of fact, Ford is going around the world and his son,[7] who is with him, was for some time an officer in the Philippines. They stopped there for a week or two. That's the thinking here on that.

There is no commission from you of any kind.

No.

Have you made up your mind, Mr. President, concerning the Philippine problem?

How do you mean "made up my mind?"

There has been a dispatch published in the last week saying that you had decided on a plan.

No, that is not true. Of course, we want to find the best plan to do what the Democratic platform says.[8]

But you have not found one?

I haven't had an opportunity to discuss one recently within the last month.

Then the matter of the personnel of the Philippine Commission is just where it stood before.
How about the industrial commission, Mr. President?[9]

Well, I have failed to get—I just hope you won't repeat it because it would reflect on whoever is chosen—I have found difficulty in getting the man I wanted for chairman. I ask you not to repeat that, simply because the man I do choose would be regarded as a second choice and it would reflect unjustly on him; but that is what is causing the delay.

Will the nomination go in this week?

If I can fix it in my mind. Yes.

I notice, Mr. President, that the confirmation of the Director of the Census is postponed, at any rate. Is there anything special to ask about that? There is no disposition on their part to hold it up?

No, I haven't heard that.

I simply thought it had not been confirmed. I thought there might be a reason that had not been indicated.

No.

Mr. President, is there any official significance [blank] in the Philippines?

No, none whatever. I didn't know he[10] had returned.

Have you determined your course with reference to the Civil Service Commission?

Well, of course, this investigation, which I assume will take place, is proposed in the civil service to meet the problem.

Is there anything new about that Boston Collector, Mr. President?

The Boston Collector?

Yes.

No there isn't. Mr. Russell[11] seems to feel that he can't accept, but that is just where it stands at present.

Will you withdraw the nomination?

Well, of course, if Mr. Russell really can't accept, then I will have to, with the greatest regret.

May I ask, have you given up hope of persuading him to accept?

No, I haven't entirely given up hope.

You are communicating with him?

I am going to try to communicate with him today.

Mr. President, once in a while you have very good questions that you suggest that we ask—

Well, I haven't [any now.] I have been on vacation a few days. I think my mind is suffering from the consequences of the vacation.

Some of the additional things we have had, Mr. President, were oversights on our part.
Mr. President, do you think you will continue to vacation this afternoon?

I am afraid not. I wish I could.

Have you decided anything, Mr. President, on the Panama situation?[12]

No, nothing has been decided on, on that.

Is there a man named Mr. Nesbit being considered for Comptroller of the Currency?[13]

Not that I know of.

Have you made any progress in selecting an Ambassador for Mexico?

I think I have, sir. I have been working on the diplomatic list, but I would rather give it all out at once.

Is that likely to come today?

No, not today.

Your attitude toward Consuls General in the civil service, have you determined that?[14]

It is not clear to me, from what I learn from the State Department, what the policy of the department has been. You see, there are different kinds of Consuls General. Some of them are really diplomatic agents.

Five of them are diplomatic agents.

They naturally would be within the civil service.

They are always appointed by their diplomatic title. Consul has been the subsidiary title.

Yes.

Mr. President, if you include an Ambassador to Mexico in your list, will that mean recognition of Mexico?

Well, I did not think of that when the other question was asked. Of course it would. I won't designate an Ambassador until something of that sort—

Will that man go in with the rest of the diplomatic list?

No, sir.

Will you give us an approximate idea when your currency message will be ready, or when the bill will be introduced?

No, I cannot. As soon as possible.

Not likely this week.

I think not.

I understand, Mr. President, that the Collector of the Port of Portland, Maine, has decided not to resign, and there is some question as to whether he will have to be removed if somebody else is to be appointed.

Well, there will have to be a vacancy if anybody is to go in, that is clear.

I didn't know whether your policy would be to remove men if their commissions are not expired?

Well, my general policy is to leave men in office until their commissions expire.

Is the report that we have generally true, Mr. President, that Seth Carter[15] is to have that place?

That hasn't been determined. I hesitated because I was trying to recall the conversation I had had with the Secretary of the Treasury on that subject. We haven't discussed it in a long time.

He announced some time ago that he was to have that place.

Did he? Well, that refreshes my recollection. He has only the problem of one to remember. I have to try to remember all of them.

Mr. President, do you know if any federal agency is contemplating an investigation of the receivership of the 'Frisco Railroad?[16]

Not that I have been informed.

Could you tell us what, if anything, is holding up the Public Printer's appointment?

Why, the indecision of the President. You shouldn't ask me such embarrassing questions.

Are you naming a Solicitor General at this time for the next Supreme Court?

I don't know, sir.

Mr. President, is Mr. Morgenthau[17] of New York being considered for some position?

You wouldn't want to go into that ambitious list, would you?

[1] Senator Lee Slater Overman, Democrat of North Carolina.
[2] Senator James Alexander Reed, Democrat of Missouri. Senator Overman was chairman of the committee.
[3] Ambassador Chinda handed the note to Wilson on June 5, 1913.
[4] See above, May 29, 1913.
[5] Professor Henry Jones Ford of Princeton spent two months in the Philippines in the spring of 1913 as a confidential investigator for Wilson. For a summary of Ford's report, which he delivered to Wilson at the White House on September 5, 1913, see PWW, Vol. 28, pp. 242-45, n. 1. See also Grunder and Livezey, The Philippines and the United States, p. 150.
[6] Bertha Batory Jones.
[7] J. Howard Jones.
[8] See above, May 15, 1913.
[9] See above, May 26, 1913.
[10] Probably a reference to the Rt. Rev. Charles Henry Brent, Bishop of the Protestant Episcopal diocese of the Philippines, who was in Washington to see the President. See the Washington Post, June 3, 1913, and Charles Henry Brent to Edward Mandell House, Dec. 28, 1913, in PWW, Vol. 29, pp. 165-67.
[11] Joseph Ballister Russell, merchant and president of the Boston Wharf Co., nominated by Wilson on May 29. See the Washington Post, May 30, 1913.
[12] That is, regarding the Panama tolls controversy.
[13] Charles Francis Nesbit, an insurance agent of Washington, D.C.
[14] That is, whether Consuls General should be covered by civil-service regulations.
[15] Seth May Carter, a lawyer of Portland, Maine, and member of the Maine Governor's Council.
[16] The St. Louis and San Francisco Railroad Company had recently gone into receivership. See the Washington Post, May 28, 1913.
[17] Henry Morgenthau, chairman of the Finance Committee of the Democratic National Committee in the campaign of 1912.

June 5, 1913

Is there any intelligence with regard to the Japanese reply?[1]

No, nothing in particular. I have just read it this morning. The Japanese Ambassador is to call on me at four o'clock and is to make his oral additions or explanations. All I can say is that the note opens a way for very interesting and further negotiations.

Does it open a way for an immediate solution, or will it take some time?

Well, I can't judge about that. The issues [involved do not] make for a very rapid discussion. How long it will take to discuss it, I can't guess.

Mr. President, then are we warranted in inferring that it does not indicate that the impending meeting and a solution are inconsistent?

Not inconsistent.

Mr. President, I hear that you are going to talk with some lawyers in New York City, also in Washington, to take it up—the question of the courts as well as the law questions. Are you asking also some lawyers who are in New York City who are up on international law who will confer with you? Of course, I don't know who they are going to be. Is that apt to be a solution, Mr. President—in the courts?

Well, of course, sooner or later, the meaning of the law will have to be determined by the courts.

I mean, will Japan take it to the courts, or we?

Well, we wouldn't. There is no process that occurs to us now.[2]

I thought you might instruct the Attorney General to intervene?

No, no instructions have been given.

Mr. President, has there been a suggestion about arbitration?

No.

Mr. President, has there been any indication on the part of Japan whether she was willing, or willing to ask on her own, that the United States should take the matter into our courts?

No, no indication at all, sir.

Mr. President, what is the point at issue?

Why, I thought everybody knew that.

I do not, sir.

Why, the point at issue is the exclusion from ownership of agricultural land, at any rate in California, of those who are supposed not to be eligible to citizenship of the United States.

And what is the attitude of Japan on that subject?

Oh well, I can't go into the roots of that.

Mr. President, is there anything you can say about Attorney General McReynolds' plan with regard to the tobacco trust?[3]

I didn't know until I saw the papers that he had a plan.[4]

I take it he hasn't discussed that?

No.

The idea of reopening the case in the Supreme Court?

We haven't discussed it, sir.

That makes it a fair assumption, does it not, to say that the Stanley bill[5] is not an administration measure?

I do not know which Stanley bill. Is there a new one?

There is supposed to be a Stanley bill to be introduced in the House and to cover the Attorney General's plan.

Well, I hadn't heard anything of it. This is the first I have heard of it.

Mr. President, has the Attorney General reported on the Weather Bureau investigation?[6]

No, the investigation was not—oh, yes it was, by an officer instead. No, he has not, sir.

What is the status of the Panama Canal tolls question?

Just where we left it.

Standing still, is it?

Standing still at present.

Mr. President, is it not true that Mr. Metcalfe[7] is going to be Governor of the Canal Zone?

No, sir, not that I know of.

I saw he was going as a member of the commission.

Well, you mustn't believe what you hear someone tell you until you hear it announced.

Not what we hear announced except from authoritative sources. Mr. Metcalfe has announced he is going to be going. We question some of the things not announced beforehand. I thought Colonel Goethals might be the first Governor.

Well, you see, there is no contemplation of changing the character of the government.[8]

Mr. President, could you tell us anything about the status of the proposed currency bill? You told us before that you had three drafts of it.

I know. I am still working on them. McAdoo is a man I feel my own judgment buttresses on, and therefore I have to go slowly in the matter.

Is it work along the lines of amalgamating these three bills into one?

The bills, as a matter of fact, are very similar in most respects, and it is largely a question of which offers the better parts of the plan.

Mr. President, could you tell us what that main similarity is, the one central idea in the three bills?

I would rather not, Mr. Oulahan,[9] until I can put the thing out as a whole. Until it is a whole, the parts are more open to criticism than if they were amalgamated in the right plan.

Mr. President, yesterday, there was a great slump in the stock market, and indications are that perhaps that sort of thing might continue. One of the reasons given was the reports that the administration was going to endeavor to reopen cases against the Standard Oil and the tobacco trust. Now, it occurred to me that perhaps in view of that suspicion you would insist that Congress remain here, and then resume the currency law after the tariff bill was out of the way.

Well, I will certainly urge that, of course.

I knew you were going to urge that, but I was wondering whether you felt quite sure you could get them to put it in effect?

I see no reason to tell you that I can, but that is the sort of thing one might not be sure about because the debates are very long, because the questions get very repetitive. No summer session—

Well, I think there is plenty of time for the House to pass a currency bill before the Senate gets through with the other bill, but it would be a question of remaining here until up to the beginning of the regular session, and I wonder whether you would consider that, or consult with the leaders regarding it?

No, I haven't been up to that point. I have a very strong hope it won't last that long, that we will get word before—sooner or later.

You are going to remain here?

Yes, sir.

Or you would until the currency bill is out of the way?

Yes, sir. If I remain here for four years.

Does that mean, Mr. President, that you hope to get through with the tariff bill in a comparatively short time in the Senate?

Well, I think the situation in the Senate is entirely satisfactory. It is a question of how many speeches are made now.

Mr. President, it is suggested that you are persuaded that this stock-market flurry is caused by sinister influences and that you are going to suggest an investigation of Wall Street methods in that regard.

No, sir, that is entirely without foundation. I have all my life been so innocent that I have never known what flurries were founded on. That is something too dark for the lay mind.

The status of the industrial commission?[10]

Well, we haven't got anything because there isn't anything constituted yet, but I am trying to give them a constitution.

Can you volunteer any remarks on the lobby investigation?

No, sir. I think that speaks for itself.

Has there been any suggestion, Mr. President, that this lobby inquiry might be made retroactive and cover the stages of the bill in the House as well as the Senate?

No, sir, I haven't heard any.

Mr. President, did you furnish a list of names to the committee?

I did.

Are you willing to appear before the committee?

They haven't asked me to, and I always don't go where I am not invited.

If you were requested to go, Mr. President?

I don't know. I never cross a bridge until I get to it.

Mr. President, I wanted to inquire, sir, if you have received many letters from Republicans in favor of just as early an enactment of the tariff law as possible, so as to put an end to the uncertainty which it creates?

Well, perhaps Tumulty could answer that question better than I can. Not very many letters of that sort have been laid before me, though some very strong letters on other legislation have been laid before me.

The *Herald* this morning had dispatches from various parts of the country, showing a very keen desire for an early enactment of the bill.

I think, of course, we can all agree that it is very desirable that it should be enacted as early as possible.

Have you any idea—

No, I haven't, but I do feel reasonably assured that the leaders of the Senate will push it as fast as they can, and I think the Finance Committee will fix the time rapidly to report.

That desirability seems to be very strongly in their minds.

I think it is, very.

Can you add anything about the free-cattle and free-wheat situations?

No, sir.

Do you still think, Mr. President, that the bill should go into effect immediately after passage, as provided in the Underwood bill?

Still think so, as of an hour ago.

I think you said, Mr. President, once before, that you had that idea, and I know there has been some question about manufactured articles. For instance, people who stocked up with woolen cloth suggest that they be given a little time.

The question has been raised with some force of argument, chiefly if not only about textiles, because it is ordinary goods in which the stock is bought, but as a matter of fact, I haven't expressed an opinion about that.

Mr. President, do you get any evidence or any reports of a curtailment of credits by bankers which might be laid to the tariff bill?

No, I haven't heard any statements to that effect.

The reports, Mr. President, are pretty fairly persistent that the railroad situation is bad, and of course the evidence is in the receivership of the 'Frisco Railroad.[11] The reports are that other railroads are similarly going into receivership before failure and that industrial credit seems to be seriously curtailed.

I had heard that general statement, but I hadn't had any specific instances brought to my attention.

No representations of that situation have been made to you at all?

No, none at all.

Is it your desire to see the currency bill put through soon? [Has it been] changed by any sort of amendments?

No, it hasn't been at all.

Have you given any attention yet to the question of good roads—federal aid—at all?

No, sir, not at all.

Mr. President, is the question of federal control of water power coming up in any tangible shape as yet?

No, sir.

A very important decision about ten days ago in the Supreme Court.[12]

Yes, I noticed that. Administratively, it has not been brought up in any concrete instance.

It is not within the power of the Bureau of Foreign and Domestic Commerce, I take it, to make any investigation of this railroad situation.[13] That would be entirely in the hands of the Interstate Commerce Commission?

I daresay, but I hadn't scrutinized the terms of the law with reference to that. But that would be my offhand—

Could you say what the artificial curtailment by banks portends? Would that be subject to investigation by the Bureau of Foreign and Domestic Commerce?

It is an entirely new question to me, so I really have no opinion about it.

[1] The Japanese government replied on June 4 to Bryan's response to its protest note regarding the California land-tenure act. See the *New York Times,* June 5, 1913.

[2] The Japanese reply repudiated the suggestion that the Japanese government pursue the matter in American courts.

[3] McReynolds was attempting to take vengeance against the reorganized components of the American Tobacco Company, which had been dissolved by the Supreme Court in 1911. McReynolds proposed a graduated internal revenue tax which would injure the larger members of the "trust" and stimulate the development of small competitors. See Link, *The New Freedom,* p. 417.

[4] McReynolds had presented the plan to the cabinet on June 3. See the *New York Times,* June 4, 1913.

[5] A measure embodying this plan was prepared by Representative Augustus Owsley Stanley, Democrat of Kentucky. It was sponsored by Senator Gilbert Monell Hitchcock, Democrat of Nebraska. See Link, *The New Freedom,* p. 418.

[6] See above, April 21, 1913.

[7] Richard Lee Metcalfe of Nebraska, associate editor of *The Commoner,* Bryan's monthly magazine.

[8] The government was changed, in accordance with a congressional mandate, in 1914, after the canal was completed. Goethals did become the first Governor of the Panama Canal Zone. See the *New York Times,* June 4, 1913, and David G. McCullough, *The Path Between the Seas* (New York, 1977), p. 608.

[9] Richard Victor Oulahan, Washington correspondent for the *New York Times.*

[10] See above, May 26, 1913.

[11] In general, railroad stocks were doing very poorly on Wall Street at this time. See the *New York Times,* June 2 and 5, 1913; and the *Washington Post,* May 28, 1913.

[12] It is impossible in this context to know to which of several cases the reporter might have been referring.

[13] The Bureau of Foreign and Domestic Commerce of the Department of Commerce was empowered to make investigations into matters pertaining to trade when requested to do so by the President or either house of Congress.

June 9, 1913

Mr. President, is the lobby investigation having the beneficial effect you expected it to have?

That is a very interesting question. I think it is having a very beneficial effect, sir.

Would you care to say, incidentally, what the results will be?

Oh, no. I can't predict what the results will be.

What do you think it has done so far?

Well, I really think that these are questions which you gentlemen can answer better than I can. You see, I wouldn't have a chance to see more than a small percentage of the things that are published about that, and that is one of the ways one could tell the effect of the thing.

I thought perhaps you had noticed some effects with regard to the Senators themselves, in your talks with them?

No, sir. My hope was to relieve those who were trying to do business in Washington of a great burden. I think it is going to do that presently—in time.

Have you received any invitation yet, Mr. President, to go before the committee?

No.

Mr. President, have you had any conferences with anybody on this question of compensatory duties that was in the dispatches?[1]

No, none at all.

Are you willing to make any comment on that?

No, because this is the first I have heard of it, in this morning's papers.

Mr. President, would such a policy of compensatory duties be consistent with the Democratic platform?[2]

Well, I haven't read the Democratic platform in the last two or three days.

Which says no duties except for purposes of revenue.

Well, reciprocity has always been an acceptable doctrine when it could be accomplished without involving extreme protectionist views.

But how would the consumer benefit from reciprocity?

The theory would be that the hand of the other government, whichever it might be, would be forced in the game, and the consumer would benefit from that result. That is the theory of it. Whether it works or not is another question. The object of course of such provisions is to get lower rates, but there is always a question whether it will work or not.

Mr. President, is there anything on currency?

No, sir. One thing is that there are two days of holiday back of me. Nothing has happened.

Mr. President, have you had any conference with Mr. Brown[3] about this West Virginia situation?[4]

No, I haven't had any conference with him.

You are not willing to say what you think of the matter?

I am really not sufficiently informed to be entitled to an opinion— I mean, as to the new developments.

The new development is a new development so far as the administration is concerned?

Yes.

Getting down to the Senate, Mr. President, can you help us as to the Collector of the Port of Boston?

Well, since Mr. Russell declined the nomination, another name has been secured, so we are just a little better off than we were about it.

The name Charles Amory[5] has been mentioned very firmly.

I know it has been, but the Secretary of the Treasury was away during the latter half of last week.

You are awaiting recommendations from him?

I will await a conference with him.

Are there any developments in the Japanese situation, Mr. President?

None whatever.

Or with reference to Mexico?

No.

Is it true, Mr. President, that Mr. Lamb of Indiana is the man to be in charge?[6] Is that—

I am not announcing the appointment yet.

Has the framing of the reply to Japan begun yet?

I daresay it has. I am not entirely informed as to that.

You have had two days for a holiday, Mr. President. Couldn't you start us with a suggestion or two?

Well, I don't know anything to start you with. I haven't anything up my sleeve.

Monday morning is a good morning to start something.

Yes, it is. When everybody feels a fresh start, it would be "fresh" to start something.

Mr. President, referring again to the currency question, have you made up your own mind, in order to be assured under the new bill, whether to use United States Treasury notes or National bank notes?[7]

I don't know that mine is the mind to make up. That is a matter about which there has been a great deal of conference and about which there is a great deal of honest difference of opinion as to whether the notes should be absolutely secured or not or justified by moral character.

Have you arranged a conference with any of the members of the House banking committee?

Only the chairman, sir.

Mr. President, is there anything to say to us growing out of the testimony before the lobby committee of Senator Townsend[8] and the other Senators?

No, sir. Nothing whatever. I don't think that calls for any comment.

[1] A proposal for countervailing duties on agricultural products equal to those charged by another country against similar American commodities. See the *Washington Post*, June 9, 1913.

[2] That is, the Baltimore platform of 1912.

[3] Wrisley Brown, special Assistant Attorney in the Department of Justice.

[4] President John Philip White and eighteen other officers of the United Mine Workers were indicted for violating the Sherman Act in connection with a coal strike in West Virginia. It was being speculated that such prosecution might violate the provisions of the sundry civil appropriations bill then under consideration. See the *New York Times*, June 8-9, 1913.

[5] Charles Walter Amory, Boston financier.

[6] Former Representative John Edward Lamb, Democrat of Terre Haute, Indiana, was reported to be under consideration for the post of Ambassador to Mexico. See the *Washington Post*, June 9, 1913.

[7] That is, whether the Treasury should issue all currency or permit National banks to issue a share. Secretary McAdoo was reported to oppose bank notes. See *ibid.*, June 9, 1913.

[8] Senator Charles Elroy Townsend, Republican of Michigan, charged on June 6 that the closest thing to lobbying that he had seen was Wilson's threat to withhold patronage to keep Democrats in line. See the *New York Times*, June 7, 1913.

June 12, 1913

Mr. President, there are rumors of a disagreement between you and the Attorney General. Is there anything in it?

Why, ridiculous.[1]

Would you care to make any explanation in addition to what the Secretary of the Treasury just said with reference to the five-hundred-million-dollar amount of money that he is ready to distribute?[2]

Well, he is not ready to distribute any money.

He says that he has his independence—

No, I think you must have misunderstood him. Those are mere dated notes, so far as that is concerned. They are merely printed notes which may be issued under the emergency currency act,[3] if an association of banks is formed and offers certain securities.

What is the purpose of his announcement, do you know?

It has nothing to do with this particular thing. He has simply been asked by a number of banks what the facts of the law were and what would be his policy in the matter. You see, there is a certain discretion lodged with the Secretary, under the act. His was a mere statement in response to an inquiry.

I understood he made it public, however. Why would he make it public? I wonder if it had any connection with conditions throughout the country?[4]

No. I don't know why he made it, but I knew he had it in contemplation.

Mr. President, isn't it a fact that the Aldrich-Vreeland currency law makes provision for the formation of an association in each state,[5] and isn't it a fact that the City of Washington has the only currency association that has been formed of that kind?

I can't answer that. I don't know.

That is my recollection.

I understood that there were numerous—

That's the first step toward making use of that five hundred million in the act.

Yes, that is the first preparatory step.

Isn't that currency subject to a tax?

Unless it is used for emergency purposes. I must say I don't remember the terms.[6]

It is an emergency act.

Yes it is—a mere emergency act.

It has one year to run.

Yes, one year more to run.[7]

It depends on the New York banks themselves. If they want it, they have got to form this association first.

But the inquiries, as I understand it, come from numerous centers—several centers—not only from New York.

My recollection is that the New York banks wouldn't go in because there was some question about a bank going in which could not get out because of the big banks. The proposition was that all the banks were to go in on an equal footing, no matter what their capital, and the big banks didn't want to come in. Have there been a sufficient number of inquiries to cause you to believe that there is any uniform opinion among the bankers?

These inquiries have been spread over a period of time. It has nothing to do with any distribution.

Mr. President, a group of Louisiana men, on the stand before the lobby committee yesterday, testified that they had assurances that sugar would not go on the free list. They left the inference that the assurance is directly traceable to the President.[8]

You notice they didn't say so at all.

No, but they left the inference very definitely, I thought. Does that—

I'll tell you a story. There was an old politician in New York who gave this advice to his son, and I hope you will ascribe the language to him and not to me. He said, "John, don't bother your head about liars. It will give you many ulcers. When there are many, don't bother to deny anything. It will only make up their minds that it is so." That is just a story. There is one special application to it.

But you are not denying this inference?

I am not denying the *inference* by my failure to deny.

Mr. President, have you considered the possibility of establishing the civil government of the Panama Canal Zone before the canal is completed?

No, not for the moment, sir.

Is there anything new with reference to currency, Mr. President?

No, there isn't, not yet.

Have you discussed with the members of the committee the question of open hearings?

No, they haven't asked anything of me.

You have no idea, Mr. President, when your message will be ready for Congress?

No, I haven't, simply because we are still working on the draft of the bill.

Have you any news from the Senate, Mr. President, with regard to the probability or possibility of passing a currency bill at this session through the Senate?

No. I know only this, that a fair number of Senators have volunteered the opinion, and the committee wrote to us [expressing] the general hope that it should be passed by this Senate.

But did they say—they did not say as to whether or not it was probable that it could be passed?

No, but they didn't express any doubt on the subject.

Mr. President, the Banking and Currency Committee of the Senate yesterday—I mean, it was stated then by several Senators—that a very heavy majority of that committee didn't think it wise to attempt currency legislation at this time.[9]

That hasn't reached me. I don't know it yet. Not because I doubt your statement. I am not officially informed.

It is not my statement, sir. It is a statement of the Senators. Could you indicate what general lines this currency bill is going to take?

It won't follow any general line. It will follow a genuine line.

Who is going to issue the money—the government?

I have already said I didn't care to indicate it in general terms.

Is there anything on the recognition of Mexico?

No, sir.

Mr. President, I understand there has been a sort of suspicious statement in the *Mexican Herald* on this question.[10] Have you got any points on that?

No, I haven't, because there has been no intervention of that kind.

You know nothing about it at all?

I know that statement appeared in the papers. That is all I know of it.

Wouldn't you care to express your views on currency? There is great interest in that.

No, sir. I have a certain number of opinions but they don't sweep the whole horizon.

Have you given any attention to the West Virginia situation?

No special attention. Of course I have been informed on what has been going on, so far as I could, from the papers.

Are you willing, Mr. President, to say anything about Mr. McReynolds' tobacco trust tax plan?[11]

He didn't have any plan that I know of.

I have been misinformed.

Yes, you certainly have.

Well, can we understand from that that there is no such plan?

There is none that I know anything about.

He hasn't made the suggestion that a graduated excise tax be imposed on tobacco products?

No, that suggestion was made and discussed for about, I suppose, three minutes, but there has been no plan of any kind.

Somebody has been mighty misleading in the last two weeks.

Yes, I have noticed that, but we are not responsible for that.

Mr. President, wasn't there some sort of agreement, understanding, that Mr. McReynolds should discuss this matter with Senator Simmons?

There was an understanding that he could discuss it with whom he pleased, yes, but he didn't propose it as a plan; and it was thrown out only as a suggestion, to be discussed by anybody that was interested in it.

You are not willing to discuss it, then, as a suggestion?

No. As I say, I have devoted about three minutes to the suggestion since it was made.

Are you going to Cornish on the twenty-ninth?

It is my present hope that I may accompany my family there and come right back.

Does that include the Fourth if you want to [stay]?

I don't know. It would depend entirely.

Mr. President, is there anything you can say at this time as to the present negotiation with Japan?

Well, it's making progress in the only sense in which it could, that is to say, the State Department has in hand the formulations of the matter that we want to lay before the Japanese government. I don't know whether there has been any further development in the past few days. No, none at all that would create a more hopeful situation. The situation has been hopeful all along. I mean there hasn't been anything to cause anxiety about it.

Mr. President, will you say anything about that sundry civil bill and the reports that have been published?[12]

No, sir, I haven't had anything to do with it one way or the other. I haven't even been consulted about it.

[1] On June 11, the *New York Times* printed a rumor that Attorney General McReynolds was considering resigning. See also the New York *American*, June 13, 1913.

[2] On June 11, McAdoo announced that he was prepared to issue, if necessary, the $500,000,000 in short-term National bank notes authorized by the Aldrich-Vreeland Act of 1908. The currency would be issued to national currency associations, formed by National banks, against United States bonds and high-grade securities. See the *New York Times*, June 12, 1913, and Link, *The New Freedom*, p. 115.

[3] The Aldrich-Vreeland Act.

[4] That is, the business recession.

[5] The act required that the additional currency be requested either by a National bank or by a currency association.

[6] The rate was 5 per cent the first month and 1 per cent for each month thereafter.

[7] The Aldrich-Vreeland Act was due to expire in June 1914.

[8] The charge was made by Senator-elect Robert Foligny Broussard, Democrat of Louisiana, and supported by Jules Godchaux, a lobbyist of the sugar growers.

[9] Democratic members of the committee predicted that currency legislation could take months to be enacted. See the *Washington Post*, June 12, 1913.

[10] Paul Hudson, editor of the *Mexican Herald* of Mexico City, published a statement on June 12 calling for recognition of the Huerta administration and claiming that intervention was the only alternative. See the *Washington Post*, June 13, 1913.

[11] See above, June 5, 1913.

[12] That is, whether Wilson would veto the bill with the amendment.

## June 16, 1913

Mr. President, we ask the absorbing question of currency legislation. The particular thought that I have in mind this morning is, can you explain to us the difference between the two lines of procedure that seem to be indicated, or rather the two lines of differences as to the issue, or proposed issue of the money, the currency—the one that the Treasury controls and the other that the banks control? Now what is the difference, in general principle, between Treasury control and bank control?[1]

Well, you will have to go to the experts to have that explained. I really don't feel competent to explain it. I have never been a banker. I have never had large transactions at banks, so that the technique of it is something I would rather leave in other hands.

That leads me to speak of the way in which we have tried to get at this thing. I don't want the impression to prevail for a moment that I have presumed to know enough to assume the authority of formulating a bill. I have been going over it to form my judgment about it as well as I could from the suggestions that were submitted to me by persons very much more competent than I am to determine the details.

And, about the details, I have had very little opinion of my own. About the main lines, I have had a considerable opinion. I think the result will be proposals that are really and genuinely the result of common counsel. No man's bill.

Mr. President, that comes back to the question of Mr. Donald Craig[2] about the main lines. There is a good deal of desire to know, and it may be that you would be willing to say what those main lines were?

The bill, I hope, will be so constructed that it will clear itself up. It is so much better to have it in definite language than in general language in which I might inadvertently mislead.

I might ask, then, this question, whether a bill which is reported substantially agreed upon follows those—I mean, agreed upon, perhaps, not with yours— whether it follows those main lines that you had in mind?

I think so, so far as I am informed of it, it does.

Mr. President, can you tell us what gentlemen are in agreement on that bill, for example, that represent your views and those of Mr. Owen and Mr. Glass?

Oh, Mr. Owen and Mr. Glass! Why I think I can say with entire truth that there is no longer any essential variation of their views.

So there will be really only one bill?

That is what I understand, yes.

The *New York Times* gives something of what purports to be the substance of the bill and the administration's program on currency legislation.

I haven't seen it. I was told, since I reached the office. I haven't read it.

Have you reason to hope for anything in the way of general assurances that there is going to be harmony on the currency?

Well, the currency is a matter about which you are bound to get perfectly genuine differences of opinion. If by harmony, you mean harmony of purpose, I am sure there will be harmony of purpose. Whether there will be entire agreement of opinion is another matter. There is no use mincing words. I have in mind all these reports that are flying about, of a great difference of opinion, irreconcilable differences. I don't take any stock in them myself. I don't take any notice because the information that reaches me doesn't support that at all.

Do you still lack direct information, Mr. President, that there will be a very sizable opposition to this currency bill?

I have enough information. Several gentlemen have said, with perfect frankness, that they oppose it, that it would not be necessary to take the matter up this session. It is not a question of whether you are opposed to the currency law. It is merely a question of whether we can undertake it at this stage and whether we can stick it out.

One of the papers this morning intimates that Mr. Bryan has taken a position against the bill.[3]

That is not true.

Is Mr. Bryan a factor in the making of the bill?

I don't know that he is. I have, of course, discussed the matter with him, but since our general discussion of it, I don't know of any part that he has played in it.

Well, if it is a fair question—I mean, it would be to take an active interest?

I don't know that he has, so far as I know.

Has it been called to your attention that Mr. Henry[4] is opposed to the bill?

I saw the speech, of course, that Mr. Henry made, demanding a full investigation of the Money Trust. Much of that speech could be interpreted as opposition, but I haven't heard anything further than that.

It might be, Mr. President, that Mr. Henry has not seen the bill yet.

I don't think he has.

Has your message been completed?

Yes, sir. That is to say, the first draft of it. I always have to put it in safekeeping a day or two, to see if it suits me.

When do you expect to send it before Congress?[5]

I will await information as to when the committees are ready. I will read it in person.

Is it your understanding that what is known as the Glass bill is actually completed?

No, that is not my information. There isn't going to be any Glass bill or Owen bill,[6] because these two bills are in conference, you see.

Well, is it a bill that may have been drawn up together? Is that bill completed?

Not entirely. I understand it will be, very shortly indeed.

Do you expect it to be introduced in the House tomorrow?

I don't know as to the exact time, but from what I learned, this week, at any rate.

Will it go to the committees, so far as you know, Mr. President, or will it be introduced in the House before it goes to the committees?

It will be naturally introduced first and then referred to the committees.

I mean, will it go to the committees for confidential information a day or two before?

I don't know whether the parliamentary procedure will be to introduce it first.

The introduction of the bill will precede the receiving of the message?

I don't know. I want to take the advice of the chairmen of the committees.

If you allow the press associations to use it in time to get it circulated, the bill that is introduced would naturally follow.

Well, I wasn't going to, where you might—simply because I have been challenged in the press.

Surely, Mr. President, we will have twenty-four hours on it?

You violated one confidence, in saying that Mr. Reed is responsible. You have had intimations as to what to expect in conference. I don't know. I will ask you not to speak further for the present because I haven't consulted Senator Kern and Mr. Underwood as to the convening of the houses, which I would wish to do in courtesy before I make that announcement.

Mr. President, are the opponents to consideration of the currency question at this time of sufficient importance to consider them an obstacle?

I don't think they will be, no sir.

You are still hoping, Mr. President, to take action this session?

Very hopeful.

Mr. President, do you have before you the sundry civil bill?[7]

It hasn't reached me.

So you don't care to say anything at this time?

I think not at this time.

Mr. President, while I can withdraw my question, I wonder whether you wouldn't accommodate us, perhaps, as that is the only piece of news we have had this week?[8]

Well now, I tell you, gentlemen, frankly, I think the courtesies of the procedure are really the essence of it. I don't want—

It was printed at some length yesterday morning.

I think it was printed from the office—

Not from this office.

Well, that, of course, is a valid presumption, but I don't want that to violate the courtesy.

Mr. President, I would like to try to make it a little easier to get this information on the currency business. We have booted it along to try to get some explanation of the thing, and I confess that I am utterly at sea and utterly ignorant to know what to say on currency. Any suggestions or lines that you can give us for public explanation would be very welcome.

Well now, I appreciate the embarrassment, and I am afraid you feel that there has been some hide and seek.

Not at all.

There hasn't been. What I have been trying to do, gentlemen, is this. I want you to know just why I handle the thing as I have handled it. When we came to Washington for this session, the Democratic party was practically unanimous as to what should be done about the tariff, not as to details, of course, but as to its revision, and its immediate revision. That was plain sailing. But the currency is a matter about which no party that I know of is of a single opinion. We had, therefore, to begin. As I think I told you gentlemen, we did begin to talk to each other very freely in all directions about the currency. Now, of course, all sorts of opinions and variations of opinion have been playing upon this thing, and we will slowly eliminate the differences of opinion—honest differences of opinion—and get down to a single plan. Now that plan never has yet been so specifically formulated as to be worth the consideration of the business community, because the business community is interested very much more in exactly how you are going into this thing than in the general thing, how you are going to trade than the machinery—the process for real, the essence of doing business. That bill will probably, from my present information, that is to say, this result of the final agreements of opinions among those who have been working hardest on them will probably be formulated within twenty-four or forty-eight hours. That is my information this morning, that being the process—that being the process of crystallization. The crystal is not yet formed.

That has been my embarrassment all along because I know there are lawyers out on the street who won't be satisfied and won't approve of the final agreement, and all this time we have been coming together and are, I believe, so far as my judgment guides me, on sound ground, except though, with several variations as to method.

That is the whole thing. That is what has made it impossible to make a statement. I sincerely hope that this apparent failure will be remedied very soon.

Mr. President, do you hope and expect an identical bill will be introduced in both branches?

I shouldn't be surprised, although I can't state that with certainty.

Mr. President, that currency legislation, shall it be party legislation or non-partisan legislation?

Although it hasn't been raised, I have of course been working entirely with my Democratic colleagues on the Hill, but I state sincerely that we will have a very considerable amount of agreement on the other side of the aisle.

Have you determined, Mr. President, on any basic principles of that bill?

Oh, yes, we are working on the basic principles now.

Could you state any now?

No. Well, again, the embarrassment is that it should not be judged by the clothes it wears.

Let's hope it isn't hobble skirts.

No, sir, it won't be hobble skirts.

Have you had any conference with Mr. La Follette[9] about currency?

No, I have not personally. I think Mr. Glass at noontime had a talk with him about it. That is my impression.

Mr. President, sometime ago, some of the Republican Senators, some on the Banking and Currency Committee, said they would welcome an opportunity to vote for some currency bill, but they would like to see it before it becomes the final administration bill. Have there been any advances of that kind made to you?

No, but I daresay that will be done.

What about the Japanese situation, Mr. President?

That is in status quo.

Do you intend to discuss that with Mr. Guthrie?[10]

No. I wrote Mr. Guthrie. I am still—

He is here to pay his respects.

No, he has a discussion with Secretary Bryan on Wednesday.

Has the Doctor Müller[11] visit any possible relation with regard to Brazil, our relations there?

Our relations are entirely satisfactory already. There is nothing pending between the governments that is even the subject of discussion.

The sealing trade[12] annoys the Brazilian government.

But the government has nothing to do with that.

With reference to the Japanese situation. The New York papers this morning state on high authority that, in the Japanese note to the American government, they note that the contents of it were being kept secret because there is a very strong tone of irritation that might tend to inflame both countries if the truth were known.

That is absolutely not true. No, there is no tone of irritation whatever.

Have you received any final decision from Mr. McCombs with regard to the embassy business?[13]

I am supposed to get one, but there has been no reply.

Mr. President, are you receiving any communications from the businessmen of the North regarding the desirability and urgency of Congress [with regard to the enactment of the tariff bill]?

Yes, I am.

I understand that there is a very great hue and cry.

There is a very general desire that it should be put through very promptly. That is coming from all quarters.

What can you say, Mr. President, with regard to similar [feeling about] currency legislation?

That is only less pronounced. The thing has not been merged. I expect they will wait to see what it is going to be like. I think a large number of bankers urge the immediate necessity of it.

I wonder whether you wouldn't say anything about the source of this thing? There's a story that it's all from the banking sources.

I can't analyze it because many of them are writing to me. I don't know them all, but they are merchants as well as bankers and general businessmen.

It will never be from the banks.

No. I have had very few replies from the banks.

Mr. President, in announcing the other day something about an insidious lobby, did you have in mind any lobby on currency?

No. I wasn't thinking of that at that time. I never—I mean at the time that this lobby was making any headway. I wanted to get rid of it as an infernal nuisance.

May we infer that you would not like to legalize the lobby by registration?

Unless legalizing it minimizes it.

They legalize it in Massachusetts.

Is it very truthful up there?

Pretty near.
Mr. President, do you believe that the arbitration treaties are in danger in the Senate?[14]

No, I don't.

Mr. President, it is announced in the morning papers that you are going to a bankers' social tomorrow.[15] Are you going?

No, sir.

[1] For a discussion of this issue, see the *New York Times*, June 16, 1913.

[2] Donald Alexander Craig of the New York *Herald* Press Service.

[3] About Bryan's opposition to some features of the proposed bill, see Link, *The New Freedom*, pp. 206-207.

[4] Representative Henry, chairman of the House Rules Committee and a close friend of Bryan, criticized the power of bankers in a speech on June 14. See the *New York Times*, June 15, 1913, and *Cong. Record*, 62d Cong., 1st sess., pp. 2049-53.

[5] Wilson addressed a joint session of Congress on June 23. His speech is printed in *PWW*, Vol. 27, pp. 570-73.

[6] A reference to the reported splintering of administration forces on the issue of currency reform.

[7] The Senate approved the sundry civil bill and sent it to Wilson on June 13. See the *Washington Post*, June 14, 1913.

[8] The reporter is returning to the subject of currency legislation.

[9] Senator Robert Marion La Follette, Republican of Wisconsin.

[10] George Wilkins Guthrie, newly appointed Ambassador to Japan.

[11] Dr. Lauro Müller, Brazil's Minister for Foreign Affairs, was then visiting the United States. See the *Washington Post*, June 12, 1913.

[12] A reference to the controversy over pelagic sealing, restricted in the North Atlantic after 1911.

[13] Wilson had offered the post of Ambassador to France to William Frank McCombs, chairman of the Democratic National Committee. See the *New York Times*, June 17, 1913.

[14] Senator Chamberlain objected to the treaty with England and demanded that the question of Panama Canal tolls should be removed from all threat of arbitration. See *ibid.*, June 15, 1913.

[15] The Washington Bankers' Association met on June 16, at the New Willard Hotel. See the *Washington Post*, June 17, 1913.


June 19, 1913

Mr. President, can you tell us anything about the Mexican situation, whether there has been any change? I ask that question because there has been a delegation here of men who represent big interests in Mexico.[1]

Well, I didn't see that delegation. So far as I know, there is nothing new in the situation. I merely state what was contained in the local papers this morning. Mr. Bryan hasn't mentioned their visit to me, so I don't know whether it had any significance or not.

There was a statement printed some days ago, Mr. President, that the new Ambassador would not be appointed until next October.

Oh, there's no authority for any statement about the matter. We are waiting.

Have you settled when you think you are going to deliver your message to Congress?

Well, the hour between them is noon. The hour will be at the convenience of the two houses. I haven't yet heard.

Mr. President, a bill will be introduced and proposed following your reading of the message?

I suppose so, although I am not controlling that.

Will you reach the sundry civil bill soon, Mr. President?

Well, I am wading through it now, but it is a long bill to examine.

Mr. President, would you care to say what action you are going to take with regard to that clause?[2]

No, I wouldn't, but I'll make a statement when I do take it.

It is a long bill to examine, Mr. President, but there is just one little provision there that you are interested in, and we have no doubt but what everything else is all right.

Mr. President, with reference to currency, I understand there has been a little polling of the Senate committee. Do you know how many Republicans are willing to stand behind the administration?

I hadn't heard of any poll. I had heard Senator Owen state they had learned something.

He asked for support of the administration, and some Republicans in the House expressed themselves that way.

I didn't know about that. Neither chairman has mentioned any-thing of that sort to me because our conferences have been entirely about the contents of the bill and not about the attitude toward it.

Would you send for the Republican members, or will they come here?

I don't know, I am sure.

You have made no special arrangements to see them?

No.

Do you still expect to get action in both houses on currency this session?

Yes, sir. I really say that with a good deal of confidence. Of course I am being absolutely confident but I see nothing, anything, that lessens my confidence.

If the Republicans show a disposition to delay the tariff bill so as to also delay the consideration of the currency bill, would you adopt the move of holding them right to it here?

If they do.

If they do?

I never discuss that.

Well, it has been assumed with pretty good authority that some Republicans, if they think the currency bill is going to get final consideration, or is likely to, at this session, will delay the tariff if possible and run the extra session into the regular session. Are you prepared to have that thing happen?

I will wait and see what happens.

Mr. President, can you tell us something about your talk today with these Japanese businessmen who were here?[3]

The visit was entirely of a complimentary nature. We didn't take up any points of controversy at all. They expressed themselves as very well satisfied at the time and gratified by the attitude that they found their countrymen to share in this country; and also I found the visit a very reassuring one, not as against trouble but as against bad feeling.

Did they say anything about the settlement of the California question?

No, they didn't, except to say that they expressed their gratification everywhere they had been received.

Did they give you any ideas, or anything new to you, about their concerns or feelings?

No, I didn't feel it wise to take that up unless they did, and they didn't.

As to the industrial commission, Mr. President.[4]

I have been delayed in that by an unusual cause. Several persons whom I had wished to have serve have declined; and, therefore, each time I have thought my list was complete, it turned out not to be complete. And I don't like to say much about that because that would imply that those who were finally appointed were second or third choices. But this explanation is for your help, as it really explains.

None of the declinings are the Illinois candidates—the Illinois men?

No, I haven't received any declination from Illinois yet.

Are there very many candidates?

No—well as many as there were last year. It is a big union.

Is there anybody from New England there?

I believe not.

From either the South or near the South?

No, I believe not.

Have you any hope for getting commissioners very soon?

I hope that I will have it in. I think the Senate meets again on Saturday.

You didn't mean that all the people had declined?

I simply meant that the list was incomplete. It is formulated. Men drop out just as you expect to send them in.

I had heard that about six of them had accepted.
You won't send in the list until you have nailed it down?

No. I don't think it's wise.

Mr. President, have you received any note from Mr. McCombs since the last cable you sent him?[5]

The matter is still open.

Mr. President, can you tell us if you have reached any decision regarding the dissolution of the Southern Pacific?[6]

No, we haven't. Mr. McReynolds has just come back and told us of the settlements which were being proposed, and we want to have an exchange of views about them. He himself has not come to any judgment about them.

Mr. President, you know the lobby committee has taken up the matter of investigating the Hamlin statements?[7]

So I saw.

Could you shed any light on that?

No. I had no information about that, so that is a lead that I didn't know about.

Do you have anything to say about the sensational revelations of the lobby investigation in the last day or two?

I think the speakers will speak for themselves, if they are determined to speak.

Would you say whether you anticipated any of these things that have been brought out?

No, not all the ramifications of them. I knew where they would lead in the general direction.

Can you tell us, Mr. President, in the original lobby statement you made some suggestions to the committee that they would be followed and that they would appear during the investigation. Some of them apparently have appeared. Has anything directly emanated from the White House? I wonder if there are still some explanations to come?

Because they don't ordinarily appear, I have done what I could to let them know what I thought—I mean, what I thought was discoverable. But there is nothing rigged about it. When you think of it, everybody knew that these things were going on, although they didn't know exactly how they were going on. What is being uncovered is the meat [of the matter], that is, really the facts of the case. I am not an original explorer or discoverer.

Mr. President, is there anything on flood prevention?[8]

No, nothing new in the last three or four weeks that I know of.

The report of the board has been called for in about three weeks, but it hasn't been sufficiently thrashed out. Have you got anything about that?

No, I haven't.

[1] On June 18, the *New York Times* reported that Bryan had received a delegation of Americans who owned property in Mexico. The businessmen complained that Bryan had not taken their concerns seriously.

[2] That is, the clause exempting labor unions and farmers' organizations from prosecution under the Sherman Act.

[3] Four Japanese commercial envoys visited Wilson and Bryan on June 18. See the *New York Times*, June 20, 1913.

[4] That is, the United States Commission on Industrial Relations.

[5] See above, June 16, 1913.

[6] Attorney General McReynolds favored dissolution to end the Southern Pacific's control by its competitor, the Union Pacific. He obtained a dissolution decree on June 30, 1913. See Link, *The New Freedom*, pp. 418-19, and *Annual Report of the Attorney General of the United States for the Year 1913* (Washington, 1914), pp. 7-8.

[7] On June 17, the Senate Lobby Committee began reading the letters of Clarence Clark Hamlin, a Colorado newspaper owner who was in charge of the Washington office of the American Beet Sugar Association. These letters yielded some sensational information about the lobbying and propaganda efforts carried out by the association. See the *New York Times*, June 18, 19, and 20, 1913.

[8] The National Drainage Congress met on April 10 and made suggestions for flood control. See *ibid.*, April 11, 1913.

June 23, 1913

Mr. President, just to start off, I wonder whether you are ready to tell us anything in answer to the criticisms of the proposal to make a purely government board in command of the currency situation. You don't say anything about that in your message.[1]

No, I don't say anything about that, because I didn't want to discuss the terms of the measure. I simply wanted to urge the necessity for action by Congress. I don't want to be quoted on this, but I want to give it to you men for your own thought: there are only two choices of course—either to give the central control to the bankers or to give it to the government. I don't see any other.

Isn't there a middle ground?

Do you mean give it to both?

Yes, with representation of the banks.

Yes, there is, but it seems to me that is not decisive. We ought to make it a clean choice. My own feeling is that governmental control is perfectly safe. I can't imagine anybody audacious enough in a political office to play politics to that extent.

We have had some.

Yes, we have, but we have never tried them out on that line. I can only reason from comparatively small things. For example, in

New Jersey the Governor appoints all the judges. Now, no Governor—the worst Governor we have had, and we have had some pretty bad ones—has ever dared to play with the Supreme Court and the Court of Errors and Appeals. We have had a uniform quality of judges, with a very far from uniform quality of Governors in New Jersey. That is because justice touches the whole community; the minute you play politics with that, the whole community knows it, and the party who dares to do it would be "chucked" and "chucked" forever—and would deserve it. I can't imagine a man even acting upon small grounds of expediency—he is a man without principle. I can't imagine anyone playing with that, because, you see, the banking system of the country will literally touch everybody.

Well, Mr. President, I was not thinking so much, and I don't think all the critics are thinking so much, of playing politics—to use that expression—with the appointments as the fact of the tremendous domination of the President at all times, through his ability to change his cabinet. And we may have a President whose views on the subject of—well, inflation, to put it roughly—were very extreme one way or the other. The fixing of the discount rate and controlling the issue of these Treasury notes, entirely apart from politics, is not a mere matter of economic theory, and his power would be enormous, and there is apparently no check upon it.

You see, there is the same extreme difference among economists as to the theory of inflation. For example, there is one school of economists, and very sober, thoughtful men they are, though I utterly disagree with them, which maintains that the credit could be inflated—I mean the issue could be inflated—so long as it is no bigger than the liquid credits of the country. Of course, the fallacy there lies in what is back of the liquid credits. The minute you get beyond definite assets and bills of lading and all the other things that are extremely definite—your hopefulness of what you are going to do—then you get to not only liquid credits, but to what I should call fluid credits. The line is a line of judgment.

Mr. President, in that bill[2] the board has the power to apportion the five hundred million dollars of the emergency currency.[3] There is nothing in that that will prevent them from giving that five hundred million to one regional bank.

I have heard that interpretation put upon it before, but I can't see it. It hasn't the power to apportion in the sense that all of it shall go here and none of it there, because the only power it has is to judge whether the credits offered are legal and sound. And any member of the regional association has the right, on a certain kind of paper, to call for these notes, and there must be some very special reason of unsoundness why they should not get them.

But if the full five hundred million dollars have been given to one regional bank on whatever assets are required, then there is no more of that for any other bank.

That raises the question whether five hundred million is enough or not. That is all that it raises. And one has to admit at once that it is a perfectly arbitrary limit. It is a guess. It isn't a mere guess; it is a guess based upon statistics. For example, in the last panic, the statistics of clearinghouse certificates—I am very poor at remembering figures, but my memory is that those certificates rose to two hundred sixty millions, but they didn't rise to anything like the level of five hundred millions. Of course, it is a debatable question as to whether that rigid limit should be set or not. I quite admit that, but aside from the supposition that that may be all taken up in one part of the country, I don't see any danger of any improper discrimination between one section of the country and another.

Only with the fixed limit.

The fixed limit—that is a conceivable outcome.

Mr. President, is this intended to be a permanent law? I mean permanent in the sense of not being amended in your administration.

Oh, well, that would depend upon how it worked.

I ask you that because in the original bill, as it was drawn, there was a provision for retiring the present bond-secured currency.⁴ Now that has all been stricken out.

Now, I want to explain to you gentlemen why it was stricken out, because I am giving you the benefit of all I know this morning, without desiring this to be a public discussion at all. All that the present bill provides for is additional currency. Let us leave out the gold certificates and the circulation now that isn't based upon the banks and think only of the bank issues. As I remember, there are seven hundred twelve millions based upon 2 per cent bonds. Now, in the case of those 2 per cent bonds of that issue, the government has no control under this bill—that is the permanent bank issue— and it remains at the same volume, no matter what the volume of business may be. The banks are making 2 per cent on the bonds, or a little less than that if they bought them at a premium, or, in addition to that, anything that they may be able to get on the currency that they lend, based upon those bonds. Now, what we are doing with this bill is to say that if the seven hundred twelve millions are not enough, then additional Treasury notes shall be issued upon such and such terms, to a sum not exceeding five hundred millions. But in respect of that issue, the central board can determine the terms of discount and control the volume by the amount of discount, and have a general power which will enable them to see to it that these notes come in again after they have done the temporary work to which they have been assigned. In the last examination of the bill as it originally stood we saw this: if you provide for the retirement of the 2 per cents—I mean for the re-funding of the 2 per cents—and base this same kind of currency on it, you are reducing the volume of the permanent currency below the seven hundred twelve millions, and, therefore, just so fast as that reduction occurs, you are making all the currency emergency currency, because you are putting it all under the control of this central board—all the rates of discount and all the general terms and arrangements made by them—unless you go to work, as the framers of this bill had not gone to work, to make another body of currency based upon the new arrangements after the 2 per cents are gone, which would be a permanent volume and not subject to exactly the same regulations as this emergency currency. Do I make myself clear? In other words, we hadn't provided the machinery by which a perfect substitution could be made below the seven hundred twelve millions limit; and, rather than work the bill out with great elaboration so as to make those distinctions, we thought it best to segregate that and regard it as a separate thing, to be treated in-dependently.

Mr. President, when the bill creating a National bank currency[5] was enacted, wasn't that intended to be a sort of an emergency currency—that is, a currency that would fluctuate in volume?

Well, I don't remember that it was. Of course, that was the orig-inal law. It was away back just after the Civil War, and the main object of the bill was to create a market for the bonds of the United States.

Reading the discussions of that time, I find it was said it would make an elastic currency, a currency that would expand or contract according to the needs of the country. But it expanded as far as it could and stopped.

I can't imagine anybody saying that who knows the processes of banking, because, you see, in order to lessen the volume of that currency you would have to sell your bonds or else merely arbitrarily withdraw your circulation.

Well, the argument was that a time would come when the income from that issue would not be sufficient to warrant the bankers to keep in it.

Well, that time has come now, if it ever was to come, because it couldn't very well sink below 2 per cent.

Mr. President, is this bill up regarded as the administration bill, or will it be subject to change—acceptable change?

Well, it is regarded as the administration bill in exactly the same sense as I hope the Underwood tariff bill will be.

In general principle subject to—

Of course, there are details which may have to be recast. I think the general principles are thoroughly defensible.

In the tariff bill, Mr. President, there will be certain sections of the bill which will not be subject to compromise. Is that so with regard to the currency bill?

I should think so; there are certain provisions built on definite principles.

Do you regard the manner of the selection of the central board of control as one of those principles?

I don't think I had better discuss that before there is discussion in Congress, because I don't want to seem for a moment to shut the doors on consideration, so far as I am concerned, of anything that is reasonable to discuss.

But it would be reasonable, would it not, Mr. President, to say that one of the principles that you feel that you would adhere to is that the government, rather than the bankers themselves, should have the dominating factor in control?

Yes, undoubtedly.

Mr. President, in that bill as originally drawn there was a provision of one-third representation of the banks on this federal board. Now the banks are compelled by this act to invest 20 per cent of their capital stock, which isn't their money but the money of their stockholders—10 per cent paid in and a liability of 10 per cent. Now, under this bill as it was changed the banks are given no right to say what shall be done with their money that they have invested themselves, and that is the thing I think some of us were somewhat mystified about.

I don't see that, because what is done with their monies is determined by the regional banks. The regional banks do not have to rediscount if they do not approve of the paper.

Yes, but the ultimate control is held by this Federal Reserve Board.

Yes, in a general way it is. It is regulative. It isn't a business regulation; it is a prudential regulation.

Mr. President, doesn't it say that the federal board may require these regional banks to rediscount for each other?

For each other, but not for the individual banks.

But there is a varying discretion in the different regions which might make one bank very reluctant to look out for another.

That seems fair, because what we are trying to do is to mobilize the reserves and make all the resources of the country available, so far as possible, to every part of it. Because one of the things that we are most bent upon correcting is the present concentration of reserves and control by the discretion of a single group of bankers or by a locality of banking interests.

Is it desirable for this central board of control to fix the discount rate or is the regional board itself to do that?

No, sir, the control ought to be a general control, in view of the possibility of inflation. There ought to be some authority that has a general view of what is going on in the country.

Is it safe to exercise that authority without the presence on the board of a banker?

I think it is safe. Of course, that is a matter of judgment. I don't see where we would get any better judgment from a large number of bankers. All we need is expert advice.

I don't know anything about the question myself, but I see that raised in the financial and commercial papers.

You see, I have this sort of feeling: a banker is in touch with the bank of his region and has the point of view of the banks of his region, but the minute he gets the general—national—point of view, he really detaches himself and ceases to be a banker.

Mr. President, the central board has no authority to fix the discount rate unless there is some emergency currency in circulation?

If none of the five hundred million is out.

Then it depends upon the individual banks.

Then it depends upon the individual banks of the country.

But it would ultimately fall upon the regional banks, because they fix the rediscount rates.

Yes, so far as the paper was rediscounted, but the individual banks would have their individual issue as now up to the bond limit and would be just as free as they are now.

Would it be correct, Mr. President, to interpret your view as regarding this Federal Reserve Board in the same way that you would the Interstate Commerce Commission in reference to putting railroad men on the Interstate Commerce Commission?

Yes, I feel that there will be, when this bill is adopted, just the same sort of change of opinion as there was about the Interstate Commerce Commission and the public-utility boards of the states, etc. They were vigorously opposed on very much such misgivings as are being presented just now about this central control, with the result that at last they were more than welcomed, because they, so to say, guaranteed the operations all along in a public way, in a way that meant the representation of no single interest or group of interests. I think that in the long run the bankers themselves will be glad of this control—this direction over which they have no control.

[1] Wilson addressed a joint session of Congress on the question of banking and currency reform on June 23, 1913. His speech is printed in *PWW*, Vol. 27, pp. 570-73. About Wilson's views on this question, see Link, *The New Freedom*, pp. 211-13.

[2] The Glass-Owen bill, introduced in both houses of Congress on June 26, 1913. For the text of this bill, see Willis, *The Federal Reserve System*, pp. 1595-1613.

[3] That is, the emergency currency provided for by the Aldrich-Vreeland Act.

[4] That is, National bank notes.

[5] The National Banking Act of 1863. See Irwin Unger, *The Greenback Era: A Social and Political History of American Finance, 1865-1879* (Princeton, N. J., 1964), pp. 18-19.

June 26, 1913

Did you see about the District commissioners, the new District commissioners?

I have given out the names.[1]

There is no further announcement to go with it?

Oh, no. The announcement is mine. It is principally my own.

Mr. President, you saw yesterday, I believe, some bankers on the currency bill?[2]

Yes, sir.

I have been told that they proposed to you, or rather suggested, I mean, that the bill should include bankers on the central board.

A minority representation of bankers.

Would you say whether your opinion has been changed at all by the representations they made?

Well, frankly, it would not be fair to express too hasty an opinion. They presented their case in a very fair way, and so fairly that I felt that I ought to say I will take it under consideration.

The reason I suggest that now is because Monday[3] you said that a board composed partially of bankers and partially of appointees and cabinet officers would be indecisive.

Yes. Well, there's something to be said for that point of view.

You could say that you have taken that matter under consideration?

Seriously speaking, I think it is my obligation to keep my mind open to proper suggestions and not simply to lock it against burglary.

I suppose that applies, then, to the other suggestions that have been made regarding the bonding of banking institutions?[4]

Oh, yes. I think we ought to say that we are willing to consider anything of that kind, whether it is possible for us to improve it or not. I think the bonding provision in the bill has been a reduction or is about to be reduced. I think that is the latest now.

Mr. Glass said so.

Oh, did he?

Mr. President, one of the very important provisions of the proposed bill is that relating to the reserves in the regional reserve associations.

Unless released for the relief of other regions.

It would not permit any bank to carry part of its reserves outside the state, certainly outside of its own association. I understood that that was desired in order to prevent the concentration of reserves in New York City, where they are supposed to be concentrated for speculative purposes.

That has proved—in a particular place where a lot of business is done—that has proved the ultimate result of the present system.

You could get them back?

Could get them back when you wanted to.

Is the breaking up of that concentration of reserves, like in New York, principally, receiving very marked attention on your part? I think it is a thing you could not determine or—

I think that all of us in conference on the matter think that it is a very essential part of it.

The bankers think that it is very essential and it should be modified.

I expected that the gentlemen who were here yesterday would bring that up, but they did not, as a matter of fact.

They did not?

Not to me. To the other gentlemen they were conferring with.

They announced they had laid great stress on it.

In their conference they—not in person, but in discussing the recommendations that they made here—they mentioned that very frankly. The only two things they discussed with me were the treatment one way or the other of the 2 per cents, and there are several ways to handle it, and the minority representatives on the central board. That is all they brought up with me.

The question of exchange, that is, the keeping of funds in the cities, not in the reserve banks, but to be used not as reserves but for the purpose of exchange, was that brought up?

No, not brought up, but I understood they spent a couple of hours with the Secretary of the Treasury.

Mr. President, in their suggestions, did any of them mention the desirability of having the 2 per cents brought up into circulating notes? That is Mr. Perrin's proposal?

I don't know, and they didn't mention it.

Well, there is, Mr. President, hope for their retirement rather than resuming—

Our chief suggestion was that they should be retired at the rate of 5 per cent of the total which, with the extra year, should make that thirty-one millions a year—twenty years.[5]

Do you hear opposition from any banks as to retiring the National bank circulation?

Well, there hasn't been very much done to give them opposition. I haven't heard any.

I heard from Mr. McAdoo the other day that he believed some bankers rather liked the National-bank provisions.

I expressed the opinion at the conference yesterday that the smaller banks, at any rate, were very well satisfied to retain them.

Mr. President, those three deleted sections back in the bill, does that mean that this additional currency will be the only currency issued by these associations or by the Treasury for these national associations?

I have just heard that these matters—that these sections—have gone back into the bill. Whether they have gone back in part or in whole as additions, I don't know.

Didn't you take the matter up yesterday, at least last night, in your conference with the Senate Banking and Currency Committee[6]—the matter of taking the limit off the amount of this new circulating medium?

We didn't exactly take it up. Almost like everything else that afternoon which was connected with the subject, it was mentioned, and it always is mentioned. As I was saying to you gentlemen the other day, of course the five hundred million is a calculation based upon experience, and therefore nobody can be certain that that is the right limit.

Five hundred million in addition to seven hundred twelve or thereabouts?

Yes. The five hundred million in addition to the seven hundred twelve.

As additional currency?

Yes.

What I was thinking of was, if you do away with the present bonded secured currency, would you then attempt to fix any limit such as twelve hundred million, or something of that sort?

Well, if the limit principle—that is to say, the definite limit principle is retained—that would naturally be a part of it, but I haven't conferred with any of the gentlemen since they put that back.

Mr. President, have you any idea that you would put a distinct floor—a definite limit, that is to say, of twelve hundred million or something like that?

Why, I accepted the judgment of men who had studied it, with experience in the matter, in the art, as to the limit, and our unanimous desire was to prevent inflation. Whether that is just the best way or not is debatable.

Mr. President, did you get any suggestions from the bankers that, if this bill should go to you in the present form, it would be necessary for them to release their National bank charters?

One of the gentlemen here yesterday made some such suggestion. I don't think he made it very deliberately or seriously.

For some banks or for all banks?

I have asked, and I find that when men say banks they generally mean all of them.

Was that gentleman from the Northeast?

I don't remember. None of them was an eastern man, unless you count New Orleans East.

Mr. President, have you had the report of the Attorney General yet with regard to the Union Pacific or the Southern Pacific dissolution plans?

No, sir.

Could you give us any idea what line you are proceeding on?

No, I could not. The question has been waiting until the Attorney General laid it before me in some way that would involve a final judgment of what was proper to do.

Don't you get an idea from him that you are going to get an agreement in a day or two?

I got that impression from him. I believe he mentioned that to me—that they were in a hopeful way of reaching a decision.

Would it be brought to your attention before there is final action by the government?

I don't know. He isn't bound to do that at all.

When will you have it sent up?

Well, of course, it could be at any time.

They have to leave here in time to get to St. Paul by the first.[7]

I didn't know there was that limitation. If I left here on the twenty-seventh, I am not going with the determination to stay over the Fourth. I am going with the hope to stay over the Fourth. But there is a string tied to me, and if it is pulled, I will come back.[8] And then there was the suggestion that the Jones liquor bill[9] would fail unless the excise commissioners are appointed by the first of July. I don't know whether that is in the interest of the law or not. I don't think so, though that has been the first suggestion I have heard that that was possible. Well, it will go in in time, anyhow.

Mr. President, one of the afternoon papers has the suggestion that the administration has in mind some changes in the Sherman antitrust law. Is there any foundation for that?

Well, you may search me, sir.

Mr. President, have you found a prosecutor for the committee that is—

No, sir, we have not. We haven't had a chance to.

Any idea that that will come within a very short time?

Yes, of course it will.

Do you expect it today?

I hope for it today. I don't know whether that is possible or not. Of course, we have got to find out who are available when we go to choose any man.

Mr. President, do you have the feeling that your suggestion with regard to the lobby had anything to do with the vote in the caucus yesterday?[10]

No. That lobby was just a burden. It wasn't doing anything except spending money—and breath.

Mr. President, have you any prospect of any action regarding the arbitration treaties which are in the Senate?

I must say I have lost track of that. I haven't seen Senator Bacon[11] in several days.

There seems to be a sufficient number of Senators opposed to the British arbitration treaty in its present form.

I don't think that is true. At least, that was not my advice two or three days ago.

I am speaking of the correspondence of the opponents. They might be able to offer a modification which would leave out the Panama Canal question.

Well, I simply can't answer that.

Mr. President, shippers who are opposed to the abolition of the Commerce Court, I understand, are to give out a statement this evening for publication tomorrow, to the effect that the chief support Mr. Sims has for his bill[12] is a letter from Walker D. Hines, chairman of the board of directors of the Atchison, Topeka and Santa Fe Railroad, intimating that the railroads are behind the abolition of the court. Has such an intimation reached you?

No, this is the first I have heard of it.

Mr. President, are there any [blank]?

I know the main ones. They have been kind enough to keep me apprised of the main ones. I haven't heard of any that cut beneath the skin.

There are none of them that would be acceptable?

I ought to leave that question to the conference committee.

Returning to currency once more, Mr. President, in the conference here last night with the members of the Senate Committee on Banking and Currency, did you get any helpful suggestions from them?

Well, I found that the time had been so short since they had received the copies of the proposed bill that they hadn't acquainted themselves with the text of it, and therefore all they were interested in was to exchange views as to the general idea of the bill, so that we didn't get anywhere.

At the conference with these bankers yesterday, was their protest as emphatic as you expected to receive from the bankers?

I would regard part of it as emphatic. They expressed a very confident opinion about the effect of the omission of what they suggested—I mean, the effect on their interests. But they expressed it in such a way that it didn't have any improper emphasis of any kind.

Mr. President, do you expect other bankers to visit you?

No, sir. You see, these gentlemen had semiofficial status. Whether they were deputized by their colleagues to come or not, I don't know. But they are members of the commission.

Do you expect, Mr. President, to have a similar conference with the House committee?

I have had one with the subcommittee last week—last Friday night. I daresay we may have future conferences, but none is arranged for yet.

Mr. President, I suppose you saw that action of Mr. Bielaski, the officer in charge of criminal investigations under the Department of Justice, in suspending Mr. Herrington who was associated with Mr. McNab in San Francisco, in criminal investigations there?[13]

No, I didn't see that.

I asked that question because I wanted to know whether you would take any action in that case? I had an idea you would be [involved]. It was on direct orders from Mr. Bielaski, according to the statements from San Francisco.

This is my first—

You remember, he was the man[14] who telegraphed you, on the removal of the district attorney—who had made the report to the Attorney General on the subject of the case and then telegraphed to protest against the Attorney General's action, and to call for his removal, on the grounds of his suspicions. He has been fired on the ground of his message to you, as I understand it.

I haven't anything further to say on it, one way or the other.

Mr. President, some of the critics of the currency bill are making a great point—seem to try to make a great point of calling it the "Bryanesque" bill, saying that Mr. Bryan is dominant in all this proposition and has entered into the political side of the discussion. Is there anything you could tell us about that?

Those things don't count. It will be called all kinds of a thing before they get through with it. Of course, they suspect his influence during these first two or three weeks while they are examining it. You can hear anything you choose to listen to, but when they get down to the solemn consideration of it, I haven't any doubt as to the result; because, you see, it's a question of suggesting something better.

Nothing has transpired to shake your confidence in getting it through this summer?

Nothing.

You really expect to get it considered this summer?

I feel confident.

Is there anything new in the Mexican situation?

I daresay there is, but I haven't heard of it.

The treaty[15] expires tomorrow.

Yes. There is no news about it.

[1] Wilson nominated Oliver Peck Newman and Frederick Lincoln Siddons to be commissioners for the District of Columbia. See the *Washington Post*, June 27, 1913.

[2] Wilson met on June 25 with members of the Currency Commission of the American Bankers' Association: George McClelland Reynolds, president of the Commercial National Bank of Chicago; Sol Wexler, president of the Whitney Central National Bank of New Orleans; John Perrin, president of the Fletcher National Bank of Indianapolis; and Festus John Wade, president of the Mercantile Trust Company of St. Louis. See Link, *The New Freedom*, p. 217, and the *Washington Post*, June 26, 1913.

[3] See above, June 23, 1913.

[4] See the *Washington Post*, June 26, 1913.

[5] The bonds were to be retired and Federal Reserve notes issued in place of the currency backed by them in twenty years. See Owen's explanation in the *New York Times*, July 2, 1913.

[6] Wilson met on the evening of June 25 with members of the Senate Banking and Currency Committee. See the *Washington Post*, June 26, 1913.

[7] The dissolution plans were to be presented to the circuit court in St. Paul by July 1.

[8] Wilson had planned to go to Cornish but later changed his mind.

[9] Senator Wesley Livsey Jones, Republican of Washington, proposed a bill (S. 2676) to prohibit the sale of liquor to Indians.

[10] The Democratic caucus voted on June 25 to support both free sugar and free wool. See the *New York Times*, June 26, 1913.

[11] Senator Augustus Octavius Bacon, Democrat of Georgia, chairman of the Senate Foreign Relations Committee.

[12] Representative Thetus Wilrette Sims, Democrat of Tennessee, sponsored a bill (H.R. 1921) to abolish the Commerce Court. See the *Washington Post*, June 27, 1913.

[13] U.S. District Attorney John L. McNab of San Francisco resigned June 20 in protest against delays by Attorney General McReynolds in prosecuting Farley Drew Caminetti and Maury I. Diggs for violating the Mann Act. The case had political overtones because Caminetti's father, Anthony Caminetti, a Democratic leader in California, had been appointed head of the Immigration Service in the Department of Labor. On June 25, Alexander Bruce Bielaski, chief of the Bureau of Investigation of the Justice Department, fired Clayton Herrington, a special agent, for criticizing McReynolds. See the *New York Times*, June 24-26, 1913, and Link, *The New Freedom*, pp. 117-18.

[14] That is, Herrington.

[15] The special arbitration treaty between the United States and Mexico expired on June 26. See the *Washington Post*, June 27, 1913.


July 14, 1913

[Did they[1] ask for a new arbitration board?]

That was the chief matter. Then they wanted an independent board of arbitration;[2] not because of any dissatisfaction with the arbitration that had heretofore occurred, because they expressed a very emphatic satisfaction with it, but because they thought that it would add to the feeling of—I don't know just how to express it—that this thing was taken seriously and was provided for independently and on a large scale on the part of both parties, if there could be a board of arbitration. You see, what happened was that the original board was independent—there was the Commissioner of Labor and the chairman of the Interstate Commerce Commission—that was the original arrangement, the Interstate Commerce Commission being an independent body, that is to say, not connected with any department, and the Commissioner of Labor being an independent commissionship. Then by various changes of the law, the commissionership of labor was included first in the Department of Commerce and Labor and then in the Department of Labor, and other duties of a very important and onerous kind being put upon the Commissioner, so that only a portion of his time, and that the minor portion, could be devoted to this important matter, so that, practically, it was a proposition to begin at the beginning again and carry out the original intention of the act. And then, in regard to the size of the board of arbitration, the act[3] originally contemplated a controversy between a single railroad and its employees; and the scope has widened and widened until now we have a situation where there is a series of railroads, though they are dealing with one or two brotherhoods or organizations in this case; so that I think the suggestions made were wholly just and reasonable,[4] and there is no reason on earth why we should not act upon them now, as it would prevent a very great inconvenience and perhaps disastrous situation for the carrying business of the country. That is the long and short of it. So the gentlemen who were present speaking for the House and Senate expressed the confident opinion that there would be no trouble at all in getting the amendments through the two houses, and it was with that understanding that we parted.

Can they get it through tomorrow night; will you be ready to sign it at once?

I will be ready to sign it whenever it is through.

Did the other parties agree to abide by the decision?

The parties have agreed to arbitrate under this arrangement, if it is passed.

Then the spokesman for the railroads volunteered the information that they were willing to accept this form of arbitration?

They were all present and spoken for by Mr. Seth Low,[5] who had brought about a number of conferences, and explicitly stated their understanding in his presence, and it is evident that he knows how to state those things, and his statement was entirely satisfactory, because no one dissented from it.

Was there any agreement as to the exact time at which this bill should be passed?

No, but the confidence expressed by both Mr. Clayton and Senator Newlands was that it would pass tomorrow. And Senator Kern was here, and it was expected, when we parted, that the Senate would not adjourn until Thursday, as it was contemplated, but until tomorrow.

Was there some agreement as to changes in the bill?

There was only a single inconsistency. It was provided in the bill that the original papers should be filed in two different places, which was a physical impossibility. It was changed so that the copies should be filed in one place and the original papers in another; and then a paragraph in the original Erdman Act had been omitted, apparently by being overlooked. It was the proviso that no mandatory process of any court should oblige an individual workman to work against his will, which is practically taken care of by the Constitution; but it was thought best not to omit it, for fear of constitutional objections that might be raised against it. But it was evidently an omission unintentionally made in the draft.

That was of the Newlands bill?

Of the Newlands bill, yes.

But there were several amendments to the Newlands bill proposed in the House which were not agreed upon today; those two were proposed?

There were two of them. One proposed a choice of a board of nine, besides the six and the three provided for.[6] That was abandoned. That had been the suggestion of the Secretary of Labor, and he said he would not insist upon that. And the other was the board itself. The amended House bill—I mean the bill as amended in the House committee—provided that the Commissioner of Labor Statistics and one other person should constitute the board of mediation, whereas, the Newlands bill—the bill that is going to be proposed tomorrow—provides that there ought to be an independent commissioner as originally intended, with an assistant commissioner associated with two other officials, acting officials, officials already appointed by and with the consent of the Senate, two of whom are to be selected by the President.

The House amendment is abandoned?

That amendment is abandoned.

Then, of course, there will be immediate appointments?

Yes, if you fellows will pray for me in the meantime.

That makes four you have to appoint, Mr. President?

No, it is only one; because the other members are already in office, you see.[7]

But whom you select?

Yes; whom I select from the existing persons.

Did Mr. Low indicate that the contending parties would wait until you had appointed this new commissioner and designated his associates?

The gentlemen who represented the bodies who had voted to strike made this representation to us, that they had promised to report to their men by Wednesday what had been done. Of course, they can't say whether their men will be satisfied with what has been done. But I haven't the slightest doubt that they will be.[8] But that was the situation.

Do you understand, Mr. President, that he spoke for both the railroad men and the companies, or for the unions?

No, he spoke for both. You see, he is president of the Civic Federation. He had brought about these conferences, and he had acted merely as a mediator. That is to say, none of the proposals were his own, or the proposals of the federation.

Might it not be possible, Mr. President, to get something he said?

It was a mere narrative statement.

It was not a formal statement of points on either side?

No. I can sum it up, I think, in a few words. He related the attempts that had been made to bring these parties into conference that had begun long before this particular crisis was reached, not only, but in view, in sight. And then he mentioned the points that were most important that had developed, and that had been embodied in the Newlands bill then, with the advice of the board of arbitration, the independent board of mediation; then he said he had represented to these gentlemen in their previous conferences the various things that had been suggested by the Secretary of Labor, for example, and others; and that the net result of their conferences was the Newlands bill. That was the substance of his speech, besides what I have already told you that he said that he was quite sure that he was speaking for them; and certain if this arrangement were accorded them, they would arbitrate this difference.

None of the merits of the controversy was touched upon?

Nothing at all; the controversy itself was not mentioned, except necessarily as pending.

These were all the conferences that had to do with trying to reach an agreement on legislation?

Yes.

Nothing on the strike itself?

If they conferred about that, he did not mention it.

This was distinctly a legislative conference?

Yes.

There was never really a controverted point at any time?

There really was no controverted point, except that the Secretary of Labor expressed his preference for a different organization, but said that he did not wish that to stand in the way of an agreement.

[1] On July 14, Wilson met with four labor leaders, five railroad men, three members of the National Civic Federation, four members of Congress, and Secretary of Labor William Bauchop Wilson in an attempt to avert a strike by over 100,000 railway employees. The basis for doing so was an amendment to the Erdman Arbitration Act proposed by Senator Newlands and Representative Henry De Lamar Clayton, Democrat of Alabama. The new arbitration bill had been passed in the Senate but was amended in the House in a manner that was unacceptable to both sides in the dispute. Thus, Wilson was looking for a formula which would satisfy all parties. See the *New York Times*, July 15, 1913.

[2] That is, one not made up of governmental officials occupying predetermined positions. The Erdman Act had placed the Commissioner of Labor and the chairman of the Interstate Commerce Commission on the Board of Mediation and Conciliation.

[3] The Erdman Act.

[4] The Erdman Act created a three-member arbitration board; the Newlands bill called for a membership of six.

[5] New York ship operator and merchant, former Mayor of New York and President of Columbia College, presently president of the National Civic Federation.

[6] The arbitration board, which would be temporary, was to have six members; the permanent Board of Mediation and Conciliation would have three.

[7] Wilson had only to appoint the independent chairman; the other members were to be chosen from appointments already made. The fourth member mentioned here was an assistant, or alternate commissioner.

[8] They were, and the strike was averted.

July 17, 1913

Gentlemen, I want to say a few words to you about the Mexican situation,[1] so that nothing might be done or said which would make it more difficult to handle than it is now, and I want to say this in our capacity as confidential friends, so that you will know exactly what is in my mind and for your guidance. The trouble is that we don't know what is going on in Mexico. I have reason to believe— I always have to say that with regard to Mexico, because nothing appears to be certain—but I have every reason to believe that the reported demonstrations in Mexico City against Americans are fomented and manufactured by a small group of persons who are trying to force this government to recognize the government of Mr. Huerta; and there is an equal artificiality attaching to a good many other things that are said to be happening in Mexico. Upon examination, they don't turn out, so far as can be ascertained at this distance, to be genuine. I will give you an instance. The other day it was reported, upon the capture of some town,[2] that a number of women were assaulted and afterwards committed suicide. We immediately tried, through the State Department, to get a confirmation of that or some means of judging whether it was true or not, through our Consuls on the spot and in the neighborhood. We could not get any verification of it at all, and in my opinion it never happened. But the very phraseology I am using shows you our embarrassment—I say, in my opinion it never happened. I don't know. And I wish you gentlemen might cooperate with me, not only in trying to get the most exact information obtainable, but also in trying to keep the public from being misled by the rumors. It has been said, among other things, that foreign governments are making representations which constitute a pressure on this government. Now, that isn't true. In the most informal way possible, they have conveyed to us the impressions as to the situation on the part of their representatives in the City of Mexico, which you see is a very different matter. And, if I may say so in entire confidence, I think that one or two of their representatives in Mexico City are very excitable and unwise gentlemen. But that is just part of the whole confusion and uncertainty of the situation. So that I can say to you that I am in search of the real facts, as is shown by the fact that we have asked Mr. Henry Lane Wilson to return to Washington at once so that we can by intimate conversation with him, instead of through telegrams, which he may feel may leak at any time, get his direct and genuine impressions in the situation. I think that that is all that I can say, because I am searching for the facts and don't believe I have got them. Now, when we get the facts, it will be possible, I hope, to formulate some definite course of action, provided things don't change overnight and throw everything into confusion after we have got the information that Mr. Wilson may be able to bring us.

Are the Mexicans fomenting the trouble?

Yes; fomenting these demonstrations, yes.

Mr. President, what form do these reports take? Are they from foreign governments—are they concerned?

As I understand it—I did not see the document itself, if there was a document—but as I understand it, three or four of the representatives of foreign governments in Mexico City did unite in an informal paper in which they embodied their impressions. They requested their several governments just to convey that to us by way of information.[3]

And that was conveyed from the capitals of the governments?

I can't say positively that it was conveyed through more than one, but at least through one.

To the State Department?

To the State Department, yes.

Mr. President, what has prevented Mr. Ambassador Wilson from supplying you with intimate and reliable information?

Well, I don't know that I can allege anything that has prevented it. I think he has been trying to supply us with information, but, you know what happens—well, at least, I will tell you what has happened. The complexion of the telegrams on one day would not be the same as the telegrams of the next. I don't criticize Mr. Wilson for that, because, I daresay if I were in his position, I would be in a highly nervous state—sitting on a volcano, as they may be sitting on one in Mexico City. The events of one day are quiet and reassuring, and the events of the next day are unquiet and disturbing; and so from day to day we get the impressions from a man who has the anxieties of the spot in his blood. That is the only reason I can give.

Mr. President, have you any other sources of information than the diplomatic and consular service in Mexico?

Well, you know I told you that Mr. Hale,[4] being a longtime friend of mine, and having gone down there in the interest of two or three papers, promised to supply me with any information he could get; and I received one or two telegrams from him. But of course they are entirely of an unofficial character—just conveying his impressions.

Mr. President, is it your intention to send Mr. Ambassador Wilson back to Mexico?

That will depend on his own advice and his account of the situation.

Mr. President, about the placing before this government of the statements made by the diplomatic representatives in Mexico City, are these foreign governments, or this foreign government, making any representations of their own indicating that they believe that something should be done?

No; simply laying before the government their impressions. Simply acting as a familiar informant.

Mr. President, can you say anything about what those impressions were?

Well, I don't know that it would be right for me, offhand, to do that, because I did not see the actual paper itself; I simply got it secondhand.

Mr. President, was the nation that conveyed this document, if it were a document, to the State Department, one of the nations that have originally signed the document?

Naturally so, because it was only through it that the document was transmitted.

Mr. President, could you tell us what those nations were?

I would if I could, but I do not remember them.

Mr. President, do you care to indicate what was the nature of Mr. Hale's impressions?

Well, mixed, like the others. Because, there again, the impressions differ from time to time.

You said, Mr. President, at least one nation had communicated this statement—the impressions of its representatives there. Could you state what nation it was?

I would if I remembered it, but I do not.

Mr. President, you spoke a while ago of these demonstrations in Mexico and other places being of an artificial character. Have you anything to indicate that they are being fomented by foreign bondholders with the object of making a better market for their bonds?

No, I can't just say that I have.

There is a dispatch this morning from, I think, Tucson, Arizona. It indicates the original source[5]—it says that the Constitutionalists there have wired to you that "We pray you not to permit the nations of Europe to make of the United States an agency to collect monies that they have advanced or agreed to advance for the support of the Huerta government." I have heard from revolutionary sources that they believe that that is the attitude of the European governments.

I, of course, had heard that; but, in answer to that question, I don't think I have any right to state it as my impression.

Do you know what day Ambassador Wilson will get here?

No, we haven't learned yet.

Mr. President, would you care to say, in the same confidential way, what you believe to be the extent of the duty of the United States towards the situation in Mexico?

No, my opinion would be conjectural until I am sure of the situation.

Mr. President, was Ambassador Wilson familiar with the purpose of the diplomats down there in making these representations to their governments?

I believe he was.

Pending further more dependable information, there will be no change in the administration policy of "hands off," pending a constitutional election?[6]

No.

So there is a determination that the government shall not be recognized there until after the election?

No, there isn't—I can't say that there is a determination about anything. I mean, we hold our minds perfectly open to do the right and necessary thing, until we find out what it is.

Mr. President, do you feel that Ambassador Wilson has been too friendly to the Huerta government?

Oh, I don't permit myself to feel anything about it.

Is this summoning of the Ambassador here in the nature of a recall?[7]

No; I have stated just exactly the nature.

Mr. President, could you say whether the first news of the administration concerning the diplomatic movements in Mexico City was from Ambassador Wilson or from the State Department?

So far as I know, it was from the State Department.

Mr. President, hasn't Mr. Wilson supplemented his cable reports by written reports?

Yes, but they have come so long after the cable reports that they were out of date before they started. You see, the means of communication are very slow now. Practically all the northern routes are interrupted; they have to come by Veracruz or other points.

Mr. President, of course, we all know you are not inclined to give any formal recognition to the Huerta government; but the Huerta government is having all the rights that we would accord to any *de facto* government outside of formal recognition. For example, they have the right to bring in arms and ammunition from the United States, and the Constitutionalists, who control, or apparently control, all of northern Mexico, don't seem to have that right. Now, I have understood that there has been no recognition of the Huerta government even as a belligerent. We have simply permitted the recognition of the Madero government to continue. Now, the Constitutionalists are anxious to have this government grant them that right to bring in arms and ammunition or else to rescind it with reference to the Huerta government. Has that matter been considered?

No, it hasn't.

Mr. President, what is done with these various individual cases of complaint that come up in Mexico City through the Consuls or through the press?

Why, they are investigated as well as they can be, and then any advice or assistance that can be given is given.

Mr. President, does this statement of impressions make any suggestion with regard to the remedy that ought to be applied, or does it try to show us our duty as a brother to Mexico?

No, I cannot say that it does.

In other words, they don't try to exert an impression upon this government?

I don't suppose they would send us the information unless they wanted to make an impression; but that isn't disclosed.

Mr. President, will this government tolerate the landing of foreign troops in Mexico?

I am not going to answer that; that is too big an "If."

We have to take that into consideration in writing.

I don't see why you have to take that into consideration, because there is no most distant intimation of that possibility yet.

I understand that there have been a good many outrages on foreign subjects down there.

I have seen that stated; there again, I don't know whether it is so or not. I doubt it myself. Of course, in a state of civil war, property may undoubtedly suffer, and the nation under which it suffered will have to render indemnity finally for it; but international law does not recognize any right other than the right of final indemnifications in circumstances of that sort.

Did I understand you to say in the early part of the interview that, after conferring with Ambassador Wilson, there will be an announcement of some definite plan?

I don't know whether our minds will be crystallized by what we hear from him.

Will Mr. Bryan, the Secretary of State, be here when the Ambassador arrives?

Oh, yes. Mr. Bryan, understand gentlemen, is within call all the time. He hasn't separated himself from the government by going off to make a few speeches. (Laughter)[8]

Mr. President, have you said, confidentially or otherwise, anything on the ethics of his absence? (Laughter)

No, sir. (Laughter)

Mr. President, there is a Mr. Emeterio de la Garza, who has been in this country about two months and a half as the personal and official representative of President Huerta. He came here a few weeks ago to try to see you and did not succeed. He is sailing today. He is very angry, and he says something about you that isn't very kind; and said you had prevented the recognition of the Huerta government in spite of the insistence of Secretary Bryan and John Bassett Moore. Can you say anything about that?[9]

Well, I don't like to be disrespectful of a departing guest. (Laughter)

Mr. President, is a man named Del Valle[10] of California furnishing you with any information?

He did indirectly through a gentleman with whom he was corresponding,[11] but not directly.

Can you state where he is now, Mr. President?

I don't know.[12]

Mr. President, have you any intention of sending anyone down to Mexico?

No present intention. I hold myself ready to do anything at any time though.

[1] On July 16, Wilson had announced the recall of Ambassador Wilson from Mexico City and set off a great deal of newspaper speculation about a change in policy toward the Huerta government. See, for example, the *New York Times*, July 17, 1913.

[2] Durango.

[3] They were the representatives of Great Britain, France, Italy, Spain, and Belgium. Their representation was conveyed to Washington by the British. See the *New York Times*, July 29, 1913.

[4] See above, June 1, 1913.

[5] Ignacio Pesquiera, Constitutionalist Governor of Sonora.

[6] Scheduled for October 1913.

[7] It did, in fact, amount to a recall. See Hill, *Emissaries to a Revolution*, pp. 55-60.

[8] The *New York Times* had that morning printed a story describing Bryan as absent from his duties, due to speaking engagements, for one fourth of the time he had been Secretary of State.

[9] See the *New York Times*, July 17, 1913.

[10] Reginaldo Francisco Del Valle, a friend of Bryan's, sent by Wilson and Bryan on a secret mission to determine the strength of the Constitutionalists in the northern Mexican states. See Link, *The New Freedom*, p. 355, and Hill, *Emissaries to a Revolution*, pp. 40-60.

[11] Del Valle sent his reports to the home address of the Chief Clerk of the State Department. Hill, p. 41.

[12] Del Valle had been ordered on July 15 to return to Washington from Mexico City. He and Ambassador Wilson, both discredited, traveled on the same steamer. *Ibid.*, p. 55.

July 21, 1913

Mexico and Nicaragua?

Well, there isn't any further progress on Mexico—I mean, we are at just at the point we were, as I explained to you the last time we were together; and as for Nicaragua, the proposal is before you,—I mean, there is nothing to be added when you write, by way of exposition, to what Mr. Bryan has suggested.[1]

Has the treaty been printed and made public?

I think not. It may turn up in the *Congressional Record*. Not presently, I don't think it will.

Could you state the points of it, probably?

I wouldn't—haven't got into that. Offhand, no.

I mean, as to what the policy with regard to Nicaragua is?

This is a proposal, you know, with regard to obtaining from them a concession on the canal route so that we may have the option of opening it if it seems wise to do so. That is the subject matter of the negotiations.

I have been away two days, and, according to the papers on which I have been compelled to rely, a much broader policy is involved. That is what I meant to ask you about.

Of course, there always is the problem with regard to those Central American states of making such arrangements as will enable them to float their loans and secure ours. I am now speaking to you gentlemen just for your information, not for the newspapers. We are sincerely desirous of finding some way by which we can render them some assistance without submitting ourselves to the suspicion of our taking possession of them or preventing them from acting. Of course, at the outset, we would be open to that suspicion. It is up to us in the long run to show that there is nothing in it.[2]

Mr. President, do you think that, in announcing that policy or in looking after our Latin American sisters, the European powers would think we are working for, perhaps, the military [advantage]?

Very possibly they would, but what we have to look at are our own purposes and our own consciences in the matter. The question

would be if any European power would have any right to object
with the Monroe Doctrine in view, and also that we have the canal
to look after—well, speaking freely to you in confidence, they would
have a right to object but— (Laughter)

Mr. President, did the suggestion for this treaty or understanding with Nicaragua originate with you or with Nicaragua?

I am sorry to say I can't answer that. I am under the impression
that it grew out of the conversations of the Secretary of State with
the representatives of Nicaragua.

One of the papers this morning states that the same proposition was submitted
to Honduras and El Salvador and that it aroused considerable excitement on
the part of the gentlemen who represent those countries here, and that Mr.
Bryan made that offer to them also.

If so, I didn't know anything about it.[3]

Of course, I don't suppose you would be willing to answer questions whether
this policy would extend over the entire of Central America?[4]

I don't want you to exaggerate anything in your minds in thinking
of it. We are not adopting a general policy with regard to Central
America. We are trying to deal in as helpful and friendly a way as
we can in each particular case as it arises. Of course, if the state
we are dealing with doesn't like the idea, we wouldn't press it for
a moment.

It would seem almost necessary for it, then, that the idea must originate with
the other countries.

At any rate, it must be thoroughly acceptable to the other countries.

Mr. President, the purpose—I don't know whether you want to say anything
about those countries or anything of that kind—the purpose with regard to
[the treaty] is really to foreclose that canal proposition with reference to any
other country?[5]

With regard to the main objective of the negotiations, yes.

Mr. President, is there anything going on with Colombia now? We had the
same sort of proposition up with Colombia in the last administration, the
acquisition of the Atrato Canal[6] rights, down near the Colombian frontier. Is
there anything going on with regard to that?

So far as I know, there is not. Mr. Bryan may have opened that matter with the Colombian Minister,[7] but I don't know.

Would it be fair to assume, Mr. President, that the administration is going as far as it can to influence and exercise relations with those countries to protect American interests?

That is to protect American interests in the large sense, to advance American interests, to show our friendliness, to help in every legitimate way. I think that is the way to help American interests, to be real friends and not try to exploit them or use them to our own selfish advantage.

Mr. President, you have approved Mr. Bryan's suggestion that a [protectorate] be included in this.

I have approved of it. The real status of this thing is under consideration by the Senate, and the matter lies in their hands. I think that is the way to conduct everything of this kind.

It is generally assumed, Mr. President, that the decision on that plan [is related to] Mexico.

It doesn't mean any more than it says. There is no colored gentleman in the woodpile. There is no joker in it anywhere.

Mr. President, are you well satisfied with the progress on the currency bill at the present time?

Yes, sir.

Do you still think it possible to pass that legislation this session?

Oh, yes, I most surely do.

There seems to be considerable doubt in the Senate about it.

In some quarters, yes.

But you haven't grown discouraged, have you?

Not in the least. Exactly what had been expected has occurred. It is a difficult subject. There are a lot of questions that excite natural differences of judgment, and it takes a good many weeks for things to crystallize and settle.

The opposition to the federal control board,[8] for instance, does that make any impression here?

That seems to have made no impression at all, and those who had first objected and criticized this outside Congress seem to have yielded that point—I mean, to have given that up.

Mr. President, are there any advices from China with regard to the uprising in the South there?[9]

Just the published information that tallies with ours, in the news-papers.

Do those reports, the conditions there, affect our policy in any way?

No, sir. Not at any rate for the present.

Mr. President, have you selected a successor for Mr. Post on that conciliation board?[10]

No. That was a stupid blunder on my part. I forgot that he hadn't been confirmed by the Senate.

The law doesn't delay things at all, because the law says "in addition to the mediator an assistant."

I shall appoint not more than two. The present number is sufficient. I am going to add another presently. I don't want to make a hasty selection.

Mr. President, referring to Mexico, there is a general feeling and I think—at any rate, I am willing to speak it for myself—that Ambassador Wilson is at any rate inclined to be favorable to the recognition of Huerta. I think that can be stated as a known condition. Are you receiving from any source the other side of the question, the so-called Constitutionalist side?

I can't say that we are. Indeed, so far as I know, we are not. By the other side, at first I thought you meant the side against the recognition of Huerta.

Well, I meant more specifically that—I mean the—*Carrancistas*.[11]

No, we are practically getting nothing with regard to them.

They are a pretty responsible element of the people there.

They are indeed. I would be very glad indeed to know exactly what is in their minds, but—

Haven't they a representative in the city here, like the Huerta representative?

If so, he hasn't been to see me.

Would you be willing to see him?

That is a question for the Department of State.

Is there anything authentic or authoritative that would lead you to believe that the dispatches are correct which state that the Huerta government is toppling?

Well, there again, I don't know. I shouldn't be surprised if that is true. I am not sufficiently informed.

The question was raised in an editorial in the New York *World* last week that seemed to me very much to the point. The administration states—in fact, I think you have said this to us—that they have not been able to get entirely trustworthy information. We have a sufficient amount of diplomatic representatives down there, and the *World* asks what the truth is.

I remember that question. It was a very pertinent one. When I covered that one, I was saying to you gentlemen the other day that local circumstances color a man's judgment on what is going on in the rest of the country, and you get one impression in one part, I mean, and in another part another impression.[12]

That would be the case with Mr. Wilson, I presume?

Yes. He has got this, that, and the other set of rumors in the different parts of the country. For example, as I understand it, fighting is constantly going on. At first, the Huerta government represents every fight as resulting in a victory of its troops. Sometimes that is true and sometimes it is not. But it changes the point of view, and so it goes from day to day. I don't think the most active inquiry on the spot would determine very much more than we get. I am beginning to get now from people who have long been resident in Mexico the judgment of persons who have been used to traveling that road and who seem to know a little bit about it.

Well, can you give us any intimation as to the general color of that information?

Well, just among ourselves, it is to the effect that the Huerta government certainly can't last.

There have been a great many reports coming here about the activities of Ambassador Wilson toward the support of the Huerta government. Have any of those been well founded?

What?

Or have you found them to be true in any sense?

I don't feel at liberty to discuss that. I don't think it would be fair to Mr. Wilson.

When do you expect the Ambassador to arrive, Mr. President?[13]

I am told that he should get here, if the boat runs as they are expecting, on Friday—whatever that is—or perhaps Thursday evening.

Mr. President, have you any information as to how our reply to Japan has been received on the other side?

No, I haven't heard at all.

The press dispatches from there indicate that there is an answer or some decision. I wondered if you had anything from our representatives?

No, sir.

Have you any information concerning the Japanese negotiations with Mexico, whether there is anything in the stories on that?[14]

Nothing, except what is obviously manufactured. It almost bears the maker's label.

---

[1] Bryan was engaged in negotiations with Emiliano Chamorro, the Nicaraguan Minister in Washington, for a treaty which would give the United States, in exchange for $3,000,000, exclusive rights to build a canal in Nicaragua, a ninety-nine year lease on the Great and Little Corn islands in the Caribbean, a ninety-nine year option to build a naval base at the Gulf of Fonseca, and what amounted to a protectorate over the Central American country. See the *New York Times*, July 20, 1913, and Link, *The New Freedom*, pp. 329-37. A draft of the treaty is printed in *PWW*, Vol. 27, pp. 527-30.

[2] Nicaragua was in desperate financial difficulty, and one benefit of the American treaty would be enhanced security for future loans.

[3] On July 21, the *New York Times* reported that Bryan had also proposed a protectorate over Honduras and El Salvador and that those countries had rejected it vehemently.

[4] This had been suggested by Senator Bacon. See the *Boston Transcript*, July 21, 1913.

[5] That is, to prevent any other country from building a canal across Nicaragua.

[6] Two routes had been proposed for a Colombian canal, both of which would follow the Atrato River and its tributaries. See McCullough, *Path Between the Seas*, pp. 29-30.

[7] Julio Betancourt.

[8] That is, the Federal Reserve Board.

[9] A reference to a rebellion in Shanghai, Kwantung Province, and other provinces of China. See the *New York Times*, July 20-21, 1913.

[10] Wilson had named Louis Freeland Post, Assistant Secretary of Labor, to the new Board

of Mediation and Conciliation created by the Newlands Act. Post had to be replaced because he had not been confirmed by the Senate in his original position as the act required. See above, July 14, 1913.

[11] Followers of Venustiano Carranza, leader of the Constitutionalists in Mexico.

[12] See above, July 17, 1913.

[13] Ambassador Wilson called at the State Department on July 26.

[14] On July 20, 1913, the *New York Times* reported the Japanese emissaries in Mexico were requesting permission to colonize the State of Morelos. This was the latest example of American fear of a "yellow peril" in Mexico. See Katz, *Secret War in Mexico*, pp. 78-79.

July 24, 1913

I think Mexico interests us all, Mr. President.

Well, there is absolutely no new development there.

Yesterday a report gained currency in high quarters that one of the things which was being considered was some form of mediation through our good offices, and the hope that it might be possible to hold the election in Mexico in the autumn.[1]

It is true that that is also being considered, but nothing has been decided on.

Mr. President, is there wisdom in asking for the cooperation of any of the great stable governments of South America?

Well, you could hardly ask anything of that sort to which my answer would not be yes, because everything the human mind can imagine has been suggested.

Have there been any further communications from Europe, Mr. President?[2]

No.

Is it true, Mr. President, that Great Britain is being asked to assist the United States?

Not that I know of.

Mr. President, could you give us any information regarding the policy of permitting the exportation of arms to both [sides]?

Senator Fall[3] was in some time ago [and discussed] repeal of the joint resolution.[4] He seemed to want to restore conditions in which arms might be sold to any [party]. What he was trying to do was to restore the ordinary situation of the matter under international law. The resolution which now authorizes the President to interdict the exportation of arms to Mexico in cases where in his judgment it would lead to disorder—I believe that the language of the resolution was not, of course, in line with that—was meant to constitute an exception to ordinary practice, which is that arms can be imported into a country where there is war, but that they of course constitute contraband of war and are subject to seizure by the other party to the war, and they go at the risk of the shipper and the shippee.

Mr. President, how much if any consideration has been given to a proposition to recognize Mr. Carranza and Mr. Huerta merely as factional chiefs in *de facto* control of certain territories, holding each responsible for the safety of the Americans in that territory?

That has the benefit of being a new suggestion that hasn't been considered.

Recently I asked, Mr. President, what was being done with regard to Messrs. Madriz and Estrada in Nicaragua a few years ago?[5]

That is another idea to digest. I am very much obliged to you.

Mr. President, they mention that the United States places an embargo on shipment to them of munitions of war.

Do you mean Senator Fall's resolution?

No, just the contrary, that will allow both sides—

At their risk.

Like any other country.

Yes.

Mr. President, have you decided to stop the exportation of arms into the hands of the government forces?[6]

No, I haven't decided anything concerning it. That was stated with great confidence in some of the papers that I saw, but there are a large number of things that people say that are not so.

Mr. President, nothing in it?

No. That is one of the things that has been talked about.

Mr. President, is your decision on these matters being deferred until the arrival of Ambassador Wilson?

Naturally, yes.

Are there any other phases of the plan you have under consideration except the matter of stopping the shipment of arms and offering mediation? Are there any other phases of that and any other points under consideration with reference to the program?

As I have been just saying, practically everything which is a matter of action has been under consideration either inside or outside official circles, so that there is hardly any phase of it that has not been discussed in order to get the whole thing in our minds.

I asked that because I had the idea you had something definite in mind.

I am trying to hold my mind entirely open, and until I converse with Mr. Wilson to discuss the plans I have got the elements of in my head, I won't attempt to be definite.

Have there been any overtures from the Constitutionalists?

None whatever. Indeed, it would hardly be regular for us to receive them.

Has the Mexican government, the Huerta people—have they made any overtures?
Mr. President, shall you talk with the Ambassador immediately upon his arrival in the city?

Well, that depends upon whether he arrives Sunday or not. I have just received a message from him that his boat won't arrive in New York until Saturday morning, so that I am afraid we can't have a real conference before Monday.

Mr. President, has there been any communication from any other Central or South American governments with regard to this proposed new arrangement with Nicaragua?[7]

Not that I know of. I read in the papers that Honduras and El Salvador are protesting, but if they are I don't know of it.

We telegraphed several of the Presidents there, and a presidential liaison in El Salvador this morning said he thought it would break up the end toward which they are all working—their formation of a Central American Union.[8] It would have that effect.

That would depend upon who proposed it. Of course, if we proposed it and pushed it, it might very well have that effect, but as a matter of fact we haven't done anything of the kind or threatened anything of the kind.

This thing could be terminated at any time or could conclude.

Yes, of course. Well, I am not sure I understood you. What could be terminated?

This proposed treaty extending the plan to Nicaragua, terminating in case there was a basis of their forming a Central American Union of the five American republics.

By mutual agreement, yes.

Otherwise it is a perpetual thing, is it not?

I am ashamed to say I can't answer that question. I don't remember. I don't remember the termination.

It gives us the exclusive right to build a canal through Nicaragua.

I remember what is involved, but I do not remember if I noticed the time element in it.

We give them three million dollars.

Then there is no provision for giving that back.

What is your attitude toward the arbitration treaties, Mr. President, that are hanging fire—the old arbitration treaties?[9]

I am absolutely, unqualifiedly in favor of their renewal.

Mr. President, are you advised as to the prospects of their being—

No, I haven't known anything about them in recent weeks. The Senators have been so engrossed in other matters that they have apparently been too preoccupied [to take them up].

Secretary Bryan told us the Italian government was expressing a rather urgent desire that they be ratified.[10]

Yes, it did.

The statement is made in the Senate, Mr. President, that there has been no pressure exerted so as to get this through.

Well, as though the Senate waited for pressure.

Sometimes.

Of course, if pressure is desired, I can produce it.

Returning to Nicaragua again, what is the status of those negotiations? Has the treaty been negotiated or completed? I know drafts have been prepared.

The formalities have not been completed, as I understand it.

That matter is now in the purview of the Senate Committee on Foreign Relations. Can you give us an idea when you are likely to act on that matter, or when the Secretary of State is likely to act? Would he wait until the Senate committee advised him?

Well, so far as I know, the Senate committee has already told him what its feeling is about the matter and said it couldn't take any action because the matter is not in shape for action; but I understand that the negotiations are going forward just as rapidly as feasible in the circumstances.

Mr. President, could you say anything as to whether you have an antitrust policy?

I have an antitrust policy, but not for this session of the Congress.

Legislative policy, Mr. President?

Oh, yes. I don't mean by that that I have policies on all conceivable subjects conceived by me, personally. But I have devoted a good deal of thought to that.

Does that include the Sherman Act?

Not necessarily. I think it is premature to discuss it. I don't think there is anything to discuss at present.

Mr. President, how about the currency bill? There seems to be a good deal of trouble in the House committee, a good deal of disagreement.[11] Is that serious enough to impair your efforts?

No. It is a naturally slow task. There is no more disagreement on currency than among the Ways and Means Committee on the tariff. They are analyzing it.

It seems to be a little more public.

It is more public, yes.

Mr. President, some of the members there want certain recommendations of the Pujo Committee.[12] Is there any objection to this?

Well, it seems to me that that is confusing two different things.

Will you stand pat on your idea of getting through a currency statute?

I am not a standpatter, sir, but I am standing where I was.

Mr. President, is this government taking any action of any kind in regard to the situation in China?[13]

No. No. No. It is not taking any action at all.

There has been a story, Mr. President, that you had agreed to take a vacation as soon as the Senate takes a vacation, as soon as the recess, as soon as the tariff is passed, and come back the first of November and discuss currency.

That has not even been proposed. I don't intend to take any vacation.

---

[1] The *Washington Post*, July 24, 1913, reported that an offer of mediation was being considered by the Wilson administration. See also Link, *The New Freedom*, p. 356.

[2] For a discussion of this issue, see the *New York Times*, July 25, 1913.

[3] Senator Albert Bacon Fall, Republican of New Mexico.

[4] A Joint Resolution of March 14, 1912, made it unlawful to export arms to any American country, except under such limitations as the President might prescribe, where the President had proclaimed that the existence of "conditions of domestic violence" would be "promoted by the use of arms or munitions of war procured from the United States." President Taft had issued such a proclamation on the day that the resolution was passed, and, since that time, the export of arms to Mexico, except to the government at Mexico City, had been unlawful. For a discussion of the law, see the Memorandum by John Bassett Moore, Aug. 22, 1913, printed in *PWW*, Vol. 28, pp. 212-15.

[5] Juan J. Estrada led a revolution in 1910 against the government of José Madriz in Nicaragua. See Walter V. Scholes and Marie V. Scholes, *The Foreign Policies of the Taft Administration* (Columbia, Mo., 1970), pp. 56-59.

[6] Wilson took this step on August 27, 1913. See Link, *The New Freedom*, pp. 360-61.

[7] The Bryan-Chamorro treaty. See above, July 21, 1913.

[8] Carlos Melendez, President of El Salvador, sent a telegram to this effect on July 23. See the *New York Times*, July 24, 1913. For a discussion of the issues, see Link, *The New Freedom*, pp. 342-43.

[9] The Senate was considering renewal of the arbitration treaties negotiated by Secretary of State Root in 1908-1909. See Link, *The New Freedom*, pp. 280-81, n. 7.

[10] Bryan conversed with reporters at Union Station upon his return to Washington on July 24. See the *New York Times*, July 25, 1913.

<sup></sup>¹¹ The *Washington Post*, July 24, 1913, reported that the currency bill might be postponed indefinitely.

¹² The so-called Pujo Committee of the House of Representatives, headed by Representative Arsène Paulin Pujo, Democrat of Louisiana, investigated the concentration of capital and credit resources in the United States. Some more radical members of the House Banking and Currency Committee were pressing to have reforms suggested in the Pujo report included in the currency bill. See *ibid.*, July 23, 1913.

¹³ Hundreds of Chinese had been killed in a rebellion at Shanghai against the government of President Yüan. See above, July 21, 1913; and the *Washington Post*, July 24, 1913.

July 28, 1913

Mr. President, are we correct in our speculations about Mexico as they appear in the papers this morning?

There have been so many, I must say I can't—

The mediation proposal[1] as a solution of the problem?

Oh, well, I am not committing myself to anything at present because I am studying the thing and I haven't even had a conference with Ambassador Wilson yet. I have only to say, as Mr. Dooley does, "I see by the papers."

You have seen his reports, though, have you [not]?

I have seen what is in the papers and his report dictated at Mr. Bryan's office.[2]

Would you care to say what recommendations—

I think it is premature to discuss that.

Mr. President, there appeared a news dispatch from Mexico City this morning that an official telegram from the United States Government had been received, and it rather aroused anti-American feeling. Can you say anything about that?[3]

I don't know anything about such a telegram.

Is there any suggestion as to Lind?[4]

I hadn't heard the suggestion.

There was.

That must be an echo of the discussion some time ago, only as a rumor.

Mr. President, have you any information that would contradict previous information with regard to the insecurity of the Huerta administration?[5]

Well, I have seen the—I have confirmatory information also. It is just a question of which reports to believe.

You are not convinced either way yourself?

No, I am not convinced either way. I don't feel clear about it.

Mr. President, can you not, in view of the rather excited condition of newspaper headlines and the public mind, permit yourself to make some sort of statement in our papers today in reference to Mexico?

Well, to tell you the truth, I don't think that the public mind is in the least excited. I think the newspaper headlines are headlines, but the exaggerations are confined for the most part to one part of the United States. And I don't think that there is any uneasiness to be arrived at except in certain quarters where uneasiness is justified, where people have employees or friends or relatives in Mexico. About their condition, you may assume us to be in sympathy with their uneasiness. I don't see anything. Nothing, certainly, has developed in the last week or ten days that increases my anxiety.

May we indirectly use that in our newspapers, and what can we say in the newspapers?

Why, I think you can just say this, that nothing has developed here which seems to make the situation either better or worse than it was ten days or two weeks ago.

And that so far as the administration of this country is concerned, what course is it pursuing?

It is pursuing a course of diligent inquiry, to see just what is the right thing to do.

When that information is gathered, Mr. President, will there be some definite and direct action on the part of this country?

That I can't say—how definite and direct—because that is just the point under debate.

When do you expect to see the Ambassador, Mr. President?

At two-thirty.

Mr. President, will any members of Congress be present at your conference with the Ambassador?

No, sir, it is not as serious as all that.

Mr. President, is there anything additional to be said at this time with reference to the Dixon matter?

No. We are simply using the utmost diligence to straighten that out.

Will it be decided today, Mr. President, whether the Ambassador is returning to Mexico?

No, I think not.

Mr. President, have you had any recent requests for permission to export arms to the Huerta government?[6]

No, they are [tapering off].

Even if you cut them off entirely from this country, they would still be able to get them.

Yes. There are abundant sources from which they can get them.

The revolutionists are in a position where it is hard to get arms that do not come from this country.

Yes. But just between you and me, it's a long border. I have my thoughts. But not everybody asks for permission.

Mr. President, how do you regard the legislative situation in the House Committee on Banking and Currency? Is the Glass bill secured?

Yes.[7]

Have you had to mediate there, Mr. President?

Nothing to do there but attend to business.

Do you think that the committee will be able to agree upon a measure?

The committee will probably be able to do that.

Mr. President, is there anything you could tell us about the developments in Nicaraguan policy?

There hasn't been anything more since I last saw you. [A break in Swem's notes here.] No, sir—checking into that, I mean, returning to that banking and currency question for a moment, I would like you gentlemen to give out the impression in some way that will occur to you as well as myself that there has not been the slightest wavering or supplicating on the part of the administration in its support for the bill as proposed, and that there is no likelihood of changes of any essential kind being made in the committee.

Mr. President, on that point, have you suggested, or is it your thought that that bill should go into the caucus of the greater House committee?[8]

I haven't suggested anything about it. I have heard that there is a general intimation suggested.

That course would make it a party measure?

That would be the natural course in regard to an administration bill.

There had been some thought at first that it might go in as a bipartisan measure and might receive some Republican support.

Well, by making it a party measure, we wouldn't mean to risk Republican support that wanted to vote for it.

Mr. President, have you got anything with reference to any protest against the sailors' action?[9]

On Friday last or two weeks ago? You mean in Seattle? No, it hasn't been brought to me.

They have made a protest.

If they have, it hasn't reached me.

Mr. President, with reference to Japan and the various exchanges up to this time, has there been anything indicated by way of a solution?

Why, I think the matter has been debated until there is practically complete understanding between the two governments. It is not so much a solution except that we should entirely understand one another. The minute we understand one another, there will be no trouble. Of course, the purposes are perfectly friendly on both sides.

Does that mean the cessation of the controversy?

Well, if the debate was concluded, that would mean cessation.

Do you look upon the debate as concluded, Mr. President?

Well, I don't know. We had the last say. We will wait and see whether they will reply or not. I don't know.

Mr. President, has there been any further negotiation or action with regard to the Panama Canal tolls?

No, nothing whatever.

Has England practically withdrawn their protest, Mr. President?

Oh, no, not so far as I know. It is just where it stood when I came into office.

[1] Wilson was at this time considering a mediation plan which called for an armistice to be followed by a free election in which Huerta would not be a candidate. See Link, *The New Freedom*, pp. 356-58.

[2] Ambassador Wilson arrived in Washington on July 26 and prepared a historical résumé of events in Mexico. See the *New York Times*, July 27, 1913. The nineteen-page memorandum is in WP, DLC.

[3] The State Department was demanding the release of Charles B. Dixon, a United States immigration inspector, who had been shot in the back by Mexican soldiers at Ciudad Juárez on July 26. See the *New York Times*, July 28, 1913.

[4] Former Governor John Lind of Minnesota, who was to be Wilson's emissary to Mexico to negotiate his scheme of mediation based on a plan first proposed by Judge Delbert James Haff of Kansas City. See Hill, *Emissaries to a Revolution*, pp. 33-34, 63-69.

[5] It had been suggested by the press and by President Wilson himself that the Huerta administration was about to collapse. See above, July 21, 1913.

[6] The White House had announced on July 23 that Wilson would soon cut off the shipment of American arms to the Huerta government. See the *New York Times*, July 24, 1913.

[7] On July 28, the House Committee on Banking and Currency voted to report the Glass bill to the Democratic caucus on August 11. See *ibid.*, July 29, 1913.

[8] That is, the Democratic House caucus.

[9] On July 18, a party of marines and sailors from the Pacific reserve fleet attacked the Socialist headquarters and Industrial Workers of the World Hall in Seattle. See the *New York Times*, July 19, 1913.

Aug. 4, 1913

I have to come to the conclusion that Monday morning is a bad morning to see you fellows because I have nothing in my mind on a Monday morning, and I don't fill it up until the week starts.

May we know why Ambassador Wilson is recalled from New York?[1]

For further consultation.

With whom?

With the Secretary of State.

Mr. President, is the withdrawing of the Nicaraguan treaty from the Senate committee to be announced?[2] Has the State Department, or have you, had anything from Latin American countries that would lead you to believe that they would not look favorably on the proposition?

With regard to themselves, certainly not with Nicaragua.

Nor any of the South American countries such as Argentina?

No.

No protest at all?

No, sir. Oh, no, they haven't said anything about it. With regard to the treaty, I think Mr. Bryan is going to say something to the correspondents this morning.

With reference to the Mexican situation, Mr. President, have the Senators conferred with you regarding their plan to call different people before the Senate committee?[3]

They have.

You haven't suggested the ones they should call?

I think that would be imprudent for me to do.

Is the House committee acting similarly?

The House committee hasn't consulted me with regard to whom they should call.

The action of Mr. Flood[4] last week, Friday or Saturday, rescinding their invitation to Mr. Wilson—

I didn't know that they had called him. As a matter of fact, Mr. Flood told me that they would not call him.

Mr. President, may we expect some action soon on Mexico?

Yes, sir. I hope I shall have something to announce within a very few hours—I mean, some procedure to announce in a very few hours—either today or tomorrow morning.

Mr. President, that would have regard to the general situation, not merely to the status of Mr. Wilson?

It will have regard to the general situation.

It has been suggested that you might decide on a plan for mediation in Mexico and not make it public until you have attempted to put it into effect.

I might. That is among the possibilities.

This information you will give us—

Of course, my preference would be not to do that. But we are dealing with a very peculiar situation, and we will just have to deal with it in the way we have been, and will be most likely to succeed.

This information you are to give us today or tomorrow will be about action?

It will be just as much as I can squeeze out.

Mr. President, are you pretty well determined now as to what your course is going to be—your initial step?

I think so, yes.

Mr. President, I will ask, has it anything to do with our interpretation of the neutrality laws?

There is no new interpretation of the neutrality laws. There is only one interpretation of the neutrality laws. But the question you are probably thinking of is the abrogation of the neutrality laws.

With respect to recognizing the government, isn't it, Mr. President?

No, the neutrality laws have nothing to do with that.

Mr. President, while that resolution of March 14, 1912,[5] is in force, would you have the authority to permit both factions in Mexico to receive arms and ammunition?

I don't know. I mean, I can't speak with confidence on the interpretation of that. I have been—I should have the right, inasmuch as it is a resolution which leaves it to my discretion. Wherever there is discretion, I suppose it can be used one way as well as the other.

You certainly would have the authority to rescind the privilege the Mexican government has now to receive them.

Yes, I think I would.

Mr. President, have you decided anything as to the future of Ambassador Wilson?

Well, that is a delicate question.

Certain newspapers are continually publishing statements that everything is pointing to armed intervention.

Well, they are dead wrong. There is no probability, I should say hardly a possibility. The pacification solution seems to be getting more practicable every day.

Mr. President, will you tell us whether you had some encouraging reports with regard to the particular plan which is in mind?

No, I can't say that I have, because that particular plan is not known to anybody.

Not with any prominent leaders in Congress?

No, sir. Of course, you understand that I have conferred with the chairmen of the two foreign relations committees. I have opened my mind to them, but it is not their plan.

You say that a pacification solution seems more practical every day. Could you develop that line a little?

No, sir. I hope to develop it in another way. I think the less I say about it the better.

Mr. President, have you taken any action with regard to Venezuela?[6]

No, none at all. We are going to send a Minister there as soon as we can. That post is vacant. We have already sent a Secretary there.[7] The Minister will follow very promptly.

Well, has any action been considered with reference to Castro?[8] You know he is a man without a country.

Well, we haven't got him. What should we do? If he were in our jurisdiction, he might be worth considering.

There is a treaty coming up again, Mr. President, with reference to wood pulp.[9]

[Break in Swem's notes]
I don't know what is being done as to the interpretation of the declaration of these several governments, because it is based on exchanges among ourselves. I may say, I heartily sympathize with it, but there have been so many expositions and simply the governments have been just waiting, and many some time; and while we are deeply interested—all Americans are deeply interested in this exposition,[10] just privately, I don't blame them. It has nothing to do with international questions and their feeling with regard to pending controversies, I am sure.

In case of trouble, it has nothing to do with the Canal tolls?

I am sure it hasn't from what has been seen in connection with it. It is just a matter of whether it is worth their while or not, and honestly I don't think it is. To return to your question, I didn't know that there was any intimation that our treaty with Panama had to be revised. I hadn't heard of that.

You mean the declaration of Panama on the wood pulp question?

I don't see how the wood pulp question—

It lends itself to the necessity of a new treaty.

That they are entitled to the privilege of a very necessary further arrangement. It hasn't been brought to my attention.

There has been nothing, then, towards the selection of the Minister?[11]

Not yet.

With reference to the Commerce Court, Mr. President, have you taken any steps in that matter? It's hanging fire between two bills on the House side.[12]

There aren't any steps to take on this end of the avenue.

That depends upon the view.

Mr. President, have you heard that Great Britain contemplates the establishment of a naval base in the Bermuda Islands?

No, sir. She always has had one there. I have visited Bermuda frequently and I know that naval station. She uses it to maintain men of—what you might call a naval yard force, men for the repair of ships. So far as I can understand it, all she is going to do now is to increase that force because it would be more of a load than it was before. And her ships naturally come there. She has always had an enormous dry dock capable of caring for any man-of-war. The naval establishment there has a big house and grounds for the naval command—a very elaborate establishment there.

Is it fortified?

Not elaborately at all. It is fortified in what I might call a superficial way. They have got guns there, but they are not buried guns, or anything of that sort, at least so far as I know. I didn't see them.

How about currency, Mr. President, is there any change in that situation?

Oh, no. It's going on all right.

In the event testimony was not favorable on this Section 11,[13] you can take it out and cancel it?

Not on that issue. That is not a possibility. We are not running the government by the suggestions of the minority.

The same report that I saw also stated that you had practically closed the doors of the White House to those who would dispute your leadership.

It is ridiculous. I can learn, gentlemen, even if I have become President.

---

[1] Ambassador Wilson was recalled from New York on the evening of August 3. On the next day, following this press conference, the White House announced his resignation and the Lind mission.

[2] On August 2, the Senate Foreign Relations Committee voted not to recommend Senate approval of the provisions of the proposed treaty which established a protectorate over Nicaragua. See the *New York Times*, Aug. 3, 1913.

[3] The Senate Foreign Relations Committee was conducting hearings on the situation in Mexico.

[4] Representative Henry De La Warr Flood, Democrat of Virginia, chairman of the House Foreign Affairs Committee, had called the Ambassador to testify on July 31. Flood rescinded the invitation on August 1 at President Wilson's request. See the *New York Times*, Aug. 1-2, 1913.

[5] The Joint Resolution of March 14, 1912. See above, July 24, 1913.

[6] Venezuela was undergoing a revolution. The cruiser *Des Moines* had been ordered there to look after American interests. See the *New York Times*, Aug. 3, 1913.

[7] On August 2, Wilson had named Henry F. Tennant of New York as the new Secretary of the American legation at Caracas. See *ibid.*, Aug. 3, 1913.

[8] Cipriano Castro, former President of Venezuela, who was behind the revolution and leading an invasion of the country.

[9] The Senate was debating the wood and pulp provisions of the tariff bill. See *Cong. Record*, 63d Cong., 1st sess., pp. 3045-49.

[10] Wilson referred here to the announcement by a number of European countries, including England and Germany, that they would not take part in the Panama Exposition to be held in San Francisco in 1915. Their stated concern was that their industrial products and processes displayed at the exposition would not be protected under American law. See the *New York Times*, Aug. 3-4, 1913.

[11] On August 6, Wilson named William Jennings Price of Kentucky as Minister to Panama.

[12] See above, April 11, 1913.

[13] Section 11 created the Federal Reserve Board and was the source of much controversy at this time.

Aug. 11, 1913

We are just as anxious to hear about Mexico as you are. We are here in large numbers.[1]

Some mornings there's nothing new. This morning, I see a good many dispatches from Mexico City in the papers, but I don't know which of them are well founded and which are not.

When do you expect to hear from Mr. Lind, Mr. President?

I can't say that there is any time we expect to hear from him. Of course, he will speak when he has something to say.

Mr. President, the proposal that he carries with him, the suggestion or whatever it is, will it be made public here or in Mexico?

I don't know, sir. Of course, you understand that our instructions to Mr. Lind are chiefly to let us know how this thing stands there, and just what the opportunities for offering our good offices in the interests of peace there are. Then anything that we instruct him to do that is susceptible of being made public will be made public, when we instruct him. So there is no fixed time.

He goes with a sort of blanket instruction to look over the ground and keep you closely advised? It may be that he will not present any—

Well, sooner or later the embassy there will make some suggestions to Huerta's government. Just when and in what circumstances, we can't yet foresee.

Has Mr. Hale reported any more that we might know?

No, he hasn't reported anything in the last forty-eight hours.

On the whole, the situation has materially improved in the last forty-eight hours?

I think it has. In other words, I think all the rather excited expectations are dissipated as to something unfortunate happening.

Mr. Huerta's attitude towards the presence of your representative there?[2] Your conference with the Foreign Relations Committee had quite a good effect on both sides?[3]

I think so, yes. In my conference with the Senators, I found they were quite ready to fall in with the program, once it was explained to them.

Mr. President, there has been a great deal of discussion lately, and it was voiced in the Senate by Senator Williams[4] on Saturday, that most of this warscare talk was an organized attempt on the part of certain American interests who had interests in Mexico to stir up a war between this country and Mexico. Are you inclined to that view at all?

Oh, I have no views as to where it's coming from. There is evidently an organized desire somewhere to have a war with Mexico, but where it comes from, I can't even [conjecture]. There could not be such colossal lying going on if there wasn't something the matter—the most colossal and impudent lying.

Is that so extensive, Mr. President, as to justify you in saying that it is an organized desire?

Organized is just a carelessly used word. It is not so extensive as to justify that as a serious statement, I should think, and of course I wouldn't say that as contravening anything Senator Williams has said, because he very likely has information that I haven't got.

He used that word in the Senate Saturday.

So I understand.

Mr. President, I think he expressed the belief that an organized monied effort was—

Mr. President, has the Huerta government made any overtures to this government at all, suggesting any alternatives?

No. None whatever of any kind.

Mr. President, have you heard in any way, directly or indirectly, from Carranza since Mr. Lind [left]?

Neither before or since. Never.

Have you had a note, as I understand it?

No, sir.

I would rather like to know what the *Carrancistas* have in mind.

I would like to know, indeed, what they have in mind.

The dispatches published in the papers said that they would advise you.

They haven't as yet.

Have there been any suggestions from any foreign governments?

Not the slightest.

Has there been any consideration of Congressman Kahn's suggestion that we invite Argentina, Chile, and Brazil to cooperate with us?

I didn't know that Mr. Kahn had made it.[5]

It was printed in all the newspapers yesterday.

There hasn't been anything of that sort.

There has been no change, has there, Mr. President, with reference to the embargo on arms?

No, none at all.

Mr. President, has your attention been directed to a statement put in the *Congressional Record* by Senator Sheppard of Texas, giving the history and purposes of Carranza?[6]

Yes. Senator Sheppard himself called my attention to it, and I read it with a great deal of interest.

It says that three fourths of Mexico is under the control of the Constitution-alists.

Yes, of course, it is very difficult to make those estimates. I dare-say that is as accurate an estimate as could be made in the cir-cumstances. I have been getting reports at various times as to the extent of the territory controlled by those forces, and I daresay that is quite correct. At any rate, with regard to the northern half of Mexico, of course. They have no hold on the south of Mexico, where the *Zapatistas* are.

A determination was made that 90 per cent of the people of Mexico are in sympathy with the Constitutionalists themselves.

You know, the peculiarity of Mexico is that 90 per cent have nothing to say about the government. It is only about 10 per cent that has been running it, time out of mind.

Mr. President, have you seen the caucus bill, the currency bill—the amend-ments?[7]

I haven't seen the latest draft at all. I know what is in it, but I haven't seen it printed at all.

Could you say, as it now stands, whether it still has the administration's approval?

Entirely. I was consulted at every step about it.

Is there a definite possibility of the recognition of the revolutionists or the Constitutionalists of Mexico?

Nothing of that sort has been considered yet.

Their movement is not strong enough to suggest even a recognition of their belligerency?

Well, I daresay that, in proportion to the power of the government in Mexico City, it is strong enough, but just as a matter of fact, we haven't taken the question up.

With reference to the currency question, Mr. President, was the suggestion of the bankers laid before you, that this advisory council be given the initiatory power instead of the other way around?[8]

No, it was not. There could be no question of laying it before me. We might as well give up. The whole central governing board has to do that.

Senator Owen said, Mr. President, that he would be in favor of modification of the reserve plan.

Just what he had in mind—I saw that in the paper.[9] Just what he had in mind, I don't know. He hasn't spoken to me about that.

You mean reducing the reserves?[10]

Yes.

The bankers were told at that meeting, I understand, that they thought that Senator Owen and Mr. Glass thought that that change could be made, but their other change would not work.

So whichever they passed, they propose, one, to change the reserves, and the other to give [initiative to bankers].

So has the disposition toward the bill by the bankers changed, has it become more friendly?

I think it has become much more. I think I can say the disposition among what I might call the little size, the little bankers, is almost uniquely so.

Whatever opposition among bankers exists is among the large banks.

In the monetary community alone.

Do you include the [interlocking directorates by] the National banks?

The bill as it now stands enables them to be trustees.

Are you still satisfied with the prospect of passage of the bill in the Senate, Mr. President?

Yes. I have been looking the field over rather carefully. I don't see any serious obstacle.

How soon do you expect the tariff bill to be through?

The Lord only knows, I don't.

[1] The main topic of the day was the Lind mission, whereby Wilson hoped to mediate the civil war in Mexico. Lind arrived in Mexico City on August 10 but did not begin conversations with Mexican officials until August 12. See Hill, *Emissaries to a Revolution*, pp. 68-75.

[2] Huerta had publicly attacked Wilson's decision to send Lind to Mexico City and had whipped the people in the capital into such a patriotic frenzy that the Governor of the Federal District feared that the American emissary might be mobbed at the railway station when he arrived. See *ibid.*, pp. 69-72.

[3] On August 9, Wilson and Bryan conferred for two hours with members of the Senate Foreign Relations Committee. Lind's mission was a principal topic of discussion, and Wilson informed the Senators that the administration would not recognize the Huerta government. See the *New York Times*, Aug. 10, 1913.

[4] Senator John Sharp Williams, Democrat of Mississippi. See *Cong. Record*, 63d Cong., 1st sess., p. 3217.

[5] On August 9, Representative Julius Kahn, Republican of California, issued a statement deploring the situation in Mexico and urging the administration to invite Chile, Brazil, and Argentina to assist the United States in restoring peace. See the *New York Times*, Aug. 10, 1913.

[6] A "Memorandum Relative to the Mexican Situation" was put into the *Record* by Senator Morris Sheppard, Democrat of Texas, on August 6. See *Cong. Record*, 63d Cong., 1st sess., pp. 3129-33. It was a memorandum by Francisco Escudero, representative of Carranza in Washington, dated July 24, 1913, printed in *PWW*, Vol. 28, pp. 70-81.

[7] That is, the bill to be presented to the House Democratic caucus.

[8] Bankers from the Midwest met with Secretary of the Treasury McAdoo on August 8 and proposed that a Federal Advisory Council, composed of bankers, rather than the Federal Reserve Board, have the power of initiative in conducting the reserve currency system. See the *New York Times*, Aug. 9, 1913.

[9] It appeared in the *New York Times* on August 10.

[10] The bankers proposed that the reserve requirement be lowered from 15 per cent to 12 per cent.

Aug. 14, 1913

Mr. President, to relieve the embarrassment, have you taken any action at all with regard to the statement that Mr. Henry Lane Wilson made yesterday, with regard to a statement from the British?[1]

No, sir, I haven't and—I mean, expecting that you gentlemen would wish to know about that, I would follow the right etiquette in the matter and refer you to the State Department, which may or may not have a statement to make later in the day. I don't know whether it will or not. I am just asking that you will go there rather late this afternoon to see if there is anything.

Mr. President, would you care to say anything about this proposed recess of Congress?[2]

Nothing, except that I mean—I mean it.[3]

Mr. President, have you taken any action this morning, or today, with reference to stopping the effort to have a recess?

No, none at all. Oh, I am confident that will take care of itself, as a matter of fact.

Your idea is, then, that Congress should stay right through until the currency legislation is completed?

Yes, that is my idea, and I think that is what is more than my idea, I think that is the idea of the country.

Have you got any communications to indicate that?

I have had, I can't say how many, but a very considerable number of communications from many parts of the country. All indicate that they think it is just as important that we should stay here and complete the tariff bill, and not take the one without the other; which is, in a sense, complete—that the business of the country needs the assistance of the currency act just as it needs to get the relief of the tariff act.

Have you had correspondence largely from bankers, Mr. President?

Not quite a large number of bankers. If I were to sum it up in one word, I would say that it was the general business feeling of the country—merchants and importers, and men of representative businesses of various kinds.

Have you been acquainted with any [an X mark by Swem here] that Congress on the part of Democrats are [here some outlines are scratched out].

I have heard indirectly that two or three Senators were opposed to it, but none of them has said so to me personally.

Mr. President, the idea of this recess is to simply take a little rest and then take up the currency bill before the regular session begins.

Yes, after the forces of opposition have gotten a little breather— got their second wind.

Mr. President, has your attention been directed to the statements frequently made on the floor of the Senate by some Republicans, to the effect that the tariff bill will take up so much time that it is very doubtful if they can get to currency legislation?

Yes, my attention has been called to that.

Do you think such a program could be carried out?

I think we could well take care of that, sir.

Mr. President, have you any hope that the tariff will be accelerated, the way it is going now?

Of course, you are privileged to say things about it that I am not.

I mean, what are the prospects of its being hastened?

I really don't know that. I can't say I have any definite expectations for it today. But it is incredible to me that the committee should continue to go as splenetically as it is now.

Mr. President, is this government communicating with foreign governments in regard to the Mexican situation?

Only sufficiently to let them know what the character of our effort is.

They say there are no exchanges, they are really communications from this government.

For information. There are no exchanges.

Mr. President, along that line, have we had any communications from foreign governments as to their attitude toward it?

No.

Can you tell us, Mr. President, anything about Mr. Lind's reports—what he has found in Mexico City?

Well, he hasn't made any reports on anything new that he has found. He has simply reported the very agreeable relations which he has already set up.[4]

Mr. President, does that indicate that we are getting closer to a recognition of Huerta, or are we getting further away from that?

I am not prophesying today. Well, that is in the nature of a prediction, and I don't think you can find any indication that things are going in that direction.

You are still in the same position with reference to that question?

Yes, sir. I have been anchored there for some time.

Mr. President, would you say, is there any prospect that this government will make a declaration that the Huerta government will not be recognized?

Oh, I can't say that. That will depend entirely on the developments, on the sort of declaration we should make.

I think—

By the way, you gentlemen, I am sure undesignedly, did me a considerable injustice the other day by reporting that I said that there was a war lobby.[5]

Now I want to call your attention to what I did say, because I am generally very careful to speak by the cards. I did not say that. You called my attention to the charge made by one of the Senators that there was an organized syndicate—I think that was the expression—intended to bring war on, and asked me if I was of that opinion. I said I had no evidence to that effect—I think you will remember that—and that all I could say was that it did look like a concerted effort in some quarters to produce a state of emergency which would have that result.

Now, any man can see, on the face of the thing itself, that I did not say there was a war lobby, and I don't want the country to get the impression that I make statements of that sort unless I have a large number of documents in my pocket.

Mr. President, that brings up a point that I would like to make and inquire about. I was not here the other morning when that occurred and my—they hadn't said anything to me about a lobby, but that you certainly shared the idea of Senator Williams.

The impressions I have are those I simply share with the public. I have no [other] impressions, no private information.

As I understand these inferences here, we are not to represent you as saying anything that is not quite right? You desire to correct the impression that you did think that there was a lobby. Now are we to use that?

No, I really was not suggesting that you correct the impression. I simply said this by way of confidence, so that—just as a more indirect way of asking you to be more careful about that sort of thing in the future. Such damage as was done has been done. I can't say it will wreck things, though it would chagrin me to read a number of editorials on my statement that there was a war lobby.

Mr. President, of course, in regard to an editor, there is a chance of a misunderstanding, and always a chance—a lot more of a certainty with editorials for misunderstanding.

I know how some editors have to be watched.

I think there were a good many newspapers which did not credit you with saying that there was a war lobby.

But some papers have a very bewildering effect on things, and they are just as likely to have editorials on them.

Mr. President, will Mr. Lind see General Huerta?

I don't know.

Mr. President, outside of the official statement that was made at the State Department, which was very brief, describing Mr. Lind's functions, would you be good enough or can you tell us more definitely what is his mission to Mexico?

Why, I don't see that I can add to what the State Department said.

That was my difficulty. I wanted to add something to it.

There isn't anything to be added. That is the literal statement of the facts. He has gone there in the only way he could go there in the existing circumstances.

Mr. President, as the imagination focuses on the questions, one of your answers, one of the possibilities now is the recognition of Mr. Huerta.

Well, you have much more advantage with your imagination, but I can't say anything to hang that imagination on.

Mr. President, I think that the time for the election—the constitutional election in Mexico—was October 25.

Twenty-six.

Now, is there any prospect, do you think, that an arrangement will be reached for elections at a date sooner than that?

I can't say that there is. I can only say that I hope there might be an earlier election than that. I think it would help to clear the decks immediately.

There was a suggestion in one of the press dispatches from Mexico City that the Constitutionalists had sent some communication to Mr. Lind.

I had not heard of that. I had not heard of that.

Mr. President, there is a good deal of confusion about your statement as taken from the State Department some time ago with regard to a communication that Mr. Lind took with him. The State Department said—referred to the President's communication being taken by Mr. Lind to Mexican leaders. When you were asked here by someone about Mr. Lind's presenting that communication to President Huerta, I understood you to say that that communication was to the Chargé,[6] or at least to the American embassy.

Well, the confusion must have arisen because of perhaps too critical attention to the language used. What I was meaning to say was that Mr. Lind, not being accredited to the Mexican government, would naturally communicate with it or at least get into communication with it through the Chargé d'Affaires down there.

The only point I wanted to clear up is what the communication was—whether it was a communication intended for the information of President Huerta or sent to this envoy with instructions to Chargé O'Shaughnessy.

It would naturally be both. It was a communication intended to fix in writing for Mr. Lind's use the views of this government. Of course, he would naturally communicate the views of this government as he got the opportunity.

Mr. President, in other words, you have a plan, but no choices?

Well, we have various ideas which we would like to suggest to the Mexican government.

Nothing inflexible about those views? They could be changed, based on investigation?

Well, they could well be changed in part.

Mr. President, was the purport of those suggestions communicated to the Foreign Relations Committee the other evening?

No, sir, except so far as I have indicated what we were after.

Are your views being communicated to Huerta or to his cabinet since Mr. Lind's arrival?

I don't know, sir.

Mr. President, what you have said just now I think has cleared up a great deal of confusion in our minds in regard to the administration's program, as I take it, from what you say.

The administration has a program. Yes, it has a definite set of views with regard to the situation down there.

And Mr. Lind has those views in writing?

Yes, sir—has them in writing. What we are really after, you see, is to make perfectly clear to General Huerta what our views are. They are entirely friendly views, and views intended to help the situation in Mexico without any intervention or meddling on our part.

The success of this program depends upon the voluntary acceptance of the views by him?

Of course. Yes.

Has Mr. Lind reported anything so far in the way of any obstacles in the way of these?

No, he has not.

Mr. President, have you ever seen any formal report from Mr. Henry Lane Wilson, or anybody else, that justified the statement that Huerta had promised that he would not be a candidate for constitutional President?[7]

No, sir.

But it is generally accepted that he did make such a statement.

You know, the dispatches I think were published at the time I was not in office and therefore I can't speak with confidence; but, as I remember, before I came into office, I had the distinct impression that, by implication, that would be part of the understanding arrived at at the outset—by plain implication. But I never understood that that was a definite, binding, and explicit promise.

Mr. President, it is announced in this morning's papers that Governor Foss intends to run in the Republican primary.[8] Can you make any comment on that?

No, sir. Some things are sufficient commentary in themselves.

Have you any idea of going and making a speech in the next campaign, Mr. President?

No.

Have you been asked about that report from Albany, that Governor Sulzer—⁹

Have I been asked? I heard about it, as I hear about various current events.

Have you any comment, Mr. President, on the Albany situation?

Oh, no.

[1] On August 13, Ambassador Wilson responded in a critical fashion to a British statement that the British government had made the decision to recognize Huerta after a congratulatory speech by the American Ambassador in Mexico City. Ambassador Wilson's remarks were an embarrassment to the administration at a difficult stage in its relations with Mexico. President Wilson issued an apology on August 14. See the *New York Times*, Aug. 14-15, 1913.

[2] Some Democratic Senators were favoring a month's recess after the Senate passed the tariff bill.

[3] Wilson had previously stated his opposition to a recess.

[4] Lind and Foreign Minister Federico Gamboa began cordial talks on August 12. See Hill, *Emissaries to a Revolution*, p. 75.

[5] See above, Aug. 11, 1913.

[6] Nelson O'Shaughnessy, American Chargé d'Affaires in Mexico City.

[7] That is, a candidate in the election to be held October 26.

[8] On August 13, Governor Eugene Noble Foss, Democrat of Massachusetts, a critic of the Wilson administration, announced that he might change parties and run for reelection as a Republican. See the *New York Times*, Aug. 14, 1913.

[9] On August 13, Governor William Sulzer of New York had been impeached by the New York Assembly for failing to report campaign contributions, for perjury, and for diverting campaign funds for speculation in the stock market. Sulzer was an alleged progressive, and there was much speculation that his impeachment had been engineered by Tammany Hall. See *ibid.*, Aug. 12-15, 1913, and Jacob Alexis Friedman, *The Impeachment of Governor Sulzer* (New York, 1939).

Aug. 18, 1913

Mr. President, to break the ice, have you any new information from Mexico this morning?

There isn't anything. I am hoping during the day to get something that will be "meat" for discussion.

Mr. President, have you heard that your views have been laid before the [Foreign Minister]?[1]

Yes.

Can you give us any ideas as to when you will make those views public?

No, I can't. As soon as agreeable to the Mexican authorities.

Will that be made in a speech, whether they are refused or accepted?

I don't know. I never can answer "If."

Mr. President, have you received any information from Mexico regarding Mr. Hale's status there?

No.

The present dispatches indicate that there is an intention on the part of some to make it unpleasant for him.[2]

I haven't the least information on that.

I believe you told us once, Mr. President, that Mr. Hale has no official standing whatever.

No, he has not.

He merely went down there?

Went down there. Before going, he got my request to keep me informed as to what was, in his judgment, going on. I have known him for a great many years and have known him to be one of the best observers.

I take it he is in this position, that if any demonstration is made against him, he will be like any other American citizen?

Yes, but I take an interest in him.

Mr. President, is Mr. Hale about to return to this country?

I don't know. He is not, so far as I know.

There is no information from there?

No.

Do the auguries continue favorable there?

It is just a big interrogatory point in my mind this morning. I
don't know whether they do or not.

Have you any kind of message from any of the Secretaries of State down there
except the Huerta people?

No.

Mr. President, have you talked with members of Congress on the Banking
and Currency Committee with regard to the so-called Representative Henry
matter?[3]

In regard to the caucus conversations? No.

So you wouldn't know what the attitude is as to compromise or suggestion of
a compromise?

There isn't going to be any.

Mr. President, may I inquire if there is any intention on the part of the administration to facilitate judicial proceedings attached to the Japanese land law?[4]

Why, we expressed our willingness to do anything that the government could properly do to facilitate a test case, but no test case
has been proposed yet.

Will the government in such case intervene on behalf of the Japanese in that
matter?

It could not intervene in a court proceeding. How do you mean?
By seeking the aid of the Department of Justice?

I mean where the construction of the treaty involves directly the Department
of Justice—

I expect we could ask to be represented. We have not formed
any plans merely because no cases have been initiated.

There were some dispatches Friday and Saturday, Mr. President, from Tokyo,
suggesting that this government agreed to indemnify Japanese subjects who
brought action under that alien-land law; further, there would be no protest
on the part of this government if the Japanese enacted a law similar to California's.[5]

Well, no, those were just speculative statements, of course. There
could not be any supposition on the part of this government about

Japan and what she has a perfect right to. I can't imagine any basis for the indemnification, except of course that the government would recognize its obligations to make indemnity if loss had been stipulated and it could be shown that Japanese citizens suffered under the treaty.

The story was not clear. I presumed from it that it stated that it meant where assessment had caused a loss or property had depreciated.

They were probably reasoning under the general obligations.

Mr. President, is any matter pending here now that would involve the Constitution regarding the complications in New York?[6]

Nothing that I have heard of. I don't see that anything could very clearly happen except an extradition from the District of Columbia.[7]

If there should be a physical clash between the two authorities there, would it be up to the federal government to see that law and order is—

All that the federal government has to do is to see that a republican form of government is guaranteed.[8]

They can have civil war there if they want it.

Yes, if they don't watch out. But you remember the language of the Constitution is that the federal government guarantees to every state a republican form of government.
There was a famous case—I don't remember the title of it—but it affected the government of the State of Rhode Island.[9] It came up in the early part of the last century, when they were under county governments, and the Government of the United States was called on. The decided position was that the Supreme Court said it had no such obligation [to interfere].[10]

Mr. President, at Newport[11] on Saturday, Mr. Daniels disclosed an hitherto unpublished statement that suggests the question as to what your view is regarding a normal increase of battleships.

Does that oblige me to form my views as a result of the inquiries? Since I did not get into the navy, I must regard myself as entirely detached from it; but I don't think that that, speaking seriously, is a matter for a difference of opinion. I haven't conferred with the naval committees of the houses about it as yet at all. I would like to know their side of it before assuming my own judgment.

The last two years have been for one battleship. The naval committee says, if permitted, they would like to finish six.

The judgment of the department has been, after it began two years ago, that there should be two a year. Since we have fallen behind, they think we ought to have four a year, simply to catch up.[12]

The General Board for a number of years has been working on a long line[13]— the department's recommendation—the Secretary's recommending to do—

But I haven't taken it up since I have been in office, and I don't know just how the matter stands at the other end of the avenue.

[1] Lind presented Wilson's message to Foreign Minister Gamboa on August 15.

[2] Mexican newspapers were conducting a hate campaign against Hale and wanted to see him deported as a "pernicious foreigner." See the *New York Times*, Aug. 18, 1913; and Hill, *Emissaries to a Revolution*, p. 87.

[3] Representative Henry, an opponent of the Glass-Owen bill, had criticized the measure as violating the Democratic platform. See the *New York Times*, Aug. 18, 1913.

[4] That is, to aid Japanese citizens who brought suits for reparations from the State of California.

[5] See the *New York Times*, Aug. 15, 1913.

[6] Following Governor Sulzer's impeachment, both he and the Lieutenant Governor, Martin Henry Glynn, were claiming to be the chief executive officer of the state.

[7] That is, an extradition case might raise the issue for the federal government as to which Governor had authority.

[8] See Article IV, Section 4, of the Constitution.

[9] The Dorr Rebellion, which resulted in 1842 in the existence of dual government in Rhode Island. See Marvin Gettleman, *The Dorr Rebellion* (New York, 1973).

[10] In *Luther v. Borden*, the Supreme Court refused to endorse either government on the ground that it was a political question and thus unfit for settlement by the court. It did recognize the authority of Congress and the President to intervene to determine which was the legal government. See Carl B. Swisher, *American Constitutional Development* (Boston, 1943), pp. 267-68.

[11] At the Naval War College at Newport, Rhode Island.

[12] Daniels recommended the construction of two battleships, eight destroyers, and three submarines. See Harold Sprout and Margaret Sprout, *The Rise of American Naval Power, 1776-1918* (Princeton, N. J., 1939), p. 304.

[13] The General Board of the Navy recommended a comprehensive building program which would include forty-eight battleships, 192 destroyers, and ninety-six submarines by 1920. See *ibid.*, pp. 305-306.

Aug. 21, 1913

Mr. President, the dispatches from Mexico give the terms of the United States or the suggestions, I believe that would be [the] right [term] for them. Can you tell us anything about those now?

Well, I tell you what I am going to do, gentlemen. At last the long-drawn-out, so far as the transmission was concerned—the long-drawn-out answer of the authorities in Mexico City has come.[1] We now know the full text of it. And it is my intention now to draw the various elements of the case together and then let the public know just as soon as possible. I can state it in a way that you won't be pessimistic about.

You won't give us the text, though?

The text? No.

The text of the Mexican—

Probably not. I will not say why I shouldn't.

You know what happened in the Senate today, I suppose?

I know the motion that was made—the resolution.[2]

It rather refuted that suggestion that you would not have the Congress or the people behind you.[3]

Yes. But I would rather—what I am trying to intimate is, I would rather make the statement as a whole than make it piecemeal, in answer to scattered questions.

When do you expect to do that?

Just as soon as I can complete it. Of course, you see, by way of explanation, I am not given any advance time to write. I am not going to give it this evening or tomorrow.

It won't be tonight?

No.

Mr. President, could you say—can you give us any idea of your opinion as to whether the outlook there now is favorable?

Oh, I don't think it is unfavorable. I think the thing is going to disentangle itself.

No more reason to be discouraged now than there was last week?

No. You have to give tangled skeins a good while to get unraveled.

It is generally stated, Mr. President, up in the Senate today, or in the corridors of the Capitol, as they debate, to keep to one purpose especially—to show that the people, when it came down to an international question, were solidly behind the President.

I want to say that Republican Senators who come to me have shown that spirit entirely. There hasn't been the slightest exhibition of partisanship in this matter. I think that the opinion in Mexico that it exists will presently be dissipated.

Mr. President, it will be at least twenty-four hours before we get any statement from you?

You see, I haven't really assembled the documents myself, and I want to make a complete thing of it.

Will it include any statement from Mr. Lind of his conversation with President Huerta?[4]

I imagine not. I hadn't thought of that. I will possibly bring that in.

---

[1] That is, Gamboa's reply to the message carried by Lind. Gamboa rejected Wilson's proposals and offered no compromise solutions. Instead, he made the counterproposal that a Mexican Ambassador be received in Washington and that Wilson send a new Ambassador to Mexico City without conditions. See Gamboa to Lind, Aug. 16, 1913, in *FR, 1913*, pp. 823-27.

[2] A reference to a resolution introduced by Senator Boies Penrose, Republican of Pennsylvania, on August 21 that President Wilson be requested to protect American citizens in Mexico. Penrose also introduced an amendment to a deficiency appropriations bill which granted $25,000,000 to the administration for the protection of American citizens in Mexico. See the *New York Times*, Aug. 22, 1913.

[3] The suggestion was made by Gamboa to Lind on August 18. Republican as well as Democratic Senators supported Wilson's position and refused to vote in favor of the Penrose resolution because it might complicate matters for the President. It was laid on the table and never acted upon. See the *New York Times*, Aug. 22, 1913; and *Cong. Record*, 63d Cong., 1st sess., pp. 3567-71.

[4] On August 19. See Hill, *Emissaries to a Revolution*, p. 80.

---

Aug. 25, 1913

Mr. President, can you tell us something about how active the foreign representatives in Mexico City have been in past weeks?

No, sir, I can't, because I haven't been there. No, I don't know. I know they have been exercising their good offices, but just how actively and just which ones, I don't know. As I say, I have read, of course, the dispatches in the papers.

Have you considered in any way a plan of intervention?

No, certainly not.

Have any of the foreign powers been approached officially or unofficially with respect to the Mexican situation—to add their moral support in our stand with Mexico?

We have informed them—we thought we ought to—of what we proposed to the Mexican government and left it to them to take what action they should choose.

Is your message going in tomorrow?[1]

Yes, if it is through, tomorrow. I mean, the circumstances apparently may change at any moment, and if they don't change, it is going in tomorrow.

And nothing in it has developed yet to change it. Will you—will you read it in person?

Oh, I suppose so, yes.

Committees here tonight?[2]

I would hope so. I haven't ascertained whether I can get all the members here tonight.

You will have all you can get to come here?

Yes.

Can you tell us how long your message is, Mr. President, approximately?

No, I can't, because I have got a new typewriter and I don't know how to count it; but it is longer than any I have ventured. Yet I daresay that doesn't mean it's very long.

How many typewritten pages?

It's about seven typewritten pages, but I don't know how many words are on the page.

Single space?
In addition to the message, Mr. President, will there be any correspondence sent to Congress?

My idea is to give them a summary of the situation.

That will be in the message?

That will be in the message.

Won't the correspondence accompany the message?

What correspondence?

Why I had a notion that the Huerta reply—

Oh, yes, that will accompany it. I thought you meant the general correspondence about the situation down there with Mr. Lind. Our proposals and their reply will of course accompany it.

Is the administration standing pat on its demand that Huerta will not be a candidate?[3]

Well, this is not a standpat administration, but if you will change the phrase, I will say that we haven't changed our attitude at all.

You don't seem to like that word, Mr. President?

No. The tone, it has sinister associations.

Mr. President, has there been anything official that President Huerta is planning to send an envoy of some kind up here?[4]

No, there hasn't. There was an intimation conveyed to us that they might wish to do that, but it wasn't official at all.

Mr. President, is there anything pending between this government and Mexico which might change your plan, or is there a possibility of something brand new happening?

Oh, there is nothing pending in the sense that we have any new proposals to make. Nothing from this end that will change the situation.

A Mexico City dispatch states that this government gave the Mexican government an ultimatum of twenty-four hours after the reading of the message.

No, we don't need an ultimatum.

Mr. President, there is a suggestion in Mexico City dispatches this morning that Mexicans thought that the next step should be a reply by this government to their reply to Mr. Lind's message.

Well, you can judge of the reasonableness of that when you read their reply. I don't think that that can be well founded, as a matter of fact, because that is a rather concave answer, an infinitive answer.

Mr. President, the American dispatches say that Mr. Lind will return to Washington after you read your message tomorrow. Anything about that?

No. I don't know what foundation that may have. Well, of course, if it's on the schedule.

Would you [say that the terms in which] your message is to be couched, that [it] will be the end of all negotiations?

Well, I think I had better wait for that because it is couched, I want to say, in very kindly terms. But I think that we ought all to recognize the fact that the situation in Mexico is appalling because it is controlled by a very small group of men, and it ought not to obscure our feeling about the Mexican people at all. We ought to remember that we are good friends of Mexico even though her affairs are being guided by a small group of people and, therefore, I wouldn't in any public utterance, or private, either, for that matter, use words of harshness or hostility.

Would you be willing, Mr. President, to say just what is the responsibility or the duty of the United States in the matter of protecting American citizens in Mexico? A great deal has been said about the dangers.

Of course, every government is obliged to hold every other government responsible to save the lives of its citizens.

Can you tell us if you have any specific recommendations to make to Congress?

Well, I think—you see, I don't know what may develop, and I think the real discussion of it is in the message, so I must wait until I am sure it is ready.[5]

Have you heard anything further today from Mexico City?

No. Mr. Forster[6] told me about an Associated Press dispatch. That is all I have heard.[7]

Mr. President, is there anything in the recommendations made by the bankers in Chicago as suggestions to the Glass currency committee?[8]

I merely saw the headlines yesterday. I wanted to be in a good humor on Sunday and I didn't read them, but as I understand it, they want us to take all the essential features out of the bill.

So that the [Federal Reserve Board] would not have major responsibilities?

So I understand.

Is there any possibility, Mr. President, that the administration will be willing to lessen the numbers of reserve banks? The bankers propose that the number be five instead of twelve.

I don't think that that will be accepted. Of course, that is really a matter—not an essential matter in one sense, though I think in another sense it is. I think there should be enough to serve the genuine economic units of the country, and my own judgment is that there are many more than five, there are—

Wouldn't that be—

You mean a central bank and branches? Yes, it could be. I don't know. I didn't mean to say central bank. Suppose you had only five other new banks, that would amount to the same thing. Usually the branch bank would have to perform the same functions. What they object to, I believe, is to divide the reserves into twelve parts instead of five.[9]

Mr. President, just before the resolution was passed by the bankers suggesting the change, Mr. Reynolds[10] told the bankers at the convention that he had just come from Mr. McAdoo in New York, and that Mr. McAdoo had assured him that the bankers would get about all they wanted in the bill. It occurred to me to ask you if you knew or suggested to Mr. McAdoo any such thing?[11]

I don't believe that either Mr. Reynolds or Mr. McAdoo said anything of the kind. That is my own judgment on that, because it is incredible on the face of it. I am quite sure that Mr. McAdoo never said anything of the kind. If he did, he hadn't the slightest notion what they were going to ask. I wouldn't say so. Now it is conceivable that certain changes of a minor sort may have been mentioned to him and he may have said that. I don't see that there would be any supposition that he made any such statement as that.

It seemed inconceivable that Mr. Reynolds would make any such a statement in a public meeting unless he had had some discussion with Mr. McAdoo to lead him to state that.

I am quite sure the thing isn't so, and I am privileged to believe that Mr. Reynolds wouldn't say it was so. I think he must have been misunderstood, because Mr. Reynolds is a very honorable man.

The sum and substance of his statement was that, if the bankers assisted the administration in passing the bill, they stood a better chance by hearty co-operation.

Yes, that is true. These resolutions, as I understood them in outline are, so far from being an assistance, they are an exact antagonism.

They present one essential feature, to take out the word "compulsory" and not compel the National banks [to join the system]. Has this been discussed?

Of course, the whole thing will go by the board.

Mr. President, what do you hear from the businessmen?

I hear not only from the businessmen but from the bankers of the country—the rank and file of the bankers of the country—the most hearty support of the bill. As it stands, there could never be any doubt about that.

[Didn't they suggest that without changes you might expect difficulty from bankers in their whole] professional number?

Exactly, and only this morning I got what might be called a tip from a banker who was present at that convention, not to pay any attention to it.

You mean, one of them speaks out and the first big banker tells the next what to say in public?

That's right.

These bankers went on and told the newspapers for publication that they were going to get exactly what they wanted and had been so assured.

What did they want?

They did not say.

If they want what is reasonable, I daresay they will get it.

There is no likelihood, Mr. President, is there, of reducing federal governmental responsibility here?[12]

You mean, there is no chance of that?

Yes.

None whatever.

Some bankers made the statement they believed they would probably get a veto.

They will not.

Is there any likelihood of reducing the number of men on the Federal Reserve Board?

I haven't heard that proposed.

Eliminate the Secretary of Agriculture and the Comptroller of the Currency, making it five.[13]

I haven't heard that before.

The bankers propose the Secretary of the Treasury and six members, three of them to be bankers. That is the proposition.

Well, I think that question answers itself. We are going to have the control exercised by the Government of the United States.

[How does Mr. Harrison feel about the Philippines?][14]

I know he feels exactly as I myself feel. He said a week ago in public that, whatever we do in the Philippines, must be done for the people of the Philippine Islands and not for ourselves, that we are trustees in the profoundest sense of the word, trustees of the Philippine Islands for the people of the Philippine Islands. That is the keynote in my mind of everything that we must do there. That is an easy part to state. It is not so easy to say how wisely you carry the trusteeship out. That is to be our study.

On that principal question of independence, it wouldn't be necessary to put it immediately into effect.

Well, no proposal has ever been made, but it has contemplated a very active preparation for independence.

We all recognize it as coming some day.

Oh, yes, and we hope very soon.

¹ Wilson addressed a joint session of Congress on the subject of Mexican affairs on August 27. He spoke of his desire to see honest, democratic government in Mexico and promised the assistance of the United States in achieving that objective. He made public his instructions to Lind and detailed the failure of Lind's mission, which he attributed to the inability of the Huerta government to understand his true intentions. After promising to exercise restraint in dealing with the delicate situation in Mexico, he invoked the arms embargo provisions of the joint resolution of March 14, 1912, thus denying the shipment of arms to both sides in the conflict. The address is printed in *PWW*, Vol. 28, pp. 227-31.

² That is, a briefing in the White House for the Senate and House foreign relations committees.

³ That is, to succeed himself as President of Mexico.

⁴ Huerta proposed to send Manuel Zamacona, a former Mexican Ambassador to Washington, to confer with Wilson. Wilson refused to receive him. See Hill, *Emissaries to a Revolution*, p. 94.

⁵ Wilson's message proposed the evacuation of Americans from Mexico. See *PWW*, Vol. 28, p. 230.

⁶ Rudolph Forster, White House head usher and factotum.

⁷ Probably a reference to an A.P. dispatch from Mexico City to the effect that European and Latin American nations were not putting pressure on Huerta to resign. See the *New York Times*, Aug. 26, 1913.

⁸ In Chicago, on August 22 and 23, the Currency Commission of the American Bankers' Association met with the presidents of forty-seven state bankers' associations and the heads of the 191 clearinghouse associations to discuss the Glass bill. The results were a number of criticisms of the measure and a list of demands to be met before the bankers would support it. See Link, *The New Freedom*, pp. 226-27.

⁹ The bankers proposed branch banks which would serve the same purpose as additional Federal Reserve banks. See the *New York Times*, Aug. 24, 1913.

¹⁰ George McClelland Reynolds, president of the Continental and Commercial National Bank of Chicago.

¹¹ On August 25, McAdoo denied making such a statement. See the *New York Times*, Aug. 26, 1913.

¹² That is, in the Federal Reserve System.

¹³ The Secretary of Agriculture was eliminated from the board in the Federal Reserve Act as passed by Congress.

¹⁴ On August 20, Wilson had nominated Francis Burton Harrison of New York to be Governor-General of the Philippines.

Aug. 28, 1913

Mr. President, have you received the last exchanges of notes from Mr. Lind?¹

I have, but I received them about five minutes ago. I haven't read them. But I want to make this suggestion to you gentlemen, if you please. If it should turn out that they are yielding to our suggestions, more or less, in Mexico it would serve the whole situation very much if you would be thoughtful not to write [so as to offend] the sensibilities of the Mexican people. We have to deal not only with a group of provisional authorities there but also with the feelings of the Mexican people. A certain proportion of them have battened up, in a way, behind the present administration in Mexico City, and they don't like to be spoken of as having "taken water" any more than we would. And if you gentlemen would help along by phrasing what you write in a way that will be careful of their sensibilities, it would help very much. I don't know yet except but what I learn from the newspapers that they are yielding, and if they are yielding, I am inclined to reopen the matter with Mr. Lind as negotiator. But if that should be true a handout from my office will be the wise way, and the way to promote success, to handle it. I thought I would take the liberty of suggesting that to you.

Has Mr. Lind gone back to the City of Mexico?[2]

I understand that he is going back or he has gone back. I am not sure which, but he is going back to Mexico City.[3]

Is it possible that you would modify your suggested good offices—that is— that there might be any moderation on your part of the proposals you make?

I think it must be evident to you all that what we suggested was extremely moderate and in a way a minimum of what would offer a basis for some kind of settlement down there.

Yes, but I thought a concession might serve diplomatic purposes and still not be very vital to the other side.

We would wish to concede anything that was not essential, certainly.

Mr. President, suppose Huerta indicates that, by remaining in the presidency, he will eliminate himself from the presidential race in October, would you regard that in any way as a compliance with your suggestion?

Well, that would depend entirely upon what we finally found he intended to do.

I mean, if he said he was going to stand firmly on that constitutional provision.

You see, just among ourselves here, you must keep this in mind. There is a danger that, by accepting that kind of assurance, we, by implication, accept that he is President by operation of law. If he is President by operation of law, he is, by the terms of the Mexican Constitution, ineligible to succeed himself. If he is not, he is not. We have to be pretty careful, therefore, in what form we accept his assurance.[4]

Yes, sir, I realize that, but he says he won't be a candidate because he is standing by the Constitution. It seems to me that that rather meets your suggestion halfway.

Yes, it halfway interprets it that he must stand by the Constitution whether he himself is constitutional or not. I think it would be very wise on his part to follow that course, because it is the only course which is consistent with his intentions.

I think he does intend, according to the press dispatches.

Yes.

Mr. President, wouldn't you consider [recognizing] him if he is willing to hold a fair election? He claims recognition under his Constitution.

No. It is a *de facto* government. *De jure* governments are a different thing. It is a *de facto* government, very much in the possession of the machinery of election as a *de jure* government.

His request for recognition is as a *de jure*, not a *de facto* government?

Yes. It is not necessarily—not necessarily, no. But I understood that that was his request.

Mr. President, if Mr. Huerta should resign, say a week before the election in October, in a judicious statement saying it was based on very good precedents under law, and then the day before election, in the interim having removed himself as the Provisional President, he therefore becomes eligible for election. The day before election he declares that he is a candidate, how then?

As you know, I don't like to answer hypothetical questions. It is a little awkward to do so and partly because it likely would not be consistent with what he intended us to understand his present assurances to be.

Is there any possibility whatever that you might—I mean, consent to his being a candidate and let him have a shot before the people?

Well, I think you can answer that by the terms of our suggestions.[5]

I know. Is there any possibility of a change in them?

You see, what we are trying to do is to bring about cooperation in Mexico, to secure a rearrangement by constitutional methods. Now, we would have to have the cooperation in that respect of the men who are now absolutely refusing to recognize the authority of Huerta.

Mr. President, have you had any assurances from Governor Carranza or any of the rest of them that they would come in on this arrangement?

I haven't had any communications with them.

The reason I asked that question is because it has been suggested that that might be the thing to try.

You see, that no longer is susceptible of discussion because, as I said, I am told in this note[6] that he is ineligible. So I want relations with Carranza to be consistent with Huerta's present intention, on which his position stands.

It said that in the message you presented to Congress yesterday.

The Constitution itself says that. I don't remember that in that note.[7]

Was Mr. Lind requested or ordered to return to Mexico City? Was he requested or ordered to return?

No. Mr. Lind is much nearer the operation than we are, and he is acting on his knowledge of what the circumstances there are.

He is going on his own initiative?

Yes, constantly keeping us in touch, so far as the slow telegraphic communication will permit.

Mr. President, I hope it is a fair assumption that he would not go back unless there was a very good opportunity.

I think that is a fair assumption.

Mr. President, I know that I, for one, am not very clear as to what the attitude and action of the foreign diplomatic representatives was in connection with the negotiations with Mr. Lind. I got the impression from the Gamboa note[8] that these foreign governments, through their representatives in Mexico City, had used their influence only to obtain a hearing for Mr. Lind.

A sympathetic hearing.

Yes, a sympathetic hearing, and that was private, of course, this reception; otherwise, there wouldn't have been occasion for it. Since then they have not done anything.

Naturally not.

That is what I want to clear up.

No.

Mr. President, are you going to issue a proclamation with reference to the export of arms from the United States?

No, that is not necessary. President Taft issued a proclamation of a general prohibition, and it made exceptions in favor of certain shipments.[9] Now I will stop making the exceptions.

How will you make your public announcement of it?

I considered my address a public announcement of it. You see, there is no way in which I could do it without reiterating the proclamation.

You could do it through having the Secretary of the Treasury issue orders to the collectors of customs and to the army authorities.[10]

That has been done.

Will you send any more troops to the border for the purpose of patrol?

Not so far as I know.

Mr. President, has there been any considerable batch of arms going from this country to the Federals?[11]

Yes. Very considerable. There was one order I remember for several million cartridges.

Mr. President, no more arms will be shipped to the Federals even if they accept our proposition?

No, although they want arms. I expect they would say they needed them to go after brigands, but I don't think they will request them if they accede to our suggestion.

Is the *de facto* government able to get arms from England?

So far as I know, they are.

Mr. President, have you had any assurances from any foreign government that they were sympathetically interested in what you said yesterday with regard to the importation of arms from abroad?

There really hasn't been. You know, it's a pretty slow business hearing from them. They speak through their representatives, not directly.

Have you made any overtures to them?

Oh, no.

We mean no overtures to them whatsoever.

No.

Mr. President, you have down on the border three thousand troops, and you have ten to twelve thousand more than can be utilized.

If it is necessary, along the neighboring areas, along the borders. The headquarters have been there, but the men are distributed.

There are a small number of troops working out.

But I hadn't heard any report from the War Department about that.

Mr. President, have you done anything with regard to helping Americans to get out of Mexico because they are unable—

We have been doing something.

But nothing since your message? Nothing in the way of—

We have sent them notes that we stood ready to help them with money as well as with transportation.

Mr. President, have you taken into consideration what those Americans would do with their property, for instance, those that have it?

Of course I have, but, you see, under the law, there is nothing we can do except to hold the authorities responsible for the amounts sacrificed and destroyed. That would involve a final accounting.

Would you assist them or permit them to drive their cattle across the border to the United States?

Very few of them are near enough to accomplish that, so far as I am informed, but I hadn't taken that particular detail up.

Mr. President, do you think all Americans should come out of the country? There are persons who are not disturbed.

No, I don't expect all of them to come out. I don't suppose it will be physically possible for all of them because the transportation is very imperfect and is interrupted.

How about the other foreigners in Mexico?

Well, of course, it would be an impertinence on our part to speak for them. Their own representatives will speak for them.

Mr. President, one of the papers said a short time ago that there were ninety thousand Americans in Mexico and now there are only eight thousand left. Do you know if those figures are correct?

I don't, but I don't think they are. I don't know anybody who has the materials for any statement approximating exactly to that statistic.

Mr. President, have you any reports, unofficial or official, whether the European powers have invited their subjects to come out?

No, sir, I haven't any information.

Mr. President, I understand from what you say that in the case of a colony of tourists, such as a group on a journey, should they become involved in difficulties in Mexico because of the situation, they would have to rely entirely on their own home government for protection.

Well, certainly. They would get all the assistance from Americans that anybody's interest may suggest; but why do you ask the question? Isn't that the case anywhere in the world?

Except as to those countries that we are supposed to be the police power over.

Are we supposed to be the police power?

They thought that was the doctrine of Mr. Monroe.

I have never heard of it before. I was reading Mr. Monroe's message today.

I haven't read it so recently.

I am trying now to find out why I read it. I went into my study in the White House and found the message, the volume, lying with the pages marked, and I can't find out who left it there. But I took advantage, in the circumstances, to read it again.

I should suspect Mr. Tumulty.

Mr. Tumulty swears he did not do it.

Mr. President, there is a suggestion in one of the morning papers that you have intimated to the Huerta government that a suggestion would be made to the bankers to let them have more funds.[12]

Well, you see, that is one of the points on which I am not fully informed from Mr. Lind yet. He was to reply to my two suggestions together, and that may be one of the suggestions I made.

Mr. President, wouldn't he notify you of the two suggestions here?

He notified us of the first one. It was the last one that I made, but I don't know the language and the terms yet.

Mr. President, is there any basis for assurance that American bankers would furnish the money?

No, we haven't asked anybody. We haven't sounded anybody about it at all.

Mr. Lind indicated that we would use our best endeavors in that line.

I suppose he meant if it proved impossible to carry out the arrangements we suggested for lack of money. In the meantime it would naturally be up to us to exercise such friendly counsel as we could in the circumstances.

Mr. President, have you heard anything as to the conditions of Mexican trade at the present time?

Nothing except what comes in as rumor.

Those rumors, you know, are very bad.

I have heard that they are very bad in quarters, but from no authorities.

Mr. President, Gamboa in his last note says you are meeting [the Constitutionalists'] representative.[13]

He said that had been done, which is not true.

He didn't say anything about the eighty thousand troops?[14]

No. No, the only thing he mentioned was a railway concession to certain Belgian investors which would not allow the government anything. He cited it merely as an instance that it was considered to be a real government.[15]

Mr. President, you spoke of having the full text of the Huerta note. Anything on the illegal [treatment of] American landowners, something as to their condition?

I haven't had time to read it yet, but expect it was the same thing they published in Mexico City which one of you gentlemen showed me this morning, or rather just before lunch. Well, we do not know if it should prove to be definitely the same in some particular matter, certainly, but I take it for granted it is the same thing.

Mr. President, are you going away within a day or two?

That depends upon what turns up. I am very anxious to get away over Labor Day, but whether I shall be welcomed as a laboring man or not, I don't know.

Mr. President, can you tell us anything about the latest Japanese note?

No, sir, I haven't seen it.

---

[1] While Wilson was addressing Congress on August 27, Lind and Louis D'Antin, a clerk in the American embassy in Mexico City, were translating a new note from Gamboa which seemed to alter the situation. Gamboa now seemed conciliatory and stated that Huerta, as the *ad interim* President, could not under Mexican law be elected President or Vice-President in the forthcoming election. Further negotiations seemed possible, perhaps with Lind returning to Mexico City to represent Wilson. See Federico Gamboa to John Lind, Aug. 26, 1913, printed in *PWW*, Vol. 28, pp. 233-39; and Hill, *Emissaries to a Revolution*, pp. 85-86.

[2] Lind had left Mexico City for Veracruz in preparation for return to the United States. See the *New York Times*, Aug. 27, 1913.

[3] He did not return to Mexico City but remained in Veracruz for the next eight months. See Hill, *Emissaries to a Revolution*, pp. 83-90.

[4] That is, because accepting Huerta's assurance might be tantamount to recognition.

[5] That is, no.

[6] Federico Gamboa to John Lind, Aug. 26, 1913. This note appeared to concede Wilson's point that Huerta was ineligible to succeed himself. See Link, *The New Freedom*, pp. 359-62.

[7] That is, Federico Gamboa to John Lind, Aug. 16, 1913—an earlier note.

[8] For this note, see the *New York Times*, Aug. 28, 1913.

[9] That is, Taft's order under the law of March 14, 1912.

[10] To stop all passage of arms across the border.

[11] That is, the *Huertistas*.

[12] Lind proposed to Gamboa on August 28 that, if Huerta yielded to Wilson's conditions for an election, the American government would ask bankers to make loans to Mexico. See the *New York Times*, Aug. 29, 1913. Gamboa seemed to reject such loans in his note of August 26.

[13] In his note of August 26, Gamboa proposed that Wilson also meet with the Huerta government's embassy personnel. See *PWW*, Vol. 28, p. 238.

[14] Gamboa had said that his government had 80,000 troops in the field fighting against the rebels. See the *New York Times*, Aug. 28, 1913.

[15] Gamboa noted that a contract had been signed with Belgian capitalists to provide for the construction of 5,000 kilometers of railway. The Foreign Minister's point here was that the fighting was not preventing progress in Mexico, as Wilson had suggested. See *ibid.*

---

Sept. 4, 1913

Mr. President, have you received any assurances from Mr. Huerta not to be a candidate?

Why the most definite sort. He says he can't be. He assures us he can't be a candidate.[1] He is in this fix. He has either got to abandon his claim to be a legal Provisional President or he has got to declare that he will stand at the election. He can't do both.

Have you had any further assurances on that?

Orally, yes. Not in writing.[2]

Does he promise not to resign and become a candidate?

No. But he couldn't play a stunt like that without forfeiting the respect of everybody, and certainly we would regard that as a distinct contradiction of the note and its explicit terms.

Why?

In that note, he says he can't in any circumstances be a candidate. If we took his word on that, they would not [omission]. He has conceded that point, too, and he has withdrawn his request to exchange representatives, which is a withdrawal of the request to be recognized, so he has conceded in that note to the principal things that we demand.

May we know any of the oral assurances that followed?

Simply that they were conveyed by the Minister of Foreign Affairs.

As to whether they cover broader ground?

They cover the broadest ground—that he would not resign and become a candidate. I don't know whether I am at liberty or not to leave you free to publish that or not. I am perfectly willing to tell you that oral assurance was given, but perhaps it would not be consistent with—

It was printed, Mr. President, that such assurances had been received.

Such assurances have been received, there is no doubt about that.

Mr. President, what are the two points you say were conceded?

He has conceded that he cannot be a candidate and that we will not recognize him as a Provisional President.

That is to say, Mr. President, that the Minister of Foreign Affairs has said so?

No, sir. He withdrew in his note a request for exchange of Ambassadors, which is a request of recognition.

I thought that the trouble was that the communications with this government have been solely through Gamboa, not directly with President Huerta, and that Mr. Gamboa's assurances on their face are all right, but would Mr. Huerta abide by them because the note was not sent by Mr. Huerta to Mr. Lind?

It wouldn't make any difference. He is the accredited spokesman of the provisional government. I don't see how there is any escape from either of those concessions. He now recognizes the fact that we will not recognize him on the presidential status and says that he cannot be a candidate. He says it in language which is meant to intimate that. I don't know anything about the Mexican Constitution, but we will let that pass.

Mr. President, in the event of an election in Mexico, would the subsequent recognition of this government be contingent in any way upon the nature of the conduct of those elections?

Manifestly. We must be sure that the constitutional machinery works as it was intended to work.

Have you any assurances up to this time that steps will be taken along that line?

Well, we have their assurances that the elections will be constitutionally conducted. If I am not mistaken, it is in that note.

In what territory?

Well, they didn't say, but presumably in the whole Mexican territory.

Mr. President, how can we scrutinize those elections to ascertain that they are honestly constitutional?

Well, I am afraid you can answer that question as well as I can.

Mr. President, how far has Mr. O'Shaughnessy or Mr. Lind gotten with the other points involved in those suggestions?

So far as I know, there is no progress on them. There is an apparent disposition to keep the door open for subsequent negotiation.

Has anything been done, Mr. President, as to how many outlying territories will participate in that election on that day?

No, sir, not by us.

It is up to them?

Yes.

The only serious thing, Mr. President, to anticipate is for President Huerta to stand, after all the assurances in the Gamboa note, which are his assurances, to stand and eventually become a candidate and run.

I suppose that is a possibility, but I think it would be very unwise.

Mr. President, can you tell us something about Dr. Hale's[3] position now, as to what his status was in Mexico with reference to this government?

Why, there is nothing new about that. Dr. Hale, as I think I said before, came to see me before he went down there, and I asked him to act as my informant as to the real situation down there. I wanted some fresh pair of eyes to look at things down there. I knew he was a trained observer, because I have known him for a long time, and I knew he would try to see things in an uncolored light and report them clearly. He has from time to time reported to me, and now he has come back, and I had a short conference with him this morning, but he has sent in regular messages which made it unnecessary for him to explain it in the way of detailed information.

Could you tell us something about his views of the situation as to the future?

No, I can't, because he has, I think very rightly, refrained from expressing views. He simply tried to transmit information and impressions, because the impressions of the situation that they make on your mind are as important a part of the information as any transaction. He has a very—I rather admired the way in which he has refrained from even intimating advice or views as to what ought to be done.

He was in Mexico on—in what capacity, as a confidential agent of yours?

Yes, sir, he was in that sense my confidential agent. But he was there in a broad capacity.

Mr. President, would it be fair to announce what he reported about the finances?[4]

He didn't report at all. I don't think he has any information about that.

Mr. President, has this government had some inquiries from foreign governments in regard to the United States using its influence?

No, sir, not at all.

Has there been anything along that line, looking to our not guaranteeing but at least giving the color of strength by acknowledging the most recent advices of the Mexican government?

No, we haven't had anything, directly or indirectly. There has been an intimation that one of the governments has helped us with our diplomatic negotiations—to have Gamboa receive Mr. Lind.[5] No, sir, nothing of the kind.

Mr. President, do you know whether there is anything in the Mexican Constitution which provides a date on which—beyond which a person cannot run for the presidency?

No, sir, I do not. My only recollection is that it bars him from the subsequent election. He can't succeed himself.

No, what I would add, Mr. President, is that these elections are to be held on the twenty-sixth of October. Candidates must announce themselves, I presume. Assuming that to be true, is there any date beyond which he could not announce himself?

I don't know of any such.

Mr. President, have you had any information generally giving notice of Huerta's successor or candidate?

None whatever.

Mr. President, is Mr. Lind taking any steps toward bringing about an armistice?

No. He could not, without the invitation or the consent of the authorities at Mexico City.

Mr. President, is Mr. Lind remaining in Veracruz indefinitely?

Yes. Well, I shouldn't have said he will remain in Veracruz indefinitely. I do not know whether he will remain, but he will be on hand.

Mr. President, currency. Is there any change in the attitude of the administration, because of Senator Weeks' resolution[6] or any other influence?

No, sir. Senator Weeks' resolution is not surprising.

Mr. President, there does seem to be such a divergence of opinion among the Republicans of the Banking and Currency Committee that those of us who have followed it for the last two or three days are sensing a very serious situation.

I am not, but you are misled because that committee consists of men, I should say, all in a way of strong individuality. They speak out their individual opinions. I mean, such things come along, but they can't represent what the country thinks. That is the policy of the Democratic party.

Mr. President, has the Mexican government shown any disposition since Gamboa's last note to receive in a favorable way your suggestion about getting money for temporary needs?

No, sir. Nothing has been said or intimated. Negotiations have been almost entirely about Huerta's not being a candidate, as they have handled it.

Mr. President, have you any information about how long the committee intends to polish the bill in the Banking and Currency Committee?[7]

No. No. No, I don't think they mean to keep it long. As I understand it, they felt it only fair, only considerate, to hold public hearings and hear what these gentlemen who represent, or at any rate think that they represent, a large association had to say.

There seems to be a desire of the members of that committee, Mr. President, even Democrats I have talked with, to have very extensive hearings that would carry them on for a number of weeks.

Well, they will have to reason with our colleagues about that.

All the Republicans and some of the Democrats feel that way.

I think the Republicans would like hearings from now to Doomsday.

Mr. President, some of the gentlemen on that committee said yesterday they would ask for a conference with yourself and some of the bankers' association. Have you granted any conference?

I haven't received any request. I saw Mr. McAdoo this morning, but I can't say anything about that.

Mr. President, there is a report current that Mr. Moore[8] has resigned. Is that true?

No, sir, it is not. If I can help it, he won't.

He told me he wouldn't resign.

I am delighted to hear it.

Mr. President, have you taken up the subject of a reply to Japan yet?

No, I have not.

Mr. President, not being personal, today is September 4, which reminds me— would you care to tell us how well you like the presidency?[9]

I have no opinions about myself or my own administration. I am sawing wood.

---

[1] This was stated in Gamboa's note to Lind of August 26, 1913. See above, Aug. 28, 1913.

[2] On August 28, Gamboa informed O'Shaughnessy orally that Huerta could not resign in order to enter the next election. See Link, *The New Freedom*, p. 362.

[3] Hale was in Washington at this time and visited Wilson at the White House on September 3. See the *Washington Post*, Sept. 4, 1913.

[4] Mexican finances were in a difficult condition. See above, Aug. 28, 1913.

[5] Wilson was hoping that Lind would be recalled from Veracruz to Mexico City for further conversations with Gamboa. This did not develop, however. See Hill, *Emissaries to a Revolution*, p. 88.

[6] Senator Weeks' resolution (S. Res. 179) of September 4 called for the Senate Banking and Currency Committee to report the currency bill on December 2, after which it would become the "unfinished business" of the Senate. The resolution was referred to the committee. See the *Washington Post*, Sept. 5, 1913, and *Cong. Record*, 63d Cong., 1st sess., pp. 4211 and 4285.

[7] The House Banking and Currency Committee finished its consideration of the currency bill on September 4 and voted on September 5 to report it on September 8. See the *Washington Post*, Sept. 4-6, 1913.

[8] John Bassett Moore, Counselor of the Department of State, who resigned on February 2, 1914. See Link, *The New Freedom*, p. 98.

[9] September 4 marked the six-month anniversary of Wilson's inauguration.

---

Sept. 8, 1913

Anything on the Mexican situation?

I have given up on that. That is quicksilver. I have no new official information of any kind.

Mr. President, have you heard anything with regard to this former Ambassador to Washington[1] who seems to be coming here from the Mexican government, as to who he is and what he is?

Yes, sir. I have heard of him. Among other things, I asked Lawrence[2] about him. Lawrence knew him, and Lawrence told me about him. He seems to be a man of character and of standing, but he is not sent as—well, the real circumstances of the man are—I will have to tell you this in confidence, because I want you to understand just how cynically we are being dealt with. We were asked if it would be agreeable to us for this gentleman to come as a personal representative of General Huerta. I telegraphed Mr. Lind to ask his opinion. Before he could reply and I could then indicate my wishes in the matter, and just as I was about to send a message to Mr. Lind, I got a message from him saying that this gentleman had started for the United States. Those are the exact circumstances.

Have you heard anything since from Mr. Lind?

No, nothing at all. It was only Saturday night that I learned from him that this gentleman had started. Now you can get the thread of the things that are being said by that narrative. It is literally true, but only literally true, that he is not coming here on any mission.

You said he was to be Huerta's personal representative?

Well, he asked if it would be agreeable to us. Before getting any answer, the man started; and therefore he started on no particular errand as they are now stating.

Now, Mr. President, did we tell Mexico that Mr. Lind was coming before he started?[3]

I don't remember.

I know the first we heard of it was about twenty-five minutes after he had left.

Well, we were sending more to Mexico than they were sending to America.

But, my word, I have forgotten, but we certainly communicated it to the embassy before he left, as I remember it. I can't trust my memory on those details.

I was thinking, they were probably taking a leaf out of our book. Have you signified, Mr. President, since, that his arrival would be agreeable?[4]

No, I haven't signified anything.

There has been no reply?

No reply. They didn't wait for a reply.

Mr. President, there seems to be some discrepancy between statements of O'Shaughnessy's advices given us here some time ago about certain assurances of the Huerta government.[5]

Discrepancy is a polite way of putting it. It is a direct contradiction. What to make of that, I can't even suggest.

Mr. President, dispatches from Mexico City this morning indicate that the American Consul General, Mr. Shanklin,[6] has sent out additional instructions to American Consuls that indicate that Americans are not to hurry out of Mexico but to take their time and make their preparations before leaving. Are those instructions based on a supplementary [instruction] from Washington?

He simply consulted us. He wanted to know if the embassy was right in construing it as equivalent to being ordered out, and we told him by no means. It was our advice to them to get out, and, so far as they could arrange their affairs, to do so. I suppose in conveying a reply to them that [he might have taken this construction].

Mr. President, he still suggests the possibility of intervention, though he says no immediate prospect of intervention is indicated.

Well, we didn't say anything about intervention to him or anybody else. That is a threatening danger, I believe. You see, it was all on the grounds of what I indicated in my address to Congress; namely, that when the contest becomes sharpened between the forces of the North and the forces at Mexico City, the danger to Americans is likely to be greater. It was in anticipation of intervention.

Have you anything, Mr. President, with regard to the alleged proposal to postpone the elections?[7]

I haven't heard anything, except what was in this morning's paper, but inasmuch as the morning papers have something new about Mexico every morning, I have ceased to be concerned about it.

There is nothing official on it?

It just shows things are in a whirligig there. Mr. Forster reminds me that several gentlemen have come in and I should repeat that I said that the detailed information about Mr. Zamacona was confidential. I repeat that.

Is there any official report about the shooting at El Paso?[8]

No. I don't expect they have made a report that would qualify as official, and they haven't communicated it to me if they have. I think what the newspapers report General Wood[9] as having said is probably premature.

Have you sent any fresh inquiry to Mr. O'Shaughnessy regarding that particular episode.

No, because I would have to send a personal inquiry every day. It is too expensive.

Do the reports vary?

Well, what I mean to say is that the reports from the telegraph office—public reports from Mexico—are different every day. I would have to ask every day. In Mexico, the published reports do not tally with our dispatches. We would have to get our dispatches to indicate the reported changes.

Mr. President, will Mr. O'Shaughnessy be asked to explain that particular statement he is reported as giving out?[10]

You understand I do not want to put too great a burden on O'Shaughnessy.

You have no official advices yet?

No, I have none at all.

Mr. President, have you gotten further along in formulating a policy with regard to trust legislation?

Well, I haven't had time to take it up since I have studied it pretty carefully in New Jersey. You of course gather from that that I have some definite ideas as to what might be done. I have simply held it in abeyance until I have conferred with the men here who know the national situation thoroughly enough to advise me. I haven't done anything.

You are not thinking of trying to do anything, even to having bills introduced this present session?

No, sir.

Mr. President, isn't there rather a serious question involved in the annual appropriation bill which would wipe out the Commerce Court?[11]

How do you mean? But they do provide for the salaries of the judges.

Because they are continued as federal judges.

Yes. Yes.[12]

The court is practically wiped out.

By the lack of money to run it.

Isn't that a rather dangerous precedent?

Well, I don't think I will comment on that.

The Commission on Industrial Relations?

Well, I am hoping every day to receive the confirmation of those nominations and—I don't know, I haven't had time to inquire what is holding them up.

Mr. President, have you given any consideration to the testimony before the Senate Committee on Banking and Currency during the past week?[13]

No, sir, because it is all in the testimony which has been contributed again and again and again before the House committee, which I read exhaustively at one time, before the bill was formulated. Then I have the elaborate memorandum from the bankers. It's an old matter, perfectly familiar.

Do you consider the matter which they have brought to the attention of the Senate this last week to practically foreclose—

I considered it all a matter that was very carefully considered before the bill was formulated.

Mr. President, a New York paper last week published a story to the effect that you had sent Secretary Garrison[14] and Secretary Daniels a certain number of statements by General Wood.

No, I did not, because I did not understand them to be war statements.

No communication from you to them at all?

None whatever, about that.

Mr. President, could you tell us something about the Japanese situation?

I would if I knew anything new, but I don't know of anything new.

---

[1] Manuel Zamacona, former Mexican Ambassador to the United States, sent by Huerta on September 1 as a "personal and confidential agent" to Washington. See Kenneth J. Grieb, *The United States and Huerta* (Lincoln, Neb., 1969), p. 103.

[2] David Lawrence, Wilson's former student at Princeton and one of his closest friends among the newspapermen.

[3] Bryan notified the Mexican government of Lind's mission in a press release on the day of the emissary's departure. Advance information went to the American embassy in Mexico City, but the telegram did not contain instructions that it should be relayed to the government. See State Department to American Chargé d'Affaires, Mexico City, Aug. 4, 1913, in *FR, 1913*, pp. 817-18, and the *New York Times*, Aug. 5, 1913.

[4] That is, Zamacona's arrival. Wilson refused to see him. See Hill, *Emissaries to a Revolution*, p. 94.

[5] O'Shaughnessy had earlier stated that he had assurances to the effect that Huerta would not be a candidate for President in the October elections. On September 7, he supported Gamboa's contention that no such assurances had been given. See the *New York Times*, Sept. 8, 1913.

[6] Arnold Shanklin, American Consul General in Mexico City.

[7] That is, postponing the Mexican presidential election to be held in October.

[8] On September 6, Lieut. Francisco Acosta of the Mexican Federal army was shot and killed by American customs and immigration officials after he began firing on the bridge over the Rio Grande at El Paso. See the *New York Times*, Sept. 7, 1913.

[9] Maj. Gen. Leonard Wood, Chief of the Army General Staff, remarked that American forces were on alert guarding the approaches to El Paso.

[10] That is, that Huerta would not be a candidate.

[11] On September 8, the House included a provision in the urgent deficiency appropriation bill which would abolish the Commerce Court effective December 31.

[12] The bill originally called for transferring the Commerce Court judges to the circuit court, but their salaries were entirely eliminated later in the day. See the *New York Times*, Sept. 9, 1913.

[13] That is, by bankers critical of the bill.

[14] Secretary of War Lindley Miller Garrison.

---

Sept. 11, 1913

Mr. President, we are still interested in Mexico, particularly about Mr. Zamacona.

Well, I am a little mystified by Mr. Zamacona. He hasn't communicated with us since he got here.

He has gone away now.

Has he?

At least I think so. Went away this afternoon.[1]

That is really all I know about him.

Mr. President, are you getting anything at all that you can tell us about from Mr. Lind and Mr. O'Shaughnessy with regard to conditions down there?

No, I am not. At least, all I am getting is simply comment on things that are occurring and comment that leaves this impression on my mind, that it is quicksand, that they have no plan down there whatever. That is the impression.

Are they showing that quicksand quality of yielding anything?

Only under the foot.

Mr. President, has Mr. Lind been instructed to stay there until after the election?

No, we haven't given Mr. Lind anything that he could call instructions at all. We are being advised by him, really, as to how long it is useful for him to remain.

You don't know whether or not it is his intention to stay after the election?

So far as I can gather, it is.

Mr. President, do you think that the election can take place on October 26?[2]

That depends entirely on the conditions on October 26.
The Mexican electors' office that performs the work would require four months for the registration of the names and for the period during which challenges may be made. Nothing of that kind has been done. I don't know whether anything like that has been done at all.

What impression do you get, Mr. President, as to whether the election would be held over?

I get no impression one way or the other. There has been absolutely no change in it, either announced or suggested. I just assumed that the election would be attempted on that date, at any rate. At least the Congress of Mexico meets next week.

If it were attempted, it would be only within that area held by the Federals, wouldn't it, as things stand now?

As things stand now, practically it would be.

You haven't any official information to tally with the reports in the papers today, that Carranza [has offered to suspend hostilities until after] the election?[3]

No, I have no reports of that kind.

If Mr. Zamacona asks for an interview, will you receive him or will you—

Well, I will have to take you into my confidence. That will depend upon what he lays down as a basis for the conversation. If the essentials are determined and the discussion is by arrangement, yes; otherwise, no.

The essential has been practically determined, hasn't it, at this time, with Huerta?

Well, we want to be sure that that is understood in his mind, that Mr. Huerta will not ask for recognition and that he will not be a candidate for election.

You have no definite assurances of that sort?

We understood that we had, sir, and I still understand it.

Did you so inform the Mexican government that his acceptance would be conditioned on that?

That is not true. We haven't informed them anything about it— a week ago, as I told you the other day, before we sent any message; therefore, we haven't sent any.

They haven't made any further requests since then?

No. They haven't communicated with us about him since then.

Well, the assurances, Mr. President, are still based on Mr. Gamboa's note?[4]

Yes.

And only on that?

Yes, but that is their official statement.

I see.
Mr. President, have you come to any further conclusion with regard to currency legislation? I don't mean regarding change of plans but to any agreement with the leaders of Congress as to how it shall be conducted?

No, they haven't suggested any change of plan. Of course, the whole thing depends upon how soon the Senate committee reports. That is the only uncertain element in the situation.

Well, my question was with reference to a conference with the Steering Committee.[5]

That conference didn't propose any particular suggestion of any sort. It was just to let me know what the situation was—I mean, what there was for the Senate to do; namely, to mark time until the conference committee report on the tariff[6] was ready and then as to how they should arrange to take up their business again, just so as to insure that the committee was able to report. But that was, as I say, the only uncertain element in it.

Well, would that mean that the Banking and Currency Committee of the Senate would not take up the currency bill until after the conference?

No, it must do it—take it up right away. It is to confer next Tuesday and go right on.

Did you get any idea, Mr. President, when the committee would report?

No, I did not.

From the Hill talk, about November first.

I know they are talking about it—until Doomsday. That doesn't hurt anything.

Mr. President, have any Senators informed you of their belief that it would be wise to pass some amendments to it?

To the administration bill, yes; they are so few in number that it does not affect the actions of the Senate at all. They have been suggesting that from the outset. There is nothing new about that— I mean, from the outset of this session.

Mr. President, to what extent may we use what you told us a little while ago with regard to the reception of Mr. Zamacona?

Well, I would rather you did not use it at all for the present. Mr. Zamacona, as a matter of fact, hasn't asked for an interview yet.

I didn't want to suggest that we should use it as coming from you or anything of that sort.

Well, you could do this: you could simply repeat what has been several times said, that it was the distinct understanding in administration circles that any further negotiations would be based upon those two assumptions.

I only want to make sure, because—
Mr. President, could we also state the attitude of the [administration toward the Mexican election]?

No. I think it is only fair that we should assume that they are going to hold it right away, even though they don't [say so].

Mr. President, in that connection, I know I am rather ignorant of what is the next step. If they hold the election in the territory controlled by them, it would be—assuming it was held in their territory—less than half the nation. What is to be the attitude of this government toward the rest of the country?

It would be less than the nation. It would be less than half the area of Mexico, but it is four fifths of the nation. Only one in five of the population of Mexico is in the more than one half which is not now controlled by the authorities in Mexico City.[7]

The area controlled by the revolutionists so far, the so-called revolutionists, with regard to area, is also sparse in population. It is just rich in territory and its resources.

Yes, resources.

There are resources in the regular part.

Yes, but the other part is very much more developed, and they are very much more thinly populated.

Wouldn't that mean that an election there would merely continue with the— I mean [the government] that has been given—

It may be. I don't know.

That has not been discussed?

That has not been discussed, but of course it is understood that we will recognize only a government which is constitutionally set up. Now the next move is up to them.

Mr. President, did you get any information—impression—this morning in your talk with Mr. Underwood, as to the length of time the tariff bill would be in conference?

No, that wasn't brought up. Wait a minute—I think Mr. Underwood did express the expectation that it wouldn't take long.

Did you gain the impression that there was a very wide divergence of opinion between the two houses and that it would take a long time?

Not upon any large, essential matter. You see, as a matter of fact, I am told there were several hundred—six hundred—minor changes made by the Senate. Of course, it will take a considerable amount of time to go over those items, item by item.

It is generally understood that there are certain big items, for instance, the income tax, wheat, and cattle—those things might take some time?[8]

These gentlemen didn't seem to anticipate that it would.

Mr. President, is there anything at all that you know that you can explain about the attitude of the foreign powers on Mexico towards Huerta's candidacy, or what their attitude is?

No. I have no means of judging what their attitude is as to his candidacy.

Mr. President, the last time we asked you, you didn't have any definite idea, or wouldn't express anything, as to how we could keep a check on the Mexican elections. Have you any more of a definite idea now?

You see, you can't have an idea until the situation develops. You would have to deal with it as it develops.

I wondered whether any tentative proposition had been suggested?

Well, there probably won't be anything new now from Mexico until the twenty-sixth of October. I don't know—I wouldn't predict anything about it.

Mr. President, have we had anything further from any of the foreign powers concerning the situation? Have they asked us what our next step is to be?

No. We have nothing, no.

Mr. President, in regard to Mr Zamacona, the belief is expressed in various quarters that possibly he is about to ask for an appointment to meet either the Secretary or yourself. This government, not having replied to the inquiry of Mexico, in that connection, would this government reply to Mexico and state on what terms he would be received and state the intentions of this government?

I would first have to know what the Mexican embassy thinks about that. That would naturally come to us through the Chargé[9] here. He hasn't said anything about it.

Mr. President, your nominations of Consuls furnish pretty good evidence that you will have a permanent consular service.[10]

That has been my declared policy from the first.

I wondered whether you could tell us any more along that line—I don't like to suggest whether you tell us whether Mr. Griffiths[11] is going to stay in the service?

I don't know. You see, I had, personally, no choice in the matter, because it must be twenty years now, long before I knew it would be put up to me, that I have preferred a permanent consular service; and before boards of trade and before every other body that was interested in that thing, I had worked on that. Even if I had wished, I couldn't have faltered because I have never had any doubt in my mind as to what I was going to do about that.

Yes, sir. In that list yesterday, there was only one man[12] who is not now in the consular service but had already passed the competitive examination.

We are trying hard to get the impression abroad, and among these men, that we really want to make this a career and that it is open to them to get in.

Mr. President, have you paid any attention to the comments of the newspapers on the literary qualities of the Secretary of State.[13]

No, sir.

They are breaking out.

I never pay any attention to anybody [who is dealing with a question that is] none of his business.

Mr. President, can you tell us anything about your antitrust program for the coming winter?

No, sir. Sufficient unto the day is the program thereof.

Mr. President, have you received any word from the Philippines as to how Mr. Burton Harrison's selection[14] has been received over there?

Why, Mr. Quezon[15] told me before he left that he had advice that it was very cordially received. Just from what sources that came, I can't say, except that he did mention the Speaker of their House. That is the only specific source.

Mr. President, have you anything to say about the death of Mayor Gaynor?[16]

No, except to express a personal regret. It is a very extraordinarily sad piece of news.

Mr. President, speaking of the tariff again, have you any information as to whether or not there is a wide difference of opinion between the House and Senate on the cotton tax?[17]

No, I haven't. I haven't.

Will you confer with the conferees from time to time, Mr. President?

That depends upon the conferees.

Mr. President, are you going to tell us what you will do with the matter of the Central American bananas? The Ministers were here yesterday.[18]

I am going to eat a few of them in the future, but I don't mind saying that, personally, I am sorry that a tax was put upon them because they constitute an article of food for so large a number of very poor people, and I don't think the tax would have been put on if the Senators had known that that tax then could be transferred to the consumer; but of course several have such an uncanny skill in transferring their costs to the consumer, I don't doubt their ability to do it.

Mr. President, are you going away?

I am going away this evening and coming back Tuesday morning.[19]

[1] Zamacona left Washington for New York on the afternoon of September 11. See the *New York Times*, Sept. 12, 1913.

[2] The regularly scheduled election day.

[3] This would be in return for the opportunity to run as a candidate. See the *New York Times*, Sept. 11, 1913.

[4] That is, the assurances that Huerta would not be a candidate given in Gamboa's note of August 26, 1913. At this time, Gamboa was contending that his note gave no such assurances.

[5] Wilson met on September 9 with members of the Democratic Steering Committee in the Senate to urge haste in considering the Glass-Owen bill. See the *New York Times*, Sept. 10, 1913.

[6] The Senate passed the tariff bill on September 9.

[7] The point here is that an election in Mexico could produce a representative government even though it could only be conducted in the half of the country controlled by Mexico City. It was, at least, so reported in the press. See, for example, the *New York Times*, Sept. 12, 1913.

[8] The Senate had amended the House bill dealing with these items, placing wheat and cattle on the free list, and adding exemptions to the income-tax provisions while greatly increasing the rates. See F. M. Simmons to WW, Sept. 4, 1913, printed in *PWW*, Vol. 28, pp. 253-54.

[9] A. Algara R. de Terreros.

[10] On September 10, Wilson nominated thirty men to consular posts, all of whom were either in the consular service or had passed merit examinations. This indicated Wilson's willingness to eliminate the use of the spoils system in the consular service. See the *New York Times*, Sept. 11, 1913.

[11] John Lewis Griffiths, Republican from Indiana, who was retained as Consul General in London.

[12] The *New York Times* said that there were two.

[13] A reference to criticisms of Bryan's lectures on the Chautauqua circuit. See, for example, the *New York Times* editorial, "Mr. Bryan's Offense," of Sept. 12, 1913.

[14] As Governor General of the Philippines.

[15] Manuel Luis Quezon, the Philippines Commissioner to the United States. See Quezon to Bryan, Aug. 16, 1913, printed in *PWW*, Vol. 28, pp. 192-93.

[16] William Jay Gaynor, Mayor of New York, died on September 10 on board a liner bound for London.

[17] Senator James Paul Clarke, Democrat of Arkansas, had proposed an amendment to add a tax on cotton futures to the Underwood tariff bill. The amount of the tax would be increased if the terms of the futures contract were not fulfilled. Clarke's objective was to regulate the trade and prevent excessive speculation. See *Cong. Record*, 63d Cong., 1st sess., pp. 4007-38.

[18] The Senate placed a tax on imported bananas of one-tenth of a cent per pound. Representatives of Costa Rica, Panama, Guatemala, and Nicaragua visited Wilson on September 10 to protest against this provision.

[19] Wilson spent the weekend at Cornish, New Hampshire, with his family.

Sept. 18, 1913

What is your pleasure, gentlemen?

Mr. President, could you tell us anything about the visit of the Japanese Ambassador?[1]

I would, if there were anything to tell that would constitute news. It was just a conversation about the last note of the Japanese government. It was merely by way of explanation of the situation on both sides. He was entirely satisfied, so there was nothing new about it.

Was Japan pressing for a reply?

No, sir. No. On the contrary.

One of the New York papers, Mr. President, carried stories this morning that the Ambassador came here and was told he could not see the Secretary of State.

He expressed his regret that any such misrepresentation should have been made.

The Chinese situation was brought up in the conversation, was it, Mr. President, the situation in China with respect to the Japanese question?[2]

No. No reference was made to that.

Mr. President, the discussion is concluded, is it not?

Oh, no.

Mr. President, could you tell us anything about that last note from Japan?[3]

Why, none of the notes has been made public, you know. It is just a thorough canvassing of all the aspects of the question, so as to see just exactly what our treaty relations will encompass.

Some time ago, Mr. President, you told us that you felt very much encouraged about the situation and looked forward to an amicable settlement of it.

I do still. I think that both governments are equally eager in their desire to come to an entirely satisfactory agreement.

Do you think you can find some definite ground for it?

I daresay we can, yes.

Have the recent happenings in Japan had any bearing upon the business of the currency bill?[4]

Oh, no. Really none that we discussed.

Does this complicate the matter any?

On the contrary, this is an interview I should have had with the Ambassador some time ago. It has been simply delayed by engagements on both sides, so there wasn't any provocation.

Mr. President, has this government made to Japan any proposition at all that an amicable adjustment could be had?

No, no definite proposition.

Mr. President, could you tell us anything about the instructions which have gone to Mr. Lind?

None have gone to him. When do you mean? Recently?

Yes, sir. I didn't hear myself, but I was told that the Secretary of State said yesterday that he sent a telegram to Mr. Lind, a long telegram.[5]

That was not in the nature of instructions. I doubt if he could have used that word. Mr. Lind was simply giving us his impressions of the day's end down there and the news of the day. That was all.

Mr. President, can you tell us how you regard that message, as to whether it was in keeping with your belief that a number of the proposals submitted by Mr. Lind would be accepted?

There was nothing in the message as it was cabled to us that was inconsistent with that last note and with the understanding which we interpreted that last note to convey.

Mr. President, there was a paragraph in one of the newspapers this morning which refers to a person formerly of Princeton as having made a confidential inquiry into Philippine affairs.[6]

Well, it was confidential in the sense that he was an old friend of mine who made it and wrote it for my eye.

And that he made some recommendations, suggesting a wider form of autonomy in the Philippine Islands?

There is no basis for that report at all.

There is no development in the formation of your Philippine policy as yet?

No further development.

Mr. President, I understood what you said just now to describe only what Mr. Lind had sent to this government. The question was, what has this government sent to Mr. Lind?

Nothing new at all.

We were all led to believe he said he got some new instructions.

No, sir. None that I know of.

He was sent a telegram.

I don't even know that.

The Secretary said yesterday afternoon, Mr. President, that he had sent a telegram, but he didn't say instructions.

If it contained instructions, of course I would have seen it. My not having seen it would indicate that it did not contain instructions.[7]

There is a question of warships being taken up, Mr. President, the suggestion made in Huerta's message about the retention of warships on the coast. Mr. President, have we asked that special permission be granted to us that we have a warship there?[8]

Of course we haven't. As we now understand it, that was done before my administration began. You see, the ordinary practice is that warships of a foreign nation have a thirty-day period of stay, and anything beyond that must be unusual and therefore, I understand, would have to be based on an understanding. But I haven't had time to look—to ask for the records in the case. I simply assume that the arrangement is correct as we got it, that some special arrangement was made, and that the arrangement was made in the middle of February, if those reports are correct. It wasn't with my knowledge.

Six months expire on the twenty-sixth of October.

It may be that some proposal to their Congress, which was reached at the time Mr. Knox was Secretary of State, was consummated, but I am only conjecturing.

At any rate, Mr. President, it was not an act of arrangement; it was based upon an act of the Mexican Congress?

Yes, sir.

Mr. President, has President Menocal presented his proposal for the ports company?[9]

Yes, it was brought to our attention some two months ago, I should say.

It was a matter of some debate before the government granted the concession, and I think the State Department then was not by any means enthusiastic over it.

I think you have got it a little wrong. I think that the only criticism of it was made by the War Department, on the ground that the improvements threatened to create an artificial barrier, as I remember it, in the channel, before the harbor of Havana is entered. My recollection has grown a little hazy on the subject.

It was during Mr. Jackson's[10] period of ministry. The concession was put through in 1911.

Was it? My attention was called to it only incidentally, so that I have only [unintelligible].

I simply remember that somebody called my attention to it and showed me a very interesting photograph, which was a photograph of the way the thing would look when it was finished.

Was any consideration given to the matter at the Justice Department?

No formal consideration.

Mr. President, Mr. Peters[11] of Massachusetts has been mentioned for Philippine commissioner. Anything you can say on the question?

No. I have a lot of suggestions about it, and we haven't come to any conclusion.

Is there anything done yet, is there any intention to answer the last Japanese note within a short time?

We will answer it as soon as possible.

Is there any change, Mr. President, in the situation in the Senate? Has there been any proposition made to you about a recess.[12]

No, none at all.

So far as you are concerned, the Senate can stay in session?

So far as I am informed, they will stay in session.

Will you stay right down here, Mr. President?

I will.

Mr. Lind is to stay in Mexico, is he?

Yes, sir.

Mr. President, have you been asked to appoint Colonel Roosevelt as a special envoy to England?[13]

That appointment was suggested, and I said that, so far as I was concerned, I would heartily acquiesce.

Would he be given diplomatic rank?

Nothing of that sort was suggested.

The *New Yorker Staats-Zeitung* said that the German government was ready to declare its intentions if we made an official invitation. Has that been called to your attention?

I am glad to know that.

Would there be such an official invitation?

I daresay there would be. Of course there is this fact to be remembered, that this is not a governmental exposition. It is not under the control of the Government of the United States. An official notice of it has generally been issued, which happened in this case, so that the government very generously cooperates in transmitting the invitations through its embassies. To make it an official invitation might involve the necessity of accepting the invitation. So it is simply a matter I haven't considered.

Mr. President, were the invitations of President Taft originally—were they merely transmitted?

I understood they were just transmitted. I would have to look that up to be sure.

Mr. President, have you taken any stand on this question raised by the Commerce Court, on the abolition of both the judges and the courts?

No, it hasn't been brought to me, sir.

Mr. President, do you understand that Colonel Roosevelt will go to England?

That was what I was not informed about. When this suggestion was made to me, I said I would very gladly cooperate. I had not read it, and I don't think the persons proposing it had learned whether it would be agreeable to him or not.

Would it be asking too much, Mr. President, to ask who made the suggestion?

No, sir. If I can remember, I think Mr. Bryan mentioned it to me as having been made to him by the gentleman usually most interested in extending foreign invitations. That is my recollection of it.

Mr. President, have you had any intimation from New York that John Purroy Mitchel was going to resign right away?[14]

I haven't had any intimation one way or the other.

Mr. President, do you know of any change that has been made in the International Joint Commission—the water commission?[15]

No, I haven't heard of any.

You haven't any resignations?

Mr. Streeter[16] is retiring on the first of October.

That is the only one?

I have heard it said that the American members were going to retire.

[1] Ambassador Chinda called on Wilson on September 18. This was viewed by the press as an expression of Japanese dissatisfaction over the slowness of negotiations concerning the California land-tenure act. See the *New York Times*, Sept. 19, 1913.

[2] Chinese soldiers at Nanking, under General Chang-hsun, had attacked and killed several Japanese citizens.

[3] On August 19, the Japanese government submitted to Ambassador Guthrie two articles which represented, in effect, the draft of a treaty. The United States Government had not yet responded.

[4] Wilson's desire for the passage of the currency bill was causing him to proceed slowly in negotiations with the Japanese. On this, see Bryan to WW, Sept. 17, 1913, in *PWW*, Vol. 28, pp. 282-83. Wilson informed Chinda of this. See Chinda to Baron Nobuaki Makino, Sept. 19, 1913, in *ibid.*, pp. 303-306.

[5] For this telegram, see Bryan to WW, with enclosure, Sept. 17, 1913, in *ibid.*, pp. 281-82.

[6] Henry Jones Ford.

[7] Wilson had seen the telegram, but it did not contain instructions.

[8] In his address to the Mexican Congress on September 16, Huerta threatened to rescind his government's permission for United States warships to remain in Tampico, Veracruz, and other Mexican ports. The warships were present for purposes of observation under an arrangement of six months' duration approved by the Mexican Congress on April 25, 1913. It thus expired on October 26.

[9] President Mario Menocal of Cuba was attempting to revoke the concession granted by his government in 1911 to the Campania de los Puertos de Cuba, a British concessionaire, for the purpose of dredging and improving the island's ports and harbors. In exchange, the company had been receiving customs duties on incoming cargo, but now Menocal was charging that the work was not being done properly. See the *New York Times*, Sept. 22, 1913.

[10] John Brinckerhoff Jackson, Taft's Minister to Cuba.

[11] Andrew James Peters, Democratic Congressman from Massachusetts.

[12] The House was planning to recess after it passed the Glass-Owen bill.

[13] It had been suggested that Wilson appoint Theodore Roosevelt as a special envoy to England and Germany on behalf of the Panama-Pacific Exposition, in which neither country was then planning to participate.

[14] Mitchel resigned as Collector of the Port of New York on October 8, 1913, in order to run as a Fusion candidate for Mayor of New York.

[15] A commission created by treaty to settle questions pertaining to international waterways between the United States and Canada.

[16] Frank Sherwin Streeter of New Hampshire.

Sept. 22, 1913

What seems to be the prospect on the tariff bill, Mr. President?

Why, I think it is very good. They are coming down to the wire. They have gotten out—only a very few items to consider now. I saw Senator Simmons this morning, and he seems to feel hopeful of an early result.

This week, probably?

Oh, yes. I don't see why it shouldn't be more than a few days.

Do you expect to sign before the week is over?

I hope so. I have got my pen sharpened.[1]

Have you been called upon, Mr. President, to decide any issue between the conferees?

No, not to decide. I have conferred with both Mr. Underwood and Senator Simmons two or three times on what initiatives have to be tried.

Mr. President, when you sign the bill, have you thought anything about the advisability of issuing a general statement as to what you think this revision does or will do?

No. I hadn't thought of that.

It occurred to me that the public might be interested in some kind of statement discussing and then summing up what you think of the tariff bill.

I would rather write history as it is than predict it before—I mean, characterizing this [bill as historic]. I think the man in the street could very well work out what the law does, or what rather it is intended to do, and whether it is going to cut the cost of living in half, or whether there is going to be a tendency to cut the cost of living where it shifts the burden of taxation.
Yes, such an analysis, if I could make it thoroughly, would be to the question. Indeed, it would make for legislating on the run, as I do, whether it would be short—

It should be short.

It is much harder to write a short one than a long one. I would like to do that, if it were possible.[2]

As to the International Joint Commission, Mr. President, can you say anything with regard to filling General Streeter's place?[3]

Why, General Streeter's resignation has not taken effect yet. It takes effect on the first of October. I don't care to say anything until his resignation is completed.

Mr. President, it has been said that there is another resignation on the board— the resignation of Mr. Tawney.[4]

If so, it hasn't been brought to my attention.

Mr. President, can you say anything about the currency situation in the Senate?

It hasn't changed except in the newspapers.

Do you expect to have any conferences, Mr. President, this week with the members of the currency committee?

No. None is planned.

Mr. President, Representative Jones, at an interview, discussed the Worcester and Phipps report with regard to slavery in the Philippines and expressed the belief that those were not honest expressions of opinion, that they were calculated to affect public sentiment here as against immediate independence on the part of the Philippines. Do you share Mr. Jones' beliefs?[5]

I haven't read those reports yet, so I don't know a thing about it.

You have no other information with regard to slavery in the Philippines than that contained in those reports?

No, none that everybody hasn't got that is published already. No.

Those reports seem to have incensed the Filipinos very much.

So I have understood. I haven't had time, really, to go over the reports yet.

Mr. President, Representative Jones intimates in this statement [unintelligible].

No sir, but my—no, it doesn't discredit Mr. Jones' statement because Mr. Jones has been a very constant student of the situation.

There was a paragraph in yesterday's papers, I think, about Mr. McCombs, that he had finally decided not to accept the ambassadorship.[6]

I saw that. I didn't pay any attention to that, because that is something that the papers will take up when there is nothing new about it. I don't think there is anything new.

Is there anything on the Mexican situation that you can discuss, Mr. President?

No, sir. I haven't any information that supplements what I have seen in the newspapers. What we get, so far as I see, is just an echo. It just reproduces the constantly changing position there. I don't know that anybody can say it has crystallized at all.

Nothing more definite about Mr. Lind's future, what he is to do?

That has nothing to do with the news in Mexico. We determine that from this end.

There is nothing to be said on it?

No, there is nothing new on it.

There is a paragraph in one of the papers to the effect that a number of the governments, including the United States, had made Argentina an offer for this new, big battleship that they built. So far as the United States is concerned, is that true?[7]

No.

I don't see how it is possible.

I don't believe any part of the story.

I think, Mr. President, under the agreement by which this ship was built, the United States can exercise an option on it before it is completed, but it hasn't been accepted yet by Argentina.

Well, but that option, I think, I have never looked into. I should say, offhand, that it was probably an option made with this in view and put in every such contract, so that if we should have an immediate need; it is a sort of war contingency.

I also was told—I got this from the last administration—that if Argentina determined to sell that ship, the United States should have the first opportunity to buy it.

That is a very natural arrangement, but you can see that it would be only on an extraordinary occasion.

[1] Wilson signed the Underwood tariff bill on October 3.

[2] For Wilson's remarks on signing the bill, see *PWW*, Vol. 28, pp. 351-52.

[3] See above, Sept. 18, 1913.

[4] James Albertus Tawney of Minnesota. Tawney did not resign.

[5] Representative William Atkinson Jones, Democrat of Virginia, was answering charges made by Dean Conant Worcester, Secretary of the Interior for the Philippines, and W. M. Phipps, Auditor of the Philippines, that slavery was widespread in the islands. Jones argued that slavery was confined to the uncivilized portions of the Philippines. See the *New York Times*, Sept. 22, 1913.

[6] That is, to France.

[7] Argentina had commissioned the construction of a superdreadnought, *Rivadavia*, which was built in the United States by the Fore River Company. It was at that time the largest and

fastest battleship in existence, and agents for the construction company claimed that Argentina had received offers for the ship from several nations, including the United States. See the *New York Times*, Sept. 17, 1913.

Sept. 25, 1913

Well, gentlemen, I should think that even those who have been skeptical among you would begin to feel that the moral influence of the United States was counting for something in Mexico.[1] I believe even Mr. Oulahan will admit that. Because you will see that really the course of events has justified my interpretation of that second note.[2] I have never varied, except for the outside news, in the impressions that I have had of what they meant, that they have yielded, of course, the two cardinal points of what we insisted upon— that General Huerta should not be a candidate, and that there should be guaranteed fair elections. Just how far the latter is practically possible, I can't judge; but they know that they must make the effort anyway. I think that the news from day to day confirms those impressions.

Would the candidacy of Gamboa be more satisfactory to the administration than that of Huerta personally?

I don't feel that we should have an opinion about candidacies outside the fact that, I may say, we have already proscribed [Huerta].

You wouldn't prejudge him as a creature of Huerta's administration?

I don't see anything that would justify our saying that.[3]

Mr. President, the Constitutionalists today announced that, under the circumstances, they can't participate in this election. If that is true and they don't participate, would the condition by us, requiring a full participation in the election, having met that condition, would that be satisfactory?

We didn't make that condition. We said that if these initial things were conceded, we would be glad to exercise our good offices to see to it that some sort of common understanding was brought about. But those good offices were declined, and there has been no opportunity for us to speak for the authorities in Mexico City at all in that matter. So that I don't think we can argue it, because it hasn't developed far enough.

Mr. President, it would be a great story for tomorrow morning if we were able to say or predict with assurance of realization that the efforts of the government would now be directed towards making the Constitutionalists tractable.

The field of prediction is very dangerous.

You have not been in communication with them[4] at all, Mr. President?

No.

Mr. President, is it likely you will make any effort to get into communication with them, without saying so to the other government?

If we did, we wouldn't say anything about it.

Mr. President, have you taken any ground with reference to the cotton-futures tax amendment to the tariff bill?[5]

I have simply done this. They have been kind enough to discuss it with me—the representatives of the Senate and House—and I have simply tried to discuss with them a fair means of dealing with this thing from the point of view of the various interests. In other words, I haven't tried to direct them.

Would you say whether you have expressed yourself in favor of the principle of that matter?

I think we are all in favor of adopting a measure which will relieve the cotton farmer from the manifest injustice of having his prices depend upon speculative operations. And the only debate is about what measures will be effective to that end. I think everybody wishes to accomplish that end. But it is open to doubt, to debate, as to which suggestion will accomplish it.

They are going to report a disagreement, I believe.

Are they?

That will leave it for the Senate to accept the House compromise or proposed House compromise. For the Senate to accept or reject the [sliding scale] I mean—[6]
Is there a positive assurance that Huerta won't be a candidate now?

As we understood it, there has been all along.[7]

I believe there are dispatches in the afternoon papers today saying that he has accepted the nomination of Gamboa and approved his candidacy for the presidency. Interpreting that proves that he will not be a candidate himself?

I think the proof will come to that effect, but as I have said to you gentlemen several times, I understood all along that we had explicit assurances to that effect, in fact that he would not [run].

Mr. President, what should we do if the Constitutionalists refuse, if we see that they refuse—

I don't think it is wise for me to discuss any "If."

Mr. President, you did make a suggestion some time ago, from which you drew the conclusion that, if an election was held in a representative portion of Mexico, it would be valid, and that you would so regard it.[8]

My answer to that, Oulahan, would be this: we have got to see what actually happens. We have got to wait and see just how far the assurances are carried out before we make up our attitude about the result.

There was a statement in one of the papers that old Don Porfirio[9] was going back to Mexico. Have you any information to that effect?

I saw that in the papers this morning. He accompanied his daughter to the port where she was to sail for Veracruz.

If Gamboa is to run for President, what is to become of Felix Díaz?[10]

Ask Felix Díaz.

Have you any advices at this time, sir?

Perhaps he has been waiting in Mexico for the election. You see, we wouldn't have any way to know that.

[What is the difficulty with the cotton-futures tax?]

You see, as a matter of fact, the amendment attached to this bill originated in the Senate, and the House has never had a chance to express an attitude on it. I think that is what is embarrassing the House conferees, that they have nothing to guide them.

Except the votes in previous Congresses.

The votes in previous Congresses, I mean, that the House has had, that the House took, except in precise connection with this bill.

Sir, on the disagreement with the Clarke amendment, to be submitted to the House for an expression—

I suppose that the matter would be taken up there, I would expect that.[11]

Mr. President, to get back to Mexico, the State Department seems to have laid down the rule that the government is not responsible for the destruction and damage of property in territory that is not controlled by the government.

Well, that is a consideration of international law. I must say I can't have any opinion on that.

Have you any new views on the currency situation?

No, sir. I am not likely to have any new ones. The currency situation really hasn't changed, except I think it is daily improving. The prospects are daily improving for action.

Have you heard anything from Japan yet, Mr. President?

No, sir. Nothing at all.

Since the assurances seem now to be answered to the full, will we change our attitude at all with regard to calling Americans home from there?[12]

You see, we will not start calling them away. I think that many of them misunderstood the message.[13] It was not meant to apply to everybody in every part of Mexico, only in those parts of Mexico where the Americans were and where the increased danger would come with the sharper conflict.

It was sent to all the Consuls.

It was sent to all the Consuls, just as an intimation that if Americans felt in danger, we were ready to assist them as much as we could.

There is no plan now that conditions are changed?

We intimated to the Consuls that we would leave that judgment to their judgment on the spot.

Mr. President, have you been able to give your attention to the appeal which comes from Boston and other places with regard to Negro segregation here in the departments?[14]

I think they misunderstand what is going on.

Will you try to enlighten them?

No, I don't know that I shall, unless some natural occasion arises. I don't think there is anything to enlighten them about. All they have to do is to come and see what is going on, and I don't think they will feel as they do.

They said there is segregation in the Treasury Department, in the Post Office Department, and in the Bureau of Engraving Department. They have a very personal plea to you.[15]

Do they?

[1] On September 24, Huerta acquiesced in the nomination of Federico Gamboa by the Mexican Catholic party as its candidate for President of Mexico and promised uninfluenced elections. For Bryan's enthusiastic response, see Bryan to WW, Sept. 25, 1913, printed in *PWW*, Vol. 28, pp. 324-25.

[2] Gamboa's note of August 26, 1913.

[3] According to Chargé O'Shaughnessy in Mexico City, Gamboa had not been involved in the Huerta coup of February 1913. Lind did not view Gamboa as Huerta's candidate. See Hill, *Emissaries to a Revolution*, p. 95.

[4] That is, the Constitutionalists.

[5] The Senate had passed the amendment proposed by Senator Clarke to add a tax on cotton futures to the Underwood tariff bill. See above, Sept. 11, 1913, and the *New York Times*, Sept. 22 and 23, 1913.

[6] The House conferees favored a compromise proposal by Representative Underwood whereby the tax on cotton futures would be retained, but the rate would not increase if the contract's terms were not met. The Senate rejected the compromise and receded from the Clarke amendment. The House accepted the Senate's action and eliminated the amendment from the Underwood Act. See *Cong. Record*, 63d Cong., 1st sess., pp. 5275-89, and the *Washington Post*, Oct. 4, 1913.

[7] On September 25, the press reported that Huerta had accepted the nomination of Federico Gamboa and would thus not be a candidate himself. Wilson contended that Huerta had been ruled out as a candidate by Gamboa's note of August 26.

[8] See above, Sept. 11, 1913.

[9] Porfirio Díaz, ex-President of Mexico, who was then residing in Spain.

[10] Felix Díaz was a coconspirator in the Huerta coup and one of Huerta's rivals for control of the government. Huerta removed him from the presidential race by appointing him special Ambassador to Japan. See Grieb, *United States and Huerta*, p. 57.

[11] The cotton-futures tax was a Senate amendment to the Underwood tariff bill and had thus not been debated in the House.

[12] That is, from Mexico.

[13] A reference to instructions issued by the American Consul General in Mexico City to hasten the departure of Americans from the country. See above, Sept. 8, 1913.

[14] The National Association for the Advancement of Colored People was protesting against continued segregation in the executive departments of the government. See the report from May Childs Nerney to Oswald Garrison Villard, Sept. 30, 1913, printed in *PWW*, Vol. 28, pp. 402-10.

[15] See, for example, Villard to WW, Sept. 29, 1913, in *ibid.*, pp. 342-44.

Sept. 29, 1913

What about this New Haven suit, Mr. President?[1]

I don't know what you refer to.

The story this morning contemplates agreeing to the [New Haven's retention] of the Boston and Maine?

Well, I had not been informed about that. Not the first I had heard of it, but the first time I had heard of that suit.

Anything new in the currency legislation?

No, sir.

Still hoping?

Still confident.

Senator Hitchcock's interview has not shaken your confidence?[2]

Oh, no.

Mr. President, is there any—has some proposal been made for a vacation of some kind between now and autumn?

No suggestion even.

Would it be entertained?

It is my [understanding that there will be no recess]. I have not heard if they want to [take a recess]. I am confident they won't, because I know their feeling in the matter, and the feeling of the Senate among the Democratic members I know is practically unanimous. They desire to go ahead with it, and to go ahead with it soon.

You haven't had yet any word from them as to whether or not they will bring it out of committee?

No.

Is there anything in the Mexican situation, Mr. President?

Absolutely nothing new. I noticed some news in this morning's paper that was news to me. I mean, a new candidate.[3] But I hadn't heard of that officially.

How about Mr. Lind's reports? Will he remain in Veracruz now until something happens, or what?

That is at his own discretion and understanding. He is at liberty to go into the Mexican situation whenever he wants to.

Mr. President, in one of the papers it is suggested that it would be well to send an emissary to the Constitutionalists.

If Mr. Lind would suggest that, he wouldn't suggest it out loud.

Well, it was printed under a Mexico City date line.

That was a useful invention when news was scarce.

Has anything been done by this government, Mr. President, in reference to meeting with the Constitutionalists or any of the other factions?

There is really no mention of those they call Constitutionalists.

What is the status of the Russian treaty matter? There is a report that Dr. Herbert Friedenwald of New York[4] has been deputized to arrange the preliminaries of a treaty with the Russians.[5]

No, sir, nothing in that.

Have steps been taken?

Not unless the State Department has taken any without my knowledge.

There is a report in New York that Governor Sulzer—that Governor Sulzer came to you in New York and told you of his financial difficulties.

[There is no reply from the President here.]

Do you think this cotton controversy will delay the tariff?[6]

No, I don't see why it should. You see, it is really an extraneous matter. It is not a necessary part of the tariff bill. And there is a very honest and rather radical difference of opinion between the two houses, apparently, as to how it should be handled. Everybody wants to accomplish the object, but the question is what measure will accomplish the object and prevent the speculative determination of prices, or rather, the determination of prices by speculative operations.

Mr. President, have you received any report of the shooting of American troops by Mexicans?[7]

No.

Are you likely to get a Collector in Boston this week?

I don't know whether we can get him this week or not, but we can get him soon.

Have the conferees submitted their opinions to you in any way so that we could know whether the conference report,[8] as it stands, would be satisfactory to you?

No, they have not. Indeed, I don't know just what the terms of their agreement were. All week up to Friday, I have known what they were doing, but I haven't known since then. But they have been kind enough to keep in touch with all the important items.

Mr. President, have you received a telegram from Dr. Adler of Philadelphia,[9] suggesting a special dispatch to Germany respecting the—

No, sir, it hasn't reached me.

Anything on Japan?

No, nothing at all.

[1] The *New York Times* reported on September 28 that Attorney General McReynolds was considering bringing suit against the New Haven Railroad for violating the Sherman Antitrust Act by acquiring the Boston and Maine Railroad.

[2] Senator Hitchcock, a Democratic member of the Banking and Currency Committee, was an outspoken critic of the Owen-Glass bill.

[3] The Mexican Labor party nominated General Felix Díaz for the presidency. See the *New York Times*, Sept. 29, 1913.

[4] Friedenwald, an author and historian, was the founder of the American Jewish Historical Association and the editor of *Termination of the Treaty of 1832 between the United States and Russia* (Washington, 1911).

[5] Negotiations were about to begin for a new treaty to replace the Russian-American Treaty of 1832. See above, April 14, 1913.

[6] That is, the controversy over the cotton-futures tax provision, the last matter on which the conferees could not agree.

[7] A detachment of American soldiers patrolling the border near El Paso was fired upon by Mexican regulars on September 28. There were no reported casualties. See the *New York Times*, Sept. 28, 1913.

[8] On the Underwood-Simmons tariff bill.

[9] Cyrus Adler, President of Dropsie College in Philadelphia.

Oct. 2, 1913

Mr. President, we are all interested in the report that you are seriously considering an idea for the government to take over the telegraphic system of the country, with a view to competing with the telegraph companies.[1]

That is one of the advantages I get by carefully reading the morning papers. I learned that this morning myself.

There is a story this afternoon to the effect that Representative Lewis[2] of Maryland has prepared a bill—he is investigating it—providing for that.

I knew that Mr. Lewis was very much interested in that. That is all I knew about it.

You haven't taken it up yourself?

No, sir.

It wouldn't be fair to advertise that as administration policy at this time?

No.

Mr. President, you say it has not been discussed in any serious way?

Not in that way. That would be implying that we have been talking about it. I have discussed it at various times with perhaps a half-dozen people who are interested in seeing our government do what practically every other government does—make that part of the postal system; but no policy has been formulated.

Mr. President, is that matter likely to be taken up before the time of your Annual Message—specific reference?

Not so far as I know at present.

Have you any idea as to—have you any information with regard to the material that is being collected?

Why, as I say, I knew that Mr. Lewis was interested, and he came in the other day. He is one of the most systematic men I have ever met in collecting material, and one of the most lucid in explaining the material he brought in—a good deal of statistical matter which we went over in a careful way, but which he did not leave with me and I did not have a chance to study.

Has the argument been strong enough for you to say whether you favor the proposition?

No, sir.

Would it be fair to say at this time whether it is likely to be in your Annual Message?

I haven't [considered that yet].

Is it one of those questions, Mr. President, to be given further consideration?

Why, naturally, just like any other question that is frequently brought to my attention.

Mr. President, has the administration had any communication at all with the Constitutionalists with a view to getting their participation in the election?

No, sir.

Has there been any other development, Mr. President, in the Mexican situation which would shed any light on what is going on there?

No, there is not, I am sorry to say. I haven't had any light within the last three days, I should say.

Nothing from Mexico City regarding the consideration of formally postponing the—[3]

No, nothing at all.

Nothing new with reference to Mr. Lind's recommendations down there?

No, sir.

Mr. President, dispatches from Tokyo yesterday and today disclose a new note based on entirely new grounds which were forwarded to this government. Have you had any word?[4]

I think that is simply based on what happened some weeks ago.[5]

Mr. President, was there any intimation about a treaty with Japan?

Not in that note.

It said Japan—the papers this morning said Japan is likely to—

I think that is simply rumor.

Has there been any discussion between yourself and Baron Chinda as to the question of a new treaty?

No, none at all.

Mr. President, have you taken any stand on the Commerce Court question, either of the court itself or the abolition of the judges?

No, except to this extent, that the Attorney General called on me before he appeared before the committee of the Senate and told me what his judgment was. I of course told him that I had absolutely no opinion to offer.

They have disregarded his views, so far as his recommendation goes, concerning both the court and the judges.[6]

Have they?

Mr. President, they have gone further than that. They have inserted in the bill the provision that a preliminary or temporary injunction may be granted by any judge in any district or circuit court. The House bill provided that, before any injunction could be granted, notice must be given the Attorney General or he must get a copy of it to study it. That House bill also provides that those judgeships shall be abolished forthwith. Is that not true?

That is the chief consideration—to make a provision for the maintenance of the court for the fiscal year. The wording of the bill abolishes the judgeships forthwith.[7]

You haven't taken any stand on it, have you, Mr. President?

No.

Mr. President, Senator O'Gorman outlined his views on the banking system before the committee the other day, in which he said he favored a single Federal Reserve bank, not the Federal Reserve bank system.[8] Have you talked with him about that? Have you anything to say about that?

No, sir. The obstacle to that is the express declaration—He explained that that was not in violation of the pledge. It was not the central bank, it was the Federal Reserve bank.

Mr. President, have you taken up actively the matter of [rural credits]?[9]

No. In a sense, I had a talk with Senator Fletcher[10] some weeks ago. They are working on the matter. I am waiting for them to seek an interview to take it up.

Mr. President, with reference to the currency question, have there been any proposals made to you, any changes in the bill, which might expedite its coming out of the committee?

No changes in the bill which the members of the committee suggested, not a one.

Mr. Glass said, two or three days ago, when he was up here, that there were two or three amendments proposed which he thought would be good. He didn't say what they were. Can you throw any light on it?

No, he hasn't indicated it to me.

The Senate Committee on Finance today has the deficiency bill, to provide that deputy United States marshals and deputy collectors of internal revenue shall be taken out of the civil service.[11] Do you consider that a serious breach?

On the contrary, that was recommended by the Civil Service Commission, if I am thinking of the same thing that you are. It was recommended by that commission.

That had referred to bonded officers.

I think so.

That is, where a deputy handled money, and the collector was really responsible for the money, the collector should have the appointment there.

It's just [to protect] the over-eager collector himself that the change was recommended by the Civil Service Commission.

This is not to be regarded as a beginning? It is not an attack on the civil service?

Not in the least.

Mr. President, was this submission of today, referring to the Postal Telegraph, was that by order of any superior officer, or was it voluntary on the part of these people?

It was entirely a private matter of Mr. Lewis'.

There is nothing new with reference to the tariff, Mr. President, so far as you are concerned?

No, sir, it seems all straightened out.

They should pass the tariff bill in the Senate tonight, or adopt the conference report. Well, how soon would you be able to sign the bill?[12]

I would [right away], if they get it to me. I hadn't been told that it was possible to get it so soon.

They were talking about trying to get a vote at six o'clock.

If I get it, I'll sign it the minute I get it.

Are you planning to go to the Capitol to sign it?

No. It will be brought down here.

Mr. President, have you dispatches from Colonel Goethals regarding the earthquake down there?[13]

I have been waiting, wondering if I should hear.

The press dispatch says there is no damage done of any consequence, except that they are still moving some of the supplies a little more rapidly, but there has been no damage to the locks.

I have interpreted no message as good news. I was startled when I saw the reports in the papers.

Mr. President, have you promised to go down to the target practice at Hampton Roads?[14]

Yes, sir, that seems one of my duties.

Have you anything from Russia yet about the prospective treaty?

No, nothing at all, at least official, that I have heard from the State Department.

Mr. President, what is the status of the Russian treaty now? Have we any further agreement with Russia with reference to rewriting the citizenship provisions of that treaty?

The whole situation is just what it was when it was abrogated.

I have been told that the citizenship provisions have been rewritten. I infer that the Russian government had given some hope to this government—

I should be very glad if they had, but if so, I haven't been apprised of it.

[1] The *New York Times*, October 2, 1913, carried a long story which described the proposed plan for a takeover of the telegraphic system and interstate telephone lines by the federal government.

[2] Representative David John Lewis, Democrat of Maryland.

[3] The Mexican Congress was at this time considering postponing the elections from their scheduled date of October 26.

[4] On October 1 and 2, the *New York Times* carried short reports from Tokyo which stated that the Japanese were proposing a new commercial treaty with the United States, one which would grant Japanese citizens a most-favored-nation status.

[5] See above, Sept. 18, 1913.

[6] That is, that both the Commerce Court and the positions of the judges be abolished.

[7] The Senate eventually decided to fund the judgeships until December 31, 1913.

[8] See the *Washington Post*, Oct. 1, 1913.

[9] Congress, in 1913, had created a Rural Credits Commission to look into the problem of excessively high interest rates on farm lands and to propose a solution. The commission, headed by Fletcher, was at this time conducting investigations. See *The Survey*, XXX (May 17, 1913), 239-40, and Link, *The New Freedom*, pp. 261-62.

[10] Senator Duncan Upshaw Fletcher, Democrat of Florida, who had introduced a rural-credits bill on August 9. See *ibid.*, p. 261.

[11] The Senate on October 2 cut the civil-service list by removing deputy United States marshals and deputy collectors of internal revenue who were required to give bond. The marshals and collectors were given authority to appoint their deputies without reference to the civil-service list. See the *New York Times*, Oct. 3, 1913, and the *Washington Post*, Oct. 3, 1913.

[12] Wilson signed the Underwood tariff bill on October 3.

[13] Two earthquakes had rocked Panama during the evening of October 1. The *New York Times*, October 2, 1913, reported that the canal locks were believed to be undamaged.

[14] The Atlantic Fleet conducted firing practice off the Virginia coast on October 18. Wilson did not attend. See the *Washington Post*, Oct. 17, 1913.

Oct. 6, 1913

I see a dispatch this morning about the probable negotiation of a new treaty with Japan. Is there anything on that?

No, nothing at all new. This whole thing in the papers puzzles me, because nothing has happened in, I guess, three weeks. There is nothing new about it at all that has been brought to my attention. Of course, it would have been brought to my attention, I think. What it is, as I suggested the other day, is simply negotiations that have been going on quietly and have been talked about.[1]

Has the Japanese embassy offered to make any explanation?

No. I haven't asked for it, at least.

Mr. President, are you receiving from the people, in any general sense, any comment of any kind on the currency bill as it stands, inquiries [that make] you think it is well understood?

I should say so, and universally desired.

In what sort of form?

It naturally wouldn't come in any analytical form—going into the features—but the country understands the main features of the bill. It naturally would not know all the details but thoroughly approves what the administration stands for.

Do you get letters from individuals?

Yes, from every quarter, and a great many different, ordinary constituents have made very interesting comments on the situation—and a great many from bankers who don't want to be quoted. You can draw your own inferences.

Are you having a new conference, Mr. President, as to whether or not and how they can bring the bill out?

No, that will be all right.

Are these bankers prominent bankers?

They range in size, so to speak. Some of them are big, but the majority of them are the middle-sized.

Bankers who are willing that they should be quoted? Do they favor the bill?

Well, only the big ones are willing to be quoted. They don't, for manifest reasons, want the absolute control of the country taken out of their hands, which no human being should desire.

No self-respecting banker.

That is right. The thing is so manifest, I wonder the country doesn't [understand].

Are you confident, Mr. President, that you will be able to sign the currency bill before this session ends?

I am.

Mr. President, has any proposition been put up to you for your consent or for your discussion, with a view to the adjournment of the House?

No, that has not been talked about with me.

How do you feel about that, Mr. President?

I don't know. I should think the House—

Mr. President, this long session is putting most of the Congressmen in sanitariums and hospitals.

When we get through, we can all go together. I don't know that it's any less hard on the President than it is on Congress, but I seem to be able to stand it.

Mr. President, there has been a great deal printed about the 5-per-cent reduction.[2] Any action taken?

There is no difficulty in construing it. The only difficulty suggested is where it does and where it does not clash with a treaty in existence. But I don't see any difficulty in determining that myself.

The logic of it seems to suggest, Mr. President, that it would lead to a 5-per-cent cut in all customs receipts from countries that are the largest carriers and have those treaties.

I wish it would. I mean, I wish from this point of view—that is based upon the assumption there are not a great many American bottoms carrying them.

They claim that if the American ships are to have that rebate, then the countries that have treaties with us, such as Japan, should receive the same privileges that American ships have got, claiming the 5-per-cent exemption also.

Well, it wouldn't work that way, as I understand it, because goods imported in American bottoms from Japan would not be discriminated in favor of against Japanese ships.[3]

That is not the way the former—

You see, that would be the natural way to interpret the treaty, in order to keep it in agreement with our previous understandings.

But that is not what they are expecting.

I think that is a mistake in their interpretation.

I was talking with—

I would have to speak absolutely offhand, without any consideration made, but I could assume that we could, just as I interpret it the other way, so as to put them on the same terms.

If we bring some goods from Japan into this country, your interpretation is that, then, whether it comes in Japanese ships or American ships, there will not be a reduction of 5 per cent?

My offhand interpretation is, I am assuming that there will be no reduction for either, so as not to discriminate.

Where the treaty exists, it would not apply to Americans?

That is my assumption. I speak purely on the spur of the moment. I have not discussed it with the State Department at all, but I should assume that they would have another interpretation, just as natural an interpretation as the other. Because, you see, the clause, as I remember it, says that there shall be this reduction provided it does not act in contravention of treaty understandings with foreign governments, which would mean that it would not operate in those cases.

But the paragraph said, Mr. President, if I remember it, Mr. President, this shall not operate to abrogate any treaty.

That is what it was intended to mean, I am sure, because whoever it was who drafted the proviso—I don't remember—and whoever it was who consulted me about it and what he intended it to say, he did not consult me about the language. But what he intended to say was that this should not be understood to be in the way of contravening a treaty.

Mr. President, do you expect to negotiate with our treaty [partners] arrangements in place of those?

Nothing is pending at present.

Well, wouldn't it be necessary to do that pretty soon?

No, sir. In some cases, certainly.

The conventional tariffs of the other countries will immediately apply upon the—following the agreement?

It may be so, but that is one of the things we haven't yet done, taken up. You see, it will be prudent to allow a certain amount of time to see how this thing is going to operate and just whom it will touch, before we can see what we will do.

Wouldn't it be necessary, then, to have a *modus vivendi*?

Yes, it may be.

Have you been memorialized by any civil-service organization with reference to a provision in the tariff bill [undermining the merit system]?[4]

Yes, there was a paper that I haven't had time to read carefully. I think it came in at the end of last week from one of the civil-service reform associations, I think the main one.

Mr. President, you told us last week that that provision was recommended by the Civil Service Commission. Did you notice that Mr. McIlhenny[5] wrote a letter?[6]

Yes, and I got a letter from him. I am a little mixed up in my mind as a consequence. It may be that the provision in the bill was given a wider scope than at first contemplated, after the members of the commission had been consulted. I think that must be the fact, because they would not say one thing one day and another the next. What was in our minds at the time that the commission was consulted was this: not the deputy collectors, but the special agents who from time to time act for the collectors and for whom the collectors are personally responsible. You see, the collector's own bonds cover these special agents in their separate, individual bonds, I am informed, and therefore he is deputizing them, in a very special sense, since he is responsible for everything that they do under his policy.

Now it was considered fair, considered fair as I understood it at the time, by the Civil Service Commission, that I should select these persons to see who occupied this specially confidential, trust-worthy relationship toward them. It may be, as I say, that the language of the bill extends them beyond what was contemplated, possibly inadvertently. I don't know. I haven't had time to look into it yet.[7]

Mr. President, would there be any opposition to the application of the civil-service rules to the special agents, applying both to the deputy?

No. But, you see, what is alleged against the whole arrangement is that it is very difficult to pick out persons you can trust by examination. It is a temperamental relationship at times.

Mr. President, can you change that provision to what it was intended by Executive Order?

I don't know. That question was raised this morning, and I had to say I don't know. I haven't had time to look it up. The whole thing in its new aspect has just come to me this morning.

Can you say anything as to the nature of the letter from the Civil Service Commission?

It certainly called my attention to the provision in the bill and expressed the opinion that it was detrimental to the service.

Is this protest against the provision in the deficiency bill or in the tariff bill?

In the deficiency bill.

You haven't had any protest against that provision in the tariff bill?

Not from the Civil Service Commission. I don't know that there have been protests from other correspondents. I have seen protests in the papers.[8]

That bill[9] can still be so—

I suppose so.

It has to go back to the House.

Yes. Has it gone to conference yet?

It hasn't passed the House with that provision in it.
Mr. President, that bill contains a House amendment prohibiting the use of any of the monies for the employment of publicity experts.[10] Have any of the secretaries complained to you about that?

No, sir.

There is a very strong feeling, I think, Mr. President, at least among knowledgeable men, that there is a lot of dynamite in that suggestion. The government stands a pretty fair chance of losing 75 per cent of excellent publicity unless that is administered very carefully. It is rather a dangerous provision.

Well, to tell the truth, I am entirely against the way publicity agents have been used and think that they [the departments] should have to provide publicity without special publicity agents.

Well, it doesn't affect [this] office, but—

Oh, it won't affect [this] office. We'll have publicity, I can promise you that.

Still, it is a fact, since the publicity agent has been employed, the publicity system has been much better than it was before, and much better work has been done by the departments.

By its being systematized under one head, I think that might be true.

The publicity agent's office, Mr. President, is a kind of clearinghouse for news for the whole department. It is one point to which you can go to get information.

You have the departments employing the special men, or simply deputizing other members to act.

There have been quite a number of special men, mostly newspapermen—I mean, men who have been newspapermen.

But have reformed.

Mr. President, it might be well to explain the point that lies in the minds of the newspapermen. Where the department employs special men, or even details one of its own men, and bottles up everything except what comes from that office, you have an uncomfortable situation. But where in some other case a man is deputized, or a special man is appointed and new avenues are opened, we have an excellent system, a system that works well. But usually it brings a great deal of criticism on the department. The question is really a pretty sizable one.

Well, isn't there, on the whole, according to that, apt to be more publicity without this nuisance than with it?

I don't think so, sir.

There might be.

It depends upon the character of the men who are assigned to this work. There would be, in the matter of spot news.

I don't see how it could be avoidable to have some one person, or some small number of persons to whom the newspapermen here can go.

In practice, these men have prepared information and given it out in a convenient form, sometimes very well and sometimes very badly.

There have been departments like the Department of Agriculture, which covers a million activities, and no newspaperman could send one third of the information they give out.

On the whole, it has always seemed to me a very valuable thing, but the efficiency depends, as any other efficiency does, on the man.

It would, necessarily.

But as Mr. [blank] says, where the head of the department insists that no information should be given, except to a trustworthy man, that, I think also, is very bad.

Then everything else of what you think and say [is prepared by] the government.

We haven't seen much of that news in this administration.

You mean, confining publicity to one channel?

Bottling up. We haven't found much abuse in the way of bottling up news, as was the case in the last [administration.][11] Anything new on Mexico, Mr. President?

No, sir, nothing at all. We had a dispatch yesterday from Mr. Lind, but it didn't disclose anything new. It was just a routine report.

You haven't had any information, then, that there will be any changes in the election plan?

None. I saw in the papers that a bill had been introduced in the Mexican Congress, proposing a change in it, but I haven't seen that verified through our dispatches, and I don't know what the contents of the bill are.

Have there been any further reports about changing the [date]?

No. None at all.

---

[1] See above, Oct. 2, 1913.

[2] A provision of the new tariff law granted a 5-per-cent rate reduction on goods imported in American bottoms. The difficulty here was that some countries had treaties with the United States which guaranteed that there would be no discrimination between their vessels and those belonging to Americans. It was feared that those countries would be entitled to the discount on all of their exports to the United States. For a long story, see the *New York Times*, Oct. 5, 1913.

[3] Wilson is offering another interpretation of the meaning of the rebate. If American ships were denied the rebate where a treaty violation might occur, there would be no need for an across-the-board reduction of 5 per cent.

[4] A provision of the tariff bill provided that, for two years, employees of the Internal Revenue Bureau could be appointed without reference to civil-service lists. See Charles William Eliot to WW, Sept. 10, 1913, in *PWW*, Vol. 28, p. 272.

[5] John Avery McIlhenny, a Civil Service commissioner.

[6] J. A. McIlhenny to WW, Sept. 25, 1913, WP, DLC.

[7] Wilson was discussing a different matter, the removal of deputy marshals and deputy collectors of internal revenue from the list of appointees covered by the civil-service law. See above, Oct. 2, 1913.

[8] There was one in an editorial in the *New York Times*, Oct. 5, 1913.

[9] That is, the urgent deficiency appropriations bill.

[10] The amendment by Representative Frederick Huntington Gillett, Republican of Massachusetts, said: "No money appropriated by this or any other act shall be used for the compensation of any publicity expert unless specifically appropriated for that purpose." Gillett argued that publicity experts were not necessary because any official ought to be able to explain his policies in plain, direct English. Such a law was already in effect with respect to the Forestry Service, which Congress believed had been wasting the taxpayers' money on publicity for its programs. The amendment was approved by the House on September 6, 1913. See *Cong. Record*, 63d Cong., 1st sess., pp. 4409-11. For a discussion of publicity concerns within the Wilson administration, see Hilderbrand, *Power and the People*, pp. 93-141.

[11] For publicity during the Taft administration, see Hilderbrand, pp. 72-92.

Oct. [9], 1913

Mr. President, can you throw any light on the situation with regard to the New York, New Haven, and Hartford Railroad and the government's ideas concerning it?[1]

No, because the things are taking their regular course. I haven't had any conference with the Attorney General.

I knew Mr. Elliott[2] had been with him this morning.

I haven't seen the Attorney General today. I understand Mr. Elliott was in the office here, but I was so preoccupied I did not see him.

Well, the idea seems to be, Mr. President, that the New Haven wants the government to consent to a plan it will propose for a practical dissolution of the lines. I don't know that. I merely heard the suggestion. I was wondering whether you had any information in advance as to what that was.

Nothing at all. I really know nothing about it.

The Attorney General said he would be satisfied with the complete dissolution along the lines the government wanted and the entering of a judicial decree in Connecticut. I was wondering whether you could tell us if the government's plan would insist on complete dissolution of the lines?

I don't know. I simply know we will have to abide by the language of the law, and there won't be any abatement, sir, of that. I don't know what plan—I mean, I don't know what decree—Mr. McReynolds would propose. I wouldn't know what the suggestion of the railroad is.

Unfortunately, I am in the same position.
Mr. President, the news today, that Purroy Mitchel has tendered his resignation—

Yes, sir—the letter reached me only this morning.[3] I haven't had time to consider the question one way or the other.

You wouldn't care to say whether—how you would rate his chances relatively?

Oh, no. I have nothing to say on that subject.

Mr. President, in that letter, there is a suggestion that he thinks this is the right course to pursue; that is, to tender his resignation but leave it to you to determine whether the resignation should be accepted or whether he should get out now. He said that the office would be run in a very competent way even if he weren't there.

Yes. I read the letter, but I don't understand that he puts the matter of judgment up to me at all.

The practical part of it is, Mr. President, if he should not resign and be defeated, he would still have an annuity, he would still have a good job.

He wouldn't have an annuity, he would have a salary, a very great difference.

Mr. President, did you construe that to mean the matter of judgment was not left to you?

That did not occur to me. I will frankly say that, when I read the letter, I just read it in a hastily minded manner. I haven't had time to read it critically.

Mr. President, I think it is pretty clear that he does, as a more or less tactical thing, he does not insist on resigning, but he feels he should present his resignation, which is how most people would get that impression.

I didn't, on a hasty reading. I will consider it very carefully.

You wouldn't want to say, then, whether you feel a man in that position ought to resign?

I will express my opinion in my action.

There will be no decision reached on it today, can I assume that?

No, sir.[4]

Mr. President, are you willing to make any comment on the suggestion that has been made, that it doesn't make any practical difference whether the currency bill is brought to you and signed on November 30, within the extra session, or on December 1, after the beginning of the regular session, since the bill would lose no legislative standing during the recess?

It makes a great deal of practical difference. Time is of the essence. The business of the country is ready to settle down to the new legislation, inasmuch as business naturally quickens and accumulates in the autumn on the approach of winter. I think it is of the first consequence that the action should be as early as possible. While it makes no practical difference from the legislative standing of the bill, it makes a great deal of practical difference to the country.

Of course, you see, what lies behind my question, not to mention the words about it, there is a feeling I have seen expressed, that there was only a technical question involved in the question—whether the bill was actually in the extra session or the next day in the regular session.

I haven't made any point of what was first, but I have made a great deal of point of the time. If the regular session began tomorrow, I would wish it passed as early as possible. It is not a question of the session, it is a question of time as being of the essence. I think it is of the first consequence that the question should be decided.

You are still as confident as you were that the result will be achieved?

Yes, sir, I am.

Has it been determined whether the bill that has come out of this committee is to be drafted by all Democratic members, or whether all of the members of the committee are to work on it?

Do you think we would get a bill if all of them do not work on it?

I don't know.

Well, you know as well as I do.

May I interpret that—that—

You are not to interpret it at all. You are to have your own thoughts about it. I will leave it to your judgment.

Mr. President, Senator Owen announced today that the hearings could not close before the twenty-fifth and that he could not tell the Senate as to whether or not the report would be made by the committee. Do you think that makes for any unnecessary delay?

Certainly it does. All that these bankers have said has been said more than once before in the committees of Congress. It is going over old ground in which they are slowly shifting their position.

Do you think, Mr. President, that the resolutions adopted by the Boston bankers[5] are any more representative of general public sentiment than the resolutions adopted at Chicago?[6]

They are not representative of the general public sentiment at all.

You don't attach any more weight to those than the resolutions adopted at Chicago?

I simply attach the weight I would attach to the utterances of men acting, no doubt, in entire honesty, who don't want their control of the business of the country altered.

Are these the large bankers?

I wasn't there. I don't know.

What do you mean by the bankers' shifting position?

I mean that some of them haven't said the same thing to the Senate that they have said to the House.

Can you give any specific instance?

No, I cannot. I have that at secondhand, because I haven't read the testimony. That is what I was told by a member of the Banking and Currency Committee of the House.

Mr. President, are you expecting to go into conference with the members of the committee in the next few days?

No. No conference is planned and I have not asked for one.

Mr. President, one of the members of the committee said if the witnesses should drop out, the committee would close today and that it would just sit there and wait until October 26, because they had said they would. Do you expect the hearings would be closed before October 25?

I don't know.

Mr. President, has anything been done today, so far as you are concerned, with regard to the 5-per-cent provision?[7]

No, nothing at all.

Has any effort been made, Mr. President, to reach Mr. Underwood[8] to suggest to him to take it up as a matter of importance, that it should be taken up presently?

I know only this: I know that one of the regular members of the State Department was seeking a conference with Mr. Underwood.[9] Whether he obtained it or not, I don't know.

I think he did, Mr. President.

Did he?

I mean, no announcement, however.

No announcement, however?

No.

I haven't heard from him since then. I simply knew he was going to sit down [with Mr. Underwood].

Do you contemplate sending a message to Congress on the subject, Mr. President?

No.

May we know, Mr. President, what is your opinion?

No, I don't care to express an opinion about that now. It is a very tangled question.

It has been suggested, Mr. President, that that can be made operative without legislative action.[10]

No. Can it?

I don't know.

I thought you had something in mind.

That would be the simplest way.

Very much the [simplest way].

Are you expecting now to make any speeches out in the country anywhere with reference to currency legislation?

No.

Mr. President, did Mr. Folk have any conference with Senator Simmons at your direction?

No. Oh, no. He came to see me, and, I remember, when he came to see me, he was going away to be at a conference, but it was not by my direction.

Mr. President, will you make a statement for the newspapers on your pardon of a man named Nolan?[11]

No, sir. If I could, I would have to go back to my notes. I could not go all over that. Pardon cases come up to me.

I was told it was with the authorization of the Attorney General.

I daresay it was.

Mr. President, we all were last night under the impression that these various recommendations made by the Solicitor of the State Department, the chairman of the Finance Committee, and the chairman of the Ways and Means Committee at least had the concurrence of what we might call the administration. He wasn't doing it on his own initiative and without consulting with the President. We assume that he was acting for the President.

Yes, sir. He was acting with my knowledge and consent. He brought the matter to my attention.

Mr. President, have the Democratic leaders of the House appealed to you to help get a quorum back here?[12]

I don't think they will need the army to make the arrest.

Have any of the departments complained to you because this deficiency bill has been held up?

No, sir.

Mr. President, have you expressed your views individually or otherwise as to whether there should be one, two, three, or four battleships?[13]

No, sir.

We have heard that England has negotiated with Colombia to get the rights for an isthmian canal.[14]

You mean recently?

Yes, sir. Recently.

I believe there were such negotiations at one time, but I haven't heard of any recently.

The new administration,[15] though.

No, nothing in the weeks past.

Mr. President, has there been any development in the Mexican situation?

There has been none whatever, son. The official dispatches from there are quite cool.

The Japanese matter stands as it did when we were here last?

Yes, sir.

Mr. President, has [a decision] been made about [assistance for] Alaska?[16]

Of course.

Probably will be sent soon?

Well, I can't tell you that. I don't know what the stage is.

Press dispatches in the last few days said, Mr. President, that Mr. O'Shaughnessy was in Veracruz for a long conference with Mr. Lind.

I did learn that Mr. O'Shaughnessy was going to pay Mr. Lind a visit. That is all I knew.

One of the [reports] said he was going to take Mr. O'Shaughnessy to wherever—[17]

Oh, that would be an equally important job.

[1] See above, Sept. 29, 1913.

[2] Howard Elliott, president of the railroad and head negotiator in talks with Attorney General McReynolds.

[3] See Mitchel to WW, Oct. 8, 1913, printed in *PWW*, Vol. 28, pp. 374-75.

[4] Wilson accepted Mitchel's resignation on October 20. See WW to Mitchel, Oct. 20, 1913, printed in *ibid.*, pp. 419-20.

[5] The annual convention of the American Bankers' Association met in Boston beginning October 6 and adopted resolutions denouncing the Glass-Owen bill. See Link, *The New Freedom*, p. 229.

[6] See above, Aug. 25, 1913, and Link, *The New Freedom*, pp. 226-27.

[7] Because this provision was causing diplomatic and financial problems, the Wilson administration favored its repeal. See the *Washington Post*, Oct. 9, 1913.

[8] He was at Atlantic City and could not be reached by telephone. See *ibid.*

[9] Joseph Wingate Folk, Solicitor of the State Department, discussed the matter with congressional leaders on October 8. See *ibid.*

[10] Wilson had proposed that the 5-per-cent reduction be repealed by joint resolution. See *ibid.*

[11] Unidentified.

[12] James Robert Mann of Illinois, Republican floor leader in the House, on October 6 called for Democratic members to return to Washington. The House had been unable to act for lack of a quorum. See the *Washington Post*, Oct. 7, 9-10, 1913.

[13] *Ibid.*, Oct. 8, 1913, reported that Wilson favored the construction of three battleships.

[14] A British syndicate was reported to be attempting to obtain a canal route through Colombia to the Gulf of Darien. The Wilson administration renewed an offer made to Colombia by Taft's Minister in Bogotá, James Taylor DuBois, to purchase the Darien canal rights for $10,000,000. See *ibid.*, Oct. 10, 1913; American Minister to Secretary of State, Feb. 5, 1913, in *FR, 1913*, pp. 287-94; and E. Taylor Parks, *Colombia and the United States, 1765-1934* (Durham, N. C., 1935), pp. 437-39.

[15] The administration of President Carlos E. Restrepo, which seemed willing to negotiate with the United States.

[16] A severe storm near Nome, Alaska, had caused $1,500,000 in damages. Representative Albert Johnson, Republican of Washington, was calling for $20,000 in aid. See the *Washington Post*, Oct. 7 and 10, 1913.

[17] Lind was at this time attempting to persuade the Constitutionalists to take part in the elections. See Hill, *Emissaries to a Revolution*, pp. 96-98.

Oct. [13], 1913

Who invented the fiction that I have abolished cabinet meetings?

I happen to be the one who wrote the story, Mr. President, that you had reason to [do so] for the summer.

No, the story I saw was in the *Sun*. It was said that I had abolished cabinet meetings and substituted individual conferences with members of the cabinet. Of course, that is done every summer, as you know.

It never has been done when the President was in Washington in the summer before.

I don't know anything about that. I know that the summer meetings have been impossible because of the absolute dispersal of the cabinet. It is one of the most magnificent fictions that has been started. While I don't want to take it too seriously, I hope sincerely, gentlemen, you won't start reports of that sort, because it looks as if I were doing things that certainly would be detrimental to the best administration of the government. Nothing is more useful to me, speaking for myself, than the cabinet meetings and the interchange of views that we take up there and the routine information that is exchanged, making it a sort of clearinghouse. I wouldn't like the impression to get out to the country that anything so amateurish and silly as that is being done. When I relieve my mind, I can relieve yours.

Mr. President, is this the state of affairs that you said presently would be revealed, the true state of affairs?[1]

Well, I didn't have so inventive an imagination as to look for it in this. No.

Are there any new advices [from Mexico] this morning or last night?

No, none at all. We got some about two o'clock this morning, but they did not throw any new light. I don't mean to say that I saw them this morning. I saw them just as I got up this morning, but they don't throw any new light on the situation.

Were there any reports made to Mr. Lind or the embassy instructing them to tell the Huerta government that the United States would look with disfavor on any harm that might befall the deputies? A story is published to that effect.

It is true that Mr. Bryan sent a message to both Mr. Lind and Mr. O'Shaughnessy, making very strong representations to the people down there, I don't know what you call them, who have those deputies at their mercy.[2]

Was that addressed to the Minister of Foreign Affairs?

No. It was addressed to Mr. O'Shaughnessy, to be communicated to him.

Will Mr. Lind return to Mexico City?

We will leave that conclusion to his own judgment.

What is the sum total, or rather, what is the effect of all this, regarding the policy of this government, your plans for—

Well, that is just what we are ourselves debating. We haven't formulated yet just how we will state our position.

Have you thought yet what effect this will have on your original plans?

Oh, so far as our original plans are concerned, they were ones that they settle their own affairs.

I had particular reference to holding the election, which was regarded as a sort of direct step toward the ending of the hostilities.

I will leave it to circumstances, as this is an election year under constitutional stipulation.

Is there anything with reference to the naval transfer that is about to be brought about of our ships that were to be taken back in connection with that expiration of the period? Are we to remove our ships?[3]

No, sir, there are no orders to that effect.

No increase in that?

No change at all.

Mr. President, during the discussion of the urgent deficiency bill in the House involving reports as to the attitude with regard to the taking of United States deputy marshals and deputy collectors of internal revenue out of the civil service, could you take us into your confidence with regard to that?[4]

I would, if there was anything definite to tell you. As a matter of fact, I have been in conference with a number of Senators and Representatives from time to time, either personally or over the telephone, about it; and there is evidently a great deal more in the matter than lies upon the surface. For example, to follow the opinions of the Attorney General, which most [certainly] will [be] read into the *Record*, into the *Congressional Record*, it is evidently a question which has been muted for some time and is not as plain sailing as it first seemed.

The whole idea, as they explain it to me, is this: that we should

not oblige officers to take subordinates, for whose faithful performance of their duties they are responsible under bond, from the civil-
service list, but that they shall be allowed to make a personal selection. It appears to be the opinion of the Attorney General of the
last administration that such officers, used in such a personal relationship to their chiefs, had not been contemplated in the civil-
service rules. So that the reason I haven't announced a definite
policy was that I was keeping my mind open.

Are those subordinates bonded?

They are bonded to their superiors, as I am informed.

Mr. President, is that both classes, both of those two classes?

I can't speak from my own examination of the law, but so I am
told.

Is this matter one that is sufficiently important to make it worthwhile as to—
Any conjecture whether or not you will sign the bill[5] when it [arrives]?

You know, the bill hasn't come out of conference. I never conjecture about that until I have completed my conferences with those
who make the bill.

Anything on currency, Mr. President?

No, sir.

There is a possibility of a recess or adjournment with your approval, Mr.
President?

I took that to be a Monday morning amusement by the newspapers.

I didn't write it.

I didn't know that anybody had, as a matter of fact.

It was Sunday morning, Mr. President.

I saw it, I think, this morning. I have forgotten what paper.

It was printed Sunday morning.[6]

As always, my calendar knows. For Monday morning is a pipe-dream morning.

Most of the government publications are released for use on Monday morning. Mr. President, haven't you left us [in the dark] really—I mean, where you stand on this question of recess?

I haven't [malpracticed] the English language for years. I may have misunderstood. I haven't said anything this morning, but I have said it so often before this morning that I didn't think it was necessary again. Speaking seriously, there hasn't been any kind of fresh proposition brought to me, directly or indirectly, as to a recess.

Is your confidence in the passage of the bill at this session still unshaken?

It is, sir.

[1] A reference to recent events in Mexico. On October 10, Huerta dissolved Congress, arrested 110 deputies, and called for a special election to be held with the presidential election on October 26. See the *New York Times*, Oct. 12, 1913, and Michael C. Meyer, *Huerta: A Political Portrait* (Lincoln, Neb., 1972), pp. 136-38, 143-49.

[2] See Bryan to O'Shaughnessy, Oct. 13, 1913, printed in *PWW*, Vol. 28, p. 399.

[3] Huerta was insisting that the United States remove its warships from Veracruz by October 26. Wilson planned to change squadrons in the port but not to remove the American presence. See the *New York Times*, Oct. 12-13, 1913.

[4] See above, Oct. 2, 1913.

[5] That is, the urgent deficiency appropriations bill.

[6] The story appeared in the *New York Times* on Sunday, October 12.

Oct. 16, 1913

Mr. President, have we had any word from General Huerta in response to the representations that have been made to him?

No, not a word. I understand from the papers he is not going to make any. I don't receive them.

Mr. President, have you any knowledge or has the State Department any knowledge of the reason for the assembling of the diplomatic corps at Mexico City, and did our Chargé d'Affaires get any instructions in relation to that matter?[1]

I was simply apprised that the matter was going to be determined in the course of events. The Ambassador[2] asked us if we had any suggestions to make. Afterwards, we authorized him to let them know, of course, what we had said.

There were no further suggestions?

No, sir.

Has he[3] reported any kind of meeting of the diplomatic gentlemen to see what practical steps their governments have to offer?

He hasn't reported at all, so far as I am notified.

Mr. President, on what conditions could Huerta procure the recognition of the United States for the election of his successor?

In the present circumstances?

Under the present circumstances?

None.

Is it the idea of this government that he ought to release [the deputies] and restore the Congress to its constitutional order?

We have no suggestions to make to them.

There isn't any alternative?
Mr. President, do you regard it important as affecting the situation with regard to Mexico, so far as the United States is concerned, of Germany's sending warships over there?[4]

Oh, no, sir.

Have the foreign governments, Mr. President, asked just what our further course will be?

No, sir.

Or have they apprised us of what our course should be?

No, they have not. I daresay the German government will apprise us of its intention in sending warships there. That is a surmise on my part. They generally adhere to the courtesy of the seas.

Have we taken any steps to secure the sympathetic or concerted action of foreign governments in our attitude toward this election?

In a sense, at the outset, when we sent the original note by John Lind, we asked for their sympathetic attitude in the matter, which we obtained. We haven't asked since then.

In a sense, you have decided the election could not be recognized?

We apprised them of the action taken.

Mr. President, there is a story published in some of the papers this afternoon from Mexico City that Mr. O'Shaughnessy took a dispatch from this government, on Tuesday, to Huerta, and then they asked to treat that as official, but the story—[5]

I know nothing as to its being official, no; simply a communication for his information. That is the reason no reply is forthcoming. All of that is fiction.

Mr. President, has there been a discussion as to the status of the recent loans that have been made by the Huerta government?[6]

I don't understand that any domestic loans have been made. Have you information to the contrary?

There has been some question in banking circles as to what would be the status of their recent loans?

That hasn't reached me.

They seem to be worrying about what would happen if this dictatorship would collapse.

Why, I should think they would.

Mr. President, has there been fairly close communication between ourselves and the important countries regarding this situation in Mexico, regarding the successive steps and the successive stages of the situation there?

We have kept them informed of every step.

Has there been very much in the way of suggestions from them?

Nothing at all.

Then it could not be described as concerted action at all?

No, there hasn't been any suggestion from them at all. We have simply kept them very carefully informed.

Mr. President, would it be correct to say that they are going to follow our lead, or that they are waiting for us to lead? Do they think any further steps will be ahead?

I wouldn't be in a position to say that.

Mr. President, what is the next step?

I am not going to discuss that at present.

There won't be anything to indicate just now that there will be any change in the policy of letting them fight it out themselves and then recognize them?

Nothing to indicate that at present.

Mr. President, do you care to suggest any event which might clear the situation?

Oh, no. I never deal in possibilities. The "Ifs" have to verify themselves.

Has there been anything yet, Mr. President, from the Constitutionalists?

No, sir.

We haven't sent them any suggestion that we would be willing at this time to hear from them, now that the Mexican situation is so—

No. I think they have known all along that we would be pleased if they would cooperate in any way for the establishment of peace.

Do you mean by stopping the fighting?

Of course, the recent events have changed the whole face of affairs.

Mr. President, has there been any suggestion from any foreign government that would like to land marines for the protection of its citizens or subjects?

No, sir. Not unless it has been made in the last few hours.

That would not be objectionable to this government though?

I don't care to answer that unless I knew the circumstances.

You know nothing whatever at all about the proposal to request Huerta to keep all his troops permanently in the capital? You haven't had any advices on that?

No, sir. None at all.

Mr. President, is the suggestion of the embargo on arms and transporting them across the border under consideration?

It is under consideration in this sense, that it is made daily.

Mr. President, have you anything at all to indicate that foreign governments would like to see an end put to the condition of affairs down there?

It is coming through diplomatic channels.

Well, all or anything?
You saw the French Ambassador yesterday.[7]

No, he did not allude to that at all. That was just his personal call on returning from his vacation.

You must have something from our Ambassadors and Ministers abroad indicating the sentiment there from [diplomatic] channels?

No, sir, not so far as I know, we haven't.

The French Ambassador told me that the policy of his government was originally the policy of this government, but it is proceeding deliberately to recognize the government down there.

I meant now; they speak of yesterday and tomorrow.

Mr. President, have you been advised of a number of protests that have been filed with the State Department against the seamen's bill[8] the Senate took up today?

No, sir. Have there been a large number?

Several.

No, I haven't, if you mean received from foreign governments.

Great Britain filed a protest.

That probably arises out of the circumstances of the time when there was the suggestion of a conference on the twelfth of November, on the subject of safety at sea; and the subjects covered by the seamen's bill are among those to be discussed by this conference. Probably it was a protest based principally on a premature determination of the question before it was discussed.

There are one or two propositions in the protest.

I am sorry to say I haven't seen that yet.

What is the status, Mr. President, of the 5-per-cent clause?

It is still in the bill.

Mr. President, can you tell us anything as to what the new attitude is on that?

My attitude is usually to find out what the law is and what the government agrees is the right administration of it and what it would make it necessary for us to do.

What do you consider it is necessary to have to do . . . ?

Well, that's a much broader question than this. The only question that arises, under this clause, since it is law, is how we ought to administer the revision of the treaties existing between us and the favored trading nations.

Mr. President, I was reading the record of the accounts of last week's meeting of the House, when Mr. Hobson detailed his charges against Mr. Underwood. Mr. Underwood threw out the same challenge to Mr. Hobson, to get your subscription to those charges. Has Mr. Hobson approached you?[9]

I haven't been asked to referee.

Do you know what the charge is? Would you care to volunteer to make some comments?

I never make any comment on those things.

You mean, Mr. President, they didn't make any?

I have forgotten.

To the effect that he was a dummy, a tool of Wall Street, as a dummy could be used as a tool of the liquor and other interests. It was that assertion on account of which Mr. Underwood issued his challenge. Mr. President, can you tell us anything about the currency situation?

I think the currency situation is daily improving, sir.

Has it improved since this morning?

Well, I don't know whether it has or not.

I notice you had three of the prominent members of the committee present.[10] Where are we to get [a 5-per-cent opinion]?[11]

Why, I haven't got it myself. I think it is under consideration in the Department of Justice, and the opinion is not ready yet.

Mr. President, referring again to the currency, has there been any further suggestion as to whether the bill now is to be a Democratic measure or whether Republicans and Democrats are working out a final solution?

It is just a matter of how far it is wise to push it. That is all there is to discuss.

Is there any assurance on the part of these gentlemen today as to the time for a final date?

I didn't ask assurances. Of course, we just discussed the situation so that I could judge whether we will lay it before the public press.

You still hope to get it through this session?

Yes. Of course, it is possible for anybody who makes use of the procedures of the Senate to find obstacles to hold it up until a year from Christmas.

You mean, so far as the committee is concerned, you think you will get it out in time?

Yes, sir, I think so.

What date do you [suppose]?

I don't know.

Did these gentlemen make any predictions this morning, Mr. President?

No, sir.

Mr. President, Mr. Underwood intimated yesterday that you would be willing to reach an agreement, evidently, as to the time, and they could take an adjournment until the regular session. Did he intimate that correctly?[12]

They don't have to get my permission to adjourn. I told Mr. Underwood that. I did make a few inquiries—I have been making them on this bill—to see what the purpose was, really, and to consult with him at the end of this week, or Monday, as to what the House ought to do, and that he should tell you about these interviews.

Has there been some pressure from the House, Mr. President, to consent to an adjournment?

Oh, not pressure exactly. A very natural impatience; an anxious hanging around, doing nothing, waiting—waiting around, not knowing exactly for what.

You can't tell us, Mr. President, what you did tell Mr. Underwood when he called up?

You won't know until I consult with him. These gentlemen are going to consult among themselves and see what progress is being made.

Mr. President, have you had any communications from people in this country showing their sentiment in regard to this action of Huerta's?

Not a great many, no. Everybody seems to take it for granted that everybody else has the same opinion.

Are you likely to communicate with Congress again on the changing Mexican situation?

No, sir. That is not part of any present plan. Of course, I have kept the Foreign Relations Committee informed.

Mr. President, with regard to Huerta's violation of Mexican rights, now as I understand it, to improve the situation, wouldn't it make it worse if he were to get—

I am tired of commenting on that. Mum is the word.

The French Ambassador said—
Anything on the Japanese situation?

Absolutely nothing.

Mr. President, have you heard anything yet with regard to Mr. John Purroy [Mitchel's] resignation last week?

No, I haven't, but that was just because I haven't had time to take it up. I can ask when Mr. McAdoo comes in about that, I presume.

Mr. President, did any of the Senators who saw you today outline any changes in the currency bill that they thought should be made?

No. Of course I discussed one or two matters of detail, but not to come to any conclusion at all. Just several of the things that were under debate.

Mr. President, Senator O'Gorman put his one-bank proposition up to us. I believe he doesn't like the way the central banking system—[13]

No, I would not.

Mr. President, have you decided on your naval bill and program? There was a report the other day—

No, sir. If I can get away to the target practice,[14] I can discuss that with the Secretary while I am under fire.

---

[1] European and Latin American diplomats were asking their governments for protection in the form of a naval and military presence. See the *New York Times*, Oct. 16, 1913, and the *Washington Post*, Oct. 16, 1913.

[2] The British Ambassador in Washington, Sir Cecil Arthur Spring Rice.

[3] That is, O'Shaughnessy.

[4] On October 15, the German government ordered a second warship to Mexican waters. See the *New York Times*, Oct. 16, 1913.

[5] See the *Washington Post*, Oct. 17, 1913.

[6] That is, to the Huerta government by Mexican banks.

[7] Jean Jules Jusserand visited Wilson on October 15.

[8] An act, sponsored by Senator La Follette, to regulate the hours and improve the conditions of American seamen. The protests came on account of a provision which abolished imprisonment for all seamen, including foreigners, who violated their contract while in American ports and which would contravene treaties with other maritime powers. See Link, *The New Freedom*, pp. 269-70, and the *Washington Post*, Oct. 17, 1913.

[9] On October 13, Representative Richmond Pearson Hobson, Democrat of Alabama, charged that Underwood was a tool of Wall Street and the liquor interests and sparked a lively exchange in the House of Representatives. Underwood invited Hobson to try to obtain Wilson's support of his charges, which related to Underwood's campaign for the Democratic presidential nomination in 1912. See *Cong. Record*, 63d Cong., 1st sess., pp. 5637-47, and the *Washington Post*, Oct. 14, 1913.

[10] Senators Reed, O'Gorman, and Hitchcock of the Senate Banking and Currency Committee visited Wilson on October 16 to discuss the Federal Reserve bill. See *ibid.*, Oct. 17, 1913.

[11] France and Japan protested against the 5-per-cent clause and asked for equal treatment

under most-favored-nation provisions in their commercial treaties with the United States. See *ibid.*

[12] See the *New York Times*, Oct. 16, 1913.

[13] Senator O'Gorman favored fewer banks than the number provided for in the Federal Reserve bill. See the *Washington Post*, Oct. 16, 1913.

[14] Wilson did not make the trip to Virginia for the naval target practice. See *ibid.*, Oct. 17, 1913.

Oct. 20, 1913

I believe that the Commissioner of Immigration did only so much as he thought remained to do yesterday, considering the situation, because it was Sunday, but he is going to have the main hearing today. The case is not before you?[1]

No, sir. It is not before me. I don't believe there is any law to bring it before me, unless I take it by the ear or head.

I suppose you can indicate the policy to be followed by the Commissioner of Immigration?

I have thought he would wish me to do so, but he hasn't consulted me yet.

Isn't it a question of policy rather than law?

I dare say it is. The law I haven't had time to examine. I dare say that it would be, just as almost any [such case would be]. We might take care of it just among ourselves. As you say, it is probably not a question of law but of policy.[2]

Mr. President, what is the situation of the currency bill at this time?

Why, I think I can sum it up in this way. I think there is very good reason to expect a report not later than the first week in November, and I find every disposition to discuss it, without any attempt to delay it when it gets on the floor of the Senate, so that I should hope that two, or at the outside three, weeks of debate would conclude the matter. I have been making some inquiries, and that is my general conclusion.

Will you have nonpartisan support for the bill?

I think there will be a very considerable degree of nonpartisan support.

Does that involve any considerable change in the bill as it now stands?

So far as I can see, no change that affects any vital part of the bill. I have found timely and unexpected agreement on the fundamental features of the bill.[3]

Do you think it is possible to obtain a unanimous report?

There are members of the committee who think that is quite possible. I, of course, don't know. I haven't conferred with a large enough proportion of the members. I have conferred with all the Democrats, but with only one or two of the Republican members.

It will be in a substantially unchanged form and not seriously amended?

Amended only in particulars, or details.

Has any proposition been suggested to you in connection with that bill running to the establishment—I don't like to use the term, the term that occurs to me—of a central bank under complete governmental control?[4]

Oh, yes, there have been such suggestions, but I don't think any considerable number of Senators have entertained them seriously.

Do you regard, Mr. President, the number of regional banks as fundamental? There is some doubt as to the number.

One number is fundamental, of course, fundamental that there should be enough. That is not a matter of debate.

Mr. President, is the presence of the Secretary of Agriculture and the Comptroller of the Currency fundamental?[5]

In the act it is a question, not of principle, you see, but of initiative, of breadth. Of course, I think we all desire that the system should have as wide and sympathetic connection with the business of the country, with the activities of the country, as possible. And that is all I think anybody is trying to work these details out on.

How about Mexico, Mr. President?

Well, I would rather ask questions about Mexico than answer them, because I don't see any change in the situation myself.

Mr. President, any comment on ex-Ambassador Wilson's statement?[6]

No, sir. I haven't read it, as a matter of fact.

Have you informed Mr. Underwood as to what he may tell the House at this time?

I have just had a little talk with him in which I gave him the same general communications as I have given you.

That the program would mean no adjournment.

Oh, yes. It would mean no adjournment. I don't hear anybody proposing adjournment.

How about a recess in the House, Mr. President?

That, so far as I can learn, depends, of course, upon the minority. It would be perfectly feasible to have one, if the minority should agree upon it. I mean, the ordinary constitutional recess.[7]

Mr. President, have you determined your attitude towards the urgent deficiency bill?

Well, I just began studying opinions this morning, before I came over here, so that I haven't reached my point of view quite yet.

Did Mr. Wilson's letter with regard to Mexico contain any matter that had not been considered?[8]

As I was just confessing, I haven't read—I [don't know whether I] read the letter. I sent it into the State Department, of course. But I don't know whether it is exactly the same as this letter or not here.

The letter of August 28.

No, sir. The second.

The one in which he chastised the Secretary of State.

Yes.

[1] The case of Emmeline Pankhurst, leader of British suffragettes, who was being denied permission to enter the United States on the grounds of "moral turpitude." See the *New York Times*, Oct. 19-20, 1913. Frederic Clemson Howe was the Commissioner of Immigration.

[2] Wilson decided to allow Pankhurst to enter the country to conduct a lecture tour. See *ibid.*, Oct. 21, 1913.

[3] Senator Knute Nelson of Minnesota, the ranking Republican member of the Banking and Currency Committee, called at the White House on October 18 to tell Wilson that Republicans accepted the basic ideas of the Federal Reserve bill. See the *New York Times*, Oct. 19, 1913.

⁴ This was the plan proposed by Frank Arthur Vanderlip, president of the National City Bank of New York, which provided for the creation of a single Federal Reserve Bank of the United States and twelve branches. Senators opposed to the Federal Reserve bill asked Vanderlip to propose this plan when he appeared before the Senate Banking Committee on October 23. See Link, *The New Freedom*, pp. 232-33.

⁵ That is, on the Federal Reserve Board. Both were dropped from the board in the Senate bill, but the Comptroller of the Currency was restored to membership in the conference report.

⁶ Speaking in Spokane, Washington, on October 18, former Ambassador Wilson said that Huerta's government was legal and should be recognized because the alternative was chaos. See the *New York Times*, Oct. 19, 1913.

⁷ Wilson informed Underwood on October 20 that a recess until November 15 would be acceptable.

⁸ On October 19, former Ambassador Wilson made public his letter of resignation to Secretary of State Bryan dated August 28, 1913. In it, he criticized Bryan for partisanship and for treating him unfairly. See the *New York Times*, Oct. 20, 1913.

Oct. 23, 1913

Mr. President, have you heard from Carden, the new British Minister, whose statement has just come up from Mexico?¹

No, sir, and I hope, for his sake, we will not.

Do you know what his remarks were?

No, sir. I haven't [been] informed.

He says that the Constitutionalists are simply brigands and evil men, that if they get control, they will control Mexico by another [dictatorship]. Would you care to say anything about that?

No, sir.

Mr. President, is it true that the British government, in the earlier stages of the present aspect of the Mexican situation, suggested to this government that there be an international conference which would induce Huerta to step down and put Gamboa in his place?

No, sir. Nothing of the kind is true.

Can you give me any idea where that comes from?

So far as I know, it is an absolute invention. But I mean to say to you gentlemen that I would be very much obliged if you would excuse me from discussing the Mexican situation for the present.

Can you give any reason?

No, sir.²

You stir our curiosity.

There seems to be nothing left but the currency, Mr. President.

There is enough of that, it ought to be said.

Mr. President, has any agreement been reached with reference to a recess of the House?

No, sir, not so far as I know.

As I understand it, you have no objection to that now, have you?

No, none whatever. It is perfectly reasonable that they should take a recess awaiting the action of the Senate.

Have you any idea what the general disposition of the Senate is with regard to the House waiting around? Will they let the House go away and play?

No, I have not. Until recently, it wasn't in a condition to be taken up in the Senate.[3] It was hanging fire in the House itself. No, I haven't heard any expressions from Senators on that subject.

Are you agreeable to the Senate's taking a recess also?

I don't think the Senate has the least idea of taking a recess.

Has Mr. McReynolds submitted to you his opinion in the 5-per-cent rebate matter?[4]

Only orally and informally, so that I haven't had an opportunity to read it as a reasoned opinion.

Would you tell us his ideas, Mr. President?

I think it would be a little premature, perhaps, because he has not formulated them. I simply asked him what conclusion he thought he was coming to, and he tried to inform me in just a few sentences.

He said that he had submitted two other papers—

I daresay they will be in my hands later.

Have you heard the latest, Mr. President, with reference to currency legislation? It is suggested that a central bank under government control is the idea of Mr. O'Gorman.[5]

No, sir. I had not heard of that. When was that suggested?

Today, in the committee. He himself came there, I understand. It looked like a new development in the whole situation.

No, sir. A new suggestion. It is not a new development.

Mr. President, Mr. Vanderlip is on the stand up there this afternoon, presenting I don't know what it is. I haven't heard. Possibly control by the government.[6]

Yes.

Mr. President, could you clear up for us the situation about the ministership to Greece? We have two men, appointed positively in stories, in the last two weeks.[7]

As a matter of fact, this thing is in the stage of negotiation so that there really isn't anything to announce yet.

Do you know Mr. Droppers?

Yes.

Do you mean, Mr. President, by negotiation, you are negotiating with Greece, or with the two men?

I mean that it is a matter yet to be determined who is to be sent.

Mr. President, is the embargo with reference to Mexico extended indefinitely?

Yes. I would rather leave the situation alone.

Could you say whether we are in negotiation with powers other than Great Britain?

No, sir, we are not. We are not in negotiation with Great Britain.

Oral exchanges then?

No, sir. I meant what I said.

I have a question, Mr. President, with reference to the seamen's bill.[8] These protests—hasn't the administration taken any part at all towards changing the course of the legislation?

No, nothing at all. You see, these protests have been made to the Congress itself, and they can act as they please about it.

Mr. President, have you taken any action yet with regard to these deputy collectors of internal revenue and deputy marshals under the new law that takes them out of the civil service?[9]

No formal action, no; but I am going to manage the thing.

Mr. President, have you discussed yet with Secretary Garrison or other authorities the question of a canal government?

Not seriously, though we have brought it up frequently in conversation, but only for a preliminary exchange of ideas.

Mr. President, what is the status of the exchanges with Great Britain in regard to the canal-tolls question?

That has been in abeyance since—practically since Mr. Bryce went away.[10]

There seems to be an idea that Great Britain is very well satisfied with present conditions. We hoped it was based on some assurances which were given by that government.

No assurances have been given. There was no occasion to speak to us. We understood, when Mr. Bryce went away, that it was naturally a matter that could not be taken up until the regular session.

Have you talked with Mr. [Houston][11] with regard to legislation [about a crop survey or] about other things?

He brought that up and made certain tentative suggestions, but nothing more than that.

Are you willing to express your views now, Mr. President, on the question of tolls? Have you thought that out?

No, sir.

Mr. President, do you regard that the President has the same right—the same right in the matter of the tolls as the Secretary of the Treasury when he suspended the 5-per-cent operation? What, for instance, when the canal is in operation and the [terms of the law] apply, would you have the right to suspend the operation of the act?[12]

I don't so understand it, no, sir. I haven't heard of what you said. I have seen the terms of the act, but I take it for granted I have no such discretion.

In fixing the maximum and minimum tolls, I think the President has discretion to adjust them.

Not to suspend the operation [of the law].

Mr. President, we are becoming rather pressed on another point, and that is with relation to the wedding next month.[13] Are you prepared to give us any ideas?

No, sir. I do not feel that is in my jurisdiction. I haven't been authorized to say anything yet.

Mr. President, is there anything about Mr. Mitchel's resignation in New York that you can give us?

No, sir. Nothing at all. I have been attempting to do so many other things, I have forgotten about it, to tell you the truth.

[1] Sir Lionel Carden, the new British Minister to Mexico, had rather ostentatiously presented his credentials to the Huerta government on October 10. The *New York Times*, Oct. 22, 1913, printed a statement by Carden defending Huerta and criticizing the United States for failing to recognize him. See Calvert, *The Mexican Revolution*, pp. 237-47.

[2] Wilson was at this time very troubled by reports from Lind that the British were behind the Huerta government. See *PWW*, Vol. 28, pp. 428-29, 434.

[3] The Federal Reserve bill was approved by the House on September 18, 1913. See Link, *The New Freedom*, p. 227.

[4] See above, Oct. 6, 1913.

[5] On October 23, the Senate Banking and Currency Committee discussed replacing the twelve Federal Reserve banks with one central bank. A number of Senators, including O'Gorman, seemed to be supporting this approach. See above, Oct. 20, 1913, and the *New York Times*, Oct. 24, 1913.

[6] Vanderlip spoke before the committee on October 23 in favor of a central-bank plan. See above, Oct. 20, 1913, and the *New York Times*, Oct. 24, 1913.

[7] The two men were Professor Garrett Droppers of Williams College and former Congressman George Fred Williams of Massachusetts. Williams was eventually appointed and replaced by Droppers in 1914.

[8] See above, Oct. 16, 1913.

[9] Wilson signed the urgent deficiency appropriations bill on October 22.

[10] Bryce presented his letters of recall to Wilson on April 24, 1913.

[11] Secretary of Agriculture David Franklin Houston.

[12] That is, not to allow the toll-free passage of American ships engaged in coastwise shipping.

[13] The wedding of Jessie Woodrow Wilson and Francis Bowes Sayre on November 25.

Oct. [30], 1913

Mr. President, could you give us an idea of how long you are going to take before making your communication on the subject of the new policy?[1]

You mean to whom?

I don't know, sir. Whether to us or to the foreign nations?

Why, as a matter of fact, what I have seen in the newspapers about my intentions was news to me. You are talking about my preparing a note for the foreign powers. Now that is not so, and I am very much instructed every day by what I learn of my intentions. But I am somewhat surprised and, therefore, that is one reason why I can't answer your question, Mr. Manning.[2]

Mr. President, not to betray the confidence of anybody at the head of the State Department, we certainly got the information over there the other day that you had asked all the powers, or all the nations, rather, that had diplomatic representatives in Mexico, to defer action as a result of the elections until this government had an opportunity of defining a policy or communicating with them.[3]

Why, that is a very different proposition.

Yes, sir. I understand as to the form.

You see, you asked me when I would be ready to make a communication. Now, whether I shall make any communication or not to anybody in particular remains to be determined. You see, there are two ways of handling a thing. You can talk or you can act. I don't mean to intimate either.

Mr. President, it is stated this morning in an Associated Press dispatch that you will present a plan or a new policy to the cabinet tomorrow.

I can hardly do that, because there isn't going to be a meeting of the cabinet.

Mr. President, I did not think we were wrong in assuming that you were going to communicate to the powers what you are going to do.

I am not trying, gentlemen, to play hide and seek with you. I am trying to convey to you the real situation—that I am waiting for things to come to me in definite shape as to the result of last

Sunday.[4] I can't communicate, even to myself, what I am going to do until I am informed.

The foreign governments understand that?

They understand that, and they are waiting for the same thing. Yes, we are entirely in touch with one another, and they are all waiting to see just what shape things take down there.

Mr. President, the United States is continuing to act independently, is it not, in this matter? It has entered into no arrangement of cooperative action?

It has entered into no such arrangement.

In other words, Mr. President, there have been a number of reports of friction with other governments over this issue. Is there anything in that?

No, sir, there is not. There hasn't been the slightest friction with any other government.

Well, Mr. President, then is it fair for us to say that the policy has not been formulated yet because it is dependent upon the result of certain things in Mexico?

Well, I don't know just how to answer that question. It would not be fair to make the statement in any such way as to imply that I didn't have very definite notions about it, but I daresay the right way to state it is that things are not in such shape as to make the announcement of our policy opportune.

In other words, you don't know, really, the result of these elections?

I don't want to set up a straw man and knock him down.

You don't know whether Huerta is going to retire or whether General Blanquet[5] is to be President or Huerta is to go to the head of the army?

You see, they haven't declared what they understand the result of the elections to be.

Mr. President, to get a little bit deeper, the foreign nations won't know formally from you, or otherwise, what you are going to do until you do it?

Well, I am not making any prediction at all.

I drew that distinction between acting now and telling people.

Naturally, they won't hear anything from us until we have something to say, but that is about all it comes to.

And there is no note?

None in my possession, nor in my head.

Mr. President, I am not quite clear yet as to whether—as to how you are going to make this known. I didn't quite understand what you meant by saying—

Of course, both the method and the action itself would have to go together. The best method of things must wait to be determined until the thing is done, as you see the form goes along with the substance necessarily.

Mr. President, are you awaiting a report from Mr. Lind on last Sunday's election?

Yes, we get reports every day from Mr. Lind. Nobody down there knows more than he does.

I saw on one of these bulletin sheets that Mr. Lind is preparing a detailed statement to be mailed to you.

I daresay he is. He follows up dispatches with letters from time to time, but I don't know that that refers to anything in particular.

I thought perhaps you were waiting for this detailed report by mail. Mr. President, with reference to the foreign nations' acting, may we know a little more definitely how far their assurances have gone, and in return how far we have gone in promises of protection?

You gentlemen seem to think that there has been a very lively conversation between us. You have heard all that I know already from the State Department, and heard it during my absence, so that I got it by telegraph just at the same time you did. It was perfectly proper that you should learn that, but just as a matter of fact.

Mr. President, isn't that expression "cooperation" a misnomer? Isn't it a fact that there isn't any cooperation, simply that they are waiting and worried about what we are going to do?

Well, of course, cooperation is mainly a matter of action and, to me, more a matter of counsel. They are certainly not standing in our way.

Mr. President, have you determined what course is to be pursued with reference to those French citizens who were at San Ignacio?[6]

Personally I have not. I know that the State Department has that intelligence and is following it up very carefully. But I can't, myself, tell you the details of it.

Is it the general policy of this government to grant protection wherever requested to foreign citizens, whenever requested by their governments?

That is rather too broad a proposition. It is our policy, and always has been, to cooperate in securing protection wherever it was possible to do so.

You see, Mr. President, this matter of detaining those citizens at San Ignacio involves, perhaps, the landing of an armed force to go overland forty miles.[7] They could hardly be protected forty miles away. What I wanted to know was whether you were likely to give that authority to the commander of the *Maryland*?[8]

I can't answer that because I don't know whether military action would be necessary.

Mr. President, has any one of the foreign nations, as we understand the terms, conveyed to this government, in any shape or form, any concrete thing that it proposed to do in Mexico?

Well, now, gentlemen, do I have to go over that ground again and again? I have given you all that I know about the subject. There hasn't been any interchange of proposals at all.

They have made none?

I understand my language to mean that. I don't know how you interpret the English language. Really, I don't think it's quite good, going from a general to a specific statement, by making me repeat it in explicit details each time.

Mr. President, I think that your remark entirely concurs with nine tenths of the people here. I don't think you ought to be subjected—

I don't like to submit a bill of particulars after I cover a thing.

Mr. President, have you replied to a letter from Representative Mann?[9]

Taking Mr. Johnson[10] back to Mexico?

I understand he had written you a second letter on the matter.

Yes, he did. Of course, the difficulty there is making discriminations between one set of persons who ought to go back and a great many others who want to go back; and it is a very difficult matter for the State Department or the Navy Department to make discriminations.

The reply to the second letter had not been received. Is that something later than yesterday then?

I think I dictated the letter yesterday.[11] It probably has gotten to him now.

Mr. President, the report is current that the War Department has a contract under which it wants to take supplies to New Mexico?

That is certainly a piece of interesting fiction. I certainly do not know. I don't know of any such thing.

Mr. President, has any decision been reached as to what this government is going to do with Mr. Díaz?[12]

That is up to Admiral Fletcher.[13] He has got him. He is the host.

Mr. President, has there been any communication with the Constitutionalists, particularly since Sunday's election?

Neither before nor since.

Mr. President, how long are you going to wait, or can you tell, before you hear from the election?

Why, we can't arrange any news, and I don't know just how they are handling it, so I can't form any calculation. I suppose, necessarily, I will be a long time learning what did happen in places far away from Mexico City.

Won't that be answered by the Mexican Congress, in the newly elected Congress? They will have the confirmation of those returns, will they not?

Yes, if they get elected.

Mr. President, are you satisfied with the currency situation?

There is nothing especially new about it. Yes, sir.

It isn't making much progress.

There was a rumor of motion, but nothing serious materializing.

[1] That is, with respect to Mexico.

[2] W. Sinkler Manning of the *New York Times*.

[3] Secretary of State Bryan had so informed reporters on October 29, 1913. See the *New York Times*, Oct. 30, 1913.

[4] The Mexican election of October 26.

[5] Gen. Aurelio Blanquet, Huerta's Minister of War and vice-presidential candidate. The election had raised constitutional issues because not enough votes had been cast to make it official. Nothing in the Constitution, however, stipulated the number of votes needed to elect a Vice-President; thus Blanquet could be elected and become President when Huerta resigned. It was then supposed that he would appoint Huerta Minister of War in the new government. See the *New York Times*, Oct. 28, 1913, and Hill, *Emissaries to a Revolution*, p. 101.

[6] French citizens in the town of San Ignacio, recently captured by the Constitutionalists, were asking for protection. See the *New York Times*, Oct. 28-31, 1913.

[7] The village was forty miles from Mazatlán on the Pacific coast of Mexico.

[8] The armored cruiser *Maryland* was ordered to Mazatlán on October 29, 1913. See the *New York Times*, Oct. 30, 1913.

[9] Mann had requested permission for employees of the United Sugar Company to return to Mexico on board a naval supply ship. Wilson declined. See *ibid.*, Oct. 31, 1913.

[10] An unidentified employee of the United Sugar Company.

[11] WW to J. R. Mann, Oct. 29, 1913, in WP, DLC.

[12] Following the election of October 26, General Felix Díaz had sought and received asylum on the United States battleship *Louisiana* stationed at Veracruz. See the *New York Times*, Oct. 29, 1913, and Hill, *Emissaries to a Revolution*, p. 101, n. 26.

[13] Rear Adm. Frank Friday Fletcher, commander of the American squadron off Veracruz. *Louisiana* was his flagship.


Nov. 3, 1913

Perhaps you can tell us something about the currency?

Well, that was not the entire object of Senator Owen's visit,[1] but I think I can say he reported progress and [came] just to inform me of what was contemplated. The committee has to adjourn over election day.

Is the four-bank plan acceptable, Mr. President?

To me? Well, I think I have answered that already.[2]

Have you talked, Mr. President, with Senator Owen, or anyone, about the proposals for public ownership of the banks?[3]

No. You mean public subscription of the stock?

Yes.

No, I have not.

Would you care to express your opinion on that?

Well, I stand for the bill. I never get on a pivot and swing around. I try to stay where I stand. The bill has an awful bony structure, but if altered would alter the whole thing. When I lay down a line, I don't mark it with chalk so that it can be rubbed out. Of course, I don't mean that there are not many debatable parts of the bill, but I say the bony structure is essential to the flesh that is on it.

Senator Owen didn't venture, did he, Mr. President, when he would bring out the bill?

No.

Is the subject of Mexico still taboo?

Well, apparently not. In reading the *Post* this morning, they, as usual, knew more about it than I did. I would be very much obliged if you would tell me what is going on in the State Department. Sometimes I get very excellent suggestions what I might do by an announcement of what I have done.

Does that apply to the suggestion this morning in the *Post*?[4]

There are a good many parts of it I couldn't recognize.

There is a dispatch from Veracruz, Mr. President, to the effect that Mr. Lind will return immediately upon the arrival of the relief squadron.[5]

That is one of the things I learned from the paper this morning.

Will it be necessary for him to do so, Mr. President?

Certainly not. You mean that the arrival of the battleships would put him in danger?

I mean, the arrival of the battleships would cause him to feel like he had to come home?

Not that I know of. He may have instances of uneasiness that I don't know anything about.

If I might, is there any report, Mr. President, of a conference with any other Ministers down there?[6]

Only to this extent: there was a conference, in which several of them came from Mexico City for the purpose of conferring with him, and they showed a disposition to cooperate with the United States.

Would you say whether they laid down any lines on which they made—

No, he did not give the conversations themselves. He just reported that general impression.[7]

Mr. President, there was a report this morning that a plea was to be made by General Carranza to be allowed to import arms from the United States. Has that reached you in any form?

All that reached me was what I saw in the paper this morning— that they desired to make certain representations to us, and we of course replied that we could not receive any representations officially from them.

That wouldn't bar them from unofficially letting you know what they wanted?

I suppose not, because it generally comes to us, you might say, one way or the other.

Has there been anything new, Mr. President, with reference to foreign governments defending their diplomatic representatives there?

No, nothing whatever. As a matter of fact, they are only slowly returning to town. The German Ambassador, for example, as I understand, has just gotten back, and the British Ambassador is detained by ill health.

Will we have the right to let Carranza have ammunitions?

Why, of course Congress would have the right from time to time to repeal that resolution, that joint resolution, thus putting the whole thing upon the ordinary footing of neutrality.[8]

Is there really a necessity for an act of Congress?

Well, I suppose, on second thought, that that joint resolution does leave discretion with the Executive as to whether arms shall be exported.

What is the status of the Judge Prouty[9] resignation, Mr. President?

Why, I haven't accepted it because I haven't found a satisfactory successor. Of course, I don't want to lame the board.

You will not be willing to accept it?

Very unwilling, from my own point of view, his splendid record on the board, but willing because he believes he can serve the board better in the new capacity he wishes to serve it in.

Mr. President, there was a suggestion some time ago, with the House sitting there doing nothing, that you might send your trust program during November, so as to give the House something to do while they are waiting for the Senate?

I have no intention of distracting the attention of the country from the banking and currency situation. It is very usefully concentrating on that subject.

Mr. President, would it be out of the way to ask whether you have any other program besides trust to suggest now?

You know, my trust program is largely fiction. I mean that I have a definite program, armed to the teeth. Of course, I have certain ideas which I am earnestly [intent] on seeing carried out, and about which I have already conferred in an informal way with Senator Newlands[10] and the chairman of the House committee.[11] And I think from those conferences, that we really are, at any rate, thinking along very much the same lines, that it is very feasible to do what I have usually done in these matters. I haven't had a tariff program. I haven't had a currency program. I have conferred with the men who handle these things, and asked the questions, and then have gotten back what they sent to me—the best of our common counsel. That is what I am trying to do in this case.

Has either Secretary Lane or Secretary Houston talked with you about the conservation program?

Not on a definite program. We have again and again discussed individual phases of the subject—administrative phases. Of course, our very important purpose has been clearly the same in those conferences.

Mr. President, getting back to currency again, there is a sort of common belief that Senator Owen, speaking before the committee, represents the administration's views on the bill. And Senator Owen, the other day, made the suggestion of a public subscription of the stock and bank control; that is, control of the regional banks on the same plan as the Glass bill. I wanted to ask whether that was representing your views?

I have already said I had not discussed that with any member of the committee. I don't think Senator Owen would want it understood that the individual suggestions were anything but his own.

I don't think he has ever said that, or understood that, but it was the general impression.

I think he would be the first to tell you that he has made a number of suggestions that he hasn't discussed with me, and it wasn't necessary that he should.

Has that 5-per-cent decision come back yet?

From the Attorney General's office?

From the Treasury Department.

[Response unintelligible.]

Did Mr. Owen predict when they would report the bill?

No. We are only predicting what will happen tomorrow.

[1] To the White House on November 2, 1913.

[2] See above, Oct. 20, 1913, and "A Statement on the Vanderlip Plan," printed in *PWW*, Vol. 28, pp. 429-30.

[3] A number of Senators were proposing that the stock of the Federal Reserve banks should be subscribed by the public, not by member banks. See the *New York Times*, Nov. 1, 1913.

[4] On November 3, the *Washington Post* reported that the Wilson administration was prepared to act in Mexico. A "supreme effort" was being made to force Huerta to retire, the report went on, after which elections could be held in which the Constitutionalists would participate. If this failed, the United States was likely to become more deeply involved in Mexican affairs, including perhaps military or naval intervention.

[5] Secretary of the Navy Daniels had ordered four additional battleships to Veracruz. Lind did not return.

[6] Lind had recently met in Veracruz with the Russian, German, and Norwegian Ministers to Mexico. See the *New York Times*, Nov. 2, 1913.

[7] Lind to State Department, Nov. 3, 1913, NA, RG 59, 812.00/9513.

[8] That is, the Joint Resolution of March 14, 1912, which allowed the President to place an embargo on the sale of arms to Mexico.

[9] Interstate Commerce Commissioner Charles Azro Prouty had offered his resignation. In the meantime, the commission had named him director of the physical valuation of the railroads which it was then undertaking. See the *New York Times*, Nov. 2, 1913.

[10] Chairman of the Interstate Commerce Committee.

[11] Representative Clayton, chairman of the House Judiciary Committee.

Nov. 6, 1913

May we know something about the Mexican situation, Mr. President?

I wish I could help you to know something about it. There hasn't been any development good, bad, or indifferent since Monday. Why, I can't explain. I don't know.

Has Mr. Lind sent up anything yet about those foreign Ambassadors?

Nothing further than we mentioned in the last interview.

Has anything developed that would relate to this report, what the communications were that were the basis for the last—

Nothing at all, except just the routine reports from day to day, which consist largely of nothing. No developments of any kind.

Has any inquiry been directed to Mr. Lind as to whether or not that statement attributed to him this morning is correct?[1]

Which do you refer to?

The statement to the effect that he had said in Veracruz that a warning was delivered to Mr. Huerta.

I saw that, but I really wouldn't attach much importance to that. No inquiry has been made about it.

This morning's *World* had a dispatch that Dr. Hale had gone to [Nogales], I believe, to confer with Carranza.

That is not true.

You mean it is not true either so far as you are concerned, or so far as he is concerned?

I believe Hale went off. I don't know just where he went.[2]

Mr. President, is this government concerned as to whether or not Mr. Huerta has replied to France's offer to serve as a mediator?[3]

No. I saw merely what you are alluding to in the paper. No, there is no confirmation of that.

Mr. President, I think last Thursday you said you were unable to say anything at all, because you were still waiting to learn what had been the development in the elections in Mexico.

Yes. So far as I have seen, there has been nothing except piecemeal announcements, so that, apparently, it is taken for granted that a Congress was elected, by what means I don't know.

Now under their Constitution, as to the election laws, there being no choice in the election, the election is supposed to devolve upon Congress.

No. I understand it, as it is advertised, to be no election. The returns are simply thrown aside under their law. I ought to say at once that I am speaking at secondhand. I haven't seen the text at all.

Don't you consider there has been either an election for President or Congress?

We have already said we wouldn't accept the results of that election.

Mr. President, is there any fixed time by which the election has to be canvassed? I mean, under the Mexican law, there is some talk about a fifteen-day period.

I am sorry to say I can't answer that question. I took it for granted that it simply provided that when the Congress met it should canvass the results.

Has Mr. O'Shaughnessy said anything further, Mr. President, as to whether or not they now expect the results to be official?

O'Shaughnessy has not said anything about the election. He seems to take the stand his government has taken—that it wouldn't make any difference one way or the other, which should be his loyal attitude.

Has there been announced, Mr. President, nothing about the note we sent down there to Mexico City?[4]

Oh, no.

The one that Mr. Bryan said was falsely called an ultimatum?

No note was sent. Simply instructions to O'Shaughnessy.

Can you give us any idea as to what that—

No. Some communications must be confidential.

Can you tell us, Mr. President, whether Mr. O'Shaughnessy was expected to communicate the contents of those instructions to Mr. Huerta?

Naturally he wouldn't be instructed to go hunting.

Has there been anything in the situation in the last few days that clears it up in any way?

No, I can't say that there has.

Is there anything in prospect that might clear it up?

That is beyond me.

Some of the papers announce that your next step is to raise the embargo and permit the Constitutionalists to get arms.

I know. But they have announced that about once a week since the thing began. I think that is set up permanently.

Mr. President, have you any idea whether you will make any communication to Congress on this subject?

No. I have no present purpose.

Can you tell us, Mr. President, about the conference with Senator Weeks last night?[5]

There isn't anything to tell, except we talked the currency situation over.

Some of us regard the situation up on the Hill as rather serious.

Do you? I don't.

Will you tell us, Mr. President, anything about the prospect of a Senate caucus on the currency bill?[6]

No, sir, I can't.

Mr. President, have you come to any conclusion with regard to the Interstate Commerce Commission vacancy?

No sir, not yet.

You haven't accepted the—

No. I have known Mr. Prouty. I couldn't accept his resignation until I have found somebody to take his place.

---

[1] The *New York Times* reported on November 6 that Lind had warned Huerta that he should resign the presidency.

[2] Hale was recognized by a reporter in Tucson, Arizona, on November 5. After preliminary conferences there on November 11, he met with Carranza at Nogales on November 12. See Hill, *Emissaries to a Revolution*, pp. 109-13.

[3] There were reports that the French were offering to mediate the differences between the United States and Mexico. See the *New York Times*, Nov. 6, 1913, and Katz, *Secret War in Mexico*, pp. 489-91.

[4] Bryan sent instructions to O'Shaughnessy on November 1 which contained the following paragraph:

"2. That, unless General Huerta now voluntarily and as if of his own motion retires from authority and from all attempt to control the organization of the government and the course of affairs, it will be necessary for the President of the United States to insist upon the terms of an ultimatum, the rejection of which would render it necessary for him to propose very serious practical measures to the Congress of the United States."

Printed in *PWW*, Vol. 28, pp. 482-83.

[5] Wilson invited Weeks, an important Republican member of the Banking and Currency Committee, to visit him at the White House on the evening of November 5.

[6] Democratic Senators were discussing the possibility of holding a caucus to determine party policy on the Glass-Owen bill. See the *New York Times*, Nov. 4, 1913.

---

Nov. 10, 1913

Currency legislation, Mr. President.

I haven't any intelligence on that. I think it is a significant circumstance that the conference for Wednesday[1] was called with perfect spontaneity by the Senators themselves, and not at my request. With my entire approval, I mean to say, but not at all at my request.

Mr. President, what about Mexico? Is there anything that has developed?

Why, no. The papers are wrong this morning in several particulars. For example, it is not my present purpose to make any address to Congress on the subject. Things are not in the shape that would give me anything definite to say. We have made certain representations to General Huerta and have received no reply of any sort yet.

Is it true, Mr. President, that Mr. Lind has recommended that all relations between this country [and Mexico] be [terminated]?[2]

Mr. Lind has made no recommendations. He has simply informed us of what was going on.

Have we set any time limit on Huerta, or anything of that sort?

No, sir.

I suppose, Mr. President, with regard to communicating anything to the other European governments, the situation remains where it was last week; that is, you don't know what you could communicate?

No. There isn't anything definite to communicate.

Have they been acquainted with our representations to Huerta?

Yes. They know just what is going on.

Then the communications with the European powers, as well as the communication to Congress, will wait upon the receipt of a reply from Huerta?

They will wait upon the development of circumstances, necessarily.

Would you care to indicate whether you are considering the step of recognizing the belligerency of the Constitutionalists there?

No. I am not ready to discuss it one way or the other yet. I would very earnestly suggest this to you gentlemen, that, having represented an act as more serious than it is, you are in danger of making it very serious, because nothing gives greater pleasure in Mexico City than to have intemperate things telegraphed from the United States as contained in our newspapers. It renders the task of the administration extremely difficult when the papers go very much faster than the administration goes.

Mr. President, has the text of the communication that Mr. Huerta is supposed to have made to the foreign representatives there been communicated to you?[3]

No. That has made me skeptical as to the communication itself. I am quite sure Mr. O'Shaughnessy would have telegraphed us the text of it immediately, and yet we haven't received any. It must be a sort of patchwork of—it may be a sort of patchwork of rumor.[4]

The Mexican Chargé has received the same information from his government—that the statement was given out down there.

I can only conjecture that there has been some delay.

He described to me, in the same general terms, that General Huerta had said that Congress would assemble and it would decide whether the election was void, particularly if some indications of public sentiment held that it was invalid, and there could be no election.

Then what about the Congress itself?

That is sort of sloughed over.

That would be an awkward situation.

Mr. President, in the light of certain happenings, is the nomination of Mr. Pindell to Russia to be regarded as assured?[5]

I hadn't considered that, no, because I hadn't informed myself of all the circumstances.

Is the nomination going in today?

No nomination is going in today that I know of.

Mr. President, with reference to this Mexican question again, has the Huerta element in Mexico City made any representations to this government as to the atrocities committed by the Constitutionalists, with a view to moving the sentiment of this government, rather than—

No, sir, and the fact that they have not leads me to hope that they have a sense of humor.

Mr. President, as a result of the proposed conference on the currency bill in the Senate, will that eventually result in making the bill a partisan rather than a nonpartisan measure?[6]

No, sir, it will not. Of course, the Democratic party is responsible for legislation, and it is also responsible for seeing that there is legislation. And only in that sense will it be a party measure at all.

The corresponding Owen bill[7] received some Republican votes in the House. Have you any information that it will receive Republican votes in the Senate?

No, I have no information on that subject at all. I should hope that it would, because, as I view it, it is not a partisan measure at all. It is either sound or is not sound. That is the only question.

¹ That is, a caucus of Democratic Senators to formulate party policy on the Federal Reserve bill. See Link, *The New Freedom*, p. 235.

² The *New York Times* reported on November 10, 1913, that Lind had suggested that the administration end all discussions with Huerta. For Lind's attitude, see Hill, *Emissaries to a Revolution*, pp. 105-106.

³ A press dispatch from Mexico City quoted an alleged note from Huerta to foreign diplomats declaring the elections of October 26 to be invalid and proclaiming his intention to continue governing until new elections could be held. See the *New York Times*, Nov. 10, 1913.

⁴ Wilson was correct here.

⁵ Wilson appointed Henry Means Pindell, editor of the Peoria, Illinois, *Journal* and an early Wilson supporter, to be Ambassador to Russia. After the Senate confirmed Pindell's appointment, the press published accurate accounts of the terms of the arrangements made by Senator Lewis with the Wilson administration. Pindell had been appointed with the stipulation that he would resign effective October 1, 1914, and he had accepted after he had received assurances from Lewis that the position would be a sinecure, with "no treaties to adjudicate, and no political affairs to bother with." This report outraged the Russian Foreign Minister, who warned that the Imperial government would refuse to accept Pindell should Wilson attempt to send him. Pindell withdrew, and it would be almost a year before Wilson would find an acceptable Ambassador to St. Petersburg. See Link, *The New Freedom*, pp. 102-103, and "The Case of Brother Pindell," *North American Review*, CXCVIII (Dec. 1913), 754.

⁶ Republican Senators were saying that it would.

⁷ That is, the Glass-Owen bill.

Nov. 17, 1913

I see by the papers this morning that Mr. O'Shaughnessy is coming back. But he has not been told to come back, and has not been given his passport down there. In short, the whole thing is a fake so far as I know.¹

Mr. President, the hopeful elements of which you spoke last Thursday have been dissipated by subsequent events?

No, sir. The mills of the gods grind very slowly, but they grind exceedingly fine.

Has this government made any representations or sent any warnings to the Constitutionalists with regard to the execution of Federal prisoners?²

We are investigating those reports. They haven't been verified yet. You notice that, in the dispatches, they vary very greatly in details and even in general import.

The newspapers reported this morning he³ didn't act with the authority of the [Constitutionalist] administration.

No sir, no—I know nothing about that.

Did Mr. O'Shaughnessy get additional instructions last night?

No, sir.

What about Mr. Lind's leaving Veracruz, Mr. President? There is a report he is about to leave there?

No, sir. We know nothing about it.

Have you information, Mr. President, from Mr. Hale, or otherwise, as to Carranza personally—what kind of man he is?

Why, no. I was reading with a great deal of interest, the other day, an article that appeared in the London *Times* from a correspondent, which gave a very interesting and apparently a rather intimate picture of the man.[4] But we have made no independent investigations or inquiries.

I have been wondering where we here could get some idea. It has been very hard for us to get a notion of the kind of man he is.

Very, very indeed. One gets varying accounts of him. It is very hard, I suppose, because he is always inaccessible due to his constant movement.

Mr. President, have you been advised that he has refused any offers of mediation from this government, with the prospect of any mediation by this government?[5]

I haven't heard of that, because he can't have refused them because none was made. I don't know where that thing got started. He is said to have made utterances declining all mediation, but no one has offered any mediation. That's a bolt shot into the air.

Mr. President, I think that, about Mr. Hale's visit there, if you could tell us something more definite with regard to Mr. Hale's purpose.[6]

Well, if I could. Mr. Hale certainly wouldn't make any offer to him. He wasn't authorized to do so.

Mr. President, has there been any change of conditions since you told us what the outlook was and you were encouraged for an immediate settlement?

I don't know that I can answer that question, Mr. Lowry.[7] The thing is kaleidoscopic. It seems to change in its detail most unexpectedly. So there have been changes, but they have been changes in the personal attitude of Huerta rather than in the circumstances. The circumstances haven't changed at all.

Mr. President, does the forced resignation of Minister Aldalpe interfere with your plans at all? Was he in your scheme?[8]

Oh, no. We wouldn't dare base a scheme on the permanency of any member of the Huerta cabinet.

Can you tell us anything about your reports from Dr. Hale?

No, sir. There is nothing to tell.

Have you received any information as to the significance, if any, of the failure of the Catholic members of the Senate to form a quorum?[9]

No. I know only that fact which was reported both in our dispatches and in the public dispatches.

There has been no step taken toward any Pan-American scheme of mediation or [similar] suggestion?

No, there has been no plan, in any direction, of joint mediation. We have kept the South American states fully informed of every step we have taken, and we have had their sympathetic cooperation.

On the same basis as the European—

Yes. You know that Brazil has never recognized Huerta.

I didn't know that. Has any other of the South American republics?

I can't speak, certainly, about that, but I know that Brazil has not.

Brazil and Chile have both stated that they were following your policy, making some direct statement to that effect.

Yes, they are.

Anything new on currency, Mr. President?

No, sir. I understand things are going all right.

Mr. President, has anything been said to you about the possibility of an adjournment of Congress?

No. No member of either house has spoken to that effect.

[1] The *New York Times*, November 17, 1913, stated that O'Shaughnessy was leaving Mexico City for Veracruz.

[2] Armies led by Francisco Villa had captured Ciudad Juárez and were reported to be executing Federal officials there. See the *New York Times*, Nov. 16, 1913.

[3] That is, Villa.

[4] [Henry Hamilton Fyfe], "Troubled Mexico: A Visit to the Stronghold of the Rebels," London *Times*, Oct. 27, 1913. This was a flattering portrait of Carranza.

[5] Carranza announced on November 13 that he would not accept mediation by the United States or any other power. See the *New York Times*, Nov. 14, 1913.

[6] Hale met with Carranza at Nogales on November 12. His instructions from Wilson were to inform the Constitutionalist leader that the United States was contemplating permitting shipments of arms, but that intervention might prove necessary if the lives and property of Americans and other foreigners were not protected. See WW to Hale, c. Nov. 11, 1913, printed in *PWW*, Vol. 28, p. 525, and Hill, *Emissaries to a Revolution*, pp. 110-14.

[7] Edward George Lowry, correspondent for the New York *Evening Post*.

[8] Huerta forced Manuel Garza Aldalpe, Minister of Interior, to resign on November 16. See the *New York Times*, Nov. 17, 1913.

[9] The Mexican Senate now lacked a quorum because members of the Catholic party were staying away. See *ibid.*, Nov. 16, 1913.

Nov. 20, 1913

Mr. President, Mexico seems to be in [the news].

Well, I sincerely wish as much as you could wish that there were some news, but we are absolutely dry today. And it was a mistake I saw in one morning paper that instructions had been sent to Mr. O'Shaughnessy. That is not true. I mean fresh instructions recently that the newspapers haven't heard of.

Were any instructions sent to Mr. O'Shaughnessy as to whether or not to attend the reception given by President Huerta?[1]

We didn't. I wouldn't know whether any were sent by the State Department or not.

The afternoon paper said Mr. O'Shaughnessy was there, they played the "Star-Spangled Banner," and Mr. Huerta embraced Mr. O'Shaughnessy.

I wish he had embraced his opinions.

Mr. President, might we know something more of Dr. Hale's mission now?

Well, you know as much as there is to know. Dr. Hale has come back, I believe, from [Nogales]. I haven't heard that definitely, but I understood he was coming.

I presume back to Washington?

I think he is coming back to Washington.

Might we know whether those negotiations have resulted in anything?

Well, don't think of them as negotiations because they were—

Communications, is that what they were?

No, they weren't communications. We simply wanted to have some method of knowing what was in the minds of the principals.

Has any information come of the result of that visit of Dr. Hale which has changed any aspects of your Mexican policy?

We were not there debating with them what we should do at all. No negotiations.

Mr. President, were possible conditions for a Provisional President in Mexico discussed?

Certainly not. Nothing was discussed, no part or intimation of a plan was discussed.

Mr. President, is it true that Carranza asked Dr. Hale for credentials?[2]

We haven't had that verified. That was in the public dispatches. I wouldn't know anything about that. I doubt if that was true. There was something done, I think, about it—brought out in the Mexican press—both from there and from persons up here.

Is there any such policy that was in contemplation under any contingency?

Oh, well, I don't look forward. I live from day to day.

Do recent reports of occurrences encourage you to believe, Mr. President, that a solution of the Mexican situation may be found through the Constitution-alists, or through using them as instruments?

Well, we haven't chosen to use anybody, either party, or anybody as instruments. And on that, all I can say is, from dispatch to dispatch, there is evidently a thing that is very slowly [developing]. About all I can say is to be drawn from the dispatches.

Mr. President, have you been notified about these reports of [blank]?

We haven't received any reports, no, about that yet.

Could you say, Mr. President, from whom you would get that report?

Why, from whoever is conducting it.

Our Department of State?

Yes, of course.

Mr. President, does the dispatch of those three English battle cruisers indicate any change in the international aspect?[3]

None whatever. That is what normally occurs in such circumstances.

There has been a great deal of suggestion that there might be some feeling of impatience from the European powers due to the lack of favorable developments.

There is no indication of that impatience at all.

Mr. President, after things have improved down there sufficiently, what can then take place? There has been considerable talk, but nothing is in sight. Even then, the condition would be even worse than it is now.

I can't discuss that.

Mr. President, in connection with the dispatch of the three British warships to Mexican waters, it was pointed out in at least one morning paper that I saw, that the Admiral[4] in command of those three ships was concerned that action of the international fleets might bring about complications.[5]

That is interesting but not important.

Mr. President, I think the most interesting question, perhaps, is whether any further action is being taken by this government in a positive way?

Well, you gentlemen will understand, of course, that it may be that if we took positive action of one sort or another, it would be wisest not to speak of it. But I can say at this hour that none has been taken, none further that you don't know about.

With regard to Dr. Hale, Mr. President, would it be fair to say he went down there to [map out a solution and to] see men, then?

The latter part would be. It would have to be an absolute negative on the other. He didn't go down there to map out anything. He went down there for information.

Was the information supplied by the Constitutionalists, Mr. President? All the indications and dispatches from down there were written as if questions about future activities were to be in the nature of pledges, but the right answers were not forthcoming.

Oh, that was largely imaginary. All the information I wanted was what he could get to us for our eyes and ears. It would not matter what they said to him at all. If you go down there and know what you are looking for, you can see it. I wouldn't know what he was looking for.

Perhaps you can tell us, then, did Dr. Hale make a report to you about the [blank] messages?
Mr. President, have you had any report of the massacre at Victoria recently, when it was captured by the rebels—some six hundred Federals killed?[6]

No, I haven't. Of course, a battle is not a massacre. We must allow for some killing in a fight.

Yes, sir, but the report was that these people were killed after—

This is an interesting circumstance. We just received within a day or two the detailed report of one of our Consuls at Torreón.[7] You know, we had the most extraordinary tales of barbarities at Torreón. I was only, this morning, reading his narrative very carefully of that series of days that preceded the capture, and, while the facts were all very sad, I don't think that anything went on that one wouldn't expect in such circumstances.

You see, we must remember that when these forces touch, there is a fringe of disloyalty in both, or treachery in both, so they naturally want to cut off that fringe when the other gets the upper hand in the contest; and there are, of course, a considerable number of persons who have played fast and loose on both sides—I mean, citizens of Mexico. But they treated Americans with respect and gave them protection in Torreón and other signals to stay.

That narrative really removed the impression from my mind that [anything wrong was done]. As I say, when there is any shooting, there is bound to be speculation.

Did the Consul report anything about the execution, after the fighting, of some thirty Federal officers?

No, he did not mention that at all. Whether that was simply an incident he took for granted or not, I don't know, but he certainly didn't mention it. The Constitutionalists were, admittedly, mentioned.

He admitted thirty officers were executed?

Well, you know, those two armies have been exchanging officers, and if a man has been with you and is found on the other side, you know the temper of the situation. And our information is that there has been that constant fluctuation of attachment.

Mr. President, it is reported from Veracruz that the *New Hampshire* has gone to the immediate neighborhood of Tampico for the purpose of protecting citizens and ships there.[8] The suggestion is made as one of the possibilities this morning of landing the marines to protect our interests.

I am sorry to say I don't know anything about that. I must say our naval officers down there are instructed to do what is necessary and feasible for the protection of American and foreign lives.

The Secretary of State told me yesterday that orders had been sent, or messages had been sent, with a view to special protection in that vicinity, because it was apparently threatened by insurgent forces.

You see, that is one of the areas where British interests are more threatened, and British property, than American, causing the dispatch of the British ships. We are affording the same kind of protection whether it is our own citizens or not.

The Mexican [military] headquarters are at [Tampico]?

Yes, I believe.

Will the instructions to the fleet down there include the landing of marines if necessary?

It would include nothing specific, according to our reports, that has not been necessary anywhere or requested anywhere.

Mr. President, have you had an opportunity to go over [Huerta's] message?[9]

I haven't seen it yet.

Have we received it?

I understand it has been received. I haven't received it.

Mr. President, has there been any complaint from the Mexican authorities—the provisional authorities—that American Consuls were assisting the Constitutionalists? I see the dispatches today mention "Mr. Yankee" particularly as being suspected by the authorities in Mexico City.

No such complaint has been received that I know of.

Mr. President, has anything been done to act to warn our citizens to leave many parts of Mexico?

Yes. They are kept constantly informed, so far as we can inform them. They are a little exacting. If we warn them that there may be trouble and they leave, then they hold us responsible if there wasn't trouble in twenty-four hours. So we are expected to guarantee the trouble.

Mr. President, have we anything new from Mr. Lind that we might know of?

Nothing at all.

Anything new, Mr. President, with reference to the adjournment of Congress, so far as you know?

No, sir. Nothing at all. I don't know whether or not there is any proposal now to adjourn.

[1] Huerta gave a reception at Chapultepec Castle on November 19 for the diplomatic corps in Mexico City. See the *New York Times*, Nov. 20, 1913.

[2] The *New York Times* so reported on November 19. Hale was finding Carranza difficult in many ways. See Hill, *Emissaries to a Revolution*, pp. 112-19.

[3] The British government had ordered two battle cruisers from its West Indies fleet to Mexican waters. See the *New York Times*, Nov. 20-21, 1913.

[4] Rear Adm. Sir Christopher Cradock.

[5] It was feared that the British might send an admiral who would outrank the American commander, Rear Adm. Fletcher, and who would be in command in the event of a joint intervention. See the *New York Times*, Nov. 21, 1913.

[6] The Constitutionalists captured Victoria on November 18, and it was reported that the Federal garrison died to the last man. See *ibid.*, Nov. 19, 1913.

[7] George C. Carothers. His report, entitled "Conditions Prevailing in Torreón from Sept. 25 to October 11, Inclusive," is in WP, DLC.

[8] *New Hampshire* was moved to Tuxpam, near Tampico, where it joined *Louisiana* to protect Americans from the fighting expected there. See the *New York Times*, Nov. 21, 1913.

[9] Huerta was scheduled to address the Mexican Congress on November 21.

Nov. 24, 1913

Fire away.

We are interested in Mexico, Mr. President.

Not so much as I, I venture to say. But there are no new developments at all that I have heard of today. I have just got into the office, but I find no dispatches of any kind. Things are just slowly crumbling, as usual.

Mr. President, Mr. O'Shaughnessy has not cabled the news of Mr. Huerta's expectation of your immediate recognition?[1]

No. I am not expecting that. That is one of the serious sides of the situation, though. They can say anything they please to in their papers and make any impression they please.

Mr. President, have you heard from Dr. Hale?

No. I believe he is returning to Washington.

Mr. President, do you care to say anything about the currency situation, the open debate in the Senate?[2]

I don't think there's anything to say. I feel that it is going to be pushed forward now as rapidly as possible.

There will be no interchange between the two sessions of Congress?

None that I have heard of.

Can you say anything as to the situation in the Interstate Commerce Commission?

No, except to express my very deep regret at the death of Mr. Marble.[3] It is a very great loss to the commission, and to me a very shocking surprise. I hadn't heard that his friends were anxious about him. It gives me the very serious problem of selecting two men, and consideration of three vacancies very near to them.[4]

Mr. President, will you deliver your message to the coming session of Congress in person?[5]

Yes, sir. That makes it a little doubtful just when I will deliver it. Of course, I will consult the convenience of the two houses in joint session.

Will that be ready fairly soon?

I am hoping to have it ready by Tuesday—by tomorrow, but some of the things I am talking about change so rapidly that I have torn pieces apart until I am certain that what I say is so.

Very long message, Mr. President?

No, sir. I hope it won't be considered so. I am making it as short as I can.

Do you outline new work for Congress when the currency legislation is finished?

Yes. I cannot decide what we want to be the most important subject.

Trusts, I suppose?

Well, I am not uttering it yet.

Do you expect, Mr. President, to discuss the Mexican situation, at any rate?

Merely to state what it is, unless of course something is done about it between now and then.

You will deal with several subjects, of course?

General matters, yes, but not with all the subjects there are.

Thank you.
Mr. President, can you give us some idea when you expect to fill these vacancies on the Interstate Commerce Commission?

No. I wish I could. I want to make the best selections possible. I feel it will be some process, canvassing the field.

There is some talk about letting this rate matter[6] go over until the commission is full.

That will mean hurrying all the more. That will have to be taken up.

That might have a bearing on it, if there are three vacancies on the commission.

I realize that. I had meant all along to get the people as quickly as I could.

Mr. President, will you fill those vacancies from a geographic standpoint?

Not anything reached. We plan to consider all men if possible.

Have you definitely decided to make Mr. Prouty [investigator] of physical values?

That is not my choice. I thoroughly approve of what he is doing, personally, but, legally speaking, it is none of my business.

If you refuse to accept his resignation?

I can't refuse to accept his resignation, but so far as that is concerned, I think it is a very wise action on the part of the commission to request him to do that.

Is there any light [blank]?

It only leaves four more candidacies. This rate case presents the possibility that we may hurry the acceptance of Mr. Prouty's resignation. There is no present likelihood of that, though, because I am delaying accepting it until I find his successor.

The mere fact that the rate matter is up wouldn't act as a stay for his resignation?

No. I think not, provided, of course, I can satisfy myself as to his successor.

Mr. President, did you receive any answer as to the inquiry in reference to the [blank]?

None, so far as I know yet. I wouldn't know why it should be delayed. I suppose it is really a difficult matter to look into.

Is there any news, Mr. President, with reference to the changed attitude toward the Mexican situation? Has any of the foreign governments sent any communications?[7]

No. None at all yet. I can say that their attitude is wholly satisfactory, wholly friendly, and shows a desire to cooperate with us.

Mr. President, could you say anything about your conference last night with Secretary McAdoo?

No. That was merely for mutual information.

[1] See the *Washington Post*, Nov. 23-24, 1913. The reports had no basis in fact.
[2] The Senate opened debate on the Glass-Owen bill on November 24. See *ibid.*, Nov. 24, 1913.
[3] Commissioner John Hobart Marble had died on November 21.
[4] In addition to Marble's position, Wilson had to fill vacancies created by the expected retirement of Judson Claudius Clements and by the appointment of Commissioner Prouty as head of the investigation into the physical value of railroad properties. See *ibid.*, Nov. 22, 1913.
[5] Wilson delivered his Annual Message to Congress on December 2. It is printed in *PWW*, Vol. 29, pp. 3-11.
[6] The Interstate Commerce Commission began hearings on November 24 on a proposed freight-rate increase of 5 per cent. See the *Washington Post*, Nov. 24, 1913.
[7] The German government had recently warned its citizens of dangerous conditions in Mexico. See *ibid.*

Dec. 1, 1913

It was a good game, wasn't it?[1]

It depends upon the viewpoint, Mr. President.
How about Mexico, Mr. President?

Well, they seem to be running their own affairs down there in a very interesting way just now. There is no development, so far as we are concerned at all.

Have you heard from Dr. Hale since his return?

No. I got a note from him this morning saying that the Doctor was at my service for a conference, but I haven't seen him.

There have been no reports from him? He hasn't written?

No, he hasn't written anything.

Have you heard anything about the visit of Señor Moheno to Veracruz?[2]

No, nothing at all, except it was in the papers. I don't know whether I saw the lead or not.

Is it true, Mr. President, that Lord Cowdray has given up his concessions in Colombia?[3]

I don't know anything more than is in the press about that.

So then there is no basis for the report that adduces, directly or indirectly, that this government was responsible in part?

Certainly not directly, and not by any indirect suggestion, of course. That the policy of this government may have had something to do with it is all I know.

It is suggested that the speech that you made at Mobile is probably responsible.[4]

I have seen that suggestion, but of course I don't know whether it was or not.

Mr. President, did you indicate to Mr. Hale when you would be willing to see him?

No, sir. I haven't had a chance to study my calendar to know when I will be free to see him.

Mr. President, going a few miles southeast of Mexico, have you given up on the idea of getting to Panama this year?

Oh, yes.

Have you made up your mind when you are going to undertake the reorganizing of the government down there?[5]

No, sir.

The Appropriations Committee got back [the day] before yesterday.[6] Mr. Sherley,[7] in a statement which he gave his local papers at least, said that the time had come when he believed the reorganization of the government there should be immediately undertaken. Have you anything to say about that?

No. I haven't taken that up.

Mr. President, in view of the fact that Congress should pass the currency bill, have you given up your idea of a vacation?

Unless they pass it in time to get away; of course I am not going unless they go. They determine my vacations as well as their own.

Have you seen the draft of the bill the Democratic caucus has been working out?[8]

Not with the results of the conference in it. I have read that the Senate had a print containing the original House [bill] and the so-called Owen suggestions[9] and the so-called Hitchcock suggestions.

Which of those do you prefer, Mr. President, the Owen—the so-called Owen bill, or the House bill?

I am in the middle of studying them. I interrupted myself to come over here this morning.

Do you get any assurances whether it will pass before Christmas or after?

No, I won't get any direct information on that subject, I suppose, until the Senate really gets down to work. As for the Senate, you can't tell. But there are not as many persons eager for opposition on the currency as on the tariff.

Does that make any difference, in the number of opponents?

I don't know. That depends upon the discretion of the members.

Can you tell us anything about the Interstate Commerce Commission, Mr. President?

I will, as soon as I know myself.

Mr. President, do you expect to read it before Congress tomorrow?[10]

Yes, sir. Two o'clock.

Mr. President, on the Mexican situation again. Is there any problem we may know with reference to Mexico?

No, no more than there was. We are awaiting developments.

[1] The Army-Navy football game of November 29 at Philadelphia, attended by Wilson, in which Army defeated Navy by a score of 22 to 9.
[2] Querido Moheno, Huerta's Foreign Minister, visited Veracruz late in November but did not see Lind. See the *New York Times*, Dec. 1, 1913.
[3] Weetman Dickinson Pearson, 1st Baron Cowdray, had been negotiating for oil concessions in Colombia, but withdrew them, he said, largely due to American pressure. See *ibid.*, Nov. 28, 1913. About Cowdray's involvement in Mexican affairs, see Katz, *Secret War in Mexico*, pp. 161-66.
[4] Wilson had addressed the annual convention of the Southern Commercial Congress at Mobile, Alabama, on October 27, 1913. He declared the United States to be the friend of Latin America and promised development there on terms of "equality and honor." Wilson's address is printed in *PWW*, Vol. 28, pp. 448-52.
[5] The government of the Canal Zone had to be reorganized because it was only empowered to build, not to operate, the canal. See Public Law 337 (H.R. 21969) of Aug. 12, 1912.
[6] The House Appropriations Committee had been in Panama on its annual tour of the facilities. See the *New York Times*, Nov. 23, 1913.
[7] Representative Joseph Swagar Sherley, Democrat of Kentucky.

⁸ The Democratic caucus in the Senate had, on November 30, completed the draft of a bill approved by the Democratic members of the Senate Banking and Currency Committee. See the *New York Times*, Dec. 1, 1913.

⁹ This was the bill approved by the Senate caucus.

¹⁰ That is, Wilson's State of the Union message.

Dec. 8, 1913

Did you accumulate any Mexican news while you were confined?

No. I didn't accumulate anything but germs. I had a very fine assortment of them.[1]

It is the same thing as to the Interstate Commerce Commission?

Well, that leads you to naturally suspect I haven't been making any progress about that, because I have been knocked out and haven't been able to do anything but the necessary routine business. I haven't finished any piece of business. I have to tackle it.

Senator La Follette makes a very strong intimation in the last column of his paper[2] that you contemplate—

I suppose he supposes that merely upon what it is generally based upon—Mr. Clements' age. He is an admirably qualified man. I haven't determined the man one way or the other.[3]

Mr. President, the federal grand jury at Pueblo, Colorado, indicted some of the officials of the United Mine Workers of America—

So I was told.

—in violation of the antitrust act, in spite of the exemption provided in the sundry civil bill. Will the Department of Justice participate in the prosecution?[4]

There is nothing in the sundry civil bill to prevent that charge. I wasn't thinking of the three hundred thousand dollars to do that. The three hundred thousand dollars wouldn't apply to the expense that might be incurred by the district attorney there. That is explicitly for the employment of special counsel.[5]

So long as there is no special counsel and they employ the district attorney for—

It doesn't affect the ordinary processes of the department at all.

Mr. President, would that case be on the initiative of the department here or the district attorney?

Not at all, sir.

But the district attorney out there—

No, not even for the district attorney. It was taken up by the initiative of the members of the jury themselves.

Do you think it is unlike the case of the business which we had in West Virginia, where the district attorney out there did start that?[6]

Yes, sir, it is different. I am speaking a little bit at secondhand, but I am quite sure I am right in what I said. It was not started on the initiative of the district attorney but on the demand of the jurors themselves.

Have there been any representations, Mr. President, asking the department not to prosecute the suit against the miners?

None that I have heard of, sir.

Mr. President, can you give us any intimation with regard to the situation in San Domingo?[7] There seem to be allegations of trouble with the elections—[8]

Well, the situation there is very confusing. I don't know that I can state it briefly. In the first place, a revolution was started against the present government, as you know, and with the provisional government itself, by representations which we were able to make through Mr. Sullivan,[9] the Minister down there, we persuaded them to postpone the election for another week and said that, so far as we were concerned, we would do everything that we had the right to do in cooperating to secure fair elections which would settle and strengthen the whole situation. Well, now, gentlemen, on the fifteenth of this month we are sending down there a few—I don't know just how many—Americans, I mean citizens who can speak the language of the island, to simply be foreign spectators so that in case there is any dispute as to what happened, there will be impartial witnesses who can testify. That is the situation in a nutshell.[10]

To work a reformation?

No, not at all. They haven't any official standing. We haven't asked the government to recognize them in any way.

Did San Domingo protest in any way?

They protested before that, on the basis that we were acting on our own.[11]

But they are satisfied, as the situation stands?

I suppose so. It has just been assumed they would be. I don't know on what grounds they could be dissatisfied.

Our information would be for the benefit of this government and then—

And for the benefit of anybody who wanted it.

They might appear, Mr. President, in local elections in Santo Domingo or other parts of the island, too?

I don't know what their process of giving testimony about the elections would be. If they have information, you see, they would be at liberty to give it.

What is the progress with reference to Central America?

We haven't any program. I didn't know of anything with Nicaragua until I took up the paper yesterday morning.

There is nothing new in the meanwhile?

Absolutely not. I read those articles[12] with the greatest interest and curiosity because I hadn't heard of anything new being started, as far as I could make out, as far as they are based upon fact at all, because nearly the whole treaty—I mean, the treaty as already some time ago proposed, the terms of which were mainly by her suggestion. We are not trying to establish any protectorate over anybody.

The conclusion is that—I mean, wasn't that her suggestion, or did she acquiesce—

My recollection is a little bit hazy, but my recollection is that it was at her suggestion that the terms of the Platt Amendment were included. But I may be wrong about that.[13]

I was thinking it was suggested in the committee, incorporated and accepted, mostly something of that sort.

I am not sure. I think that you asked me some time ago about that.[14]

The currency. Can you tell us something more about that?

No, sir. I think things are going very well.

Has there been any intimation from the Senate as to whether or not they think—

They are hoping to have it[15] by the twentieth, but I haven't seen it so far.

Are the House amendments and the Senate amendments nearly ready?

I don't know. That is a large order.

I notice Mr. Glass is scheduled to visit you today.

I haven't looked at my schedule, but I don't think it's about that. I can tell by the "eye" time that he is going to stay—

[Tumulty] Only ten minutes.
Could you suggest in ten minutes that he bow out gracefully?

He could if he wanted to.

Mr. President, if the currency bill is to be passed by the Senate by the twentieth of December, would there be any opposition to their being ready to adjourn, letting Congress start again after the holidays?

I am very embarrassed, because the implication is that I am running this show, which I am not trying to do. I don't see anything necessarily standing in the way of an adjournment, and I don't think that the—what we may call the Owen phase of the bill—is far enough away from the Glass phase of the bill to make it likely that the conference will take a very long while in getting together.

Mr. President, have you determined when your trust message is to go to Congress?[16]

No, I haven't. I daresay very soon after the recess, if there is one.

Mr. President, could you say when you are expecting to go on a vacation?

No. I believe that will be settled in the upper house.

Mr. President, has Dr. Hale been in?

No. I didn't know Dr. Hale was here until I was in bed with this cold. I haven't had a chance to talk with him yet.

There is no change in that situation, so far as you are concerned?

No, sir. We are tending to our own affairs.

Mr. President, have you worked out any complete plan of presidential primaries? It was suggested in your message.[17]

No, sir. That was—

As to the details of it?

My mind strongly—

You don't know, Mr. President, whether a bill on that subject is ready to be introduced?

No, I do not.

---

[1] Wilson had been in bed for several days with a cold.

[2] *La Follette's Weekly*.

[3] Commissioner Clements' term was about to expire. Wilson reappointed him.

[4] On December 1, the grand jury indicted twenty-five officers of the United Mine Workers for restraint of trade under the Sherman Act. See the *New York Times*, Dec. 2, 1913.

[5] An amendment to the Sundry Civil Appropriations Act for 1913 had forbidden the use of the funds provided for the purpose of prosecuting labor leaders under the Sherman Act. Thus none of the $300,000 provided in the bill could be used to employ special attorneys for labor prosecutions.

[6] See above, June 9, 1913.

[7] For a discussion of American policy in the Dominican Republic in this period, see Dana G. Munro, *Intervention and Dollar Diplomacy in the Caribbean, 1900-1921* (Princeton, N. J., 1964), pp. 269-81, and Sumner Welles, *Naboth's Vineyard: The Dominican Republic, 1844-1924*, 2 vols. (New York, 1928), II, 713-23.

[8] Elections were scheduled in the Dominican Republic for December 15, 1913.

[9] James Mark Sullivan, American Minister to the Dominican Republic.

[10] The three American representatives were Hugh Gibson, Jordan Herbert Stabler, and Fred Sterling, all officers of the State Department.

[11] For the Dominican Republic's protest, see the *New York Times*, Dec. 7, 1913; and the Minister of the Dominican Republic to the Secretary of State, Dec. 6, 1913, in *FR, 1913*, pp. 441-43.

[12] The press was suggesting that Wilson wanted to apply the Bryan-Chamorro Treaty, which established a virtual American protectorate over Nicaragua, to all nations in Central America. See, for example, the *New York Times*, Dec. 7, 1913.

[13] Wilson was correct. See Munro, *Intervention and Dollar Diplomacy*, pp. 269-81; and WW to Bryan, Feb. 20, 1914, printed in *PWW*, Vol. 29, pp. 274-75.

¹⁴ See above, July 21, 1913.
¹⁵ That is, the Federal Reserve bill, which was moving rapidly through Congress at this time. See Link, *The New Freedom*, pp. 235-37.
¹⁶ That is, a message about revision of the antitrust laws, the third part of Wilson's New Freedom reform program. For its origins, see *ibid.*, pp. 417-27.
¹⁷ In his message to Congress of December 2, Wilson urged the passage of a law for primary elections throughout the country to select presidential nominees. See *PWW*, Vol. 29, pp. 7-8.

Dec. 22, 1913

What have you heard from the conference committee, Mr. President? Will they get the bill?

I haven't all the details at all. I have heard that they sat up to five o'clock this morning, and that they have reached an agreement that there are no points of difference left; and further than that my information doesn't go, except that I once again was called up on the telephone yesterday about particular points. But, so far as I can learn, it is a very satisfactory settlement all around.[1]

There will be no delays in signing the bill?

None whatever, sir. As soon as I can get my hands on it.[2]

Mr. President, can you give us any indication of when you are likely to announce the names of the [members of the] Federal Reserve Board?

Well, you see, one of the points that the conference has determined, I understand—and I am very happy that they determined it—is the organization committee. The original bill provided for an organization committee which would proceed at once to get the thing in operation. And I was anxious for that, because I wanted the work to begin at once, and I also wanted to know the timing of their investigation, to make sure of my appointments on the permanent board; and therefore this conference agreement gives me the time that I need so that I shall be very careful, indeed, in that selection. I regard them as some of the most important posts that I have to select, of course.

Who are the organization committee?

I can't tell you offhand. It is an *ex officio* list. The Secretary of the Treasury, the Comptroller of the Currency, the Secretary of Agriculture, they are on it, the original *ex officio* members proposed for the Federal Reserve Board, and perhaps one or two others, but I can't be sure in my recollection of that.[3]

Mr. President, you don't have to designate any others?

No, they are designated by the bill *ex officio*.

That leaves sixty days in which to complete the organization of the Federal Reserve Board.

The sixty days is not a limit on that so much as on the preliminary stages of the organization. I probably will have sixty days, however, although we are going to curtail it as much as thorough work will permit.

Do you suppose they will permit the deputy Comptroller of the Currency to act on that?[4]

I expect they would. That point has not been raised.

Would they, Mr. President? He has not been confirmed by the Senate.

Perhaps. In that case, we will have to get busy and appoint a Comptroller.

Will you appoint a Comptroller before you leave, Mr. President?

I intend to see the Secretary of the Treasury today. I will raise that point with him.

Mr. President, last week the Republican National Committee was here and raised, you know, the calamity howl quite loudly, and the howl has been taken up in the papers all over the country, particularly Republican papers. It has also been expressed on the floor of the House by Republicans.[5] I wanted to ask you if you would care to say anything for publication as to what you believe is the condition of the country, and what you hear and also what you think will happen when the currency bill goes into effect?

No, except that I shouldn't raise your interest with the expressions of these gentlemen. That is their regular employment.

Will you make a statement when you sign the currency bill?

I don't know whether I will or not. Probably I shall.[6]

Mr. President, in the American Telephone and Telegraph suit last week, you expressed a belief that the business of the country was more nearly conforming to the law. Is there anything in that suit that led you to that statement?[7]

I think the Attorney General would tell you that there seems to be a very general disposition to inquire what will be expected of them and to comply with it.

Would other corporations?

Yes. I could give you specific instances. As I said in that regard, I get that impression more and more from what I learn from day to day.

Might you say whether it is the policy of the administration—

We have already shown that we certainly don't want to put any barriers in place of anybody who wants to obey the law. We will naturally cooperate very heartily to encourage the impulse on their part to take the initiative.

I think the business world is interested, with some help, to obey the law when they see how the law is broken.

Oh, I think that everybody will see that we are ready to help in every way we legitimately can.

Mr. President, have you heard anything from Mexico that we might know?

Nothing at all. Things seem to be in their usual, unstable equilibrium down there.

Has anything come to the government officially with reference to this Roosevelt affair at Santiago?[8]

No. The only thing I know is what is in the papers this morning.

Have you expressed yourself at any time, or would you care to express yourself, on the matter of governmental ownership with respect to telephones?[9]

No, I have not.

There is another matter pending before Congress you might not want to mention, concerning the literacy test in the immigration bill. Have you said anything on that, Mr. President?[10]

No, sir.

Mr. President, can you tell us anything about the Interstate Commerce Commission?

No, sir, further than that we are taking the time to canvass the thing, very slowly, but really very diligently, so as to satisfy myself as to the choices.

Mr. President, before you leave,[11] will you have any statement on the Carabao dinner?[12]

I don't know. Perhaps so.

Mr. President, may we expect some Interstate Commerce Commission appointments before you leave?

I want to, before I leave, but won't because the Senate always adjourns very promptly and there wouldn't be time to confirm them.

Will you receive any visitors during your southern trip?

Not so far as I know. I haven't made any appointments—anything of the kind. I am going to try to be very quiet.

[1] In an all-night session, the conference committee resolved differences between the House and Senate currency bills. See the *New York Times*, Dec. 22, 1913, and Link, *The New Freedom*, p. 237.

[2] Wilson signed the bill on December 23.

[3] The Reserve Bank Organizing Committee consisted of the three officers listed by Wilson. See Willis, *Federal Reserve System*, p. 1667.

[4] The office of Comptroller of the Currency had been vacant since April. Wilson nominated John Skelton Williams of Richmond, Virginia, on January 13, 1914.

[5] Republican complaints about the depressed and uncertain state of the economy came during debate on the Federal Reserve bill in the House. See *Cong. Record*, 63d Cong., 2d sess., pp. 1293-1307.

[6] Upon signing the federal reserve bill, on December 23, Wilson said that it represented a great step forward for American business. He described it as a measure of "accommodation" and said that those who supported it did not do so in the interest of any class. The remarks are printed in *PWW*, Vol. 29, pp. 63-66.

[7] On December 19, the Justice Department reached agreement with the American Telephone and Telegraph Company whereby the company would voluntarily divest itself of the Western Union Company in order to comply with the Sherman Act. The statement referred to was in a public letter on the agreement issued by Wilson. See the *New York Times*, Dec. 20, 1913, and the American Telephone and Telegraph Co. to the Attorney General, Dec. 19, 1913, WP, DLC.

[8] On December 21, during a ceremony at the University of Santiago in Chile, Theodore Roosevelt clashed with Dr. Marcial Martinez, former Chilean Minister to the United States, over the meaning of the Monroe Doctrine. After Martinez referred to the doctrine as a dead issue, Roosevelt responded that it was still a foundation stone of the foreign policy of the United States. See the *New York Times*, Dec. 22, 1913.

[9] See above, Oct. 2, 1913.

[10] On December 15, the House Immigration Committee reported a bill (H.R. 6060) to restrict immigration by application of a literacy test to those who wished to enter the United States. See *Cong. Record*, 63d Cong., 2d sess., p. 937, and see the *New York Times*, Dec. 16, 1913.

[11] To vacation at Pass Christian, Mississippi, and to meet Lind for consultations regarding the situation in Mexico. See Hill, *Emissaries to a Revolution*, pp. 138-39.

[12] The Washington branch of the Military Order of the Carabao, a society of veterans of the Philippine campaign, held its annual dinner on December 11, 1913, and members sang anti-Filipino songs and made fun of the administration's Philippine policy and of Secretary of State Bryan. Wilson was angered by this behavior and asked the Secretaries of War and Navy to consider courts-martial for the offenders. The Secretaries recommended a reprimand instead, and Wilson issued a stinging rebuke of the officers on December 22. It is printed in *PWW*, Vol. 29, pp. 54-55. See also the *New York Times*, Dec. 23, 1913, and Link, *The New Freedom*, pp. 78-79.

# 1914

This has been a real "much ado about nothing," as a matter of fact, because I think I earned your gratitude by presenting you with a live opportunity to make copy;[2] but, as a matter of fact, and speaking seriously, what I gave out at first was literally true. Of course I bluffed you. Lind has been sending us constant dispatches, but you can get in a conversation of two or three hours what two weeks of dispatches wouldn't give you—all the color of the situation, the points of view of different people.

Now, there was no special reason of any kind to bring him up, no causes of excitement, or new questions. It was simply our desire to have conversation. He is not even coming ashore. He is going back this afternoon on the *Chester*, after he has seen his sons. Our conversation was just conversation—the whole field of conditions in Mexico. We didn't discuss any particular measure or plan or anything of the kind. It was just a get-together talk. We learned each other's minds, and the situation, and everything connected with it. Now, that is literally the whole truth.[3]

Will you care to say this morning whether you are more hopeful of a speedy settlement of conditions?

I would put it this way—that in my view the situation down there has not changed.[4]

Your plans have not changed?

No. As I say, we really did not discuss plans. It was for information.

Of course, you might have a different point of view, Mr. President, if things change before you leave?

No, sir. Oh—I—we didn't discuss alteration of policy.

Was there anyone else on the visit that came up from down there?[5]

None but Mr. Lind.

[Is Mr. Lind enjoying his long stay in Mexico?]

No, I won't say he has enjoyed it, but he is so deeply interested that he is perfectly willing, of course, to stay down there. He has no other idea.

With regard to lifting the embargo—

Nothing specific was discussed.

Any likelihood that anything particularly new will come about as a result of this conference?
Is he going to Veracruz or Mexico City?

No, he is going to Veracruz. I am so much nearer to him here that I only consider this as a neighborly visit. We knew I wouldn't have this chance again. I don't think you can use direct quotations, but I think you fellows understand.

Intimate or paraphrase will not be objectionable?

Well, just say that the President explained, and so forth.

[1] This conference was conducted at Gulfport, Mississippi.
[2] Wilson had met with Lind on board U.S.S. *Chester* on January 2, after giving the reporters the impression that Lind was coming ashore for the meeting. See the *New York Times*, Jan. 3, 1914.
[3] For a memorandum on the meeting, which suggests that the main topic of the Wilson-Lind conversation was to find ways to help the Constitutionalists, see *PWW*, Vol. 29, p. 110.
[4] As Wilson informed Bryan, Lind had nothing new to offer that persuaded Wilson to change his views on Mexico. See WW to Bryan, Jan. 6, 1914, in the Papers of William Jennings Bryan, DLC.
[5] It had been reported that Huerta or other Mexican officials were coming with Lind. See Hill, *Emissaries to a Revolution*, p. 139.

Jan. 12, 1914[1]

Well, this is, strictly speaking, no formal conference—not arranged for—but I daresay you will desire it. That may be one thing.[2] But, as I say, that is for Tumulty to find out from the Hill. What are you ready for?

Is the message ready?

I have sketched it out. Got it ready to put in shape [when I get] back.

Is it very long?

I don't know how long it will be.

Mr. President, have you digested the rural-credits report which the committee has brought in?[3]

I read most of it. There were parts of it that had information that I was familiar with already, so I didn't really read all of it. I read the parts that were [new]. I wanted to get hold of it. I read the bill, and I subsequently wrote Senator Fletcher that I had read it and would be glad to have a conference with him when I got back.

Does the bill, in its general scope, meet with your approval?

Well, it seems to me a sound bill, with some additions that ought to be made.

Have you made up your mind on the Federal Reserve Board? Have you made out a list?

Oh, no. I took a real vacation down there. I didn't tackle any job.

Did you see the story about your vacation—that a man who had been to see you had gotten a remark from you about a prospective place for Judge Taft?[4]

I didn't see that.

We of course assumed that was not true.

Absolutely wrong.

I just want to confirm the denial. It went out from New Haven.[5]

No, I didn't see a soul down there, or talk politics with anybody, until I saw Colonel Ewing of New Orleans, who lingered a few minutes, and even that was not anything but general talk about how things were going.

Is the time of your trust message contingent on arrangements Secretary Tumulty is making?

No, sir—contingent on a good many things. I understood when I left that there was some idea of [Congress'] taking a somewhat longer vacation than the usual. I have forgotten just what that was. I will have to address a joint session, so it is up to them to determine.

We could assume, Mr. President, that the trust legislation will be the paramount question now?

Well, I promised them a special talk on that.

Have you been advised of Mr. O'Shaughnessy's [arrest] on the Mexican-Veracruz railway, at a place called Orizaba? The railroad has been cut. His [arrest] there?[6]

I have heard a good many things. That is absolutely untrue. I won't believe that until I hear from him. O'Shaughnessy has been "threatened at the front" when nothing has happened to him of any kind.

Has the War Department consulted with you about the refugees on the border?[7]

No, sir. There is already a considerable number, you know, of refugees here that have been taken, one way or the other, into the army posts down there; but if there are twenty-eight hundred of them, that is a serious problem on the border.

There will probably be Red Cross funds issued?

I suppose so.

What did we do with the ammunition that we have got?[8]

I didn't understand that we have got the ammunition. You will have to consult Major McNamee.[9] He is the one that belongs to. I don't know. Well, I hope you fellows had a reasonably interesting time.

---

[1] This conference was held on the train trip to Washington.

[2] A reporter had apparently asked a question about Wilson's forthcoming address to Congress on antitrust legislation.

[3] A commission headed by Senator Fletcher had studied the rural-credits problem and proposed the creation of a system of county banks and credit associations. See the *New York Times*, Jan. 14, 1914; and *Agricultural Credit*, 3 parts, 63d Cong., 2d sess., Senate Document 380 (Washington, 1914).

[4] It had been reported that Wilson was considering appointing former President Taft to the Supreme Court when Chief Justice Edward Douglass White retired. See the *New York Times*, Jan. 12, 1914.

[5] Taft's residence. He was at this time Professor of Law at Yale University.

[6] Rebels had cut the railway between Veracruz and Mexico City at the time that O'Shaughnessy was returning to the capital following a meeting with Lind. See the *New York Times*, Jan. 12, 1914.

[7] Following Villa's victory at Ojinaga on January 10, 2,800 Federal soldiers and six of their generals had fled across the border near Presidio, Texas. See *ibid.*, Jan. 11-12, 1914.

[8] Over 200,000 rounds of ammunition were turned over to United States officials by the Federal soldiers.

[9] Maj. Michael M. McNamee, U.S.A., commander of the American border patrol.

Jan. 15, 1914

I think there was a misunderstanding about the hour, Mr. President.

This is the right hour.

Did you recognize the antitrust legislation this morning from the accounts in the paper?[1]

No, I can't say that I did. It had a strong family resemblance.

Is there anything you can tell us about developments with regard to legislation that you favor?

No. You see, what I have been doing is the usual thing. I have been conferring with the men who are going actually to frame the bills and get their angle of view, more or less correcting mine by that angle. In other words, we are going through the process of comparing views. They are immensely helpful to me, I am sure.

Have you fixed a time for the delivery of your message?

No. There are one or two other groups of men I want to see, but I take it for granted that it can be arranged for the early part of next week.[2]

Has there been a decision yet as to whether the legislation is to be in one bill, two, or several?

I suppose naturally in several.

Would you say anything about this amendment exempting labor unions?[3]

No. We haven't discussed that side of it.

Is there anything, Mr. President, you would care to say about the Mexican situation, especially with reference to the financial state of affairs?[4]

No. When one does say anything about Mexican affairs, it turns out to be untrue the next day.

It seems to be certain that they have stopped the payment of interest.

I know, but I have nothing to say about that.

In your talk today with the Earl of Kintore, who came here in connection with

that exposition, was there anything promised as to the government's participation in that?[5]

No. I simply expressed my genuine interest in it and said I would
be very glad to do what I could to obtain participation.

Mr. President, when do you expect to take up the Panama government?

Very soon. I am planning to have a conference with the Secretary
of War about it.

No selection has been made?

No, nothing beyond the arrangements for the conference.

Anything about the new commander of the Marine Corps?[6]

No. The Secretary of the Navy hasn't brought that to me yet.

Will it be several weeks before the nominations to the Federal Reserve Board
will be made?

I suppose so. Of course, I feel that is almost like constituting a
whole Supreme Court. It's almost equal in importance, and I want
to make it—I want to be sure I am selecting from the whole field
before I make the final choice.

Mr. President, did anybody ask whether there would be any amendments to
the antitrust act, or merely additions? I didn't know. I didn't get here until
late.

I don't think anybody has contemplated changing the Sherman
Act.

Mere additions to it?

Yes, in one sense, in another, not additions.

I didn't know. What I had in mind particularly was that rule of reason—the
expression used by the Supreme Court—and if the language of the statute
was to be changed.[7]

My rule of reason is not to divulge my policy before I read my
message.

Mr. President, have you laid down any lines for the appointments on the Federal Reserve Board? Are they going to be geographical as well as otherwise?

Naturally, I would seek to distribute them geographically but [not in] any hard and fast division.

Any bankers that the law requires? Anything of that kind?

The law doesn't specify bankers.

Question of banking experience.

No, I haven't gone far enough in choice to come down to a settled opinion about that, just whether I will choose actual bankers or not.

There is one case for [blank].

No, that's one case, you see, where the organizational process is going on and necessarily will take some time. The time is very welcome to me. While the bill was pending, I didn't have leisure time enough to study the personnel.

What is the preliminary machinery that is set in operation now with respect to rural credits?[8] Is it being framed by the committee?

It is being framed by the committee.

The committee of the House, is it not?

The committee of the Senate, that Senator Fletcher is on.[9]

Of course. That would be handled by the Banking and Currency Committee.

I suppose so.

Do you know whether they consulted him or not?

No, they have not.

Mr. President, will that legislation proceed faster than trust legislation?

I don't know, sir. That depends on unpredictable circumstances.

You have no policy as to that?

I don't think it is of consequence which one leads.

Mr. President, the House is debating the system of postmasters[10] this afternoon. Have you submitted any views to the Congress?

They haven't asked me for any, no.

Without being asked?

No. But I think it's pretty well understood.

Is there anything new at all in the Mexican situation that you can tell us?

No. Every day there are new details coming to notice, but nothing important.

I mean, anything new, a new policy on the part of the government?

No. The situation is unchanged. That is to say, the drift is taking place in Mexico, as was observed before.

What is the situation after your conference with Mr. Lind? Was that left as before?

What I gave out to the press was literally true. It was merely a conference for information, to let him know what was in my mind, and to let me know what was in his mind.

Have there been any communications from foreign powers with respect to the default on Mexican bonds?
Mr. President, have you any knowledge about the peace treaty that Mr. Bryan has conferred with the Senate on?[11]

No, sir.

Mr. President, have you stated when you were going to deliver your message?

No. I said just now I hoped it could be arranged for the early part of next week.

Has anything been done, Mr. President, to hold the Third Hague Peace Conference?[12]

No, nothing has been done by this government.

Is there likely to be something done before long, do you know?

I haven't taken it up with any people at all, sir.

Mr. President, have you any information that leads you to believe that Great Britain and Germany are united in a trade war with the United States?

None whatever. That is pure fiction of the imagination.

Have you any information as to any agreement between Germany and Great Britain as to exhibiting in this exposition?[13]

No. I don't think there is any foundation for supposing that there is one, tacit or explicit.

Mr. President, could you tell us anything about the possibility of presidential primaries at this session?

No. That is one of the things I want to take up with the appropriate committee, but I haven't had time to do it directly yet.

Are you hoping that there will be legislation along that line at this session?

Oh, naturally so. That is one of the things I recommended.

Mr. President, is this report, about Congress wishing to adjourn early in June—will the program still include presidential primaries?

Why, like everybody connected with business in Washington, I hope we will get it through without its being changed. I don't want Congress to adjourn before it gets through.

Is it your idea, Mr. President, that the presidential-primaries law should be passed at this session?

I don't think that is essential, but I think we ought to get to work on it and get the opinion of the country, and of everybody whose opinion is significant—I mean because they will really study it— so that we can get a law passed that is universally satisfactory.

Do you feel the same way about the trust legislation?

We have been thinking about trust legislation for a whole generation. We don't have to back and fill much longer about that.

Senator Kern said today, in reply to a question by Senator Cummins,[14] that his Committee on Privileges and Elections would take up direct-primary matters as soon as they were finished with these [hearings] next week.
Mr. President, are the delegates to the Safety-at-Sea Conference at London[15]— are they asking any instructions as to details over there?

No, sir.

They have full authority over there?

Yes, they are at full liberty to sign any report that they wish to sign.

You have heard nothing, have you, from Mr. Furuseth[16] since he came back?

I have had only a note from the Secretary of Labor about his return. I have heard nothing directly about his return. The Secretary told me, recently, that he was returning.

There is nothing contemplated to mollify him?

I haven't heard that he was clamoring to be mollified. He is a man of very strong opinions and naturally doesn't doubt them.

Have you heard anything since your return about the reported visit of the President of France to this country?[17]

I think that is just for the interest of the readers.

[1] The *New York Times*, January 15, 1914, carried a front-page story with elaborate details about Wilson's alleged antitrust program.
[2] Wilson read his message to Congress on January 20. It is printed in *PWW*, Vol. 29, pp. 153-58.
[3] The American Federation of Labor was pressing for administration support of the Bacon-Bartlett bill, which would have exempted labor organizations from prosecution under the antitrust laws. This issue was a continuation of the dispute over the exemption granted labor in the Sundry Civil Appropriations Act of 1913. A modified version of the Bacon-Bartlett bill was later included in the Clayton Act. See Link, *The New Freedom*, pp. 427-33.
[4] The Mexican government had defaulted on the payment of interest for six months, and Huerta had declared a bank holiday until March 1, 1914. The newspapers saw this as an indication that Wilson's pressure on Mexico was beginning to be effective. See, e.g., the *New York Times*, Jan. 15, 1914.
[5] The Earl of Kintore, chairman of the executive committee of the Anglo-American Exposition to be held in London to commemorate the centenary of the Treaty of Ghent, visited Wilson on January 15. Kintore favored British participation in the Panama-Pacific Exposition to be held in San Francisco. See *ibid.*, Jan. 16, 1914.
[6] Wilson appointed Col. George Barnett to replace Maj. Gen. William Phillips Biddle as Commandant of the Marine Corps.
[7] The "rule of reason," as set forth in *Standard Oil v. U.S.* (1911), 221 U.S. 1, accepted the common-law doctrine that monopolistic behavior that did not "unreasonably" affect interstate

commerce should not be construed as restraint of trade under the antitrust act. Wilson wanted a more precise definition of unlawful business activity. See the *New York Times*, Jan. 17, 1914.

[8] See above, Jan. 12, 1914.

[9] The Senate Commerce Committee.

[10] One provision of a post office appropriation bill then being debated would have removed 2,400 assistant postmasters from the civil-service list. Wilson opposed this provision and was threatening to veto the bill if the provision was not deleted. The House eliminated it. See the *New York Times*, Jan. 13 and 15, 1914, and Link, *The New Freedom*, p. 175.

[11] A reference to Bryan's treaties of conciliation, whereby five-member joint commissions would endeavor to solve disputes and prevent wars. The Secretary of State negotiated thirty such treaties, and twenty-eight were ratified. See Link, *The New Freedom*, pp. 280-83, and, for example, *Treaties and Agreements Between the United States and Other Powers, 1910-1923*, 64th Cong., 4th sess., Senate Document 348 (Washington, 1924), pp. 2666-67.

[12] The Third Hague Peace Conference was scheduled to meet in 1915 but was postponed by the European war and never held. See Calvin D. Davis, *The United States and the First Hague Peace Conference* (Ithaca, N. Y., 1962).

[13] That is, the Panama-Pacific Exposition.

[14] Senator Albert Baird Cummins, Republican of Iowa.

[15] The International Conference on Safety at Sea had been meeting at London since November 12, 1913. It concluded its deliberations on January 20, 1914. See the *New York Times*, Jan. 21, 1914, and Link, *The New Freedom*, p. 271.

[16] Andrew Furuseth, president of the International Seamen's Union, who had been working for twenty years for the passage of a comprehensive seamen's bill. He was an American delegate to the London conference but withdrew and returned to the United States to oppose the treaty because its standards fell below those of the seamen's bill which he was then supporting. See Andrew Furuseth, "Report to the President of the United States," Jan. 12, 1914, WP, DLC, and Link, *The New Freedom*, pp. 269-71.

[17] Probably inspired by the visit to France of the Sayres, Wilson's daughter and son-in-law. They had an audience with President Raymond Poincaré, who sent greetings to President and Mrs. Wilson.

Jan. 22, 1914

Mr. President, can you tell us something about the Japanese situation?

Why, so far as I know, what appeared in the papers this morning pertaining to the Government of the United States is not founded on anything that I know of.[1]

Well, we have not replied to the last note to Japan?[2]

No, we haven't sent a formal reply, but we are, of course, in constant touch with the Japanese Ambassador. I think I can say, with confidence, there is no trouble of any kind.

Well, will we do anything now? Is there anything more to be done? What else could come from the Japanese government?

In one sense, there is always something we could do to show our real attitude towards the Japanese people. Just what it would be, I can't say.

Mr. President, has the Japanese Ambassador said anything to the government here?

Nothing whatever.

There has been no pressure from the embassy for an answer to that note?

No, there has not.

Do you know whether Mr. Guthrie[3] has made a report on it?

No, none that has been shown me, and all the dispatches of importance are brought to me within twenty-four hours after they arrive.

Are you negotiating for a new treaty?

That hasn't been formally taken up. I see so much work to do from day to day, my mind hasn't gotten that far, to tell you the truth.

Mr. President, does the legislation which proposes to put the finances of the railroads under the Interstate Commerce Commission[4] take the place of any proposal to regulate the stock exchanges?[5]

Those, of course, have nothing to do with one another.

I thought possibly the proposal to regulate the issues of the railroads might in some way affect the stock-exchange legislation?

Oh, no. Those are entirely separate subjects, just as production and rigging the market would be two different things.

Then might I ask whether you intend at a later time to recommend legislation?

I am not going to recommend anything that is not in the Democratic platform, and I don't find that there.

Your reference to Japan, Mr. President. If a certain state refuses to recognize the terms of one treaty, would the negotiation of a new treaty or the replacing of that treaty help the situation any?

I don't say that it would. Of course, you are assuming in that question, California. I suppose you have in mind that it would act inconsistently with the existing treaty with Japan. That is a debatable question.

That is debatable?

Yes. Of course, that is debatable. A new treaty could make everything more specific. I am just answering your question. I have no
such matter in mind.

Mr. President, has a suggestion for a new treaty come from Japan?[6]

No, it has not.

It has been said that some time ago Mr. Bryan suggested to the Japanese
Ambassador that a new treaty might solve the difficulty.

I daresay. I don't know.

With reference to this legislation concerning railroads, Mr. President, is the
plan to make it retroactive in any way as to past issues, or will it affect only
future securities?

I haven't heard any suggestion to make it retroactive. That would
be contrary to all the precedents in legislation.

That would compel the railroads to write off past issues wherever the property
values wouldn't come up to par?

I don't know anything about that.

Is the plan regarding railroad-securities legislation a part of your antitrust
program?

Now don't go too fast. I mean, I haven't any plans, properly
speaking, with regard to these things. I make as specific suggestions as I can when the plans are brought to me from the congressional committees. The proposals are theirs. I mean, the formulated
proposals are theirs, and no such proposal has been brought to me.

Will the Republican members of Congress have a chance to cooperate in the
framing of this legislation?

I suppose so, sir. I think they are quite willing to cooperate, from
what I can learn.

I understand they are willing.
Are they invited to the White House conferences?

What I do is to invite the chairman, and he brings anybody with
him that he chooses. I don't select.

Mr. President, has General Huerta made any proposals to you through this envoy he sent to see Mr. Lind?[7]

Not that I have heard of. General Huerta hasn't been audible for some time.

We are told that this man, Magon, had gone to the conferences with Mr. Lind at Veracruz, and had represented Huerta. So it was stated in the papers.

Why, he didn't make any proposals to him that Lind has reported.

Does the situation remain the same? Is Mr. Lind audible yet, Mr. President?

Oh, yes. Mr. Lind is audible, every day. His voice just doesn't extend all over the country.

Mr. President, are there going to be any public hearings on the trust bills?

I understood from the committees I have been consulting that the fullest opportunity will be offered for suggestions and criticisms by businessmen of the country. I think that is everybody's desire and understanding.

Would there be a double set of hearings before the Interstate Commerce Committee and the Judiciary Committee also?

Well, there will not be, because they won't handle the same bills. There is a common misunderstanding there.

But what I was wondering is whether both of those committees would grant hearings for the parties interested in their particular bills?

I don't see any other bills in which they could be given an opportunity for suggestion and criticism. I take that for granted.

Are those hearings likely to be repeated in the Senate, after the House committee has heard them?

I don't know. Of course, that depends a little bit upon how the bills are handled. If they are considered at the same time in both houses, I suppose the hearings would naturally be final. But that is a detail of handling it that I don't know anything about.

You haven't heard any talk of a Democratic caucus on these bills?

No, sir.

Do you expect action on all the features of this program that has been outlined before the adjournment of this session?

Oh, yes. I don't hear any doubts expressed about that. After all, it's a reasonably homogeneous group of bills. I mean, they are all in the same field. I think they will make about equal—I suppose they would make about equal progress through the two houses.

Mr. President, you suggested a question concerning the ownership or control of stock—a question whether a man should be able to vote on both [boards of directors]. Have you any answers to that question?[8]

You understand, I handled it in that way because the answer to that question, confidentially, is no. It is not original with myself, but my mind is clear, really, on the subject.

Have you found whether the Congress seems to favor it—in your conferences?

Our conferences have not touched on that particular feature.[9]

Mr. President, do you think that the Senate or House will take up these bills initially?

There again, I can't say. The procedure has not been touched upon in the conferences I have had. It has been merely the plans for having the bills, at any rate, drawn in professional form so that they will be the object of criticism and the period of examination [will be] gone through with as promptly as possible.

Mr. President, when do you expect to announce the Federal Reserve Board?

As soon as I find them.

Is there a limitation?

There is no necessary limitation in the law itself. I ought to have decided on them at the latest, I should say, by the latter part of next month. But it is a pretty responsible choice. The only thing I am certain about is that those who are candidates for the positions will not get them.

Your hope is to get those in before the first of March?

I would like that to be generally known. It would save a good deal of correspondence.

Evidently there has been a great deal of correspondence, Mr. President?

No. I would be misrepresenting my feeling, candidly, if I said a great deal. There has been some.

Picking out someone that would be a good man?

Oh, no. But after you have sat in the Governor's and the President's office for a little while, you can easily tell the difference. There is an organized campaign on the one hand, and, on the other, "spontaneous" letters from "fronts," but the spontaneity is generally detectable.

Mr. President, is Mr. Garrett[10] going back to the Argentine as Minister?

He is on leave now. He is going immediately to Switzerland.

Is he going to remain in the diplomatic service, or will you accept his resignation?

I haven't accepted it yet. I am trying to persuade him to remain in the service.

Interstate Commerce Commission?

I am always ashamed to say no, but I have to say it yet.

Do you know, Mr. President, if there will be a Federal Reserve Bank in New York?

No, sir, I do not. Thank the Lord I don't know anything about it. That is one job that is not up to me.

[1] The Japanese Foreign Minister, Baron Nobuaki Makino, said in his annual message to the Diet on January 21 that Japan was not satisfied with the response of the United States to its protests against the California land-tenure bill. See the *New York Times*, Jan. 22, 1914.
[2] The note of August 19, 1913, proposing the negotiation of a new treaty between the United States and Japan which would clear up the issue. See Link, *The New Freedom*, pp. 302-303.
[3] George Wilkins Guthrie, American Ambassador to Japan.
[4] A bill proposed by Representative Sam Rayburn, Democrat of Texas, gave the Interstate Commerce Commission the authority to superintend and regulate the bond and stock issues of all interstate railways. See the *New York Times*, Jan. 22-23, 1914, and Link, *The New Freedom*, p. 426.
[5] Senator Owen had introduced a bill to regulate the stock exchange, but Wilson refused

to support it because it was not a part of the Baltimore platform. See the *New York Times*, Jan. 22, 1914.

[6] The Japanese had submitted on December 13, 1913, a new draft of a proposed most-favored-nation treaty with the United States. See Link, *The New Freedom*, pp. 302-303, and WW to Bryan, Jan. 15, 1914, printed in *PWW*, Vol. 29, p. 133.

[7] Huerta sent Jesús Flores Magon to Veracruz on January 19 to consult with Lind. See the *New York Times*, Jan. 20, 1914.

[8] A reference to a feature of the antitrust legislation prohibiting interlocking directorates. This became part of the bill introduced later by Representative Clayton. See Link, *The New Freedom*, p. 425.

[9] The question of interlocking directorates had come up at this time because of an announcement by the House of Morgan that it was withdrawing from the directorates of thirty railroads, banks, and industrial corporations. See *ibid.*, p. 424, and the *New York Times*, Jan. 3, 1914.

[10] John Work Garrett, former Minister to Argentina, served as a special agent for the State Department in Geneva until August 6, 1914, when he moved to Paris in the same capacity.

Jan. 29, 1914

Mr. President, can you discuss the Japanese situation?

I could discuss it more intelligently if I understood what it was. I am learning all that I know about state affairs now from the newspapers.[1]

Mr. President, there is a good deal in the newspapers which seems like rumor, and some of it more or less mischievous. Of course, we can't dissipate it without some knowledge. I don't know how far you can go or want to go in giving us this knowledge. If you could discuss the situation with us—

The rumors are mischievous because they are unfounded. I meant what I said playfully just a moment ago almost literally. I don't know anything about the things that the papers are now talking about. They are not founded on fact.

This alleged sale of Japanese arms to the Mexicans, what about that?

That is an old story. That is at least seven months old. It is certainly not fresh news.

Mr. President, has this government any objection to Japanese commercial firms selling arms to Mexico?

It can't have under the laws of nations.

Have we ever asked Japan to try to check that?

Certainly not; it is a perfectly ordinary operation of commerce that is permitted by the rules of international law.

Mr. President, isn't it so that most of the nations who were asked by this government to wait until we had defined a policy in Mexico before they took any action are really showing a friendly feeling by not permitting the shipment of arms?

No, sir, that isn't true. They are showing the most friendly spirit— that part is true—and doing all that governments can do, but governments cannot, legally, at any rate—they have no legal authority to—stop commercial transactions of any kind.

We have.

By special joint resolution of Congress,[2] yes; but they have no such legislation. I would not if it were not for the joint resolution of Congress, which is just now the law of the land. In ordinary circumstances, I couldn't interpose any obstacles, the only rule being the rule of international law that the shipment of contrabands of war is made at the risk of the shipper and of the person to whom it is assigned, that is to say, the risk of being taken by the other side. But the only limitations on sales of arms anywhere to Mexico has been the ordinary commercial limitations of whether they could get the money or not.

There are two points in that connection, Mr. President; one of them is the statement that has appeared that the government of Japan is directly selling these arms to Mexico, and the other is that the government of Japan is not to be included in the list of nations to which Mr. Oulahan has just referred— that is, Japan was not notified of our intentions with regard to Mexico.

Neither of those statements is founded in fact. I have to speak from a somewhat imperfect recollection now, because, as I say, this is several months old—the matter of the shipment of arms from Japan—and I can't be sure what the details are. But I remember this with great distinctness—that we learned from our Ambassador in Japan that the report that the Japanese government had anything to do with it was absolutely false.

That Japan was not included in the list of nations?

That is not true. We have been notifying her just as we have notified other powers.

Did that information from the Ambassador at Japan come from the Tokyo government?

Of course, that must be true. I have not the direct recollection of that that I would have if it were a recent transaction. This was the assurance of Mr. Guthrie who had looked into it and who was speaking by the card.

Recently, Mr. President?

When it happened. It is old news now, about seven or eight months old.

Mr. President, I don't think that there has been any claim that this government purposely overlooked notifying Japan, but there has been a report that, through an oversight, Japan was not included in the list of nations that were asked to suspend any action until after we had decided upon the course of action we would take.

If that is true, I had not heard it before; and I don't think it is true.

Mr. President, in this present situation of the United States forbidding the shipment of arms and ammunition across the border or into Mexico, aren't we really favoring the Huerta party in that it can receive arms from abroad, whereas the insurgents have been almost entirely disabled by our very action?

I daresay that is the practical operation of it.

In that connection, Mr. President, can you say anything about the reports that the embargo will be lifted?

No, sir, I have nothing to say about that. That is a report that has been recurring, as you remember, for several weeks.

Mr. President, have you any information as to whether there are any arms now being received by Huerta from Japan or whether the contract has been filled?

I remember it was said that the shipment was set up in two installments, so to speak. I think, when I received that information, that one shipment had already been made and the other was to be made, if I remember rightly, the next month, in February. That is my present recollection, but I wouldn't depend on it.

Is Huerta getting arms from any other country?

Oh, yes, and he has a very large assortment of arms which are not in use, and enough ammunition to do business with for a long time, but there is no business doing.

Mr. President, at present, then, you are going to continue your policy of simply watching things down there and letting them take their course?

Yes, sir, that is the settled part of my policy.

Well, I meant that there is nothing to indicate any particular change such as the lifting of the embargo?

Well, I won't say about that except from day to day, because I don't want to make any predictions at all.

Mr. President, can you tell us anything about your information concerning the visit of the Japanese sailors to Mexico City?[3]

Why, I understood that the captain and a number of officers, I think about fifteen, from the *Idzuma*, the Japanese cruiser that has just arrived, were to go up to Mexico City and present their respects to the government there, just as the British admiral did when he arrived—you remember, the British Admiral Cradock; and the German did the same. So there is nothing novel in that or unusual.

Mr. President, when the new British Ambassador goes to Mexico City, the British government will be confronted again with the question of according recognition to the Huerta Government.

Do we know for certain that there is going to be a new British Ambassador?

No, sir, I do not.

Neither do I. I really don't know. Of course that question would arise again in that case.

I thought you had that information from Mr. [Walter Hines] Page.

No, we simply learned from Mr. Page what the newspapers contained—that that was reported. He apprises us of what is being reported as well as of what he knows to be true.

I saw a newspaper dispatch—I think it was an Associated Press dispatch—from London several weeks ago saying that, when Mr. Page was asked about the report that Sir Lionel Carden was to be recalled, he admitted that he knew it and readily named his successor.

Well, I should receive that with several grains of salt.

The morning papers say that the London *Times* has announced that Sir Lionel starts home very shortly.[4]

I understand that that is true on business but not necessarily for the other reason.

Mr. President, can you tell us something about your information with regard to the present condition of the Huerta government, financially and otherwise?

Why, I understand that he is getting absolutely no money from the outside and that he is living, as the paper expressed it this morning, "on the country," by forced contributions of every sort and increased taxes.

And that of course is causing a great deal of dissatisfaction?

Yes, I think it is.

Do you know whether that extends to Mexico City?

Whether the dissatisfaction extends to Mexico City?

Yes.

No, I don't; I can't say that I know anything about the state of mind in Mexico City.

Mr. President, can you say anything with regard to the progress towards the settlement of the California land controversy in Japan?[5]

The California land controversy is past history. They are not trying to settle that.

Is it to be left as it is?

Well, have you anything else to suggest? What are we going to do about it?

I don't know.

The Government of the United States cannot tell the State of California what its land laws are to be.

The question is, Mr. President, what is Japan going to do?

I do not know. You will have to ask Japan. There is nothing pending, if that is what you mean.

Mr. President, Japan has suggested that her citizens and subjects in this country be given the [same] rights of naturalization as American citizens as other immigrants have. That was included in her note, I understand; has anything been done by Japan to push that plan?

No, and I do not remember that that was proposed. There again, the matter is many months old, and I cannot speak with perfect confidence.

Is it a fact, Mr. President, that there are negotiations looking to either a treaty or protocol to eliminate these points in dispute?

It is a fact that we are discussing the various proposals so as to make our friendship and attitude toward Japan perfectly evident, but nothing has been formulated, if that is what you mean.

Mr. President, have you ever expressed yourself publicly in regard to the matter of making treaties the law of the land?

They are the law of the land.

I mean the laws of the country override the rights of the states.

No, because that is a legal question in which my opinion would not be of very much value. The language of the Constitution is very interesting. I cannot recall it exactly, but it says that "this Constitution and the laws made in pursuance thereof and the treaties of the United States shall be the supreme laws of the land."[6] In other words, it does not seem to limit the treaties by the Constitution. It says that the Constitution and the laws made in pursuance thereof, that is to say, in pursuance of the Constitution, shall be the supreme laws of the land, and that the treaties shall also be. Now, whether that means that the United States can exercise treaty powers to a greater extent than it can exercise domestic power is the legal question which I suppose that language leaves open to debate.

In other words, the Constitution gives the states certain rights with regard to making laws?

Yes, clearly; that is to say, imposes certain limitations on the federal government.

Mr. President, you could not by treaty do anything that you cannot do by statute, can you?

That is just the question.

Because otherwise you could override the Constitution with a treaty.

Yes, theoretically you could. Of course, we are opening here a purely theoretical question—I mean here now in what is being asked. Theoretically, it might be maintained that the Government of the United States, being given the exclusive treaty-making power, could make any kind of treaties that any other government could make. And, on the other hand, it would probably be maintained that the general character of the treaty-making power was not unlimited, and that the general limitations on federal action applied to the federal government under the Constitution [when it made treaties].

The Supreme Court has held that treaties and laws are paramount—that a treaty can be repealed by a law and that the law can be repealed by the treaty, but it does not place the treaty in a higher position than the law.

No; it might put it in a different position, however.

What action would be necessary to make it clear?

Why, a case at law in which the Supreme Court would hold one way or the other.

Is there a difference between a federal and a state statute in that matter of treaty rights? Is the state statute given a higher plane?

Of course, as Mr. Low[7] says, the Supreme Court has held that a law passed, let us say, this year that is inconsistent with the preceding treaty may henceforth abrogate it, since they are upon the same level with each other; but the question whether the treaty will in all cases take precedence over a state statute has never been raised, so far as I know.[8]

Mr. President, is there any prospect that that matter will be brought up in connection with the settlement of the Japanese controversy?

No; you see it is like constitutional questions in England. The British Parliament can do anything that it pleases, but it will never please to do anything that British opinion does not approve. So it is purely a theoretical question.

Mr. President, has the Mexican situation served to group the Russian treaty matter and the Japanese situation and the Colombian interchanges in your mind?[9]

No, not at all. They have absolutely no connection with one another.

Mr. President, has the United States Government any suggestions whatever to give Mr. Pindell[10] to secure [the rights of an American citizen] when he goes to Russia with a passport?

No, sir; at least, I have not thought of any. Now, I want to make this suggestion, gentlemen: the foreign policy of the government is the one field in which, if you will permit me to say so, you ought not to speculate about in public, because the minute the newspapers in any large number state a certain thing to be under consideration by the administration, that is of course telegraphed all over the world and makes a certain impression upon foreign governments, and may very easily render the things that we really intend to do impossible. The rumors that I have seen in the last couple of days[11] are absolutely unfounded, and they are embarrassing the government. That is the long and short of it. And I feel the thing very keenly. I do not think that the newspapers of the country have the right to embarrass their own country in the settlement of matters which have to be handled with delicacy and candor. I have seen it stated, in one or two papers at any rate, that I, as the Executive, was considering certain things that had never come into my mind as courses of action. Now, if in dealing with the representative of the government concerned, I state an entirely different proposition and let it be inferred that the other course never occurred to me, there is some danger that I be regarded as disingenuous, that I am not saying what I really have up my sleeve, when I have nothing up my sleeve. It is a very serious disservice to the country to embarrass the foreign policy of the government in that way. I say that without any feeling of criticism but in order that you may know how seriously these things affect public policy. With regard to domestic matters, it is a very different question, because we are all on the inside, and we can all exchange suggestions as to possible courses of action. But that is not true with regard to the foreign policy of the government. For example, you take the Japanese question or a Russian question or a German question or an Italian or French question, and there is no such interchange of editorial and other knowledge between us and them as there is, for instance, between us and England. A great deal more of what is being thought in the United States—because it is thought in English—is known in England than is known in the other countries. I can illustrate it in this way: I once said at a dinner, when we were welcoming to New York one of the representatives of the English government, that I doubted whether it was a very valid argument to say that our cordial relations with England were based chiefly upon our speaking of the same language, because when, for example, a French newspaper was disagreeable about the United States, most of us did not know it, but that we all read the *Saturday Review*, and that, therefore, we knew the uncomfortable opinions which were entertained about us in some quarters of England very much more than we did the uncomfortable opinions of us in foreign countries.[12] Of course, I said that in entire pleasantry, because I knew one of the editors of the *Saturday Review* to be present, but I meant, and mean now, the point seriously. Things that affect foreign countries are telegraphed; the main body of our opinion goes unnoted amongst them; and therefore a vast deal of damage can be done by such speculations as I have seen in one or two papers, at any rate, during the last day or two, since that conference at the White House with the Foreign Relations Committee.[13] I take it that the newspapers do not want to render it impossible for me to confer with the Foreign Relations Committee; but it will be rendered impossible if every time I confer with them there is mischief to pay somewhere. As I told you gentlemen with the utmost frankness after that conference, there is no crisis that I know of anywhere, unless you consider the Mexican situation as a perpetual crisis. There is no new phase or situation.

Mr. President, it seems to me that the papers have been almost unanimous in reflecting just that view.

Almost unanimous, yes; and a very large majority of the papers have handled the thing with discretion.

Certainly, Mr. President, a number of gentlemen there that night carried away the impression that a number of the questions that were discussed there were interrelated.

Yes, they were all interrelated; because I naturally do not confer with the Foreign Relations Committee except upon subjects that we ought all to be forming a judgment about for action. In other words, I do not bring up things that are not pending.

Mr. President, can you say anything about the pending arbitration treaties?

I understand that they are in a fair way to be reported out. That is my information, though I did not get that directly from the committee.

You impressed upon a number of the committee your desire?

Yes, I expressed it very earnestly.

Mr. President, are you expecting any action by the committee in regard to the Nicaraguan treaty?

I do not know what the stage is that that has reached.

Mr. President, have you expressed yourself with regard to the merits of the literacy test in the immigration bill?

No, I have not put my mind strongly on the subject.

Mr. President, might I ask that, if it appears up here with that test in it, you will still give hearings to people who might be opposed to it?

I suppose I should, if they applied for them. I don't know.

Mr. President, have you made any progress toward the selection of members of the Federal Reserve Board?

The progress being this, that almost every time I have a lucid interval in my day I turn to it. My mind is beginning to center on certain men, but I am leaving myself entirely at liberty to jump to somebody else if he looks better.

Can you add anything to the Panama tolls question?

No; there is nothing at present to add.

Mr. President, have you given any consideration to a suggestion to modify the Federal Reserve Act and make it a little easier for some of the trust companies and savings companies to come in?[14]

My attention was drawn to what the gentlemen who were in conference on the bill seemed to admit was an oversight. The first provision of the bill, which was that all the reserves should be put in National banks, was left in there after it had been taken out in the Senate. I understand that that was but an oversight. What they are going to do about it I do not know.

Aren't the requirements of capital pretty onerous for the smaller trust companies in the smaller cities—the amount of capital they would have to have?

I have not heard them complain. No more onerous for them than for the National banks.

Except that the National banks have had considerable advantage in getting in capital. A good many trust companies have started with smaller amounts.

That is true of the smaller ones.

[1] Newspaper stories had reported that relations with Japan were deteriorating as a result of Japanese arms sales to Huerta. See the *Washington Post*, Jan. 27-28, 1914.

[2] A reference to the Joint Resolution of March 14, 1912.

[3] The Japanese cruiser *Idzuma* was calling at Mexico's Pacific ports. When a delegation of sailors traveled to Mexico City to pay their respects, they were fêted with a five-day celebration. See the *Washington Post*, Jan. 28, 1914.

[4] See *ibid.*, Jan. 29, 1914.

[5] The Japanese government was being criticized by its opposition for not protesting against the California land-tenure law more strenuously. See *ibid.*, Jan. 27, 1914.

[6] Article VI.

[7] Alfred Maurice Low, chief American correspondent of the London *Morning Post*.

[8] This issue had been raised in a number of cases and decided in favor of the primacy of the federal treaty-making power. This was the opinion of the Supreme Court in the case of *Hauenstein v. Lynham* (1880), 100 U. S. 483, when it held against the right of the State of Virginia to make a law denying property rights to Swiss citizens secured by federal treaty.

[9] The *Washington Post*, Jan. 27-29, linked these issues in a series of stories.

[10] The Senate confirmed Pindell as Ambassador to Russia on January 26. See *ibid.*, Jan. 27, 1914.

[11] That is, that the Wilson administration was worried by potential difficulties with several foreign nations simultaneously.

[12] For Wilson's remarks, see *PWW*, Vol. 15, pp. 147-49.

[13] Wilson met with the Senate Foreign Relations Committee at the White House on the evening of January 26. The newspaper accounts about a crisis in foreign policy linking Mexico and Japan resulted from that meeting, and from an interview that followed with reporters, in which Wilson said that the United States found itself now estranged from virtually every major power in both hemispheres. Wilson described the combination of difficulties as being related to each other only in that they were occurring at the same time, but he warned that the situation with Mexico, which was not really related to any of the other problems, could aggravate them all. The *New York Times*, Jan. 28, 1914, carried an exclusive report based on an interview which Wilson gave to Charles Willis Thompson; it is printed in *PWW*, Vol. 29, pp. 180-84. See also the *Washington Post*, Jan. 27-28, 1914.

[14] Trust companies and state banks had two major complaints against the new Federal Reserve System: they had difficulty meeting minimum reserve requirements under their present capitalization, and they thought that banks in Federal Reserve cities had an unfair advantage because of their proximity to reserves. See the *Washington Post*, Jan. 30, 1914.

Feb. 2, 1914

Isn't this Ground Hog Day?

Yes it is. I always forget, sooner or later, whether he goes back if he sees his shadow or doesn't see it.

Mr. President, is Mr. Underwood's visit today with reference to the legislative program?[1]

To tell the truth, I don't know. Mr. Underwood is coming today, is he? I don't know what the object of his visit is.

There is a story that he was to set up a definite program.

Well, he always does. I mean, the caucus always adopts [one], as I understand it.

Have you received word from businessmen generally, expressing a desire or willingness to appear before either of the two committees with regard to the trust measures?

I have been surprised that I have not, and the committee has advertised—I mean, judging by all the correspondence—has advertised that it would conduct hearings, and it has had very little response to it. I don't know whether the businessmen of the country are merely willing to trust us to frame the measures or whether they haven't taken notice.

One of the papers suggests this morning that they are afraid their appearance here may cause misunderstanding, that they might be branded as lobbyists.

Of course they wouldn't be branded as lobbyists if they came on invitation. And the invitation is out. And besides, I am not in the branding business.

Mr. President, returning to this visit of Mr. Bulkley,[2] he is the chairman of the committee which was appointed by the House to draft rural-credit legislation?

As chairman of the subcommittee which was appointed by the House Committee on Banking and Currency to take charge of it.

This bill[3] was introduced the other day as an administration bill. As was reported in some of the other papers, Mr. Bulkley is out of the job. If you will pardon me for saying so, that is bad reasoning.

On the contrary, the bill introduced was not a bill formulated by that committee, and that committee, before introducing its report and before introducing the bill, did bring the bill to me, and I said, so far as I can judge, it is a sound bill. And it is to go, of course, to the judgment of the House committee, and it will depend on whether they think it is a sound bill.

Mr. President, have you expressed your opinion to the members of Congress with regard to the literacy provision of the immigration bill?[4]

No, I haven't. I feel this delicacy about all such cases. I think it is bad manners, at least for the President, to say, before he is asked, whether he agrees with Congress or not when a definite bill is under discussion. Of course, if he is consulted beforehand, that is another matter.

Have you been informed, Mr. President, that the Senate is about to consult you?

I recently saw that in the papers. I haven't learned of it. They haven't notified us.

You wouldn't care, at this time, to express yourself?

No. I think I ought to see, first, if they consult me.

Would you care to say, Mr. President, whether there could be some restrictions placed by the Senate?

I think we are all agreed that we should carefully study the restrictions to assess their effect on immigration.

Mr. President, is there anything you can tell us about foreign affairs—Mexico and Japan?

Since I saw you gentlemen last, nothing that I recall your asking about has turned up. Our dispatches have been very few—just of the routine sort. So there is nothing new that I know of.

Has there been anything from Salvador indicating a condition of unrest down there?

No, sir, not that I have heard.

What is the status, Mr. President, of the Russian treaty matter?[5] There were three gentlemen here last week who said they discussed it with you and shed further light—Mr. Marshall[6] and one or two others with him.

I don't remember that those gentlemen discussed a possible treaty with me. No. It comes back to me now. They discussed the literacy test. That was their errand.

They didn't comment on the treaty themselves?

No. They did not discuss the Russian treaty.

Mr. President, with reference to the commercial treaties, it is suggested in one of the morning papers that there is a movement in which you intend to broaden the scope of some of the treaties. Mr. Underwood, some weeks ago, gave an interview in which he said that the present treaties were inadequate, that they hampered trade, and then another suggestion was renewed, that there may be some attempt to broaden the range, perhaps, of certain features. Is there anything to that?[7]

I saw what you allude to in the *Washington Post* this morning, but it was the first that I knew of it. I often learn things for the first time in the *Washington Post*, particularly things that concern me. Of course, it was linked in that article, apparently, to the headlines. I seldom get beyond the headlines. As for the arbitration treaties, of course, it had nothing to do with them.

I think the article distinguished—

Perhaps the article did. For the rest, I simply know nothing of the thing you allude to, though it is quite possible that the State Department may have expressed some opinion to the leaders upon the Hill that the reporter may have confused with something from myself.

Mr. Underwood's position itself was very astonishing. He practically suggested the denunciation of the present commercial treaties and the redrafting of them in a form acceptable to the United States. Of course, that is rather difficult.

Yes. It would be a big task, at any rate.

Mr. President, do you know whether Dr. Gulick[8] was to talk with you today to discuss the Japanese situation or his plan to restrict immigration, in which he is interested?

He simply asked for an interview. He didn't state the subject. He is interested in that, then, is he?

He is interested in restricting it to 5 per cent of the naturalized citizens of whatever nation it might be. He is after a settlement of the immigration question, particularly in relation to Japan.[9]

No, I don't know. Possibly he may discuss either or both.

Mr. President, some of the newspapers in the Middle West are saying that [support] is being asked of you in the interest of Sullivan[10] and that means that it is a situation that you are interested in.

I hope you gentlemen will understand that no candidacies are approved officially by me, because it is none of my business.

I was going to ask that question, whether in any primary contest—[11]

No, I haven't, in any instance, and I don't expect to in any instance.

Has there been any development in Haiti, Mr. President, that demands action on our part?[12]

I don't know how fast it is developing there, to tell the truth. The President, I suppose, if he is still being called that, has left the island, and there are three candidates at the head of three armies who are seeking to rally the populace behind them. That is the present situation. I don't know of any new development.

Senator Vardaman delivered a very interesting lecture on Negro rights in the Senate the other day.[13]
Mr. President, have you settled on the Commandant of the Marine Corps yet?

Well, I will leave that to the Secretary of the Navy to announce. He consulted me the other day.[14]

Have you had anything to worry about because a number of these peace treaties are stymied in the Senate, or is there some reason for delay?[15]

I can't answer that. I don't know of any delay. They are almost identical in terms. It may be the Secretary's idea [that] it will save the time of the Senate to consider them in groups. I think he told me the other day that there were eleven countries now that had expressed their willingness to enter into the agreement. He may be waiting for the negotiation of other treaties.

Those peace treaties?

The treaties he agreed to submit. There are a couple of disputes to investigate.

Mr. President, have you given any consideration to the recommendations of certain of the cabinet [members] about the retirement of superannuated employees, this first measure for that retirement?

I think that that question has come up about every other time in cabinet meetings because it is, of course, one of the serious questions. Everybody feels disinclined to throw the oldest employees on the cold world. Yet it is a problem what to do with them. But it hasn't come to me with any definite proposition.

Have any of the cabinet officers suggested two-term employment, which was suggested here in Congress several seasons ago—a seven-year term—a civil-service appointment?

No, sir.

---

[1] That is, in his capacity as House Majority Leader.

[2] Representative Robert Johns Bulkley, Democrat of Ohio.

[3] A bill sponsored by Senator George William Norris, Republican of Nebraska, and Representative Ellsworth Raymond Bathrick, Democrat of Ohio, which would have involved the federal government directly in the business of lending money to farmers. Wilson preferred another bill written by Senator Fletcher because it promoted privately controlled rural banks under federal charter. See the *New York Times*, Jan. 29, 1914, and Link, *The New Freedom*, p. 261.

[4] Wilson was known to disapprove of the literacy test to determine the suitability of potential immigrants to the United States.

[5] That is, the negotiation to replace the Convention of 1832, abrogated during the Taft administration in protest against Russian treatment of American Jews.

[6] Louis Marshall of New York, president of the American Jewish Congress. The other two callers were Dr. Cyrus Adler and Abram Isaac Elkus, of Philadelphia and New York. These prominent Jewish leaders, who wanted protection for American Jews in Russia, visited Wilson on January 29 and were reported to have discussed the prospective treaty with the President. See the *New York Times*, Jan. 30, 1914.

[7] See the *Washington Post*, Feb. 2, 1914. The *Post* story referred to Wilson's desire to renegotiate expiring arbitration treaties, not to the need for a general renegotiation of commercial treaties.

[8] Dr. Sidney Lewis Gulick, missionary and lecturer at the Imperial University of Japan, Kyoto.

[9] Gulick proposed a quota system whereby annual immigration from any country would be limited to 5 per cent of the naturalized citizens and their children originating in that country. As Gulick pointed out, this would favor immigration from northern Europe. See the *New York Times*, Jan. 30, 1914.

[10] Roger Sullivan, Democratic leader of Illinois.

[11] Sullivan was engaged in a bitter primary battle for the Democratic senatorial nomination in Illinois, and the reporter wanted to know if Wilson would interfere. For a discussion of this issue, see John Morton Blum, *Joe Tumulty and the Wilson Era* (Boston, 1951), pp. 82-83.

[12] A revolution in Haiti had forced President Michel Oreste to seek shelter on a German warship. Power resided in the armies of Generals Davilmar Théodore, Oreste Zamor, and Charles Zamor. See the *New York Times*, Feb. 1, 1914; and for background, see Hans Schmidt, *The United States and the Occupation of Haiti, 1915-1934* (New Brunswick, N. J., 1971), pp. 42-51.

[13] Senator James Kimble Vardaman, Democrat of Mississippi, made several statements on

January 31 in opposition to the application of progressive principles to black Americans. See *Cong. Record*, 63d Cong., 2d sess., pp. 2650-53.

[14] The Secretary of the Navy announced the appointment of Col. Barnett on February 2.

[15] Eight of Bryan's "cooling off" treaties had been approved by the Senate Foreign Relations Committee on January 30. See the *New York Times*, Jan. 31, 1914.


Feb. 5, 1914

Mr. President, can you say something about the conference you had with Mr. Palmer and State Chairman Morris yesterday with reference to the Pennsylvania situation?[1]

Well, I do not know that there is much to say. They were kind enough to consult me as to my judgment about giving up my Secretary of Labor[2] and I told them that that would be a very serious thing for me to do; and they readjusted their plans partially on the basis of that. Of course, I told them, as I would in any case where state politics were involved, that I would leave it entirely to their judgment what they were to do. I would not intervene.

Well, this is not to be taken, then, as a ticket with your O.K. on it?

The ticket was, of course, made up by consultation among themselves, and it is made up of men whom I very thoroughly and absolutely believe in.

I understood that they came back here at six o'clock with a view to getting your O.K. on the ticket.

They came back with a view of telling me of the rearrangement they had made in view of my disinclination to give up Mr. Wilson.

Might I ask whether the other candidates who are running for other offices out there will be able to presume that you are not going to interfere in the fight?

They will be able to presume what all the world knows. Of course, everybody in the United States will know that, so far as the two gentlemen already named are concerned, I absolutely believe in them.

But you don't want this to be known as your ticket?

I do not want any ticket to be known as my ticket. You must not pin me down that way; I am back of the men I believe in, but I do not want any ticket labeled my ticket. And I am "agin" the men I do not believe in.

Have you picked out those you believe in, in Illinois?[3]

I am not picking out. I am not in that business. But when they are picked by somebody, then I have an opinion.

Have you decided on anybody who has been picked?

I did not know that anybody had been picked.

Mr. President, will the troops along the border be reduced now as a result of the lack of the necessity of watching so closely?[4]

Of course, they have not all along been agents of the Treasury Department to prevent smuggling, though they have incidentally kept an eye on that, and I do not know of any immediate reason why the number should be reduced. Perhaps their assignment to stations might be altered, but I do not know anything about that. That is left entirely to the War Department.

I understood that you had considered the matter of reducing the number.

That is not true; I have not considered that.

Mr. President, is there any other step which you can tell us of—the next move?

None that I can tell of.

I put it in that way purposely.

I know you did, and I do not want to leave the impression on your minds that there are steps impending, for that would not be true. We are moving step by step to see what effect will be had.

Mr. President, have you received any advice from Mr. O'Shaughnessy as to how the Mexican authorities took the notice of the lifting of the embargo on arms the other day?

No, the news that has been conveyed to us has been negative, namely, that there had been apparently no excitement and that it had not affected the situation in Mexico City, so far as he could see one way or another—just what the newspapers themselves had corroborated this morning.

Mr. President, has there been anything of late from Mr. Lind?

No, not, I think, for a couple of days.

He is still at Veracruz?

Oh, yes.

Mr. President, it is reported today that Mr. Bryan is planning, with your approval, a trip to Europe in the next few months.

I had not heard of it.

Mr. President, are you likely to announce anything on the Panama tolls controversy?

I did not know that there was anything to announce.

There have been a number of conflicting reports as to your position on free tolls.

I do not see why there should be any conflicting reports. My position is perfectly well known.

Mr. President, Senator O'Gorman said yesterday, following a talk with you, that it was his impression that the Panama tolls question might not come up at the present session; and, inasmuch as ships are supposed to go through the Canal before the next session, I wonder how you feel about it.[5]

All I can say is that Senator O'Gorman did not get that impression from me.

Mr. President, in the British note of protest it was stated that the British government had some doubt as to whether they had any reason to object if the exemption provision could be confined absolutely and exclusively to our coastwise ships; but they intimated that there might be some difficulty in distinguishing between our coastwise trade and our foreign trade. Have you any thought of seeing that the regulations were framed so as there would be no doubt at all about their applying to our coastwise ships only?[6]

It has been some time since I read that note. My recollection of it does not correspond with yours that they intimated that that was a debatable point.

I think they said they might concede the point if it could be kept exclusively to our coastwise trade.

That "If" has not been debated.

Mr. President, is it true, as it is reported, that you favor a two-battleship program this year?

I am naturally back of the recommendation of the Secretary—I mean in specific matters like that.

Mr. President, would you mind telling us what your position is on the Panama tolls question?

I earnestly hope that the provision exempting American coast-wise ships will be repealed.

Well, now Mr. President, are you going to attempt to have Congress take any action at this session with regard to that? There are two bills pending, or, rather, one bill pending and one suggested.[7]

I shall use any legitimate influence I have to bring that about, yes—to bring about the repeal.

At this session?

Oh, of course.

Mr. President, what has been done lately towards the convening of the Hague conference?

I am afraid I am a little vague on that subject. Mr. van Dyke, who is our Minister at The Hague, made a suggestion the other day as to the practical first step, which Mr. Bryan brought to my attention. As to just the form of it, I am ashamed to say at this moment that I do not remember it; but the first step has been taken towards the calling of the conference.[8]

I understood that all other foreign governments refused to take that initiatory step.

I did not understand that they had refused. I understood that they had not taken it.

Mr. President, are there any conferences set on the immigration question with members of Congress?

No.

Mr. President, might we know what your attitude has been towards this literacy test in the immigration bill?

I do not think I had better talk about that. I do not like to say with regard to a pending bill what my attitude is. It is not very respectful to the houses.

Might I ask whether you have expressed any opinion about taking it up further at this session?

No, I have expressed no opinion about that.

Mr. President, there has been a suggestion that you may read a message on the Panama tolls controversy. Are you contemplating that?

If you have attended some of the conferences I have been holding recently, you would know that it has been suggested that I send a message on everything under heaven; but I am not in the message business as a profession.

[1] On February 4, Wilson met with Representative Alexander Mitchell Palmer and Roland Sletor Morris to discuss the political situation in Pennsylvania. See the *New York Times*, Feb. 5, 1914.

[2] To be a candidate for United States Senator from Pennsylvania. Wilson persuaded Palmer to run instead, with Vance Criswell McCormick as candidate for Governor.

[3] See above, Feb. 2, 1914.

[4] Wilson issued a proclamation on February 3 lifting the arms embargo against Mexico and recognizing the Constitutionalists as a belligerent party. The *New York Times* reported on February 5 that troops were being withdrawn from border patrol duty in Douglas, Arizona. See also the *New York Times*, Feb. 4, 1914; WW to Bryan, with Enclosure, Jan. 31, 1914, printed in *PWW*, Vol. 29, pp. 206-208; and Press Release, Feb. 3, 1914, printed in *ibid.*, pp. 216-17.

[5] After a meeting with Wilson on February 4, O'Gorman said that he doubted that the Panama Canal tolls controversy could be settled during the current session of Congress. See the *New York Times*, Feb. 5, 1914.

[6] In a protest note of November 14, 1912, the British argued that the exemption would not violate the Hay-Pauncefote Treaty if it applied only to American coastwise shipping, but that it would be virtually impossible to limit the exemption. See the Secretary of State for Foreign Affairs of Great Britain to the British Ambassador, Nov. 14, 1912, in *FR, 1912*, pp. 481-89, and Link, *The New Freedom*, p. 305, n. 100.

[7] The pending bill was sponsored by Representative Adamson of Georgia and would have suspended the exemption provisions for two years. See the *New York Times*, Feb. 6, 1914.

[8] Henry van Dyke, American Minister at The Hague, had communicated with Queen Wilhelmina of the Netherlands, which had led to the placing of the matter before other foreign diplomats in the Dutch capital. See *ibid.*, Feb. 5, 1914.

Feb. 9, 1914

Mr. President, could you say anything about the conference you are going to have with Governor Glynn of New York?[1]

No, sir, I cannot, because I do not know what he is going to talk to me about.

Are you interested in the reorganization of the Democratic party in New York?

I would naturally be very interested in that.

Could you give us any ideas about that?

No, I could not. The ideas originate in New York State.

Mr. President, have you interested yourself at all in this matter of taxation and taxation bills for here in Washington?

No, frankly, I have not, in one sense. That is to say, I have not interested myself in the sense that I have been studying them, because I have not had time. I am interested in them and have picked up all that I could by the wayside.

How do you stand on the half-and-half proposition?[2]

I do not stand at all, because I have not studied it. I am "walking."

Mr. President, is it true that you have given your views on immigration to Senator Smith of South Carolina, the chairman of the committee?[3]

Yes.

On the literacy test?

Yes.

Could you give them to us, Mr. President?

Well, I would rather leave that to the Senator and the committee, because when men seek my advice, I think, so far as I am concerned, it is confidential.

Mr. President, there has been some discussion of your position with regard to canal tolls and its relation to the Baltimore platform.[4] Could you take us into your confidence?

Why, certainly; I think that a platform declaration on such a subject as that is necessarily related to the circumstances, and the circumstances arise all over the world as well as in the United States. In other words, when there are elements which we cannot control in the situation, only those elements which we can control bind us, and I think that a change of circumstance changes the attitude of the government and will change the attitude of the country towards it.

You mean change of circumstances with reference to the attitude of Europe on the question?

Well, that will be involved, yes—the whole international situation and the point of view of the governments, and everything of that sort.

Since the Baltimore convention, Mr. President, have you changed your mind with reference to the exemption of tolls or exemption of American coastwise ships from paying tolls?

From the first, personally—speaking only for myself—I have regarded it as an unwise policy.

Your position at this time, however, Mr. President, is based on the international aspect rather than national aspect?

Well, I cannot say rather than the national aspect, because that plays a very important part in it.

You think it unwise with regard to the treaty provisions or as an American policy?

Well, I have already expressed in a letter, which Mr. Marbury published, my personal opinion about the treaty aspects of it.[5]

Mr. President, can you tell us whether there have been any representations from other foreign governments otherwise than England on the subject of canal tolls?

No, sir, there have not.

Have there been any intimations conveyed to Great Britain since the last note as to our attitude other than the announcements of the press?

No, and I have not been approached concerning it by the British Ambassador since Mr. Bryce left. Just before Mr. Bryce left, we exchanged half a dozen sentences about it, and since then it has not been brought up.

May I ask whether Villa has made any satisfactory representations with regard to the Spaniards in Torreón?[6]

Of course, as a matter of fact, we are not in communication with Villa. But, indirectly, through the officers on the border, I understand that his attitude is becoming a very correct one, indeed, about the whole question of the safeguarding of foreigners, the Spaniards included.

Have we had any information, Mr. President, that might shed some light on the situation in Mexico City or Veracruz?

No, I cannot say that I have.

Is there anything connected with the conference with the Secretary of State yesterday that you can tell us?

That was just with regard to minor matters which had to be attended to at once. It did not concern anything critical at all— some business in Santo Domingo and one or two other matters.

Are you ready to announce a new Ambassador to Russia, Mr. President?[7]

No, sir, I wish I were.

Are you not ready to announce the Ambassador to Paris?

No, sir.

Mr. President, is the fifth antitrust bill now in contemplation the one placing the stocks of railroads under the Interstate Commerce Commission?[8]

Not that I know of. I have not counted them. I have heard that they are called the five brothers. Is one of them missing?

Yes, one of them is missing.

On what subject?

On the placing of the stocks and financial operations of railroads under the Interstate Commerce Commission.

You know, there have already been introduced into Congress several comprehensive bills on that subject, and I do not believe that any new bill is going to be planned.

Is there any particular bill that you have in mind that would fit in with your program?

Do you mean that is not yet formulated?

Yes.

No.

Among those that are pending that would fit in with your program covering that one point?

You mean introduced by individual members?

Yes.

I do not know that one bill is preferable to another. They all have excellent features. A sort of combination would be the best.

Mr. President, in connection with the Panama tolls question, have you determined yet that you will go to Congress yourself with a message?

I do not see that that would be necessary. It is a simple point, and my position is so clearly known it would look like a sort of—

Do you think you can accomplish just as much by taking counsel with individual members?

I hope so. I do not know that my spoken word in the Congress has very much importance.

Mr. President, does that mean that you will not write anything at all?

I am not binding myself on anything. I am ready to break loose at any minute.

Mr. President, in the Haitian affair, the Congress down there has selected one of the Zamor brothers as President;[9] is there anything in your mind right now that would indicate whether you are going to support him or not?

We will wait and see what happens—see how they handle it. We found that we had made a mistake the other day. We thought there were five candidates with armies, but we have found that one of them has two names and we were counting him twice.

---

[1] At a conference later on February 9 with Governor Martin Henry Glynn and William Frank McCombs, Wilson gave his approval to their attempts to reform the Democratic party in New York by reorganizing the party's structure and promoting William Church Osborn for the state chairmanship, with the ultimate goal of ridding the party of the Tammany boss, Charles Francis Murphy. See the *New York Times*, Feb. 10, 1914.

[2] Under the Organic Law of 1878, Congress provided that the federal government would pay half of the expense of running the capital city. This "half-and-half" provision was changed in 1919, when the federal contribution was scaled down. See Constance McLaughlin Green, *Washington: Capital City, 1879-1950* (Princeton, N. J., 1963), pp. 4-5, 274.

[3] Senator Ellison DuRant Smith, Democrat of South Carolina, chairman of the Immigration

Committee, told reporters, after a meeting with the President on February 9, that Wilson favored amending the literacy-test provision of the immigration bill. See the *New York Times*, Feb. 10, 1914.

⁴ The Democratic platform of 1912 favored exempting American coastwise shipping from payment of Panama Canal tolls. See Schlesinger and Israel, *American Presidential Elections*, III, 2175.

⁵ Wilson's letter to William Luke Marbury, which stated that the tolls exemption was a clear violation of the Hay-Pauncefote Treaty, had been published in the *New York Times* and other newspapers on Feb. 7, 1914. The letter is printed in *PWW*, Vol. 29, pp. 220-21.

⁶ Villa announced on February 8 that he would protect Spanish citizens and other foreigners in Torreón, then under siege by rebel forces. See the *New York Times*, Feb. 9, 1914, and Hill, *Emissaries to a Revolution*, pp. 160-61.

⁷ Wilson was having a difficult time finding a replacement for Ambassador-designate Pindell, who had withdrawn after the terms of his appointment became known publicly. The President's first choice was Charles Richard Crane of Chicago, but he refused finally on May 18, 1914. Wilson's next choice, Representative William Graves Sharp, Democrat of Ohio, was not appointed because the Russian Ambassador in Washington expressed dissatisfaction with his role as a member of the House Foreign Relations Committee in 1911, when the committee had recommended the denunciation of the Russian-American Commercial Treaty. On June 20, 1914, the President finally appointed George Thomas Marye, a former banker and Democratic leader in California, who was acceptable to the Russian government. Marye was succeeded in early 1916 by David Rowland Francis, a former Governor of Missouri. See Link, *The New Freedom*, p. 103.

⁸ This part of Wilson's program would be put in final form in the Rayburn bill, which was introduced by Representative Rayburn on May 7, 1914. See *ibid.*, p. 426.

⁹ Orestes Zamor was named President on February 8.

Feb. 16, 1914

Mr. President, with reference to the Mexican situation, the British government sent some machine guns and ammunition to Mexico City to protect the legation. Is that contrary to any principle?¹

No. Not at all. They notified us before they did it.

Is there any likelihood of our taking such steps?

I don't see any occasion for it in sight. Everything seems to be very quiet there. The minds of some persons are disturbed. More than anything else [Mexican affairs] seem to be in a state of [decay].

You think the process of decay will require treatment?

Well, sir, I would have to be nearer the patient to diagnose that. The process is certainly going on, yes.

Mr. President, have we recognized the government of Peru?²

The provisional government, yes.

In what way does the accession to power of this new party conform to the direction of our South American policy?

Why, nothing. The President, who was removed, had practically abrogated the power of Congress. The power of Congress was sustained by the Congress, the Supreme Court, and by all the constitutional authorities of the country. There seems to be a clear constitutional process in the land, in short.

It has been said, Mr. President, that that approval, though, was secured by a show of armed men without the approval of the Congress.

There is no evidence of that. On the contrary, my information is that the Congress approved of the show of arms. In other words, that the army acted with the approval of the Congress. That is my information. I was of course very careful to inquire, and that certainly is the version of it which I believe to be true.

Is there anything you can say, Mr. President, with regard to our probable position toward the new government in Haiti?

Well, it is hardly safely settled yet, is it? I gather that it is not, though I haven't read the most recent State Department dispatches from there. I haven't had time.

Before we can take any action there, I suppose you would have to await further developments?

Yes.

Have you had any late advices from Ecuador?[3]

No, sir.

Argentina?[4]

None that have been sent over.

This conference due, Mr. President, in the Japanese embassy, of Ambassador Chinda and Consul Iijima of New York and Consul Numano from 'Frisco, had you heard anything of it at all?[5]

No, sir.

They are very reticent up there as to the purpose.

No, I don't know what that is about.

Have there been any complaints, Mr. President, with regard to our treatment of Japanese in this country?

I haven't heard any.

That is supposed to be the purpose of that meeting, to inquire—

No. I haven't heard of anything at all.

Are you ready, Mr. President, to take us into your confidence with regard to your position on the literacy test?[6]

Has the bill passed the Senate?

It has not.

I thought it might have passed while I was asleep. Why, no, I still feel a strong conviction—it is a compulsion of honor itself— not to speak while a bill is pending about my own attitude upon it, except to those who consult me.

When you said you thought it might have passed while you were asleep, that might mean if you are awake it won't pass?

No. I meant literally asleep. I was speaking literally of being in bed.

Mr. President, can you give us any inkling as to your personnel for the Reserve Board yet?

No. My thoughts are not so much about that yet. I haven't gotten them crystallized.

There has been more or less talk of Secretary Houston leaving the cabinet.

So I have noticed. There is nothing in that. I wouldn't like to break this team I have got. I would feel very much at a loss if I did.

Mr. President, Secretary Bryan came out with an attack on Mr. Roger Sullivan last week. That doesn't change your attitude with reference to the Illinois senatorial fight?[7]

My attitude has been the same as it has been all along the line. I have nothing to do with that matter or any other except my own.

It is reported from time to time, Mr. President, that the South American republics look upon our Mexican policy with fear and trembling. Can you tell us how far the South American republics do approve of our policy in Mexico?

I think I can say with the utmost confidence that I am right that they don't look upon it either with fear or trembling or disapproval, and that they have supported us in it without hesitation.

Have the great nations of South America declined to recognize the Huerta government, Argentina and Chile?

I wish I were able—not sure. My impression is that either Argentina or Brazil has recognized it.

Mr. President, do you intend to urge further action with regard to the Panama toll provisions?

Further action—there hasn't been any yet.

Do you intend to urge further action?

Oh, certainly.

Have you had any conferences on the subject that would cause a disposition to take up that matter?

The conferences I have had make me feel confident that they will be taken up.

Mr. President, if it is a fair question, have you heard that Mr. Underwood is opposed to the repeal?

No, I have not.

Mr. President, is there anything new in your trust program?

No, sir, unless something has turned up that I haven't heard of. I get numerous letters about the subject.

Have the businessmen been showing a greater interest in it than they did?

Yes. They are showing greater interest in some quarters, a very helpful interest, though the interest is not in the—the active interest is not as widespread as I had expected. It makes the impression on me of having been discounted beforehand, and rather taken for granted. That is the general impression I get. The legislation will be taken care of without their taking any interest. I mean, that is, the legislation they expected but was not ready. That is the general impression I get.

Mr. President, the Chamber of Commerce of the United States proposes to take a referendum vote of its members on the five bills.[8] Their rules require forty-five days—between forty-five and fifty days—before they can get that. Would you be willing to urge Congress to hold back on the passage of those bills long enough to permit that?

Of course I could not do that. We are all attempting to bring about the completion of the work of the session and give them a rest not later than a given time, so I shouldn't be justified in urging that they take an interest in that.

What is the given time?

It is generally spoken of as the fifteenth of June.

The results of this referendum might be in in time to assist the Senate.

Yes, although the Senate might act first. Both houses are considering the bills at the same time. There is no telling which will act first.

Has there been any disposition, Mr. President, in conferences with you, to amalgamate these bills and put them in one?

No. I remember in one of the conferences it was said that a number of them might otherwise be united, but that was not spoken of as a plan, just a possibility, to simplify the process.

Mr. President, is this helpful, this public criticism of the sections of the trade commission bill?[9]

Yes. I should say that there was perhaps more interest in it than in any other because, you see, there are two different schools of thinking about that. One is, of the two, a great deal more than we are proposing, making sort of immunity-power arrangements, and the other is more a matter of investigation, so that there are a great many suggestions as to what powers might be given the commission. There are, I think, no serious criticisms as to the powers that are proposed in the bill.[10]

Relatively little criticism to the other features of the bill?

Relatively less.

There have been questions that these conferences favored not making public trade secrets of corporations which are perfectly good.

I think a good deal of the criticism and apprehension about the publicity is based upon an ignorance of the present laws of the United States. The present Bureau of Corporations has very great powers in that direction, and the powers granted this commission are not a very great enlargement upon those. It has been some time since I read the statute creating the bureau, but that is the impression I retain. Certainly that bureau has felt at liberty at any time to report on conditions in numerous corporations.

Mr. President, there has been an amendment to the consular appropriations bill, setting aside a certain five thousand dollars for the entertainment of the Interparliamentary Union next year in this country.[11] Do you favor that?

Oh, yes, sir. It is a very routine operation of courtesy. You see, we started that union, as I remember it. It will be our turn to entertain it in natural rotation next year.

Mr. President, in the hearings on the Owen stock exchange bill, the suggestion was made that could very well receive the committee's approval; that is, the functions contemplated with respect to which publicity might very well be lodged with the proposed trade commission.[12] Have you interested yourself in that at all?

No. I haven't heard that suggestion.

Mr. President, a bill has been proposed providing for the creation of an additional federal judgeship, and adding a provision demanding publicity on recommendations. Is that in contravention of the spirit of the Baltimore platform declaration?[13]

You mean adding it? I ought to be embarrassed at asking just how the platform phrases it. I always thought of that as favoring the policy of disclosing what influences were back [of an appointment]. We would have to buy space in the whole of an edition of some newspaper if we were to publish those who recommended particular persons for office. Our files will hardly contain them. They sag. They groan under them. Most of them are of no significance whatever, at least so far as I know. They come from persons—someone I never heard of.

Mr. President, do you reason from that, as an administrative function, that whether it directs you to do it or not, you may make public the endorsements?

I daresay I might, at any time, so far as my constitutional powers are concerned.

Mr. President, have you received any communications that might show the condition of business throughout the country?

Why, they are constantly coming in, yes. And all of them are encouraging—reassuring.

Have you received any trustworthy information that they are bad?

Why, none showing any widespread conditions that are unsatisfactory. There are spots.

Not affecting a whole trade?

No, not affecting a whole trade.

Mr. Walsh's statement in the papers this morning is rather of a pessimistic nature.[14]

With regard to the unemployed? This is always the unemployed period of the year, and the conditions are always such as to call for some action, if any is possible, to relieve them.

You wouldn't regard the fact that three hundred and fifty thousand people were out of work as unusual at this season of the year?

That is not an established fact, though.

I am only quoting Mr. Walsh.

That has been denied. I don't understand that Mr. Walsh's speech came from his unofficial tour, only from what he had heard.

---

[1] On February 14, the British sent in a legation guard of marines with machine guns from the cruiser *Suffolk*. See the *New York Times*, Feb. 15, 1914.

[2] A revolution in Peru had deposed President Guillermo Billinghurst and replaced him with a governing board led by Col. Oscar Benavides. See *ibid.*, Feb. 4, 1914.

[3] Then undergoing a rebellion led by Gen. Carlos Concha. See *ibid.*, Feb. 12, 1914.

[4] A new cabinet had been appointed amid unrest in Argentina on February 15. See *ibid.*, Feb. 16, 1914.

[5] Ambassador Chinda called the meeting with Kametaro Iijima, Consul General at New York, and Yasataro Numano, Consul General at San Francisco, to gather information about

Japanese-American business and the treatment of alien Japanese in the United States. See the *Washington Post*, Feb. 16, 1914.

[6] The *Washington Post*, February 17, 1914, reported that Wilson would veto the Burnett bill if it contained the literacy test.

[7] For Bryan's attack, see "Sullivan, Senator? No!" in *The Commoner*, XIV (Feb. 1914), 2. Democrats opposed to Sullivan, who was then campaigning for the party's senatorial nomination, formed the Wilson-Bryan Democratic League of Illinois. Wilson, however, refused to take part in the campaign. Sullivan won the Democratic nomination handily, but was defeated narrowly by the Republican candidate, Lawrence Yates Sherman, in November.

[8] The Chamber of Commerce decided on the referendum at its convention in Washington on February 12. See the *New York Times*, Feb. 13, 1914.

[9] The criticism of the Covington bill (about which, see the next note) came during hearings in the House Interstate Commerce Committee. Critics attacked the measure as excessively restrictive and asked that the commission control only larger corporations. See *ibid.*, Feb. 16, 1914.

[10] The bill to create an Interstate Trade Commission, proposed by Representative James Harry Covington of Maryland, empowered the commission to investigate corporate practices, determine violations of the antitrust statutes, and recommend procedures to bring corporations into compliance with the laws. It did not go as far along the lines of federal control as some advanced progressives desired because it created only a new version of the Bureau of Corporations with broader investigative powers. See Link, *The New Freedom*, pp. 425-26.

[11] An amendment to the diplomatic and consular appropriations bill to provide funds for the Interparliamentary Union for the Promotion of International Arbitration. The amendment was rejected by the Senate on June 15, 1914. See *Cong. Record*, 63d Cong., 2d sess., pp. 10472-74.

[12] The bill providing for regulation of the stock exchanges, proposed by Senator Robert Latham Owen of Oklahoma, required full publicity of all facts relating to the value of stocks and stock transactions. This bill, which contained provisions almost identical to those of the Truth-in-Securities Act of 1933, failed to receive administration support and died in the Senate. See Link, *The New Freedom*, p. 426.

[13] The Democratic platform of 1912 favored publicity about recommendations. See Schlesinger and Israel, *American Presidential Elections*, III, 2169.

[14] Francis Patrick Walsh of Kansas City, Missouri, chairman of the Commission on Industrial Relations, reported that 350,000 workers were unemployed in New York City alone. Walsh promised to look into the possibility of governmental action to alleviate the problem. See the *New York Times*, Feb. 16, 1914.

Feb. 26, 1914

Well, I will start the ball rolling by saying that these stories about sending marines to Mexico City are nothing but yarns. There isn't a word of truth in them. We have not been advised by Mr. O'Shaughnessy that it was necessary to do anything of the kind; on the contrary, he has advised us that it was not necessary. These things that I entertain myself by reading in the papers are pure inventions. Only last evening I had a conference with the Secretary of the Navy, who showed me the latest dispatches from Admiral Fletcher, and there was nothing of the kind alleged in his dispatches. It is a mystery to me how these things get started.

Can you say, Mr. President, what the Admiral did say?[1]

Why, it was a dispatch about all sorts of details of the business that he was charged with down there. He simply stated the pros and cons of the argument for and against the sending of marines and that he saw no occasion to do so.

Then, of course, Mr. President, there has been no request on our part for Mr. Huerta's permission to land marines and no refusal on his part?

Certainly not.

Admiral Fletcher, I understand, Mr. President, was opposed to it even if the marines went in civilian clothes.

My recollection isn't as specific as that, but that is my impression, too.

Did he state specifically that it was his recommendation that marines should not be sent to Mexico?

He did not mention it one way or the other. We simply asked him to state the circumstances, and he stated them fairly and dispassionately.

Has the Navy Department ever submitted to the State Department plans for sending a thousand marines to Mexico City?

No, sir, so far as I know.

Mr. President, have we ever given any consideration to sending troops across the border to recover Benton's body?[2]

No, sir.

Could that be done without construing it as an act of war?

Oh, no; that would be an act of war.

Did we not send troops down to Nicaragua, Mr. President, to take charge of the railroad there some years ago to restore order?[3]

I don't remember.

In 1912, Mr. President, I think there was some trouble in Nicaragua.

It must have been done with the consent of the Nicaraguan government.

By invitation of the Nicaraguan government.

That is a very different matter.

Mr. President, one of your predecessors did suggest this very thing—that troops be sent into Mexico for the purpose of establishing order without declaring war, and he did it in a message to Congress.[4]

Yes, I know, but he did not suggest at that time under what theory of international law he was doing it. I saw that message. It was just like saying, "We will come in under arms, but please consider this just a polite call."

But couldn't we do that now?

We could go through the motions, but it would be war all the same.

Mr. President, one of the papers have cited the sending of troops at the time of the Boxer Rebellion as a parallel of the present case, but it is not a parallel, is it?[5]

Not at all a parallel, so far as I can see.

At that time the Chinese government—the central government—frankly admitted its inability to deal with the rebels.

And the embassies at Peking were known to be in immediate danger from these disorderly rebels. I mean they were not under the command of any ordered government or control of any kind. That was an utterly different situation.

Isn't that true of Villa's following.

No, it certainly is not. There are wandering independent bands, as I understand it, in northern Mexico, about whom that would be true, but there is no danger of their getting near Mexico City.

The relief was a light column made with the consent of the Chinese government, was it not?

It was explicitly so.

Mr. President, in Mexico we haven't any recognized government of any sort.

Yes, so far as we are concerned, there isn't any.

Mr. President, have you had any answer from Carranza in regard to the communication sent to him the other day about Benton's body?[6]

No; if so, I have not heard of it.

Could you give us any idea of what is going to be done or what is the present status of the Benton matter?

Why, I think we are slowly finding out the details, after the mist clears away. At first there were all sorts of excited rumors that turned out not to be true; and we are pursuing a necessarily patient course of inquiry, because the process is so slow. It is very difficult. You see, Villa is moving from place to place, and it is very difficult to get into communication with him. Telegraphic communication is, I believe, by a single line and that not always available. So it is a slow process, but we are slowly separating rumor from fact, and I hope within a day or two to know exactly what happened.

Have you had any modification of the terms that we made, that is, as to whether they will permit an additional American representative and a British representative to see the body?

We have not been able to reach him with that; we have not got any reply to it.

Do you know where he is, Mr. President?

The last time I did know he was in Chihuahua.

Mr. President, do you know whether a medical examination would be satisfactory to the British government?

The British government has not made any representation to us on that subject. It has taken the very generous attitude of leaving the investigation to us, and it was at our suggestion—Mr. Bryan's suggestion—that Villa was asked the question if a British representative might accompany our representative. That was not at the suggestion of the British government.

Have you anything showing the character of the man Benton, whether he was peaceful or warlike?

He seems, so far as I can gather, to have been a very aggressive sort of person. Warlike would not be the right term; aggressive, self-assertive.

Mr. President, do you know where Benton's body is?

No, sir, I do not.

Mr. President, has your failure to reach Villa been due to his refusal to see our representative or merely our inability to locate him?

He has been unable to see our representative because of his preoccupation with what he was doing; moving from place to place, he was unable to appoint a place and time, and it has been difficult for us to follow him up, or, rather, for the Consul to follow him up.

He hasn't refused.

Oh, no.

You have asked him to give up the body, have you not?

We have, yes.

Suppose he positively refuses, Mr. President?

Well, I am not answering that question yet. There are so many "Ifs" in this case.

You haven't heard from him then since you did ask him?

No, we have not.

Mr. President, have you modified that request at all to the extent of permitting us to see the body on that side?

We haven't modified it, because we haven't got an answer yet.

The second request was that a medical officer accompany the American Consul, was it not?

Yes, sir.

That is one you have no answer to?

We have no answer to that.

He did answer the first one, did he not?

I am a little confused about that, because the answer you have in mind was not direct from him. In that he seemed to say, not that he refused, but at the proper time he would grant our request. It was couched in very polite language; and then subsequently it was almost immediately learned that he was willing that the widow and some representative of the government should see it.

Should see it, but not have the body?

No, that was not expressly stated, at any rate; so that we have only to conjecture what he meant, whether it was merely to view the body and then reinter it or not. We do not know for a certainty that it was interred.

Mr. President, are the other Americans and Englishmen reported missing yet accounted for?

I believe all but one is, and I am not sure but that the dispatch I have just read does not cover him.

Mr. President, there is a feeling by the British government that if the British Consul goes to Juárez, his life may be in danger. Have you anything to show that that is so?[7]

I do not think there is the slightest foundation for that. I was just reading a dispatch an hour or two ago from one of our Consuls who spoke of the rumor that most Americans were afraid to cross the river to Juárez, but he stated in the telegram that there was no ground for that as far as he could discover.

Was that from General Bliss[8] or Consul Edwards?[9]

I think it was from Edwards.

Mr. President, have you given any consideration to the idea of the formation of another republic of the northern states of Mexico? Has that come before this government in any way?

Certainly not; on the contrary, I have every reason to believe that that is an idea expressly rejected by the Constitutionalists. I mean that they disavow any intention or thought of that sort.

That suggests something that was in the papers yesterday, that there was a dispatch from Mexico City about two weeks ago that this government had made that suggestion to Carranza, or rather it made the suggestion to Carranza that we should send troops into Mexico for the purpose of protecting foreigners in northern Mexico, and he said if we crossed the border it was an act of war and would be resisted.

There was no foundation for that at all.

Mr. President, when you say the idea of forming a northern republic was rejected, can you tell us on what you base that—whether or not Carranza has communicated with this government?

No. I simply base it on what I have heard from men who I am sure know Carranza's mind on that matter and had heard that matter discussed in his presence, and that it was rejected with emphasis—that they were not after merely establishing a local independence; they were after redeeming Mexico from the stain that Huerta had put upon it.

Mr. President, did I understand you to say that you asked Admiral Fletcher for his views on the question of marines?

As to what he understood the situation to be.

Did that follow a discussion of that question here in Washington?

No, sir; except to this extent—that when one or two of the other governments thought that it was necessary to send some sort of guard to their embassies we simply asked O'Shaughnessy whether he felt it was necessary with ours. He said no. As a matter of fact, Mexico City is perfectly quiet. Nobody there would know that anything unusual was going on unless he were behind the scenes.

Mr. President, why were those foreign marines sent there?

I do not know; I can only conjecture. The other governments may have had information that I do not possess, or they may have just thought that the situation in general made it wise.

We were notified, I understand?

Oh, yes.

Have you an idea of the size of the foreign legation forces in Mexico City?

No, but they are very small; eight or ten men, I suppose something like that.

Mr. President, have you any information to show that Huerta's financial resources are any less now than they were last summer?

Well, yes and no. They are less in this respect, that he has absolutely exhausted all the ordinary means of getting money and he is now making arbitrary exactions that are rising in percentage and in character; he is doing simply what amounts to confiscation of property.

Have you heard that there have been any serious objections on the part of the Mexicans to his method of raising money?

Oh, very serious indeed, but they do not dare express them out loud.

Mr. President, have you any knowledge how Carranza and his people are getting money?[10]

No, sir, I have not.

There is a story afloat that he is being financed by certain people in return for private concessions?

Well, I answered your initial question too positively. I don't know where he is getting his money. I was rendered uneasy by those very reports you refer to, and I made a careful investigation and am convinced that it is not true.

They don't center in New York?

No. I am convinced that he is not getting them by private concessions.

Of course, he must be getting it, because we have very good knowledge that he is buying ammunition.

He is getting money, but he is getting it in part, and I daresay in chief part, by levying on the people within his part of the country.

Has he got much actual money that he could live on?

Well, I can't answer that.

Because he probably has to pay cash for what he buys abroad.

Of course, I suppose he has to.

[1] For a paraphrase of Fletcher's report, see the *New York Times*, Feb. 26, 1914. Lind was proposing intervention and had developed a scheme for using marines to capture Mexico City. See Hill, *Emissaries to a Revolution*, pp. 142-44.

[2] William Smith Benton, a British subject engaged in cattle ranching in Chihuahua, was shot by Villa on February 18 for allegedly attacking Villa. This caused a great deal of excitement in England and the United States about the need to intervene to protect lives and property in Mexico. See *FR, 1914*, pp. 842-54; the *New York Times*, Feb. 21, 1914; Hill, *Emissaries to a Revolution*, pp. 148-54; and Kenneth J. Grieb, "El Caso Benton y la diplomacia de la Revolucion," *Historia Méxicana*, XVIII (Oct.-Dec. 1969), 299-301.

[3] During a rebellion in Nicaragua in the summer of 1912, President Adolfo Díaz had invited American intervention to protect lives and property. The Pacific Railway of Nicaragua was taken over by United States marines on September 4. See *FR, 1912*, p. 1043, and U. S. Department of State, *A Brief History of the Relations Between the United States and Nicaragua, 1909-1928* (Washington, 1929), pp. 8-10.

[4] Under similar circumstances in 1859, President James Buchanan had recommended that a law be passed authorizing the President "to employ a sufficient military force to enter Mexico for the purpose of obtaining indemnity for the past and security for the future." Congress failed to take any action on this proposal. See James D. Richardson, ed., *A Compilation of the Messages and Papers of the Presidents, 1789-1897*, 10 vols. (Washington, 1896-99), V, 563-68, and J. Fred Rippy, *The United States and Mexico* (New York, 1926), pp. 212-13.

[5] During the rebellion of the so-called "Boxers" in China in 1900, the United States joined other western nations in sending a relief column to rescue foreigners besieged in Peking. See Kenneth E. Latourette, *A Short History of the Far East*, 3rd edn. (New York, 1957), pp. 434-37.

[6] Secretary of State to Vice-Consul Frederick Simpich, Feb. 24, 1914, in *FR, 1914*, pp. 849-50.

[7] Charles A. S. Perceval, British Consul at Galveston, was ordered to the border on February 24, 1914.

[8] Brig. Gen. Tasker Howard Bliss, U.S.A., Commander of the Southern Department and the cavalry division at Fort Sam Houston in San Antonio.

[9] Thomas D. Edwards, American Consul at Juárez.

[10] Carranza's money came primarily from the revenues of estates in northern Mexico and from ransom paid for the return of captured *hacendados*. See Katz, *Secret War in Mexico*, pp. 253-55.

March 2, 1914

Mr. President, there is some doubt in the morning papers about the question whether this expedition to Chihuahua[1] was halted by the rebels, or by the American ,Consuls, or by the government, or by whom. It doesn't seem to be straight.

It is halted for the time being by Mr. Carranza's sense of his personal dignity, so far as I can discover.

I meant specifically whether orders to the commander at Juárez had stopped it, or our folks had just realized it was some—

It was simply that Carranza wanted to take the matter in his own hands, and we are waiting for a message from him.

The prospect of the expedition going on?.

I take it for granted, yes. Carranza is only wishing to assert himself personally.

Mr. President, what interpretation do you place on this letter to Mr. Bryan? Nothing but a sense of dignity?[2]

Nothing but that he is one of that despised kind known as an academic person. He wants to stand on the letter of the law, whether the facts justify it or not. In other words, he wants every transaction with a foreign government received through his foreign department, and to observe all the bureaucratic procedures.

Do you feel that in the end you will prevail and that the commission will go down there?

I am assuming, of course, it will. I can't imagine accepting a final rejection.

Does Villa submit himself to this authority?

Yes, he does.

Has that been indicated since yesterday?

That was indicated yesterday. That came along with the rest of the dispatches. He simply said, of course, that Carranza was the supreme authority.[3] You will notice in every turn where that question has been raised, he has taken that position.

What about his[4] position that we, the United States, can't make inquiries about British subjects?

He makes it by that statement, that it is none of our business. Of course, we can't insist on acting for England in any case. He has us there, I suppose. If it were an American, of course, we would insist upon satisfaction. We were acting as the nearest friend and as the friend who was in a position to act, and he says we had no right to do so.

But that doesn't mean that we will let it go by the board.

Of course, we were acting largely on the action of the British authorities themselves.[5]

Are the British authorities to negotiate directly with Carranza on that matter?

Not that I know of. Of course, I would like to know what their plans are, but I haven't heard.

If they do, does that mean that this would be dropped?

You realize what it would mean if they did? It would mean their recognition of Carranza as a belligerent, and they have already recognized Huerta. So there you are.

What I am trying to get at, if they don't do it, will this mean following through?

I can't predict. It's a very mixed affair, to tell the truth.

Isn't there a general impression that we have entered into some sort of understanding or agreement with the powers to look after their subjects?

Yes. It is understood that they desire that—if we will, of course. They haven't any right to demand it, and don't demand it, but they desire us to act with all foreigners as we have acted in the case of Benton.

Is there anything new in the Vergera case?[6]

No. We have had two or three dispatches from Mr. O'Shaughnessy yesterday, saying that he had full assurances from Huerta's authorities saying they would follow it up as rapidly as possible.

Have you anything to add to the situation of those going down to Torreón?[7]

No. I don't think that that is at all unnatural. We need time to equip the expedition.

In connection with that, Mr. President, have you kept track of the number of arms that are going across the border?

Oh, no.

Mr. President, this refusal of Carranza has given rise to the story again that it might mean a change of policy on the part of the administration. Are you thinking of a change of policy now?

Well, no I am not. A country of the size and power of the United States can afford to wait just as long as it pleases. Nobody doubts our power and nobody doubts that Mr. Huerta is eventually to retire. There need not be any hesitation in forming the judgment that what we wish to accomplish in Mexico will be accomplished. But these people who are in haste to have things done, as they say, forget that they will have to do them themselves. They will have to contribute brothers and sons and sweethearts and the rest to do it if they want something done right away. If they are willing to wait, that won't be necessary.[8]

Mr. President, has there been any reply to the note that Huerta says he sent to you last week about lifting the embargo on arms?

I have never seen such a note, or seen it in the newspapers.

The British Ambassador said their government had received a copy of it.[9]

We haven't, so far as I have received it.

That was a peculiar message last week.

You must remember that the only thing that Huerta is successful at is being a consummate politician. He issues these things, not to us but for the consumption of Mexican opinion and foreign opinion. It is all a game. There is nothing in it. He is playing to the gallery.

There was also a report last week, Mr. President, that the Secretary [of State] had told the Foreign Relations Committee of the Senate that, but for a friend's interference, there would be a coterie of Germany and France openly against the American policy, but for England's interference.

He couldn't have made such a statement.

Wasn't it that the British attitude prevented a loan being made by Japan and France, something about six or eight weeks ago?

If Mr. Bryan said that, of course he knew what he was talking about. He could certainly have mentioned other circumstances.

France, Belgium, Japan and others had asked Great Britain regarding her attitude to their making a loan, and the government had declined to enter into any arrangement, therefore the banking powers of the other nations retired.

I haven't heard anything of that. This is the first I have heard of it.

Mr. President, are you able to tell us anything about the facts in the Benton killing, as they have been gathered?

No.

That is, have they been finally gathered?

No, sir. Every time you gather them, you gather a fresh crop of rumors, and the thing has a different story.

Mr. President, I'm afraid I didn't get your point about going on with the example of this commission going down there—in view of what Carranza said, we would have to agree that he would have us, whether or not the British government asked us to go, or he could [prevent our going]?

I suppose that is a hypothetical question. He hasn't said that we could go on with it. He simply said what must be done must be done through his authority.

I thought he said that the British government would have to take it up directly with him?

Yes. He said that after this had been assured. He hasn't said that this[10] must be called off, so I don't know just exactly what the circumstances are.

Has the British government communicated with Carranza on that question?

Yes. They are waiting on an investigation.

That was the report, that the commission of their own accord realized the train could not be gotten on. It is not clear whether it was true that they were refused admission to the train and followed instructions or stopped of their own accord.

As a matter of fact, both things happened, although not quite as you put it. That is because they were apprised by us of this position taken by Carranza.[11] They were advised by us and saw themselves that they had better wait and see developments. And then they failed to get permission. It was not that they were forbidden, but they failed to get permission to take the regular train. There wasn't rolling stock enough to make up a special train, as they expected. They were holding the regular train to get permission from Villa, explicit authority to come down, and they didn't get it. And it was told to us that it was because of this dispatch from Carranza.

Then the orders came from Villa and not Carranza?

I would say yes, but I'm not sure just how that happened or how they learned of it.

Is there anything new on the Russian post, Mr. President?

No, sir.

Anything about the trust bills, Mr. President?

No, sir. I suppose I will have conferences this week on the bills. Of course, you all understand that no difficulty has arisen about them. We are simply trying to get counsel from every direction, to see the bills from every point of view, before we finally cast them.

Have you been informed, Mr. President, where the initial action will be begun on the trust question, whether in the House or the Senate?

No.

Mr. President, is the Committee on the Merchant Marine preparing the report today and asking that the Interstate Commerce Commission's authority extend over lake rates, as well as over certain features of international shipping?[12] We will be glad to have the report made available today.

They gave it out yesterday.

That hasn't been brought before you?

No, sir.

[1] A six-member international commission to examine Benton's body at Chihuahua was turned back at Juárez on March 1. Carranza had ordered the commander at Juárez, Colonel Fidel Avila, to refuse the commissioners access to the train to Chihuahua because arrangements for their investigation had not been approved by him. See the *New York Times*, March 2 and 3, 1914, and Collector of Customs Zach Lamar Cobb to the Secretary of State, March 1, 1914, in *FR, 1914*, pp. 857-58.

[2] Carranza wrote to Bryan on February 28 to protest that the United States Government was acting improperly and ought to be negotiating with him rather than Villa in the Benton matter. See the *New York Times*, March 1 and 3, 1914; Hill, *Emissaries to a Revolution*, p. 153; Vice Consul Simpich to the Secretary of State, Feb. 28, 1914, in *FR, 1914*, pp. 856-57.

[3] Collector of Customs Cobb to the Secretary of State, March 1, 1914, in *FR, 1914*, pp. 857-58.

[4] That is, Carranza's, made in his letter to Bryan of February 28.

[5] Ambassador Spring Rice had requested that the State Department undertake an investigation of Benton's disappearance. See the British embassy to the Department of State, Feb. 22, 1914, in *FR, 1914*, p. 847.

[6] Clemente Vergera, a Texas rancher, had been put to death by Mexican Federal soldiers near Hidalgo. See the *New York Times*, March 1 and 3, 1914.

[7] To take part in the Benton investigation.

[8] This statement was given to reporters as a press release by the White House on March 2. It is printed in *PWW*, Vol. 29, p. 302.

[9] It was presented to the State Department on March 3. See the *New York Times*, March 4, 1914.

[10] That is, the commission to investigate Benton's death.

[11] While at Juárez, the commissioners were informed by Bryan that Carranza had questioned their authority. A later British report stated that Bryan feared for the safety of the commissioners

if they went on to Chihuahua. The commission was thus both refused passage and decided on its own not to proceed. See the *New York Times*, March 2 and 3, 1914.

[12] The House Merchant Marine and Fisheries Committee, having completed its investigation of the "Shipping Trust," reported on March 1 that all foreign and domestic shipping combinations should be placed under the supervision of the Interstate Commerce Commission. See *ibid.*, March 2, 1914.

March 5, 1914

Mr. President, in your message today[1] there was an implication that the foreign policy of the government depended more or less upon this tolls exemption. Are you willing to take us more into your confidence than you did Congress by way of detail?

Of course, one cannot discuss these things without doing more harm than good, and I do not want any of you to draw the implication that there is anything critical that has assumed shape at all. It is just this: it is very awkward to deal with foreign nations no one of which believes that you will keep your promises and thinks that it has proof that you will not. That is the situation in a nutshell.

That is the only feature to which you referred in your paragraph?

That is the only feature to which I referred.

Didn't you say in a message to somebody in Baltimore, Mr. President, in a direct quote that the foreign nations did not think that we were keeping our promises?

You refer to my letter to Mr. Marbury.[2] I don't think I used that expression. I don't remember it.

You said a couple of weeks ago that other nations were rather suspicious or were becoming so, but that you had no direct communication, did you not?

I have information so much as that, when you deal with people, you know what they think of you, without anything being put in words or action.

Mr. President, what is the status of the inquiry into the Benton case by our commission?

I do not know; since yesterday I have not seen Mr. Bryan or heard anything from the department.

Is it the purpose of the administration to go ahead and have the Consuls make inquiry, forgetting this other end of it?

I must say frankly I don't know of any change of plan on the part of the State Department. All along we have been trying to make use of every means of independent inquiry. I mean independent of every partisan form of inquiry.

Mr. President, you have no intimation yet of any change of Carranza's attitude as expressed in this note?

No, I do not think that he meant to be offensive at all.

He was looking after his own interests.

Yes.

Mr. President, has there been any suggestion from him that either we or England be represented at the time his commission makes its investigation?[3]

Not so far as I know.

And we have not suggested that we would like to be present?

Oh, no. I do not think we have suggested anything about that commission of his.

Has he sent us official word, Mr. President, that he is sending such a commission?

I believe I saw a dispatch from either Mr. Carothers[4] or Mr. Letcher[5] that he had been told by Carranza that such a commission was contemplated. I suppose that was for the purpose of official notice.

Are Mr. Carothers' instructions general or specific in any one particular connection?

They have been specific from day to day as to what he should do, when he asked for instructions.

May we ask what his mission is then?

You know what Carothers is. Carothers is a consular agent. He isn't assigned to any one place; he is simply to be serviceable to us in any way he can.[6]

I wanted to find out, if I could, just what he was going to see Carranza about.

Well, there isn't anything that you don't already know.

Mr. President, it has been about two weeks now since Bauch[7] disappeared. The last we heard of him, as far as the State Department says, was about a week ago saying that the Consul had seen Bauch about a week previously. Are we making any investigations or getting any reports about him?

We are following the case up just as fast as it is possible to follow it up.

Can you say at this stage whether you think the man is dead or not?

I have no thoughts about it. I am going to wait and see.

Is General Carranza's attitude on information about it satisfactory?

So far as I know, entirely.

Mr. President, Carranza left for the interior today. Is it Mr. Carothers' purpose to keep in touch with him? Is that why he is given this mobile assignment?

He has always had the assignment as a mobile commissioner. That is what the consular agents are for.

I meant will he keep in touch with Carranza on this overland trip?

I don't know. I didn't know he had left.

Mr. President, is it too early to inquire whether you have anyone under consideration for Mr. Moore's position?[8]

Yes, it is too early to inquire. It is a very difficult place to fill. It requires something more than mere theoretical knowledge of international law.

Mr. President, one of the morning papers carries a dispatch of last night to the effect that three Attachés of the German embassy have gone to Mexico City.

I have not heard of that. Three Attachés of this embassy?

The Military Attaché—

I do know this, that the Military Attaché called to say good-by the other day and said he was going to Mexico City; but they assign those Attachés to several capitals, for example, to Washington and one or two of the South American countries. So that it is not a special mission at all. He is going his rounds. I am glad you brought that up.

Mr. President, can you tell us anything of your interview with Sir Lionel Carden?[9]

Yes, sir; I am perfectly willing to tell you all I know. Sir Lionel did not come with any suggestions or proposals of any kind, and you know the interview was of his seeking. So I was ignorant of what it was about until he came, and, judging from what happened, it was only to inform me as far as he could of conditions down there as he observed them and to answer any questions I might have to ask. It was a very interesting interview on that account, but altogether of an informal sort.

Did he dissipate in the interview the impression, if it was in your mind, that he was antagonistic toward the United States?

When did you discover that that was in my mind?

I said if it was.

In my present office I am not entitled to views of that sort.

Did he make any statements in reference to the criticism of him or his official conduct?

Oh, no; it was not alluded to one way or the other.

I understand he told you something in connection with the population down there in Mexico City, the manner in which they were voting—the Indians. Is that so?

I remember his saying that the Indians had no conception of what it meant to vote and that, as a rule, when there were elections, they did not vote. That is all I remember.

Did he make any statement about the percentage of the voters down there, the percentage of the people who did vote?

No. Besides I knew that already.

Mr. President, will you say whether what you learned from Sir Lionel or any other foreign source was responsible for the last paragraph of your message today?[10]

Before you came in this afternoon, Mr. Oulahan, I had been explaining that and I am very glad to state it again, because I want it understood that nothing particular gave rise to that paragraph— nothing that was not as true a month ago as it is now. As I was saying to the gentlemen who were present then, just as I said in the message, there is a general impression on the other side that we sail as close to the wind as we choose in interpreting our promises, and of course that embarrasses the administration at every turn. There is no pressure of any government or anything specific.

Outside of the British communication, there has been no exchange of communications between this government and Great Britain regarding the tolls matter?

No; none whatever of a formal character with this administration. The exchange of notes between the two governments occurred before I became President, and since then there has been nothing except an informal conversation between Mr. Bryce and myself.

Mr. President, had you had assurances that this message would practically clinch the repeal of that clause?

Oh, no. I am convinced that the clause will be repealed, but I have had no assurances that this message would make it certain.

Some of the leaders down there thought that that was all that was necessary to assure it.

What occurred, and what they probably had in mind, was this: You know that persons who want to defeat a thing are apt to go around and say, "The President isn't very much interested. The fellows say he is, but he isn't; he doesn't care." And I remember that that has been reflected in some of the questions that have been asked me here. One or another of you have asked me if I was going to insist on this, if I was very keen on this subject. I always had to say yes, but the very question showed that somebody was handing around a doubt as to whether I was or not. One of the members of the committee charged with this matter did say to me that he thought it would be very useful to remove that doubt absolutely,[11] and nothing but a message could do that. That is probably what is at the bottom of it.

Mr. President, in the second note of protest by Great Britain on the Panama Canal tolls question,[12] the statement was made by Sir Edward Grey that it also would be wrong for the United States to subsidize its ships to the extent of the tolls of the Panama Canal, because that would be the same thing; and Mr. Knox took the view that the United States had a right to subsidize its ships in any way it chose. Has that question come up now?

It has not come up at all in this administration.

Mr. President, can you tell us anything about the negotiations for friendly relations with Japan?

There hasn't been anything active in that field for a good many weeks, and I will have to refer you to the Secretary of State. I don't know anything about it.

Mr. President, has the government learned anything since the recent dispatch about Great Britain's attitude on the Panama-Pacific Exposition?[13]

I was very much interested in that dispatch. I think it was a petition signed by a large number of the members of the House of Commons, wasn't it? We have not, so far as I have been informed, received any message about that. Naturally, we would not, because, you see, that was not an official paper. It was the privately signed petition of a large proportion of the members of the House of Commons.

Was that topic mentioned, Mr. President, in your discussion with Sir Lionel Carden?

No, not at all.

Mr. President, getting back to Mexico, have you had any advices from Chargé O'Shaughnessy about this threat purported to be made against his life?[14]

Yes, he referred to it, but he did not make anything of it.

He did not say anything about the guard being increased?

He said it was not necessary.

Mr. President, is the government doing anything in the way of making suggestions to the contending factions in Mexico toward bringing about peace?

No, sir.

Have Governor Colquitt's requests been taken up?[15]

No, the last communication from Governor Colquitt that I saw simply set forth that there were two persons claiming to be Governor of the state to which he wished to direct communications. (I refer to it in that way because I can't pronounce the name of it.)[16] That, of course, was a legal question for the law officers of the Department of State.

Mr. President, I understand Mr. Felix Díaz was in town today?[17] Have you tried to see him?

No, sir.

As a result of this threat on Chargé O'Shaughnessy, do you know, Mr. President, whether anything will be done in regard to sending a guard to Mexico City?

Not unless he indicates the absolute necessity of it. And that is a peculiar feature of the situation down there. While the other governments, or at least one or two of the other governments, have sent guards to their embassies, O'Shaughnessy has repeatedly said there is no occasion for us to send any.

Mr. President, have the House and Senate committees on trust legislation asked your views concerning the interstate trade commission—whether there should be three or more members?

Individual members have asked me, and I ventured to express the opinion that it wouldn't make any difference whether there were three or five.

As to the question of limiting the publicity which is to be given to their work, have you taken any stand on that?[18]

My judgment—and I think I am speaking the judgment also of those who spoke to me about it—is that we ought not to limit the publicity of it except in regard to matters like legitimate trade secrets and things of that sort which it would not be fair to make public.

There is also a report coming from the House, Mr. President, that this plan[19] to define violations of the Sherman law may finally be given up for fear of endangering the entire statute. Has that been taken up with you?

Yes; that is the difficulty we recognized from the first. That is the reason we threw these things out so freely for discussion. Definition is always a risky business, because if you define you not only include, but you are in danger of excluding.

You haven't determined what it is too risky to attempt?

No, we haven't. I say "we" because the best advice we can get is being taken on just how far the definition may be carried without risk of rendering the statute less, rather than more, effective. But if you will look at the language of that bill as it was last brought to me, you will see that the prohibition runs like this (I am not quoting it exactly), that the prohibition of the Sherman Act shall be held to include the following, which plainly means that this definition must not be meant to exclude anything, but for fear the courts might overlook this, we will just mention it in passing.

Can you tell us anything about the Federal Reserve Board, Mr. President?

Nothing more than that, as I said, I have been given grace until about the first of April.

You will not make any selection—

Not before the first of April.

Mr. President, have you any information as to when the new system may be instituted?

Just as fast as the organization committee can organize it. Just now, as I understand it, the secretaries who went around with them are collating very voluminous material which they collected and digested, so that they can determine the results of the various hearings and come to their conclusions. I suppose they will remain in seclusion a week or two after deciding which cities shall be the reserve cities. If I were in their place, I would take to the woods.

[1] Wilson addressed a joint session of Congress on the question of the Panama Canal tolls exemption. He asked for repeal of the American exemption as "in plain contravention" of the Hay-Pauncefote Treaty. See the *New York Times*, March 6, 1914, and *PWW*, Vol. 29, pp. 312-13.

[2] See above, Feb. 9, 1914.

[3] On March 3, Carranza named a commission of his own to investigate the Benton Affair. See the *New York Times*, March 4, 1914, and Consul [Marion] Letcher to the Secretary of State, March 4, 1914, in *FR, 1914*, p. 859.

[4] American consular agent at Torreón.

[5] American Consul at Chihuahua.

[6] Carothers was assigned to remain in contact with Carranza. See the *New York Times*, March 5, 1914, and Hill, *Emissaries to a Revolution*, pp. 133-35.

[7] Gustave Bauch, an American citizen, had disappeared in Mexico and was presumed to be

dead, probably killed by *Villistas*. See the *New York Times*, March 1 and 4, 1914, and Hill, *Emissaries to a Revolution*, p. 148.

[8] John Bassett Moore tendered his resignation as Counselor of the State Department on March 2. See the *New York Times*, March 3, 1914.

[9] Carden, the British Minister to Mexico, called at the White House with Sir Cecil Spring Rice on March 3. Their meeting, according to Spring Rice, was "friendly" but "decidedly dull." Carden argued that elections would not work but had no advice for Wilson other than that he continue to wait. See C. A. Spring Rice to Sir William Tyrrell, March 9, 1914, printed in *PWW*, Vol. 29, pp. 324-25.

[10] This paragraph caused much controversy because it referred to "other matters of even greater delicacy and nearer consequence" that would be impeded if the tolls exemption was not repealed. For the text of Wilson's message, see *ibid.*, pp. 312-13.

[11] In a letter of February 23, 1914, Representative Adamson informed Wilson that the chances of passing the Sims bill for repeal of the Panama Canal tolls exemption would be enhanced by a presidential message to demonstrate Wilson's interest in the matter. W. C. Adamson to WW, Feb. 23, 1914, printed in *ibid.*, pp. 282-83.

[12] That is, the note of November 14, 1912.

[13] A memorial signed by 350 members of the House of Commons on March 4 urged the British government to participate in the Panama-Pacific Exposition. See the *New York Times*, March 5, 1914.

[14] On March 1, Huerta offered additional protection for the American Chargé. See *ibid.*, March 2, 1914.

[15] Governor Oliver Branch Colquitt of Texas requested authorization for Texas Rangers to pursue Mexican marauders across the border. He argued that, only in this way, could American life and property be protected. See *ibid.*, March 4, 1914.

[16] Nuevo Leon.

[17] To testify before the Senate Foreign Relations Committee about affairs in Mexico. See the *New York Times*, March 5, 1914.

[18] It had been suggested in the House and Senate Interstate Commerce Committees that the Federal Trade Commission should avoid revealing trade secrets. See *ibid.*, March 6, 1914.

[19] An early version of the Clayton bill. See Link, *The New Freedom*, p. 425.

## March 9, 1914

We haven't anything except an Associated Press dispatch. Would you care to say what complications this will raise, if any?[1]

No. Really, the thing is so fresh and new, I don't see just what its ramifications are.

The morning paper stories suggested, Mr. President, that the Washington government may have known something of the recommendations the Consul[2] there was to receive—

It certainly did not.

Mr. President, the dispatches also indicate that possibly the local Federal authorities had given permission for such information.

They certainly did not. Of course, that oughtn't to need an answer.

I presume—I meant the Mexican local authorities. There was a story which said that the Consul had permission from the Federal commander.

I thought you meant our federal authorities. I have no information about that. I didn't see that mentioned.

There was a dispatch that intimated, several days ago, that the Consul obtained permission. They weren't at first to go there, I am sure. The dispatch also spoke of the Rangers availing themselves of that permission.

I missed that. I simply don't know about that.

Could they have gone, under those circumstances, without authority from Washington?

Oh, I suppose so. It would have been more formal to have authority.

Mr. President, Mr. Edwin Hood[3] of the Associated Press says that fact has been denied.

Oh, I see. I think it unlikely.

Mr. President, it is substantiated that this man who was killed[4] was an American?

Oh, yes. That has not been denied at any time that I have seen.

Have there been any new developments with reference to Benton?

None at all. No.

That Mexican commission hasn't made any reports?

Hasn't reported, no.

Mr. President, what position has the Huerta government taken with reference to Vergera?

Simply that it was going to inquire. I believe the State Department had the impression that Vergera had escaped and probably joined the Constitutionalists.

Has the government any information as to whether Carranza—as to whether he is the real Carranza or the brother of the real Carranza?[5]

We haven't heard that there was any need of identification, so that report that he is not the genuine article—

It appeared in the *Congressional Record* that this is the brother of the original Carranza, who is now dead.

A good many queer things are now read into the *Congressional Record*.

Has he got the same whiskers?

A family resemblance, I believe.

Mr. President, did the Secretary of State have any information at all on this problem?

No. He came directly from his residence to this office. He had not been to his office, so far as I knew. There hadn't been any new official dispatches.

Mr. President, will this government inquire of Governor Colquitt as to these reports?[6]

Yes, we have full correspondence with him.

Will it be in order for the federal government to repudiate the action of private citizens?

I don't know what will be in order.

Will you wait for a report from Governor Colquitt on this, or will you inquire on your own immediately?

Oh, if he doesn't report immediately, we will eventually inquire.

Mr. President, has word been sent to our patrols on the border to guard against repetitions of things of this kind?[7]

No, we haven't had time to do anything, I was asleep when the dispatch came last night. I didn't know anything about it.

Mr. President, those resolutions that were introduced in the United States Senate by Poindexter and Jones,[8] directing certain inquiries to you, do they call for any more of a reply or explanation than you made to the newspapermen at your last meeting?

Oh, they haven't been adopted yet.

Not if you don't want them to be, I don't suppose they will be.

So the request hasn't reached my ears yet.

Mr. President, has any step been taken looking to the selection of an Ambassador to Russia or, rather, have you determined upon—

A number of steps have been taken, but we have been canvassing a number of men I wish to [consider], so—

Has Governor Cox of Ohio endorsed the candidacy of Mr. Sharp?[9]

Yes.

Did he bring up any other matters of general interest or policy?

It was the only thing we discussed, except personal conversation. We didn't discuss any policies.

Mr. President, have you any information that Mr. Morgenthau[10] wishes to leave his position in Turkey?

No.

There was a report in the New York papers that you were considering him for the Federal Reserve Board.

I didn't see that. I haven't had any information from Mr. Morgenthau that he would care to be removed or transferred.

Have you made any selections at all, Mr. President, for the Reserve Board?

Well, I have got a few in the back of my head, but they are not in the front of it yet.

Can you say, Mr. President, whether there is any intimation that the New Haven company will stand suit rather than settle?[11]

I haven't heard that.

That story has come from Boston.

I heard that rumor, but I have no reason to think that it is true. I haven't any intimation from the Attorney General to that effect. When I last spoke to him about it, about four days ago, everything seemed to be going as per program. Of course, there were points being debated along the way, but nothing serious. [We are] hanging fire a little, I think, on it.

Is the opposition to the Panama Canal tolls repeal in the West seriously embarrassing the administration?

No, sir.

Have you any conferences on the trust bills this week?

I have just been told that Judge Clayton wants to see me today, and I hope I shall be able to arrange it.

Mr. President, is there any information in the State Department or here with reference to the reported attitude of Germany in the matter of protecting her own nationals?[12]

No, nothing whatever.

Nothing to indicate that they would be true?

Nothing. Not the slightest.

The newspaper that reported, that sent word that we had better look out after German citizens who were molested, that they wouldn't stand for any foolishness. Hasn't that been their attitude all along?

Not that I have heard of.

I heard last night that the German Ambassador took the precaution to demand indemnity, and got an indemnity of three hundred thousand pesos or a threat to—

You mean recently?

Not recently, but that was in the Madero administration.

I don't remember anything about that, but that has not been the attitude of the German government at all. I don't think it is true to say that of the German government.

The Consul in Mexico City said that—the Minister.

The German government has occupied a most dignified position in the matter. It hasn't gone around with a chip on its shoulder.

Mr. President, Mr. Carden didn't bring back any word to change your attitude about permitting foreign governments to use force in Mexico.

April 7, 1913

The first four pages of Swem's shorthand notes of the press conference of April 7, 1913. The circle on this page indicates that Swem did not transcribe these notes.

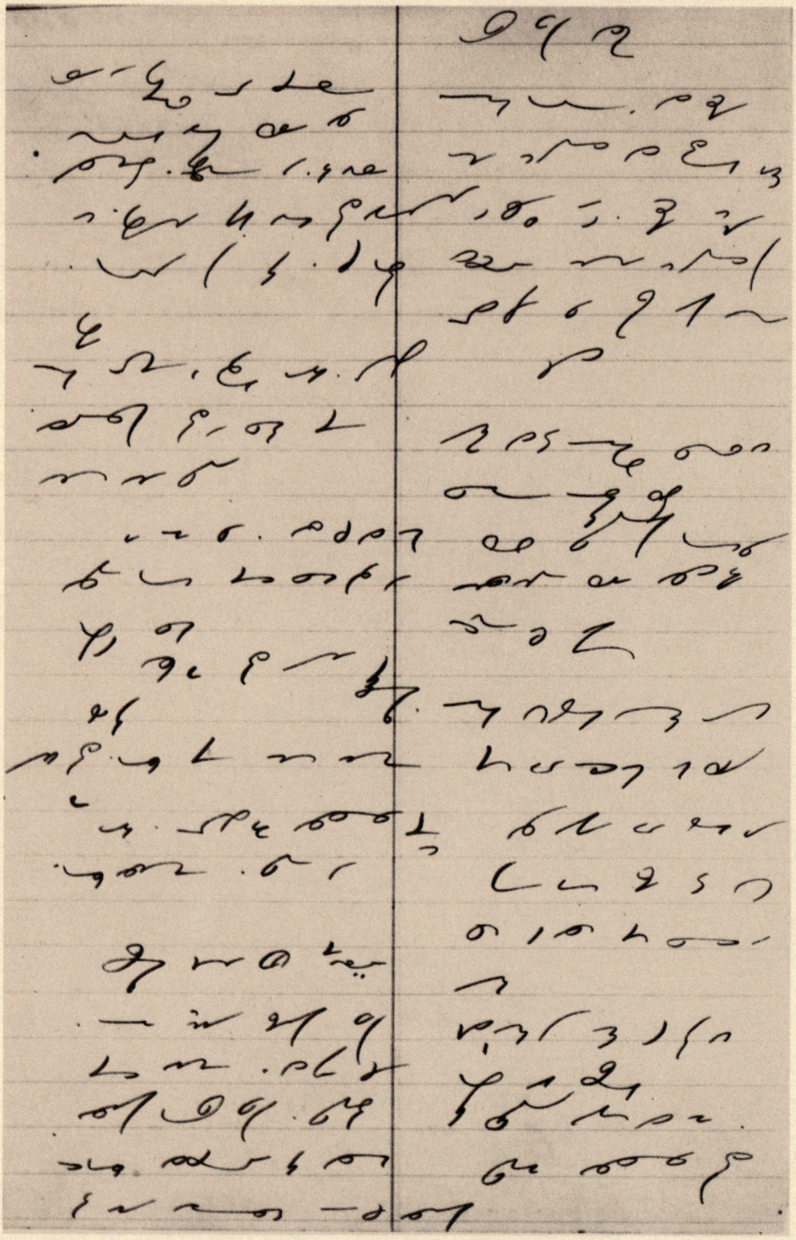

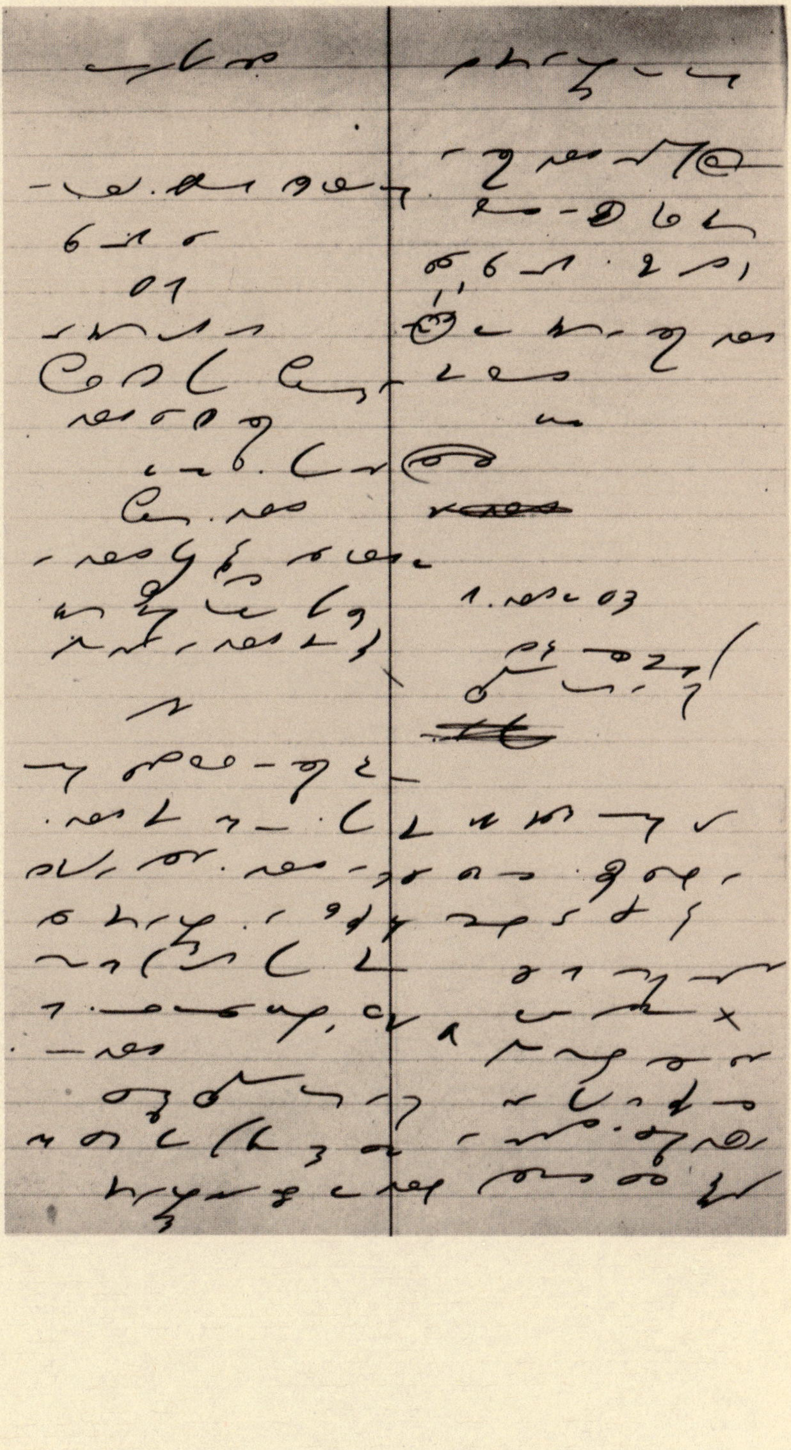

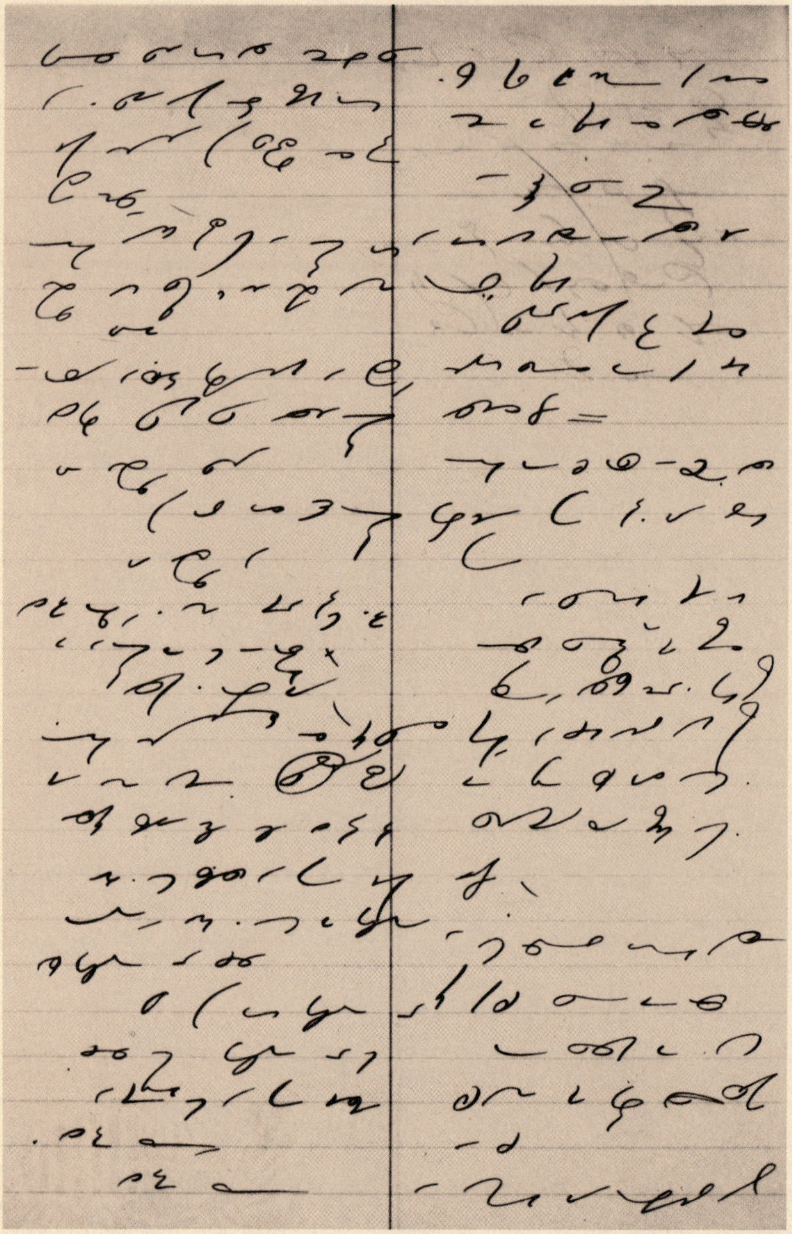

No sir, he did not.

Have you decided to abandon that commission[13] yet?

To tell the truth, I don't know what has become of that commission.

Mr. President, if it is a proper question, it might clear the atmosphere a good deal if you could tell us just what the attitude of this government is as to the protection by this government of [British] nationals in Mexico?[14]

There is nothing secret in that. Having recognized Huerta, they can't deal with Carranza. That is clearly—that is all there is to it.

Mr. President, can you give us the name of Mr. Moore's successor today?

No, sir. I wish I could.

The foreign governments, then, Mr. President, would have to look to Huerta for their protection, not to us? We will still do all in our power to protect their nationals?

Yes, of course we will.

But that will be only by courtesy.

That has been the case all along.

[1] The newspapers reported on March 9 that Texas Rangers had crossed five miles into Mexican territory to retrieve the body of Clemente Vergera. There were no reports of any opposition by Mexican forces. See the *New York Times*, March 9, 1914.

[2] United States Consul Alonzo Garrett of Nuevo Laredo, who made arrangements for the retrieval of the body.

[3] Edwin Milton Hood of the Associated Press' Washington office.

[4] That is, Vergera.

[5] It was suggested at the time that Venustiano Carranza was dead and was being impersonated by his brother, Jesús Carranza.

[6] Colquitt reported that his men had not crossed the border, but that the body had been brought to the Texas side by Mexican authorities. See the *New York Times*, March 10, 1914.

[7] That is, for United States Army patrols to prevent similar action by Texas Rangers in the future.

[8] Senator Miles Poindexter, Republican of Washington, on March 6 introduced a resolution (S. Res. 289) inquiring of the President what "other matters" he referred to in his address on the Panama tolls exemption question. On the same day, Senator Wesley Livsey Jones, Democrat of Washington, introduced a resolution (S. Res. 288) to inquire which other nations had protested against the tolls exemption. See *ibid.*, March 7, 1914, and *Cong. Record*, 63d Cong., 2d sess., p. 4393.

[9] Governor James Middleton Cox was recommending former Representative Sharp of Ohio for the post of Ambassador to Russia.

[10] The *New York Times* suggested on March 8 that Ambassador Henry Morgenthau might be appointed to the Federal Reserve Board.

¹¹ Following a meeting in New York of the board of directors of the New Haven Railroad, it was suggested that the company might not divest itself of the Boston and Maine Railroad without a federal suit. See the *New York Times*, March 9, 1914.

¹² It was being reported that Germany might decide to take matters into its own hands in Mexico if atrocities were committed against German nationals. See Katz, *Secret War in Mexico*, pp. 227-32.

¹³ To investigate Benton's death.

¹⁴ See above, March 2, 1914. For Carranza's views, see Vice-Consul Simpich to the Secretary of State, March 11, 1914, in *FR, 1914*, pp. 859-60.

March 12, 1914

Mr. President, two more regiments have moved.¹

Yes, so I understand.

Is there any special significance in that?

No, that was simply because the people on the border were uneasy, and we thought their fears might as well be quieted.

Mr. President, has any effort been made by any of the foreign nations to get this government to define exactly what its attitude is toward Mexico in the way of exercising a fatherly protection or in the way of defining the Monroe Doctrine as applied to Mexico?

No. We haven't waited for them to ask us to tell them what our attitude was. We, at each important turn of affairs, sent them a note.

Did you see what Mr. Page, the Ambassador at London, said at the dinner last night in London?²

I did not read it. I just glanced at the headlines and something drew my attention away, so that I didn't finish reading it. What did he say?

He said that the Monroe Doctrine simply meant that the United States preferred that the European nations should not acquire any territory in America, which was only another way of stating the Monroe Doctrine in a polite way.

He is evidently learning the diplomatic language.

That suggested to my mind whether this government had done anything in the way of more explicitly defining the Monroe Doctrine with reference to possible foreign intervention in Mexico.

No, we haven't done anything except send these notes as to our attitude with regard to a particular situation.

Have you found a successor yet, Mr. President, for Professor Moore?

It is not difficult to find one; it is difficult to select one. We haven't selected one yet, no.

Mr. President, you say you have sent notes at each stage. Have you been able to send notes to the other governments with regard to General Carranza's attitude with regard to receiving complaints through the United States?

No, he made that public; it was not necessary for us to communicate that.[3]

Mr. President, have we had anything from him since then that indicated a change of attitude?

No; nothing that I have heard of. I saw some intimation in the papers that he had changed his attitude, but whether that is based on a communication to the State Department or not, I don't know.

Mr. President, what do you get from Mr. Carothers with regard to his conversations with General Carranza?

I haven't seen anything from Carothers this week, I think; at any rate, not since our last interview on Monday.

Mr. President, has the intention to send a joint British-American commission to Chihuahua been—

I must simply plead ignorance on that. Mr. Bryan has not said anything about it in the last three or four days.

Mr. President, in the notes to the foreign governments, has the principle of the Monroe Doctrine been reiterated or has it not been discussed at all?

The Monroe Doctrine has not been mentioned one way or the other.

Would you care to state now what the policy of the government is as to that, because there is a good deal of discussion about the Monroe Doctrine, about its being obsolete, and so forth?

There is a good deal of discussion as to what it means but no doubt.

Does the Doctrine stand?

I haven't heard of its falling, sir.

Mr. President, could you tell us something about your conferences with Senators and Representatives with regard to the tolls question?

Yes, if there were anything to tell. All that has happened is that I have seen various Senators and Representatives, chiefly because I sought interviews in order to ascertain just what the sentiment is in each of the houses and in order to inform them on any point that they were in doubt about.

Did you discuss that with Speaker Clark?

What I discussed with Speaker Clark was the time at which the parliamentary openings should be made for the bill. That was all.

They paved the way for that yesterday.

Yes, sir, I know they did.

Have you had any polls made by the leaders?

I haven't had any; but polls have been made which showed a very distinct majority in both houses.

There will be no occasion, Mr. President, to use the compromise suggested, merely giving you discretion?

I see no occasion to use that at all.

Have you had any confirmation of the reports that the northern wing of Carranza's army has been defeated, Mr. President?[4]

No, sir.

Has there been any news from the Huerta government about the Vergera case since we made our last inquiry?

Not that I know of.

Mr. President, in what shape is the antitrust program?

It is in very good shape. The committees of both houses are working at perfecting the bills. I think that most of them are ready or about to be ready to be introduced.

You spoke the other day about the danger of specifying certain things which were to be prohibited. Has there been any decision as to whether they shall amend the Sherman Antitrust Act in that regard or not?

No, there has been no intention to amend the Sherman law. On the contrary, there is every intention to avoid amending it. The only serious debate that there has been has been on the point of whether we should attempt definitions, and we have tried to avoid attempting them where we are sure of definitions already covered. We don't want to interfere with a certainty already existing and create a new uncertainty. Every time you make a new definition you make a new series of cases to interpret the definition. I think the intention of the committee of the House is to avoid definition as much as possible and to bring this other thing about—to fix personal responsibility for those things which have been determined to be illegal. If you will examine the so-called definition bill,[5] you will see that the object of it is to fix individual responsibility for the specific acts which are regarded as acts intended to establish monopoly or restrain trade.

How will that affect, Mr. President, the so-called rule of reason?[6] Will there be any attempt to interfere with that?

There has been no suggestion to interfere with that. You cannot in the nature of things. It in itself is unsusceptible of definition.

Mr. President, has it been determined what the holding-company law shall be?

I had a draft submitted to me the other day, and I have not yet had time to really come to a mature judgment about it. It is a very difficult thing to define.

But it is not likely that that will be dropped from the program?

No, I don't think it is at all likely to be dropped from the program. You see, the difficulty is this—the difficulty of finding language in which to draw the distinction. But there is a distinction between holding companies, that is to say, companies formed for the purpose of controlling a group of corporations, and what I would call owning companies, necessitated by the variety of laws in the states. For example, if a corporation in New Jersey chooses to build a factory in Pennsylvania, it has to be reincorporated in Pennsylvania, because no foreign corporation can own real estate under the laws of Pennsylvania. In that case, it would have to duplicate itself, so to speak, on the other side of the state border. Here would be two companies with the same directors and apparently constituting a holding company. Now, it depends upon the circumstances whether that is a holding company under the prohibitions of the Sherman Act or whether it is a company of a perfectly legitimate sort merely extending its operations into another state.

There is no intention of interfering with that?

No, there is no intention of interfering with that.

That brings you back to the intent of the act.

This is, of course, our difficulty. I daresay terms can be found which will define the differences in the processes of the two companies. I should think they could be found—that a business, for example, which was actually administered as a unit was not a holding company in the sense of the companies whose stocks are held for voting purposes and not for administrative purposes.

Mr. President, the same difficulty lies in the directorates bill.

No, I don't think the same difficulty exists there. I mean, I think that it is possible, by hearing enough criticism and getting all the likely cases in your mind, to frame a definition there which would be quite workable.

Mr. President, you said in your message, as I recall it, that everybody agrees that holding companies should be prohibited?

Yes.

But that there was another form of holding company that had to do with the personnel of the various concerns—rather an underground, insidious sort of ownership. Does this new bill provide for reaching organizations of that sort?

You see, that is not an organized company, and that constitutes its difficulty. For example, let us take a very violent hypothesis. Suppose that I hold a majority of stock in two companies that were in the same business and that were independently organized and had been independently developed, but in which I had acquired a controlling interest. There is there what in the case of two kingdoms would be called a personal union—the same person controlling by ownership, by perfectly legitimate and bona fide ownership of the stock, the chief power in both corporations. Of course, the owner could put in directors, even if he did not put in the same persons in the two corporations, who could virtually set aside competition between the two companies, by dividing territory, or resorting to any of the ordinary devices for destroying competition. That is the thing that is difficult to get at, because we don't want to stop the free right to buy stock.

I understand that is what you are after—

But it is a very difficult thing to get at—to say how to forbid without interfering with perfectly legitimate business.

In connection with stock ownership, Mr. President, is it possible under the Constitution to restrict ownership of stock that way?

Of course, the law can determine the voting power of stock. That is a matter—

Just, for instance, in that very case you illustrate—one man controlling the bulk of the stock in the two corporations. Is it possible under the Constitution to enact a law that will prevent a man from voting that stock in whatever way he pleases?

I never raised that question in my own mind, but I assume it is. If it is possible to make charter restrictions, it is possible to do a thing of that sort.

The restriction must be in the charter, in the organic law of the corporation?

Or in some law governing the general operation of the corporation which is not inconsistent with their charter.

It has been prohibited, I think, already, Mr. President—something of that sort—where there would be a community of interest, for example.

Yes, in part it has been. The thing hasn't been gotten at entire.

Mr. President, would you give us an idea of how far you have gotten in the matter of determining Federal Reserve districts and the selection of members for the board?

I haven't gotten anywhere; it is none of my business. I understand that the organization committee7 has been delayed by Secretary Houston's illness. He came back with a very able-bodied germ on board of him and the germ has been in command, I think until yesterday, when he got out for the first time. Meanwhile their secretaries have been collating the really extraordinary mass of testimony that they collected.

Was it your understanding, Mr. President, that they are simply collating this evidence in order that the board might take it up; that is all that has been done up to this time?

That, I think, is absolutely all that has been done at this time.

You haven't gone deeply into the matter of selecting the board?

No, I am waiting until they tell me that the actual operation is in sight.

There have been a number of suggestions made about Mr. Morgenthau being appointed?

That was perfectly gratuitous, I am sure, so far as both he and I are concerned.

---

¹ On March 11, Wilson instructed Secretary of War Garrison to move the Ninth and Seventeenth Infantry Regiments to the Mexican border. His apparent purpose was to prevent further raids across the border by Texas Rangers or other Americans. See the *New York Times*, March 12, 1914.

² Speaking to the Association of Chambers of Commerce in London on March 11, Page interpreted the Monroe Doctrine to mean that the United States would "prefer" no further colonization in the Americas. He also jokingly remarked that the United States was pleased to know that Great Britain would profit most from the construction of the Panama Canal. This caused an uproar in the American press and in Congress, where a resolution (S. Res. 298) introduced by Senator Chamberlain was passed unanimously on March 12 which requested the Secretary of State to furnish details of the speech. See the *New York Times*, March 12, 13, and 15; Ross Gregory, *Walter Hines Page: Ambassador to the Court of St. James* (Lexington, Ky., 1970), pp. 41-43; John Milton Cooper, Jr., *Walter Hines Page: The Southerner as American, 1855-1918* (Chapel Hill, N. C., 1977), p. 264; and *Cong. Record*, 63d Cong., 2d sess., p. 4721.

³ The Department of State did communicate this information two days later. See the Secretary of State to the Italian Ambassador, March 14, 1914, in *FR, 1914*, p. 860. The information was also sent to the embassies of Austria-Hungary, Germany, France, Great Britain, Japan, and Spain.

⁴ An exaggeration of the results of an offensive then being launched by Huerta. See the *New York Times*, March 13, 1914.

⁵ That is, the Clayton bill.

⁶ See above, Jan. 15, 1914.

⁷ See above, Dec. 22, 1913.

---

March 16, 1914

Mr. President, what looks to you like a beginning?

I haven't been thinking from that point of view this morning. I have found sometimes it weakens me.

Anything you would like to change public opinion on?

Nothing that I know of. That is a large job.

Mr. President, will there be anything in the trust program with reference to the exemption of labor unions from the Sherman law?[1]

That hasn't been brought to me. You see, the line we are working on doesn't touch them.

Is the American Federation of Labor insistent that that shall be in the bill?

Not so far as I know.

Well, their publications are full of it, but I wondered whether they had urged it personally?

Not upon me, certainly.

Mr. President, can you tell us what the object of the visit of Mr. Clayton and the subcommittee of the House committee this evening is?[2]

Just to go over a redraft of one of the bills.

Is that the definitions bill?

No. I think it is the—to tell the truth, I have forgotten. There were several we discussed last time. I do not know which it is he is going to bring.

Mr. President, is there anything in the Mexican situation that indicates a change?

No, sir. I found a number of dispatches on my table this morning that I haven't had time to read.

Mr. Lind hasn't said anything that would be of interest?

Not in any dispatch that I have yet read.

Is there anything with regard to the burning of that post office of the government from Governor Johnson?[3]

I don't believe that is so. I have seen only two newspapers. I have seen it in only one.

It was in both. It looked like it was credible.

I would regard that as falling under the heading of "important if true." It hasn't been confirmed, certainly.

Mr. President, will your conference this afternoon with the Attorney General relate to the New Haven matter?

No, sir, not so far as I know. He sought the conference and I don't know what he is going to bring before me, but I am quite sure it has nothing to do with that.

Mr. President, have you done some thinking since your statement [about Tennessee] was prepared?[4]

No, I have not.

Mr. President, is that thinking to apply to all the citizens down there and in other states? Is it going to be generally that way?

No, sir. I attend to only one piece of business at a time. I don't fire a revolving Gatling gun.

Mr. President, did the trade commission bill which came in this morning represent your views as submitted to you for approval? The trade commission bill was given out last night and introduced this morning.

I don't know. I haven't seen that copy. I suppose so. I say I suppose so because I haven't heard of any important modifications. Which committee did it come from, the House or Senate?

Mr. Covington's.[5]
Mr. President, is there any indication that the appointments to the Federal Reserve Board will come rather earlier or a little later than you expected?

No, sir. I have consulted with the organization committee. It seems to me that there is no need that it should come before they get ready to start the system. Because, you see, there is nothing for the board to do until the work of the organization committee is entirely completed.

As soon as the first?

Oh, no. They don't hope to be finished as soon as that.

Mr. Hamlin's name is suggested as a prospect for being on the Board.[6]

I hear every day of appointments to positions, but they don't take place.

The Union Plaza,[7] Mr. President?

I hope to decide that within twenty-four hours.

I didn't quite catch one thing. Did you indicate as to when the work of the organization committee would be through?

I merely said there was no prospect of its being completed by the first of April and there won't be any announcement of any reserve districts before the first of April, not that I have heard.

Anything with regard to the Russian ambassadorship, Mr. President?

No, sir.

The Counselor of the State Department?

No, sir, not yet.

Anything new on the third Hague Peace Conference?

No, sir.

Is there anything new, Mr. President, with reference to Ambassador Page's recent speech?

That was all due to an absolute misunderstanding as to what he said. In the versions that I have seen printed, he was not correctly reported. For example, in one passage he was made to say that "I recommended the repeal of the tolls not merely to please Britain but also." He did not say that at all. He said "I recommended not to please Britain but also." Whoever put that "not merely" in, made a mistake, to say the least. In other words, he made an absolutely accurate statement of the facts.[8]

[1] The American Federation of Labor was at this time backing the Bacon-Bartlett bill to exempt labor unions from antitrust prosecution. For a discussion of this topic, see Link, *The New Freedom*, pp. 426-33, and the *New York Times*, March 17, 1914.

[2] Representative Clayton, chairman of the House Judiciary Committee, visited Wilson at the White House on March 16. He brought with him Representatives Charles Creighton Carlin and Flood of Virginia. See the *New York Times*, March 17, 1914.

[3] On March 15, three men said to be Mexicans burned a general store in Tecate, California, which contained a United States post office. The postmaster died in the fire, and Governor Johnson declared martial law in the area. See *ibid.*, March 13, 1914.

[4] A reference to Wilson's statement following a meeting on March 14 with leading members

of the Democratic party in Tennessee, in which he called for party unity. See *ibid.*, March 15, 1914.

[5] Representative Covington was chairman of the subcommittee of the House Commerce Committee which was preparing the trade commission bill.

[6] Charles Sumner Hamlin of Boston, who was later nominated for the Federal Reserve Board.

[7] A reference to awards to owners of land condemned for the construction of the Union Station Plaza in Washington. Wilson decided that they were too high and did not approve them. See the *Washington Post*, March 19, 1914.

[8] See the *New York Times*, March 17, 1914, and W. H. Page to WW, March 31, 1914, printed in *PWW*, Vol. 29, pp. 388-89.

March 19, 1914

Gentlemen, I want to say something this afternoon. In the first place, I want to say that I know that in saying this I am dealing here in this room with a group of men who respect and observe the honorable limitations of their own function, but there are some men connected with the newspapers who do not. I am a public character for the time being, but the ladies of my household are not servants of the government and they are not public characters. I deeply resent the treatment they are receiving at the hands of the newspapers at this time. I am going to be perfectly frank with you. Take the case of my oldest daughter. It is a violation of my own impulses even to speak of these things, but my oldest daughter is constantly represented as being engaged to this, that, or the other man in different parts of the country, in some instances to men she has never even met in her life. It is a constant and intolerable annoyance. These things are printed without any attempt to verify them by communication to the White House, and when explicit denials are received from persons who are known to tell the truth and to feel bound to tell the truth, those denials are not respected in the least. On the contrary, they are represented as avoidances.

Now, I feel this way, gentlemen: Ever since I can remember I have been taught that the deepest obligation that rested upon me was to defend the women of my household from annoyance. Now I intend to do it, and the only way I can think of is this. It is a way which will impose the penalty in a certain sense upon those whom I believe to be innocent, but I do not see why I should permit representatives of those papers who treat the ladies of my household in this way to have personal interviews with me. They are entitled to all the news there is, and so far as even the ladies are concerned they are welcome to all that is true, but beyond that there is something that I cannot and will not endure, so far as I can handle it. My daughters have no brother whom they can depend upon. I am President of the United States; I cannot act altogether as an individual while I occupy this office. But I must do something. The thing is intolerable. Every day I pick up the paper and see some flat lie, some entire invention, things represented as having happened to my daughters where they were not present, and all sorts of insinuations. When they are told that the person who is nearest to me in all the world is not seriously ill and is steadily recovering from a fall, they go about to create rumors that something is being concealed.[1]

Now, if you have ever been in a position like that yourselves—and I hope to God you never will be—you know how I feel, and I must ask you gentlemen to make confidential representations to the several papers which you represent about this matter. I do not want to take any action, particularly an action which will embarrass you gentlemen, and I am perfectly honest in saying that I do not believe you are in the least degree responsible for these things; yet I would not respect myself if I permitted this thing to go on. Every day in my own household, we have to recite to each other with embarrassment and resentment things that have appeared in the newspapers that are utterly false. I know you would like to cooperate with me in preventing that, for in some way it must be prevented. If you will report to us whenever you hear rumors of any kind, we are perfectly willing to tell you anything that is true. For it is not a household in which there is anything to conceal. You would be welcome, so far as anything in the house was concerned, to see the inside of all the correspondence that goes in or out of that house. Now, put yourselves in my place and give me the best cooperation in this that you can, and then we can dismiss a painful subject and go to our afternoon's business.

Mr. President, if I could have a copy of your remarks and send them confidentially to the editor of the paper I represent, although this paper has at no time offended in the way of which you complain, I know it would dissipate all possibility of anybody ever taking any course in this matter that would annoy you or cause you resentment. I think perhaps every member here, if he could send those remarks to his paper, would give you the fullest amount of protection which he is capable of giving.

I am perfectly willing except in one sense. The only objection I can see is this. You men see me twice a week and you know what my attitude is, and you know my personality, as far as that counts for anything, and you know the tones of voice in which I say these things. That could not be conveyed with the written page. It is possible that I might give that in some such form as would be serviceable to that purpose. Here I have just, without premeditated forms of wording, laid my mind bare to you, because I know I can do so. But I am very much obliged to you for the suggestion.[2]

Mr. President, have you any information that Mr. Huerta's Minister of Foreign Affairs, who is now in Veracruz, has any proposals to lay before Mr. Lind?[3]

No, I haven't at all. I simply saw what you have seen, that he had gone there and that there was some conjecture that he had gone for the purpose of seeing Mr. Lind. I have no information to that effect. I hear him represented to be a man of fine character.

Mr. President, in the morning papers today there was a report of 149 mutineers shot as fast as they could shoot them down there. Isn't there some question about the authenticity of that? Has there been any official confirmation of that?[4]

No, I had not heard of that. I haven't had time to read the dispatches today. I have not received any official ones.

Mr. President, have you arranged a method of fixing the route of the Alaska railroad?[5]

No, I am acquainting myself with the geography of Alaska. In order to be a railroad man, I have got to know what I am about, and I am taking such time as I can find in the evenings to know where the suggested routes are. I have a very serviceable map made in connection with the former surveys that were made by government engineers, showing practically all the feasible routes and plotting out the different mineral deposits of the state and the available arable land. I am trying to get that in my head before I undertake the extraordinary responsibilities of the Alaska railway bill.

Do you purpose sending a commission of engineers to Alaska to look it over?

You see, until I study this other report, I can't see just what we would send them for, just how much of that work would have to be attempted over again.

Have you studied, Mr. President, Representative Ferris'[6] or the bill that has come out of the Public Lands Committee on Alaska?

No, I haven't. Is it along the lines of Mr. Lane's suggestions?

Yes.

I have gone over it very thoroughly with Secretary Lane, but I haven't seen the bill itself.

I think it was drafted largely in the Interior Department.

I am thoroughly in accord with that policy.

Mr. President, following your conference yesterday with Mr. McCombs, it has been announced that you may take the stump in the campaign.

So I saw, but there was no suggestion of that in our conference at all. We were not talking about the campaign. We were simply talking about a score of different things in connection with getting ready for the campaign. No plans for my participation, or for the participation of anybody in particular, were discussed.

Mr. President, have you been able to take up matters of taxation and other matters within the District?[7]

No, I am sorry to say I have not. I have to admit I do not know anything about the subject.

Has it occurred to you, Mr. President, the advisability of a commission, a nonpartisan commission, such as was suggested by Mr. Underwood, a non-congressional commission on that subject, possibly to be called by yourself, to either serve without pay or to be municipal experts?

That suggestion hasn't reached me.

There seems to be a good deal of question in resolving the facts involved—as to what facts are involved.

Yes, I would like to be on the commission and find out myself.

Mr. President, can you tell us anything about your conference yesterday with the Secretary of Agriculture and Senator Swanson[8] about good roads?

Yes, if I can recall just what ground we did go over. You see, the Secretary of Agriculture had made very explicit recommendations at the hearing of the committee about the matter, and Senator Swanson wanted to see him and me at the same time to find out if we all three could not come to a common mind in the matter, a common plan, and I think we came within hailing distance of it, at any rate.

There has been some talk as to the dropping of the Shackleford bill[9] as passed by the House; have you any—

Nothing was said about dropping it. I understood that Senator Swanson himself was in favor of modifications.

Did you discuss Senator Swanson's own bill, which for some time has been before the committee?[10]

I discussed it in so far as the points were concerned that he brought up, but they were very few. You see, Senator Swanson, while Governor of Virginia, took the initiative in bringing about a change in the whole system of state subvention of the roads in Virginia and instituted a very excellent system there. We took the head of their roads commission for our department here—a man with the respectable name of Wilson.[11]

Mr. President, have you heard any complaints from the railroads of their financial condition at the present time?

No; I have heard what everybody is talking about, of course— the uncertainty of their position.

Some of them have been pointing out that their net revenues have been decreasing very, very largely, on account of their increasing operating expenses. The last year, I think, the net revenues of the railroads have decreased about thirty-three million dollars, and I wondered whether the administration was giving any consideration to that condition.

Well, we are giving consideration to it at every point where we can help at all, and those general facts had been brought to my attention, of course.

I believe the law which created the Interstate Commerce Commission gave the President authority to consult with them about such matters. You haven't done so, so far?

Not with the commission as a whole. Individual members of it have called on me from time to time. We discussed everything that they brought up very frankly.

Mr. President, have you yet been informed as to whether the trust bills are to carry a provision exempting organized labor?

That matter has not been brought to me, for some reason.

Have you heard that the labor men of the House in some sort of a conference last night agreed that such a provision should be embodied in the bill?[12]

I heard merely from Senator Hughes this morning that there had been such a conference, and this being a busy morning we did not have time to discuss it. He is coming back as soon as we can make an engagement to talk it over.

Mr. President, have you heard Judge Pou's name suggested in connection with the successor of Justice Clabaugh?[13]

Yes.

Mr. Clayton[14] has spoken to you about the thing?

I don't remember whether Mr. Clayton did or not. A number of gentlemen have.

I suppose you have not reached a decision on that?

No.

Mr. President, can you give us the name of Mr. Moore's successor?

No, I can't yet. I am trying to find out whether the gentleman I have in mind will take it or not. I don't want it to be known that I was turned down if he should not take it![15]

---

[1] This is the event which apparently prompted this outburst by Wilson. On March 19, newspapers reported that Mrs. Wilson, who had recently fallen on the polished floor of her bedroom, was seriously ill and that this was the reason for the cancellation of social engagements by other members of the Wilson family. See, for example, the *New York Times*, March 19, 1914.

[2] The remarks were given out, along with the rest of this press conference, marked "confidential—not to be published."

[3] José López Portillo y Rojas, Huerta's Foreign Minister, traveled to Veracruz on March 18, reportedly to open negotiations with Lind. See the *New York Times*, March 19, 1914, and Hill, *Emissaries to a Revolution*, pp. 171-72.

[4] Over 1,000 of Huerta's soldiers had mutinied at Jojutla, and some were killed in subsequent fighting. See the *New York Times*, March 19, 1914, and the *Washington Post*, March 19, 1914.

[5] Wilson signed a bill on March 12 providing for $35,000,000 for the construction of an Alaskan railroad. See the *New York Times*, March 13, 1914, and Edwin M. Fitch, *The Alaska Railroad* (New York, 1967).

[6] Representative Scott Ferris, Democrat of Oklahoma, chairman of the House Public Lands Committee, who had proposed a bill (H.R. 13137) for the leasing of coal land in Alaska. See *Cong. Record*, 63d Cong., 2d sess., p. 3244.

[7] See above, Feb. 9, 1914. The Johnson-Prouty plan for shifting the tax burden on residents of the city was introduced in the House on March 18. See the *Washington Post*, March 19, 1914.

[8] Senator Claude Augustus Swanson, Democrat of Virginia.

[9] Representative Dorsey William Shackleford, Democrat of Missouri, introduced a bill (H.R. 11686) on January 15 to provide federal aid for the construction and maintenance of rural post roads. The bill passed the House on February 10, but was not acted on in the Senate. See *Cong. Record*, 63d Cong., 2d sess., p. 1749.

[10] The Joint Committee on Federal Aid in Construction of Post Roads. Shackleford was vice-chairman and Swanson was a member of the committee.

[11] Philip St. Julian Wilson, assistant director of the Office of Public Roads and Rural Engineering in the Department of Agriculture.

[12] Prolabor Congressmen met on March 18 and voted not to support any antitrust legislation which did not exempt labor unions from its provisions. Senator William Hughes, Democrat of New Jersey, carried this message to Wilson. See the *New York Times*, March 21, 1914.

[13] Chief Justice Harry M. Clabaugh of the District Supreme Court died of a heart attack on March 6. Representative Edward William Pou, Democrat of North Carolina, was among those suggested as his successor. See the *Washington Post*, March 7, 1914.

[14] Representative Clayton was also among those under consideration to replace Clabaugh. See *ibid.*, March 11, 1914.

[15] Wilson appointed Robert Lansing to be Counselor of the State Department on March 20, 1914.

March 23, 1914

Mr. President, can you tell us anything about your conference yesterday on the tolls question?[1]

You mean with Mr. Burleson?

Yes.

We were simply counting up to see where we stood, and it was very satisfactory.

Does the situation in Congress look good to you?

Entirely. The only thing we are anxious to do is to bring it to a vote. That is the only thing we are conferring about.

Have you identified any particular interests that are fighting against your program for the repeal?

No. To tell the truth, I haven't looked around to find any. I don't want to find any.

Mr. President, is there any intimation in some quarters that Judge Gray of Delaware is about to retire?[2]

No, sir.

Mr. President, you say you don't want to find it. Would you mind elucidating?

Well, this is a difference of opinion, so far as it goes, among Democrats. If I saw any reason to believe that influences of an improper kind were actively at work, of course I wouldn't hesitate about looking them up. But I don't see any, and I am not looking for any, in the sense that I am not expecting them.

You do not notice any insurgency among shipbuilders?

There are no shipbuilders in Congress! You see, this is a peculiar situation. A majority of Democrats never did vote for the tolls exemption in the House. There was always a large majority, so far as the Democratic votes went, against the tolls exemption in the House. So there is no new situation now, and I am simply trying to go the way of the majority.

Have you made a canvass, Mr. President, of the Republican votes that will be cast against the tolls exemptions?

No, I have not done that. I have understood that there is a considerable number of Republicans that will vote for the repeal of the exemption.

I wonder if you know just how many?

I do not.

When do you expect the vote to come in the House, Mr. President?

Just as soon as the rivers and harbors bill is out of the way.

Are there any influences at work to prolong the debate on the rivers and harbors bill in order to[3]—

I can't say. Yes and no. It would certainly look as if there were a filibuster. Minorities always filibuster. That is the way they disclose themselves.

Mr. President, have you asked that this rule be adopted, to limit debate?[4]

No. I haven't had any part in suggesting the rule at all. I mean, the character of the rule, of course. I hoped that there would be a rule to bring the thing in.

As to Mexico?

Things are happening in Mexico, but not anything I am responsible for, fortunately.

Nothing for publication?

Well, I have nothing to do with it, so far as the publication is concerned—I mean with what is now going on in Mexico.

It is said that a full report has been made of what is taking place in Veracruz, for example, and I wonder whether you could say anything?[5]

That is not true, so far as I am concerned. What do you mean? About the alleged negotiations?

Yes, sir.

So far as I know, they are all imaginary. I don't mean that O'Shaughnessy hasn't probably met with Lind, and Lind has seen Señor Portillo y Lopez[6] so far as I know, but nothing of the nature of negotiations between the two governments has developed because of those conferences.

Mr. President, have there been any propositions presented to Mr. Lind?

No, none that he has reported to us.

Is Mr. O'Shaughnessy to resign?[7]

I hope not. I hadn't heard of it at all. If he does, it will be on account of ill health. I have heard some report that his health is not very good. That would be the only ground, and I hope that that isn't true.

Is Mr. O'Shaughnessy under fire of any character?

No, sir. Not that I know of.

One of the papers this morning is saying he wouldn't resign under fire. Those words "to be recalled" are in direct quotations.

He must have gone to Veracruz by way of Torreón.[8]

As to the New Haven settlement, Mr. President, have you any intimation as to Governor Walsh's position, or that of the commonwealth's?[9]

Governor Walsh, I understand, has been cooperating in the matter very heartily. I don't know just what you have in mind—

It is necessary for the commonwealth to release the Boston and Maine stock.

Governor Walsh will cooperate in that, so far as he can.

Mr. President, has there been any change in the trust program—any progress?

I daresay there has been progress, though the gentlemen haven't consulted me within about a week, and I don't know just what it has been.

Has any suggestion reached you from either house that they would like to postpone the trust legislation until fall?

Not the slightest.

That the [blank] wouldn't be favorably looked upon?

Well, "Ifs" are dangerous things to argue, gentlemen, but I have no reason to believe there would be any such.

Has that labor exemption come up, Mr. President?

No.

Have you had any reports on the military situation around Torreón? Anything from Mr. Carothers?[10]

No, sir.

Mr. President, do you intend to participate in any of the state fights this fall? Some state fights, like Pennsylvania?

No, sir. Sometimes you reach the age of discretion.
No. But to speak seriously, I think it would be very improper for the President to make any attempt to guide.

I mean to make speeches, Mr. President, to go around to any one of them to make speeches in certain states when the fight came to a [climax]?

I haven't been invited to, yet.

We can fix that up, Mr. President.

I wasn't fixing.

Mr. President, have you taken any interest in the proposed stock-exchange legislation?[11]

No more than I hear, no. There again, I have been discreet. I know so little about the operations of the stock exchange, I don't feel that I have any judgment as to what sort of regulation would go through.

[1] In a rare Sunday meeting, Wilson discussed the Panama tolls question at the White House with Postmaster General Burleson, Tumulty, and leading Congressmen. See the *Washington Post*, March 23, 1914.

[2] The *New York Times*, March 24, 1914, reported that George Gray of Delaware, age seventy-four, a judge on the Third Federal Judicial Circuit, was to retire.

[3] Representative Sims charged on March 21 that Republican Congressmen were intentionally prolonging debate on the rivers and harbors bill to forestall consideration of the Panama Canal tolls exemption repeal bill. See *Cong. Record*, 63d Cong., 2d sess., pp. 5259-61.

[4] H. Res. 437, a special rule to limit debate on the Sims bill to twenty hours, was proposed by Representative Henry on March 26. It was adopted on March 27. See *ibid.*, pp. 5554, 5619. Cong., 2d sess., pp. 5554, 5619.

[5] The *Washington Post*, March 23, 1914, reported negotiations at Veracruz among Lind, O'Shaughnessy, and Mexican officials.

[6] Lind rejected suggestions made by Portillo y Lopez and did not continue the conversations. See Hill, *Emissaries to a Revolution*, pp. 171-72.

[7] The *New York Times*, March 23, 1914, reported that O'Shaughnessy had clashed with Lind and had been asked to resign.

[8] Torreón was the scene of the current fighting in the Mexican civil war.

[9] Under the terms of a dissolution agreement reached on March 21 by the Justice Department and the New York, New Haven, and Hartford Railroad, the company promised to divest itself of its Boston and Maine Railroad stock. Because this stock was owned by a holding company, the Boston Railroad Holding Company, which under its charter could not divest itself of the Boston and Maine stock, a special law needed to be passed by the Massachusetts legislature. This required the cooperation of Governor David Ignatius Walsh. See the *Washington Post*, March 22, 1914.

[10] For reports of the fighting, *ibid.*, March 23, 1914.

[11] What eventually became the Owen bill to regulate the stock exchanges. See Link, *The New Freedom*, p. 426.

March 26, 1914

Who is in possession of Torreón in our understanding?[1] What is the answer to that first question, Mr. President?

That is what I want to know.

No, I was asking for information. The morning papers seem to be a little contradictory and doubtful on the subject. Any dispatches, Mr. President?

None whatever.

Have you had any dispatches, Mr. President, concerning the situation in Mexico City?

No. With respect to what situation?

Our relations or possible changes?

No, nothing at all. Nothing to support the public dispatches.

Have we had any information, Mr. President, as to what is behind this new loan that Huerta was able to raise, whether that was based on confiscation?[2]

No confiscation of the kind as I understand it, though the information is a little fragmentary. They intended to set up a national bank of some sort, and the banks entered into an arrangement with him in order to avoid a radical change. It is an entirely local arrangement, so far as I can make out.

Has there been anything new in the trust situation, Mr. President?

No, nothing at all. They are still continuing their hearings, are they not? A gentleman came in today and said he had just been before the Judiciary Committee of the House, so I assume they were continuing their hearings.

That labor exemption hasn't been brought up to you?

No. Not in any form at all.

Anything about tolls, Panama tolls? Can you tell us anything there?

Nothing, except that the exemption is going to be repealed. Tumulty reminds me that I have been correcting as far as I could a partial misapprehension about what I am asking Congress to do in regard to the tolls. I meant my message very literally. You remember my message was to this effect—that in my opinion it was a mistaken economic policy and a breach of the treaty, but that I had not come to urge my opinion on Congress; that I had come merely to state a situation which had nothing to do with the question whether it was a good economic policy or a breach of the treaty or not. So that what I am asking the men on the Hill who voted for the exemption to do is not to reverse their opinion as to whether it is a correct policy or a breach of the treaty or not, but merely to correct an international situation which has arisen because of this exemption and which need not exist. So that the men who base the whole thing upon the question whether it is a breach of the treaty or not are off the mark, in one sense; in another sense that is very pertinent to the discussion.

You could not say anything further, Mr. President, what you mean by correcting an international situation that has arisen?

Why, simply this, that now that the South American republics, if their editors speak for them, have voted in the matter,[3] so to speak, the opinion is unanimous in the world against us. I mean in this particular transaction; and so long as that is the case, of course they are not very enthusiastic about entering into new agreements with us.

You mean unanimous in belief that it is a violation of the treaty?

Yes.

Mr. President, your embarrassment is in making new treaties—difficulty is in making new treaties?

Well, let us just suppose that we were in the habit of entering into very handsome arrangements which we said were for the benefit of the whole world and of which we wished to take no selfish advantage, and then Congress were to take any advantage that it pleased, whether it was contrary to the agreement or not. What impression do you think it would make on the rest of the world?

Mr. President, did you receive the text of Ambassador Page's speech? Have you any comment to make on it now?

None, except that it was a perfectly proper speech.

There has been some suggestion, Mr. President, that some compromise action might be possible to answer the situation—not a flat repeal, but by turning it over to the President, or some other compromise.

What is there to compromise? It is going to be repealed.

They want to avoid compromising their attitude.

But they are not to compromise their attitude. The situation, as I have stated, is perfectly plain and involves no compromise of previous attitude. It is based upon considerations which were not in their mind at the time the original action was taken.

(When asked if his preceding remarks might be quoted, the President said:)

I would prefer that they should not be quoted. I am speaking to you gentlemen without studying the phrases at all, just as freely as I would in conversation with anybody else. I do not want to seem to be expounding upon the duty of Congress, except to those who consult me from Congress. I think that is rather an offensive attitude to be in, and certainly not the attitude which I am in towards

Congress, because I think my attitude is fully understood by the individual members. But I thought it would be serviceable for your own guidance in explaining the situation. My statement of the situation is so simple and plain that I do not think you will have any difficulty in carrying it in your mind.[4]

A good many members think they haven't a sufficient reason, that you have not given them a sufficiently explicit reason, in the matter, and this might clear it up.

Well, this isn't any more explicit than I have given them both publicly and privately. I have simply repeated my recent message to Congress with an altered phraseology.

Mr. President, this is a question that might be embarrassing to you, but would it satisfy this international situation that has arisen if, instead of repealing this act, to modify it in accordance with the suggestion of the British government, that this exemption be limited exclusively to bona fide coastwise trade?

It is alleged that that was their suggestion. I haven't had the documents shown me to prove it. Moreover, why should we desire to satisfy the situation less than generously? Why should we want to be cheese paring about it? We are big and powerful enough to do anything we please. Now, aren't we big enough to do the thing generously? That is what I want to know. We are too big to say, "We will do just as little as possible."

If you think I am embarrassing you, I will take it back and ask no more questions. You are still not searching for motives?[5]

No. That is an invidious game. If you have to search after what is on the surface, that is another matter.

Is the administration aware that there are any sinister influences on the borders of this country stirring up the war spirit?

The administration is aware that there have been, for a great many years. The interesting thing about the situation on the border is that it is better now than ordinarily. I have had a series of editorials sent me from authoritative papers, like the *Dallas News*, for example, saying that, as a matter of fact, the conditions down there are very much more peaceful and regular than is ordinarily believed to be the case. You know, the Texas border is very like what the English and Scottish border used to be in the Middle Ages. It is part of the regular business of the day to raid one way or the other for cattle, and those raids are, for the most part, stopped, and fewer men are being killed than in the ordinary course of business.

Mr. President, there was something in the morning papers printed in connection with your visit with Senator Stone[6] saying that Argentina had considered protesting against the tolls exemption repeal? Has there been any protest made?[7]

On the contrary, the Latin American press is unanimous against the tolls exemption.

Have they considered making a formal protest against the Panama Canal [tolls exemption]?

No.

Mr. President, have you considered this situation: in considering the Danish treaty taken up in the Senate yesterday,[8] concerning the Danish islands in the West Indies, if we entered into a new treaty, that the suggestion might be made to exclude our protest against the sale of the islands to some other power, in contravention of the Monroe Doctrine?

That hadn't been brought to me. It is novel to me.

The Federal Reserve Board. Is there anything there?

No. I think I am getting warm on the subject. Very near the goal. But I think it is safer just now to keep the thing in my own head.

Can you tell us anything about the probable time you will make the announcement?

No. It will be just as prompt, following the organization of the regional reserve banks, as possible.

The committee has not informed you yet, Mr. President, when they expect to announce the districts?

No, they have not.

[1] The *Washington Post*, March 26, 1914, reported that Huerta's forces had won a major victory over Villa's at Torreón.

[2] After resumption of interest payments on foreign debts, Huerta received a new loan of 50,000,000 pesos from branches of European banks in Mexico. See *ibid.*, March 26, 1914, and Katz, *The Secret War in Mexico*, p. 194.

[3] See the *Washington Post*, March 26, 1914. Most South American editors favored repeal of the exemption.

⁴ Reporters liberally paraphrased Wilson's remarks. See, for example, the *New York Times*, March 27, 1914, and the *Washington Post*, March 27, 1914.

⁵ Senator O'Gorman suggested on March 25 that selfish interests were behind the fight against repeal of the tolls exemption. See the *Washington Post*, March 26, 1914.

⁶ Wilson visited the ailing Senator Stone at the Senator's home on March 25. See the *Washington Post*, March 26, 1914.

⁷ The *Washington Post*, March 26, 1914, reported that Argentina and Brazil opposed repeal because they hoped that their own coastwise shipping might be the beneficiaries of the tolls exemption.

⁸ Opponents of Secretary of State Bryan's "cooling-off" treaty with Denmark charged that it might require the United States to arbitrate the possible sale of Danish possessions in the Caribbean to Germany or Great Britain, thus undermining the Monroe Doctrine. See *ibid.*

March 30, 1914

Mr. President, Mr. Knowland, who is proposing a resolution to be introduced, made a statement that you had some deal with Sir William Tyrrell, secretary to Sir Edward Grey. Will you say anything about that?[1]

Of course, that answers itself. It is just the crowning of a number of insults which have been introduced into this debate. That is all I can say about that. In that connection, I want to express my regret that what promised to be a dignified contest, where there were genuine differences of opinion, has seemed to degenerate into an attempt to discredit the administration. It is a great pity that important public affairs should be handled in that way. It makes all the more certain the result, but it is a great pity. I do not mean that that is the effort on the part of even a majority of those who did not agree with the committee, but there are symptoms that that is the coloring that some are attempting now to give it.

Does that originate from political motives?

I don't know how it originated, sir.

I would like to ask, Mr. President, if you care to say anything about the idea as to free tolls being a subsidy?[2]

It certainly is a subsidy; and as between the principle of the party and a policy which violates that immemorial principle there ought not to be much difficulty in choosing. This whole thing reminds me now of a story I used to be fond of telling of a very effective debater—I need not say where this happened—who sent a challenge down into a county very hostile to him to debate. The people down there did not like the challenge very much, but they put up the man they liked best and who was generally put up on such occasions, a great big husky fellow whom they all called Tom. The challenger was given the first hour of the two hours allotted to the debate, and he hadn't got more than halfway through his speech when it became evident that he was convincing the audience; and one of Tom's partisans in the back of the room cried out, "Tom, Tom, call him a liar and make it a fight." That is the stage this has reached.

Are you going to fight, Mr. President?

I don't have to.

Mr. President, in that connection, it has been stated editorially in a number of places that you have abandoned the first high plane you had taken as the principle of carrying out an honest bargain, and had attempted to put it on some rather ambiguous grounds—will you say anything about that?

The only reply to that is, it isn't so. That is easy.

It is still insisted that the real principle is we have made a bargain and should live up to it?

Yes; but the only thing that may have given some excuse, if there be any at all, for the coloring you have spoken of is this: I said that in my opinion the thing was a plain violation of our agreement with Great Britain, but that I was not seeking to impose my opinions upon the Congress. I was stating to them a situation which was to this effect—that, however we might differ in this country, there was no difference of opinion anywhere else in the world as to its being a breach of contract, and that we couldn't afford to be regarded by all the rest of the world as not living up to our contractual agreements, particularly when we profess to make those contractual agreements in the interest of the whole world. If that isn't a high plane, I don't know where higher I could climb.

The editorials apparently were based on the last paragraph of your address to Congress with reference to other matters of greater delicacy.

Some editorial writers would base it on a single syllable if they could find the right syllable—if it were sibilant.

(When asked about Senator Lewis'[3] bill for compromising—instead of repealing the exemptions, to give the President power to suspend them—the President said:)

He has not consulted me at all about that.

Would you be willing to comment on that at this time, Mr. President?

I will have to tell you another story. A friend of mine, or rather, in view of the story, I should say an acquaintance of mine, was chairman of the local campaign committee in one of the Oranges in New Jersey, and on election day, towards the end of the day, an old colored man came in and stood, and shifted, and shifted, and finally my friend looked up and said: "Well, what do you want?" "Is dis Mr. Annin?"[4] "Yes." "Is you de chairman of de Republican Committee?" "Yes. What do you want?" "Well, Mr. Annin, I think dar is a lot ob dese niggers agoin' to vote de Democratic ticket." He said, "Well, what are you going to do about it." The darkey said, "I think if I had about two dollars apiece for dem niggers, I could fix 'em." Annin said, "Look here, what you are proposing is in any case wrong, but when you don't need the votes, it is a crime, and I don't need them." I don't know whether you can draw the moral or not.

Mr. President, would you care to repeat what you said once before about the party platform planks? You said something a couple of weeks ago about that plank relating to the tolls.

Why, if you examine the platform, you will find that there are two planks in it, one directly, as all other declarations of a party have been, against subsidies, direct or indirect, or any additional burden laid upon the people for the sake of encouraging shipping;[5] and the other with regard to tolls. Now, it ought not to be difficult to determine which should take precedence—a long-established principle of a party or what now seems to be an exception from that long-established practice. That is perfectly plain sailing to my mind; I don't see any escape from it.

Well, then, even if this international situation had not arisen, you still would be opposed to that declaration of the platform?

Yes, as inconsistent with the other, which takes precedence over it by a long series of declarations.

You wouldn't have been opposed to it to the extent of asking for the repeal?

No, because the act that I am now asking them to repeal was enacted by a Congress with which I was not associated. Of course, I am not going back trying to correct mistakes made before I had anything to do with the administration; but I should still have held that it was utterly inconsistent with Democratic practice. And one of the proofs is that a large majority of the Democrats in the House voted against the exemption to begin with. It never has been a policy of the Democrats in the House of Representatives.

Mr. President, in the last few days there have been dispatches from Berlin telling of instructions sent to Ambassador Gerard to protest against the German oil-monopoly bill. What feature of the bill is he protesting against? The German newspapers seem to think it was against the bill itself. I understand it was against certain features.[6]

The answer to that is he hasn't protested.

His instructions, then, were merely to inquire?

Yes, merely to inquire; and if there was a discrimination, he was to let us know what the nature of it was and whether there were any grounds for our protesting.

In that connection, Mr. President, do you know who made the complaint, the Standard Oil or the independents?

There were communications from the Standard Oil and from the independents, and from other quarters—on the other side of the water, Americans on the other side of the water, also. Just what their line of argument was, I don't know, because all that I was interested in was to have the Ambassador inquire whether there was any ground for complaint, whether it was an unjust discrimination.

You haven't seen a copy of the bill?

No, I have not. I saw an analysis of the bill, and, so far as I could make out from the analysis, there was nothing to protest against.

Is it true that the independents have said they are not particularly interested in it, that it wouldn't affect them at all?

It may be. To tell the truth, I paid so slight attention to the points raised before getting the information from the Ambassador as to the exact text of the bill, I can't answer that question.

His instructions were not to be regarded as a protest, just as an inquiry?

Just as an inquiry.

Some of the newspapers took it as a protest.

I don't know what he did, as a matter of fact; that hasn't been reported to me. His note may have been open to that construction, but it cannot have been intended as such.

You have not heard from him yet?

I have not. The department may have received dispatches that I have not seen.[7]

---

[1] Representative Joseph Russell Knowland, Republican of California, stated in the House on March 28 that Wilson had made a deal to repeal the Panama Canal tolls exemption in exchange for British cooperation in Mexico. See the *New York Times*, March 29, 1914, and *Cong. Record*, 63d Cong., 2d sess., p. 5707.

[2] That is, to the American shipping industry.

[3] Senator Lewis' bill (S. 5086) authorized the President to suspend the Panama Canal tolls when he regarded it to be in the national interest to do so. See *Cong. Record*, 63d Cong., 2d sess., p. 5649.

[4] Robert Edwards Annin of New Jersey.

[5] See Schlesinger and Israel, *American Presidential Elections*, III, 2175.

[6] Ambassador James Watson Gerard inquired in Berlin about the petroleum-monopoly bill then being considered by the Reichstag. This bill to create a German oil monopoly would have forced the dissolution of a subsidiary of Standard Oil, and Bryan instructed Gerard to inquire whether the American company would be adequately compensated for lost equipment and business. See the *New York Times*, March 29, 1914.

[7] Wilson permitted reporters to quote from this press conference, which was not his usual practice. See, for example, *ibid.*, March 31, 1914.

---

April 2, 1914

Mr. President, there is a story today to the effect that you had given your approval to a bill by Mr. Crosser of Ohio for the municipal ownership of street railways in the District?[1]

I haven't heard of the bill yet.

Has he consulted you about it?

No.

Have you any opinion on that question, Mr. President?

Well, I haven't had time to form one yet. I haven't been spoken to about it.

Mr. President, is there anything to say about any negotiations in regard to arranging things in Mexico? You remember we recently had a number of reports with regard to it.

Well, there is not; there is nothing to say about any negotiation.

Mr. President, have you expressed any opinion as to the request of the Poindexter resolution to have you submit to the Senate in executive session—

No, sir; all I know about it is what I have seen in the newspapers.

Would you favor doing that?

I don't meet occasions before they arise.

Mr. President, what is your information in regard to the prospect of an early action on the tolls bill?

I haven't really anything to go by. I am hoping and, from what I hear from various Senators, I think hoping with reason, that there will not be factional delay. I mean filibustering delay. Probably there will be a long discussion.

There seems to be very good opportunity of getting it out of the committee—

Yes, I think so.

At an early date?

I think one or two members of the committee, at any rate, who will not vote for the repeal are perfectly willing to have it reported out and settled in the open Senate. Somebody on "mischief bent" invented the statement that I had sent the Senate some kind of an ultimatum. I don't know whether it meant I was going to use the Army of the United States or not, but it was a most interesting and silly invention. I never sent any branch of the government an ultimatum about anything.[2]

I saw a story to that effect, Mr. President, but it spoke of Senator Owen's ultimatum; I didn't quite see what it meant.

I suppose so. The story was that he had consulted me and then had gone to the Senate and delivered this ultimatum. As a matter of fact, he didn't even see me. I was reminded of a man who lived in a ten-story building and who read a report that there had been a murder on the second story. He said the only truth in the report was the word "story"; there had been a theft on the third story.

Senator Owen made a statement yesterday morning, Mr. President, but I doubt whether it was supposed to have come from you; it didn't refer to you.

Well, it was misinterpreted, evidently, because several of the papers I saw said that he had consulted me and then had gone up and read the riot act to the Senate.

There was no authority for that in anything Senator Owen said?

Of course not; there couldn't have been.

Mr. President, have you voiced any view that the bill should go through the Senate unamended? There are still other propositions for compromise.

I haven't seen any of the Senators about that one way or the other, and I haven't heard any proposition from our side to amend it.

Mr. President, the Speaker, in his speech, made a very interesting point in a complaint that he had not been taken into your confidence with relation to the reasons that moved you to ask for a repeal. Would you care to discuss that?

No, I don't think it would be proper to discuss that.

Has any suggestion been made to you, Mr. President, of a caucus of the Senate Democrats on this question?

No, sir.

Mr. President, have you heard anything lately from Governor Lind in regard to his talks with various officers of the Mexican government who are in Veracruz?

Not recently, no. I had a dispatch from him just after his talk with the Minister of Foreign Affairs, and that didn't amount to anything. I mean the Minister didn't have any suggestions or proposals to make. It was just a friendly talk, apparently.

Nothing that could be construed by this government as a suggestion that they might meet us halfway—nothing like that.

No; nothing at all. By the way, I want to tell you gentlemen, for fear you should think something was happening, that Mr. Lind, as I understand, sails tomorrow on the ship *Solace* for the United

States because he is worn out with his labors down there and wants a vacation. I don't blame him. He is not being recalled; he is coming at his own request.[3]

Is he going to Minnesota?

I think he is going to the French Lick Springs.[4] It is only for a vacation.

Is it indefinite, Mr. President?

Well, indefinite in respect of the time that it will require him to rest.

He will surely come to Washington?

I suppose so, though there is no special reason why he should. His dispatches are really very remarkable. I wish they could be published as literary productions.

So do we.

I don't think you want them merely as literary productions. I mean he has a great faculty for setting things forth clearly. That is what makes me think there is no special reason why he should come to Washington, because we know his mind very fully. And Washington is not a good place to rest.

Mr. President, there was some suggestion that your rural-credits legislation is to be given precedence over the trust program.

Nothing of that sort has been suggested.

Mr. President, Senators have begun to talk of the session lasting until September or October. Has there been some process suggested of condensing the program, or something of that sort?

We can easily dispose of the present program by the time we all want to get away—the middle of June or the first of July.

That will include the trust program?

Yes.

Have you any knowledge of or ideas regarding the proposals to reorganize the Indian Bureau?[5]

No, sir, I have not. Is there a proposal pending to that effect?

There is quite a merry row on in the Committee on Indian Affairs. Mr. President, there has been some misunderstanding as to the time when the Federal Reserve Board will be appointed. There is some story to the effect that it wouldn't have to be appointed until the districts and the banks are organized and in full operation. That, of course, will take a couple of months or more.

Well, it wouldn't have to be. As for the time when it will be, I haven't settled that at all.

It might be a matter of months?

It might be as far off as I could postpone it, and it might be much sooner. What I mean to say is I am simply taking all the time I can, because I haven't satisfied myself in the search for men yet.

Mr. President, in reference to the legislative program, is it contemplated at this session to pass a Philippine independence act?

I have lost track of that legislation—I don't mean of that question. I don't know what stage the Philippine bill is at.

It hasn't been reported to any committee yet?

No. My mind is "to let" on that subject. I do not know anything about it.

Mr. President, have you any information as to when a decision in the 5-percent freight rate cases would come?[6]

No, sir, I do not know where that statement that was in the papers this morning came from, that it would probably be within the limits of this month.

The commissioners are expected to say something on that very soon, Mr. President?

Yes, I had heard that mentioned, but I had not heard that a statement promising action had been made.

Have you given any special consideration to the bill looking toward the abolition of interstate commerce in prison-made goods?[7]

No, sir.

Would you favor such a prohibition?

I couldn't say in such-and-such a form. I do not favor any bill except when I know the terms of the bill.

Mr. President, have you given any consideration to increasing the scope of work done by the Children's Bureau? The House Committee had cut the appropriation from one hundred and sixty-four thousand dollars down to twenty-five thousand dollars.[8]

Yes, I am very sorry for that.

It has been suggested that, under the act which created the bureau, that it would take another act in order to increase its scope. Would you recommend that?

Well, I haven't studied the act. I would not be entitled to an opinion on that. The act, as I remember it, provides that the bureau should study all questions affecting the life and labor of children, which would certainly seem to be broad enough to cover anything.

There is a limitation on the number of persons that can be employed to study them.
It is limited to fifteen.

Well, an appropriations act could easily change that.

Mr. President, have you determined the Alaskan railroad route?

I think I have, but I am not ready to announce it.

Have you decided upon the men?

No, not yet.

---

[1] Representative Robert Crosser, Democrat of Ohio, introduced a bill (H.R. 15191) to provide for municipally owned street railway lines for the District of Columbia. Wilson did not endorse the measure. See the *Washington Post*, April 3, 1914.

[2] On April 2, 1914, the *New York Times* reported that Senator Owen, a member of the Committee on Inter-Oceanic Canals, said, while leaving the White House, that "strong measures might be necessary to get the bill before the Senate." The *New York Times* stated on April 3 that Owen intended to introduce a resolution to discharge the committee if it did not act promptly to report the repeal bill. In fact, Senator Owen did not see Wilson on the day that he went to the White House.

[3] About Lind's visit to the United States, see Hill, *Emissaries to a Revolution*, pp. 174-76.

[4] In Indiana.

[5] The bill being debated (S. 4164) provided for more efficient administration of Indian affairs through the creation of a commission and had been introduced by Senator Joseph Taylor Robinson, Democrat of Arkansas. See *Cong. Record*, 63d Cong., 2d sess., p. 2256.

April 6, 1914

I see you are trying to get an increase in the railroad rates.

Oh well, you know, I explained to you gentlemen before that I couldn't express any opinion about that because the commission is a semijudicial body and it wouldn't be proper for me to do so.

Speaking of the Interstate Commerce Commission—this is just for your private consumption—I don't want anybody to get a false impression of Mr. Daniels.[1] I have known Mr. Daniels intimately for nearly twenty years. I have fought alongside him for the things I think are best, at any rate, for the life of the country. There is not a more just or enlightened man in the United States, if I am a judge of men, than he is. I think that this is the principle we ought all to go on in selecting public servants, not to select a man who you think beforehand will decide this way or that, but a man whom, so far as you can judge him, you know to be just.

I want to say, gentlemen, that justice is the hardest thing in the world. It takes more courage, it takes more strength, it takes more conscience than anything else. Now this is a just man, if I know him, and I ought to know him, because I have been intimately associated with him, and we have fought for all sorts of things together. I don't want anything that might have created misapprehension in the minds of some Senators to get a reopening in your minds.

Mr. President, speaking of confirmation, have you looked into this McNally case at all?[2]

I don't even know what it is.

It will be too long to explain. That fight out there—a man who was nominated, from Tsingtau. Finally from the incumbent, Newmann, comes charges of embezzlement and bribery and for other things like that.

It hasn't come to my attention.

Can you say anything about Secretary Daniels' order, Mr. President, on the liquor—[3]

I have nothing to say about that. That is a departmental matter.

Mr. President, does the correspondence that you are receiving show any widespread opposition or widespread popular opposition to your position with regard to the Panama Canal tolls?

No. Quite the contrary. Very much to the contrary.

The reason I asked was, although the press of the country seems generally to be favorable, some people who are visiting here from various sections of the country seem to indicate other feelings, and I wondered whether that had reached you?

Of course, it may be that people want to send me favorable impressions, but I haven't got any such impressions as that. On the contrary, friends who have been traveling have sent me just the opposite. In the railroad trains and buses, in casual and overheard conversations and comment, I think it shows that feeling is very much behind me.

Is it your opinion—information—Mr. President, that the country is particularly excited one way or the other?

No, it is not.

Do you believe that there is any plot to buy the canal?[4]

No, I didn't know it could be bought by a plot.

Well, a scheme or plan.

By whom?

By several European nations.

That could be commented on in pearly language.

That story was known yesterday before the *Post* was published. That is the reason it was asked.

Well, you know, there are all kinds of fools in this world. It wouldn't do to classify them publicly.

Do you think that the canal question will enter largely into the campaigns of this fall? Do you think it will be one of the issues?

It will be entirely over then.

Have you got any information, Mr. President, as to the progress in the Senate on the program that is being followed?

Nothing that I can call definite information. I just get impressions and all are favorable.

Mr. President, have you heard of the action of the Huerta government in refusing to continue to recognize Carothers, one of our Consuls in Mexico?[5]

No.

There is a story to that effect, charging him with being biased in confirming the reports of the fall of Torreón. They still continue to deny that the city has been taken.

I am not at all surprised that they would not recognize the people who tell the truth. Their recognition has nothing to do with Carothers. He operates in the northern states, where they don't control at all.

Mr. President, in that connection, dispatches Saturday, and yesterday, stated that General Carranza desired recognition now but the United States has held to belligerency [until it becomes] the *de facto* government. Has the administration considered that at all?

He hasn't expressed that desire to the administration.[6]

Has the administration taken that up in any way?

No.

Mr. President, has there been any effort to interest you in changing the decision of the Federal Reserve Bank organization committee?[7]

No. Of course there has to be unhappiness with the decision in some quarters, but I want to say that it was absolutely none of my business under the law, and it would be improper for me to make any suggestions of any kind. But I do know how thoroughly and conscientiously the organization committee considered the facts. Not the facts with regard to any one city, but the facts of the regions as they related themselves to one another. So that their choice was based upon actual conditions of financial exchange, trade, capitalization, lending, and everything of that sort. I believe, from the statistics that I have seen, that the thing is very solid indeed.

You wouldn't be ready to say now when the Federal Reserve Board will be named?

I don't know yet.

Mr. President, do you still anticipate that your trust program will be completed and passed before Congress adjourns?

Yes, sir.

And that they will adjourn in June?

I hope so.

There is a story, Mr. President, printed this morning, to the effect that there was quite a bash in the Judiciary Committee of the House and that you were going to be called upon to wave the olive branch?[8]

Where did you get this report?

I don't know, sir. It didn't say. Just that you had been appealed to—you were going to be appealed to.

If it was in that form, it had no foundation in fact. I mean, I have not been appealed to, or heard of anything.

Mr. President, have you had any confirmation of the Torreón report—about Villa?[9]

No.

In connection with Mexico, Mr. President, is it the purpose of the administration not to recognize anyone until order among the people is restored, or is that more or less a practical—

You mean, to recognize?

Any government as *de facto*?

That will depend upon the course of events.

There has been some discussion of the point that the government here would not recognize anyone down there until law and order had been restored—until a fair election was held.

That has been the practice of this government. For example, when old Porfirio Díaz became President, this government waited, I think, eighteen months, at any rate, a period of almost two years in length, before it recognized him at all.[10] So that we have always been very slow to recognize a government that was in the making.

You wouldn't care to say whether you would follow that precedent or not, or whether you would depend entirely upon circumstances?

We will depend entirely upon the development of events there.

[1] Winthrop More Daniels, a former Professor of Economics at Princeton, who had been nominated by Wilson for the Interstate Commerce Commission in January 1914. Progressives led by La Follette protested against the nomination because they regarded Daniels as a "reactionary" who would approve the 5-per-cent rate increase, but the Senate confirmed the appointment on April 3. See Link, *The New Freedom*, pp. 449-50, and the *New York Times*, April 3-4, 1914.

[2] James Clifford McNally, formerly Consul at Tsingtau, was being considered by the Senate for the position of United States Consul at Nuremberg. He was being attacked by J. F. Newmann over a real estate transaction at Tsingtau. McNally was not confirmed by the Senate. See the *New York Times*, April 8, 1914.

[3] Secretary of the Navy Daniels had ordered a ban on shipboard liquor or wine in the navy, to become effective on July 1. See *ibid.*, April 6, 1914.

[4] The *Washington Post*, April 6, 1914, reported that the repeal of the Panama Canal tolls exemption was the first step in a plan for internationalization of the canal. Under this alleged plan, several European nations would reimburse the United States for its expenses in constructing the waterway.

[5] Following Villa's victory in the battle of Torreón, Huerta claimed that Carothers' reports were biased against his forces. He charged the American Consul with unethical behavior for siding with the revolutionaries, withdrew his exequatur, and declared him *persona non grata* in Mexico. The State Department ignored Huerta's charges, and Carothers remained in Mexico. See the *New York Times*, April 4-6, 1914, and Hill, *Emissaries to a Revolution*, pp. 162-64.

[6] For a clear statement of Carranza's desire to obtain recognition, see the *New York Times*, April 7, 1914.

[7] Federal Reserve districts and bank cities were named on April 2, and some cities were naturally disappointed. See *ibid.*, April 3-4, 1914.

[8] On April 6, 1914, the New York *World* reported that Democrats on the committee feared a deadlock over an exemption for labor in the Clayton bill which could only be settled by Wilson's intervention. See also Link, *The New Freedom*, pp. 427-29.

[9] After capturing Torreón, Villa announced that he would deport the 600 Spaniards living there. See the *New York Times*, April 6, 1914; Hill, *Emissaries to a Revolution*, pp. 165-66; and the Secretary of State to Special Agent Carothers, April 6, 1914, in *FR, 1914*, pp. 796-97.

[10] Porfirio Díaz became President on May 2, 1876, and was recognized by the United States Government on April 8, 1878.

April 9, 1914

Mr. President, you had a conference with Mr. Malone[1] yesterday; did he indicate anything that might be said as coming from you?

No, except that I have been distressed at the color given everything concerning Mr. Malone by some reports. Mr. Malone is one of the closest friends I have, and anything that represents me as rebuking Mr. Malone in any respect is just pure fiction. Now, that is just for your own ears, for your own guidance. I do not want to be quoted in this matter because the minute you contradict something that plainly isn't so, you give color to it. I am not going to contradict anything, but anybody who tries to make trouble between Dudley Malone and me is going to get nothing whatever for his pains. My friends and I cannot be separated by fiction.

Does that mean, Mr. President, that you approved of Mr. Malone's view of Governor Glynn's administration?

I don't know what Mr. Malone's view of Governor Glynn's administration is.

He has been quoted once or twice in criticism of it.

Well, quote him; he generally knows what he is talking about.

Mr. President, it was intimated in a number of newspapers yesterday and today that when the occasion arises you expect to show the animus of the newspapers whose criticisms of your Panama [tolls] policy you have regarded as unfair.

I don't think that is necessary. I think it shows itself. I don't undertake unnecessary jobs.

It was intimated that you would go a little bit further than that.

No, I never discourse on the obvious.

What do you understand the obvious animus to be, Mr. President?

Just what you understand it to be.

You haven't lost any confidence in the passage of the bill?

Not the slightest. On the contrary, I have gained more. If some gentlemen want to play with boomerangs, who are not accustomed to handling them, I always know what is going to happen.

Mr. President, can you discuss the proposed treaty with Colombia?[2]

No, sir, because it hasn't reached me, and I don't know the terms of it.

Do you know whether or not, Mr. President, that twenty-five million dollars is the correct sum?

It may be, but I am not definitely informed that was finally accepted down there. I only know what propositions were to be discussed.

Do you know whether Colombia demanded an apology or not?

She did not and was not given one.

Mr. President, some dispatches this morning said that you had sort of softened the blow, so to speak—that you had told Colombia, or rather your embassy had, that we were wrong in acquiring possession of this territory in the manner which we did.[3]

I didn't express any opinion about it one way or another. No, that is all "guff," pure "guff." I hope that is universally intelligible language.

Mr. President, do you understand that the treaty will contain anything that could be called an expression of regret? That is the phrase that is used by certain parties.

How many forms are you going to ask the same question in? I have answered it.

Mr. President, is there an agreement of some kind to have this treaty published on a certain date, based on any action by the Colombian Senate?[4]

There is no agreement like that that I know of.

I think there is a dispatch from down there that there is an agreement between the two governments to have it published after the holidays?

There is so much information that is not so coming from down there that I don't think you might attach any more importance to one item than to another.

Mr. President, does your knowledge of the negotiations contain any information about the rights and privileges which Colombia was to be accorded on the canal?

To tell you the truth, I haven't been following the details of the negotiations. I remember very clearly the main lines that were laid down for the negotiations and the limits within which changes were regarded as admissible, but just the final form has not been brought to me.

Mr. President, have you made any progress at all with Russia with regard to negotiating a new treaty?

We haven't begun. I am waiting until I find an Ambassador.

Could you say whether you are going to have a new Ambassador soon?

I hope so.

Can you give us any intimation who he is?

No, because I am puzzling between two or three.

Mr. President, the situation in Mexico with reference to the Spaniards is somewhat perplexing to us newspapermen. I don't know whether it is to the administration or not. If it isn't, we would like to know.

I don't think that there is anything I can say about it.

In face of the unofficial representations made by this government through the State Department to General Carranza and Villa, quite a number—six hundred and some odd—of Spaniards were expelled from Torreón.

So I understand.

And almost simultaneously the British commander of the warship *Hermione* announced to Admiral Mayo that he had been instructed to take care of the Spanish refugees.[5] I wonder if that has any direct connection with the situation in northern Mexico.

So far as I know, it has not, though one would naturally connect the two. But I have no knowledge that they are directly connected.

How has Carranza's attitude in this case been accepted or interpreted by this government—as a rebuke or merely as a political, or diplomatic, maneuver?

I can only speak entirely unofficially about that. I know only what everybody else knows, namely, that from the outset the Constitutionalists have shown a distrust, a particular distrust, of the Spaniards. What they have based it on, I don't know, but they have in every city that they have entered shown an inclination to discriminate against the Spaniards. That really is all I know about it, and that is, as I say, what everybody else knows.

Mr. President, have you been getting any information as to how far the Spanish government has gone in entrusting her subjects to Great Britain?

No, I have not.

Does General Carranza's refusal to grant the request tend to complicate the relations between the governments?[6]

Grant which request?

Why, day before yesterday, or night before last, the State Department made a second or third request with regard to the Spaniards, and General Carranza replied yesterday that he did not propose to interfere and General Villa carried out his instructions by sending out all Spaniards whom he mistrusted.

Of course, the only authority the United States Government would have with regard to the nationals of another country would be to make a protest.

It wouldn't tend to force an issue between this government and the Constitutionalists, then?

I don't see how it could at present. You understand that in a state of war everything awaits subsequent settlement. It doesn't mean that, when nothing further happens at the moment, there will not be a final settling up of claims.

Is there anything about the Federal Reserve Board?

No, sir; we will have to keep that as a perennial topic.

Can you say anything about Andrew Carnegie's call on you today?

Yes, sir, anything you want me to say.

Can you tell us what he wanted?

He didn't want anything. He is quite removed from want. No; it was entirely a friendly visit. He was passing through and he came in to pay his compliments. He didn't ask a thing or discuss a single public question.

Mr. President, did Congressman Buchanan[7] call today?

He did call.

Was it about the Children's Bureau?

No, sir, it was about a post office somewhere. But it was Congressman Buchanan from Texas.

Miss Lathrop's[8] call, I suppose, was about the Children's Bureau?

Yes, of course.

Did you reach any conclusion with regard to what action to take?

About what?

About trying to get that appropriation she desires?

That wasn't the subject of her call. I had some time ago written to the Commissioner of Education and to Miss Lathrop suggesting the possibility of cooperation between those two bureaus in certain matters, and it was with regard to that. I have spent such time as I could devote to it to the interesting task of trying to draw the different pieces of this government together so that they would be cooperative.

Mr. President, have you had any information to indicate what are the objects of the visit of the Queen of Bulgaria[9] here, other than a mere visit to the country, whether she is going to look into welfare work and things of that sort?

No, I know only what was in the papers. I don't know anything more about the subject.

---

[1] Dudley Field Malone visited Wilson on April 8 to discuss New York politics. Malone had recently been critical of the Glynn administration, and the press reported that the President had reacted strongly to his criticisms. Wilson reassured Malone that these reports were not true, and Malone emerged from the meeting in good humor. See the *New York Times*, March 30 and April 9, 1914.

[2] A treaty was signed in Bogotá on April 6 which restored cordial relations between the United States and Colombia, provided for an indemnity of $25,000,000 to Colombia for the loss of Panama, and gave Colombian citizens free use of the Panama Canal. See the *New York Times*, April 9, 1914; Link, *The New Freedom*, pp. 321-23; and Minister [Thaddeus Austin] Thomson to the Secretary of State, April 6, 1914, in *FR, 1914*, pp. 154-55. For the text of the treaty, see *ibid.*, pp. 163-64.

[3] Article I expressed "sincere regret" that anything should have occurred to interrupt or mar good relations between the United States and Colombia. See *FR, 1914*, p. 163.

[4] The agreement called for the treaty to be published on May 14 or 15. See Minister Thomson to the Secretary of State, April 6, 1914, in *ibid.*, pp. 154-55.

[5] As the British commander informed Rear Adm. Henry Thomas Mayo, the American commander at Tampico, the Spanish government had placed its citizens there under the protection of the British fleet. See the *New York Times*, April 9, 1914.

[6] When Carothers protested to Carranza against the treatment of the Spaniards, the First Chief denied the right of the United States to intercede on behalf of foreign citizens. On April

12, Carothers succeeded in negotiating an arrangement with Carranza whereby American intercession would be accepted if the agent's instructions stated specifically that the nation involved had requested the United States to intervene. See Special Agent Carothers to the Secretary of State, April 9 and 14, 1914, in *FR, 1914*, pp. 801 and 806, and Hill, *Emissaries to a Revolution*, pp. 166-67.

7 Representative James Paul Buchanan, Democrat of Texas.

8 Julia Clifford Lathrop, head of the Children's Bureau.

9 Queen Eleanora of Bulgaria was scheduled to visit the United States in May. Her spokesman stated that she was coming to study American hospital administration and charitable work. See the *New York Times*, April 10 and 14, 1914.

April 13, 1914

Mr. President, there was a story in several of the papers this morning to the effect that Congress would adjourn without passing the trust program unless they thought they really had to.[1]

That is put in, gentlemen, I must assume, in some minds, because "the hope is father to the thought," but there is no such thing contemplated.

One suggestion was that one bill would go through.

I saw what you are alluding to, but there is no foundation to it whatever. I haven't heard anybody even suggest that we hesitate about our program.

There has been some suggestion that Senator Robinson and other Senators would talk to you about curtailing it to some extent. Not entirely?

No, that is not true. I had a talk with Senator Robinson about the trust bills, but no suggestions whatever were made about curtailing the program.

Are you determined that the trust bills should be passed?

I think it is absolutely necessary, yes, to keep faith with the country.

If the trust program can be carried out, do you think we can get away from here in July?

If they will adopt the express schedule instead of a freight schedule, yes. And I don't mean by that cutting short the necessary discussion, but getting at the procrastinators.

What is your information as to the status of the program as far as the Judiciary Committee is concerned?

I am going to meet with the subcommittee of their committee today at 11:30.[2]

Is it right what the insiders say, that they are rather dilatory?

That is not fair to them. They have really been working at it very hard.

Ten weeks, right?

Yes, but ten weeks is not a long time in which to understand the business of the country or to try to understand it.

Is there any [reason for bringing Lind] back?[3]

Not that I know of, sir. To tell the truth, I didn't know he was coming until I saw my schedule this morning.

Mr. President, will you say anything about last week's events at Tampico?[4]

No. I am just busy learning the details. I haven't caught up with all the dispatches since I got back this morning,[5] so that at present I have no mature opinion on the subject.

Mr. President, has the salute been made by the Mexican authorities?

Not that I know of.

Do you think it will be?

I think it will be.

Does the Mexican government show any tendency to refuse to comply with our demand?

I would rather not discuss it at all until I get more fully informed, because I can't answer those questions without full knowledge.

Mr. President, this urgent situation in Torreón where Villa is still insisting that the Spaniards must go.[6]

Well, again I haven't caught up. I took a real vacation while I was at it.

Could you tell us, Mr. President, whether Spain has made any direct request of us in the matter?

No, I cannot. I don't know whether she has or not.

Will Mr. Lind be here tomorrow?

Either today or tomorrow. I hope today. But there has been a hiatus in his information since he left there.

Have you any information as to the sentiment in Colombia with respect to this treaty, as to whether they will agree down there to accept it. Some stories seem to think it might be rejected.[7]

I understand that it had been accepted, or was to be, before it had been considered by the authorities here, but I can't say that authoritatively.

Mr. President, can you say anything about the tolls repeal situation?

Why, I think it is constantly improving, from my point of view. Apparently, the gentlemen who were going to appear at the hearings are getting "cold feet"—in the vernacular.

Mr. President, the question as to whether our repeal of the law at this time is to be an interpretation of the treaty[8] or whether it is merely to remove a possible difficulty—

It couldn't be an interpretation of the treaty, because the repeal is a legislative act and not an interpretation of the treaty authoritatively done in consultation with the Senate. It is only a legislative act.

Mr. President, do you care to comment on the criticism that has been made of the Colombian treaty, inasmuch as it would permit Colombian war vessels to go through the canal free?[9]

I am not going to say much. Criticize the treaty process and you are automatically criticizing the treaty. I always think that is a necessary preliminary.

Have you seen that poll that has been made of the delegates to the Baltimore convention on the tolls question?[10]

I saw what was in the Baltimore *Sun*. I think it was this morning.

Mr. President, are we to judge from that remark—may we conclude from that remark—that there has been some misunderstanding with regard to the details of the Colombian treaty?

Just that its full text is not here.

Has Mr. Carnegie approached you with reference to getting a federal charter—which Mr. Carnegie indicated? It was said that he was trying to forestall investigation of governmental expenditures never ordered. Are those statements true?[11]

Absolutely false. He didn't mention either subject to me, in person or by letter. I didn't realize that the field of fiction was so large.

Mr. President, has it been decided as to whether or not it would be necessary for you to give your approval to Secretary Daniels' [order]?[12]

That profound question hasn't been put up to me. I suppose, theoretically, strictly speaking, every order of every department is subject to the approval of the President. I don't know whether that is true or not.

The distinction was made between the mere draft on the part of the Secretary and a change of regulation. It was pointed out that you would have to approve an order before it would become effective.

If so, he will report it to me. He hasn't brought it to me yet.

Mr. President, is it a fair question, is there objection to amending the repeal bill slightly, in the form suggested?[13]

What form do you refer to?

The one containing a declaration of no surrender of rights—

I have simply heard people declare that. It hasn't been proposed to me.

There has been a suggestion, which I think is being more or less seriously considered, Mr. President, that the Norris amendment be accepted; and I understand that Senator Norris is willing to waive the last few lines of it, which would direct the President to take steps toward arbitration that would simply leave an expression of opinion, and if anybody wanted to arbitrate it, we had no objection.

The Norris amendment hasn't been seriously suggested to me at all. And I don't see any anxiety among the Senators who will constitute the majority to amend it. It is so obvious that a legislative act is not an interpretation of a treaty that—

The point is made that this would increase your majority slightly.

Oh. I am not working for numbers.

Mr. President, some of the papers have published statements to the effect that the name of Mr. Sharp[14] has been submitted to you recently, but that it has not been favorably received because of some objection.

That is absolutely false. It hasn't been submitted. I haven't made a choice. That is most unfair to Mr. Sharp.

Have you anything to say about the Federal Reserve Board yet?

No, sir.

[1] The *Washington Post*, April 13, 1914, reported that Democratic leaders in Congress did not intend to press for antitrust legislation unless Wilson insisted.

[2] For a report of this meeting, see *ibid.*, April 14, 1914.

[3] Lind arrived in Washington April 13 for meetings with Wilson and Bryan. See *ibid.*, April 14, 1914.

[4] At Tampico on April 9, 1914, the crew of a whaleboat from U.S.S. *Dolphin* was arrested and detained by Mexican officials. Admiral Mayo responded by demanding an apology and a salute to the American flag by Mexico. See the Secretary of State to President Wilson, April 10, 1914, in *FR, 1914*, p. 449, and Robert E. Quirk, *An Affair of Honor: Woodrow Wilson and the Occupation of Veracruz* (Lexington, Ky., 1962).

[5] Wilson had spent Easter with his family at White Sulphur Springs, West Virginia.

[6] See above, April 6, 1914.

[7] See above, April 9, 1914.

[8] That is, the Hay-Pauncefote Treaty.

[9] Senator O'Gorman, an opponent of tolls repeal, made this charge on April 12. See the *Washington Post*, April 13, 1914.

[10] Thomas Jones Pence, "director" of the Democratic National Committee, issued a report of a poll taken by Senator Thomas Pryor Gore, Democrat of Oklahoma, which indicated that delegates to the Baltimore convention now favored repeal. See *ibid.*, April 14, 1914.

[11] The *Washington Post*, April 11, 1914, reported that Andrew Carnegie was attempting to obtain a federal charter for the Carnegie Endowment for International Peace to forestall an investigation into the organization's use of federal funds to distribute speeches.

[12] It had been suggested that Wilson needed to approve Daniels' order prohibiting alcoholic beverages on shipboard. Daniels argued that his order was only an instruction, not a regulation, and thus did not require presidential approval. See *ibid.*, April 12, 1914.

[13] Senator Norris, on April 1, proposed an amendment to the tolls repeal bill which stated that the United States was not surrendering any of its treaty rights with Great Britain. See *ibid.*, April 14, 1914, and *Cong. Record*, 63d Cong., 2d sess., p. 6097.

[14] Sharp was being considered at this time for the position of Ambassador to Russia. See Link, *The New Freedom*, p. 103, n. 30.

April 16, 1914

Mr. President, is it true that you have official word that Huerta is going to authorize the giving of that salute?[1]

All I can say at present is that the advices are very encouraging.

Mr. President, can you tell us along that line whether it is customary for a government that is receiving a salute in reparation to return that salute?

It is invariable, that is my information; there is no known exception.

On the theory that you touch your hat to a man if he apologizes to you?

Yes, and you take his hand if he extends it.

Mr. President, under the peculiar circumstances which exist, would that involve recognition of the Huerta government?

No, it is the return of a recognition. I mean it is a return of a courtesy.

Mr. President, can you tell us anything, now that we seem to be getting down to what has been happening, what proposition was made by the Mexican government with reference to saluting the *Dolphin* or the flag of Admiral Boush[2] or some proposition of that sort?

As a matter of fact, no proposition was made, Mr. Oulahan. Those propositions, I think, were speculative, and if made by anybody were made by subordinate officials on the spot.

There was no offer, Mr. President, to fire a salute of five guns, was there?

No, not that I heard of.

That was based on the idea, Mr. President, that the commander of the *Dolphin* was entitled to five guns.

I simply hadn't heard of that.

That, of course, would have been a personal salute to the commander of the *Dolphin* and not a national salute?

It would be a personal salute.

Mr. President, if Huerta does fire this salute, will you keep all those fleets there, or will they be withdrawn?[3]

Our thought hasn't got that far. They were due, I think, to arrive tomorrow, but you see, they had been at Hampton Roads and were due to be ordered somewhere; they will naturally be disposed of according to the circumstances.

Mr. President, will the firing of the salute be considered reparation for the other incidents[4] which have been mentioned as well as the one at Tampico?

The other incidents were all apologized for, you understand, and the only thing asked in this particular instance in addition to the apology was the salute.

Mr. President, can you add a little to what you said a minute ago to the effect that your advices were encouraging?

No, because that is as far as it goes. As a matter of fact, I was trying to put in a single phrase my general impression.

That is, you have no details in mind as to where or by whom the salute is to be fired?

Nothing final, no.

Mr. President, is there anything official on just what is happening in the fighting about Torreón in the last few days?

No, I haven't heard of anything beyond what is in the public dispatches.

There is no official information at all of results there?

No, I haven't heard of anything beyond what is in the public dispatches.

Has there been any official confirmation that Villa has won the last battle?

I haven't heard of any official confirmation of that. I did see a letter from Torreón which spoke very favorably of Villa's treatment of the wounded and of his prisoners.

Mr. President, there was a story published in several New York papers the other day to the effect that Chargé O'Shaughnessy's conduct was not satisfactory to the administration and that he might be recalled.[5]

I noticed that that has sprung up two or three times. There is no basis to that.

Mr. President, can you tell us something about the situation in regard to the representations which we have made to General Carranza on behalf of the Spanish Government?

No, I have not been informed about that within the last day or two.

Mr. President, can you tell us something about the conditions in the City of

Mexico? We are not getting any press dispatches from there; there is a very strict censorship on.

I can't tell you anything except that we occasionally, or repeatedly—twice a week—get assurances from O'Shaughnessy that everything is perfectly quiet there, with no apprehension or disturbance or inconvenience to foreigners.

Is the Congress in session?

I judged from one dispatch that the Senate was in session, but whether that is true or not I couldn't tell. It was an incidental reference. It was only an inference of my own on the spot.

Mr. President, can you tell us anything of your conference with Governor Lind?[6]

I am quite willing to tell you all there is to tell. It was just a conversation to supplement his dispatches, a discussion of what he understood the situation to be from several points of view. There was nothing new in it, if that is what you mean.

There was no intimation of a new policy that might be adopted?

No, he hasn't recommended any policy.

Mr. President, would you care to say whether the negotiations now hinge on the question of whether we will return Huerta's salute?

I have already answered that; the salute is invariably returned.

The report is current that the German and French governments would lend their good offices in negotiating the salute [with Huerta].

I don't know whether that is true or not; I hope it is.

Mr. President, to return to Governor Lind, has it been decided whether or not he is to go back?

That depends upon his personal convenience. He is pretty tired.

Is there anything in the present situation that will prevent his going back?

No, nothing at all.

Mr. President, does Mr. Lind believe that the Constitutionalists will win?

I don't know; you will have to ask him.

I will put it in another way. Does he believe that Huerta can stay?

I didn't ask him; I think we are about as able to conjecture about it here as he would be there.

Mr. President, when Villa took Torreón, he found a lot of cotton there. It was the property of Spanish and British citizens and I understand both the Spanish and British governments have protested about it. Is there anything being done?

I suppose so. You know, what happened with me is that dispatches appeared under my eye, and in reading them I took it for granted that the thing was being attended to. I didn't make any inquiries.

I don't suppose there is any way of enforcing payment for that cotton?

Not at the present; it goes on the books.

It is claimed that Villa is proceeding on what was done in the United States half a century ago,[7] when cotton was found and seized as contraband of war.

I will have to look that up.

The Senators and Representatives who talked to you yesterday[8] gained an impression that this government would not resort to any force, unless circumstances made force immediately necessary, until you had gone before Congress and explained your position in the matter and obtained the sanction of Congress for whatever program you had in mind.

That would naturally be the course I would take. I hope and believe that it is not a matter that will need discussion. Nobody doubts, as I understand it, that the Executive would have the right to take the immediate steps necessary in a case like this just to obtain the recognition of the government's dignity, but when the Congress is actually in session, it would be natural for the President to keep in close cooperation with it, no matter whether he had the authority to act without it or not.

I understand that yesterday you cited the precedents of the bombardment of Greytown, Nicaragua, in President Pierce's administration[9] and the firing on Japanese forts[10] as giving you authority.

I did, and I didn't. What I mean to say was I was reading from a memorandum prepared by the Department of State.[11]

Well, a pacific blockade wouldn't be considered an act of war.[12]

It doesn't amount to much either.

By what right, Mr. President, do you say it doesn't amount to much?

The very fact that it is pacific, that is to say, [the fact that] it isn't based upon a declaration or a state of war makes it questionable what the blockading nation has the right to do with regard to ships of other nations entering and leaving the ports. Those questions always arise and, so far as I can learn of the precedents, have never been answered satisfactorily.

The last case, I believe, was in the Venezuelan blockade by Great Britain, Germany, and Italy.[13]

I suppose; I don't remember.

Didn't the United States take a position at that time that there is no such thing as a pacific blockade under international law?

I don't remember; I didn't have my ears open then.

Mr. President, it has been said that Mr. O'Shaughnessy reported that the approach of the Constitutionalists toward Mexico City—nearer to Mexico City— was almost certain to cause anarchy there in the capital. Do you recall seeing anything about that?

I didn't see anything about that.

Mr. President, you appointed, I think, in the last few days Mr. John Campbell White to be Third Assistant Secretary of the embassy?

Yes, sir.

There was no suggestion of a recognition of the government in appointing this man?

That isn't involved in any way. Nobody but the Ambassador and the First Secretary are accredited to the government. The others are merely assigned by routine, and Mr. White had passed the examination of the highest grade.

Mr. President, can you tell us whether there will be any forcible action taken at Tampico or Veracruz before Admiral Badger[14] arrives at either of those ports?

That is based on conjecture, which I don't think need be discussed. No action, I think, can be necessary.

Mr. President, it was printed, I think, Sunday night that the Mexican authorities had demanded this return of salute from us?[15]

That isn't true.

Mr. President, did this question of the return of the salute come up between the State Department and the Navy Department at all?

No, except inquiry for information as to what is customary.

Mr. President, has sending of the Pacific Fleet down to the West Coast of Mexico any special significance?[16]

Most of the vessels of that fleet have been there all along.

They are sending another regiment of marines down there.

That has no more significance than this other has.

Mr. President, by way of encouragement, can we expect something more definite today?

I don't know when—it is your phrase, I think—the news will break.

May I ask if we return that salute whom we would be saluting?

You may ask it, sir, but you will have to answer it. I don't know any more than you do.

Mr. President, may I ask this: if he makes the salute and we return it, will that end the incident?

Why, of course.

Under international law we can land marines without that being construed as a declaration of war?

Oh, yes.

[1] To the American flag. See above, April 13, 1914.

[2] Rear Adm. Clifford Joseph Boush, commander of the second division of the Atlantic Fleet. The Mexican Sub-secretary of Foreign Affairs proposed that the salute be made to the flag on the *Dolphin* to avoid the demonstrations that might arise from the hoisting of the American flag on Mexican soil. See Chargé O'Shaughnessy to the Secretary of State, April 12, 1914, in *FR, 1914*, p. 453.

[3] Wilson had ordered the entire Atlantic Fleet to Tampico. See the *New York Times*, April 15, 1914.

[4] In a press statement of April 14, Wilson said that the situation at Tampico "must not be thought of alone" and listed other Mexican offenses against the United States. The statement is printed in *PWW*, Vol. 29, pp. 433-34.

[5] This was an expression of a longstanding problem. Wilson thought that O'Shaughnessy's judgment was sometimes clouded by his intimacy with Huerta. See the *New York Times*, April 16, 1914, and Hill, *Emissaries to a Revolution*, pp. 172-73.

[6] Lind visited Wilson at the White House on April 14. The *New York Times* reported on April 15 that Lind expressed a desire to take strong measures against Huerta. See also Quirk, *Affair of Honor*, pp. 49-50.

[7] That is, during the American Civil War.

[8] Wilson met at the White House on April 15 with members of the Senate Foreign Relations and House Foreign Affairs committees to tell them his reasons for sending the fleet to Tampico. An account of what he told them is printed in *PWW*, Vol. 29, pp. 440-43. See also the *New York Times*, April 16, 1914.

[9] During a controversy at Greytown in 1853, the American Minister was insulted. President Franklin Pierce ordered U.S.S. *Cyane* to Greytown, and its captain demanded an apology and threatened to bombard the town. When the apology was not made, *Cyane* bombarded the town for forty-five minutes.

[10] An American merchant steamer was fired on in 1863 in the Straits of Shimonoseki. U.S.S. *Wyoming* retaliated, and the Japanese eventually paid an indemnity of $10,000.

[11] This memorandum is printed in *PWW*, Vol. 29, pp. 437-38.

[12] In his meeting with the congressional committees, Wilson had suggested the possibility of a peaceful blockade if Mexico did not render the salute. See the *New York Times*, April 16, 1914, and *PWW*, Vol. 29, pp. 442-43.

[13] In December 1902, Great Britain, Germany, and Italy had proclaimed a pacific blockade of Venezuela over the nonpayment of claims of their subjects stemming from a Venezuelan revolution. The United States Government claimed that such a blockade did not apply to its ships. See Chester Lloyd Jones, *The Caribbean Since 1900* (New York, 1936), pp. 219-28.

[14] Vice Adm. Charles Johnston Badger, commander of the Atlantic Fleet.

[15] Huerta stated that his reason for refusing to render the salute was that he feared that the United States would not return it. He proposed that this problem be solved by a simultaneous salute. See Chargé O'Shaughnessy to the Secretary of State, April 15, 1914, in *FR, 1914*, pp. 463-64.

[16] The Pacific Fleet, commanded by Rear Adm. Thomas Benton Howard, was ordered to Mexican waters on April 15. See the *New York Times*, April 16, 1914.

April 20, 1914

I want to say to you gentlemen, do not get the impression that there is about to be war between the United States and Mexico.[1] That isn't the outlook at present at all. In the first place, in no conceivable circumstances would we fight the people of Mexico. We are their friends, and we want to help them in every way that we can to recover their rights and their government and their laws; and for the present I am going to Congress to present a special situation and seek their approval to meet that special situation. It is only an issue between this government and a person calling himself the Provisional President of Mexico, whose right to call himself such we have never recognized in any way, so that I had a feeling of uneasiness as I read the papers this morning, as if the country were getting on fire with war enthusiasm. I have no enthusiasm for war; I have an enthusiasm for justice and for the dignity of the United States, but not for war. And this need not eventuate into war if we handle it with firmness and promptness.

Is it possible, Mr. President, to deal with a *de facto* government—a dictator— by the navy without precipitating war?

Why, certainly. It has been done. You have only to search the precedents to find it done by the score of times. For example, on one occasion the United States, perhaps with unnecessary emphasis, almost wiped out the town of Greytown[2] on just an occasion of this sort.

Is the seizure of a customhouse or of a port equivalent to war or a declaration of war?

No. You may remember that ports have been seized as security for the payment of debts without that being taken as a declaration of war at all.

A declaration of a blockade—is that war?

That depends upon how far the blockade is carried.

Mr. President, there will be no declaration, as far as Congress is concerned, more than a mere granting of the authority to act, leaving it to your judgment?

No. You see I am simply going to go [to Congress] on an occasion when, strictly speaking, I am advised it is not necessary for me to go. Of course, it is my desire to have their full cooperation both of thought and of purpose, and I am very glad to take it to them. But as I understand my powers as President, I could take the steps necessary in a matter of this sort, because it would fall very short of a declaration of war, which lies only with Congress.

Mr. President, following up on your very clear statement at the beginning to allay the public feeling and excitement in the United States, would you care to give some indication at this hour in advance of the meeting of Congress as to what steps you had in contemplation.

No, sir, I would rather think that out very carefully before I do that. Of course, the events of the day may change the whole aspect of things, and I am just going to act on the necessity from hour to hour.

The main purpose is the elimination of Huerta?

Not of this act, no sir.

To compel the recognition of the dignity of the United States?

That is all we want, a full recognition of that dignity, and such a recognition as will constitute a guarantee that this sort of thing does not happen any more.

Of course, I understand that, but I was thinking of the steps that might follow.

Oh, well, that would depend on developments entirely.

Mr. President, is there still any lingering hope that Mr. Huerta may at the last moment accede to anything of that sort?

Well, to tell the truth, I have found my mind so different from General Huerta's that it has been impossible for me to forecast what he is going to do. I haven't any standard of calculation. Of course, I hope so, but that is a different matter from expecting.

Mr. President, have there been any communications, even indirectly, in the past twenty-four hours from representatives of foreign governments tendering in any way their good offices in the hope of bringing about a peaceful solution?

No, sir, merely the information from Mexico City that such offices had been voluntarily tendered. I mean that efforts have been made to induce General Huerta to accede to our demands, but no representations were made to this government.

What time do you go to the Capitol, Mr. President?[3]

That depends on the arrangements up there.

You will be prepared to go as early, Mr. President, as they are ready?

Yes, sir, I would like to have time for a cabinet meeting first; but they naturally will not convene before noon.

Somebody suggested three o'clock this afternoon.

Any time will suit me perfectly. I am ready with my message.

Mr. President, will there be any advance copies of your message?

I am afraid not, because I want to keep it under advisement to the last minute.

Mr. President, have the forces of the army or navy made any further movements than were ordered last week?

No.

Then they are, while in a state of readiness, held pending the developments as you see them?

Yes.

No order has been issued affecting the militia?

No, sir; I wouldn't have a right to do that for anything out of the country without action by Congress.

There is a bill pending—I believe it has passed one branch—that seeks to give you the right to send the militia out of the country.[4]

But that did not originate in this situation.

Mr. President, has any consideration been given to a restoration of the embargo?[5]

Oh, no.

What information is there available about the Constitutionalists and their attitude toward this matter?

None, so far as I know.

Mr. President, you said that your main purpose was to simply enforce the recognition of the dignity of the United States in connection with this salute proposition?

And to guarantee us against subsequent indignities.

So that if at any time Huerta should now give the salute and give these guarantees, that would close the incident?

I suppose so; it would depend altogether upon the circumstances. I want you gentlemen to get this point, if you will. I have not lost my patience. I think it is an act of weakness to lose your patience, particularly when you are strong enough to do what you please when it is the right thing to do it. I just saw this happening: if these incidents went on, they might go from bad to worse and lead to something which would bring about a state of conflict; and I thought it was wise, in the interest of peace, to cut the series of such incidents off at an early stage. That is the spirit in which I am acting.

[1] The White House issued a statement to the press on April 18 which said that, unless Huerta yielded in the matter of the salute by 6 p.m. on April 19, Wilson would take the matter to Congress on the following day. The statement is printed in *PWW*, Vol. 29, p. 460. See also the Secretary of State to Chargé O'Shaughnessy, April 18, 1914, in *FR, 1914*, p. 468.
[2] See above, April 16, 1914.
[3] Wilson addressed a joint session of Congress at three o'clock on April 20 to ask its approval to use the armed forces to secure recognition of American rights in Mexico. It is printed in *PWW*, Vol. 29, pp. 471-74.
[4] The volunteer army bill, which would have allowed the President to press the state militia into regular service, had passed the House in December. See the *New York Times*, April 20, 1914. The Senate passed the bill on April 20. See the *New York Times*, April 21, 1914.
[5] Wilson was contemplating a naval blockade which would constitute an effective arms embargo against Huerta. In fact, the President's timetable for action was materially affected by information from the American Consul at Veracruz to the effect that the steamer *Ypiranga* of the Hamburg-American Line would deliver a large load of ammunition for Huerta there on April 21. *Ypiranga* later discharged her cargo at Puerto México and eventually carried Huerta into exile. See Link, *The New Freedom*, p. 399.

April 23, 1914

Mr. President, what do you get from O'Shaughnessy?

We haven't anything directly from him, except the news that he has been handed his passports and will probably be leaving within twenty-four or forty-eight hours.[1]

Not until then?

No.

Mr. President, can you tell us to what government the American interests will be entrusted there?[2]

That hasn't been arranged yet.

Have you had any communication from the Mexican Chargé here as to the interests of Mexico or the *de facto* government being placed under anybody's charge?

He has merely asked for his passports, and they are being prepared for him.

Will they be granted to him?

Of course.

As the representative of the Huerta government or as the Chargé d'Affaires of Mexico?

As the Chargé d'Affaires of Mexico from which he was accredited before any of this began.

Mr. President, I don't think the boys want to ask a great many questions this afternoon. They feel that you are overloaded with work now; will you be good enough to tell us what you have in mind, especially about the embargo[3] and the Carranza note?[4]

Of course, gentlemen. I feel this way. This is a very serious business that has come upon us, and I think that it is my duty to confine my communications at present to facts. Now, all the facts that we have are at your disposal, as you know. We have withheld nothing; but what the first steps of policy will be, I don't think it is wise to discuss. That is my instinctive feeling in the matter, because, of course, we might have to alter our course from time to time, and it is not wise to let everybody concerned know just what we have in mind. So that just the only comment I have for the present to make on General Carranza's statement is that which I gave out this morning.[5]

Has the embargo on arms been reestablished?

No.

Have you done anything, Mr. President, to hold up any shipment of arms to the Constitutionalists?

No, sir, I don't know of any.

Have any further orders, Mr. President, gone out to the army or the navy today?

No, sir; none except the arrangement of details.

Mr. President, do you happen to know whether the statements in the morning papers are true that ten million rounds of ammunition have gone to the Constitutionalists?

I have been unable to verify that.

Mr. President, do you still regard this as not a state of war with regard to Mexico?

So far as my authority is concerned, it is not a state of war.

The giving of passports to the Chargé—is that a preliminary of war?

That is an act which always precedes war, but war does not always follow it.

Mr. President, I suppose now Huerta will undoubtedly notify the governments which have recognized him that this condition of war exists?

Well, will he? I don't know whether he will or not.

This being a sort of act of war—

Oh, no, you must not go beyond the facts. While diplomatic communication is always broken off before a war, war does not always follow, by any means, the breaking off of diplomatic relations. His purpose hasn't been disclosed yet.

Mr. President, Mr. Knox handed passports to the Nicaraguan Chargé d'Affaires and yet we had no break in our relations at that time.[6]

It frequently happens that war does not follow the breaking off of formal diplomatic conditions.

Mr. President, have you any present plans of going again before Congress with the situation as it now is?

No, sir.

Mr. President, could you tell us what efforts are being made to assure General Carranza that we have no quarrel with him?

No direct efforts. The statement that I issued this morning was meant as a clarification, or as rather a restatement—a little more explicit—of my position.

Mr. President, was that sent to Mr. Carothers?

It was sent to Mr. Carothers; of course, we have no diplomatic relations with the men in the northern part of Mexico.

Then Mr. Carothers has not replied that he has any further word?

No.

Mr. President, I perceive a warning to Carranza in that statement. Is that reading something in it that you did not intend?

I will not interpret the statement. Anything that you find there is possibly there; I don't know what you find.

Mr. President, have you compared the telegram from General Carranza, which was delivered officially to this government, with the translated copy that was given out at El Paso and which was printed in the newspapers?

No, I have not; I have read only the one sent to this government.

There is said to be a great discrepancy between the two, and we have begun to feel—

My attention hasn't been called to that. Have you called Mr. Bryan's attention to that?

I compared some of it last night, Mr. President, and, while there was some difference in meaning, the general purport of the thing was the same, according to the representatives here who had both the official and unofficial copies.

It is probably a difference in the translation, because it was obvious in some parts that I read that the translation was somewhat imperfect, and I think the meaning was very obscurely conveyed. For example, when he said—I can't remember the whole phrase, but the point was that "friendly relations had obtained until today"— I think that was an imperfect translation of "even yet," not meaning to intimate that there was a termination of friendly relations "today" but that they "even yet" existed, notwithstanding this misunderstanding.

Mr. President, that is the very reason we should like to have your own official copy that was translated by very careful translators.

I don't believe that the Spanish original has reached us. That is coming to us by mail, so that we have nothing but the telegraphed translation, if I am correctly informed, and we don't know whether that is perfect or imperfect. I can only conjecture.[7]

By whom was that made, Mr. President?

I don't know.

Could we have that telegram?

That would rest with Mr. Bryan.

Mr. President, are you prepared to say how far we are going to notify the foreign powers?

We haven't notified them of anything but the facts.

That is, the facts about the occupation of Veracruz?

Yes.

Have there been any communications from the foreign powers regarding their citizens and asking us to do anything particularly?

None that I have heard of.

Mr. President, has any action been taken yet with regard to our Consuls?

No; that is part of the arrangements we are trying to make. We were taken somewhat by surprise by the breaking off of diplomatic relations, and therefore we haven't completed the arrangements. We have to get the consent of the other government. We have to consult the government to which we want things handed over.

Have you reason to think that Mr. O'Shaughnessy will get to Veracruz safely?

Oh, yes; I don't doubt it.[8]

Mr. President, you said a moment ago that Mr. O'Shaughnessy might remain there forty-eight hours. We understood early this morning, when his dispatch arrived, that he would leave at nine o'clock this morning.

No; as a matter of fact, in his dispatch to us he said this evening or tomorrow morning—leaving it vague.

Meaning this evening?

This evening, yes, or tomorrow morning.

Have you heard of conditions in Mexico City from him, Mr. President?

No, sir.

Is communication open between Mexico City and here?

It is more or less interrupted. I don't know why. Sometimes things get through promptly and sometimes they do not.

Mr. President, will it be necessary for you to go back to Congress?

That depends upon the circumstances entirely.

Mr. President, have you heard anything about the conditions to the southeast and southwest of Mexico City?

No, sir; of course, the dispatches stated that General Maass[9] was likely to receive reinforcements from the State of Pueblo, but I don't know what importance to attach to that.

Mr. President, how far has our military action extended in Mexico? We know, of course, that marines and bluejackets have been landed at Veracruz, but I thought perhaps a blockade might have been established on the West Coast.

Nothing except what you know of has been done.

Nothing has been done yet, Mr. President, with regard to Tampico?

Nothing at all. We understand that there is a rather large number of refugees going on merchant ships at Tampico, who will be carried to Galveston, probably.

That is, at their own desire?

Oh, yes.

Mr. President, Mr. Bryan spoke last night about the third section of a train from Mexico City to Veracruz as being missing or not accounted for.[10]

I suppose it has arrived. I have not heard anything more about it; I think I would have if it had not arrived.

Mr. President, the dispatches this morning stated that the American commander of the ships at Tampico had ordered all vessels out of the harbor until further notice.

I don't think that is true; I have not heard of it.

All of those ports are still open?

Yes, all of them, including Veracruz.

So there is actually no blockade?

A blockade which excluded neutral vessels would be a state of war.

Before you could do that you would have to notify the world at large, would you not?

I suppose so, yes.

Mr. President, have any statements come from the other governments similar to the statement of Japan that she would remain neutral?[11]

I didn't know that Japan had made that statement. I don't think that is necessary. It is always assumed that foreign governments will remain neutral.

Mr. President, at the present moment there are actually no military operations going on?

None whatever. I am told that there are breastworks three miles out of Veracruz along the line of the railroad occupied by our men, keeping the enemy beyond.

Mr. President, have we got the bridge across the ravine down there?

No, that is twenty-seven miles out.

You mean with the exception of the breastworks there is nothing being done?

Nothing.

So far as military operations are concerned, it is just at a standstill?

Yes, sir.

May I ask what, then, is pending?

You may ask, but I can't answer.

Mr. President, you still regard all your actions in Mexico City as in the nature of a private act?

Yes, sir, so far as they have gone.

¹ On April 21, 1914, United States naval forces took possession of the Mexican port of Veracruz. This military response to the diplomatic impasse caused by the Tampico affair resulted in fighting on Mexican soil between American and Mexican troops. On April 22, Chargé O'Shaughnessy was handed his passports by Mexican officials. See the *New York Times*, April 22-24, 1914, and Quirk, *Affair of Honor*, pp. 78-120.

² Brazil eventually handled American interests in Mexico.

³ Wilson's announced purpose in seizing Veracruz was to prevent the landing of arms for Huerta's forces. See the *New York Times*, April 22, 1914, and above, April 20, 1914.

⁴ Carranza's response to Wilson's action was an angry note of April 22, denouncing the "invasion" of Mexican territory. It is printed in *PWW*, Vol. 29, pp. 483-85.

⁵ Wilson's statement expressed his friendship for the Mexican people. It is printed in *ibid.*, p. 488.

⁶ To express disapproval of Nicaraguan President José Santos Zelaya, Knox dismissed his government's Chargé on December 1, 1909. See *FR, 1909*, pp. 455-57, and Scholes and Scholes, *The Foreign Policies of the Taft Administration*, pp. 45-55.

⁷ Carothers telegraphed the translation and sent the original by mail. See Special Agent Carothers to the Secretary of State, April 22, 1914, in *FR, 1914*, pp. 483-84.

⁸ Huerta's son accompanied O'Shaughnessy to guarantee his safety. See Chargé O'Shaughnessy to the Secretary of State, April 22, 1914, in *ibid.*, pp. 484-85.

⁹ Gen. Gustavo Maass, commander of Mexican forces at Veracruz.

¹⁰ A refugee train was late in arriving at Veracruz. See the *New York Times*, April 24, 1914.

¹¹ Japan issued a statement of neutrality in the matter on April 22. See *ibid.*, April 23, 1914.

June 1, 1914

Adjournment?¹

I didn't know there was going to be any.

There is an effort to pass a conservation bill at this session, Mr. President. Have you any attitude as to that?²

Why, I was deeply interested in that group of five bills, all of which I heartily support, and was fearing that they could not be considered at this session because they need careful consideration, and yet hoped that they might be. That was my attitude. You see, they were completed after the program of the session was also completed, and I didn't feel at liberty to urge that they put them in the way of the program, but I am just as interested in them as I was in the program itself.

Mr. President, is the Ransdell bill³ in that group of five?

The Ransdell bill is not in that group of five, no. I am heartily in favor of that bill. That, of course, has much the same principle in it, but it is very much more restricted in the part of the country it affects.

Mr. President, is there movement in the House looking toward asking for a special rule so that these conservation resolutions might be passed by the [end of the session]? Can you give us an idea as to your attitude on that?

I haven't been consulted about that yet, and I don't think it would be right for me to give an offhand opinion about it. I can only say that I am most heartily in favor of the bills. You see, the West has been waiting, I wouldn't know how many years, while this has been held up, as if the federal government couldn't make up its mind what it was going to do with the public resources. Nevertheless, those resources ought to be released upon some equitable principle, and I think these bills contain an equitable principle. It is the first successful effort at a constructive program.

Mr. President, what do you hear about the future of the seamen's bill?[4]

I have been so much engrossed in other matters, I hadn't heard anything about it. I hadn't asked about it, to tell the truth.

Mr. President, the amendment to the Clayton bill, defining the status of labor under the Sherman law, that amendment is said to have been agreed to by you and representatives of the House. I wonder whether that agreement in any way involves any compromise of your position when you approved that rider to the sundry civil bill, in which you said you would not favor any measure that would limit the opportunity or the power of the Department of Justice to prosecute under the Sherman law?

No, sir. I consider it perfectly consistent. You see, ever since the antitrust legislation—ever since the Sherman Act—was passed, it has been understood that the meaning of the act was not that labor organizations were themselves illegal. They have been complaining—and I think their complaint was not clearly sustained by the decisions of the Supreme Court, but it might be implied from them— that they existed by the suffrance of the Department of Justice. Now that clearly was not intended.

I think the whole country approves of the right of laboring men to organize and to present their claims for just treatment by means of organization. And it was in order to remove all doubt as to whether they were in themselves illegal under the Sherman Act that clause number seven, I think it was, was put in, and the amendment added for perfect clarity.

Doesn't paragraph number eighteen go farther than that, however? Wouldn't it make it open to a different construction—to legalize the secondary boycott?[5]

I think paragraph eighteen was very carefully drawn as part of the antiinjunction bill and has been recognized as practically the legislation that had already been passed by one or the other of the two houses, but not at the same time, with regard to injunctions.

You will notice that the acts are very carefully specified in that bill and cover those things which have generally been recognized to be the legitimate means of insisting upon the rights of labor. That was the intention, at any rate.

Then does the amendment confer any right upon labor under the Sherman law that it does not already possess?

I don't think that it does, but some of the decisions of the Supreme Court would leave that open to doubt. At any rate, it is open to doubt in some minds.

The purpose of the amendment, then, is to remove that doubt?

The purpose of the whole legislation is to remove all doubt as to whether these are legitimate organizations, whether they are disobeying the laws of the United States in carrying out their legitimate objects. That is the way I understand it. I think the justice of that is manifest.

Without any specific wording, the same law, then, would permit businessmen or employers to organize under similar conditions, would it not, without any other specific amendments?

I hadn't thought of that. I don't know. I suppose so. You see, clause number seven describes these organizations. They are organizations for mutual aid, not joint stock organizations and not for profit.[6]

I had in mind, for instance, chambers of commerce, boards of trade, or the Hardware Manufacturers' Association. They have occupied so high a social plane that their existence has never been challenged. The law would permit them to do some things that would be illegal for other organizations.

I don't understand that it would, no.

If they transgressed the law, they would be liable just the same.

Yes. That is understood all around.

Mr. President, in your conversation with the Ohio manufacturers and the Illinois manufacturers, you said in the statement that was given out, you were quoted as saying that you were as aware of the depression of business as we were. So that if you can tell us what does—if you can tell us what are the causes as your correspondents report them to you?[7]

I am afraid that is too large an order. I should say that the depression was confined. These are merely impressions. They need to be very carefully confirmed. I wouldn't like them quoted as my views because they are merely impressions. My impression is that there is no depression in business—in what might be called the business of the country. For example, you take wholesale houses—houses that send their salesmen out for miscellaneous sales of all sorts of goods throughout the country—they are not finding depressed conditions. The average purchases of the country, the ordinary purchases of the country, are going on just as usual.

There is a depression which seems to radiate from the railroad offices. I am not saying that in criticism at all, but merely to mention this. Of course, a great part of the steel industry depends upon the extent of the purchases made by the railroads. If the railroads feel themselves embarrassed and don't place their orders, there is a considerable contraction in the steel business, and that affects all the allied or related manufacturers—all the number of things that are related to the general steel and iron industry of the country; and that, in turn, has its effect upon the credit market—I mean, the market of lenders, because they are a little afraid that business is not quite good enough to put their money out, and they are timid.

Yet, in spite of that, you will notice that Mr. Gary[8] and somebody else—Mr. Farrell[9]—have stated that the outlook in the steel industry is excellent, which means that in other fields, then—other than the railroad field—the country is going forward and has full heart in its business.

So that, in spite of the fact that, on the face of it, the steel business is affected by the prosperity of the railroads and there is depression, there is not depression in the steel industry. Taken as a whole, now, I construe that to be a very interesting and, indeed, a remarkable circumstance which is quite reassuring. What I said to those gentlemen meant this: if they believed that prosperity was coming, it would come, and come with a jump. That is the reason I said it was psychological. They are in a depressed state of mind. And as long as you are in that state of mind, you don't undertake very much.

Has the tariff very much to do or anything to do with it?

I don't think the tariff has anything to do with it. As a matter of fact, I recently had a long conversation with the Secretary of Commerce, who said that our exports were increasing more rapidly than our imports, which would show that the tariff certainly hadn't had a depressing influence on our [business].

Mr. President, has the Secretary given you any information showing these conditions are more or less worldwide?

He has spoken of that, but that is very well known, that the business depression is worldwide. That is a well-known fact. The interesting part of it is that the depression is less felt in the United States than anywhere else. That also is clearly established.

Mr. President, is it your impression that, if the rates are advanced for the railroads, business would improve immediately?

I have explained that I don't feel I have any right to comment about a pending decision of the Interstate Commerce Commission.

Mr. President, what has been your attitude toward the investigation of the New Haven going on by the Interstate Commerce Commission?[10]

I haven't had any other attitude than that of the interested public.

Can you tell about the Reserve Board yet, Mr. President?

I am waiting for the Secretary of the Treasury to come back. He ran away with somebody's daughter.[11] I want to have a final conversation with him. He will be back some time this week.

Mr. President, any comments to make on Colonel Roosevelt's remarks?[12]

Oh, no.

Mr. President, do you feel that these investigations against the railroads have in any way affected their business?

I don't learn that they have.

Mr. President, have you any comment to make on the suggestion to curtail action in the Senate on the interstate trade bill in order to let Congress go home earlier?

Perhaps you don't know that the Senate interstate trade commission bill has all the rest of the program in it. Perhaps you don't know that it is loaded to the gunnels. It was, when I saw it. I handled it very gingerly.[13]

It differs slightly from the House bill?

Yes it does, in a number of particulars. What I meant was, it covered the entire subject matter.

Mr. President, has any violation of the civil-service law in the matter of the selection of fourth-class postmasters been called to your attention?

No, sir. Various accusations have been made about it, but nothing applying to the civil service.

[1] Leaders of Congress were hoping to adjourn by July 20. See the *New York Times*, June 2, 1914.

[2] Conservation proved to be too difficult a question for Congress to deal with in 1914. For a discussion of the problems and the measures proposed, see Link, *The New Freedom*, pp. 125-35.

[3] Senator Ransdell introduced a bill (S. 5683) on May 27 to restore to the public domain all naval reservations not needed for naval purposes. See *Cong. Record*, 63d Cong., 2d sess., p. 9283.

[4] This question about the La Follette bill to promote safety at sea was probably prompted by the sinking on May 29 of the liner *Empress of Ireland*, in which 964 persons perished. See the *New York Times*, May 30-June 1, 1914.

[5] Section 18 of the Clayton Act said that restraining orders or injunctions should not be issued against peaceful strikes, boycotts, or picketing, nor should those acts be construed as illegal. See Link, *The New Freedom*, pp. 427-33.

[6] Section 7 of the Clayton Act defined the exempted organizations and said that they should not be regarded as illegal combinations in restraint of trade.

[7] Wilson met with officers of the Ohio and Illinois manufacturers' associations at the White House on May 28. In a White House press release, Wilson was reported as describing the cause of the depressed business conditions as "merely psychological." See the *New York Times*, May 29, 1914, and *PWW*, Vol. 30, pp. 93-96.

[8] Elbert Henry Gary, chairman of the board of directors of United States Steel.

[9] James Augustine Farrell, president of the United States Steel Corporation.

[10] An investigation of alleged illegal business practices by the New Haven Railroad. See the *New York Times*, May 27-29, 1914.

[11] Secretary McAdoo married Eleanor Randolph Wilson in a White House wedding on May 7.

[12] Before sailing for Europe on May 31, Roosevelt criticized the Wilson administration for failing to solve the nation's economic problems and contended that the only solution was the implementation of the Progressive party platform of 1912. See the *New York Times*, June 1, 1914.

[13] Wilson was pursuing a strategy designed to win Senate acceptance of his antitrust program by including a strong trade commission in the Senate bill. See Link, *The New Freedom*, pp. 436-39.

June 8, 1914

Gentlemen, I will have to tell you, for your information, confidentially—though this is a rather large group—I say confidentially, because it hasn't come very directly or directly from his government, that we have learned that General Huerta has suspended his order for a blockade of Tampico.[1]

What is on your minds this morning?

Mr. President, have you ever expressed any disapproval at any time of the so-called Norris amendment?[2]

I haven't been given an opportunity to express a favorable or unfavorable opinion.

Mr. President, when you asked for the repeal of the exemption, you said something to the effect that you hoped it would be given in such ungrudging measure as to enable you to meet without embarrassment certain other questions. Will the repeal bill with the amendment kill that hope?

No, it does not. It does not alter the repeal in the least degree, of course. But as you understand, and as I interpret the whole matter, it is quite unnecessary. Legislation doesn't waive treaty rights and can't conceivably waive treaty rights, so that it doesn't alter the character of the legislation at all.[3]

It doesn't really raise the question, then, of whether we are right or wrong, which you hope will be avoided?

It doesn't necessarily raise it at all. It is a strong intimation that, at any rate, some of the gentlemen who voted for the repeal don't wish to be understood as settling the question of right or wrong by their vote. That is the point, I understand, it is intended to make. And, of course, any one of them could have done that by a personal statement on the floor.

You won't object, Mr. President, to its going through? You have no particular objection to it?

Well, I'm not saying.

Mr. President, can you tell us anything with regard to the form that the Philippine legislation is expected to take?

The form—you mean the character of it? No, I can't. Mr. Jones has a bill which I understand he is about to introduce, which he was kind enough to bring to me, and I have been reading it over very carefully and am just now consulting with the men in the War Department who have been most familiar with Philippine affairs, to see what details of the matter need to be restudied, so that it is now just in that shape when I am forming an opinion about it.[4]

Do you expect any action on that by either House or Senate, or both, at this session?

Action on anything additional is, of course, dependent upon the state of business in the Senate.

Is there anything about the conservation program, Mr. President, in the House?

I understand from one conference which I held that there is a very good prospect of the conservation bills passing the House. I sincerely hope so.

Is that the old Jones bill?[5]

No. It is an entirely different bill.

Has it been introduced so that you could—

It hasn't been introduced yet, and I don't feel at liberty to discuss the features of it yet. It may be modified before it is introduced.

Mr. President, is there anything you can tell us about the Colorado situation?[6] Is there any change? Are the troops to be left there?

The troops are to remain there for the present, pending developments, which I think are hopeful. That is why there are some rifts in the clouds that hang over the attempt at a settlement by conference. And I am waiting to see how that develops—I mean a conference between the operators and the miners.[7]

How about the Federal Reserve Board, Mr. President?

I hope I shall be ready in a day or two to announce my nominations.

The ratification of the Colombian treaty—is that urged at this session?[8]

That is a matter upon which I haven't talked with the Secretary of State recently, and I can't say. He is in conference with the Foreign Relations Committee and will know better than I whether they will be ready to take it up or not.

The Nicaraguan treaty?

Of course, we desire that all treaties are [unintelligible].

[1] Huerta had ordered a blockade of the port by Mexican gunboats to prevent a shipment of arms for the Constitutionalists from being landed by the Cuban ship *Antilla*. The Wilson administration made known its intention to keep Tampico open, and Huerta rescinded his order on June 8. See the *Washington Post*, June 7-9, 1914.

[2] The Norris-Simmons amendment to the Sims bill. Introduced on June 6 by Senator Furnifold McLendel Simmons, Democrat of North Carolina, this amendment stated that the Sims bill was not a "waiver or relinquishment of any right the United States may have under the

treaty with Great Britain." The original amendment, introduced on April 1 by Senator Norris, had been a stronger statement of the same principle. The Senate approved the amendment on June 10 and passed the Sims bill on June 11. See *ibid.*, June 7-12, 1914, and *Cong. Record*, 63d Cong., 2d sess., pp. 10127-58.

[3] For a discussion of this issue, see the *Washington Post*, June 9, 1914.

[4] Representative William Atkinson Jones of Virginia, chairman of the House Insular Affairs Committee, introduced a bill (H.R. 17856) on July 11, 1914, to declare the intentions of the people of the United States toward the future status of the Philippines and to provide for a more autonomous government there. See *Cong. Record*, 63d Cong., 2d sess., p. 12001, and Francis B. Harrison, *The Corner-Stone of Philippine Independence: A Narrative of Seven Years* (New York, 1922).

[5] The earlier Jones bill (H.R. 28026) had been introduced on January 14, 1913, and called for the independence of the Philippines within eight years. See *Cong. Record*, 62d Cong., 3d sess., p. 1530.

[6] The United Mine Workers called coal miners out on strike in Colorado on September 23, 1913. Violence erupted when the operators brought in strikebreakers and heavily armed guards while state and federal mediators worked in vain to find a compromise settlement which the owners would accept. On October 28, the Governor of Colorado, Elias Milton Ammons, called out the National Guard to keep order in the strike zone, an action which resulted in tragedy when guardsmen charged and burned a tent colony of strikers at Ludlow on April 20, 1914, killing twenty-one men, women, and children. The strikers responded violently, and conditions in Colorado approached civil war. Since all sides appealed to Wilson for help, the President asked John Davison Rockefeller, whose Colorado Fuel and Iron Company was a major employer of miners in the area, to accept federal mediation to avert the necessity of sending in federal troops. Rockefeller refused, and Wilson, on April 28, 1914, ordered the army to occupy the strike zone. See Link, *The New Freedom*, pp. 457-59, and George P. West, *Report on the Colorado Strike* (Washington, 1915).

[7] The House on June 8 approved a joint resolution introduced by Senator Owen and Representative Edward Keating of Colorado authorizing the creation of a commission to resolve the Colorado strike. See the *Washington Post*, June 8, 1914.

[8] The Thomson-Urrutia Treaty with Colombia was approved by the Colombian House of Representatives on June 9 and signed on June 10. See *ibid.*, June 10, 1914.

June 11, 1914

Well, I haven't anything to say. Have you?

Mr. President, can you tell us anything more of your attitude toward the amendment to the tolls bill that was adopted yesterday?[1]

Oh, no. I have nothing more to say.

Mr. President, have you any idea of appointing an Ambassador to France or Russia?

Of course, that matter comes into my mind frequently. I hope, within a couple of weeks, to settle that matter.

Mr. President, I think you saw Mr. Stevens of New Hampshire[2] yesterday with regard to his amendment to the interstate trade commission bill. Is there anything you can tell us about that?

No. That was merely for the purpose of discussing and getting thoroughly acquainted with what his proposals were—just the rough [outlines].

Mr. President, we were told that you approved his proposals as embodied in section eleven of the bill he introduced some time ago.[3]

I approved his bringing it to the attention of the Senate committee and leaving it to their action.

You wouldn't signify that you intend to support cease and desist?[4]

I haven't studied the detail of it [enough] to be confident about that part of it.

Anything on the Federal Reserve Board, Mr. President?

No. I am going to have a conference this evening about that.

Mr. President, have you made any plans yet for participating in any of the state campaigns—Pennsylvania, Iowa, and so forth?

No, sir.

Mr. President, there was a paragraph in the morning papers from Europe that said Mr. Williams, our Minister to Greece, had sent out a circular offering American assistance to settle the Albanian situation. Have you heard anything about that?[5]

No. I inquired of the department, and they had not heard anything about it. I think there must be some mistake somewhere.

Mr. President, has there been any complaint from Norway as to the treatment of Norwegian immigrants in Ellis Island?[6]

No, sir. Not that I have heard of.

I saw a related story in one of the papers quite a few days ago.

That they were discriminated against?

No, that there had been some mistreatment of these Norwegians.

I hope that is not true.

It was raised in the Norwegian Parliament. Nothing has reached you through any official source?

No, nothing at all. That would be for you down at the Department of Labor, I should think.

Mr. President, have you been consulted by the House Committee on Merchant Marine and Fisheries with regard to changes in the seamen's bill?

No, sir. I saw a committee of gentlemen this morning headed by Mr. Furuseth, but it was only—[7]

That was not a congressional committee?

Just a committee of seamen.

Mr. President, last Monday you expressed some hope that there might be a settlement in the coal strike situation. Has that gotten any further?

I don't know whether to say yes or no. The little news I have had since Monday continues to be encouraging; that is to say, continues to indicate that there is a possibility.

Mr. President, do you know that the sundry civil bill carries the same exemption of labor unions that it carried last year?

The same special limitations?

Yes.

No, I didn't.

[1] The Norris-Simmons amendment to the Panama Canal tolls repeal bill. See above, June 8, 1914, and the *New York Times*, June 11, 1914.

[2] Representative Raymond Bartlett Stevens, Democrat of New Hampshire, a member of the House Interstate and Foreign Commerce Committee.

[3] Stevens had proposed a strong federal trade commission with broad powers of investigation and injunction, which Wilson was coming to accept at this time. The Stevens bill was incorporated into the federal trade commission bill on June 12. See Link, *The New Freedom*, pp. 437-39.

[4] The Stevens bill gave the new commission the authority to prevent unfair competition by issuing cease and desist orders, which would be enforced by federal courts.

[5] Minister George Fred Williams had been sent to Albania to investigate conditions in that troubled new country, where the United States had no representative. See the *New York Times*, June 11, 1914.

[6] For conditions at Ellis Island, see Henry Noble Hall, "Great American Hold-up at Ellis Island," in New York *World*, Nov. 30, 1913.

[7] Wilson had been visited by Andrew Furuseth and members of the International Seamen's Union, who asked his support of the La Follette seamen's bill.

June 15, 1914

Mr. President, have you selected the Reserve Board Governor yet?

I would never select the Governor at the time of the nominations. I designate him subsequently.

Have you reached any decision?

Yes. The names will go in today.[1] The blanks aren't quite ready. I make it rather a point of courtesy not to announce nominations before the Senate is apprised. But that will be some time today.

We will know, then, who is to be the Governor?

No. Not until the board is confirmed.

Mr. President, has there been any opposition raised to the appointment of Mr. Jones?

No. I haven't heard anything.

Apropos of the question as to whether the President would present the reasons for his interpretation of the nation's psychology, I am going to let you gentlemen see copies of correspondence that has come into my notice, showing you how the psychology is created. So, if later in the morning, you will inquire for these copies, you will be supplied information about an interesting and elaborate process.

Are you going to add anything of your own to these?[2]

No. I don't think it is necessary.

These copies show where the psychology comes from?

In this case, from a publication called *The Pictorial Review*. I don't know anything about it.

Mr. President, have you attempted in any way to trace the boom for immediate adjournment of Congress? There seems to be a piling up of letters. They have a similar ring. They all ring in the same tone.

That is part of it. That is part of the campaign. It won't have to be faced. You will just have to expose its face.

It commenced about two weeks ago in the Senate.

It may possibly be. If so, it escaped my notice.

Mr. President, have you gone behind the actual publications? You say this was from *The Pictorial Review*. Have you gone further back than that?

No.

Mr. President, businessmen whom I talk with say that the condition is this—that autumn business is good, but there is no new business. The real trouble is in the matter of new business. Is that your understanding?

No. Broadly, there is the normal amount of new business, and in some lines of business more than the normal amount of new business—more than just what might be called the normal growth—something more.

Mr. President, generally, have all the leading Democrats of the House and Senate approached you submitting the proposition that there be an adjournment after the passage of the appropriations bill, to reconvene in November?[3]

No. On the contrary, some of them have said to me very earnestly that there should not be.

This is attributed to Mr. Underwood.

I have discredited that. I saw a notice of that in the paper, but so far as I know, there is nothing in it. I saw that about Mr. Underwood. We all will meet to work out the business. It will work out. This same discussion has occurred after the passage of every bill. It is not needed and it is not novel. And I predict that, when the gentlemen on the Hill think it over, this will end in the same way.

Mr. President, has there been some suggestion that, after reporting these [appropriations] bills out of the committee in the Senate, and reporting out the trust bills, then to adjourn, with an agreement with the Republicans to take a vote in December?

I had not heard that. Has there ever been one suggestion somebody could not think of? That is one I had not heard of.

The only suggestion we need pay much attention to is that they remain in session until the trust program is passed?

I think that is the thinking of the men who have considered the matter most thoroughly—that we ought to seek to adjourn as soon as possible, but not before we finish the business at hand.

Don't they think they can get fairly quick action?

I think they do. I happen to think of only one or two that have expressed an opinion on that subject. I don't see any reason why they should not. The minute it is known that we are going to finish the program, everybody will be interested in finishing it.

Do you think, Mr. President, that there has been a good deal of unnecessary delay up to the point where they realize that?

It is perfectly obvious to the whole country that there was unnecessary delay on the tolls bill.

Mr. President, the impression has been pretty general that some influence here is at work to try to hold up the trust legislation. They have been suggesting that all along the line. I thought you might say something a little emphatic that might convince us if that is true. I talked with a gentleman in Chicago yesterday, and he said that throughout the country there was the idea that, even though they hear that you are going to be willing to take action on this proposition at this time, they are still apprehensive. But if they can get a little cheerful word from you at this time, it will be helpful.

I think the prospects of the business being finished is much more cheerful than the prospect of its being left unfinished. And I think it is much more sensible. I would think the worst thing that can happen to business is to be in doubt for another six to eight months as to what the legislation of Congress is going to be; and that is the worst possible thing for business.

It is quite reasonable to assume that you will continue to press on earnestly for trust legislation?

It is more than reasonable. It is certain. Just so far as my influence goes, it will be for completion of the program.

Mr. President, is there any further so-called business legislation in contemplation when the trust bill is out of the way?

Not that I know of. There is nothing pending, unless those conservation bills[4] are business measures. They can hardly fall in that category.

Mr. President, in that connection, the Chamber of Commerce announced last night that it sent a protest to you against the Clayton bill and the sundry civil bill.[5] Have you received them?

Yes.

Will you make any comment on the sundry civil bill, particularly?

No.

Has any decision been made on the appointment of a Russian Ambassador? Is anybody in mind?

No. No decision has been reached there.

We understood that the conference with Mr. Bryan this morning—it had something to do with that. Was that matter taken up with Mr. Bryan?

I haven't had a conference except over the phone.

Have you seen Mr. Owen today?[6]

No, sir.

Mr. President, have you expressed any view on the Crosser bill? It has been reported out of the House favorably and provides for governmental ownership of the streetcars of the District.[7]

No, I haven't. I haven't had any opportunity to study the bill at all.

Would you care to say whether you would sign the District bill if it abolished the half and half?

I wouldn't care to say anything, honestly.

Can you say anything about the half and half?

Oh, no.

Did Representative Johnson[8] have anything new for you—have you any new schemes for ending—[9]

Mr. Johnson came to see me merely on the matter of information he desired about the plaza rents.[10]

I thought maybe he cooked up something new?

He is a very honest gentleman, and a terror to crooks.

Honest men can be good crooks just the same.

[1] Wilson named Charles Sumner Hamlin of Boston, Paul Moritz Warburg of New York, Thomas Davies Jones of Chicago, William Procter Gould Harding of Birmingham, and Adolph Caspar Miller of Berkeley, California.

² Wilson released to the reporters copies of a circular letter from William Paul Ahnelt, president of *The Pictorial Review*, dated May 1, 1914; two enclosures to the circular letter; and a circular letter from the Simmons Hardware Company, dated June 9, 1914. The Ahnelt letter called for businessmen to appeal to the President, Congress, and members of the Interstate Commerce Commission for a delay in antitrust legislation. The enclosures offered sample letters and telegrams which might be used. The letter from the Simmons Hardware Company called upon Congress to adjourn because political agitation was preventing improvement in the conditions of business. These materials were published in the *New York Times*, June 16, 1914. See also WW to Tumulty, June 12, 1914, printed in *PWW*, Vol. 30, p. 173.

³ Representative Underwood, among others, had suggested that an adjournment until November might be advisable. See the *New York Times*, June 15, 1914.

⁴ See above, June 1, 1914.

⁵ The Chamber of Commerce of the United States had conducted a referendum in which members opposed the exemption of labor unions. See the *New York Times*, June 12, 1914.

⁶ Wilson met with Senator Owen and eight other Senators at the White House on the evening of June 15 to discuss nominations to the Federal Reserve Board. See the *Washington Post*, June 16, 1914.

⁷ See above, April 2, 1914.

⁸ Representative Ben Johnson, Democrat of Kentucky, chairman of the House District of Columbia Committee.

⁹ Probably a reference to ending the deadlock over the District appropriation bill, then in conference. See the *Washington Post*, June 14, 1914.

¹⁰ That is, the new Union Station plaza.


June 18, 1914

Have you any plan yet as to any speaking tour this fall?

No.


Have you any further information about business conditions?

Nothing except this, that evidences abound in my mail of improving conditions. I suppose you saw, for example, the statement the other day of James J. Hill¹ with regard to it. I do not know why some of the newspapers did not carry that statement. Mr. Hill is certainly informed of conditions over a large part of the country; and men who are in a position themselves to collect information write to me and say I am entirely right about the position I have taken. I want you gentlemen to understand what apparently was not quite clearly understood the other day. I gave out that letter of *The Pictorial Review* as a very interesting example as to the way in which the psychology was made up. I do not care how it was made up, provided the country knows how it was made up. Everybody has a right to his opinion. I have no quarrel about that.


Did that letter have the desired effect?

What was the desired effect?

I suppose that is more definitely defined—

The desired effect was exactly what I intended—to let the people know that the impression was being systematically worked up. It is being put into the minds not only but in the correspondence of persons who otherwise would not have the thought [to do so].

I rather take it that the effect was designed to reach Congress.

No, I can reach Congress myself.

I thought it was an indirect way.

I thought it would be useful to everybody concerned to know what was going on. I do not mind anything that everybody knows about. That is my position about all public affairs. If everybody understands how the game is being played, I am satisfied.

Is there any change as to the Colorado situation?

No, I wish there were. I continue to hear hopes expressed that the way is opening for the arbitration or settlement by understanding, but I have not, I am sorry to say, anything definite in the way of things accomplished.

[1] James Jerome Hill, president of the Great Northern Railway, who stated that depressed business conditions had been exaggerated and were improving.


June 22, 1914

Mr. President, can you give us any information as to whether the negotiations with Japan have been resumed?

No, they have not been resumed.

You said, I believe, in one of the conferences last fall, that the last note needed no answer, or to that effect, that the federal government could not override the rights of the state in that matter, and that the treaty had not been violated.

Yes. That was our contention. There is a new ministry in Japan, and they apparently wish to discuss the whole matter again. There has been no active interchange of notes.

There is some intimation, Mr. President, that previous correspondence might be given out simultaneously by the two governments.[1]

No, sir. I am not apprised of any such purpose.

Could Turkey take any position, Mr. President, as to the question of selling these two ships to Greece?[2] I notice the—

I authorized the Secretary of the Navy to make the suggestion to Congress.

It is intimated, Mr. President, that that is really a peace proposal, that it would make for stability.

I am convinced that it is not a war proposal, or else we couldn't have had anything to do with it.

In what way does it make for peace between Greece and Turkey?

That is a matter that the Greek Chargé[3] can explain to you. I really don't feel prepared to make a full statement, because it was conveyed to me some time ago.

At least, that is the position the Greek Chargé takes?

Oh, yes. He assures us that there is not the slightest purpose or intention of war.

Mr. President, it is reported that the Senate committee had made certain changes in the Clayton bill which would eliminate [the prolabor] proposals that have been discussed as such. Do those changes meet with your approval?[4]

They haven't been brought to my attention yet. I don't know what they are.

One in section eighteen, the injunction section.

Yes, sir.

Has the letter of Mr. Bush,[5] the president of the Ohio Manufacturers' Association, been brought to your attention? I don't know whether it is a statement or an open letter, but unquestionably it is designed to reach your eyes.

No, sir, it has not.

There is some discussion, Mr. President, that there is some filibuster in the House against the conservation program?

I haven't heard of that. I think it is most unlikely. A filibuster is not easy to conduct in the House.

It can be done. In that connection, has the inability of the Democratic leaders to maintain a quorum in the House been brought to your attention?

They really can't maintain a quorum. They haven't, up to this time. It is just what happened last summer, at vacation time; it was difficult to have a quorum. I think if I were to be divided up as is the Congress, I would take a vacation sometime. Being indivisible, I haven't.

There is nothing new, yet, on the Colorado situation?

No. I wish there were, but I can say that my last conversation with the Secretary of Labor continued to show encouraging signs of a possibility of a conference that would settle things.

Isn't there some plan to have some delegation of miners come here and see you?

Someone did speak of the probability of that, and asked me if I could not see them. I of course said yes; but I haven't heard anything further.

Have you heard anything from Governor Walsh relative to the status of the New Haven emergency bill?[6]

No, I haven't, recently.

It appears to be believed that if the bill fails, the Department of Justice will sue for dissolution.

I suppose that will be the course.

Mr. President, in connection with this Bush letter, Mr. Bush complains that the manufacturers have been criticized for petitioning against the Clayton bill, and that no protest has been made against the propaganda of the farmers and laboring men. Has any such protest reached you?

No, sir. As a matter of fact, no criticism was made of anybody's petition. The only criticism I made was of a systematic plan of writing letters for other people to sign. That is the only thing that was criticized. Everybody has a right to come direct either to me or to the Congress. It is a very interesting matter, to say the least, to send broadcast all over the country letters which you are seeking other people to copy on their letterheads and sign. That is all that has been criticized. That is an artificial way of making a protest, which is certainly open to criticism.

The labor unions have done it.

If they have done it in the same way, certainly. I don't know that they have done it.

Is there anything you can tell us, Mr. President, about either the Nicaraguan or Colombian treaties?

No, sir. They are under consideration by the Committee on Foreign Relations. I saw in the paper that Mr. Bryan was to meet the committee again today. I think that the more those treaties are canvassed, and the better they are understood, the more certain they will be to be ratified.

[1] The *New York Times*, June 22, 1914, stated that the entire correspondence over the California land-tenure law would soon be made public by both governments simultaneously.

[2] The Turkish Ambassador, A. Rustem Bey, did protest against the proposed sale of two battleships, *Idaho* and *Mississippi*, to Greece. This was a period of strained relations between the two Mediterranean countries, but Wilson maintained that the ships would be used to preserve the peace, not to make war. See *ibid.*, June 23, 1914.

[3] Alexandre C. Vonros.

[4] The Senate Judiciary Committee removed some of the prolabor provisions of the bill, such as the prohibition against the use of injunctions to halt picketing. See the *New York Times*, June 21, 1914, and Link, *The New Freedom*, p. 432.

[5] Samuel Prescott Bush of Cincinnati, Ohio, answered Wilson's charges that there existed a business lobby by citing similar activity among other interest groups. See the *Washington Post*, June 21, 1914.

[6] The Massachusetts legislature was dragging its feet on the passage of a bill to permit the New York, New Haven and Hartford Railway to dispose of the Boston and Maine. Because this disposal had been part of an antitrust consent decree, the Justice Department planned to take the matter to court if the legislature did not act. See the *New York Times*, June 23, 1914.

June 25, 1914

Mr. President, it is being said that you would like Philippine legislation at this session—that the Jones bill[1] be acted on at this session of Congress?

Well, I haven't consulted with the leaders of the House about it. No, I have been consulting with Mr. Jones about the bill, which he was kind enough to bring to me, and which I think is being gotten up in fine shape.

He also said that you rather hoped for legislation along that line at this session?

Of course, with the program that is now before the Senate, I am rather modest about hoping for anything in addition, but I don't know, of course, what will be the decision of the leaders.

Mr. President, did you read this morning the remarks of Colonel Roosevelt on the Colombian treaty?[2]

I never have time to read the morning papers until evening.

He claims that this payment of twenty-five million dollars is merely blackmail. Anything you would care to say?

No. I have no comment.

Mr. President, have you heard about Claflin?[3]

I have heard of that.

Have you had any communication with any New York businessmen with regard to that? Has anybody asked for governmental aid?

No, nothing like that at all.

Mr. President, has there been any suggestion of a federal investigation of that matter? There is some report in New York to that effect.

You mean, of the Claflin firm—I hadn't heard of it. I don't know anything to investigate. I am afraid the heat has taken the questions out of it.

You had a visit from Missourians today, Mr. President.[4]

A very interesting and creative visit.

The whole delegation?

Only three were here, but they brought a paper signed by the whole delegation.

Did they take anything away, Mr. President?

No, they didn't ask for any quid pro quo.

Mr. President, has the name of Murphy J. Foster[5] been presented to you yet?

No, sir.

No successor to Postmaster Leonhardt?[6]

The one in New Orleans?

The postmaster resigned yesterday.

No.

Mr. President, there is a protocol agreed to there in [blank].

The thing is still in a formative shape.

Mr. President, have you taken any steps toward changing the name of Culebra Cut to Gaillard Cut?[7]

No, sir. I have merely been inquiring what my legal authority would be in a matter of that sort.

You have not determined what you would do yet?

No.

Has any decision been reached, Mr. President, on the [blank] judgeship?

No, no final decision. I hope it will be reached shortly.

Mr. President, can you say anything about your conference today with Mr. Fuller?[8]

Mr. Fuller called. It appears that Mr. Fuller is unusually well acquainted with the leading people and with conditions in general in Central America. He very generously called to tell me very many interesting things he knew about the attitude of individuals there, the general impressions obtained in South America about questions of policy. He didn't call on any special errand.

He didn't call representing the bankers?

No, sir, he didn't call representing the bankers.

Mr. President, have you heard from either the governments of France or Germany about the reports on the amount of indebtedness that Haiti owes?[9]

Not a word.

There is a persistent rumor that they are going to take some steps.

That was, I think, just a rumor.

It has been published very broadly in the German newspapers.

Yes. I daresay they have rumors as well as we do.

[1] See above, June 8, 1914.

[2] Roosevelt characterized the proposed payment of an indemnity of $25,000,000 to Colombia under the terms of the Treaty of Bogotá as "blackmail" and contended that, if the new treaty was "right, then our presence on the isthmus is wrong" and the canal should be restored to Colombia. He viewed the Colombian treaty as the climax of the foreign policies of Wilson and Bryan, "which have been such as to make the United States a figure of fun in the international world." See the *New York Times*, June 25, 1914, and Link, *The New Freedom*, pp. 321-23.

[3] H. B. Claflin Company, a large New York wholesale dry goods concern, went into receivership on June 25. See the *New York Times*, June 26-27, 1914.

[4] Democratic Congressmen from Missouri visited Wilson on June 25 to pledge their support for his antitrust program. See *ibid.*, June 26, 1914.

[5] Murphy James Foster, of Franklin, Louisiana, United States Senator, 1901-1913, was appointed Collector of Customs for New Orleans. See the *Washington Post*, July 10, 1914.

[6] Alexander F. Leonhardt, postmaster at New Orleans, resigned June 24 at the request of Postmaster General Burleson. See New Orleans *Times-Picayune*, June 25, 1914.

[7] The Culebra Cut in the Panama Canal was renamed in 1915 for Lt. Col. David Du Bose Gaillard, the American engineer who conquered it. Gaillard died of a brain tumor in 1913 after suffering what appeared to be a nervous breakdown in Panama. See McCullough, *Path Between the Seas*, pp. 573-74.

[8] Paul Fuller, a prominent New York lawyer, whom Wilson sent to meet with Villa in August and Carranza in September. See Hill, *Emissaries to a Revolution*, pp. 229-44.

[9] The *New York Times*, June 24, 1914, reported that the French and German governments were threatening to seize Haitian customhouses unless debts were repaid. See also Arthur S. Link, *Wilson: The Struggle for Neutrality, 1914-1915* (Princeton, N. J., 1960), pp. 520-22, and Schmidt, *United States Occupation of Haiti*, pp. 51-53.

June 29, 1914

Mr. President, there are two or three conservation bills up there.[1] Each claims presidential favor.

That is a definite exaggeration of [my position on] the bills. Of course I am very much interested in them, and I have had several conferences about them. Was there something special about them you had in mind?

There is some supposed conflict between the Adamson bill and the bill prepared by Secretary Lane—on the preservation of power on our public lands.

So I learned last week. I am going to try to bring about a conference on the subject between the two committees and the two departments, which will eliminate any disharmony, if there is any. I am not perfectly clear, yet, that there is any.[2]

They have been lining up in the House, getting ready for legislative committee meetings on the two bills.

I learned that on Saturday.

The Adamson bill is opposed by the conservation organizations.

I think that may be due to a misunderstanding. At any rate, whatever it is, it will have to be cleared up.

Mr. President, is there anything to be said about George Fred Williams?[3]

No, sir. I know nothing more than what has appeared in the papers. We haven't heard direct from Mr. Williams at all.

May I ask if he is going to hear from you?

He hasn't, so far, heard from me. I am waiting to hear from him.

Have you asked him for a report?

I have not. I think the Secretary of State has been in communication with him, though I am not certain about that.

It is stated that a report has been received.

It is stated this morning?

Yes, sir. I think so.

I haven't heard of that.

Mr. President, can you lift the lid on Mexico sufficiently to talk on anything that concerns the reports on big business?[4]

No. I don't think I had better comment on anything about Mexico.

Is there anything to say on the Santo Domingo situation, Mr. President?[5]

No, except it is very obvious it is very mixed, very difficult to see the threads of.

Mr. President, has the speech that General Evans made at the banquet been called to your attention?[6]

Yes, sir.

Does that call for any investigation?

I have simply asked the Secretary of War if General Evans made that speech.

You haven't heard?

No. I just sent the inquiry today. Indeed, the letter has only been dictated. It has not been sent.

Mr. President, is there anything to say with respect to the Japanese situation?

No, sir. That published correspondence disclosed all there was.[7]

Has it been decided, Mr. President, whether federal troops will be sent to Fort Vancouver, or is it Missoula, Montana?[8]

I am awaiting advices from Governor Stewart.[9] The difficulty there is a very peculiar one, as you know. It is not a difficulty between the mine owners and the miners. It is a difficulty between two opposing groups of miners. While there has been somewhat serious disorder there, it is still under control, so far as I have learned. The Governor has not asked us to send troops to back him. He has asked us to have troops in readiness.

Mr. President, do you know whether there is any chance for safety-at-sea legislation in the House before adjournment?

I don't—I think there is.

Special rule?

I suppose it would [be necessary], but I just had a word with Judge Alexander[10] the other day, in which he handed me some memorandum,[11] which I haven't had time to look at, except to glance at, but I understand that it is not beyond hoping for.

Mr. President, have you had any further assurances concerning the work of Democrats in the Senate on trust legislation? Some time ago, you were talking about getting together.

I don't know anything to the contrary. The last I heard, the two parties were working in the committee with a very fine spirit of cooperation.

Mr. President, will you do anything in relation to the District Commissioner, pending the appeal?[12]

No.

Has he sent in his resignation?

No.

Is there anything further as to business conditions, Mr. President?

Not that I know of, no sir.

[1] The two conservation bills dealt with the construction of hydroelectric projects. One, H.R. 16053, introduced by Representative Adamson, chairman of the House Interstate Commerce Committee, was supported by Secretary of War Garrison and opposed by conservationists. The other, H.R. 14893, sponsored by Representative Ferris, chairman of the House Public Lands Committee, had the support of Secretary of Interior Lane and conservationist groups. A struggle was developing in the House and the cabinet over this issue. See Link, *The New Freedom*, pp. 129-30.

[2] A meeting of the four men on June 29 failed to resolve their differences. Wilson called them to the White House for a second meeting on July 2, this time with better results. See *ibid.*, p. 130.

[3] Williams, United States Minister to Greece, announced publicly on June 27 that he was resigning to aid the Albanian uprising against Greece. See the *New York Times*, June 28-29, 1914.

[4] As a result of continued difficulties between the United States and Mexico, American oil and mining interests there were in jeopardy. See, for example, the Secretary of State to the British Chargé d'Affaires [Colville Adrian de Rune Barclay], June 24, 1914, in *FR, 1914*, pp. 718-19.

[5] Following general instructions to protect the lives and property of Americans and foreigners in the Dominican Republic, the United States gunboat *Machias* on June 28 fired on and silenced a government battery bombarding the rebel town of Puerto Plata. See the *New York Times*, June 29, 1914, and, for the background of the incident, Link, *Struggle for Neutrality*, pp. 496-511.

[6] Brig. Gen. Robert Kennon Evans, U.S.A., commander of the Department of the East, delivered a speech to the Sons of the American Revolution on June 26 in which he described America's foreign policy as "meddlesome" and called for an expanded army. See the *New York Times*, June 27, 1914.

[7] Correspondence concerning the California land-tenure law was made public in Washington and Tokyo on June 25. See *ibid.*, June 26, 1914.

[8] To help keep the peace in fighting near Missoula, Montana, between the Western Federation of Miners and insurgents seceding from the union. See *ibid.*, June 24, 1914.

[9] Governor Samuel Vernon Stewart of Montana, Democrat.

[10] Representative Joshua Willis Alexander, Democrat of Missouri.

[11] The memorandum is missing, but it probably concerned the substitute seamen's bill largely drafted by Representative Alexander and reported out by the House Committee on Merchant Marine and Fisheries on June 19. See Hyman Weintraub, *Andrew Furuseth: Emancipator of the Seamen* (Berkeley and Los Angeles, Calif., 1959), pp. 127-28.

[12] A jury on June 26 found that District Commissioner Newman had failed to meet the residency requirements for the position. See the *Washington Post*, June 27, 1914.

July 2, 1914

Can you tell us something about Mr. Morgan's visit?[1]

I can tell you anything that there is to tell. Mr. Morgan just came down on a visit of courtesy. I have known Mr. Morgan for a good many years, and his visit was lengthened out chiefly by my provocation, I imagine. Just a general talk about things that were transpiring.

Mr. President, what did he say about the conditions of business in the country?

We didn't go into that. Not that I felt that I knew as much about it as he did, but the talk didn't turn in that direction. It was one of those discussions that just drifted of its own volition. It wasn't about anything in particular, in short.

Is this to be the forerunner, Mr. President, of a series of talks with men high in the world of finance?

No, there is no plan about it. I am hoping I may have a visit from Mr. Ford,[2] but that is the only one in prospect. No, I believe there is a committee that wishes to see me—the Chicago Chamber of Commerce—next Wednesday.

Mr. President, do you find more acquiescence of spirit among the businessmen in the country to the trust program?

Yes, I do. I think they feel the force of what has been urged as to relieving business of its uncertainty and getting through with a well-known program. Because, of course, there is nothing new in this program. It is what has been implicit in practically every party platform for two or three campaigns.

Insofar as that matter now stands—the objections and suggestions looking to an adjournment of Congress on the ground that the trust program would influence the business of the country—in any of your correspondence, was there any specific explanation given as to how the trust bills, and what provisions of the trust bills, would influence the business of the country?[3]

No, that is the peculiarity of it. It has been fairly like what preceded the currency bill—the objections have all been general. None of them has been specific. I can only conjecture that the same thing is happening now that was happening then. They haven't read the bill.

I have some letters from a Cincinnati merchant that the objections were all too general.

That has been true all through our correspondence.

Did Mr. Morgan express any opinion on business conditions, Mr. President?

No, he did not. Our talk was purely reminiscent of the warm friendship we had had, and our summer meetings.

He didn't happen to mention the Claflin failure?

No, not at all.

The talk next week with Mr. Ford will relate to business conditions, will it not?

I suppose so. There is no specific plan about it.

Mr. President, is it proper to be connecting these Morgan and Ford visits and the Chicago Chamber of Commerce [visit] you were mentioning to us just now?

They have absolutely nothing to do with one another.

Mr. President, has Mr. Williams, Minister to Greece, resigned?

I declare, I don't know. I have been meaning to ask Mr. Bryan, and I have neglected to do so.

Has any statement from him been submitted to you, Mr. President?

No, sir.

Mr. President, can you tell us anything about Haiti?[4]

No. I say "No" chiefly because of my ignorance. It is a very conflicting situation, and I haven't been able to catch up with it in the last three weeks.

Do you think that there is a danger of our being compelled to intervene down there in some way?

Oh, I don't think that there is any danger of our intervening in the literal sense of the word. Of course, we are trying to exercise such influence as we can now to quiet things and accommodate things down there.

Has there been any suggestion about taking charge of customhouses?

That is always suggested, but that has not taken any concrete form.

Mr. President, do you understand the reasons prompting Mr. Vick to resign?[5]

Yes. I understand them because he stated them. It is his wife's health. And his own, Mr. Tumulty reminds me. He has suffered. It is a pretty trying climate to live in down there.

Has General Evans submitted any explanation of his speech yet?[6]

No. I am promised a report from the War Department but I haven't received it.

Do you understand, Mr. President, the amended water-power bill—the Adamson bill? Is it satisfactory to the administration?

We had a conference last week that I think resulted very satisfactorily to everybody.

You don't expect any difficulty in agreement on those amendments in the House?

No. The Republicans in the House who were present—and three or four of them were present—didn't intimate that there would be any difficulty at all.

Did they represent both sides?

Yes. There was the chairman of each committee, Mr. Adamson and Mr. Ferris, and their Republican colleagues, Mr. Stevens[7] and Mr. Lenroot.[8] We all feel, of course, that it is not a partisan matter at all.

Have any steps been taken towards a new treaty with Russia, Mr. President?

Of course, we are waiting for our new Ambassador to get over there and get into harness.

Will the new Ambassador carry any instructions with him on that matter?

There are formal instructions, of course. The first thing he would have to do would be to inform us as to how things stood.

Mr. President, has Japan made reply to our last note?

No, sir.

Is there any change in the Montana or Colorado situations?

No, none at all.

---

[1] J. Pierpont Morgan, Jr., visited Wilson at the White House at 12:30 on July 2. Morgan refused to discuss the meeting, except to describe it as "very cordial." See the *New York Times*, July 3, 1914.
[2] Henry Ford, the automobile manufacturer.

³ See above, June 15, 1914.

⁴ See above, June 25, 1914.

⁵ Walker Whiting Vick resigned on July 2 as Receiver-General of Customs for the Dominican Republic. Dominican customs were at this time under the jurisdiction of the Bureau of Insular Affairs of the War Department. See the *New York Times*, July 3, 1914, and Link, *The New Freedom*, pp. 108-109.

⁶ Evans reported to Secretary of War Garrison on July 2 that he had been misquoted on his speech. See the *New York Times*, July 3, 1914.

⁷ Representative Frederick Clement Stevens of Minnesota.

⁸ Representative Irvine Luther Lenroot of Wisconsin.

July 6, 1914

Mr. President, can you tell us anything about George Fred Williams?

Nothing more than I am sure you know, sir. We felt obliged to disapprove the attitude he had taken as in any way connected with instructions from this government.[1]

He doesn't seem to know whether he had resigned or not.
Mr. President, to whom was that disapproval made known?

It was made public and sent to the representatives of the various powers.

On Saturday?

On Saturday, I believe. It must have been on Saturday.

Mr. President, have you requested his resignation?[2] The stories sent out from Philadelphia[3] read to that effect, the other reports all being in effect that you had not.

I think for the present that had better be a confidential matter.

Mr. President, as a step toward the continuing independence of the Philippines, has there been substantial agreement on the bill which will make for an elective Senate?[4]

There has been a substantial agreement, more than a substantial—entire agreement—in the House committee on a bill framed by Mr. Jones and modified by consultation. But, so far, the Senate committee has not taken the matter up at all and, therefore, it is only half in shape so far as the Congress is concerned.

Well, does that meet with your general idea on the subject?

Yes, sir, that bill does.

Does your program go any further than that?

Well, of course, I don't suppose you have seen the bill, have you? I would rather wait until the bill is published so all features can be discussed together.

It may be regarded as the administration's views on the subject?

Yes, sir. I want you gentlemen to understand, if you please, that when I say that with regard to a House bill, I don't mean to be understood as attempting to preclude any consideration of the details that will be undertaken in the Senate. I mean, I don't want it to look as if I am trying to ram it down the Senate's throat, because I have no such attitude towards it at all.

What do you think the chances are this session?

I hardly think it is possible that it will pass the two houses this session.

Mr. President, has there been any complaint from France with regard to the action of the Treasury agents over there?[5]

No official complaint that I have heard of.

But you are informed, are you not, that there is resentment?

I am informed through the papers. Only in that way.

Is the General Evans incident closed now?[6]

Yes, sir, I believe so.

The Philadelphia dispatches said that you had determined upon a public reprimand.

Well, public reprimands are not given. There is no way of giving one.

Your letter to the Carabao Club[7] was in the nature of a public reprimand.

Yes, because that was not a single individual. You can't give any other sort to a group of persons unnamed.

Mr. President, about the adjournment of the [conference] in Niagara Falls.[8] Is that still a barred subject?

You see, it is not an adjournment; it is a recess, in the hope that it and all the Mexican factions may come together, and therefore, so far as that part of it is concerned, it is still barred.

Does that bar any comment from you on the election in Mexico?[9]

I don't think any comment is necessary, do you?

Have you any definite information, Mr. President, as to the plans of General Huerta personally?

No. I am not his confidant. You remember Mr. Dooley's[10] remark? He said, "It was understood."

I see. Nothing on Santo Domingo?

Nothing that I know of.

Mr. President, have you been informed as to the position of the Senate committee on the confirmation of Mr. Jones, as to what they intend to do?[11]

I don't think that that is serious.

---

[1] Secretary of State Bryan issued a statement on July 3 repudiating Williams' position on Albania. See the *New York Times*, July 4, 1914.

[2] *Ibid.*, July 5, 1914, reported that Wilson had done so.

[3] The news came from Philadelphia because Wilson was there to address a gathering at Independence Square on July 4. The address is printed in *PWW*, Vol. 30, pp. 248-55.

[4] The Jones bill.

[5] French authorities were complaining about the secret methods used by American Treasury agents to prevent smuggling. See the *New York Times*, July 3, 1914.

[6] *Ibid.*, July 5, 1914, reported that Wilson was not satisfied with Evans' explanation.

[7] See above, Dec. 22, 1913.

[8] In a conference at Niagara Falls, Canada, which began on May 20, the governments of Argentina, Brazil, and Chile attempted to mediate the dispute between the United States and Mexico. At Wilson's insistence, the conference also endeavored to resolve Mexico's internal political problems. The conferees failed to reach agreement, exchanged final notes, and recessed, never to meet again, on July 2, 1914. See the *New York Times*, July 3, 1914, and Link, *The New Freedom*, pp. 405-13.

[9] An election was held in the federally controlled parts of Mexico on July 5. Because the voting was very light, the election was generally regarded as meaningless. See the *New York Times*, July 6, 1914.

[10] A character created by the humorist, Finley Peter Dunne.

[11] The nomination of Thomas Davies Jones for the Federal Reserve Board had run into serious difficulty with progressives in the Senate as a result of his position on the board of directors of the International Harvester Company, the so-called harvester trust, then under indictment as an illegal combination. Jones, an old friend of Wilson, had been called before the Senate Banking Committee for further investigation. Following a bitter battle, Jones asked Wilson on July 20 to withdraw his name from consideration. See the *New York Times*, July 5, 1914, and Link, *The New Freedom*, pp. 451-56.

July 9, 1914

Can you tell us anything about your talk with Mr. Ford today, Mr. President?[1]

It was just a pleasant get-acquainted and an exchange of general impressions about the business of calming the attitude of businessmen, and so forth. It was, to me, a very reassuring conversation. Mr. Ford himself is in a very happy frame of mind.

Mr. President, may the same be said with regard to your conversation with the gentlemen from Illinois?[2]

Yes, though that conference had a more businesslike aspect. They had come down to say that they were not at all opposed to the general character of the trust legislation we were contemplating, but wanted to point out certain features which they thought would be better if modified. And I think that, after I explained some of the changes that were in contemplation, they felt that their points were, most of them, met. At any rate, it was a cooperative thing and not a critical thing. They did not come down here to criticize but to cooperate.

Mr. President, can you tell us briefly what some of these contemplated changes are?

Well, nothing that I don't think you know already. You knew all along that the uneasiness of the businessmen has been about attempting to express the definitions that would be reached, that might cover more than we intended to cover in the prohibitions of the law. Everybody sees that the most difficult thing to do is to make a definition which will cover just what you want it to cover— not more, not less. What they were pleading for was some method of adaptation to the varying circumstances of different cases, which we all desire, and it is furnished, I think, in what is now, I believe, the fifth section of the trade commission bill, of the Newlands bill, which makes illegal unfair practices in trade and gives the commission the right to check those practices when they regard them as unfair.[3]

Will any change of phraseology in the paragraph defining the rights of labor result from this conference?

Well, they didn't speak of that. I mean, they didn't speak in any way that would suggest a change. They simply referred to it as one of the debatable parts of the measure, but what they said didn't go beyond that.

If that measure means what you explained to them that it does mean, I suppose they are fully satisfied?

They are fully satisfied.

It is only the other interpretation?

It is only the other interpretation which I don't think in the least is there.

Mr. President, the fifth section, will not that make it more indefinite about unfair competition?

It will, in a way. You see, this is a very close analogy. The law forbids fraud, but nobody can define fraud. No lawyer has ever attempted to define fraud, and when, in that vague field of fraud, the court undertakes in specific instances, where fraud is alleged, to determine whether there was any fraud or not, fraud is found elusive, a thing that may be committed in a myriad different ways. Some things may bear the appearance of fraud which upon examination don't turn out to be such at all. So there are certain competitive practices which in some circumstances are restrictive of competition and in others are not—the very same practices. I can give an illustration. Take the case of an exclusive agency forbidding anyone to deal with an agent that had handled the goods of competitors. In certain rural districts, that might shut out competition altogether because there are only one or two men with whom it could make the exclusive arrangement. But in a big city, making an exclusive arrangement with one dealer doesn't seriously interfere with competition, if it interferes with it at all, so that the very same kind of contract of the exclusive agency would, in one neighborhood and in one set of circumstances, constitute restraint of competition and in another would not. I don't know of any means in a law of foreseeing or discriminating between those cases.

Didn't the Supreme Court, in the decision of the grocers case, in the handling of certain patented goods, lay down a specific ruling?[4]

Yes, but that was in the case of a patented article. That was in a case of articles, the prices on which were fixed by manufacturers.

Mr. President, is it that the businessmen are trying to make sure that the trade commission will be a sort of clearinghouse for those problems; that is, they will have somebody to whom to go to resolve the doubt whether a certain practice is fraudulent?

A great many of them do [want that]. It is that part of the legislation, as it stands, that does not put the commission in quite that position. It puts it in the same position that the Interstate Commerce Commission is in, of checking certain practices, but not of okaying them before they have occurred.

Do any of them suggest they [would like to] have somebody to go to with a certain business problem, to find out whether it is illegal?

Yes. Some of them want immunity powers beforehand.

That is at the bottom of their uncertainty, as to what is fraud and what is not fraud, and that is all you are trying to clear up?

Yes, but of course there are two methods of clearing it up—one after a practice has been entered into and [one] before it is entered into—and I don't think it is safe to say beforehand whether a practice is going to be good, bad, or indifferent. You don't know until the effects are clear.

The idea is to have the same effect as the Interstate Commerce Commission's hearings on complaints?

As the bill stands, there is no provision for complaint. You can readily understand how, in the business world, a great many men might deliberately make trouble by constantly lodging complaints, provided the law said that the complaint had to be acted on. Of course, they can always call the businessman upon investigation, if they think the information is important, either upon investigation or, more often, on their own initiative.

Mr. President, during the winter, the House Judiciary Committee and Mr. Lucking,⁵ the attorney of Mr. Ford, argued for the setting of resale prices, upholding the practice which is now prohibited by law. Did Mr. Ford talk with you—

He did not talk about that.

Mr. President, as a result of this conference, can you say that it might change your attitude as to having legislation at this time?

No, I wouldn't say that they have changed my attitude. I will say that I know more about their attitude than I knew before, and their attitude is not hostile to having legislation at this time, and that the average businessman of the country appreciates having things done upon a definite plan.

Mr. President, have you been given any information as to when the Interstate Commerce Commission will finish the rate case?

No, none whatever.

Do you still get information from various parts of the country that that is holding up—

Yes, and I think we also get information that the railroads are going ahead with their necessary expansions and taking on their men again.

Has Mr. Warburg requested to have his name withdrawn?[6]

Not yet. No, sir. I am hoping he will not.

You haven't heard from him?

I have heard from him,[7] but I won't accept it as a final answer. I think the whole country approves of his appointment and desires his confirmation. That is enough for me.

The statement given out by the Committee on Banking and Currency dealing with the testimony of Mr. Jones[8]—does that in any way shake your conviction as to the accuracy of your own characterizations of his purposes in joining the harvester trust company?[9]

No, sir. It shakes my faith in the accuracy of the statement given out by the committee. I mean that if it conveyed any impression contrary to the estimate I put upon it, it was inadvertent and was not essentially contradictory at all.

I think the statement of the committee rather made it appear that Mr. Jones is in sympathy with the purposes of the harvester company as at present constituted.

Well, if it does, why of course it was an imperfect statement. The fact is that Mr. Jones said that in his opinion the actions of the company since he had been connected with it were legal and proper, and I think that is true, from all I can learn. You see, there are some companies—I don't know enough about the harvester company to know whether it is one of them—but there are some companies which, though they may have been organized in contravention of the law, have not used their organization in a way to contravene the law, or that, although their very organization may be, in itself, tainted with illegality, their operations have been legitimate.

They have the power for evil without using it.

Exactly. The Supreme Court has said, as I understand it, that the Sherman law forbids businessmen putting themselves in a position where they can monopolize the market, whether they do so or not. So it may be that the initial step was illegal.

Mr. President, do you know whether Mr. Jones was opposed to voluntary dissolution in the suggested [settlement]?

I don't know anything about that.

It was said by a member of the committee that he said that.

I simply know that I would rather trust Mr. Jones' judgment than mine. I have been associated with him for twenty years. There have been occasions when I would have made mistakes if I had not had Mr. Jones by [my side]. I don't mean since I got into politics, but before. He is one of the sort of men that doesn't offer his advice. He is not trying to run things. He is one of the best persons [I know].

Mr. President, the London *Express* asked and has now an article to the effect that an American member of Congress cabled you with regard to the situation in Albania and had suggested intervention on the part of the United States, and as a result of that cable, Mr. Williams was sent on to make an inquiry. Do you recall anything of that kind?

No. If I did, it wouldn't get any further than the State Department. Oh, no. That is an invention.

Mr. President, do you know whether Mr. Sullivan[10] will go back to Santo Domingo?

No, I don't. I haven't seen Mr. Sullivan yet. He hasn't got here. He can't go back until he gets here.

Well, Mr. Vick is back. You have got others back who can go back.

Mr. Vick has resigned.[11]

Was that a voluntary resignation?

Entirely.

I understand that there was some sort of communication which reached you here with reference to Mr. Sullivan?

You mustn't believe everything you hear.

Mr. President, it was stated yesterday that you were still hopeful for a solution of the New Haven situation without filing a suit.[12] Could you tell us anything about your hopefulness?

No. I am not familiar enough with the details to discuss that. I was basing that hopefulness—I didn't know I had expressed it, I felt it, but somebody must have expressed it for me—I think that the hopefulness was based upon a conversation I had with the Attorney General.

Did Mr. Walsh tell you anything along that line that you might tell us?[13]

No, sir. He really didn't tell me anything that threw any light on the situation at all—the circumstances that surround the legislation. He had a little time left to tie a small string to it.

Did he say whether he had discussed with any New Haven officials with regard to their attitude on that legislation?

He didn't and admitted he had not.

Mr. President, there is considerable agitation among the exporters of France regarding what they term the unfair activities of American customs agents there.[14] Has that come to you?

Only through the newspapers.

Do you know whether there is any disposition on the part of the government to modify their activities?

I have not heard it discussed at all.

Is there any change in the Santo Domingo situation, Mr. President?

No changes.

Mr. President, have you any new protests from Japan?

No.

Have you heard whether or not one of them has been sent in to the State Department?

If so, I have not heard of it.

[1] The automaker visited Wilson at the White House on July 9.

[2] A delegation from the Chicago Association of Commerce visited Wilson on July 8 to ask for the adoption of legislation to establish a strong trade commission. See the *New York Times*, July 9, 1914. Wilson also met with a delegation from the Illinois Bankers' Association on July 9. See *ibid.*, July 10, 1914.

[3] Section 5 of the federal trade commission bill empowered the commission to prevent unfair competition by issuing cease and desist orders which would be enforced by federal courts.

[4] *Virtue v. Creamery Package Mfg. Co.*, 227 U.S. 8, 33 S Ct 202.

[5] Former Representative Alfred Lucking of Detroit, a Democrat.

[6] Warburg had refused to appear before the Senate Banking and Currency Committee and, on July 3, had asked Wilson to withdraw his name. See the *New York Times*, July 9, 1914, and Warburg to WW, July 3, 1914, WP, DLC.

[7] On July 3, reiterating his desire to have his nomination withdrawn. See Jones to WW, July 3, 1914, *ibid.*

[8] Following Jones' appearance before the committee on July 6, a summary of his testimony was released to the press. Jones was reported to have stated that his purpose in becoming a director of the International Harvester Company was only to oblige Cyrus Hall McCormick, Jr., his lifelong friend. He also was supposed to have said that he "fully approved all acts of the company since he became a director in 1909, believing them proper and within the law." See the *New York Times*, July 7, 1914, and Link, *The New Freedom*, p. 454.

[9] In a letter of June 18 to Senator Owen, chairman of the Senate Banking and Currency Committee, Wilson defended Jones' service on the board of directors of the International Harvester Company and said that he joined the board "for the purpose of assisting to withdraw it from the control which had led it into the acts and practices which have brought it under the criticism of the law officers of the Government." Jones' testimony did not confirm this interpretation, which Wilson appears to have invented. See WW to Owen, June 18, 1914, printed in *PWW*, Vol. 30, pp. 191-92, and Link, *The New Freedom*, pp. 453-54.

[10] James Mark Sullivan, American Minister to the Dominican Republic. Sullivan's corrupt and incompetent behavior was at this time being revealed to Wilson by Walker W. Vick. See Link, *The New Freedom*, pp. 108-10, and Dana G. Munro, *Intervention and Dollar Diplomacy in the Caribbean, 1900-1921* (Princeton, N. J., 1964), pp. 275-301.

[11] See above, July 2, 1914.

[12] Governor Walsh, on July 7, signed a bill which separated the Boston and Maine from the New Haven Railway. The terms did not satisfy the New Haven's board of directors, however, and they were threatening to fight dissolution. See the *New York Times*, July 8, 1914. Wilson was reported in *ibid.*, July 9, 1914, as being still hopeful for a settlement without prosecution.

[13] Governor Walsh visited Wilson on July 8. See *ibid.*

[14] French officials were now reported to be threatening to expel American Treasury agents. See *ibid.*, July 6-7, 1914.

July 20, 1914

Mr. President, are you now in agreement with Adamson about the general dam bill?[1]

Well, what we are trying to do is to get the Adamson bill and the

conservation bill—what might be called the Ferris bill[2]—into un-
questionable harmony with one another. I don't think there is any
necessary contradiction between them, or conflict, but we are trying
to make the language such that there will be no reason to doubt
that.

There have been several amendments proposed, I believe, but Secretary Lane
of late has agreed to an amendment in conformity with the conferees' bill to
go to Secretary Garrison. I am not able to say that they have gone any further
than Secretary Garrison.

I am hoping to have another conference about this thing, to see
just where it stands. I am a little mixed in my mind just what
decisions have been reached. I don't think it is a matter of any
fundamental difficulty, but it is very difficult, I have found out, to
find the phraseology that will be [acceptable] to both sides. We are,
we will agree, all after the same legislation.

I suppose you gentlemen understand what the real difficulty is.
It is very difficult to manage it in the statement of a law. The
Department of War is to have immediate jurisdiction over navigable
waters, and is to have the right to say whether obstacles shall be
placed in navigable waters or not. If they are emplaced under protected conditions, they can be permitted there. But in some parts
of the country, there are navigable streams that would be very much
more important to spread abroad for the irrigation of the country
than to use for navigation. And there is one feature which is not a
feature of navigation but which is most important to parts of the
country, and that is its use as a source of supply for water for the
reclamation of arid lands and the prosperity and general living
conditions of the community.

Now this is the law that will maintain the proper jurisdiction of
the Department of War, and when you give to the authorities of
the government the right to divert navigable streams, and even
disperse them, so to speak, for other purposes, it is very difficult
indeed.

Haven't the courts decided that any ordinary stream which will float a log is
a navigable stream?

Not that I have heard of.

I understood that was one of the court definitions of a navigable stream.
Doesn't the [situation require leaving out] some [rivers] necessary for navigation rather than for irrigation?

I think that is for Congress to determine.

These conferences haven't raised the point whether the Secretary of War should be the last resort?[3]

They have, to some measure, but it is recognized that some questions are more important in one part of the country than they are in another.

And someone will have to say that?

Someone will have to say that.

Isn't there a bill that creates a water-power commission—the Secretary of War, the Secretary of Commerce, and the Secretary of the Interior?[4]

I don't know what bill you can be referring to, unless it be the bill which contemplates a study of water conservation throughout the country, particularly to prevent floods.

Mr. President, are you informed that it is the intention of the Senate to dispose of the Colombian treaty at this session?

I am not informed one way or the other. I have taken it for granted that it was agreed that both bills[5] were entirely approved by the administration, and the amendments were merely added to reconcile their apparent conflicts. I think that [the differences] were only apparent, myself, but they have been entirely obviated now.

Mr. President, do you understand that this is satisfactory to the conservationists?

Why, so I understand it. I haven't that direct from anybody.

I was told Saturday by them that it was absolutely not, that there were fundamental points that they demanded in the bill which were not included, as they were told they would be in the conference.[6]

I don't know what that can refer to. I learned from the chairmen of both committees afterwards that, as a result of the conference, the bill had been improved, but I am uninformed as to particulars.

The conference has cleared up the conflict between the Ferris bill and the Adamson bill, but the real, fundamental purposes that the conservationists demanded, one of which is federal compensation for water power,[7] was not included, as they were given to understand it would be.

Of course, there is a very considerable difficulty there. The general dam bill has to do with the jurisdiction of the United States over navigable waters. The theory of the bill is that all that the United States is parting with is its sovereign right to forbid obstacles [to navigation]. It is not parting with any property. It is not parting with anything except the right to interfere. That seems a very abstract way to put it. That is all. It is granting a permit to erect a certain kind of obstacle in a navigable stream under such and such conditions. Now, in the field of conservation—I mean in the field in which conservation is of the greatest consequence to us in the earlier stages, for example, in that general region the government is parting with a great deal more than a right to object. It is granting the use of its property, and there is an objective basis there for direct compensation to the government itself. The safeguards in the general dam bill are of a very careful sort; namely, that the construction and conditions of the operation of these water powers shall be held under the control of state public-service commissions, where such commissions exist or, where they do not exist, under the regulation of the Department of War acting as a sort of national public-service commission so far as those water powers are concerned.

There is no limit placed by the bill upon the regulation which may be imposed through those channels. Now just what part of that they regard as debatable, I don't at present know.

The fundamental opposition of the conservationists there is that they think the United States should exercise the right to demand payment for the use of that water, as disposing of the water power as property of this government. That is just the point. In most of the places governed by the other bill,[8] it is the property of the government, but in matters covered by the general dam bill, it is in no case that I now know of the property of the government.

Mr. President, the conservationists claim that the United States spends a large amount of money in developing the headwaters, which increases the power in the navigable streams. They claim that there should be compensation for that.

I want to know, whom do you mean by the conservationists? I don't want to be excluding myself. I am a conservationist myself.

That is the claim of the National Conservation—[9]

Who has been speaking for them recently with regard to those bills?

A brochure put out by Mr. Pinchot[10] recently.

Now, do these gentlemen, so far as you know, who were in the conference the other night, also feel that the arrangements at that conference were not satisfactory?

I don't know.

We had two very earnest friends—everything of that sort present. You see, our view of these bills is the obvious view—that they are not partisan measures in any sense. The other night Judge Stevens and Mr. Lenroot were present and I understood—I asked them just before we parted—I understood that they had acquiesced in the conclusions that we reached.

Mr. Lenroot said the bill is much better than it was when they started, but it is not entirely satisfactory.
Mr. President, did your recent conference with the Kansas City bankers and businessmen bring out any new points with regard to consideration of the trust legislation?[11]

No, sir, I can't say that it did. From all those conferences, I did not derive a great deal of information by reason of the fact that I don't think that their object was to urge any particular course, but merely to speak of certain aspects of business as it appeared to them.

Did they at all discuss the tariff as a factor in business conditions?

It has been rather interesting to me that in none of these conferences has the tariff been brought up except incidentally. They generally mention the difficulties, of course. Some period of adjustment to the tariff is necessary. None of them criticized the tariff.

Mr. President, Captain White[12] was one of the Kansas City men who said after the conference that he was under the impression that the trust program would be considerably better.

Well, I suppose he got that impression from this. They came here with the Clayton bill after it passed the House in their minds. I pointed out that the Senate was proposing various modifications in the Clayton bill, not changes in the sense of changing the purpose of the thing, but in the character of the provisions. I told them, so far as I was informed, what those changes were like, that the program therefore was still to be developed because just the form in which these things would finally come out of conference could not be foreseen. And that was on the order of what they had in mind.

Mr. President, with reference to the tariff, I see that the manufacturers' association of Montgomery County—I think it's in the Schuylkill Valley—has written you a letter indicating their dissatisfaction over tariff conditions.[13] I wonder whether that was an isolated case?

I don't know of any other case.

(Mr. Tumulty) It is the only letter of such a kind that has been received. Is the trust legislation in the committee making satisfactory progress?

Yes. I learn from various quarters that this is the situation: as you know, the commission bill is before the Senate, and inasmuch as any number of Senators, however small, can keep things retarded, two of the Republican Senators, I am informed, have said that they would not be willing to vote on any one of these three bills until all three are before the Senate and they can know what the whole program is. Senator Culberson's[14] Committee on the Judiciary is ready on practically twenty-four hours' notice to report. That would be its report on the equivalent of the Clayton bill. The railroad securities bill is, I am told, not yet ready to be reported. So I suppose if these two bills can make good their opposition, things will go slowly until that bill is reported.

But there has been no doubt on the part of the committee?

None whatever.

Mr. President, is it your understanding that section five of the trade commission bill makes unnecessary any definitions of the Sherman law?[15]

Yes, sir.

Mr. President, have you heard whether the sentiment in the House is for or against the Rules Committee's reporting out anything when it reaches the end of the session?

I haven't heard about it.

A number of things haven't come up, [could come up] only under a special rule?

Well, I understood that the House felt that its work for the rest of the session was cut out for it already. It wasn't longing to do any more.

Mr. President, is there anything to be said on the Jones nomination at this time?

No, sir. I don't know of any development in it.

Anything about Warburg, Mr. President?

No, sir. That is in the same condition. In limbo.

Have you taken up the question of Mr. Justice Lurton's successor?[16]

No, sir, I haven't. Some of the newspapers reminded me of the widow who was proposed to just as soon as she reached the house, after attending her husband's funeral, and she said she was sorry but another man had proposed at the grave. They reported the very next morning my having certain persons in mind.[17] I had been too genuinely distressed to have anybody in mind and haven't been going very fast in the matter. It happens that he was an old friend of my father's,[18] and one of the justices whom I personally knew well.

Mr. President, there is a report this morning that China has asked this government to help obtain a seventy-million-dollar loan through our State Department. Has that come before you?[19]

I don't know anything about it. I hadn't heard of it.

[1] Adamson's bill (H.R. 16053) provided for the licensing of dams on navigable rivers. See Link, The New Freedom, p. 129.

[2] The Ferris bill (H.R. 14843) provided for fifty-year leases on hydroelectric projects constructed in the public domain and national forests. See ibid.

[3] The Adamson bill granted final authority to the Secretary of War.

[4] An amendment to the Adamson bill proposed by Senator Newlands provided for a regulatory commission to consist of the three named cabinet members. See the New York Times, July 8, 1914.

[5] That is, the Adamson and Ferris bills. Wilson has returned to the previous subject.

[6] Conservationists feared that the Adamson bill would permit the granting of nearly perpetual leases. See Link, The New Freedom, p. 129.

[7] That is, that the power companies compensate the federal government for the right to build dams.

[8] The Ferris bill.

[9] The National Conservation Congress.

[10] Gifford Pinchot, conservationist and president of the National Conservation Congress.

[11] Wilson met with a delegation of businessmen from Kansas City on July 15.

[12] John Barber White, a Kansas City lumber dealer.

[13] The Business Association of Montgomery County, Pennsylvania, made public its letter on July 19. It described the Schuylkill Valley as "paralyzed" and blamed poor business con-

ditions on the Underwood tariff and other antibusiness legislation. See the *Washington Post*, July 20, 1914.

[14] Senator Charles Allen Culberson of Texas, chairman of the Senate Judiciary Committee.

[15] See above, July 9, 1914.

[16] Horace Harmon Lurton, Associate Justice of the Supreme Court, died on July 12, 1914. See the *Washington Post*, July 13, 1914.

[17] See, for example, the *New York Times*, July 13, 1914.

[18] Lurton had been a resident of Clarksville, Tennessee, when Dr. Joseph Ruggles Wilson had taught there.

[19] The Chinese government was attempting to obtain a loan from a four-power consortium. See the *New York Times*, July 8, 1914.

July 23, 1914

Mr. President, can we ask you anything today about Mexico, what you think of the situation there?

I can't say that anybody that I know knows with certainty just what the status of things there is, but I should say, on the whole, that it is quite encouraging.

We understand that General Carranza is going to Tampico to meet with Carbajal.[1]

I understood that he had gone there, but I didn't know that was his purpose.

Mr. President, have you heard anything about General Villa's attitude?

I have heard more things than I can recall.

But it isn't clear what he is going to do.

I think it is perfectly clear that he is not going to get into trouble.

Had you noticed in the papers, the dispatches from the border stating that Villa refuses to move his troops south? And then there was a story this morning that he was entering into some sort of compact with Carbajal for the purpose of opposing Carranza?[2]

You may rest assured of this, that everything that comes from El Paso is not so. That is the greatest exchange for gossip, that is made up on the spot, that I know of on the borders of a distracted country. If it comes from El Paso, dismiss it from your minds.

Mr. President, would you tell us something about your conference with Mr. Brandeis?[3]

That was a very businesslike conference on some features of the railway securities bill, just discussing a number of details in the bill which he wanted to discuss with me, in order that I might be apprised of the point of view of some of the men who are most intelligently interested in it.

Mr. President, as a result of that conference, is there any suggestion from you as to how far the government's obligation might lie?

There really was no suggestion from me. It was a conference that I was glad to hold for my own information. I only have them to learn something, and I take note of all that I get.

Mr. President, Mr. Fitzgerald, in his statement this morning, complained that he and his colleagues from New York City had been pictured to you as the representatives of crooks, grafters, and political buccaneers—I think that's the language he used—upon which statement he bases the opinion that the situation will be adjusted in the conference with you. Do you know anything bearing on that situation? Why Mr. Fitzgerald gave out an interview in which he declared that he and his colleagues from New York City had been misrepresented to you in various ways and, as a consequence, they didn't have the standing here which they ought to have as Democrats and which they felt they needed in the next campaign which was to come; and this situation, generally described in that manner, is the situation which he thinks should be adjusted for which purpose he is to arrange an interview with you?[4]

Well, I am glad he is. I don't know how he got that impression because, for one thing, I happen to know more than he thinks. People can't describe Mr. Fitzgerald and others unjustly to me without my knowing it, so that he didn't have to be under the impression that I innocently sit here and believe everything I hear.

I am selective about what I believe, and I don't remember that anybody has come to me and shown those gentlemen in a false light. I don't readily listen to mischief of that sort, so that I am sorry he had got the impression that those impressions have been conveyed to me, for they have not. It should not be difficult for him to remove them.

That was the question I had in mind, as to whether his assumption was justified?

No, it is not. Of course, various people do say things in public and otherwise, intending to create an impression.

Mr. President, what is your attitude in the [antimachine political battles]?

I ain't got none.

That applies to both [New York] and Illinois?

There are no exceptions that I know of.

Mr. Hennessy,[5] the traditional—

I am not saying anything, but I am doing a lot of thinking this morning.

Mr. President, Secretary Bryan has endorsed a candidate in Illinois by a telegram to Governor Dunne. Is that purely an individual action?[6]

Oh, yes.

Has the administration any plan to give official recognition to or celebration of the signing of the Treaty of Ghent?[7]

So far, there is no program in the making at all. It is rather a matter for Congress than the administration.

Congress has refused the appropriation?

Yes.

I wondered if the administration had planned to give any other official recognition?

No, sir. Not at present.

Mr. President, in connection with that question Mr. Henning[8] asked—that Illinois situation—can you say if you are going to keep your hands off?

I can say what I please, but I am not going to say anything.

Mr. President, can you tell us something about the government's attitude in the Haitian situation? I refer particularly to the fact that announcement was made by the War and Navy departments that several marine regiments were going to be sent to Guantánamo to be held in readiness there for eventualities in Haiti and the Dominican Republic, although we understood that Haiti was meant particularly. That indicates that the administration certainly has some policy in view that might involve the use of force.[9]

No. It indicates only that the administration has some anxiety with regard to the case. It is one of those situations that is just bristling with interrogation points. I don't know what is going to happen from day to day. We didn't feel at liberty to be so far away that if it should appear with regard to some lives, for example, or interests that ought to be protected, that we could not act, but it doesn't in any way seem plain [now].

Could you say, Mr. President, whether any negotiations are afoot now for taking over the customs revenues of Haiti under the—

No, sir. There are no negotiations.

Mr. President, has this government sent anything to the government of Haiti and the Dominican Republic about the necessity of restoring order?

Yes, sir. We have been very eloquent on that.

Do the representations approach an ultimatum?

We can't get the audience to sit still long enough to hear us, like some other audiences that I have addressed.

Could you tell us, when you catch them, what you are going to say to them?

No. That's too conjectural.

Can you tell us when the arbitration treaties are to be presented to the Senate for ratification?[10]

Why, just as soon as they are made ready. Most of them have been. Forthwith.

I understand they have not been submitted for ratification in the Senate.

What took place, I believe, was that Mr. Bryan informed the Foreign Relations Committee of the probably immediate readiness of a certain number, knowing he had only one. When Mr. Bryan has them in shape, he will take them up to the Senate.

Mr. President, have there been referred to you any complaints of violation of the civil-service law by the discharge of Spanish-American war veterans?[11]

No, sir. I have heard nothing of it. Are there such statements?

They were printed several days ago and have been taken up by the press associations here.

I hadn't heard of that.

Mr. President, do you intend to have the treaties acted on in this session as a part of the program?

I sincerely hope they will be. My intention in that matter is not the intention of the Senate.

[1] Huerta appointed Chief Justice Francisco Carbajal as Minister for Foreign Affairs on July 10 and then resigned; Carbajal became Provisional President on July 15. It was understood that Carbajal, a Constitutionalist sympathizer, would yield the presidency to Carranza. See Link, *The New Freedom*, p. 413.

[2] Rumors were beginning to develop of a dispute between the Constitutionalist leaders. See the *New York Times*, July 23 and 25, 1914, and Katz, *Secret War in Mexico*, pp. 260-68.

[3] Brandeis visited Wilson at the White House on July 22 to discuss the Rayburn bill, then being considered by the Senate. See the *Washington Post*, July 23, 1914.

[4] Representative John Joseph Fitzgerald of Brooklyn, the dean of the New York Democratic congressional delegation, called on July 22 for Wilson's support of New York Democrats in the November elections. Fitzgerald's concern was occasioned by Wilson's apparent support of the anti-Tammany forces in New York and resulted in a meeting between Wilson and New York Democratic Congressmen on July 29. See the *New York Times*, July 23, 1914, and Link, *The New Freedom*, p. 170.

[5] John A. Hennessy, a progressive Republican running as an anti-Tammany candidate for Governor of New York. See Link, *The New Freedom*, pp. 170-71.

[6] In a telegram to Governor Edward Fitzsimons Dunne of Illinois, Bryan had opposed the candidacy of Roger Sullivan for the Democratic senatorial nomination. See the *Washington Post*, July 24, 1914.

[7] On June 29 Representative Flood proposed a bill (H.R. 13922) to create a commission to plan a celebration for the centennial of the signing of the Treaty of Ghent with Great Britain on December 24, 1814. The measure, which also called for an appropriation of $25,000, was defeated, fifty-two to 187. See *Cong. Record*, 63d Cong., 2d sess., pp. 11325-27.

[8] Arthur Sears Henning of the Chicago *Tribune*.

[9] The *New York Times* reported on July 23, 1914, that 400 additional marines were being sent to Guantánamo to join the 500 already there.

[10] Twenty treaties were sent to the Senate on July 24. See the *Washington Post*, July 25, 1914.

[11] It had been reported that Spanish-American War veterans were being dropped from the Philippine civil service under the new administration. Secretary of War Garrison denied the charge. See the *New York Times*, July 24, 1914.

July 27, 1914

Mr. President, is there anything you can tell us about your plans with regard to Mr. Warburg's nomination?[1]

No. There really isn't anything, really.

Have you heard from Mr. Warburg yet, Mr. President?

No, I have not.

Mr. President, will there be any further conferences to reconcile Mr. Adamson and Mr. Ferris in their differences on the general dam bill?

Well, they still—

They are split on the Sherley amendment.[2] It is proposed that the government should reserve the right to exact payment for our [water].

That is a fundamental difference of opinion between them. I think that will just have to be settled by vote.

Mr. Ferris and Mr. Lenroot both appear to be opposed to the Adamson bill.[3] As a result of the conference, both have declared in speeches in the House that they are not satisfied.

Still, to say that they are not satisfied, and to say that they are opposed, are two different things.

Mr. Lenroot said he would rather see no bill passed than that bill—in the speech he delivered.
Mr. President, have you seen that bill since it was reprinted?

No. I merely know what was to go into it.

Part of the propositions agreed to in conference are printed in brackets, and then there are a great many lines printed in italics which weren't discussed in the conference at all. Those are the parts that are objected to.

Well, of course, I don't know anything about that.

Mr. President, the Adamson bill, is it regarded as an administration measure, or merely the result of the conference?

I don't know whether they will call it an administration measure or a party measure. Generally, what is called an administration measure is a party measure. There is nothing of a party nature about any of these bills. As the bill left the conference, it had my support and approval.

Has the opposition of the conservationists made any difference in the situation?

No, I don't see that it has. I don't think that some of their objections are well founded. Others simply show a fundamental difference of opinion. I don't find anybody in the House contending for provisions which would, so far as I understand them, put the government at a disadvantage, or the people at a disadvantage. I think I said in a previous conference that the question fundamentally at issue is a very difficult question—whether the government is obliging those who receive permits to erect dams to pay for the government's refraining from objecting; that is to say, to pay for the government's refraining from exercising its sovereign right.

That is a very difficult and in some ways an abstract question, although very practical in the form it has taken in this discussion.

Well, then, that bill with the proposed Sherley amendment will not have your approval?

I never can say until I see the amendment. I don't know what its terms are.

I just meant any fundamental change.

Well, I can say that I am perfectly open to discuss the matter. But as it left the conference, that—as I understood it—had been laid aside as impracticable.

One of the conservationists' objections, Mr. President, is that the bill seems to protect the consumer against "*extortio* justice"[4] and then goes on in the next paragraph and works in a "joker" which doesn't extend protection to the consumer at all.[5]

What joker?

I understand one paragraph seems to protect the consumer against "*extortio* justice"—one of the things they have been trying for some time. But the next paragraph, I understand, as presented yesterday, seems to take that back.

I don't know of any such paragraph. The bill was gone over very carefully, and I would know of any such paragraph.

The second paragraph is one of those in italics—suggestions put in by the committee—and wasn't put in it at the conference.

I don't know anything about it.

You would be in favor of protecting the consumer, Mr. President?

Oh, absolutely. And I understand that was one of the main intentions of the bill, because one of its fundamental principles is that in states where there is a commission which can regulate such matters, the regulation is to be left to it, and in other states it is to be left to the Secretary of War.

Mr. President, have you given your approval to the plan to defer action on the various pending treaties?[6]

I don't know that there is any such plan.

I only get my information from the newspapers.

That is the reason I doubt it, because I haven't got it from any other source.

You haven't been party to any such agreement?

No, sir.

Mr. President, I don't know whether you deem it wise to say anything at all on the subject, but I would like to ask you whether the United States is in a position to maintain the peace of Europe at this time?

Well, that is a matter which it would be perhaps unwise for me to say anything about. I can only say that the United States has never attempted to interfere in European affairs.

Will you fill the Jones vacancy, Mr. President, before Mr. Warburg has indicated—

Not necessarily, but I am taking steps to send in a nomination.

Mr. President, it is being said by the Senators that you would welcome the defeat of the rivers and harbors bill.[7]

I haven't discussed that with any living soul—or dead one, either.

Mr. President, have you any position with regard to that bill?

I haven't read the bill.

Mr. President, have you a definite expectation as to the date when Congress will adjourn?

No, sir. I find it's not worthwhile to entertain definite expectations. It leads to too many [disappointments]. But I enjoy the climate.

There is a very sad story about you this morning, saying that you were very anxious to get away. It's very hot here.[8]

I'm not fond of fiction, so I don't read the Post.

---

[1] The New York Times, July 25, 1914, reported that Wilson was nearly ready to withdraw Warburg's name from consideration.

[2] Representative Joseph Swagar Sherley, Democrat of Kentucky, proposed to amend the general dam bill (H.R. 16053) by authorizing the Secretary of War to prescribe the amounts

to be paid by power companies receiving rights. These could be adjusted at ten-year intervals, thus giving the Secretary of War some control over the profits earned by the power companies. See the *Washington Post*, July 26, 1914, and *Cong. Record,* 63d Cong., 2d sess., pp. 12759-78.

[3] That is, the general dam bill.

[4] That is, justice by extortion.

[5] Gifford Pinchot charged that the bill was "full of jokers" and did not protect the public interest. See the *Washington Post*, July 26, 1914.

[6] The newspapers reported that the Senate had postponed consideration of twenty "cooling off" treaties, along with the Colombian and Nicaraguan treaties, because there was no time to discuss them. See the *New York Times*, July 26, 1914, and the *Washington Post*, July 26, 1914.

[7] Wilson was worried by charges that the bill (H.R. 13811) was a Democratic "pork barrel" measure. See Samuel P. Hays, *Conservation and the Gospel of Efficiency* (Cambridge, Mass., 1959), pp. 236-37, and the *Washington Post*, July 18, 1914.

[8] The *Washington Post*, July 27, 1914, reported that Wilson was "tired out" by the "wrangling" over legislation.

July 30, 1914

Mr. President, could you give us any more—some of the details—of the talk yesterday to the New York members?[1]

I would, with pleasure, if there were any to give. There really were no details. It was just a free expression of views as to the situation in New York. The individual members told me what they thought were going to be their difficulties in their districts. That was about all that it came to. It was a sort of "spa" meeting.

As I understood it, you told them that persons who were claiming to have the [authority] of the administration in New York were not authorized to say that.[2]

I didn't say exactly that. I don't remember, Mr. Oulahan, that I said anything on the subject, but I have frequently said, of course, that I don't constitute anybody my spokesman.

Mr. President, is there any likelihood that you will make any other statement than you gave out yesterday in regard to that conference?[3]

That was really all there was to say. There was not any significance in it of any other sort. Of course, conferences of that sort always have more read into them than is intended, and it is difficult to make people believe that that happens.

Mr. President, did they make any specific complaints at all?

No. None whatever.

There weren't any names mentioned, I understood, Mr. President?

No. I think not. I think none at all.

Mr. President, have you taken any action at all on behalf of this government in connection with the war in Europe?

No, sir.

Mr. Bryan told us yesterday that formal notice of a declaration of war had been received from Austria and he thought you had issued a neutrality proclamation?[4]

I don't think we have. We don't have, at this distance, a sufficient key as to what the situation is.

Has there been any suggestion, Mr. President, from any of the governments of the world, that we might offer our services?

None at all that have reached me.

Mr. President, have you considered offering such services on your own initiative?

I have practically answered that question. I don't see the key yet to the situation, or what lock to insert it in.

Mr. President, yesterday you told these wholesalers[5] that you thought that the trust bills and everything else would be out of the way in about six weeks. Have you any assurance in that regard? I am only seeking information about the situation.

No. I was simply making a calculation of my own. I have no assurances of any sort, except I believe that, since I saw this bill, the Republican Senators have held a conference which I think makes it hopeful that we shall get trust legislation without any hard and fast delays, at any rate.

Senator Smoot rather expressed the hope this morning that we would get away by the twentieth of August.

He mentioned the twenty-eighth to me. I don't know why he picked out the twenty-eighth. It may be the end of the week. I haven't looked at the calendar.

Senator Kern, Mr. President, said this morning that they will vote on the trade commission bill details this week surely.

I think that is the general expectation.

Mr. President, would you tell us whether there is a likelihood that you will nominate a successor to Justice Lurton before the present session ends?

Oh, yes. I certainly shall. Otherwise, I would have to make a recess appointment which I don't think—

That is not the way, I understand, in the case of the Supreme Court.

No, and I don't want to do that in any case where it is not necessary.

Mr. President, can you tell us what the status of Mr. Warburg's case is, as you understand it?

Well, I understand, just as I have seen it reported, that Mr. Warburg is coming down and will certainly meet with the Senate committee, as I understand it. His message to me[6] was practically the same as that the papers contained this morning.

In [that he said he would] merely have an informal conference with some of the Senators, preliminary to going before the committee?

I don't know about that. You see, I don't know what Senator Hitchcock or Senator O'Gorman may have said to him, or what expectations they led him to have about it.

Mr. President, in view of the expectation of the six weeks before adjournment, has there been any change in the attitude toward the Colombian and Nicaraguan treaties, or any treaty pending?

No. There has been no change of attitude at this end at all. I don't know of any at the other end.

Have you chosen a successor to Mr. Jones?

No. I hope to do that within a very short time.

Have you decided on the locality from which he will come?

I am trying to find a man from the same general region.

Mr. President, is there any news from the visit of Mr. Crane?[7]

No, nothing at all. I saw Mr. Crane both yesterday and today. He had no special errand.

The passage of the trust bills [blank] the administration, or together with the administration program?

Oh, yes. Of course, what I have been expecting was that the conservation bills might get through. That, I suppose, will depend entirely upon the circumstances.

Mr. President, it was announced yesterday that Judge Alexander of the Merchant Marine and Fisheries Committee would discuss with you certain features of the seamen's bill and the London Safety-at-Sea Convention.

That was to save time. I have received a number of letters from men who evidently knew what they were talking about, calling attention to the qualifications of some of the crews; and I had sent those letters to Judge Alexander, and he came in to discuss the question whether these gentlemen understood thoroughly the operation of the bill or not, just to clear up doubts about it.

Does it appear from yesterday's talk that the measure will be passed this session?

It wouldn't appear whether it will or not. Of course, it has no place on the agenda of the calendar. It may be it will be crowded out. I don't know. You see, questions of this sort arise: the bill provides that the crews of vessels shall be made up of men who can understand the orders of officers, as well as that they themselves understand and speak the same language, to that extent, at any rate; and that affects the shipping on this side of the continent in a different way from which it would affect the shipping on the Pacific coast. There are difficult questions of that sort which have to be canvassed.

Mr. President, have you gone at all into the probable effect of the European war on business conditions in this country?

Not at all yet. I have been hoping and praying there may not be any general European war.

Mr. President, have you made any plans for the fall campaign tour?

No, none at all.

Did you give Mr. Gordon any answer to his invitation to participate in the Ohio campaign?[8]

No. Except Cleveland would be very delightful to speak in, if I may say so. They have a most interesting arrangement in Cleveland, you know. They had had—perhaps they have made more of the business [of speaking] in Cleveland than any other place in the country. One thing that particularly struck me when I spoke there, they always cover the floor of their meeting places with sawdust. It not only made the arena orderly but it made it singularly quiet. That, of course, was the object. There's always a lot of talking around, and so forth. It made a good place to speak in.

Has your attention been called to the fact, Mr. President, that the Music Hall in Cincinnati is carpeted?

That is a luxury I haven't dreamed of. Is it carpeted under the seats?

We could fix it that way.

It would have to be velvet carpet to be as silent as sawdust.

Mr. President, have you expressed yourself on the senatorial primaries in Kentucky?

No, sir, I have some discretion.

Mr. President, any itinerary that you may make will be very largely dependent on what Mr. McCombs says after [his trip].[9] Is it anybody's—

It will be dependent upon the situation, when the time comes. Of course, we will just have to determine whether I shall speak at all, and if so, where.

Mr. President, do you care to say what Mr. Chalmers reported on conditions?[10]

I am quite willing to say anything that I recall that was significant. Mr. Chalmers said that his business for the year had been better than in previous years. I am speaking from memory—I don't remember how many years he said. At any rate, that business was everything he could desire, though he did say that during the last two months, I believe it was, there had been somewhat more than the seasonal falling off in sales—still leaving the average for the fiscal year, however, above previous years.

He explained to me that, so soon after new models are announced, people are apt to stop buying, because they want to wait for the next year's models. That always happens, but it has gone a little further this year than previously. I think that was the sum and substance.

Did he support you in passing the [antitrust] legislation before the end of the session?

Very heartily. Strangely enough, although one was led to believe that the preference of the business community was the other way at one time, it seems unmistakably in that direction now. I think reflection has shown that it, incidentally, is just the very thing they want to get passed.

Mr. President, did you get that from the wholesalers yesterday also?

Yes. They didn't come to offer the least objection to the legislation. On the contrary, they came to express support, but they came to offer detailed and express objections to the Clayton bill. I hope I was able to throw a little new light on the sections that they referred to.

Mr. President, did you take any definite action in the Dominican Republic or Haiti?

That is not in a position lately to be discussed, because it is in flux in both places.

Is there any prospect or has any progress been made in the efforts to send the—to send Americans to the Dominican Republic?[11]

No.

Mr. President, a great deal has been published in the Philadelphia newspapers regarding—about your interest in the Pennsylvania state fight, and there has also been a good deal said about dissatisfaction in the Democratic party over there. Has that been discussed with you recently?[12]

No, it has not. And I daresay the speculations are wide of the mark. I don't appear to see them.

Mr. President, is there anything you can say on the developments in the Mexican situation?

No. The news we get from there is entirely encouraging. One knocks on wood when one says that, but that is the fact.

Coming back to the seamen's bill, Mr. President, do you expect the London convention to be ratified at this session?

I must admit I have lost sight of the progress of that. I don't know.

Can you say whether these letters come from the shipowners or from the seamen's union?

One of those that I discussed with Judge Alexander yesterday came from a gentleman whose connections I don't know. I don't know whether he was a shipowner or not. But his criticisms—his pointing out what the effects would be—were so detailed that he evidently had the facts in his possession.

He opposed that provision that you spoke of, about understanding the orders of the officers?

He didn't exactly oppose it, but he simply pointed out what the effects would be. You see, a great many of the Pacific steamships, not our own ships, but foreign ships, employ Asians and East Indians generally.

[1] Thirteen members of the New York Democratic congressional delegation called at the White House on July 29 to ask Wilson for support in the coming campaign. See the *New York Times*, July 30, 1914.

[2] A reference to Dudley Field Malone, who was criticizing Tammany Hall ostensibly in the name of the Wilson administration.

[3] The statement was printed in the *New York Times*, July 30, 1914. It said that the meeting had been a "free and frank expression" of opinions about the political controversy in New York and had been characterized by a "spirit of cordiality."

[4] Austria declared war against Serbia on July 28; the Wilson administration had not yet issued a proclamation of neutrality. See the *New York Times*, July 29-31, 1914.

[5] A delegation from the National Trade Association of Wholesalers visited the White House on July 29. They discussed business conditions with Wilson and proposed changes in the Clayton bill and the trade commission bill. Wilson attempted to reassure the businessmen; he informed them that the administration was not "running amuck" but was attempting to achieve constructive legislation. See *ibid.*, July 30, 1914.

[6] Warburg telegraphed Wilson on July 29 to say that he would consult with Senator Hitchcock and members of the Senate Banking and Currency Committee about making an appearance to answer questions. Wilson had urged Warburg to reconsider his decision not to appear. See *ibid.*, and WW to Warburg, July 25, 1914, in *PWW*, Vol. 30, p. 304.

[7] Charles Richard Crane of Chicago visited Wilson on July 29 and 30 to discuss the Federal Reserve Board. See the *New York Times*, July 29, 1914.

[8] Representative William Gordon of Ohio had asked Wilson to speak on behalf of Democratic candidates in Ohio. See *ibid.*, July 31, 1914.

[9] McCombs, the chairman of the Democratic National Committee, was touring the West to assess Democratic chances there in the fall elections. See *ibid.*, July 28-29, 1914.

[10] Hugh Chalmers of Detroit, an automobile manufacturer, visited the White House on July 29. See *ibid.*, July 30, 1914.

[11] Wilson sent a message to "various Dominican leaders" on July 27 in which he called for free elections and the establishment of regular constitutional procedures in the Dominican Republic. He said that the United States would send representatives to observe the election. The message is printed in *PWW*, Vol. 30, pp. 307-309.

[12] See above, Feb. 5, 1914.

Aug. 3, 1914

Gentlemen, before you question me, I want to say this: I believe it is really unnecessary, but I always want to tell you what is in my mind. It is extremely necessary, it is manifestly necessary, in the present state of affairs on the other side of the water that you should be extremely careful not to add in any way to the excitement. Of course, the European world is in a highly excited state of mind, but the excitement ought not to spread to the United States. So far as we are concerned, there is no cause for excitement. There is great inconvenience, for the time being, in the money markets and in our exchanges and, temporarily, in the handling of our crops, but America is absolutely prepared to meet the financial situation and to straighten everything out without any material difficulty. The only thing that can possibly prevent it is unreasonable apprehension and excitement.

If I might make a suggestion to you gentlemen, therefore, I would urge you not to give currency to any unverified rumor or to anything that would tend to create or add to excitement. I think that you will agree that we must all at the present moment act together as Americans in seeing that America does not suffer any unnecessary distress from what is going on in the world at large. The situation in Europe is perhaps the gravest in its possibilities that has arisen in modern times, but it need not affect the United States unfavorably in the long run. Not that the United States has anything to take advantage of, but her own position is sound, and she owes it to mankind to remain in such a condition and in such a state of mind that she can help the rest of the world. I want to have the pride of feeling that America, if nobody else, has her self-possession and stands ready with calmness of thought and steadiness of purpose to help the rest of the world. And we can do it and reap a great permanent glory out of doing it provided we all cooperate to see that nobody loses his head. I know from my conferences with the Secretary of the Treasury, who is in very close touch with the financial situation throughout the country, that there is no cause for alarm. There is cause for getting busy and doing the thing in the right way, but there is no element of unsoundness, and there is no cause for alarm. The bankers and businessmen of the country are cooperating with the government with a zeal, intelligence, and spirit which make the outcome secure.[1]

Can you elaborate a little, Mr. President, on the subject of shipping, beyond the mere fact of the introduction of the bill?[2]

Of course, so far as we are concerned, our national interest in shipping is not merely to sell our crops—the surplus crops—but to be serviceable to Europe in getting foodstuffs to her in this emergency. We owe it not only to our own farmers, but we owe it to the world at large to release the surplus foodstuffs that are in sight in our present enormous crops; and we are going to do everything that is possible to find ships and to get ships for that worthy purpose—for that purpose which is as much unselfish as selfish.

I am wondering, Mr. President, if you can say anything of the possibility of converting coastwise ships into trans-Atlantic carriers?

I think from what I can learn that will be done to a very considerable extent. Of course, many of the coastwise ships are built for particular services which render them relatively unserviceable for grain shipments, without internal alterations or arrangements, so that how many of them—how many of the fruit ships, for example— could be used for that purpose, I am not yet informed.

Has there been any thought of using sailing ships?

Yes, sailing ships will be used so far as available. I was going to say that, according to statistics, we have a larger proportion of sailing ships than other countries have. It just shows that we are behind the times, as a matter of fact; but as a matter of statistics, we have more sailing ships in proportion. I guess—for I have no means of knowing—that they consist largely of these large three- and four-masted schooners which are used for the most part in the coastwise trade, but they can be used for trans-Atlantic trade. They are absolutely seaworthy and, except for their slowness, will be suitable for that purpose.

Do you regard the rate decision[3] as being favorable to the domestic financial situation?

I can only judge by what I saw in the papers this morning, which calculated that it would add to the income of the railroads, to whom the advance was granted, some ten or fifteen million dollars—and, of course, that ought to be helpful. But I am speaking now at third hand. I haven't personally gained any knowledge of it.

Have you, since your conference with the railroad men on Saturday, heard anything further from them?[4]

No, but I have every reason to believe that the railroad managers will take a satisfactory course of action in the matter.

Can you say whether Germany or any other nations have transferred their interests to our diplomatic representatives?

No, I cannot. Mr. Bryan can give you that list. Of course, we are going to be in the very singular position of being one of the very few neutral powers to which the various governments can turn over their interests. We will, of course, be of any service that we can.

Do you expect to be able to complete the Reserve Board this week?

I hope so. So far as I am concerned, it will be completed this week.

Will the nominations go in today?

I am not sure. I am waiting to hear from one gentleman whom I wish to nominate.[5]

Is it true, as reported, that the Queen of Holland[6] invited the United States to join her in an attempt to avert the European situation?

Not so far as I know. That is the first I have heard of it. I haven't seen anything about it.

Have you had any advices from Secretary McAdoo in respect to the New York situation?[7]

Mr. McAdoo was on the phone just a little while ago—he had Mr. Tumulty on the phone. He was very much encouraged and felt that it would work out very successfully.

I understand some suggestion has been made that Mr. Carnegie is proposing a plan to the administration.

None has reached me.

How soon can the Federal Reserve System be in working order after the nominations are acted upon?

The time would be different in different parts of the country. There are several steps to be taken. You see, not all the regional banks have elected their directors. They elect their directors and then the Reserve Board completes the directorate; and then they have to establish their physical headquarters.

Do you feel that the quick organization of the Federal Reserve Board would help the situation?

Very much. The Federal Reserve Board by itself cannot perform its useful functions; it must perform its service through the regional banks. As soon as the regional banks are in operation, they can control the rates on call money and things of that sort and help govern the market.

Would the inauguration of the Federal Reserve System be complicated by the use of emergency currency?[8]

No, not at all. If you look at this feature, you will see that the emergency act is to serve until next June in order to give time for the organization, and therefore the Aldrich-Vreeland Act is really a part of this act, making money much more available. It is part of the intermediate machinery. The rate[9] that the banks will have to pay is 3 per cent of their capital stock, and that will not tighten up the money market.

Have the shipowners or shipbuilders indicated their attitude toward the proposed legislation about ships?

I do not know whether they have or not; not to me.

Has this government taken any formal or informal action toward the offering of its good offices?

No, sir.

Will the European situation make it necessary for Congress to remain in session?

Oh, no. I do not see why it should alter their plans.

Do you think it advisable or necessary to act on the suggestion that ships be sent to bring Americans back?

Mr. Tumulty tells me that, in a telephone conversation he had with Mr. McAdoo this morning, Mr. McAdoo said he had been consulted by the New York banks as to the means of assisting our people, our tourists, through their correspondents on the other side of the water, and that he thought it could be arranged.[10] As for sending ships, that is easier said than done—where are the ships? Of course, we will do everything of any sort that is necessary. We are looking around now to see just what is at hand in the way of available means of getting them here.

Could transports be spared for that service?

Yes, they could; they are highly suitable.

Has the suggestion been taken up of neutralizing the liners held here?

That does not appeal to us. The matter has been discussed, but no plan has been suggested. Neutralization has to be bona fide. It cannot be make-believe; and it is a violation of neutrality merely to hoist the American flag over the ship when she is not an American ship. There might conceivably be some understanding about it, but when the European governments are so much engaged, it will be hard to manage a detail of that sort; and we could not commandeer them.

Have any of the shipping interests suggested that they will purchase these foreign ships?

I haven't heard of that suggestion, but I have very little doubt if American registration were open a great deal of that would be done. It would be profitable.

[1] Wilson permitted quotation of the above statement.

[2] The ship registry bill (H.R. 18202), which amended the Panama Canal Act to permit American registry of foreign ships prior to five years after launching and streamlined the process of reregistration, was introduced in the House and passed unanimously on August 3. The bill passed the Senate on August 17, and Wilson signed it on the following day. See Link, *Struggle for Neutrality*, pp. 82-84, and *Cong. Record*, 63d Cong., 2d sess., pp. 13173-90.

[3] On July 29 the Interstate Commerce Commission granted a rate increase of 5 per cent to railroads operating in Illinois, Indiana, Michigan, Ohio, and parts of western Pennsylvania and New York. See the *New York Times*, Aug. 2, 1914.

[4] Wilson met on August 1 with a delegation of railroad managers and labor leaders to discuss ways to avoid a strike on the western roads. See *ibid.*, Aug. 2, 1914.

[5] Frederick Adrian Delano of Chicago, president of the Monon Railroad, who was confirmed by the Senate on August 7.

[6] Queen Wilhelmina of the Netherlands.

[7] That is, the financial crisis engendered by the European war.

[8] Congress passed an act on August 4 which permitted banks to receive an additional billion dollars in "emergency" currency beyond the $500,000,000 limit set by the Aldrich-Vreeland Act, See the *New York Times*, Aug. 4-5, 1914, and Link, *Struggle for Neutrality*, pp. 78-80.

[9] That is, the tax on currency issued under the Aldrich-Vreeland Act.

¹⁰ Wilson sent a message to Congress (H. Doc. No. 136) on August 3 requesting an appropriation of $250,000 to assist American citizens stranded in Europe and to transport them home. See *Cong. Record*, 63d Cong., 2d sess., pp. 13190-91.
¹¹ That is, German liners which remained in American ports.

Aug. 17, 1914

Mr. President, there was a suggestion in the papers this morning that England is displeased at this legislation we are about to pass regarding shipping?[1]

I don't know anything about that.

There has been nothing from any other government?

There has been nothing from any government that I know of.

Mr. President, will you discuss the Japanese ultimatum now in the Far East?[2]

There is nothing to discuss about it. I feel one of the duties of neutrality to be to have no opinion about what other governments are doing.

Will you say whether this government is satisfied with Japan's assurance of the eventual restoration of German possessions over there to China?

Well, I daresay she has made the same assurances everywhere. We are satisfied with her good faith, certainly.

With reference to the ship registry bill, Mr. President, there is an intimation that there is to be a conference today. We don't know what your attitude is.

My attitude was expressed in the original House bill. That was framed after a conference[3] in which I was asked to participate, and I am entirely satisfied with it. It just happens that I have not had an opportunity to follow closely the subsequent changes.

Do you share the apprehension, Mr. President, that this legislation is destructive of American control of coastwise trade?

No, I don't share any apprehension.

Mr. President, does the administration contemplate any legislation looking toward the permanent upbuilding of the merchant marine?

This registry bill is, of course, not a temporary measure, and one of the things that I have held as most important and have been

talking about for fifteen years has been to find the right means for
building up our merchant marine. I haven't any very great confidence in my own judgment as yet whether we can find the right
way or not, but we shall certainly diligently seek it.

In that conference of the Secretary of the Treasury the other day with the
sixty-two businessmen,[4] it was pointed out that the ships would go back to
the flag from which they came as soon as the war was over, unless there was
legislation tending to remove restrictions on the operation of American ships.

That, of course, is a matter of opinion.

Mr. President, has any decision been reached as to the proper attitude of this
government toward censoring cable messages?[5]

Not as yet. I am trying to discover what is very difficult to find—
an absolutely impartial treatment of the subject. I am consulting
now with international lawyers and the Department of Justice as
to what the power of the administration in that matter is and hope
in twenty-four hours or so to work out something that is really
impartial.

You haven't any opinion yet of the real powers of the United States?

No, for the reason, as I understand it, that the United States
Government has the right to do anything that is necessary to enforce
neutral action within its territory, but just what the detail of that
would be—how far it can be carried—depends upon developed and
partly upon undeveloped principles of international law. Since that
part of the field is new, we have to feel our way all along.

Would the strict censorship of the wireless depend upon our ability also to
impose a strict censorship on the cable?

I think so. That is just what we are trying to figure out—what
kind of control, if any, of the cable is required of us in an impartial
treatment of this matter. The difficulty is this: the cable can deliver
any message from this side to the other side of the water. The
wireless can deliver messages at least half way across. I don't know
whether this is scientifically true or not, but I am told that vessels
cannot be reached, with the apparatus that they have, directly from
either shore more than half way across, so that there is a very
considerable difference between the cable in the objective point of
its communication and the wireless. How far, if at all, that should

differentiate the two in treatment we are just now trying to determine.

Would the ability to get uncensored messages over to Canada have any bearing on that question?

I don't know whether it would or not. Of course, the only means of communication with foreign shores is the cable or the wireless, whereas there are a score of means of communication in American territory—the ordinary telegraph, and so forth—and I should imagine that the practical difficulties there would be insuperable.

Mr. President, has any agreement been reached yet with regard to the revenue measures to be proposed to Congress?

No, I am going to have a conference presently with Mr. Underwood and Mr. Simmons.

Have you any suggestions in that regard that you could tell us of?

No, I haven't. My mind is entirely to let on that subject.

Can you tell us as to when the law might go into effect?

I have been so interrupted in my duties that I have lost track of it. I am going to take it up.

The Treasury could issue Panama bonds for any urgent needs.

It has the right now for a deficiency of the Treasury to issue bonds. The Panama Canal leaves a large balance in the Treasury.

Is that in contemplation at all?

No, not at present.

Mr. President, do you think Congress will adjourn during September?

I haven't stopped to think anything about it. It depends so much upon the development of events. So far as the program—the old program we used to talk about—is concerned, I think that will be finished tolerably soon.

Mr. President, referring to Mexico for a moment, now that Carranza has taken hold of the new government there, have any plans been made about Veracruz?[5]

No; no plans as yet.

Mr. President, the trade commission bill is in conference now. The Senate added the section about unfair competition to the House bill; have you taken any stand as to whether that should remain in the bill or not?[6]

I am very much in favor of that.

That is, in favor of the definition?

No; I think the definition so difficult as to be undesirable.

[1] That is, the ship registry bill. See above, Aug. 3, 1914.

[2] The Japanese government informed Germany on August 15 that Germany must remove its warships from the Far East and evacuate Kiaochow by August 23, or else Japan would take action. See the *New York Times*, Aug. 17, 1914, and Ambassador Guthrie to the Secretary of State, Aug. 15, 1914, *FR, 1914-WWS*, pp. 170-71.

[3] Wilson had called Democratic congressional leaders to the White House on July 31 to discuss the potential shortage of ships caused by the European war. The result was the Ship Registry Act. See Link, *Struggle for Neutrality*, pp. 82-83, and "A News Report," July 31, 1914, printed in *PWW*, Vol. 30, pp. 324-25.

[4] Secretary McAdoo met with bankers and shippers on August 15 to gather information about the merchant marine. See the *New York Times*, Aug. 16, 1914.

[5] That is, about the American forces in Veracruz.

[6] That is, Section 5. See Link, *The New Freedom*, pp. 438-41.

Aug. 20, 1914

Mr. President, is the war tabooed?

Well, any expressions of opinion by myself are tabooed.

What I had in mind is this, Mr. President. It is in line with what you said the other day in your address to the people.[1] Could you tell us whether the government has had any assurances from either Great Britain or Japan with regard to limiting the area of the hostilities between Japan and Germany?[2]

No, sir. Not so far as I know.

Or that the Japanese government has asked us to take over Japanese interests in Germany?[3]

I don't know about that. Perhaps they can tell you at the State Department, but I haven't been informed.

Is there anything about the conference with Mr. Bryan today, Mr. President, that you can tell us?

No. That was about interesting matters. Several associations have been planning this, that, and the other thing with regard to peace demonstrations, and so forth, and they were kind enough to ask me if I saw anything in them conflicting with the advice I gave the other day in the letter to which Mr. Oulahan has just referred. It wasn't anything of more than domestic significance.

Well, would you indicate what they were going to do, whether you approve it, whether it will meet your idea of the situation?

It always depends upon the particular thing planned. It encouraged me very much to see the spirit they displayed, that they wished to ask my advice as to whether it was proper or not. I think it is. A very wonderful response has been made to that letter.

How far has Great Britain gone regarding the neutralization of any foreign ships that we might charter for returning Americans?[4] The State Department gave out something this morning to the effect that a limited approval had been given out since.

I am sorry to say I don't know anything about it.

Have any representations been made at all regarding this proposed legislation for buying foreign ships or ships of any kind?[5]

No representations against it. I have received a number of messages approving of it.

Are those domestic messages, or from abroad?

Oh, domestic.

Mr. President, the idea would be to use such ships as the government might buy only in trade with neutral governments, would it not?

Well, that would depend. You see, our object is to get our goods to such markets as we can properly get them to and minimize so far as we possibly can the effects of the war upon our own commercial position.

Have you, in that connection, heard whether any of the countries of the world might object to the United States Government's taking over ships of other countries?

No, sir. I don't see any grounds on which they could object to our buying ships and using them according to the well-known rules of international law. You see, we are very much in this position. We are the great department store which has been using trade wagons of other department stores, and now we haven't any trade wagons.

Mr. President, is there anything you can tell us with regard to the censorship of the cables?

No, because we are looking as carefully as possible into every legal aspect of that—just what my powers are in the matter, and just what the obligations of neutrality are in detail. There are a good many novel elements associated with it, and I haven't got full advice yet.

Mr. President, Mr. Bryan sent a telegram yesterday to Tuckerton, New Jersey, telling the persons in charge that they had no license to operate the wireless station.[6]

That is true.

Have you taken any measures in that connection at all?

Well, none has been taken that I know of, Mr. Oulahan. I learned only yesterday that they had not taken out any license.

Was that true, about the Sayville plant?

The Sayville plant has a license.

Mr. President, is there anything you might tell us with reference to the proposed war tax, to make up the deficit?

No. We are simply still in the position of determining just what the probable means of the government will be, and just what taxes, if any, would be the least burdensome and most equitably distributed.

Mr. President, do you see any hope of escaping a war tax altogether?

We are still hoping that that will be possible, but I don't know. I mean, I haven't any opinion on that subject yet, because it is entirely a matter of the facts.

Mr. President, you saw Mr. Covington today, I believe?

Yes.

Did he give you any idea with regard to the passage of or getting the trust program out of the way?

No. Our conference was entirely confined to the trade commission bill. Mr. Covington sought the interview in order merely to acquaint me with the questions that have been raised in the conference and the progress being made. And I think that everything he told me was very encouraging.

The conference has been going slowly, but I understood that to be because there were a number of Senators who wanted to have both the Clayton bill and the trade commission bill in the final shape that the Clayton bill was in before voting finally on the conference report.

Mr. President, have you any idea as to the probable time that it will take for you to get this law for the purchase of those ships?

No, I haven't, but I have heard such universal assent to the principle of it, from gentlemen on the Hill whom I have talked to and heard from indirectly, that I should think it would be accomplished somewhat promptly.

Mr. President, did you see the proposal of Mr. John Wanamaker[7] in regard to using the postal savings fund to purchase the ships?

No, I didn't.

About 30 per cent to be used for that purpose.

Well, it is impossible, yet, to calculate the returns on any investment of that sort.

Mr. President, has it been determined what amount of money would be necessary to purchase these ships?

No. That is a matter which the Ways and Means Committee will probably determine.

It is, but I understood you considered yesterday the matter of purchasing ships with some Panama Canal bonds and a first appropriation?[8]

Of course we discussed the various alternatives, but what we first discussed was the organization, that is, how we could accomplish the best results. First of all, the principle of the bill, whether it was to be proposed at all or not, and then the form in which it was to be carried out. Regarding the method of raising the money, it didn't play any important part in the discussion at all?

Mr. President, did you get far at all in the matter of what sort of company would be [chartered]?

No. It seemed, I think, to all of us in that conference that the most convenient way to manage it, all things considered, all legal aspects considered, was through a corporation, but a corporation which would be entirely controlled by the government.

Mr. President, do you intend a message to Congress with reference to that or any of these emergency measures?

No, sir, I don't think that that is needed.

Mr. President, has it been determined whether Panama bonds are to be sold to make up any possible deficit in the Treasury?

No, that has not been determined.

Mr. President, have you received a report on the food-price investigation?[9]

No, sir. I looked into it recently and I found that it has been very thoroughly conducted. They come in to meet I don't know when. They are pushing it just as fast as they can.

[1] On August 18, Wilson issued an "appeal to the American people" in which he requested them to be "impartial in thought as well as in action" during the European war. See the *New York Times*, Aug. 19, 1914, and *PWW*, Vol. 30, pp. 393-94.

[2] Although Wilson feared that Japan's military involvement in the war against Germany might threaten the territorial integrity of China, he had no alternative but to accept the Japanese assurances that it would not. See Secretary of State to Ambassador Guthrie, Aug. 19, 1914, in *FR, 1914-WWS*, p. 172.

[3] Japan had asked and Secretary of State Bryan had accepted. See Bryan to WW, Aug. 17, 1914, printed in *PWW*, Vol. 30, p. 390.

[4] Wilson hoped to use German merchantmen in American and Italian ports to return Americans stranded by the war in Europe. The British agreed provided that the ships flew American flags, carried American crews, and returned to their neutral berths after completing their mission. The French balked at the suggestion, and it was never carried through. For correspondence on this matter, see *FR, 1914-WWS*, pp. 474-85.

[5] At a meeting at the White House with congressional leaders on August 19, Wilson proposed that the federal government charter a corporation to purchase foreign ships. The corporation, which would be controlled by a shipping board composed of the Secretary of the Treasury, the Postmaster General, and the Secretary of Commerce, was to be granted a capital stock of $10,000,000 and empowered to sell Panama Canal bonds to raise another $30,000,000. The measure was proposed in a bill (H.R. 18666) introduced by Representative Alexander and Senator James Paul Clarke, Democrat of Arkansas, on August 24. See the *New York Times*, Aug. 20, 21, and 25, 1914; Link, *Struggle for Neutrality*, pp. 86-87; and Jeffrey J. Safford, *Wilsonian Maritime Diplomacy, 1913-1921* (New Brunswick, N. J., 1978), pp. 35-66.

[6] Shortly before the war, German companies had constructed wireless facilities at Tuckerton, New Jersey, and Sayville, Long Island, which were capable of communicating with Europe.

When hostilities began, the stations were used to direct German warships and merchantmen at sea, thus employing American territory as a base of naval operations. On August 15, Wilson issued an Executive Order forbidding all stations to transmit unneutral messages, and a month later he took official possession of the stations under the Radio Act of 1912 and ordered the Navy Department to operate them or to regulate their operation. See the *New York Times*, Aug. 20, 1914; the Executive Orders, in *FR, 1914-WWS*, pp. 668, 678; and Link, *Struggle for Neutrality*, pp. 58-60.

 7 John Wanamaker of Philadelphia, a Republican merchant and Postmaster General in the Harrison administration.

 8 The possibility was being discussed of selling bonds to be repaid by Panama Canal toll revenues in the future. See the *New York Times*, Aug. 20, 1914.

 9 Wilson had called for an investigation of rising food prices to be conducted nationwide by United States district attorneys and special agents of the Department of Commerce. See *ibid.*, Aug. 15-20, 1914.

Aug. 24, 1914

I see by the papers, gentlemen, that an impression has gotten abroad that we are going to drop the suggestion of the government's buying ships.[1] I learned that for the first time from the newspapers. It is an entirely wrong impression, absolutely wrong impression, created, I daresay, in interested quarters. It goes without saying we are not only willing but desirous that private capital should go into the purchase of ships, but private capital, so far as we are apprised of its purposes, is not willing to go in unless the government guarantees the securities of whatever company is formed.

Well, that is for the trans-Atlantic trade, isn't it, particularly?

I haven't been informed which it is for, but that is the only proposal, the only plan of private capital that has come to my attention. Now, of course, as between that plan and the plan of the government's buying the ships and operating them, there is in my mind absolutely no choice. I am for the purchase of the ships by the government. By saying there is absolutely no choice, I mean that there is no debate in my mind which is preferable.

Mr. President, it has been said, in the first place, that private capital might not be able to get money, private money, to invest in ships, that the government is going in to compete with them, and that the administration may qualify this bill so as to make it [conditional], to use the power to buy the ships only in case private capital wouldn't do it.

It isn't going to be modified at all, so far as I am concerned, not in the least particular. That is of course absurd. It may be modified in any part, but not in any essential matters. It is not the idea of this bill to compete with private capital, but to develop trade where it will not otherwise be developed, but must be developed and developed to handle trade.

Do you anticipate that it will be possible to pass this bill in two or three months?

Mr. Essary,[2] it will be possible to pass it within two or three weeks.

Mr. President, does your reference to government-guaranteed securities mean that the government will own part or all of the company?

I mean, the plan proposed by me—not directly that, but the plan as I was informed—was that a company could be formed successfully if the government would guarantee its bonds. That is the only proposal of private investment that has come to my knowledge.

The proposal made during the [blank] the remainder to be left open to private enterprise?

One of the plans being debated is governmental ownership of a corporation by the ownership of the government of a majority of the stock. That is one of the plans under discussion to carry out what I am interested to see done, but then the government would own the corporation, as you should understand.

Will the purchase of these ships by the government, Mr. President, tend to encourage or discourage private capital in the future?

I should expect that it would be encouraged. Certainly it would be pursued by my administration in such a way as not to discourage private capital.

Have you any suggestion as to what way it will encourage them?

Well, for one thing, it might be used for developing lines of trade in undeveloped markets into which private capital could not be expected to go.

Mr. President, suppose that between now and the time that the bill passes, private capital should develop enough interest to provide enough ships to provide for the present developed trade. Then would this government line simply be used in undeveloped fields?

Well, that would depend on circumstances. It would depend upon how well the other fields were taken care of. I don't think the government ought to bind itself in that respect. But it ought, in the public interest, to be careful not to discourage private capital.

There seemed to be a general notion that, according to the newspaper statements, this line of ships could not be used in the trans-Atlantic trade or elsewhere because of the very nature of such trade being contraband, and that it could only be used in South American trade.[3]

I don't know where they got that.

On the theory that they were subject to capture, just like private ships.

They would not be. They would be under neutral flags. They would not be carrying contraband. Understand, there are two kinds of contraband. There is absolute contraband, and there is conditional contraband, which is contraband in certain circumstances. If it is being shipped to a British port, for example, if it is consigned to unknown purchasers, it is adjudged to be for belligerent governments. If it is consigned to such a place so obvious that it is intended for a belligerent area—circumstances of that sort—it makes it contraband. But in ordinary circumstances, it is not contraband.

Foodstuffs are of that class. The government's ships would not carry things of that nature?

Certainly not. It would not be dreamed of, carrying anything that either—I mean, it wouldn't carry anything that was conditional contraband under circumstances that would make it contraband. It would accept the condition.

It would carry anything to a neutral port?

Oh, yes. But those are questions which I think it is premature to discuss, and I hope that you won't discuss them as coming from the White House at all. I am perfectly willing to tell you men all that I know about it, but I think that all I ought to authorize you to discuss as a result of this interview is the purpose of the administration to push this bill.

Mr. President, we learned from the Treasury Department this morning that the situation is very rapidly being relieved as to the congestion of products in American ports.

I think it is, at any rate, in some parts of the country. Apparently it is hopeful on the North Atlantic seaboard. It is improving in New Orleans. It is not showing much improvement in Galveston, I know, where there is a very great railroad warehouse congestion.

Have you an appointment with the subcommittee of the Committee on Naval Affairs?

Yes, sir. At half-past eleven.

Can you tell us something about it?

It is about the Weeks bill.[4]

Will you take up at the same time, Mr. President, do you know the Talbott[5] suggestion of building additional naval auxiliaries for this trade? The Weeks plan, I think, is to use old-type vessels now in the navy. The Talbott scheme is to build additional auxiliaries to be used in time of peace.

I daresay he will bring that up, but I don't know just what it will be.

There is a most diligent effort inside and outside—presently outside—of Mexico, to make trouble between Carranza and Villa. That effort is in the interest of those persons who would profit by intervention. We are constantly receiving direct information from those associated with Villa and those associated with Carranza, and the reports which I see in the newspapers are false.[6]

Can you intimate what Villa's plans are?

I am not in his confidence as to his plans. I am not in his confidence in any respect, but it is perfectly evident to me that he does not intend to present unreasonable proposals of any kind. And I think that Carranza is already showing that he knows how to manage some people in Mexico City.[7]

Is it correct, Mr. President, that John Lind is going to Mexico?

No, sir.

Mr. President, do you want to be any more specific about these people who would profit by intervention?

I don't need to be. The world knows about it.

Mr. President, have you seen Mr. Fuller since his return?

He is coming back this week from New York. I hope to see him again.

Mr. President, has this government received any assurances as yet to the restriction of the war zone in the Far East?[8]

No. None, so far as I know.

So far as you know, then, we have no assurances that it will be limited to the attack on Kiaochow?

No. We have no assurances of any kind, so far as I know.

What about the registry of ships under the new law, Mr. President? Can you tell us anything about that?

It is passed—but what do you want to know?

I want to know whether there is any considerable movement on the part of the shipping to come in?

There is none at all that I have seen. This is from Mr. Sweet,[9] the Acting Secretary of Commerce. I have reason to believe that all the foreign ships now contemplating United States registry will come in immediately. I think the total number will be slightly over one million tons under the plan.

How much has any of the proposed changes in navigation laws entered into this question of the ships? Are they making it a condition—

I don't think I understand you.

Are the foreign shipowners making it conditional, this concession, that the navigation laws should be suspended so that they can operate ships immediately under the American flag?

Some could already operate them under the American flag.

No. It seems that the present regulations in the navigation laws might keep out some vessels.

I think I know what you are referring to. There is a very slow process of inspection that some of them wish to escape.[10] It is slower, merely—not because their ships could not come up to test, and they are asking, or desiring, at any rate, that those conditions should be waived; that is to say, they should be permitted to take the registry before the inspection is completed.

Mr. President, Mr. Drake[11] of the Panama Railway Company also suggested a provision of five years requiring watch officers to become American citizens. He thought within that time they could become naturalized.

I receive conflicting information about that. I am told in some quarters that there are officers, not enough, but almost enough, available who do speak English and are Americans. I want to be very careful to know what is true about that before I suspend that requirement, because I want all the American officers available employed first.

Mr. President, reverting again to the ship-purchase bill, this may be a hypothetical question, but if private capital were to embark in the enterprise of purchasing ships, would that forestall the necessity of passing the bill now pending?

Well, I don't know. It would depend altogether on the skill and character of their enterprise.

Isn't the bill practically a mere enabling act?

Yes. It is an enabling act.

You can act on your discretion as to whether or not you put it in operation?

The bill, as a matter of fact, hasn't been drafted. What I mean to say, it is not in the form of a law and just what the terms of it would be in that respect, I don't know. But of course the extent to which we enter into the thing would necessarily be dependent upon the discretion of the government.

Mr. President, do your reports on the investigation of food prices show any reason for some of these increases, such as sugar, for instance?

Well, I can't speak with any knowledge about that, I am sorry to say, because the results of the investigation haven't been laid before me, and therefore I can't say what they show. But there is information which shows some marked combinations for the purpose, and I am hopeful that we may be able to get at some of those combinations very promptly.

Partly so, but as far as it has gone, the retailers don't seem to be to blame for that.

I have to say I don't know whether they are parties to it or not.

Do you favor the silver-purchase bill, Mr. President, that passed the Senate Saturday?[12]

I am not ready to discuss that. Did it pass the Senate?

Yes, sir.

[1] Unnamed Congressmen had given this story to the press, probably to relieve the pressure that they were receiving from Wilson for passage of the bill. See the New York *World*, Aug. 23, 1914.

[2] Jesse Frederick Essary, Washington correspondent of the Baltimore *Sun*.

[3] See the *Washington Post*, Aug. 24, 1914. The ship-purchase bill provided for the purchase of vessels to be used in trade with Latin America "and elsewhere."

[4] Senator John Wingate Weeks, Republican of Massachusetts, had introduced a bill (S. 5259) to authorize the use of naval transports to establish mail lines to South America. See *Cong. Record*, 63d Cong., 2d sess., pp. 13134-41.

[5] Representative Joshua Frederick Cockey Talbott, Democrat of Maryland, a member of the House Committee on Naval Affairs.

[6] See, for example, the *Washington Post*, Aug. 22, 1914.

[7] Following the Constitutionalist victory, Carranza made a triumphal entry into Mexico City on August 20. Villa was absent, however, and was threatening to break with the First Chief. See Link, *The New Freedom*, p. 416.

[8] Following its declaration of war against Germany, Japan notified the United States Government that its war zone would be limited to the Far East. See the *Washington Post*, Aug. 24, 1914, and Ambassador Guthrie to the Secretary of State, Aug. 15, 1914, *FR, 1914-WWS*, pp. 170-71.

[9] Edwin Forrest Sweet, Assistant Secretary of Commerce.

[10] The Ship Registry Act authorized the President to suspend regulations governing the inspection of ships being brought into the foreign trade of the United States.

[11] Edward A. Drake, vice-president of the Panama Railway Company, testified on August 21 before the House Committee on Naval Affairs. See the *Washington Post*, Aug. 22, 1914.

[12] S. 6261, sponsored by Senator Reed Smoot, Republican of Utah, authorized a one-time purchase by the federal government of 15,000,000 ounces of silver. See the *Washington Post*, Aug. 23, 1914, and *Cong. Record*, 63d Cong., 2d sess., pp. 14124-27.

Aug. 27, 1914

Mr. President, can you say anything about the call of the French Ambassador?[1]

He was really calling just to pay his respects, as always happens after reaching his post again. We had a conversation about the war, but it was nothing of any political significance.

Anything with reference to the alleged [protests] on the part of these governments?[2]

No.

Will this government take any cognizance of them, any more than to receive them—those protests?

Where will the protests come from?

The Belgian Minister[3] lodged one in the State Department. I understand that the Belgian government [blank].

I hadn't heard of that. I would have to consult the international lawyers as to our rights about that. I don't know. Fortunately, the circumstances are novel.

Mr. President, will there be any curtailment of the antitrust program? Some Senators talk about putting the railroad securities bill in cold storage this session. They are saying so with some emphasis.[4]

They have consulted with me about it. Of course, our reason is to make new financial arrangements with regard to the railroads. While their finances, which are disturbed by the conditions throughout the country, will probably be improved, there is a great deal of weight in their argument.

That doesn't apply to the terms of the Clayton bill?

No, not at all.

Mr. President, we understood from Senator Newlands yesterday that you were going to have a conference with the conferees of the House and Senate on the trade commission bill. Has that been postponed?

You must have misunderstood him. I haven't expected to have any such conference. I have conferred with Mr. Covington, who is the chairman of the House conference, and with Senator Newlands, who is the chairman of the Senate conference, but that is as far as I expect to go, unless they desire a conference, and I haven't heard that.

Mr. President, has it been decided to postpone action on the railroad securities bill?

Nothing has been decided, so far as I know.

The conference on the trade commission bill will still await action on the Clayton bill, isn't that the situation?

No. Senator Newlands told me that they would go ahead today and tomorrow, and he expected to finish by the end of the week.

Mr. President, have you decided on the regulations regarding the registration of ships?

No, sir. There is some difference of judgment, and some are manifestly more qualified to judge just what ought to be done. I have several memoranda which I am going to take with me this afternoon and study carefully before I act.

Are they regulations similar to the canal regulations?

Well, of course, under the act, I am authorized to waive certain requirements of the existing law, and I will have to name the time and the conditions under which the waiver will be made.

That will have to be done by proclamation?

That will have to be done by Executive Order, I suppose.

Has there been any protest from any foreign government on the proposed purchase of ships by this government?

Not that I know of.

Can you tell us anything about Mr. Fuller's visit, Mr. President?[5]

It was a visit preliminary to going to Mexico City. And just a conference. There was nothing especially to discuss. No particular points, I mean.

Mr. President, could you tell us just what the situation is there between Villa and Carranza? Villa has just issued a statement and refers to the Torreón Agreement,[6] and we know nothing of Carranza's purposes.

I don't want to discuss that, although I can say this, that I have every confidence now that any disagreement there may be between Carranza and Villa will not result in anything serious which will upset the country again. I feel reasonably confident of that.

Can you say anything yet with regard to recognition, Mr. President?

Oh, no. That would be premature.

Mr. President, has Japan sufficiently outlined her purposes to this government so far, to the satisfaction of this government?

Mr. Tumulty refers you to a statement that got published in the papers this morning, which is very explicit.[7]

Has there been any complaint, Mr. President, of the activities of Brand Whitlock in Belgium?[8]

Oh, no. There have been some very fanciful inventions as to what he did.

It is difficult to tell if they are true.

I only know that what was published was not true.

He is still at Brussels?

Yes, he is still at Brussels.

Have we communication with Brussels?

Intermittently, yes.

Mr. President, may we take it from that that he is not protesting in this matter?

Is declining to interfere.

With Belgian negotiations?

He has no right to interfere with any negotiations. I am only quite sure that he is minding his own business, that is all I know.

Mr. President, can you tell us anything with regard to the situation in Turkey? Some questionable stories have been denied, and still—[9]

What situation do you refer to?

There is a general unrest throughout Europe. As a result of this, they are a little down on Turkey, and there has been some apprehension that, if Turkey became involved, the Christians there would suffer as a consequence at the hands of the Turks. Has there been any of that fear?[10]

No.

Can you say anything, Mr. President, about an emergency revenue measure?

Not until it is ready, I can't.

Mr. President, would it be possible to say now when it would be?

I understand that it will be possible to get it ready by the first of next week.

Mr. President, you spoke of Mr. Fuller returning to Mexico City. Can you tell us what his mission will be there?

No, sir, I couldn't.

Mr. President, do you think that the foreign situation will make it necessary for Congress to remain here after the trust program and emergency bills are out of the way?

No, sir.

Mr. President, will it be possible that the regular—have they told you when they might be expecting to complete this program?

I am told that the Clayton bill will probably be voted on before the end of this week, in which case the program, with the exception of that bill, would be already virtually completed. Then they would be only waiting for the conference report on the Clayton bill, and Senator Newlands hopes that the conference report on the commission bill would be ready by that time.

The rivers and harbors bill up there is partly finished. Will that be part of the program?

Is it part? Ask them about that. We have no trouble about that bill.

[1] French Ambassador Jean Jules Jusserand visited the White House on August 27.

[2] The French and Belgian governments had lodged protests against German activities in violation of the Hague conventions. See the *New York Times*, Aug. 26-27, 1914, and *PWW*, Vol. 30, pp. 457-58.

[3] Emmanuel Havenith.

[4] A reference to the Rayburn bill to grant the Interstate Commerce Commission authority over the issuance of new securities by the railroads. It had passed the House on June 5, 1914, but was dropped from consideration in the Senate. See the *New York Times*, Aug. 28, 1914, and Link, *The New Freedom*, p. 426.

[5] Fuller, Wilson's special agent to Mexico City, visited the White House on August 26 to report on his recent trip to Mexico. See the *New York Times*, Aug. 27, 1914, and Link, *Struggle for Neutrality*, pp. 242-45.

[6] This was the truce signed by Villa and Carranza on July 8, which provided for a conference

of revolutionary generals to establish a new constitutional government. See Link, *Struggle for Neutrality*, p. 236.

[7] This was a paraphrase of Wilson's note to Japan of August 19. See above, Aug. 20, 1914.

[8] The *New York Times*, August 26, 1914, reported that Whitlock, the American Minister in Belgium, had played a part in persuading the Belgian authorities not to defend Brussels against the Germans. See also Brand Whitlock, *Belgium: A Personal Narrative*, 2 vols. (New York, 1920), I, 268.

[9] It was speculated that Turkey was about to enter the war against the Allies. See the *New York Times*, Aug. 26-27, 1914.

[10] *Ibid.*, August 27, 1914, reported that Henry Morgenthau, American Ambassador to the Sublime Porte, had expressed this fear.

Sept. 3, 1914

Can you tell us, Mr. President, about the conference with the German Ambassador?[1]

He just came to pay his respects on returning. We didn't discuss anything that the public is interested in.

Do you know whether or not, Mr. President, he has lodged any protest with reference to certain firms in this country shipping arms to England?[2]

No, he has not.

Has there been any protest or any charges in which the question of neutrality is involved in the *Adriatic* [case]?[3]

I haven't heard anything. The only people who are astir there are our own officials, to find out what our duties are.

Mr. President, there have been conflicting reports with regard to the attitude of Great Britain and France toward the proposed purchase of German ships by the United States. Has there been any complaint on the subject from them?

No, there has not. I understand that that whole question is merely a question of bona fides on the purchase of a vessel in the existing circumstances, but a prize tribunal would make inquiry merely until the bona fides is established. Of course, that would be easy to establish in case we should purchase, but of course you also understand that the pending bill in Congress is not for the purchase of German ships. It is for the purchase of ships. We don't have to purchase anywhere.[4]

You expect that bill to pass this session?

Yes, certainly.

Mr. President, can you say when you will issue your proclamation on the Ship Registry Act?

I am hoping to issue it tomorrow. I have got it practically ready.

Mr. President, is it a fair question, are other ships in contemplation—the German, French, and English?

I don't know the listing. I could say that they are French and English, but there are other ships in our choice.

It has been intimated, on what seems to be very good authority, that we should split up our purchases, and there would be no complaint from anybody.

Yes.

Mr. President, can you say just to what extent these inquiries have been—

Those—it has merely been a perfectly informal discussion between the Ambassadors and the Secretary of State.

Have they laid out in any way the attitude of their governments?

No. They expressed, I believe that they have expressed, their own opinions as to what that attitude would be, but in the most informal way, or personally so.

The view from London, Mr. President, is that Great Britain would not feel that she should be exempt from capturing ships which carried the things which the British Admiralty had announced, not necessarily as contraband, but as prohibited to German commerce—and there are very few articles that can be carried by German ships.[5]

That is mere talk.

Mr. President, the purpose of these ships is to carry at this particular time commerce to Europe, South America, or Asia?

To carry commerce wherever it needs to be carried.

Generally?

Yes. Also to get our own products to market. Probably I should say just a personal opinion. The shipments to Europe will take care of themselves. That is my guess about it, because things are becoming much more normal in that field.

You mean those countries themselves are carrying it in their own ships?

Those that have ships, yes.

Mr. President, have you had any suggestion with regard to this government and the violation of Chinese neutrality?[6]

No, sir, not so far as I know.

Mr. President, has any arrangement been made for a conference with the Belgian commissioners who are on their way to this country?[7]

No. I haven't officially learned they were on their way. I have seen that in the newspapers. So far as any announcement may have reached the State Department, I haven't heard of it.

Has there been anything that can be construed as a protest on the part of Ambassador Herrick in the matter of the—[8]

No, sir. Those first reports seem to be corrected by the dispatches that I have seen.

Mr. President, can you say at this time whether your attitude toward receiving these Belgian commissioners—

No, sir. I can't say what my attitude will be five minutes from now about that. Everything depends upon the whole case at the time. Of course, one would naturally expect to receive them with cordiality.

Can you say anything, Mr. President, as to your attitude relative toward the rivers and harbors bill?

No, sir. I have had so many things to have an attitude about, that I haven't had time to study that bill, to tell the truth.

Mr. President, could you say something about the results of the food investigation by the Department of Justice?

No. That is going forward. I think there are some leads in it, but I can't speak of any definite results yet.

No suggestion has come to you yet for additional legislation to react to the question legally.

No, not yet. Of course, that is a little difficult. The field of legislation in that matter really lies with the Congress, except so far as it concerns interested groups. It is pretty hard to get at, but we are studying it out.

Mr. President, has the wireless question been settled?

Yes. I agreed with the Secretary of State on a memorandum this morning. I can't repeat the exact terms of it, but he will be giving it out today.[9]

Mr. President, has Congress laid before you the war-tax program?

Only in a very general form. Not in any particularity.

Has there been any final decision reached as to the amount to be raised?

Approximately one hundred million. If we had not lowered the tariff, it would have been much greater. I mean to say that the deficit would have been much greater due to the falling off of the imports and the customs duties. Fortunately, the tariff is a smaller part in all the general revenues and therefore there is a smaller deficit due to the falling off of the imports.

Mr. President, right along that line, without saying anything specifically about the rivers and harbors bill, I presume it could be said that the administration intends to economize wherever it is possible?

That goes without saying, yes.

Is there any specific item, Mr. President, in which the administration may insist in this war revenue measure?

Any direct suggestion? No. I think that it is peculiarly the province of the House of Representatives to choose the objects of taxation.

You expect to make no direct recommendations?

No. I am going to deliver a message tomorrow, but make no specific recommendations.[10]

Will the law become operative shortly after its enactment?

I assume it will be operative immediately, yes.

Mr. President, there has been some suggestion, because of the lasting effects of this war, that the tax may have to apply for a number of years. Do you understand it that way?

Nobody knows or has the least idea about anything in the future, whether it will last or not. It certainly will not last a great length of time—I mean, the tax.

Did you read the remarks in Congress today with reference—

I read everything that is intended for the salvation of my soul.

Mr. President, is it in order to ask about Ambassador von Bernstorff's statement the other day, that Germany was ready for peace at any time? Did it please you to read that?

I didn't see that, as a matter of fact. Was that authoritative?

It was in direct quotes. As I understand it, he denied it the next day.
Mr. President, has there been any suggestion from President Carranza that the time was right for withdrawal of American troops?[11]

No, sir. By the way, there isn't any such person as President Carranza. He is First Chief of the Constitutionalist Army. He is not talking English—

General Funston feels that they [the new government] are making a big difference in food supplies [for Mexico City]. Has there been anything further on that?[12]

No. There is nothing further at all.

Have you had any new ships, Mr. President, that are going to take out American registry?

I simply know—I am told—that there are a considerable number awaiting the Executive Order I am going to sign.

Mr. President, what is your opinion about the adjournment of Congress?

I haven't any.

[1] Wilson met with the German Ambassador, Count Johann Heinrich von Bernstorff, at the White House on September 3, 1914.
[2] Bernstorff made this charge publicly. See the *New York Times*, Sept. 4, 1914.
[3] The *Adriatic*, a White Star Liner, arrived in New York on August 29, carrying American

refugees. A controversy arose as to whether or not she was a warship because she was armed with four six-inch guns. The ship was allowed to sail for Liverpool on September 3. See *ibid.*, Sept. 1, 3-4, 1914, and the documents in *FR, 1914-WWS*, pp. 605-607.

[4] The British were opposed to any American purchase of German ships that might be temporary and not completely bona fide. They argued that, in such circumstances, the ships might be treated as German by their prize court. See the *New York Times*, Sept. 1, 1914, and Ambassador Page to the Secretary of State, Aug. 21, 1914, *FR, 1914-WWS*, pp. 489-90.

[5] For a list of the items that the British, on August 5, 1914, declared to be absolute and conditional contraband, see *FR, 1914-WWS*, pp. 215-16.

[6] The Japanese landed troops on the Shantung peninsula on September 3, 1914.

[7] King Albert sent four commissioners to lay before President Wilson protests against German activities in Belgium. The head of the commission was Henri Carton de Wiart, Envoy Extraordinary and Minister Plenipotentiary; he was accompanied by Louis de Sadeleer, Paul Hymans, and Emil van de Velde. See the *New York Times*, Sept. 1-3, 1914.

[8] *Ibid.*, Sept. 3, 1914, reported that Ambassador Myron Timothy Herrick in France had passed on to the State Department a protest by Americans in Paris against the dropping of bombs from German airships.

[9] Secretary Bryan issued a statement on September 3 saying that the wireless stations would be allowed to operate in code. American censors were to be supplied codebooks to insure that neutrality was not violated. See *ibid.*, Sept. 4, 1914.

[10] Wilson addressed Congress on September 4 and requested passage of a war tax to provide approximately $100,000,000. See the *New York Times*, Sept. 5, 1914; the address is printed in *PWW*, Vol. 30, pp. 473-75.

[11] That is, from Veracruz.

[12] General Funston, the American commander at Veracruz, was concerned about reports that Carranza had ordered the port closed. The First Chief also demanded the withdrawal of American forces. See the *New York Times*, Sept. 1, 1914, and Hill, *Emissaries to a Revolution*, pp. 240-43.

Sept. 10, 1914

Mr. President, have you got any response from your letter to the Colorado people yet?[1]

No, not at all. There has hardly been time.

They might telegraph.

They haven't telegraphed. I hardly think there has been time for a letter. They probably have received mine. They couldn't have considered it before Tuesday.

Mr. President, has Ambassador Page advised you of England's position towards peace?[2]

If so, I haven't received the telegram.

Have you had any intimation from Germany or Austria or the other belligerent countries with reference to their attitude towards mediation?

No, sir, none at all. I have heard the expression of opinion of Germans in this country—one or two—but nothing official.

Mr. President, unfortunately, I came in late. I don't know whether anybody asked about the alleged telegram from the Kaiser?[3]

There has been such a telegram received. When I was asked about it, when it had not been placed in my hands, I knew nothing about it.

Can you say anything about it?

I don't think that I ought to.

The text has been published today.

Not my reply.

Have you replied at all?

No, sir, I have not, yet.[4]

Do you intend to?

Oh, yes. I am obliged, in courtesy, to reply to it.

Mr. President, you said that you had discussed this with a few German citizens in this country.

I said that one or two of them had written suggestions to me.

Could you say whether you have received any suggestions from Mr. Oscar Straus?[5]

No, sir, I have not.

Has Mr. Schiff taken the matter up at all?

He has not.

Is there anything in the Kaiser's letter, Mr. President, that would persuade you to renew your activities looking toward mediation at this time?

The Kaiser's letter was not about mediation. It was a protest about certain alleged facts.

So I understand, but I thought perhaps from those known—

I didn't see in it any opinion of any kind, but I wouldn't like to be quoted even to that extent, because I don't think it would be proper for me to make any comment except my answer.

Mr. President, is there anything you can say about the visit of the railroad presidents yesterday? Did they make any impression on you with their statement?[6]

Yes, sir, naturally. I think their letter was a very striking document, and I have written an answer to it, copies of which are going to be supplied to all of you at once.[7]

Mr. President, do you feel that there is anything in that situation as bearing on this idea of the suggestion of the Ways and Means Committee today—to put a tax on railroad freight?

No. One thing wouldn't affect the other. Of course, that would be merely a tax added. That wouldn't affect the railroad situation at all.

This tax is a tax on the shipper, isn't it?

It is a tax on the shipper altogether. At least, the proposal is to put it on the shipper.

Mr. President, there have been some stories this morning that there is something in the air on peace. Is there anything official?

No, sir. I am afraid it's all in the air.

Do you think, Mr. President, it will be necessary to put an embargo on the export of sugar or any other product?

Not so far as I can see. How do you mean, necessary?

I understand that large quantities of sugar, for instance, are being shipped to New York for England, or have been. That means a lessening of the supply.

I don't know whether it necessarily means that, because we are not shipping from any place from which we ever get sugar. The sources of sugar are just as open as before.

Could you place an embargo on anything, Mr. President?

Why, no. Congress would have to do that.

Could that be done except as a tax?

Congress could enact an embargo of any kind it chooses. It has done so in the not very distant past.

It was done in time of war.

Yes. It was done in connection with war, at any rate.

Mr. President, do you care to comment upon the nomination of Mr. Sullivan?[8]

No. I don't comment on nominations.

Mr. President, the federal trade commission bill is about to be passed by the House.[9]

The conference report.

The conference report. Does it meet with your approval?

I haven't actually read the conference report, but I think I know what is in it, and if I do, I approve it.

Have you given out anything concerning the makeup of this commission?

No. I am not going to name the members of that commission until the December session. It is a matter of such consequence to the country that I want to have time to look around. You see, I haven't known at these final stages whether there would be three or five commissioners, for one thing, and the bill, fortunately, provides, if the phraseology hasn't been changed—and I don't think it has—that the present Bureau of Corporations shall merge into the commission, when the commission is constituted and organized. Therefore, there is no interruption, no lapse in the operation of the Bureau of Corporations, and they can continue until December, if I take that interval to make a choice.

Mr. President, in your reply to the railroad men this afternoon, you took the position that their request for support and cooperation is a—that it is proper for governmental agencies, wherever possible, to cooperate and render it when it can be rendered. Will you take any further steps, then, than simply this letter—I mean, in the way of an address to these various governmental agencies and the public generally?

I think that that is a sufficient statement of my position about it. It would hardly be proper, in one sense, for me to advise other governmental agencies what their duty was.

You will confer, will you not, with the members of Congress on the meeting on—with the commission?

I will be glad to confer with anybody who seeks a conference.

Was there any suggestion made about a precedent, Mr. President—whether the conference with railroad [presidents will set a] precedent?

You mean with me?

Yes, sir.

No, sir. I want to say with regard to the conference that I was very much impressed with the entirely reasonable attitude of the men who were present, not only reasonable but a very big sort of attitude. They had no word of criticism for the Interstate Commerce Commission, or for anybody. They said that they wanted it understood that criticism was left out, that they were simply trying to state the facts without color; and nothing that was said contained, so far as I could see, any prejudice or feeling of a questionable kind.

Mr. President, did you discuss the rivers and harbors bill with Senator Simmons?

Yes, sir.

Do you know whether there is a plan to cut down the amount of that bill at this time?

I believe there is. We discussed only the possibilities of cutting down. Of course, Senator Simmons was not in a position to state any conclusion about it.

Mr. President, you conferred this morning with Congressman Henry? Was there anything to take up in the way of special rules for this legislation they have for the war tax?

No. He came to see me about certain other legislation which I am bound to admit I had lost sight of, to ask just how necessary it was to get that in at this session.

Mr. President, is this government disposed to complain to the Turkish Ambassador about this interview, as published in the American press?[10]

I would rather not comment on that now.

Mr. President, the cutting down of the rivers and harbors bill materially would cut down the necessity for the tax[11] to that extent, would it not?

Yes. I assume that it would. Of course, it is very difficult to cut down the rivers and harbors bill without stopping good improvements undertaken somewhere.

The chief opposition at the present time is against the new projects, is it not?

Yes, I know it is.

[1] On September 7, Wilson sent a letter embodying a plan to end the Colorado coal strike to the operators and labor leaders. The plan, drafted by Hywel Davies and William R. Fairley, Commissioners of Conciliation, called for a three-year truce, during which striking miners would be rehired, intimidation of union or nonunion men prohibited, troops withdrawn, and picketing disallowed. See the *New York Times*, Sept. 8, 1914; the letter is printed in *PWW*, Vol. 30, pp. 485-88.

[2] The *New York Times*, September 10, 1914, reported that Sir Edward Grey had informed Page that England would enter into negotiations only if the Germans agreed to pay reparations for invading Belgium. See Ambassador Page to the Secretary of State, Sept. 10, 1914, *FR*, *1914-WWS*, pp. 100-101.

[3] The Kaiser's telegram of September 8 complained of the use of dum-dum bullets and guerrilla warfare by Belgians. See the *New York Times*, Sept. 10, 1914, and Ambassador Gerard to the Secretary of State, Sept. 8, 1914, *FR*, *1914-WWS*, p. 794.

[4] Wilson acknowledged receipt of the Emperor's telegram on September 16 and expressed his hope that the war would reach a speedy conclusion. See the Secretary of State to Ambassador Gerard, Sept. 16, 1914, *FR*, *1914-WWS*, p. 797.

[5] Oscar Solomon Straus, former Ambassador to Turkey and American member of the International Tribunal at The Hague, had dined with the German Ambassador on September 5 at the New York home of Jacob Henry Schiff. When the subject of their conversation turned to peace in Europe, Straus asked if the Ambassador thought that the Emperor would accept a mediation offer extended by Wilson. Bernstorff replied unofficially that he thought that he would, if the other belligerents were also willing. Straus informed Bryan on September 6, and the Secretary of State began the United States Government's first serious attempt to mediate the European war. On September 7, Bryan instructed Gerard in Berlin to offer mediation to the Emperor, while he discussed the proposition in Washington with the British and French Ambassadors. See the *New York Times*, Sept. 13, 1914; the Secretary of State to Ambassador Gerard, Sept. 7, 1914, *FR*, *1914-WWS*, p. 98; Oscar S. Straus, *Under Four Administrations: From Cleveland to Taft* (Boston, Mass., 1922), pp. 378-80; and Link, *Struggle for Neutrality*, pp. 196-200.

[6] Six railway executives, led by Frank Trumbull, chairman of the Chesapeake and Ohio Railway Company, visited Wilson at the White House on September 9. Their statement said that the railroads were in an "emergency of a magnitude without parallel in our history" and called for the government to support the railroads with credits. See the *New York Times*, Sept. 10, 1914.

[7] Wilson's letter of September 10 called for public cooperation in the emergency. It is printed in *PWW*, Vol. 31, pp. 20-21.

[8] Sullivan, head of the Illinois Democratic machine, had won the party's senatorial nomination in a primary election. For a discussion of Wilson's reaction, see *PWW*, Vol. 31, p. 232, n. 2.

[9] The House approved the conference report of the federal trade commission bill on September 10. See the *New York Times*, Sept. 11, 1914; Link, *The New Freedom*, p. 442; and *Cong. Record*, 63d Cong., 2d sess., pp. 14919-43.

¹⁰ The Turkish Ambassador, A. Rustem Bey, issued a statement on September 7 complaining about what he regarded as attempts by the British to draw the United States into the war. He argued that the United States had no right to complain about the possible massacre of Christians in Turkey because of American treatment of blacks in the South and alleged American atrocities during the Philippine Insurrection. See the *New York Times*, Sept. 8, 1914. Wilson rebuked the Ambassador publicly on September 11. See *ibid.*, Sept. 12, 1914.
¹¹ That is, the special war tax then being proposed.

Sept. 17, 1914

Mr. President, have you received any reply from the Kaiser yet?[1]

No, sir.

There has been a persistent rumor that the Kaiser had replied in some form indicating that it might be a basis for mediation?

We had an acknowledgment from the Imperial Chancellor,[2] but nothing from the Kaiser yet at all.

Is that an acknowledgment of the original offer of mediation?[3]

No, sir; of the formal inquiry.

Did it say that they had merely received it—no comment at all?

It simply made a perfectly noncommittal comment. I don't remember what the terms of it were.

Has there been any report, Mr. President, from our Ambassador at Berlin with regard to the timeliness of the suggestion?

No, there has not. He has made no comment at all, so far as I know.

Mr. President, was he asked to give his views—the Ambassador at Berlin?

No; he was only asked to ascertain the views of the government.

Is there any report, Mr. President, with regard to the alleged protest of Great Britain and the refusal of Brazil to grant clearance papers to the *Robert Dollar*?[4]

I must say I had not heard of that at all. I don't know anything about it.

Mr. President, will you receive this German-American delegation that Senator Lewis wishes to bring before you? They have some reply to make to the Belgian Commission.[5]

I am getting a lot of information. I hadn't heard of that at all.

Are reports from Turkey of such a character as to occasion anxiety here or to require steps on our part?

No, sir. The statement that appeared in a paper yesterday morning to the effect that Doctor Mott had come to tell me of the dangers in Turkey was an absolute invention. Doctor Mott did not even so much as mention Turkey in the conversation. I would like to say what I think of such things, but I won't. Any man that would write anything calculated to get this country into international trouble just now can never lay claim either to honor or patriotism. I mean any false statement, any unverified statement.[6]

Mr. President, can you take us into the inside of Mexican affairs at this time?

As far as I can go myself.

It would be interesting.

I don't know of any inside thing that is disturbing in the least. On the contrary, just today I got what I consider to be official corrections of statements that had been made to make it look as if trouble were afoot there. These are perfectly explicit statements to the effect that the other allegations were unfounded, so that I don't see any difficulty that wasn't to have been expected in the final settlement. I think things have gone off with remarkable peacefulness.

Have our representatives in Mexico been able to approach the authorities at this time with a view to ascertaining their ideas of the future?

No. You see, our only representatives there now are consular representatives and, of course, all that they could learn would be that what is to be done remains to be determined by the conferences and results of the election. Nobody can speak for the future in anything but the most general terms.

Mr. President, what were the actual reasons for the abandoning of the proposed tax on railroad freight?[7]

I don't know, because I didn't abandon it.

You had never been committed to it, had you?

Mr. Underwood, I am told—I know this only secondhand—made

a statement in the caucus which was as frank as it was creditable to his character. I would prefer, gentlemen, not to be quoted on this, because I don't want it to seem that I am even making a comment on it, but you are perfectly welcome to the facts for your own thoughts. Mr. Underwood told, of course, the exact truth— that he had brought the matter to me and I said very frankly that I did not like that tax but, I said, I do not desire to dictate to the Ways and Means Committee, and if that is the tax preferred by the committee and the caucus, I won't stand in the way. And he has, I know, frankly stated that exactly to the committee and stated it the other night to the caucus, that that was exactly what I had said and he had done, so that everything is perfectly understood, I think, at the Capitol.

What was in my mind was whether you regarded the tax merely as unpopular or unsound?

I don't think I ought to argue it now, because it is in the past tense.

Mr. President, does this bill[8] as now suggested meet with your approval?

I cannot say that I know the details of it, but what I have heard of it, it does.

Mr. President, can you tell us about the visit of Mr. Knox today?[9]

Anything that there is to tell. He was a gentleman from New York who called on some private business.

Mr. President, within a short time now the departments will be making their estimates for next year.

They are making them now.

Is there any understanding—has any word been sent out by the administration to hold the estimates down in view of the—

No such word was necessary. It has been mentioned once or twice incidentally in cabinet, and the general understanding is that the estimates are to be held down to the lowest figure compatible with the efficiency of the departments. You see, we are undertaking by current legislation new tasks all the time, and certain measures that require additional expenditures are unavoidable.

Mr. President, have you any expectation of being able to recognize the Mexican government soon?

I can't say that I have any expectation one way or the other. I see no reason to doubt that they will form a government successfully.

You don't regard the present government as a regularly established government? Perhaps they do not themselves.

They do not. They frankly describe it as revolutionary, temporarily so.

Mr. President, could you give us any idea of whether Carranza is going to retire very soon in order that he may be a candidate for the presidency?

I know absolutely nothing about that. I simply understood that he has called a conference of the military leaders and, I believe, the Governors of the states for the first of October, and I suppose that they will lay plans immediately to be carried out for an election.

The withdrawal of the troops would not be followed, then, by recognition. We would have to wait until some sort of a more formal government was set up?

I really haven't formed any plans about it. I simply wanted to show my recognition of the fact that they were in charge of their own affairs and that it was no longer any of our business.

Mr. President, could you say whether an Ambassador is likely to be appointed within a very short time?

All that would depend upon the intervening events.

Mr. President, can you give us any idea as to what is going to be done with regard to the troops on our side of the border?

No, that is a question we haven't taken up either. Of course, there is normally a considerable body of troops in Texas anyway.

Has the time been fixed for the withdrawal of the troops at Veracruz?[10]

No date, except that the order was to take effect as soon as possible.

I notice that General Funston in the dispatches today recommended October 10.

That must be for some practical reason; but it is to take place immediately, as soon as it is practicably possible. You see, we have to await such arrangements as the Mexican authorities will make to take over the port. We have to make an accounting for the revenues we have received in their name and which belong to them, and we have to wait for the processes of their law by which a new municipal government will be set up, at least so far as it was set aside. All that will take time.

Mr. President, have you made any response yet to the message from the President of France?[11]

No, sir.

Mr. President, how much longer will the refugee camps be maintained on the border?[12]

To tell the truth, I had forgotten about the refugee camps. My impression is that the men in those camps have been in process of being distributed already. I vaguely remember some conversation I had with the Secretary of War about that. I have forgotten just exactly what was done.

Mr. President, have you had anything indicating an alarming disorder in Mexico City itself?

Not a thing.

Mr. President, you spoke of receiving some assurances that there was no danger; could you tell us from where you received them?

I meant assurances from the circumstances. I didn't mean that anybody in particular had assured me.

---

[1] That is, regarding Wilson's offer of mediation of September 7.

[2] Theobald von Bethmann Hollweg replied on September 12, rejecting mediation because "it would be interpreted by our enemies as a sign of weakness and not understood by our people at all." See Link, *Struggle for Neutrality*, pp. 199-200, and Ambassador Gerard to the Secretary of State, Sept. 14, 1914, *FR, 1914-WWS*, p. 104.

[3] That is, Wilson's general offer of good offices of August 4.

[4] The *Robert Dollar*, formerly a British steamer recently transferred to American registry, had been denied clearance at Rio de Janeiro because the British Consul objected to its release. See the *New York Times*, Sept. 17, 1914, and the documents printed in *FR, 1914-WWS*, pp. 492-99, 501.

[5] Senator Lewis' group wished to respond to charges of German atrocities in Belgium. See the *New York Times*, Sept. 17, 1914.

[6] Mott visited Wilson on September 16, and the afternoon newspapers reported that he had called on Wilson to take measures to protect missionaries in Turkey. Wilson denied this strenuously. See *ibid*.

[7] The proposed tax on railroad freight in the war revenue bill was dropped after a White House conference with Democratic leaders on September 15. See *ibid.*, Sept. 16, 1914, and Link, *Struggle for Neutrality*, pp. 103-104.

[8] That is, a war revenue bill to provide for a stamp tax and excise taxes to raise revenues lost due to the war. See the *New York Times*, Sept. 16, 1914.

[9] George William Knox of New York, a clergyman with experience in Japan.

[10] Wilson, on September 15, ordered that preparations be made for the withdrawal of American forces from Veracruz. See the *New York Times*, Sept. 16, 1914; WW to Garrison, Sept. 15, 1914, printed in *PWW*, Vol. 31, p. 33; and Link, *Struggle for Neutrality*, p. 248.

[11] Raymond Poincaré sent a telegram to Wilson on September 10 protesting against German atrocities in Belgium. This followed the protest by William II that the Allies had been using dum-dum bullets in violation of the Hague conventions. See the *New York Times*, Sept. 17, 1914, and the President of France to the President of the United States, Sept. 10, 1914, *FR, 1914-WWS*, p. 794.

[12] That is, with Mexico.

Sept. 21, 1914

I have read only one paper this morning, gentlemen, but that says that it is understood that the President intends to call a world congress and do a lot of very foolish things.[1] I want to know, who understood that, and from whom? I am not as big a fool as I look, and if you will just go on the assumption that I am not a fool, it would correct a good many news items.

I think, Mr. President, you can act on the assumption that we are wholly acting on that assumption.

But regarding items like that, elaborately set forth, a column long of it—"it is understood to be the purposes of the administration"— coming from Washington makes an impression and will probably be transmitted to the other side, and other things that I am earnestly, let me say, prayerfully, trying to do for the peace of the world may be blocked by all this talk of things that are impossible and unwise, and in themselves unworkable. That is what disturbs, gentlemen, but here we are, in the presence of a world crisis. This is no child's play. We may make it impossible for the United States to do the right thing by constantly saying that she thinks of silly things to do. Let us at least propose things that grown-up people would think of. I think that is very important, that we should be of age in our plans. Please, do your best not to let that happen again. I am not accusing or even suspecting anybody, but I know that by cooperation you can prevent that kind of thing from happening. I saw it in a form that didn't look like special correspondence, and therefore I am afraid it has appeared in a number of papers.

Mr. President, the attitude of the press generally has been satisfactory, hasn't it?

Admirable. I haven't anything to complain of. And the attitude of the article is all right. I don't think the person who wrote it intended to do any mischief. But I just wanted, if I might, to point out to you how mischief may be done without intending it.

What paper was it in, Mr. President, do you recall?

Well, it may not have appeared only in that paper. I don't want to pick out a particular paper.

How about the rivers and harbors bill, Mr. President?[2]

I don't know anything about it, except what I see in the papers.

Do you expect to discuss it with Senator Simmons this morning, Mr. President?

No. He is coming on other matters.

How about Senator Shields?[3]

I notice on my calendar that he just wants a couple of minutes. It's no errand of great importance.

Mr. President, Mr. Fuller is back in this country.[4] Do you expect to see him?

I expect to see him on Wednesday.

Mr. President, have you any new information you can give us about conditions in Mexico?

No. There's a great deal of new information from El Paso, but none of any importance.

Is there any date set for removal of the troops, Mr. President?

I am going to see the Secretary of War today. My instructions were simply to effect it as soon as it could be effected, taking care of everything that has to be taken care of in the process.

That situation in Veracruz, Mr. President—will you send a delegation there? The representations that have been made by the Mexican priests[5] and the recommendations of General Funston—

I wouldn't know. I mean that—

He merely recommended that the number be reduced somewhat until these refugees could be taken care of.

Tumulty says the State Department is handling that. I hadn't been brought directly into contact with it.

Mr. President, is it necessary or at least desirable that the immigration bill should be passed at this session?[6]

Well, there are a great many features. Most of the features in that bill are specific administrative features which, to tell the truth, I have entirely lost sight of.

Mr. President, are you considering as to whether or not the situation in Europe makes it more or less desirable to act on this measure at this time?

No. I don't know that it would be very much affected by that. I can only conjecture what the result would be with regard to immigration.

Is there anything new about the ship-purchase bill, Mr. President?

No, sir, not that I know of.

Has the case of the *Robert Dollar* that was held up in some South American port come to your attention?

It was spoken of at our last conference on Thursday, but that is all I know about it. It hasn't come to my attention at all.

---

[1] The Editor could not find this news report, but the idea of calling a world congress of neutrals was discussed frequently at the time. See, e.g., the *New York Times*, Sept. 22, 1914.

[2] A filibuster in the Senate against the rivers and harbors bill ended September 21 when the bill was returned to committee. The bill passed the Senate with its appropriations greatly decreased on September 22. See *ibid.*, Sept. 20, 22-23, 1914, and *Cong. Record*, 63d Cong., 2d sess., pp. 15475, 15528.

[3] Senator John Knight Shields, Democrat of Tennessee.

[4] Fuller returned from Mexico on September 19. See the *New York Times*, Sept. 20, 1914, and Hill, *Emissaries to a Revolution*, pp. 243-44.

[5] Approximately 300 priests and nuns had fled to Veracruz and asked the protection of the United States. Provisions were being made to remove them from the country by the time of the American withdrawal. See the *New York Times*, Sept. 22, 1914.

[6] That is, the Burnett bill to restrict immigration by use of the literacy test. See Link, *The New Freedom*, pp. 274-75.

Sept. 24, 1914

Is there any suggestion as to the negotiation of the new treaty with Russia?[1]

We have all along been asking Russia to conclude a treaty similar to those we have been concluding, and, while I do not know anything officially about the matter, I saw in this morning's paper that she had indicated her willingness, which is pleasing. I hope it is so.

The new treaty will take the place of the old one?

I was thinking of the peace treaty. We haven't any information as to that treaty.

I understand that the Russian Ambassador[2] will take that up with Mr. Bryan as soon as he gets back.

I am very pleased to hear that. I had not been informed.

Does the ship-purchase bill remain a part of the legislative program or has there been an agreement to defer action on it?

It remains a part of the program. I think it is very necessary in order to handle things that private enterprise cannot be expected or asked to handle.

Do the number of applications for registry under the ship-registry law come up to the expectations of the administration?

I have not even inquired about that.

Have you been informed of any disinclination on the part of the House—

I have heard of the opposition of individual members.

Have you any information as to the *Robert Dollar* incident?

The same question was asked about it several days ago.
I do not know anything more about it now than I did then.

It was reported that she sailed several days ago.[3]

I do not know anything about that.

Is there anything new with reference to the Colorado situation?

No, the conference yesterday[4] did not come within length of a conclusion of any kind. Mr. Welborn wanted to lay before me, and I was glad to have him do so, all the conditions as he saw them as affecting his company, but he did not state any conclusions.

Have the other operators of the group sent you a reply?

They sent me a telegram expressing regret that the meeting was held too late to meet with Mr. Welborn and that they were mailing a letter. The letter has not yet reached me.[5]

Have you taken any action with regard to Villa's refusal to recognize Carranza, that is, in the way of sending representations to Villa?[6]

I haven't taken any action at all. I am not sure that I understood your inquiry, Mr. Oulahan?

Have you sent anybody down to see Villa on account of his refusal to recognize Carranza?

No, sir.

Has there been any change in the matter of the shipment of arms?

No.

Do you expect to send Mr. Fuller back?

That is not my present intention.[7]

Does the conference report remove your objections as to some of the definitions of the Clayton bill?[8]

You will notice that in Sections Two and Three of the conference report the definitions are relieved of rigidity by saying that whenever those practices substantially lessen competition or tend to create a monopoly, those conditions are left to the judgment, by a subsequent section, of the trade commission. That gives the elasticity that is desirable.

Do you still expect to sign the bills together?

I do not know. My time on the trade commission bill is Saturday and I do not want to miss the pleasure of signing it, but I do not know whether I shall have the Clayton bill so soon as that or not.

It has been stated that if you sign the trade commission bill before the other, all the definitions in the Clayton bill might be regarded by the courts as amending the previous legislation.

That must have been some person whose study was unprofitable; it is too ingenious.

At any rate, you are not going to let the bill go without your signature?

No, I do not want it to become a law without my signature.

Have you had any conference with the Secretary of the Treasury regarding the hoarding of money by the banks?[9]

No, sir. He read me his statement before he issued it, and he knows what he is talking about, as usual.

Do you still expect the adjournment of Congress?

I am very hopeful of it. Of course, I hope that it will be able to adjourn very soon.

How soon do you expect to send in the nominations for Argentina and Chile?[10]

Those have already been signed. They are going in today.

Is someone going to take Mr. Garrett's place?[11]

Mr. Garrett has no place at present.

I understood you were going to nominate Ambassadors.

Yes.

Who is going to take Mr. Garrett's place?

Frederic J. Stimson of Boston. He is rather a very eminent lawyer, who has written some volumes that I have often consulted on comparative legislation, particularly of this country.[12]

He is not "J. S. of Dale"?[13]

I have often asked and got an answer to that question and have habitually forgotten it. My impression is that he is the same, but I would have to verify that.

Is it too early to say what place Mr. Garrett will take?

It is too early to say that.

[1] The Russians had recently accepted Secretary of State Bryan's request for the negotiation of a conciliation treaty. This gave rise to hopes that a new Treaty of Amity and Commerce might also be possible. See the *New York Times*, Sept. 24, 1914, and the Russian Ambassador to the Secretary of State, Sept. 24, 1914, in *FR, 1914-WWS*, p. 8.

[2] George Bakhméteff.

[3] The *New York Times*, September 24, 1914, reported that the *Robert Dollar* cleared on September 23, flying British colors.

[4] Jesse Floyd Welborn, president of the Colorado Fuel and Iron Company, visited Wilson on September 23 and informed him that his company could not accept some of the terms of the proposed compromise agreement. See the *New York Times*, Sept. 23-24, 1914, and Welborn to WW, Sept. 18, 1914, printed in *PWW*, Vol. 31, pp. 48-54.

[5] Forty-seven other companies also protested and stated their unwillingness to comply in a letter to the President dated September 23 that accused the Secretary of Labor of partisanship toward the strikers. They argued that the goal of any agreement should be to protect the miners now peaceably at work, and that the President's plan amounted to making a bargain with lawbreakers. See the *New York Times*, Sept. 28, 1914, and John Cleveland Osgood *et al.* to WW, Sept. 23, 1914, WP, DLC.

[6] Villa declared his independence of Carranza, renounced the First Chief as leader, and proclaimed open hostilities on September 23. See the *New York Times*, Sept. 24, 1914, and Link, *Struggle for Neutrality*, p. 250.

[7] Fuller did not return to Mexico.

[8] The conferees agreed on the Clayton bill on September 23. See the *New York Times*, Sept. 24, 1914, and Link, *The New Freedom*, pp. 443-44.

[9] Secretary of the Treasury McAdoo issued a statement on September 23 which accused banks of hoarding money and charging excessive interest rates. He also threatened to publish the names of offenders in the future. See the *New York Times*, Sept. 24, 1914.

[10] The United States legations in Argentina and Chile were being upgraded to embassies.

[11] Garrett had been Minister to Argentina.

[12] Frederic Jesup Stimson was nominated as Ambassador to Argentina and Henry Prather Fletcher, the current Minister to Chile, was named Ambassador to that country.

[13] Stimson wrote several novels under the pen name of "J. S. of Dale."

Sept. 28, 1914

Mr. President, is the reply of the Colorado coal operators final or is it one to be considered further?[1]

I think it is one to be considered further. I have just arranged to consult the Secretary of Labor about it. He is in touch with the whole situation.

Did Mr. Welborn make a reply?

No, he really did not make any reply. He simply made a number of interesting representations as to the situation out there. I do not understand that his company has come to a conclusion. The conclusion of this group of operators is on the whole favorable.

Can you tell us what further steps you expect to take, Mr. President?

No, I cannot now, because I am discussing it in my own mind.

Mr. President, with reference to the shipping bill, do you share the general feeling that the urgency is passed?

No, not in the least. The urgency has increased.

Mr. President, Judge Alexander said Saturday that his advices were that the emergency for it was over; that there were plenty of ships for it.

For the ordinary trade, yes, but that is not what it is for. It is chiefly for the development of American trade where it will be unprofitable for private capital to develop it and where I know for a certainty that private capital will not develop it. It could not be expected to.

Mr. President, you told us last week that the opposition to the bill was rather negligible.

So I was then informed.

Don't you think that it has grown?[2]

Apparently it has. I don't know whether it is apparent or real. You know a few persons can make a great deal of noise sometimes, particularly a few persons who are interested from an investment point of view.

Does that alter your views or position any?

No, sir, because the circumstances are not altered. Opposition does not alter me; circumstances, I hope, do.

Mr. President, isn't that opposition chiefly toward taking it up at the present time rather than toward the proposition?

That may be. I don't know. I am going to confer with some of the members of the House just as soon as I can find space on my calendar. I will find that out; that may be all there is in it.

Can you say anything of the visit of Mr. Alexander or Mr. Underwood today?

It was about that subject.

Your present judgment is, Mr. President, that it ought to pass at this session of Congress?

Unless I learn something that changes my judgment in the matter. I don't mean something about the opposition to it, but something about the urgency.

How is the Philippine bill, Mr. President?[3]

I don't understand that there is any trouble about that passing the House of Representatives.

Mr. President, to go back to the ship-purchase bill. The seamen's bill, in a good many minds, is somewhat of a first step toward any action upon the shipping bill. Is there any plan to pass the seamen's bill at this session?

I don't know. I have fallen out of the conference on that.

Mr. President, is there anything you can say on the Mexican situation?

No, nothing intelligible. I don't know just how it is developing.

Is the opposition to the conference report on the Clayton bill among Democrats in the Senate confined to Mr. Reed, do you know?[4]

No, I don't know; but it is confined certainly to a very small group.

The group is not large enough to endanger the adoption of the report?

Oh, no; not so far as I know.

Is adjournment in October likely?

I should say so, though I have now stopped committing myself, having proved a false prophet. Still, I think Europe is more responsible for the false prophecies than we are.

Mr. President, do you expect all of these measures to go through both the House and the Senate this session?

I don't expect the Philippine bill to go through the Senate.

Do you expect the shipping bill to go through?

Well, I am waiting for these conferences. I don't know just what can be done with that.

Mr. President, has your attention been drawn to the opposition of western bankers to that provision in the conference report about interlocking directorates?[5]

Yes, but there is a clear judgment among us that that ought to be done, and it is clearly pledged in the platform of the party.

Is it your intention to send Mr. Fuller back to Mexico at this time?

No, sir.

Are Mr. Silliman and Mr. [Carothers] doing anything to patch up this difference?[6]

I think they have exerted their best influence in that direction all along.

Are any new steps being taken?

No, sir; I don't see that there is any opening just now. Tumulty tells me that there is a meeting between representatives of the two groups or factions taking place today. I did not know about that. That is, representatives of Villa and of Carranza.[7]

There is nothing new in our offer of mediation to Europe?

No, sir.

Mr. President, has Mr. McAdoo's word of warning to the bankers in the country who are hoarding money had the desired effect so far as you know?

Well, it has stirred up the embers considerably. Just what result it will have, it is too early to say. Of course, the Secretary of the Treasury always speaks from the facts, and we will see if it has the desired effect.

Mr. President, do you expect to have another conference in the near future with Mr. Henry over this cotton plan?[8]

No, sir, I have not been asked to.

---

[1] See above, Sept. 24, 1914.

[2] The *New York Times*, September 29, 1914, reported that approximately seventy Democrats in the House opposed the bill. See also Link, *Struggle for Neutrality*, pp. 87-91.

[3] On September 26, House Democrats limited debate to eight hours on the Jones bill. See the *New York Times*, Sept. 27, 1914.

[4] Senator Reed was at the time delivering a two-day speech criticizing the conference committee's removal of specific definitions from the Clayton bill. See *ibid.*, Sept. 30, 1914, and Link, *The New Freedom*, pp. 443-44.

[5] George McClelland Reynolds, president of the Continental Commercial Bank of Chicago, telegraphed Vice-President Thomas Riley Marshall on September 26 to protest against the provision of the Clayton bill which prohibited a person from being a director of more than one bank in a city of over 200,000 in population. See the *New York Times*, Sept. 27, 1914.

[6] John Reid Silliman and Carothers were Wilson's special agents to Carranza and Villa, respectively. They were at this time attempting to "patch up" the dispute between the two Mexican leaders. See Hill, *Emissaries to a Revolution*, pp. 225-90.

[7] Representatives of Carranza and Villa were making arrangements for a meeting to compose their differences at the Convention of Aguascalientes. See the *New York Times*, Sept. 28, 1914; Hill, *Emissaries to a Revolution*, p. 259; and Robert E. Quirk, *The Mexican Revolution, 1914-1915* (Bloomington, Ind., 1960), pp. 101-31.

[8] A delegation of cotton men led by Representative Robert Lee Henry, Democrat of Texas, met with Wilson on September 24 to discuss the problems caused for the industry by the war in Europe. Within a week after the outbreak of the war, the German market was eliminated and the Allied and American cotton exchanges closed their doors. As buyers for cotton almost ceased to exist, the price fell to half of its July rate of 12½ cents per pound, and cotton spokesmen in Congress searched for a workable plan to prevent an economic disaster from befalling the South. For Wilson's remarks, see *PWW*, Vol. 31, p. 79; see also Link, *Struggle for Neutrality*, pp. 91-102.

Oct. 1, 1914

Mr. President, can you tell us anything about your hope for an adjournment of Congress or a recess?[1]

That is a subject upon which I have so often discoursed that I know nothing new to say. I think the leaders on the Hill hope for an adjournment by the tenth of the month.

An adjournment or a recess?

An adjournment.

Mr. President, have the circumstances changed your opinion as to the urgency of the ship-purchase bill?

No, but I have assurances that it will be very promptly taken up.

Promptly taken up at the next session or this?

At the next session.

You think, then, that, when they do adjourn, they will adjourn until December—or November 15?

Well, as I understand it they will adjourn, and then it will be left for us to counsel together as to when the next session should occur.

That is as to whether there will be an extra session?

Whether Congress should convene earlier than December or not.

Are there any developments, Mr. President, in the matter of the investigation of the high prices of food products which was in progress some time ago?

None that have been called to my attention.

I saw a paragraph from Cincinnati to the effect that the district attorney there did not find any evidences of criminal conspiracy. Do you think that that applies generally?

No, that would not apply to other places. I had not seen that, as a matter of fact. The action of the federal government would altogether depend upon evidences of that kind—of some combination to control prices.

What is the latest word from Mexico, Mr. President?

I have no information that I think you have not received already. Apparently the prospects for an accommodation there are good.

Mr. President, have you any comment to make on the New York election at the primaries?[2]

No, sir.

If there should be an adjournment on or about October 10, do you still stand by your declaration in the Doremus letter that you will not enter into any of the campaigns personally?[3]

Oh, yes. What is keeping me here is not only, perhaps not chiefly, the business of Congress, but the whole situation of the world.

Even if Congress should adjourn, do you intend to remain here?

Yes.

Mr. President, with regard to those protests from the Catholics regarding the situation in Mexico, have you taken any action on that?[4]

There isn't any action to take. We have been doing everything that it was possible to do in that matter, and I am afraid that there isn't anything at present that can be done beyond what we have already attempted. Mr. Tumulty tells me that Mr. Bryan has taken it up.

Mr. President, about the Colorado situation, are you still working along the lines of that tentative basis of settlement, or is there something new?

I am working along those lines still.

Do you expect to see the Secretary of Labor about that situation soon?

As soon as he comes back. He is in Pennsylvania now.

Mr. President, do you contemplate doing anything soon about the withdrawal of federal troops?

Well, all that is part of the problem I am trying to solve. I am trying to bring about a settlement which will make the presence of the troops unnecessary.

Mr. President, Mr. McAdoo has issued an order withdrawing some three million dollars from certain national banks; has there been any discussion as to how far the Treasury may go in the withdrawal of funds and still remain within the limits of safety?[5]

How do you mean of safety?

In your address to Congress, in which you asked for the imposition of a war tax you rather [implied that the alternative was] the withdrawal of the seventy-five million dollars.[6]

There is no danger to a bank that is keeping a reserve of 45 per cent, for example, when 15 per cent is all that is required by law. Of course, he isn't withdrawing them where it is unsafe to withdraw them, as it would be if the bank were running close to its reserve, for example.

What I had in mind was how far you could go toward the withdrawal of the seventy-five millions without incurring any danger?

You see, the real ground for his withdrawing them is that they are not making any use of them for the public, and they are not deposited to adorn the vaults.

Do you think that that is generally true, that there can be a safe and larger withdrawal of the funds?

That I could not answer. In those particular instances where he is withdrawing them, he is doing it where it is safe because the banks make no use of the deposits.

He is dealing now only with the crop-movement deposits which total only thirteen million dollars up to date. He has just removed a part of that.[7]

I don't know whether that is what he is doing or not.

Mr. President, Senator Smoot introduced a resolution yesterday concerning the treatment of contraband goods. Has there been anything new with respect to that?[8]

No.

Can you say anything, Mr. President, as to just how far that discussion has gone between the State Department and Ambassador Spring Rice?[9]

It hasn't gone as far as the newspapers report. As a matter of fact, I think it can be summed up in this way, that the British government is most friendly in its attitude and most willing to discuss anything to which this government enters an objection, and I have no doubt that a satisfactory arrangement can be arrived at.

Have we had any communication, Mr. President, with the government of Holland with reference to the [smuggling] issue?[10]

None whatever. I am informed—I mean through the newspapers, not officially—that the government of Holland laid an embargo on certain shipments itself.

That is, across its frontier?

Across its frontier, yes.

The contention of Great Britain, as I understood it, was that anything sent to Holland would find its way across the frontier. That was its original objection.

I can't answer that specifically. I would say, just among ourselves here for your information, that, as I understand it, they are not trying to interfere with trade that is as a matter of fact neutral, but that they are anxious to prevent such shipments through Holland as are in fact unneutral. That is what it comes to. Of course, it is very difficult to state a rule that will cover that without the rule working as if it were a general interference with neutral trade. I think that is the difficulty they are trying to work out.

[1] Leaders in the House were at this time discussing taking a series of three-day recesses from October 10 to November 15. See the *New York Times,* Oct. 1, 1914. They eventually decided on an adjournment, however. See *ibid.,* Oct. 2, 1914.

[2] In the New York primaries, held September 28, the Democrats nominated Governor Glynn for Governor and James Watson Gerard for Senator. See *ibid.,* Sept. 29, 1914.

[3] Wilson wrote Frank Ellsworth Doremus, chairman of the Democratic Congressional Campaign Committee on September 4 to inform him that he would not campaign personally in the fall elections but would undertake an extensive letter-writing campaign. The letter is printed in *PWW,* Vol. 30, pp. 475-78.

[4] Following a speech by the Most Rev. Joseph Schrembs, Bishop of Toledo, on September 27, the convention of the American Federation of Catholic Societies, which met in Baltimore on September 27-28, called upon the Wilson administration not to recognize any Mexican government which did not guarantee religious liberty. A delegation presented this request to Wilson at the White House on September 30. See the *New York Times,* Sept. 28 and 30 and Oct. 1, 1914, and Link, *Struggle for Neutrality,* p. 468.

[5] McAdoo removed $3,000,000 in funds that had been deposited in the National banks for the purpose of moving the autumn crop. See the *New York Times,* Oct. 1, 1914.

[6] In his address to Congress of September 4, 1914, Wilson said that, without taxation, the Treasury might be forced to withdraw the $75,000,000 on deposit in the National banks, which would cause irreparable harm to business. The address is printed in *PWW,* Vol. 30, pp. 473-75.

[7] Because bank reserves were so high, McAdoo had deposited only $13,000,000 of the $34,000,000 he had announced as available in August. The $3,000,000 withdrawal was part of the $13,000,000 deposited. See the *New York Times,* Sept. 30, 1914.

[8] Senator Smoot of Utah introduced a resolution (S. Res. 458) on September 30 calling on the State Department to report on whether the British were interfering with American copper shipments to Rotterdam. It passed unanimously. See the *New York Times,* Oct. 1, 1914, and *Cong. Record,* 63d Cong., 2d sess., p. 15933.

[9] The British Ambassador, Sir Cecil Spring Rice, called at the State Department on September 30 to announce that the British might begin seizing conditional contraband if it was believed to be bound ultimately for Germany. See the *New York Times,* Oct. 1, 1914, and Link, *Struggle for Neutrality,* pp. 114-18.

[10] The Dutch government declared martial law on its border on September 26 to prevent smuggling of food to Germany and to protect its neutrality. See the *New York Times,* Sept. 27, 1914, and the Minister in the Netherlands [Henry van Dyke] to the Secretary of State, undated but received Oct. 2, 1914, *FR, 1914-WWS,* pp. 317-18.

Oct. 5, 1914

Is there any progress yet in the Colorado matter, Mr. President?

Not since last week. Things are in a state of inquiry.

Have the attacks on the conference report on the Clayton bill changed your views of it at all?[1]

Oh, no, not in the least. They confirm it.

Mr. President, has any information come to you regarding conditions in Mexico? You remember the bishop that came over from that Catholic conference on Thursday, Bishop Currier?[2]

No further information at all. Of course, he didn't bring any fresh information.

No, but he understood that you had told him that you would make inquiries regarding their allegations.

No, I didn't say that. I said, of course the government would continue to do everything it was possible to do to check such things as he was complaining of. We receive information constantly, you know, of what is going on, so that further inquiries are not called for.

There are stories in some of the papers this morning that Mr. Silliman is on his way to see you.[3]

Yes, I see. I don't know what for. He simply telegraphed us that he was coming up.

There seems to be a man named Cole who is coming here to ask the recognition of General Carranza.[4]

I hadn't heard about him yet.

Has Mr. Silliman been in San Antonio till recently?

He may have reached there. I don't know.

He has been there for some time?

Oh, no, not for some time, certainly. Within the last four or five days, he has been on his way from Veracruz. I mean, he was in Veracruz some four or five days ago.

Has the deadlock on the part of the conference over the Alaska coal-leasing bill reached—I understand that they are still in a deadlock. The House and Senate won't yield to each other.[5]

I hadn't heard about that.

Mr. President, the adoption of the conference report on the Clayton bill and the passage of the war-tax revenue measure, will that conclude the session's performance?

Yes, sir.

Is there anything else?

I can't think of anything else. Nothing else is pending. Of course, this Alaska bill would be one of the things.

Is the safety-at-sea bill—is that still in conference?

That is still in conference, but it is not necessary to act on that before adjournment.

Did you notice the remark of Chairman Henry, that Congress would not be permitted to adjourn before it had supplied the South with the five hundred million dollars?[6]

I should think the House would determine that, and not Mr. Henry.

Mr. President, there has been some suggestion that if the Congress adjourns until the middle of November, the next recess will be in the middle of December.

That is a matter for the conference committees—their decisions on anything that might be left over.

But it is not a program, though—there is no program that would look to an extra session after the fourth of March?

No, sir. The reason I laughed was that I think Congress has had so much sitting that it would necessitate a very large reason for calling any extra session.

Outside of the appropriation bills, there is quite a bit of the program remaining.

There are three very important things. There are two conservation bills[7] which passed the House without a dissenting vote, you remember, which, I should imagine, would pass the Senate without a great deal of difficulty. Of course, I am speaking entirely without any conference with them. Then there is the Philippine bill and the ship-purchase bill. The House ought to have passed, at any rate, one of those by that time, and the Senate has the time, before the maturing of the appropriation bills, for the consideration of those measures.

Those are the only three that strike you at this time?

Those are the only ones that occur to me just now as unfinished business.

The presidential primary bill?

I have been very much interested in that. I have had one of those conferences, not recently, but some months ago, with Judge Rucker[8] and others on that subject. And there is a very great complexity in framing the thing. And while there appears to be no serious difference of opinion as to the desirability of the legislation, there is a very reasonable difference of judgment as to the details. And whether that bill can be matured satisfactorily or not, I don't know, for this Congress.

Mr. President, would you include the securities bill in that list, or do you think that that is going over into the full session?

I think that is going over.

Would you suggest some points of difficulty [about the presidential primary bill]?

One is the very great variety in the laws of the states. Another is the imposing of a uniform system, for example—the matter of the time—on the states. Of course, it would be desirable that the primaries should take place on the same day throughout the country, just as the national election would. And that is very difficult to arrange, under the great variety of electoral laws in the states, and the arrangements for registration. There is a possible conflict of federal law [with state law].

The federal law at times supersedes all those arrangements?

Of course, we ought not to put on the states, if we can avoid it, the burden of entirely separating the electoral process, which would be very expensive. It might lead, for example, to a presidential primary, a state primary, and a state election, which would be a tremendous burden.

The states themselves could readily meet that.

They could, if their legislatures were in session.

But then the bill would not have to take effect for a few years.

Yes. It might be done that way, I daresay.

Well, if feasible, it would naturally take some years to institute that system, wouldn't it?

I shouldn't think so. I shouldn't think it would take more than a year. But I am now speaking without the facts before me.

Is that water-power bill, Mr. President, the general dam one, is that one of the measures you expect Congress to act on?

Yes.

Is it the one on the construction of the dams?

Yes, sir, the so-called dam bill, and the general leasing bill are the two.

Not the public lands?

And the public-lands bill.[9] The dam bill is not in the conservation program, understand, though it is of equal importance.

Mr. President, would you like to make some comment for publication on your meeting yesterday with Mr. Harvey?[10]

I would like to, if there was anything to indicate. It was just a friendly call. And we discussed, as I see the papers are calling it, the general political situation and particularly the European situation. Colonel Harvey has recently been in Europe and has a good deal of information that it was very serviceable to get.

Is Colonel Watterson[11] also to meet with you?

I hope so, some day. There is no present arrangement.

Mr. President, have the automobile manufacturers made any direct protest to you on the proposed tax?[12]

No, sir. None that has come to me.

[1] In spite of the attacks, the Clayton bill passed the Senate on October 5. See the *New York Times*, Oct. 6, 1914.

[2] The Most Rev. Charles Warren Currier, Bishop of Matanzas, Cuba, visited Wilson and Bryan on October 1 and made representations against the seizure of property belonging to the Catholic Church in Mexico. See *ibid.*, Oct. 2, 1914.

[3] *Ibid.*, Oct. 5, 1914, reported that Silliman had passed through St. Louis on his way to Washington. See also Hill, *Emissaries to a Revolution*, pp. 267-68.

[4] Richard H. Cole, a personal friend of Carranza, was on his way to Washington to seek the recognition of the *Carrancista* government. See the *New York Times*, Oct. 5, 1914.

[5] The Alaska coal-leasing bill (H.R. 14233), which provided for the opening of Alaskan resources, was approved on October 6. See *ibid.*, Oct. 7, 1914.

[6] Representative Henry had introduced a cotton-relief bill (H.R. 18916), which called on the Treasury to deposit $500,000,000 in southern banks for loans to cotton planters affected by the war. See *ibid.*, Oct. 3, 1914.

[7] The general dam bill and general leasing bill.

[8] Representative William Waller Rucker, Democrat of Missouri, chairman of the House Committee on Election of President, Vice-President, and Representatives in Congress, visited

Wilson on October 5. They concluded that it would be impossible to enact a presidential primary law for a nationwide primary in 1916. See the *New York Times*, Oct. 6, 1914.

9 The general lands bill (S. 2883), to dispose of land under federal control.

10 Colonel George Brinton McClellan Harvey, editor of *The North American Review*, visited Wilson at the White House on October 4. He and Wilson "buried the hatchet" over difficulties arising from the preconvention campaign of 1912, when Harvey pretended to believe that Wilson had rejected his editorial support. See the *New York Times*, Oct. 5, 1914, and Arthur S. Link, *Wilson: The Road to the White House* (Princeton, N. J., 1947), pp. 367-70.

11 Colonel Henry Watterson, editor of the Louisville *Courier-Journal*, had also felt insulted by Wilson's attitude during the preconvention campaign of 1912. He was invited on October 6 to visit the White House. See the *New York Times*, Oct. 5 and 7, 1914, and Link, *Road to the White House*, p. 365.

12 Thirty-three Michigan automobile manufacturers sent a telegram drawn up by E. R. Benson of the Studebaker Motor Car Company to the Michigan members of Congress protesting against the proposed tax on gasoline in the war revenue bill. See the *New York Times*, Oct. 4, 1914, and Link, *Struggle for Neutrality*, p. 104.

Oct. 8, 1914

How is the cotton situation, Mr. President? Have you reached any solution of the problem in your mind?

No, sir. I wish I had. I have been trying to, very hard, but I haven't seen anything yet which seemed to be workable. Of course, as I said the other day, the cause of the problem is the European war, and we can't account for that. It's the large proportion of our cotton generally bought abroad and the fact that we depend for our gold balance in so large a part from the cash sale of cotton.

There is no chance of a corner—I don't mean corner exactly, but suppose those men put up their hundred and fifty million,[1] is there no chance of their buying cotton enough to control cotton in any dangerous way?

I don't see it. Really, the cotton pool, so called, this fund, would be so generally subscribed for that there wouldn't be any one group or person who could operate and control it. If it were all operated from a small number of banks or a particular group of persons, that might be involved; but if it is not being managed, there isn't any possibility.

Mr. President, will you see that committee from St. Louis tomorrow?[2]

I didn't know there would be a committee.

Yes, there will be a committee.

I don't know, sir. I haven't, so far as I know, an appointment with them.

They have an engagement with the Federal Reserve Board at three o'clock. You haven't approved any of these various bills that have been submitted to you?

No, sir. I have simply taken them all under consideration, so far as I can, to determine the matter.

Have you expressed disapproval of any of them yet, Mr. President?

Only in the sense that, as I have said, I didn't see anything yet proposed that would be feasible.

I believe, for my part, to use the phrase, what is uppermost in our minds, that at present the mobilization of the currency of the country, the treasure of the country, will suffice if that mobilization will be effected, and I don't see any reason to doubt that it can be. It is not the lack of sufficient currency, because there is more currency in the country than there ever has been, but the lack of means, so far, of putting it at the disposal of the persons who most need it in this particular situation.

Mr. President, what is the grain situation? Grain is being exported in unprecedented amounts.

I don't know that there is any difference, any difference as to these exports, except, of course, if men do not receive cotton they can wear old clothes, even if they are rags. And the cotton situation is partly an anticipated situation. Only in Texas has the cotton been gathered, as I understand it, and it is yet to be gathered in most of the cotton belt.

Well, if the Federal Reserve Board assisted in the operation,[3] wouldn't the situation be very much improved?

It would be very much improved, yes. And for that reason, the directors who are now chosen, so far as the southern region is concerned, are very active. You know, they have been consulting and were, within the last forty-eight hours, very active in trying to get the system under way.

Mr. President, are there any features of the tax bill as it now stands in the Senate that you can comment on?

To tell the truth, I don't know just how it does stand. I have had so many other things to occupy the foreground that I am not informed in detail at all. Of course, it will have to go through conference yet.

The leaders of Congress have not informed you as to whether or not they expect to get away?

No, sir.

The subcommittee of the Senate Committee on Commerce, to which the seamen's bill has been referred, is planning to meet very shortly to reconsider the seamen's bill. Is there any intention to push that this year?

I don't know. Of course, I have pledged myself not to coerce anybody. I don't know what their plans are.

Mr. President, have you anything special in mind besides the ship-purchase bill that you want passed in the next session—the short session?

The two conservation bills that are of the five that remain unconsidered.[4]

And the water-power bill?

The water-power bill and the leasing bill.

The water-power bills?

Yes, but the other one is a navigation bill. You mean now the Adamson bill, the general dam bill?

The general dam bill and the public lands bill.

Yes, and there is the general leasing bill, which is more properly than some of the others called conservation.

You said the Philippines bill too?

Yes, the Philippines bill.

You are not going to do the rural credits in this session?[5]

I would be very glad to, but no plan has matured yet, and I am afraid it's past hoping for with the campaign interfering and the committee with no mature plan yet.

Is it necessary—is rural-credit legislation urgent at this time?[6]

Well, it is urgent in a way, since it is extremely desirable. And I don't know that it is considered more urgent right now than it has been for a good many years except by, I think, the farmers of the country who will be very much surprised to find how much rural credit there is in the new Federal Reserve System. I don't think that is at all realized yet.

If anything, it is rather less than more urgent than it was at the time you [took office].

It is less in proportion as the Federal Reserve Act includes provisions for it.

There is no special session next spring in sight, is there, Mr. President?

Lord, don't get another spring on my mind, too.

Mr. President, have you any information that you could tell us regarding the financial situation of the railroads?

I haven't anything at all, no sir.

Mr. President, have you heard anything of a plan of the bankers—something of an international credit bureau, similar to the New York Clearing House Association?

No, sir. I hadn't heard about that. Nothing is brought to my attention that is going well, only those things that are going badly.

How about Mexico?

Well, I haven't any new information. So far as I know, it is going reasonably well.

Can you say anything about Mr. Silliman's long conference with you the other evening?[7]

There is nothing to say, except that he came up to tell us all that he knew about what was going on. It did not alter the general aspect of affairs at all.

There is a persistent report that he urged recognition of Carranza. Is that true?

No. He didn't urge anything.

He made no representations on behalf of any faction?

Oh, no. No.

Mr. President, have there been any exchanges between this government and Japan with regard to the Japanese military operations in China?[8]

No, none that have been brought to my attention. I have seen from the newspapers that they have, at each step, given assurances that they are doing the temporary things that it is necessary for their objectives in the war.

Was there ever any assurance on the part of Japan as to the limitations on her activities?

You mean geographic limitations? I am not clear on that point. There seems to be what was abundant assurance that she was not going to take advantage of the country.

I meant specifically on that point, because it has been reported both ways. I have never been able to get it straight.

I think the assurances have been satisfactory. As a matter of fact, I have just learned of them in a general way. There again, if anything had been going wrong, I am sure I would have known it.

You haven't heard the reports of the operations of the Japanese outside of their territory in China,[9] in which they originally intended to operate, and the protest of China against their operations along the railroad running to Tsingtau?[10]

I have simply learned of those things. There is nothing official.

Mr. President, are you going to take a vacation after the Congress adjourns?

No, sir. I don't think so. I don't see any chance.

Is there anything new in the Colorado situation?

No, sir.

---

[1] In an effort to solve the problems caused by the collapse of the cotton markets, Festus John Wade, president of the Mercantile National Bank of St. Louis and head of the St. Louis Clearing House Association, proposed that bankers combine to provide a fund of $150,000,000

to be lent to southern farmers. Such a loan program would permit cotton farmers to hold their crop for at least a year, and Wilson adopted it as the cornerstone of his southern relief program. After a struggle with cotton-state Senators and Congressmen, who favored the more interventionist plan proposed by Representative Henry, the program went into effect on November 30, only to be rendered useless by the restrictive policies imposed upon the loans by the Federal Reserve Board. See the *New York Times,* Oct. 8-9, 1914; Link, *Struggle for Neutrality,* pp. 97-101; and *PWW,* Vol. 31, pp. 129-30.

² A committee, led by Wade, visited Wilson on October 9 to promote the cotton-pool idea. See the *New York Times,* Oct. 9, 1914, and Link, *Struggle for Neutrality,* p. 99.

³ That is, by making funds available. The Federal Reserve System began operations on November 16, 1914.

⁴ See above, Oct. 5, 1914.

⁵ Wilson remained unable to resolve his differences with agrarian leaders on the question of rural credits. Many Congressmen still favored the bill (S. 5542) introduced by Representative Robert Johns Bulkley, Democrat of Ohio, and Senator Henry French Hollis, Democrat of New Hampshire, which Wilson regarded as providing for too much government involvement in the economy. See Link, *The New Freedom,* pp. 261-64, and *Cong. Record,* 63d Cong., 2d sess., p. 8426.

⁶ That is, because of the war in Europe.

⁷ Silliman visited Wilson at the White House on October 7. See the *New York Times,* Oct. 8, 1914.

⁸ The Japanese had declared war against Germany and were attacking the German leasehold in China. See the Japanese Embassy to the Secretary of State, Oct. 1, 1914, *FR, 1914-WWS,* pp. 182-83.

⁹ The Japanese had attacked Jaluit, the seat of German government in the Marshall Islands, and Yap in the Caroline Islands. See the *New York Times,* Oct. 7-8, 1914, and the Ambassador in Japan to the Secretary of State, Oct. 6, 1914, *FR, 1914-WWS,* pp. 183-84.

¹⁰ The Chinese were protesting against the Japanese occupation of the Shantung Railroad running to Tsingtau. See the *New York Times,* Oct. 8, 1914, and the Minister in China [Paul Samuel Reinsch] to the Secretary of State, Oct. 2, 1914, *FR, 1914-WWS,* p. 183.

Oct. 12, 1914

Mr. President, is the Alaskan coal-leasing bill still part of the winter program?

Yes. I understand that that is going back to conference.

Mr. President, is there anything about adjournment?

No, I haven't heard anything definite at all.

Anything further about the Colorado strike situation, Mr. President?

Nothing at all. I understand that Governor Ammons is reorganizing the militia of the state so as to relieve the federal troops of their duty, but just how far that has gone, I don't know. There is no change in the situation.

Has the international credit bureau situation reached you, except through newspapers?

Not even that way, sir. I don't know anything about it. What is it?

Sir George Paish and other financiers expect to discuss it with the New York financiers.[1]

I knew about that, but I didn't know that they would be received any particular time. That hasn't taken shape yet.

Mr. President, on the financiers who are coming in from England—do you know, is there any scheme to invite representatives of other countries to a conference?

I don't understand that these gentlemen were invited. I understand that they are coming of their own volition.

Mr. McAdoo has been of the impression that they had been invited.[2]

Has he? I simply wasn't informed. I did not know. Of course, one has to take hard facts into consideration. Some countries are free to send representatives, and others are not, just as a matter of fact, not as a matter of law. What we are seeking to do is to keep that part of the commerce of the world moving which is movable, which is free to move.

At the risk of [breaking] over a straw, Mr. President, you have taken no action or steps with reference to European peace except as to that first note?

No. A good many are taken for me.

Have you heard anything from Mr. Carnegie, Mr. President?

No, not a word.

Anything from Mexico?

No. I saw some dispatches in this morning's papers which surprised me. I didn't know that there was any firing over the border. Apparently there is some local difficulty.[3]

Have you received anything from there, Mr. President, as to the requests on the Veracruz situation—the protection of those merchants down there, those merchants who have supported the municipal government?[4]

Nothing definite has come about that.

Has any time been fixed for the definite withdrawal of our troops?

Well, we are anxious to get away immediately. We are simply

waiting for the things that are necessary to arrange to have some-body to hand over the authority to. We can't simply drop the city and leave it to take care of itself.

Doesn't that hinge on that reply?[5]

It hinges in part on that. Of course, we can't exact anything of the Mexican authorities with regard to their own citizens, but we have a right to expect, of course, that proper arrangements will be made to transfer authority.

Mr. President, do you expect to sign the Clayton bill today?

Yes.

There is some idea that you might not sign that bill until you can get out a statement?

No, sir. I don't want to have statements becoming chronic.

Mr. President, have you any choice between the House and Senate revenue bills?

To tell the truth, I haven't read the Senate revenue bill. Has it been reported out of the committee?[6]

Yes.

I haven't read it yet. I shall begin to get deeply interested when it gets to conference.

Mr. President, have you any information regarding business conditions throughout the country after the first flurry of the war?

I haven't any systematic information I can think of, no, but from what I can learn, the great bulk of business is going very normally, as much as it is disturbed by the cotton situation; and the lack of adequate international exchange is of course disturbing. But I have every reason to hope that that will be facilitated and put on as good a footing as is possible in the circumstances.

Imports improving?

They are improving.

The war tax?

It hasn't shown any such marked increase as to affect that increase, unfortunately.

Have you received any intimation from the British government relative to the embargo on wool, except the telegram from Consul General Skinner?[7]

No, sir. Nothing at all.

Is that conditional contraband list righting itself?

I think it is righting itself. I get that impression. Of course, it hasn't come to any definite conclusion yet. Understand, of course, that under the practices of international law, nations at war have the right, within certain limits, to increase the lists of the things which are to be considered contraband or conditional contraband, as the case may be, because of the circumstances arising in the war itself, and the use that is being made of what is shipped. So it is bound to be a little bit fluid for a time.[8]

The question of neutral ships and neutral ports, that has been eliminated? But the revamping of that list by the British government—they revised their list on certain foodstuffs, whether countries such as Holland could transport to neutral ports, and would that apply to all those nations—Turkey, Sweden? Isn't there a danger of merchants being a little overfearful? Take, for example, the sending of that ship in ballast to bring back the cargo and supplies. It is suggested to me from pretty high quarters that they haven't got the government[9] backing for it.

They have certainly got the government backing it to the limits of all our rights, of course; and I don't think our rights will be interfered with.

Has Great Britain called any attention to the export of grain to Sweden and Norway?[10]

There are always exports to those countries.

It was particularly heavy.

That might be, because those countries always draw on the Russian grain fields.

Mr. President, have you received any note from Ambassador Jusserand about German atrocities?[11]

Yes, sir. The State Department sent me over a formal representation of the French government about it.

It will be handled the same way as the other?

Yes.

Was that recently?

Yes. Within five days. At a guess, some time last week.

You have merely filed them?

Of course, we acknowledge them in the proper way, but we can't form any conclusions with regard to the matter.

There isn't anything the government can do at all about this matter?

Except reserve judgment.

---

[1] Sir George Paish, editor of *The Statist* and adviser to the British Treasury, was visiting the United States along with Basil Blackett, representative of the Chancellor of the Exchequer, to confer with Secretary of the Treasury McAdoo, members of the Federal Reserve Board, and prominent New York bankers about the adjustment of credits between the United States and England. See the *New York Times*, Oct. 12, 1914.

[2] They had been invited by McAdoo.

[3] On October 9, an American soldier named John Wilson had been killed near Naco, Arizona, by a stray bullet from across the border. One day later, American troops had fired on a portion of Villa's army which had strayed on to American soil. See the *New York Times*, Oct. 10 and 12, 1914.

[4] Merchants in Veracruz feared that, following the American withdrawal, they might be forced to pay new duties on goods already taxed by American customs officials and that the Carranza government might take reprisals against those who had cooperated with the Americans. See War Department to State Department, Sept. 21, 1914, *FR, 1914*, pp. 601-602, and Hill, *Emissaries to a Revolution*, p. 269.

[5] On September 22 and October 1, the Department of State had asked José M. Cardoso de Oliveira, the Brazilian Minister in Mexico City, who was handling American interests there, to obtain assurances from Carranza against mistreatment of the merchants. The reply of October 5, made by Isidro Fabela, Mexican Foreign Minister, did not, however, address this question. For correspondence on this matter, see *FR, 1914*, pp. 603, 608-10.

[6] There was considerable debate in the Senate over the emergency war revenue bill, with Republican Senators attacking the administration for excessive spending. See the *New York Times*, Oct. 12, 1914, and *Cong. Record*, 63d Cong., 2d sess., pp. 16418-23.

[7] As Consul General Robert Peet Skinner at London had reported, the British government had forbidden the export of wool outside the Empire. See the *New York Times*, Oct. 11, 1914.

[8] With respect to copper, the British government had agreed not to seize conditional contraband items unless clearly destined for a belligerent. See *ibid.*, Oct. 10, 1914. Copper, along with other strategic raw materials, was added to the list of absolute contraband in the Order in Council of October 29, 1914. See Link, *Struggle for Neutrality*, pp. 114-26, and the Ambassador in Great Britain to the Secretary of State, Nov. 3, 1914, *FR, 1914-WWS*, pp. 260-63.

[9] That is, the United States Government.

[10] The British were considering placing exports of food to Sweden and Norway on the same footing as to Holland. See the *New York Times*, Oct. 17, 1914.

[11] See the President of France to the President of the United States, Sept. 10, 1914, *FR, 1914-WWS*, p. 794.

Oct. 15, 1914

Mr. President, you will sign the Clayton bill today, I understand? Are there any comments you care to make on it?[1]

No, sir, I believe not. I am going to make some general comments on the session which will include that.

May that be taken to conclude the business legislation that is desired for some time to come?

Of course, there is still to be determined just what legislation will be enacted with regard to railroad securities. That is an unfinished question, but I believe it is a question which the committees in Congress are not ready to deal with yet.

The present situation doesn't require any legislation on that subject, does it?

I suppose not.

Mr. President, Mr. Walters saw you today on the cotton situation?[2]

Yes, one may say it was on the cotton situation. It was about the general effects of the cotton situation on the business situation. Mr. Walters wasn't by any means pessimistic about it.

Mr. President, you expect to have Congress take up the railroad-securities bill at this next session, do you not?

I can't say that I have any definite opinion about it, because I haven't consulted with them about it for some months now.

Can it be considered as part of your program now?

Not part of the immediate program, no.

Mr. President, in view of the fact that the next session is a short session and will have to busy itself in large part with appropriations bills, is there any particular program, such, for instance, as the adoption of a budget system looking to greater economy in the public expenditures?

Well, I am afraid it is past hoping for that we can do anything so systematic as that at the short session, but I think that is in everybody's mind to accomplish as soon as possible.

Has there been any conference looking to the cutting down of estimates?

Well, so far as I am concerned, there has been; that is to say, in cabinet we have gone over the matter repeatedly, very carefully, and with a view to studying every possible economy, and there are going to be reductions proposed. The trouble is that with each additional piece of legislation there is some additional function which necessarily involves the expenditure of more money. But aside from new functions it will be possible, I think, to keep expenses down all along the line.

You think, then, that the appropriations of next year will be below those of this year?

I have every reason to think so, yes.

Mr. President, has any figure been set as a maximum over which they should not go at this short session?

You mean in the appropriations?

Yes.

That would be quite impossible until the whole thing is coordinated.

What is the news from Mexico today, Mr. President?

None today. The news of the last forty-eight hours is very encouraging, indeed.[3] I think Mr. Tumulty was discussing that with some of your number.

Are there any new developments on the Colorado strike situation?

None at all, sir.

Mr. President, is there anything new in the foreign-trade situation?

No, except that there is a constant though slow improvement in everything except the movement of cotton, but even that cannot be considered as definitely bad, because the movement of cotton hasn't begun.

We are sending all the cotton they will take?

They have bought very little so far. One element of the situation, you see, is that a very large part of the crop is not picked yet, not ready for market, and so the buying has not definitely begun. I have surmised, without knowing, that that was due to the fact that, with the cotton exchanges closed, it was very difficult for any systematic buying to occur, because they would not know at what price to buy it.

Mr. President, have you heard anything at all about any demand for American goods, any unusual demand, in countries that have been dependent on Europe heretofore?

I haven't had any official information to that effect. I have got it in letters and in conversations that the demand is considerably greater than it was.

Does that apply to South America?[4]

That applies to South America. It applies to Spain. It applies, I believe, to the Scandinavian countries, though I am speaking out of a recollection that would have to be verified.

Do you recall, Mr. President, what classes of goods are wanted? I know those countries you mention have taken a considerable part of the cotton that has been shipped out.

Well, it was chiefly in cotton fabrics, as this information reached me.

Had you heard anything from Japan on that question?

No.

Mr. President, is there anything you can tell us of the possibility of reopening the stock exchange?[5]

No, I know nothing about that.

Mr. President, what have been your latest reports as to the ships coming in under the American registry?

Well, I haven't had any very lately—not within three weeks. At that time it was about one a day coming in, an average something like that.

Mr. President, in the development of commerce with foreign countries, especially with South America, isn't the difficulty less an unwillingness to buy than an inability to pay?

That is one of the elements; not so much their inability to pay as their habit of having long credits extended to them. I believe in their trade with other countries they have had credits of from six months to a year. That was impossible for us to manage because their banking connections were foreign connections and not American. So that our problem is to establish the machinery of credit at the same time that we are establishing the trade itself.

There are some steps being taken in that regard?

Yes, there are.

That is, they are being taken by private bankers?

By private banking institutions, yes, sir. Or, rather, by National banking institutions. Those that I happen to know were National banks.

Mr. President, can you tell us something about your engagements after Congress adjourns? I know you are going to Pittsburgh, at least I understood so.[6]

That is in fulfillment of an invitation extended long ago when I was less prudent than I am now. That is the only engagement ahead of me.

Have you made any response yet to the invitation of the City of New York to attend that celebration of the three-hundredth anniversary of—[7]

No, that group of clergymen who were here the other day pressed it upon me very cordially. I could not give them any definite answer.

You haven't made any political engagements?

No, none at all.

Mr. President, Congressman Gardner of Massachusetts has introduced a resolution calling for a special commission to inquire into the preparedness of the United States for war?[8] Would you care to express in advance an opinion on that?

No.

Mr. President, is it your desire or intention to make public the letter to Mr. Palmer in which you discussed the presidential term plank of the Democratic platform?[9]

You mean that old letter?

Yes.

No; I am not thinking about that just now.

Mr. President, you had quite a long talk with Mr. Stimson;[10] I was wondering whether you had any particular ideas in mind with regard to increasing our trade relations with the Argentine.

So far as I recollect now, trade wasn't mentioned. We wanted to talk over our general policy with regard to establishing the real foundations of friendship between the United States and the Latin American countries, in which he was very deeply interested.

Mr. President, the State Department made a statement as to commerce with belligerent nations.[11] Do you understand that loans to belligerents would be in the contraband category?

I would prefer that what I say now should not be quoted, because it is an offhand opinion. My own information is that loans stand in the same case as anything else—loans from private individuals. You see how wrong it would be for me, so far as I can speak for the government, to have any attitude about it of any kind. All that we can do is what we did yesterday, namely state what is international law.

Is the situation any different now than it was a few months ago at the time of the outbreak of the war?

The situation hasn't changed at all so far as I know, but I don't want to express any opinion about it.

[1] Wilson signed the Clayton bill on October 15.

[2] Henry Walters of Baltimore and New York, chairman of the board of the Atlantic Coast Line Company.

[3] Reports indicated that Carranza had resigned and that General Antonio J. Villareal, chairman of the conference at Aguascalientes, had been accepted by both sides in Mexico as the new Provisional President. See the *New York Times*, Oct. 15-16, 1914.

[4] *Ibid.*, October 15, 1914, printed a story about improved trade with South America.

[5] The New York Stock Exchange had been closed on July 31; it reopened on a limited basis on November 28, 1914. See Link, *Struggle for Neutrality*, pp. 76-77.

[6] Wilson spoke on October 24, 1914, at the seventieth anniversary celebration of the Pittsburgh Y.M.C.A. The address is printed in *PWW*, Vol. 31, pp. 220-28.

[7] A delegation from New York, which included Oscar S. Straus, the Rev. Frank Oliver Hall, the Very Rev. Edward G. Fitzgerald, and the Rev. George Unangst Wenner, visited Wilson at the White House on October 12 to ask him to address the New York Tercentennial Celebration at the Hippodrome on October 25. Wilson accepted the invitation on October 15 but was unable to attend. See the *New York Times*, Oct. 13, 16, and 23, 1914.

[8] Representative Augustus Peabody Gardner, Republican of Massachusetts, introduced a resolution (H.J. Res. 372) on October 15 calling for a national security commission consisting of three Senators, three Representatives, and three presidential appointees. Gardner wanted the commission to examine and report on America's defenses, which he thought were not prepared for war. "In my opinion," Gardner said, "the effect of the vast sums of money spent by Andrew Carnegie in his peace propaganda has been to blind Americans to the fact that our national security from a military point of view is undermined." The United States should be prepared, Gardner concluded, "when the day of necessity comes." See *ibid.*, Oct. 16, 1914, and *Cong. Record*, 63d Cong., 2d sess., pp. 16694, 16745-47.

[9] Wilson wrote a letter to Representative A. Mitchell Palmer on February 3, 1913, expressing opposition to the plank in the Democratic platform of 1912 which called for a constitutional amendment to limit Presidents to one six-year term. At that time, legislation was being proposed to effect such an amendment. See the *New York Times*, Oct. 13, 1914; WW to Palmer, Feb. 3, 1913, in *PWW*, Vol. 27, p. 97; and Schlesinger and Israel, *American Presidential Elections*, III, 2170.

[10] Stimson, the new Ambassador to Argentina, visited Wilson at the White House on October 14.

[11] This general statement of October 15 cleared the way for a revision of previous policy by placing loans on the same footing as other goods. It is printed in *FR, 1914-WWS*, pp. 573-74; and see the *New York Times*, Oct. 16, 1914, and Link, *Struggle for Neutrality*, pp. 132-36.

Oct. 19, 1914

Mr. President, are you still adhering to your plan of not appointing a Federal Trade Commission until the December session?

Yes, sir, chiefly because I haven't time to make a careful selection before that time.

On Saturday, Mr. President, Senator Stone said something in the Senate.[1] Had he discussed that with you before he said it?

No, sir.

There is nothing you could add to it?

Oh, no.

Mr. President, in that connection, one of the British vessels outside of New York, Tuesday—I think it was—seized the tank steamer *Brindilla,* formerly a German vessel but now owned by the Standard Oil Company.[2]

So I saw by the papers this morning.

Under the general rule of international law, isn't it true that a vessel, even carrying contraband from one neutral point to another neutral point, is exempt from seizure?

That is the general rule. So far I know nothing of the official circumstances of this seizure. Indeed, the only thing I do know about is what I saw in the papers this morning.

Mr. President, we haven't taken any official cognizance of the nearness of foreign warships to our ports either at New York or elsewhere?

We have no right to do that.

In the Franco-Prussian war we took it seriously. The French government withdrew their ships.

I don't know anything about that. Any ship has the right to come no closer than the three-mile limit.

Mr. President, have you an engagement to meet Sir George Paish?[3]

No, sir. I understood that he was in town. I would like very much to see him. I had it in mind to send word that I would like to see him, but I haven't done so yet.

Can you give us an idea, Mr. President, of what matters are going to be taken up by Sir George Paish and the Secretary of the Treasury?

No, I cannot, because I don't know fully the circumstances that brought him over here. I judge from what I have heard unofficially that it is to ease the methods of exchange between the two countries.

Mr. McAdoo told us that he discussed the cotton situation.

Yes, sir.

Mr. President, you said at the last conference that you heard that some National banks in this country were trying to establish a basis of credits with South America. Has that gotten any further?

What I meant was that one or two banks were establishing branches in South America. I haven't heard anything about that recently.

Have you been advised of any move by the German government to have Mr. Whitlock removed from his official position and retained as a private citizen?[4]

No, sir, I haven't heard that.

Mr. President, there were some reports last week that the government had now changed its attitude on the matter of foreign loans by private individuals; is there any foundation for that?

None whatever.

Is it opposed to neutrality to lend to foreign nations?

I won't discuss it. I will just say that the government has not changed its attitude.

Do you know, Mr. President, what the chances are of getting the seamen's bill into conference?

No, I do not. Amidst the many other things that we have been handling, I haven't been asking about that recently.

Are there any new developments in the Colorado situation, Mr. President?

None at all that I am informed of.

Are negotiations still going on with the operators?

No, not strictly speaking. They have declined to accept the plan that I suggested to them, except with modifications that would take all the essential features out of it.

Mr. President, from something you said last week, I was in doubt whether you intended to include the Adamson bill—the water-power bill—in your conservation program?

I think I said that it was not, properly speaking, part of the conservation program. That is a sort of what one might call an historical accident. By conservation, we mean the handling of the public domain, really, and its resources. The Adamson bill referred to the navigable waters in those portions of the United States not owned by the government. That is the reason that, technically speaking, it is not part of conservation at all, though in the broader sense it is a very important part of conservation.

The Adamson bill is regarded as a very important part?

Yes, because of its collateral effect on the whole conservation policy.

Do you favor the bill in its present form?

It was pulled about a good deal in the House, and I haven't read its present form; but so far as I know it is satisfactory.

It is satisfactory to conservationists?

I am a conservationist. It ought to be satisfactory, if it is to me.

Is there anything you can tell us on the Mexican situation, Mr. President?

No, sir, except that I hear a good many things being told that are not so. Apparently somebody is still interested in having things occur down there that do not occur.

There was a report a few days ago that Mr. Silliman arranged with General Aguilar those details about Veracruz. Has that been finally decided?[5]

No. I received a dispatch to that effect—that he had a conference.

That must be, of course. Whatever Aguilar might—

Yes, of course. The authorities in Mexico City are in a fluid condition just now.

Has there been any reply from Carranza as to his attitude on several points this government wanted to know about?

No direct reply. I understand that—this was indirectly, and I will just have to give it as rumor—that he referred to those matters about what I take leave to call the "Hot Springs" conference.[6]

Mr. President, this morning's papers say there is a schism in the administration on the armament question. Is that true?

I can answer that, gentlemen. There is no schism in the administration over armaments or anything else.

About armaments in Europe or here.

I didn't know we had any, in the European sense.

The leading article in one of our morning papers sets forth that there is a decided division of opinion in the administration over the question whether we should or should not increase our armaments.[7]

I say there has been no discussion of the subject, and there hasn't been a chance to be a schism.

Mr. President, did you notice the propaganda that Mr. Gardner of Massachusetts has stirred with reference to that? Have you ever expressed yourself at all in regard to the army and the navy—a proper army and navy, or anything of that sort?

No, not at all.

And that hasn't been put down as one of the articles in your next year's program?

Not so far.

Would you care to say anything about it?

No; it is something that has been discussed a long time. I remember it being discussed just the way it is now ever since I was ten years old. I remember that far back, so I am quite familiar with it as a subject.

Do you intend, Mr. President, to recommend to Congress that an appropriation be made for a larger number of auxiliary vessels?

I have no such present purpose. As I say, we have not discussed the matter, much less formed any policy.

Mr. President, do you think it is a good thing to discuss those things right now?

As a mental exercise, I don't think it does any harm. Have to be joshing some in this regard!

Does the same hold true with regard to the cotton bill—the cotton-bond bill?[8]

You mean the one in the House?

Yes.

Yes, I don't see any harm in discussing that. I think every possible thing that can be done to relieve the situation in the South ought to be thoroughly discussed.

Mr. President, going back to cotton a moment. You saw Colonel Ewing[9] this past week, I believe. This morning he has got a suggestion in the papers about restricting the acreage of cotton next season to 50 per cent of the present crop. I was wondering whether he discussed that with you.

We did not discuss cotton at all. We discussed the management, the carrying out of the protection against floods in the lower Mississippi entirely—carrying out a thoroughgoing policy about that. Of course, the suggestion about a limitation of the acreage of planted cotton is being discussed everywhere.

That would be a state question?

I don't see how it could be anything else.[10]

(A question was asked about warehouses that the stenographer did not hear distinctly.)

I have been very much in hopes that the House would pass the so-called Lever bill.[11] The Senate has already passed it.

That is almost necessary?

I think so, yes. You see, we want to help by means of warehouse certificates, and if there are no warehouses there cannot be warehouse certificates, of course. There are warehouses, but I mean not enough.

Will the element of federal supervision satisfy the government as to the conditions, et cetera, of the securities—involving their soundness?

Yes, oh yes.

---

[1] On October 19 Senator Stone denounced the search of the United Fruit Company's steamer *Metapan* and the "paroling" of five German passengers by officers of the French cruiser *Condé*. Stone said that "it is well for other nations to know that we will not look with indifference upon a violation of the rights of our Government or our own people," and warned that the neutral rights of the United States had to be respected. See the *New York Times*, Oct. 18 and 20, 1914, and *Cong. Record*, 63d Cong., 2d sess., pp. 16765 and 16769.

[2] The tanker *Brindilla* was seized and taken to Halifax as a prize on October 18 by the British auxiliary cruiser *Caronia*. The ship, owned by the Standard Oil Company, had been transferred to American registry from one of the oil company's German subsidiaries. See the *New York Times*, Oct. 19, 1914, and Lansing to WW, Oct. 20, 1914, printed in *PWW*, Vol. 31, p. 193.

[3] Wilson saw Paish on October 19. See the *New York Times*, Oct. 20, 1914.

[4] The *New York Times*, October 20, 1914, reported that this story about Brand Whitlock, American Minister at Brussels, was not true.

[5] The reports were that Silliman had met with General Cándido Aguilar on October 17, and that Aguilar had agreed to American conditions for the withdrawal of troops from Veracruz. See above, Oct. 12, 1914; Hill, *Emissaries to a Revolution*, p. 270; and the *New York Times*, Oct. 18, 1914.

[6] That is, the Convention of Aguascalientes.

[7] The Editor could not identify this article.

[8] That is, the Henry bill. See above, Oct. 5, 1914.

[9] Robert Ewing of New Orleans visited Wilson at the White House on October 14.

[10] Senator Luke Lea, Democrat of Tennessee, was proposing a federal plan to eliminate the entire cotton crop for 1915. His plan called for the President to assemble a congress of cotton growers to establish a voluntary association which would agree not to plant a crop. Senator Hoke Smith of Georgia was proposing a two-cent-per-pound tax on cotton to limit production. See the *New York Times*, Oct. 17, 1914.

[11] The Lever-Smith warehouse bill (S. 6266 and H.R. 18359) to establish federal inspection and licensing of warehouses for cotton, grain, tobacco, and other agricultural products, and to facilitate borrowing by farmers against warehouse receipts. See Link, *Struggle for Neutrality*, pp. 98-99, and *Cong. Record*, 63d Cong., 2d sess., pp. 16189-90.

Oct. 22, 1914

Mr. President, can you tell us something in regard to the seizure of the *John D. Rockefeller*?[1]

Nothing that is at all authoritative or conclusive about it. We have asked for an explanation and for the particulars, but they haven't reached us yet, so far as we know.

Have you got a report yet, a report that was asked for in regard to the facts concerning the capture of the *Brindilla*?[2]

No, sir. That's not the same case.

Can you say anything generally, Mr. President, in regard to the whole question?

No, sir.

Mr. President, the Senate has just appointed a committee to take that up with the State Department. Has that been laid before you?

No. I didn't know that they had.

Have you heard anything from Mexico today or yesterday?

No, except that the eighteenth was the [unintelligible].

Is it true, Mr. President, that Villa has some forces at Aguascalientes?[3]

So far as I know, he does not, unless there were forces that were already there when the convention assembled.

What is the status of the administrative questions relative to the withdrawal of troops?[4]

I understood that Carranza had left it to the convention, but I have lost sight of it in the last day or two.

Mr. President, do you know any of the details in regard to the arrangement in London for the American committee to take charge of the relief of the Belgians?[5]

No. I heard something through London from Belgium to the effect that a committee of that sort had been formed, but I thought in Belgium.

Mr. Hoover, who has been head of the American relief committee in London, seems to have charge of it.

I simply learned that there was no opposition by any government to the attempt to relieve those who were in danger of starving there.

Mr. Tumulty just tells me that the British Ambassador has just telephoned that the *John D. Rockefeller* has been released.

That Belgian matter, Mr. President—that is purely a private matter, not governmental?

Not governmental at all. We did receive some inquiries as to whether there was any opposition to our consular officers acting to transmit the supplies, but if they did it would be merely as individuals, not as representatives of the government.

Mr. President, there have been some statements from abroad with regard to the status of Mr. Whitlock, the American Minister to Belgium, as to whether he still held the office of American Minister while the Germans control the capital and most of the country. Could you tell us something about that?

Well, if Mr. Whitlock should come to Washington, he would still be Minister to Belgium.

Is he performing any functions at all?

Well, of course he can't perform the ordinary functions of communicating with the Belgian government, because it isn't there to communicate with.

Mr. President, did Mr. Tumulty say whether the crew had been released as well as the *John D. Rockefeller*?

The objection had been, it seems, that it was a cargo of oil not assigned to a particular government, so that if it is released, this means that the crew are released also. I assume so. That is only a conclusion.

Mr. President, a letter received in New York said that Mr. Sharp, the Ambassador to France, had left France, and that Mr. Herrick was attempting to do the work there.[6]

What letter was this?

A private letter received in New York which said that that was the understanding. This letter came from London.

The writer didn't know what he was talking about.

Mr. Sharp is still in France?

So far as I know.

One of them is in Bordeaux and one is in Paris?[7]

I think not.

I thought Mr. Sharp went to Bordeaux?

If so, I haven't been informed of it. I was talking with his personal friend, Senator Pomerene,[8] only this morning, and he gave no intimation of that.

Mr. President, I was going to ask you about Senator Pomerene. Was the discussion anything more than the general talk about political conditions in Ohio?

It was hardly that. It was partly about Mr. Sharp and the rest I think about senatorial contests.

Did he make any suggestions?

No.

Mr. President, when you think incidentally of the adjournment of Congress, have you made any new plans for going to Pittsburgh?

I think it is clear that they will adjourn before I know when I am going to start.

Mr. President, has anything come up to your mind to settle whether there will be a special session in November?

No, sir. That is still a perfectly open question.

Mr. President, have you furthered your plans at all about spending the interim between congressional sessions—

No.

Your idea is to stay here?

Yes. I am tied by the leg. I can't get away. I saw Mr. Burgess,[9]

I think from Texas, this morning, and he said he was going to make an address in Texas, and he would show me how, if I went, by starting from New York to Galveston, I would have four free days. I explained to him that I didn't dare have four free days.

Mr. President, did you know about the informal conversations between Mr. McAdoo and the Reserve Board with Sir George Paish—they come from him—as to the definite proposition of settling the government's—

No, I did not know. I have generally kept informed, but Mr. McAdoo has been in bed, and I have lost track there a bit.

I understand that Sir George Paish has been convinced that, while we have a tremendous amount of gold, more than England has, and we really need it here, and it is tied up by law in some cases, and necessity in others, they are willing now to make some sort of arrangement by which this government, on return of the—I mean the directors of the Bank of England will liquidate their obligations and take our short-term notes, or something of that sort.

I am sorry to say I can't—I am not informed as to the results of the conference.

They are also perfectly willing to stimulate cotton exports to England.

Yes. Sir George Paish intimated as much as that to me. Because, you see, their factories presently will be standing still unless the cotton begins to be shipped.

I know it has also been suggested, Mr. President, that the British factories would pay for a very large amount of American cotton immediately, and store it, in order to reduce the balance of trade. Have you heard anything of that sort?

No, I haven't. I only heard somebody—I have forgotten who it was now—say that of course if the price of cotton was very low, they would naturally buy as much as possible at a low price and store it against the needs of another season.

Have they some cotton on hand?

I don't know. Of course they have a little. I don't know how much.

The trouble about buying cotton, I understand, on the other hand, is that nobody knows what its bedrock price is, because it may go still lower.

Yes. That's the trouble with everybody. I really don't see why that should hold anybody back, because no matter what price they buy at now, they are going to get high prices for the goods, so that even the man that bought it at a relatively high price would certainly cover his operations, though he would not make as large a margin of profit as the man who bought at the lower price.

Mr. President, after the cotton shipments—of course that will consume a large part of this debt that the United States owes England. It won't balance it. And there is some intimation that England would be willing to take some short-term securities for the balance. Can you give us any idea of the nature of those securities?

No, sir.

Mr. President, I understand that a letter was read on the floor of the House this morning, from you, asking that the warehouse bill be passed before the adjournment.[10] I was wondering whether the same thing would apply to that last amendment of the currency act?[11]

I ought to have included that in the letter. In hurriedly writing it, I omitted it. I do stand for that. It would certainly facilitate other things we are trying to do to help the cotton situation in the South.

[Question not written down by Swem.]

Expect so. I have never been in Washington when Congress adjourned and, therefore, I don't know what the possibilities are.

The President usually goes over to the Capitol.

I shall go, of course, and sign bills, as soon as the hour is set.

Has that committee been appointed?

[1] The British seized the *John D. Rockefeller*, a tanker owned by the Standard Oil Company, in early September. The State Department protested against its capture on October 21, and the ship was released on October 22. See the *New York Times*, Oct. 22, 1914, and *FR, 1914-WWS*, pp. 324-25.
[2] See above, Oct. 19, 1914.
[3] Villa created a stir by appearing personally at Aguascalientes on October 17. See Hill, *Emissaries to a Revolution*, p. 265.
[4] That is, the withdrawal of American troops from Veracruz.
[5] The Commission for the Relief of Belgium, to be directed by Herbert Clark Hoover, was at this time being created. See Herbert C. Hoover, *An American Epic*, 4 vols. (Chicago, Ill., 1959-64), I, *Introduction: The Relief of Belgium and Northern France, 1914-1930*, 1-90, and the *New York Times*, Oct. 22, 1914.
[6] Sharp had been sent to France to replace Herrick as American Ambassador.
[7] Because the Germans had driven near Paris, the capital had been moved to Bordeaux.

[8] Senator Atlee Pomerene, Democrat of Ohio.

[9] Representative George Farmer Burgess, Democrat of Texas.

[10] Representative Henry read the letter from Wilson in the House on October 22. See the *New York Times*, Oct. 23, 1914, and WW to Henry, Oct. 22, 1914, printed in *PWW*, Vol. 31, p. 205.

[11] A reference to S. 6505, a bill to amend Sections 16 and 19 of the Federal Reserve Act. This bill would have made rediscount facilities available immediately instead of after three years. Its supporters argued that it would strengthen reserve banks in the cotton- and tobacco-growing states and expand credit facilities in the South. The bill died in the House. See *Cong. Record*, 63d Cong., 2d sess., pp. 16945-53, and 63d Cong., 3d sess., pp. 31-33.

Oct. 26, 1914

Mr. President, do you think that the various developments of recent days have to some extent cleared up the cotton situation so as to obviate the necessity of emergency legislation?[1]

Yes, I do. I thought all along it was likely to clear up. Not, of course, completely. The only way to restore the cotton situation is to stop the war; but the most that could be done financially to help the situation is in course of being done, and every day makes me more certain that that is true.

Have we now virtually a clear market in Europe? There is a story this morning about the willingness of Great Britain to let cotton go into Germany.[2]

I had not heard of that feature of it. You see, it is an absolutely necessary thing, and, as it happens, it heads the list of the things that are not contraband, and there is every reason why all the ports possible should be opened to it, and I think they will be.

With Great Britain not interfering with the shipment of cotton and the possibility of getting cotton into Germany, wouldn't that furnish a very marked measure of relief?

I should think so, though I am not informed as to the mills in Germany—as to just how far they are being operated—but I should assume that that would make a great deal of difference.

As a matter of fact, the cotton exports are already increasing, are they not?

Yes, but increasing by a very small figure.

Mr. President, can you give us any clear insight into the Mexican situation today other than the newspaper accounts furnish?[3]

I haven't seen the morning papers; being away on Saturday,[4] I have been clearing my desk at the house. What is the latest news?

The newspaper accounts this morning indicate further disturbances between Carranza and Villa.

I am sorry to say I haven't any light to throw on that at present.

Is there anything you can tell about the Colorado situation, Mr. President?

There is no new development there that I know of.

Are there any plans about removing the federal troops?

Not at present; no sir.

Mr. President, do you expect to get to the appointment of the commissioners on the Plaza awards soon?[5]

I am going to take that up the very first moment I can. I haven't had time yet to read the resolution in its final form, though I signed it. I just know in a general way what it provides. There are to be three commissioners?

Yes, sir. I suppose you will discuss it with the Attorney General.

Yes, I will.

Is there anything unsigned, Mr. President?[6]

No, sir, nothing at all that I have heard of. You see, when they thought they were adjourning on Thursday I rushed in and signed everything in sight, and they haven't had a quorum since then to pass anything else.

Mr. President, is there anything new you can tell us about the tank steamer *Brindilla* belonging to the Standard Oil Company?

No, except that that matter is being handled in a very friendly way, and that it will come out all right.

Is there any information to show that the change-of-registry question is being considered in connection with the release of the *Brindilla*?

No, I think not.

So far as you know, it is not being considered in this case?

I think not. That is my information, but I am not perfectly clear on that.

Mr. President, have you any plans for getting early consideration of some of the leftover legislation, like the immigration bill and the seamen's bill?

I am going to discuss, after the election, of course, when I can get hold of them, with the leaders of the Senate what program will be possible. Of course, we don't want to attempt an impossible number of bills at the short session, because the Senate will have only the time before it receives the appropriation bills from the House. I should say at a guess that would be until about the first of February, perhaps.

Can you say as to whether the bills which have passed either one or both of the houses will have precedence over the bills which have not been taken up at all; take, for instance, the seamen's bill?

We will have to consider what their order of importance is. You see, there is a very important general leasing bill, the general dam bill, and a number of large measures of that sort of general policy; and the Philippines bill, which would naturally occupy the foreground.

You feel fairly certain that they will get away on the fourth of March next?

They have got to. There is a constitutional limitation. They cannot sit longer than noon on the fourth of March.

Mr. President, have you any information from the South to the effect that they share the hopeful feeling with regard to the cotton situation that you just expressed?

I haven't any information at all one way or the other from the South, but I have received a variety of impressions. I haven't found businessmen from the South very deeply apprehensive about the situation. It may be that those who were apprehensive did not come to me, but those who did, and a good many people who were apprehensive did come to me, were not businessmen, strangely enough.

There is cash available to cover all safe loans in the South, isn't there?

Oh, yes. The trouble is not the amount of money available, but the basis on which it is to be loaned. Of course, you have to ascertain a probable price for cotton before you can establish a basis for credit.

What is the status in your mind of the ship-purchase proposition?

Why, it hasn't any different status in my mind from that in your mind. It hasn't been brought up yet.

Is it going ahead?

I expect it to, unless there is something else of greater importance. As I just said, in a short session precedence is given to those things that are of the greatest consequence.

Mr. President, there was something said about devising a navigation law at the time these emergency measures were taken up?

That is quite out of the question.

[1] The Federal Reserve Board gave its approval on October 24 to the creation of a cotton loan fund of $135,000,000 to assist cotton growers in the war emergency. See the *New York Times*, Oct. 25, 1914, and Link, *Struggle for Neutrality*, pp. 99-100.

[2] Sir Edward Grey announced on October 26 that "cotton is not contraband and so far as the British Government is concerned will not be." See the *New York Times*, Oct. 26-27, 1914; Link, *Struggle for Neutrality*, p. 131; and the British Ambassador to the Acting Secretary of State [Robert Lansing], Oct. 26, 1914, in *FR, 1914-WWS*, p. 290.

[3] The armies of Carranza and Villa were reported fighting near Parral. See the *New York Times*, Oct. 26, 1914.

[4] Wilson had been in Pittsburgh.

[5] The Plaza awards were made to holders of property condemned for the construction of Union Station Plaza in Washington. The original awards had been excessively high in Wilson's opinion, and a commission was being created to revise them. See the *Washington Post*, March 19, 1914.

[6] Congress adjourned on October 24.

Nov. 10, 1914

Mr. President, have you any personal comment to make on the election?[1]

No, sir. It is very evident that the Democrats are retaining control of the government.

As the head of the party, Mr. President, wouldn't you like to make some more extensive comments than that?

No, sir. My comment will, I hope, be the action of the next two years. I am very much more interested in doing things than in talking about them.

Can you explain the embargo situation to us, Mr. President?[2]

Which embargo?

With reference to the British embargo on exports from her colonies. There is a very strong effort to get wool shipments to the United States.

No. I can't explain that any further than it has been in the public prints. Because, of course, that is domestic policy and there is no reason why she should explain it to us.

There are very strong efforts made to get the State Department to take some action, such action as it could. It is a question as to whether anything could be done.

It would naturally be. Of course, if anything were done, it would be only by influence. We have no rights in the matter.

Mr. President, have you given any thought to the trade commission appointments?

Yes, sir, I have given a great deal. I haven't made any selections yet.

There is a report in the morning papers that Mr. Redfield[3] is to be one.

If you had had the experience I have, you wouldn't believe what you see in the papers. I mean about matters of that sort. Of course, there will be speculation of all sorts, but I have made no selections.

There is a point of view that no member of the present House can be appointed.

Certainly. Until after the fourth of March. The Constitution exempts them during the term they were elected.[4]

I ask because Mr. Palmer's name has been mentioned.

To tell the truth, I haven't noticed whose names have been mentioned in the papers because that, of course, is pure speculation. I only smile when I learn that I am considering some name that I am then hearing of for the first time.

Mr. President, when do you hope to send those names to the Senate?

Just as soon after the convening of Congress as possible.

Mr. President, Mr. Gardner this morning—yesterday—in discussing his resolution,[5] said that there would be a number of civilians who would testify at the hearings on the resolution, and that there would be many army and navy officers, provided their departments let them. Can you say anything?

I can't say anything. Hypothetical questions I can't answer.

Mr. President, how about the Plaza commission?[6]

I hope to have that within a day or two.

Mr. President, have the apparent difficulties among the members of the Philippines Commission been brought to your attention?[7]

I began to read about them in the paper this morning. That was the first time. I don't understand that there are any difficulties except such as naturally arise in any case where there may be some conflict of jurisdiction, and that has to be settled by the superior authority, that is all.

Mr. President, could you tell us what the status is of Mr. Herrick, and also the status of Mr. Sharp in Paris?

In what respect?

What I have in mind is the report that Mr. Herrick is going to remain there as Ambassador.

That would be impossible, of course, because we can't reverse the appointment and the confirmation. We have wished to leave him there as long as he could be serviceable to the French government.

Mr. President, doesn't he hold until his successor succeeds him?

Until his successor presents his credentials.

He hasn't done so yet?

No.

Mr. President, there is no thirty-day limit after confirmation, or anything of that sort?

Not that I know of.

Mr. President, is there anything you can tell us with reference to your program?

No, sir. Nothing new. Of course, there is a bit of unfinished business, as you know.

You have said something about that soon after the Congress adjourned.

I want to make a definite recommendation with regard to that in my Annual Message.

Mr. President, could you say whether or not you expect the immigration—the enactment of the immigration legislation at this session?

I don't know of any prospects for it. You see, this is a desperately brief session.

The—

You mean that—

The government support for roads?[8]

Oh, yes.

Mr. President, have you had estimates from any of the departments yet on which to base their appropriation bills?

I have had most of them.

Are they more than they were last year?

Most of them are lower. Several of them are necessarily higher because of the new things that Congress has mandated, which has to be done. But except where functions have been increased, I think there is no increase. There is a slight increase, I believe, in the State Department's estimate, because of the unusual things that it has been necessary for it to do.

Has there been any increase in the naval appropriations?

No, sir.

The program is going to include the conservation bills?

Yes, of course.

Are you likely to give any special attention to District matters, District affairs, in the next two years?

I can't say. I can only think of the front of the stage. The play is very complicated.

Are you committed to any particular program for naval construction for the coming year?

No, sir, just the particular changes outlined in the Secretary's report.

That is a two-battleship program?

It has a great many details, and until the Secretary's report is published, I think I shall reserve comment upon it.

Mr. President, there is not likely to be any reduction in the naval construction program of last year?

We have set out our program which, so far as I expect, will not be broken.

Do you expect the cotton and warehouse bills this winter?

You are asking me in detail what you asked me in general a moment ago, and I think that's not quite fair.

Mr. President, the Mexican situation?

No, sir. I wish I could. I feel confident it will work out.

Did you ever get an explanation of that report that marines were landed in Acapulco?[9]

No. Just that it was not so, if that is an explanation.

Have you determined, Mr. President, on the successor of General Wotherspoon as Chief of Staff?[10]

No, sir. I will, in two or three days.

[1] In the state and congressional elections of November 3, 1914, Democrats lost many of the gains that they had made in 1912. The Democratic majority in the House was reduced from seventy-three to twenty-five, and Republican candidates won in a number of key states. See the *New York Times*, Nov. 4-5, 1914, and Link, *The New Freedom*, pp. 468-69.

[2] The British embargo prohibited the shipment of wool from the colonies to any place but England. See the *New York Times*, Nov. 21, 1914, and the Secretary of the National Association of Wool Manufacturers [Winthrop Lippitt Marvin] to the Secretary of State, Oct. 29, 1914, in *FR, 1914-WWS*, p. 419.

[3] Secretary of Commerce William Cox Redfield.

[4] Article 1, Section 6, of the United States Constitution forbids the appointment of any member of Congress "during the time for which he was elected" to any office created during that time.

[5] See above, Oct. 15, 1914.

[6] See above, Oct. 26, 1914.

[7] The *New York Times*, November 9, 1914, reported that Governor General Harrison was in a dispute with Clinton L. Riggs, Secretary of Commerce and Police, over the implementation of Wilson's new policy for the Philippine Islands.

[8] The American Road Conference, meeting in Atlanta, called for federal assistance to the construction and maintenance of highways. See *ibid.*, Nov. 10-11, 1914.

[9] *Ibid.*, November 10, 1914, reported that United States marines had been landed at Acapulco to protect foreign inhabitants endangered by the Mexican Revolution.

[10] The army Chief of Staff, Maj. Gen. William Wallace Wotherspoon, was succeeded by Brig. Gen. Hugh Lenox Scott, who had been his assistant. See *ibid.*, Nov. 8, 1914.

Nov. 17, 1914

What are the facts in Mexico, Mr. President?

I don't know anything more than I take it for granted you already know. We have understood that General Carranza is willing to retire on the terms named,[1] but we haven't heard directly from him, of course, and are only receiving the reports that are gathered in the northern part of Mexico.

Do you prefer to hear from him directly?

I don't expect to hear from him directly.

Is there intimation, Mr. President, with regard to the information on Villa?

None that hasn't come direct to you.

So that, so far as you know, there hasn't been any agreement between Carranza and Villa, though the dispatches would seem to indicate that there had been, not between them but each of them communicating with the new Provisional President[2]—whatever his name is. I can't pronounce it. Has the new Provisional President asked this government to recognize him? Do you so regard that letter, that telegram?[3]

No. There's no suggestion of that in that message.

Well then, Mr. President, under the circumstances, it is not quite clear, is it, as to whom we will turn over the city of Veracruz?[4]

No. But of course that is one situation that is not our responsibility, now that we have the promises that nobody will be molested who shouldn't be.

You don't look for a condition of anarchy, then, even though—

No. No, sir. You see, as a matter of fact, as we understand it, the men who were formerly in civil office are still there. They can merely resume their functions.

The customs which we have collected will remain in our custody?

Until there is some authority to turn them over to.

There is one story that they would be shipped to France?

No. They will be shipped to the Mexican government, when there is one.

There is less danger of turning over Veracruz than turning over the customs.

You see, one of the things we wanted assurance about was that the customs which we have collected wouldn't be collected all over again.

That assurance has been given?

Yes, that assurance has been given.

Mr. President, have you replied to the telegram of the new Provisional President?[5]

No. That was, as a matter of fact, addressed to the Secretary of State, conveying these assurances to the—

Mr. President, what is the purpose of an inquiry into the alleged breach of neutrality on the part of the Latin American countries?[6]

I don't understand that we have made any inquiry.

I so understood from the statement attributed to Mr. Bryan this morning.

I saw that, but I haven't had a chance to see Mr. Bryan.
But I took that merely to mean that the Ministers of those governments had gotten wind of this and merely informed Mr. Bryan. I don't know of any inquiry that this government has made.

It hasn't made it, but I thought that they made it clear that it has been directed.

I don't think it does make it clear. At any rate, I don't know of any circumstance to justify that inference.

Our interest in the neutrality of these countries is more or less of an academic character?

Yes. Literally speaking, it is none of our business. But it is evident from what you are referring to in the papers this morning that they are very anxious to have it known that they are doing their very best to maintain neutrality, just as we are. And of course we have the interests of a neighbor, and genuine friendship, that that should be the case.

That statement, in itself, if it is accurate, would just about satisfy the situation then, wouldn't it?

I think so. I hope so.

Mr. President, have you requested any conference with the legislative leaders concerning the program?

No, I haven't, simply because they have had so late a vacation that I have hesitated to bring them back here for a conference. Senator Kern was in the other day, and I had a few words with him.

It says in some of the newspapers that Mr. Gerard may retire from his position as Ambassador because he feels that his influence has been, to some extent, impaired by virtue of his defeat in New York.[7]

That is somebody's ingenious invention. There is nothing in that at all.

Mr. President, have you taken up yet the question of appointing a committee to have charge of arranging Belgian relief?

I am taking it up before rejecting it. I have been urged to name some person through whom they might communicate with one another, or something of that sort. I haven't entirely rejected that idea. You see, there are a good many groups, and so forth, and it may be necessary to do something to facilitate our common action, but what that is hasn't yet become known.

Mr. President, has any suggestion been made to change the immigration law, so far as Belgian immigration in the near future is concerned?

No, sir. No such suggestion has reached me. There are a good many efforts being made to get Belgian refugees places of settlement. In the South I know of some efforts, and elsewhere.

Does that necessitate any legislation?

No. My attention has not been called to any feature of the law that would be violated.

Mr. President, is it not true that most of the refugees, so far, have come from the cities, and are in the class of engineers, artisans, and workers in the trades, rather than farmers?[8]

I think not. At any rate, not if we are to credit the estimates of the number of those who are out of employment and have no shelter or home. I don't know what the total population of Belgium is. A reporter told me it was seven million, and it was estimated at one time that as many as five million of the seven million were homeless. I sincerely hope that is an exaggeration. But if anything like half of the population are homeless, that would mean, of course, that the wealthy population was involved very largely indeed.

Have the immigration officers much discretion with regard to the admission of paupers, as these people virtually are?[9]

They have practically no discretion with regard to the definite provisions of the law. Now I will have to speak with a very vague knowledge of the law, to tell you the truth, but my impression is that the pauper provision merely means that if the commissioners, the immigration authorities, are convinced that there is no one to take care of these people, and that they are likely to become a public charge, that they must not admit them. I take it that if they are not, and if you know that they are going to be placed and that they will not become a public charge, you are at liberty to admit them. But I must repeat that that is spoken with only a vague knowledge of what the law is.

These employment bureaus are in operation at the various ports, and it seems that they might be used.

Engaging them if they got over here. They would not have the right to bring them over under contract.

Mr. President, do you know of any general movement to provide work for them?

No general movement I know of. Several local movements.

Mr. President, has Japan expressed any uneasiness on account of the election of legislators in San Francisco, California, who are reputed to be hostile to their aspirations there?

No. Some apprehension was expressed during the campaign because of the apparent effort to revive the land issue out there, but I could not follow the thing very carefully in any one place. But it seems that it has subsided—that attempt to revive the agitation has subsided.

Can you report progress on the trade commission, Mr. President?

Not a great deal, but things will crystallize suddenly, I hope, when I get the whole field looked over. I can't afford to make a mistake on that.

Can you tell us anything about—

I can't tell you anything new. It[10] started yesterday.

Will the effect on the system be unduly against the Sub-Treasuries?[11]

None that I know of.

Won't it put the money into the Federal Reserve banks instead of into the Sub-Treasury?

The Secretary of the Treasury is so authorized under it. It is now in the Sub-Treasury.

That will be the effect, or will it not?

That is left, as I understand it, to the discretion of the Secretary.

There is now about seventy million in the various Sub-Treasuries, and I thought perhaps all of that would be put in the Federal Reserve banks.

I haven't heard the Secretary of the Treasury say what his action would be.

If they held all the cash, it would make the Sub-Treasuries' practically nil.

They are sometimes, only more so.

Mr. President, there is a report in one of the morning papers that inquiries had been sent to our Ambassador in London to discover who was responsible for the mining of the North Sea.[12]

Of course he will have to inquire who was responsible. The question would seem to be who was responsible for starting it rather than who is doing it now.

Mr. President, has the cotton situation improved in recent weeks?

I was reading in this morning's papers that conditions in the cotton exchanges, which opened yesterday, were very encouraging;[13] some seven and three quarters and some figures still over that. Eight and a fraction. The paper stated that that was quite as good as had often happened in normal times. I mean, it was no worse—it has often happened in normal times.

Well, do you receive any direct reports as to whether the situation has improved?

I haven't received anything one way or the other.

You don't know whether Mr. Henry, or those who are as interested, I should say, as he is, intends to renew the agitation?

I don't know anything about that.

There is an intimation that they might insist upon a preferential position for their bill, thereby threatening some of the appropriation measures?

That is not in their hands. That is in the hands of the House of Representatives itself.

Yes, but they are part of the House.

They will have to find out how big a part.

Is there anything new on the Colorado situation?

No, nothing at all.

Mr. President, have you had any conferences with any members of the Committee on Rivers and Harbors, relating to this new rivers and harbors bill?

Mr. Sparkman,[14] the chairman, came to see me some three weeks ago, and we had a very brief talk about it, just to talk over the general policy about it. We didn't come to any conclusion. It was just an exchange of ideas.

[1] On November 16, Carranza agreed to resign provided both he and Villa left the country and a convention would later assemble in Mexico City to elect a new Provisional President. See the *New York Times*, Nov. 17, 1914, and Link, *Struggle for Neutrality*, pp. 256-57.

[2] Eulalio Gutiérrez, who had been elected Provisional President by the Aguascalientes Convention on November 1. Gutiérrez was a *Carrancista* but was acceptable to the *Villistas* and *Zapatistas*.

[3] Gutiérrez sent a telegram on November 13 announcing his assumption of power and asking for good relations with the United States. He did not formally request recognition. His telegram is printed in *FR, 1914*, pp. 620-21.

[4] American forces left Veracruz on November 23, 1914.

[5] Bryan sent congratulations to Gutiérrez on November 16. It is printed in *FR, 1914*, p. 622.

[6] Great Britain and France complained on November 15 of breaches of neutrality by Ecuador and Colombia which included permitting Germany to use wireless stations and to supply German warships with coal. Bryan stated that the United States would not intervene. See the *New York Times*, Nov. 17, 1914, and the Secretary of State to the Chargé d'Affaires in Colombia [Leland Harrison] and the Minister in Ecuador [Charles S. Hartman], Nov. 14, 1914, in *FR, 1914-WWS*, p. 686.

[7] Gerard, the Democratic nominee for Senator in New York, was defeated in the election of November 3 by the Republican, James Wolcott Wadsworth. See the *New York Times*, Nov. 4, 1914.

[8] The Rev. J. F. Stillemans, head of the Belgian Relief Committee, issued a statement on November 16 about the impracticality of settling Belgian refugees on farms in the United States. See *ibid.*, Nov. 17, 1914.

[9] The Immigration Act of 1882 denied admission to paupers or anyone likely to become a public charge.

[10] That is, the Federal Reserve System.

[11] The Sub-Treasury System, established in 1846, provided for the conduct of Treasury business in major cities throughout the United States. The Sub-Treasuries would be weakened if Treasury funds were deposited in the Federal Reserve banks. See Willis, *Federal Reserve System*, pp. 1130-40.

[12] The British government had announced that, after November 5, the entire North Sea would become a war zone and mines would be sowed there. It argued that this had been made necessary by the indiscriminate laying of mines by Germany in the area. See the *New York Times*, Nov. 17-18, 1914; Link, *Struggle for Neutrality*, pp. 131-32; and the British Ambassador to the Secretary of State, Nov. 3, 1914, in *FR, 1914-WWS*, pp. 463-64.

[13] The New York Cotton Exchange reopened November 16. See the *New York Times*, Nov. 17, 1914.

[14] Representative Stephen Milancthon Sparkman, Democrat of Florida, chairman of the House Rivers and Harbors Committee.

Nov. 24, 1914

I see that somebody has been unfailing in finding interesting things for me to do. I don't think of half the things to do that other people think of. I understand that I am going to visit the Senate in secret session, and introduce the members of the cabinet in the House, and a wealth of interesting things I have not heard of, I suppose, in addition to the conference of neutrals.[1]

Now that they have been suggested to you, how do they appeal to you?

I am like the Scotch caddie. You remember the old caddie. He was caddying for a person who was a very poor player; at least he was playing very badly that day. And he nodded in confidence, and he said, "I daresay you have seen a worse player on this course?" The old fellow didn't say anything, so he thought he hadn't heard. He repeated, "I daresay you have seen a worse player on this course?" The old caddie said, "I heard you the first time. I was thinking!"

Somebody in this morning's paper recalled the fact that in one of your early books,[2] Mr. President, you favored the budget system, and suggested that the Secretary of the Treasury should be in the House, at least to explain the appropriations.

Well, as a matter of fact, that is an old story. Though very few people seem to remember, committees of the Senate themselves have, I believe, three times—twice certainly—reported in favor of that, that is, in favor of high cabinet officers being given seats— the right to be present in the houses and take part in the debate, answering questions, though of course not to vote. Nothing but the Constitution can give them that.

It has not been voted on in the Senate?

I believe one of the reports that I recall was made by a committee of which, I believe, Senator Pendleton[3] was chairman, so it is not a new matter. It is a matter which has been talked about intermittently for thirty years, to my certain recollection.

Senator Stone, in the *Star* yesterday, suggested in an interview, after having been quoted elsewhere, he said he thought it would be a good idea for the President to come into a session to explain international diplomatic subjects; other than that, he did not think it was good.

The question really has not been raised. As a matter of fact, it is not going to be, so far as I know.

Isn't it a fact, Mr. President, that President Washington went to an executive session?[4]

Oh, yes. He went to several.

Have you anything from Mexico this morning?

Yes, I have just read several telegrams, all of which are reassuring, I mean, as to the preservation of order and the control of any forces that might give foreigners trouble.

Mr. President, what, in your opinion, has been the big thing achieved by the taking and the evacuation of Veracruz?

Well now, do you mean my own? If I speak to you, not for publication only, that is the only way I can speak about it, because in the first place we are in there because of the action of a naval officer. Understand that we didn't go on the choice of the administration, strictly speaking; but a situation arose that made it necessary for the maintenance of the dignity of the United States that we should take some decisive step; and the main thing to accomplish was a vital thing. We got Huerta. That was the end of Huerta. That was what I had in mind. It could not be done without taking Veracruz. It could not be done without some decisive step, to show the Mexican people that he was all bluff, that he was just composed of bluff and show; and that is all they ever got.

That part is not for publication. I am sure I can trust you. But it is important that it should guide your thought in the matter, because apparently we are in there for nothing in particular, and came in for nothing in particular, and I don't wonder that people who don't look beneath the surface couldn't see that the objective was to finish Huerta, and that was accomplished. The very important thing, the thing I have got at heart now, is to leave those people free to settle their own concerns, under the principle that it's nobody else's business.

Now, Huerta was not the Mexican people. He did not represent any part of them. He did not represent any part. He was nothing but a "plug ugly," working for himself. And the reason that the troops did not withdraw immediately after he was got rid of was that things were hanging at such an uneven balance that nobody had taken charge; that is, nobody was ready to take charge of things at Mexico City. I have said all along that I have reason to feel confident, as I do feel confident, that nothing will go seriously wrong with Mexico City, so far as the interests we are surely responsible for are concerned. Of course, we can't protect Mexican citizens. That is another matter. That is the whole thing. I am very glad, in confidence, to let you know just what is in it.

Mr. President, upon what basis do these foreign nations from time to time ask us to look out for their interests there? I mean, for instance, yesterday the French and British Ambassadors made inquiries and several days ago the

Spanish Ambassador asked us about protection of Spanish citizens, and we gave them some reassuring information. Are we assuming that task?[5]

Not exactly, no. I think that it is simply a recognition on the part of some countries, without any suggestion from us, that we are Mexico's nearest friend, that we are the neighbors who can—the only powerful neighbor who could be looked to—to exercise influence in such matters. I think that is the whole of the truth. They are a long way off. They would find us, in most instances, doing what we could, and perhaps doing it easily. At any rate, more easily doing it—that is all there is to it.

All they ask us is just to use our good offices, not to attempt to dictate in any way to Mexico how she should act?

I think what they really expect is this: that any representations we make to Mexico, she will naturally feel are the most important that could be made to her. I think that is all.

Mr. President, have you considered the proposal, and its feasibility, of the American Federation of Labor, to place the coal mines under federal receiverships?[6]

That suggestion was made to me; and Mr. Wilson, the Secretary of Labor asked, I believe, the Solicitor of the Department[7] about it. There is no precedent in law for any such action. So, without any, I didn't take it up.

Do you mean by that, that it is not being seriously considered at this time?

Oh, it couldn't be if it weren't legal.

You didn't say it was not.

I should say that there is no legal warrant for it in the precedents and in the decisions of the courts.

There was a report from [Denver] several days ago that Governor Ammons was considering sending you word asking you to remove the troops. Has that been received yet?[8]

No.

Mr. President, there is a report coming in this morning to the effect that a disagreement has occurred in the Federal Reserve Board during their consideration of the desirability of the bank deposits.

So I heard. We called up the Treasury Department, and there isn't a thing in it.

Anything new from Turkey?[9]

No. We got a dispatch about another matter from Mr. Morgenthau that was dated previous to the one we had received, the one I gave out about the *Tennessee* incident. I don't know what the trouble is in communications with Constantinople, but it apparently takes a week or ten days to send a message and get a reply. You see, it's nine days now since the incident, and we haven't heard anything since. We sent a message to Morgenthau, but evidently the whole thing is cleared up now as to exactly what happened.

Mr. President, can you give us any further information on the legislative program this winter?

No, sir. I am consulting as many people as I can get hold of as to a feasible program, in view of the message I am writing a few sentences at a time.

Do you expect to get some legislation besides the appropriation bills?

Yes. I think that the Senate will certainly complete legislation that was begun by the House.

The conservation bills?

I hope so.

Mr. President, did you receive a copy of a remarkable letter of Mr. Frank O. Smith of Maryland's Fifth District,[10] that was sent to everybody, in which he wants to sell to Great Britain what is called the panhandle of Alaska. He wants to sell that to Great Britain as an instance of a model concession, as an instance of the love of man for his fellow man, and in that way he wants to produce a very good feeling and in that way bring about Great Britain's—You were asked a moment ago about the budget program for Congress. Have you any decided views about that in the way of establishing a budget system?

I have very decided views, but one man's views have to become several men's views before they amount to anything. I haven't had a chance to consult with the leaders of Congress about what plan would be feasible, if any. We have had so many things to do that I have never touched on that except in a casual conversation.

Mr. President, a number of suggestions have recently been made that this would be an opportune time to establish a tariff board, for a scientific study of it.

That has been proposed ever since—the earliest I think is '79. It hasn't come to me in any tangible form.

Mr. President, did Senator Pomerene urge that Mr. Sharp speedily take the place of Ambassador Herrick?[11]

Not at all. Mr. Herrick had handled his post admirably, and it is so satisfactory to have somebody familiar with the situation that we have left him there just as long as it was legally possible to leave him there. You see, after the Senate has confirmed a successor, we are in a way taking the law into our own hands to postpone the substitution, and it has been done in constant consultation with Mr. Herrick and without any friction or splintering or anything of that sort. Mr. Herrick has been very anxious all along, you know, to be relieved.

Mr. President, as a result of your recent conference with the two Maryland Senators and Governor Warfield, is there any prospect of an adjustment?[12]

It seems to be the impression that Governor Warfield came to talk about federal patronage. He didn't mention—he didn't bring that subject up. He came about an entirely different matter, to tell me about experts—I suppose you would call it—that his company is getting up, a group of merchants and manufacturers, and university men and representatives of the various sides of our life to go to South America. That was the entire object of his visit. The other two gentlemen did speak about patronage, but we didn't propose or adopt a method.

Can you report on anything regarding the Interstate Commerce Commission?

Not as much as I should like to report. You see, when you are trying to find the very best men, you want to be very sure that you have found them.

Mr. President, have you been advised of the negotiations on the part of the Russians for the purchase of the *Minnesota*, the American ship?[13]

No, sir, I hadn't heard of it. We wouldn't be at liberty to sell a ship to a belligerent. I simply saw a report of that in the newspaper.

Mr. President, has the protest of Germany regarding contraband additions yesterday been brought to your attention?[14]

Nothing official. Through the newspapers.

Mr. President, several days ago there was a dispatch from Petrograd saying that there was an expectation over there that we would begin overtures for negotiation of a new commercial treaty?

No, sir. I don't know.

They had expected that we would do so, and I wondered if there was anything afoot?

Not so far as I know. Nothing official. Of course, we have been anxious all along to negotiate the treaty.

Mr. President, the Department of Commerce officials seem to think that the new registry law has resulted very satisfactorily in bringing in a large number of vessels under the American flag.[15] Will that have any effect on your wishes regarding the purchase of a number of ships?

That will depend. I haven't seen the results yet. I haven't seen the statistics. There are so many channels of trade in which we are in need of ships that we need a very great number. But I haven't received any recent information. For example, the last I heard— about five or six days ago—there were plenty of orders for cotton but no ships to send it in from the southern ports—for example, Galveston. They may be over it now, but when I last heard, that was the trouble.

[1] See the *New York Times*, Nov. 24, 1914.

[2] Woodrow Wilson, *Congressional Government* (Boston, 1885).

[3] Senator George Hunt Pendleton, Democrat of Ohio, in 1879 introduced a bill to give cabinet members a seat in Congress with the right to take part in debates. See Link, *Road to the White House*, pp. 18-19.

[4] Washington appeared before the Senate in the summer of 1789 to discuss a treaty being negotiated with the southern Indians. The experience was so unpleasant for the President that he did not appear again. See Andrew C. McLaughlin, *A Constitutional History of the United States* (New York, 1935), pp. 249-50.

[5] The British and French Ambassadors called at the State Department on November 23 to inquire about the protection of their citizens in Mexico during the renewed fighting there. See the *New York Times*, Nov. 24, 1914.

[6] The American Federation of Labor at its annual convention unanimously approved federal receivership for the coal mines if the Colorado owners refused to accept the President's plan of settlement. A delegation from the United Mine Workers, including John Philip White, president, Frank J. Hayes, vice-president, and William Green, secretary-treasurer, visited Wilson and presented this proposal on November 19. See *ibid.*, Nov. 19-20, 1914.

[7] John B. Densmore.

[8] Governor Ammons and Governor-elect George Alfred Carlson were reported on November 22 as favoring the removal of federal troops. See the *New York Times*, Nov. 23, 1914.

[9] A launch sent from U.S.S. *Tennessee* was fired upon by Turkish forts at the entrance of Smyrna harbor. Capt. Benton Clark Decker of the *Tennessee* demanded an explanation, as

did Ambassador Morgenthau. They were informed that the forts had been attempting to warn the launch of the presence of mines in the harbor. See *ibid.*, Nov. 18-19 and 22, 1914, and telegram from the Ambassador in Turkey, Nov. 17, 1914, in *FR, 1914-WWS*, pp. 771-72.

[10] Representative Frank Owens Smith, Democrat of Maryland. Smith was referring to the concession by Great Britain in the dispute between Alaska and Canada over the area known as the panhandle. In 1903, a Joint High Commission was formed to resolve the conflict, and the British commissioner, Lord Alverstone, voted for the American position. See Howard K. Beale, *Theodore Roosevelt and the Rise of America to World Power* (Baltimore, 1956), pp. 109-23.

[11] Herrick left France on November 28, 1914. See the *New York Times*, Nov. 29, 1914.

[12] Wilson's visitors were ex-Governor Edwin Warfield and Senators John Walter Smith and Blair Lee.

[13] Russia was negotiating for the purchase of the liner *Minnesota*, owned by the Great Northern Steamship Company. See the *Washington Post*, Nov. 22, 1914.

[14] Ambassador von Bernstorff made public on November 23 his government's earlier protest to neutrals about the treatment of contraband by England and France. The Germans claimed that their enemies were violating the Declaration of London and asked the neutrals to defend their rights. See the *New York Times*, Nov. 24, 1914, and the Ambassador in Germany to the Secretary of State, Oct. 21, 1914, in *FR, 1914-WWS*, pp. 263-65.

[15] See [Secretary of the Treasury and Secretary of Commerce] *Increased Ocean Transportation Rates, Letter from the Secretary of the Treasury and the Secretary of Commerce*, 63d Cong., 3d sess., Senate Document 673 (2 parts, Washington, 1914-15), pp. 17-19.

Dec. 1, 1914

Mr. President, have you got any word from Mr. Low and those other gentlemen, when they expect to come to Washington?[1]

No. There is no immediate occasion for them to come to Washington.

It was stated in one of the New York papers that they would be here.

It may be an arrangement they have made with the Department of Labor. There is no special occasion for their organizing immediately. Their appointment, you understand, had nothing to do with the present strike but with future difficulties.

Mr. President, could you explain what is to be done out there in Colorado, pending any action by this commission?

There is nothing to be done. Of course, I am waiting for an official announcement from the Governor of the state that he is ready to take over the guard, the militia there, to keep the peace that it is necessary to maintain.

As soon as he announces that, you will withdraw the federal troops?

I expect to.

What is the status of Congressman Gardner and his resolution? He is excited.

I don't determine his status. That is a matter for Congress, of course.

Do you expect to have a talk with him?

I hope I shall.[2]

Are you in general sympathetic or unsympathetic with his resolution?

I won't discuss that now.

Mr. President, some time ago, there was an intimation in different parts of the country for movements afoot to get Belgian farmers to come to this country. I think you spoke of having some knowledge of some such movement.

The only direct knowledge I have on that matter is that I had a visit from Mr. Hugh MacRae of North Carolina,[3] who has already been instrumental in bringing about some very interesting settlements of immigrants on lands in North Carolina, and he expressed a desire to cooperate, I believe, with other southern companies in taking care, in that way, of any Belgian immigrants who might— who were farmers and might wish to find settlements of that sort. That is the only knowledge I have of it.

And Belgians, or anybody else coming to this country, even though they were going to settle or take up farming, are all of them on the same basis as other immigrants coming here for the purpose of any kind of work? There could not be anything done, there is nothing in the law which would allow them to come in, any more than men of any other class?

No. There was no suggestion of discrimination in these plans.

I thought probably there could not be, under the law.

There could not be, so far as the terms of admission are concerned. Of course, farmers could voluntarily form themselves to take care of a particular class, if it comes to that.

Under the law, no immigrant can be assisted at the departure time; immigrants could be assisted after they got here. It would not be possible for philanthropic societies to pay the fare of immigrants?[4]

I can't, offhand, answer that.

The only provision I have in mind at present is that nobody can be brought

over with—under the contract to labor. I don't know of any other provision of
the law. I know that there was a discussion in certain states that wanted
farmers to come and settle, about the possibility of paying six thousand fares
of Belgian families, or other families in other countries who wanted to come;
and the question arose whether or not that would be against the law.

I don't think so. It constantly happens that the friends and relatives of immigrants send them the money to pay their passage
over.

There would be, perhaps, a violation, though, of the spirit of the contract labor
laws, and of course—

It may be, but I would refer that to the lawyers in the Labor
Department. I couldn't give an opinion that would be worth anything on that.

Mr. President, do you know whether any officials of the Department of Labor
have arranged to confer with the Belgian Consuls, or anyone else?

No, not so far as I know.

Mr. President, do you desire action on the Burnett bill this session?

You mean the immigration bill?

Yes.

I have no desire one way or the other about that.

Mr. President, is it a proper question to ask, Mr. Theodore Marburg, who was
formerly our Minister to Brussels, has an interview on Thursday, and he is
very active in Baltimore. Have you any information?[5]

So far as I know, he is merely coming to pay his respects upon
returning to this country.

Mr. President, are you giving any encouragement to the proposed amendment
of the Sherman law which would enable exporters to cooperate to meet the
competition of foreigners?

That has been brought to my attention a number of times—I
mean, that subject. I must say that my mind is straying on the
subject. I haven't yet satisfied myself with a judgment about it.
There are two very good sides to the argument.

Reports were published recently that you had made some informal, unofficial protests regarding the dropping of bombs in Europe. Could you tell us exactly what you did?[6]

Well, if your information is correct, perhaps the best thing to do would be not to discuss it.

I had no information on the subject.

I mean, if the information that is current in the newspapers. I didn't mean you.

Mr. President, could you give us any of the high spots of your coming message to Congress?[7]

No. I am afraid the light might fade from them if I test them beforehand.

Will it be a long message?

No. I hope not. I am trying to be moderate.

Anything from Mexico, Mr. President?

No. Mr. Tumulty says that there are dispatches he just referred to the State Department which are quite hopeful in character, so far as they show complete order in every place where foreigners might be concerned—in Veracruz and Mexico City.

Have you had any communication from Gutiérrez?

None whatever. Of course, you understand that it is better to be on your guard about the reports from Mexico. There are a very large number of our fellow citizens determined to have trouble down there, whether it exists or not, and the safe thing is not to believe anything you hear—from anybody.

Mr. President, have you had—I am curious—to consider suggestions from South American countries, with a view to establishing neutral zones?[8]

I have had an occasion merely in this passing way. It has been brought to my attention, and I have had a brief discussion of it with Mr. Lansing and also with the Secretary of State. But just what was feasible as to the way of acting on the suggestion, we hadn't formed a judgment about. Of course, it is highly, manifestly a thing in which the act would have to be voluntary on the part of the belligerents. Outside the three-mile limit, nobody has jurisdiction.

Mr. President, anything on the trade commission?

No, not yet.

Mr. President, do you favor the rivers and harbors bill at this coming session?

Well, there will be one, I suppose, whether I favor it or not. I thought the rivers and harbors bill was like a law of nature—it is an annual event.

You are to see Mr. Sparkman today?

I am to see him today. I don't know just what the scope of the discussion will be. He said he wanted to see me before Congress convenes.

Mr. President, there is a great deal of talk now on this question of a larger army and navy, in connection with this Gardner resolution. On the other hand, I notice this morning there are some mysterious high officials near the White House quoted as being opposed to it.[9]

So I saw. That interested me very much. I don't know anything about it. It is astonishing how much is going on inside the government that I learn from the newspapers.

Mr. President, are you able at this time to tell us something about your visit with Mr. van Dyke?[10]

That I think has no special purpose. Dr. van Dyke and I are old friends and colleagues, and he has come down to take lunch with me and report on things before lunch.

Have you any information that he bears a special message?

I have no information that he does. I think not.

Mr. President, is there still any time for this ship-purchase bill?

Oh, yes.

You have recently given that further thought, have you?

It is not a case of again but still. I have been thinking about it all the time.

The last time we talked with you about it, you said that you had no late information as to the number of ships.

That is true, but I am getting more and more information.

Do you expect to pass the Philippines bill at this session?

I certainly hope so.

Mr. President, have you taken up with the Senators the question of ratifying the Safety-at-Sea Convention?

Not recently, no.

Anything on the interstate trade commission?

No, there is nothing yet.

Mr. President, have you had any conference yet about the definite establishment of the legislative program at this session?

No. You see, the leaders haven't been in town. I don't know whether they are here yet or not.

It would have been done in the Senate, wouldn't it, except insofar as the House would take up the appropriations bill?

The shipping bill, for example, has not passed either house. The Philippines bill and the conservation bill and the general dam bill.

It won't be necessary to establish a definite program before the holidays?

I suppose not. The program is already settled in itself.

Mr. President, it has been suggested that there be an amendment to the ship-purchase bill under consideration, whereby the government would lend 100 per cent of the purchase cost of the ships to the operators.

That is an interesting suggestion. I hadn't entertained it.

---

[1] On November 29, Wilson appointed a commission to help settle the Colorado coal strike. Its members were Seth Low, president of the National Civic Federation; Charles Wilson Mills, a Pennsylvania coal-mine operator and principal owner of the Climax Coal Company; and

Patrick Gilday, president of the second district of the United Mine Workers. See the *New York Times*, Nov. 30, 1914, and Wilson's statement, printed in *PWW*, Vol. 31, pp. 367-69.

[2] Wilson invited Gardner to the White House on December 7 to ask him to abandon his resolution calling for a National Security Commission. See the *New York Times*, Dec. 8, 1914.

[3] Hugh MacRae of Wilmington, founder of Penderlea Homesteads in Pender County, N. C. See Paul K. Conkin, *Tomorrow a New World: The New Deal Community Program* (Ithaca, N. Y., 1959), pp. 277-80.

[4] The Contract Labor Act of 1885 forbade the importation of labor under contract or the advance payment of immigrants' fares.

[5] Theodore Marburg of Baltimore, executive head of the Maryland commission for relief of Belgium. See the *Washington Post*, Dec. 2, 1914.

[6] The reports appeared in the New York *World*, November 27, 1914, and the *Washington Post*, November 27, 1914. Secretary of State Bryan issued a statement on November 27 which described the inquiries as only requests for information about injuries to Americans. See the *New York Times*, Nov. 28, 1914.

[7] Wilson delivered his Annual Message on December 8. It is printed in *PWW*, Vol. 31, pp. 414-24.

[8] Argentina, Peru, Chile, and Uruguay had requested that the Pan American Union create neutral zones off the coasts of the Americas. This would require the removal of belligerent warships from the American waters thus designated. See the *New York Times*, Nov. 27-28, 1914, and the Chargé d'Affaires in Argentina [George L. Lorillard] to the Secretary of State, Nov. 18, 1914, in *FR, 1914-WWS*, p. 438.

[9] The *New York Times*, December 1, 1914, reported that Wilson was opposed to the Gardner resolution.

[10] Henry van Dyke, Minister to the Netherlands, visited Wilson on December 2 to discuss the prospects for peace in Europe. See *ibid.*, Dec. 3, 1914.

Dec. 8, 1914

Mr. President, Colonel Roosevelt, in his article on Mexico,[1] presented the testimony of certain individuals with regard to conditions that existed or are supposed to have existed there. Could you tell us, please, whether or not these persons made any private effort to submit this information to you?

I can't say, because I didn't read the article. I don't know whom it refers to.

Then you don't know, of course, as to whether or not it agrees with the reports that you have?

No. I didn't read it at all.

Mr. President, does your correspondence manifest any opposition to the military propaganda?

I should say it does.

We find some evidence in the office of the *Star*. The letters we are getting there regarding Veracruz shows something of that sort. I don't know if you—

It indicates it very clearly. Mr. Tumulty suggests that one of the indications is that article in last evening's New York *Evening Post* by Mr. Nicholas Murray Butler, president of Columbia.[2]

We have definitely in our possession a set of letters, all militant in tone, of men coming to this country to avoid military service abroad. The letter I forwarded to you, you might have more on that?

I haven't had anything of that particular sort, but my correspondence has been very emphatic on that point.

Is the suggestion of the Civic Federation for the creation of a national council of defense rather in line with Mr. Gardner's idea?[3]

I don't think it is in line with Mr. Gardner's idea. It is an idea not at all new. Of course, the whole question just at present is the proper method of action, and everybody wants the facts known very clearly and the policy discussed with the greatest frankness. But I think, for myself, there is a right way and a wrong way to go about it.

Do you regard the agitation as one part of the political campaign? Do you think it is a partisan matter?

Well, I wouldn't like to say. I wouldn't like to say, for this reason, gentlemen. Whenever the foreign relations of the country are concerned, I think party should be left out of the question. Even in comment. At any rate, by anybody who represents the government.

Mr. President, do you think there are many instances of outside influences being used in favor of the increase of armaments?

Well, no more evidences than words. I think you see, then, don't you, in short, what I am trying to say: I don't know any more about it than would be known by anybody. I have no special knowledge of it.

I meant, as taking the form of a lobby here? That is what this article I referred to charges.

As I said, I have no special information whatsoever.

Mr. President, I understand that Mr. Sullivan has made a request for an investigation on his behalf.[4] Are you taking any steps?

Yes, I have taken steps.

Will you make any comment, Mr. President, regarding the bill, I think, of Senator Hitchcock, prohibiting the selling of munitions of war to foreign governments?[5]

I haven't heard of it.

I think the bill was introduced yesterday.

I had just begun to look over the *Record*.

Mr. President, could you tell us what steps you are taking to investigate the Sullivan charges?

Well, I can't take the steps. I have instructed the department to take them.

Mr. President, there is a publication to the effect that orders are to go forward to the troops to withdraw from the Mexican border. Is that true?[6]

That is premature, although the fighting out there will probably be called off this morning.

Have you received any information about that?

I had heard they are going to meet to consider it.

Did you notice the charge of Senator William Smith that Carranza sent you an ultimatum, that if you didn't get out, there would be trouble down there?[7]

I did not.

Mr. President, is there anything with reference to the trade commission?

No. I am almost ashamed to say there is not. I have been working at it, but I haven't yet finished my list.

In that connection, Mr. President, have you anything to say on Mr. Fahey's visit?[8] He said that he had presented to you on behalf of the United States Chamber of Commerce the request that certain legislation be enacted amending the Sherman law, pending organization of the trade commission.

You must have misunderstood him. He didn't mention any legislation.

He said that he proposed an amendment to the Sherman law which would permit common selling agencies to be formed.

I beg your pardon—he did ask me if I had considered that subject, and I said I had and my own mind had been on both sides of it and I hadn't come to a conclusion.

That is what I understood him [to say].

He was chiefly talking about a banquet they were going to have, at which he was anxious I should be present; and discussing the general business conditions of the country as he had found them.[9]

Did he propose to you, Mr. President, that there should be at least one or two businessmen on the trade commission?

Perhaps he did. Everybody has. I don't remember individual cases. Very likely he did.

Mr. President, have you taken any action on the request of local merchants for a half-holiday?[10]

I have replied to them that I haven't any legal power. You know, as a matter of fact, the summer half-holidays are actually a breach of the law. I have followed that custom because not only was I winking at it, but Congress was winking at it. But Congress hasn't winked on this subject, and I am not at liberty to break the law.

May we have a copy of that letter, Mr. President?

Certainly you can.

Mr. President, there has been many a suggestion from Congress about the program we understood you wanted. One suggestion is, if it is necessary to have an extra session, it would not be necessary to have the appropriation bills.

I think that is true. I have conferred with Senator Kern and Mr. Underwood yesterday. Besides, you haven't heard the program yet.

We will get an intimation of that this afternoon?[11]

Yes, sir. A very plain intimation.

[1] Roosevelt's article, "Our Responsibility in Mexico," was harshly critical of Wilson's policy in Mexico and accused the administration of responsibility for creating some of the political turmoil there. See the *New York Times*, Dec. 6, 1914, Section IV, p. 1.

[2] In his article, "War Preparedness," Butler argued that the war in Europe disproved the thesis that armaments prevent war. In fact, he contended, agitation for preparedness was dangerous to the United States, and excessive fear of attacks might produce "not only an act of folly, but national suicide." See the New York *Evening Post*, Dec. 7, 1914.

[3] The National Civic Federation in its annual convention unanimously approved a resolution by Talcott Williams, editorial writer for the Philadelphia *Press*, for the creation of a council of national defense. See the *New York Times*, Dec. 6, 1914.

[4] Sullivan, American Minister to the Dominican Republic, asked for an investigation of charges that he had illegally used his influence for corrupt purposes. Wilson, on December

8, ordered Garrison to investigate. See *ibid.*, Dec. 9, 1914; Link, *The New Freedom*, pp. 108-109; and the New York *World*, Dec. 7, 1914.

⁵ The Hitchcock bill (S. 6688), introduced on December 7, would have widened the neutrality laws to forbid the sale of arms and ammunition for use against a country at peace with the United States. Similar bills were introduced by Representatives Richard Bartholdt, Republican of Missouri; Henry Vollmer, Republican of Iowa; and Charles Otto Lobeck, Democrat of Nebraska. See the *New York Times*, Dec. 8, 1914, and Link, *Struggle for Neutrality*, p. 164.

⁶ Because of casualties being suffered by American citizens across the border in Arizona, Governor George Wylie Paul Hunt asked for assistance. On December 8, Wilson ordered the cavalry back one mile from the border and moved artillery companies nearer to Mexico. See the *New York Times*, Dec. 8-9, 1914.

⁷ Senator William Alden Smith, Republican of Michigan, charged that Wilson had decided to remove American forces from Veracruz after Carranza had given him a twenty-four-hour ultimatum. See *ibid.*, Dec. 8, 1914.

⁸ John Henry Fahey of Boston, newspaper publisher and president of the United States Chamber of Commerce, 1914-1915.

⁹ Wilson addressed the meeting of the Chamber of Commerce at the New Willard Hotel on February 3, 1915. The address is printed in *PWW*, Vol. 32, pp. 178-87.

¹⁰ The Washington Retail Merchants Association requested two half-holidays in December to allow government workers to do Christmas shopping. See the *Washington Post*, Dec. 6, 1914.

¹¹ Wilson delivered his Annual Message to Congress at 12:30 on December 8. This press conference began at 10 a.m.

Dec. 15, 1914

Mr. President, can you tell us something about this Panama situation? There seems to be some misunderstanding as to what Colonel Goethals wants to do with these destroyers?[1]

There is no misunderstanding; we simply have not been informed. We are just waiting for information.

There is some suggestion of a possible conflict of jurisdiction between the War and Navy departments over the matter of wireless stations.[2]

Well, all I can say is that there are not going to be any conflicts of jurisdiction, because there is a clearinghouse. I have not heard of any difficulty of any kind, as a matter of fact.

Will hearings be held on the ship-purchase bill, Mr. President?

I don't know what the plans are. The matter is in the hands of both committees.

Mr. President, will that clearinghouse be able to settle the conflict of jurisdiction over the water-power bills; there seems to be quite a good deal of difficulty over the navigable rivers bill?[3]

Where is the difficulty? Difficulty on the Hill?

Mr. Lane advises one thing and Mr. Garrison advises another.

The clearinghouse for that is Congress. I am not the clearing-house for that.

You have urged the passage of them; I wondered if you had any views as to how you wanted the bills framed.

I want them framed the way they are.

It is said that certain concessions to the states have been made with the approval of the Secretary of War.

Made where, in the bills as they stand?

Yes.

All I know is that the bills as they passed the House were satisfactory to me. I don't mean that they are not susceptible of amendment; what I mean is I have no criticism of the bills as they passed the House.

We understood, Mr. President, that the Senate committee had laid aside the House bill and were proceeding on an entirely different basis.[4]

I had not heard of that.

Mr. President, is there anything you can say about the Mexican situation, especially at Naco?

There is nothing really to say. There is no change in the situation.

When do you expect to be able to name the trade commission?

I don't know, sir. I am doing my best.

Is it likely to be named before Christmas?

I can't say whether it is or not. I may finish any day; I don't know.

Mr. President, is there any truth in the report that you are opposed to Mr. Kitchin's leadership?[5]

Of course not. It is none of my business one way or the other. I haven't formed an opinion.

Mr. President, are you formulating any plan looking to the enactment of legislation which will give the United States—the federal government—greater authority in the enforcement of treaty obligations wherever state laws conflict?

No; I don't see that there is any occasion or room for legislation. The whole thing is a question of treaty obligation and of the relative authority of treaties and state laws. In other words, nothing that could be put in legislative form would affect the matter one way or the other.

Are you formulating any plan that would look to a more satisfactory relationship between the federal government and foreign governments in matters of that kind?

No, sir. It is a mere matter of handling the case in the most satisfactory way. No plan, it seems to me, could be worked out.

Isn't it true that if a state insists upon what it regards as its own sovereign rights, it can embarrass the government, and the government is practically without any recourse in the matter?

Yes, theoretically, that is true. You will notice, if you have the California case in mind, that the California legislation explicitly states that nothing in that law is to be considered in derogation of the treaty obligations of the United States.

I was thinking more of the Arizona case, the 80-per-cent bill.[6]

You see, so far as I am now informed, we have no treaty obligations involved there.

Under the most-favored-nation clause, they would probably demand the same rights as other countries.

There is no discrimination in the Arizona law between one [country] and another.

No, but certain countries have treaties with the United States which would make it impossible to carry out such an 80-per-cent restriction against them, whereas other countries with whom we have no direct treaty on that particular subject would have to look for their protection to the most-favored-nation clause.

I think that is only a theoretical case. My impression is that all nations affected stand on the same treaty basis, because we have been rather generous in our treaties with foreign countries, and they are all pretty much on the same basis.

Has any foreign country brought the matter to the attention of the administration?

Yes, I understand that several of them have called attention to the law for the purpose of inducing an inquiry, but there have been no formal protests of any kind, so far as I am informed.

Mr. President, we had an occasion in point in 1892, I think it was, when some Italians were killed in New Orleans,[7] and at that time, of course, it was supposed to be the duty of the state to have protected those men. That was the supposition, and the Italian government, as I remember, made protests, and the United States Government paid money to the widows and children of those Italians. The state did not pay it at all. I wondered if afterwards the state did not reimburse the federal government.

That is an entirely different case. That is one case that rests on the general obligation of the United States to protect the lives of citizens of foreign countries. That was not a case with regard to any legislation, as in Arizona.

I understand that, but I thought it was a case where in a way the federal government said to the state government, "If there is an indemnity, you should pay it," but the United States Government paid it out of some fund without any legislation of any kind.

I don't remember the details of that. I merely know that we did pay.

Do you know of any replies, Mr. President, that have been received from Ambassador Page with reference to a dispatch sent him asking about the license for the sailing ship *Aryan*, loaded with wool at Sydney, Australia, bound for America?[8]

I never heard of the case before.

That case was taken to the State Department, and I think the dispatch was sent; at least, assurance was given that it would be sent; and the point was made under the circumstances that a refusal to grant a license could be construed as a violation of the treaty of 1818.[9] I don't know whether the State Department has sent it with that view, but that was the point made by the attorney for the New England Woolen Company, which had bought the wool.

Those cases are never brought to me unless some difficulty of a diplomatic sort arises, and I don't know anything about it.

Mr. President, have you taken any stand with reference to the proposed legislation concerning an embargo on munitions of war?

No, sir.

Did you notice that Mr. Ridder makes rather a savage attack in that connection—Mr. Herman Ridder?[10]

No, I did not.

Have you expressed an opinion on the immigration bill that is pending?

Very often. Not in public though.

Have you anything to say in public now on it?

It is so full of items, good, bad, and indifferent, that I could not give a blanket opinion about it.

How about the literacy test, Mr. President?

It is very well known that I think the literacy test is a bad test. I mean is a test that does not test quality.

Is that objection so serious, Mr. President, as to overweigh the value of the good features of the bill?

I don't know. I have not got to that yet.

Mr. President, has the Secretary of State asked you to use your influence to get his Nicaraguan and Colombian treaties passed by this session?

No; I have several times expressed the hope that they would pass to the members of the committee—not since this session began, but in the last session. Yes, I did write to the chairman of the committee this session.

Have you decided yet, Mr. President, whether to withdraw the federal troops from Colorado?

No, sir; we are going to let things settle down there.

I understand that Governor Ammons is coming here during the latter part of the week. Will you see him?[11]

I hope I shall. I think he is not coming for the purpose of seeing me, but coming on some other errand.

Mr. President, a delegation saw you yesterday to ask you to change your proclamation allowing foreigners to become mates on American ships.[12]

I have read the memorandum they left with me. I don't think that was exactly their idea. Their idea was in case the present shipping bill passed we should give preference to American mates and captains.

Through legislation?

No, as I understand the memorandum, administratively; not by legislation, because, of course, there is nothing in the legislation to prevent it. There is nothing in the order which I issued under the recent legislation that would prevent it. That is a matter of administrative management.

That would have been done, anyway, Mr. President?

Oh, yes, that would have been done anyway.

Mr. President, do you favor any change in the London convention so that the seamen's bill should be enacted?[13]

I am just now seeking advice from legal quarters as to whether any change is necessary for the passage, at any rate, of most of the provisions of the seamen's bill. I have not yet got that advice. I have an idea that that convention, if properly construed, does not prevent additional legislation in the same spirit by any of the contracting parties. It is merely meant to establish a minimum, so that each nation will see that at least those provisions are lived up to, because they are above the standards of some of the nations which were present at the conference, though they are somewhat below our standards.

---

[1] Col. Goethals had requested on December 12 the dispatch of two destroyers to the Canal Zone to prevent breaches in the area's neutrality which included the use of wireless facilities and illegal activity by colliers and warships near the isthmus. The destroyers were sent. See the *New York Times*, Dec. 13-16, 1914.

[2] Wilson had ordered the Navy Department to oversee the operation of wireless facilities at Sayville and Tuckerton. See Link, *Struggle for Neutrality*, pp. 59-60.

[3] About this continuing controversy, see Link, *The New Freedom*, pp. 128-32.

[4] That is, the Senate committee was now considering the Shields bill (S. 6413), introduced in January 1915 by Senator John Knight Shields, Democrat of Tennessee.

[5] Representative Claude Kitchin of North Carolina, the likely Democratic floor leader in the next Congress, to succeed Oscar W. Underwood, who had been elected to the Senate. See the *New York Times*, Dec. 20, 1914.

[6] The Arizona law provided that no firm with more than five workers could employ more

than 20 per cent aliens. Great Britain and Italy protested against the measure. See *ibid.*, Dec. 15, 1914, and Jan. 7-8, 1915.

[7] See above, April 11, 1913.

[8] *Aryan* had contracted to carry wool purchased by Americans in Australia before the outbreak of the war. Although Secretary of State Bryan guaranteed that the wool would not be reexported, he did not succeed in winning its release. See correspondence in *FR, 1914-WWS*, pp. 426-28.

[9] The questioner meant the Treaty of Peace and Amity Between the United States and Great Britain of 1816. See David Hunter Miller, ed., *Treaties and Other International Acts of the United States of America*, 8 vols. (Washington, 1931-1948), II, 574-84.

[10] Publisher of the *New Yorker Staats-Zeitung*. See the excerpt from Ridder's editorial in the *Washington Post*, Dec. 15, 1914.

[11] Ammons visited Wilson on December 23.

[12] A delegation from the Masters' and Pilots' Association asked Wilson to support an amendment to the ship-purchase bill which would permit only Americans to be employed as officers on government-owned vessels. See the *Washington Post*, Dec. 15, 1914.

[13] The seamen's bill went beyond the London Safety-at-Sea Convention by freeing foreign sailors in American ports from bondage to their contracts. The bill's supporters wanted to place a reservation on the convention to bring the two items into conformity. This was accomplished in a reservation proposed by Senator John Sharp Williams, Democrat of Mississippi, stipulating that the United States had the right to abrogate treaties providing for the arrest of deserting seamen and to "impose upon all vessels in the waters of the United States, such higher standards of safety and such provisions for the health and comfort of passengers and immigrants as the United States shall enact for vessels of the United States." The convention was approved by the Senate with this reservation on December 16. See the *New York Times*, Dec. 15 and 17, 1914, and Link, *The New Freedom*, p. 272.

Dec. 22, 1914

Mr. President, there has been more or less discussion in the newspapers recently about appointments. Can you tell us anything about them?[1]

So I see. It has been chiefly in the newspapers, let me say. I have learned with a great deal of interest that there is a fight between me and the Senate. I wasn't aware of it. The Senate has a perfect right to reject any nominations it pleases. I have no criticism. You may be sure that nobody can get up a row on the matter of patronage. We are engaged in very large affairs in this government, much larger than patronage. You won't find any harangues in this office on that subject.

Well, Mr. President, isn't it a fact that the stories discussing a row between the Senate and the President are based on what it is expected you will do, rather than what has been done?

Exactly. Anybody is at liberty to speculate about what I will do, but I would advise you to wait and see. I don't know of any fight. It often gives me a very good idea of what not to do.

Mr. President, it is understood in the House that the ship-purchase bill is ready to put on the track and be slipped through when the proper moment comes.[2] Do you know anything about that?

Perhaps it would be more appropriate to say "put on the ways." No, I don't know, speaking seriously, just what are the details of the plan of handling the bill in the House, but I am glad to hear that it is ready to be launched.

There was a statement that you had a conference with Mr. Gregory last night about some of these appointments that are being discussed in the papers?

That is not true. It was about future appointments.

In that connection, Mr. President, what is the status of the Maryland appointments?

Why, simply that I haven't gotten them all ready.

You are waiting to send them in all at once?

I prefer to do that in every case, so as not to leave any speculation.

Is the Newlands river-regulation bill[3] a part of the conservation program?

Our judgment was, last night, that it would not be right to take it up this session, because of the shortness of time, and so forth. But last night's meeting was not a conference with regard to that; it was a talk covering the whole matter. Senator Newlands wanted Mr. Maxwell,[4] who was with him, to be heard, but the heads of the several departments, whose bureaus would be affected by such a bill, also wanted me to hear them. So it was a meeting to hear the whole case stated from his point of view and not to determine anything. That is the reason we had an evening meeting, so we could keep on as long as the subject lasted.

Can you say, Mr. President, whether you agreed to the main features of the proposition?

I never say those things until we get ready to launch a thing. It is not a matter of this session.

How is rural credits, Mr. President?

Well, I have nothing to add to the message on that.[5]

Well, is there likelihood of the bill being reported out?

I haven't heard that there was. I don't know.

Mr. President, a local committee saw you yesterday about this loan-shark law which has caused a great deal of talk in the District.[6]

I feel a great deal of interest in it. In New Jersey, when it was brought up, up there, I found time to read the papers and the bill that they left with me, but I have not done so here.

It has caused a lot of trouble. They have raised loans above the 10-per-cent mark.

We are bound—when people come directly and ask my support for additional legislation at this session, I feel bound to tell them that it does not look possible or even right to crowd Congress.

Mr. President, some in the House and Senate have stated that the Williams clause on the Safety-at-Sea Convention has practically nullified it.

I sought advice on that myself and have received it, but I have not had time to look it over. It got to me late last night. I mean, as to whether it does nullify it.

Mr. President, a bill has been introduced in the House which would make it an offense against the federal government to violate the treaty rights of an individual by a state. Is there any time for such legislation?[7]

I shouldn't think so. I don't know anything about the bill you speak of.

The bill was introduced by Mr. Bartholdt.

It is to what effect?

If the treaty right of an alien has been violated by a state heretofore, it was necessary to try that as a state offense. Bartholdt's bill makes it an offense against the federal law.

Makes the jurisdiction in the federal courts? It is a matter I haven't heard anything of.

Mr. President, some of the members of Congress are urging a larger navy, presenting the argument that, because Congress last year and the year before provided one battleship, and the Secretary of the Navy urged a program of two battleships, now there is a shortage of two battleships, and they would like to have four next year or three this year and next year. How do you view that suggestion?

I view it from afar.

Mr. President, have you decided whether the Alaska Railroad is to be controlled by the government's engineeers or by a private contractor.

I haven't yet received the report of those who were sent out there. I understand it is in our hands. It will be in my hands shortly.

Mr. President, have you anything to say about the Federal Trade Commission?

No, sir. I am still in a state of mind about it.

Anything on Mexico?

No, sir. I believe nothing has come in this morning at all.

Mr. President, regarding the recordership of the District of Columbia, there is some interest in that in Washington.

Yes, there has been a good deal of interest in it.

There is some suggestion that your view of the platform pledges on home rule[8] is in conflict with your promise to give new laws—

Really, Mr. Price,[9] it is not in shape to be discussed.

Mr. President, have you taken any interest in the question of the Chinese loan, one way or the other?[10]

How do you mean, taken an interest in it?

China is trying to get a loan.

I know that.

And some of the interests there are trying to prevent her from getting a loan. I understand that they appealed to you to strengthen the military there against revolution.

They must have been absorbed in the State Department. Not all the protests that are made reach me.

Mr. President, have you told any members of Congress your position on those bills to prohibit exports of ammunition?

No, sir.

Mr. President, have you given any further consideration to the proposal to have an expert tariff commission?

Well, it is called to my attention about once every twenty-four hours, so it's a continuing performance. As a matter of fact, you will notice in the law that the trade commission is authorized to report and advise Congress upon these, as upon all such matters.

Mr. President, former Ambassador Herrick saw you last week[11] and, while he was here, he discussed with us his proposition for more centralized relief work, and he said he had mentioned it incidentally to you. I was wondering whether he had asked you to appoint a committee, or to approve that idea of a central clearinghouse committee?

No, he didn't. He discussed the desirability of it with me, but as I now remember the conversation, he rather agreed with me that it was working itself out, at any rate, with some improvement.

[1] The Senate on December 14 rejected unanimously the nomination of John R. Lynn to be federal district attorney for the Western District of New York because Lynn was opposed by Senator O'Gorman. This raised the issue of Wilson's attempts to appoint nominees opposed by Democratic Senators from the states concerned. At the time of this press conference, the Senate was discussing the nomination of Ewing C. Bland to be United States marshal for the Western District of Missouri against the wishes of Senator Reed. Bland's nomination was rejected on January 5, 1915. See the *New York Times*, Dec. 19 and 21-22, 1914, and *Cong. Record*, 63d Cong., 3d sess., p. 979.

[2] See the *New York Times*, Dec. 22, 1914.

[3] The Newlands bill called for the coordination of work on the nation's rivers by the creation of a commission of departmental heads. It also provided for an annual appropriation of $10,000,000 for ten years to deepen channels and conserve river heads. See *ibid.*, Dec. 24, 1914.

[4] George Hebard Maxwell of Chicago, executive chairman of the National Irrigation Association.

[5] Wilson's Annual Message of December 8 said that the "subject of rural credits still remains to be dealt with, and it is a matter of deep regret that the difficulties of the subject have seemed to render it impossible to complete a bill for passage at this session." It is printed in *PWW*, Vol. 31, p. 419.

[6] S. 4850, introduced by Senator John Walter Smith, Democrat of Maryland, to regulate loan brokers in Washington. See *Washington Post*, Dec. 23, 1914.

[7] H.R. 20196, introduced on December 19 by Representative Bartholdt, to confer jurisdiction on the federal courts in cases of this type. See *Cong. Record*, 63d Cong., 3d sess., p. 430.

[8] That is, for the District of Columbia.

[9] William Wightman Price of the Washington *Evening Star*.

[10] Two Chinese emissaries, Wong Chiu-fau and Fai Chou Tong, were in the United States attempting to obtain a loan for their government. See the *New York Times*, Nov. 17, 1914.

[11] Herrick visited Wilson on December 16. See *ibid.*, Dec. 16, 1914.

Dec. 29, 1914

Mr. President, what time did that note of protest go to Great Britain yesterday?[1]

I wasn't informed just when it went. I supposed that it went on Saturday last.

You have had no reply to it?

No, we have had no reply to it. You understand, of course, that each case that has been called to our attention has been the ground for a protest also, and the way the thing works out is that if the government concerned is in the wrong, damages have eventually to be paid.

Then this is not the first protest?

No.

Were they made public?

They were protests of individual cases. If we made public everything we do, you wouldn't have space for anything else.

Is there any question of a treaty violation in this in any way?

No, it is just a question of the rules of international law.

Does it have any bearing on former protests that we have made in other times; I mean, for example, in 1812?

Oh, no, the protest itself refers to precedents, but not to any former controversy between this government and that.

Is there a possibility of extended correspondence on this subject, Mr. President, or does this protest which we have sent represent fully our final position in the matter?

It represents fully our position, and really, so far as the theory of the position is concerned, there is no debating it, at least in our judgment.

Mr. President, the note as published this morning[2] contains a sort of threat in it; that is to say, we say, as I read it, that we want England to give up her position so that we might take steps to protect American interests.

There is nothing of that kind in the note. The text of the note was not published, was it?

No.

Diplomatic correspondence isn't conducted that way.

Mr. President, are the reported conditions in the Philippines such as to shake your faith in the expediency of the pending legislation?[3]

Not in the least. The incident has been ridiculously exaggerated.

Mr. President, has the recent meeting of the Pan American Union any connection with the note we are sending?[4]

None whatever.

Their objections seem to be about the same?

Their object was their own commerce; of course, this note had nothing to do with that.

Our position would apply naturally to any neutral country, wouldn't it?

Yes, it would apply to any neutral country. There is nothing in it peculiar to our view of international law. The great embarrassment to the government in dealing with this whole matter is that some shippers have concealed contraband in cargoes of noncontraband articles, for example in a cargo of cotton. So long as there are *any* instances of this kind, suspicion is cast upon every shipment, and all cargoes are liable to doubt and to search. This government can deal confidently with this subject only if supported by absolutely honest manifests.

Mr. President, are you prepared to say whether we will adopt the suggestions of Germany regarding the United States Consuls in Belgium?[5]

I don't know anything about that yet. It hasn't been brought to my attention officially. I merely saw what was in the papers, so that I don't know yet just exactly what it is they are proposing.

Mr. President, can you tell us anything further about that Canadian incident?[6]

No, I read of that with a great deal of distress only last evening, and I don't know anything about it except the public news.

Has any word reached the State Department?[7]

No. Of course, there may be some explanation for it that we don't know about. I sincerely hope there is.

Mr. President, is it your intention to take any formal notice or make any formal reply to the Manufacturers' Association of Montgomery County, Pennsylvania?[8]

I am sorry to say I did not know about it.

Well, it appeared in the form of an open letter. I didn't know whether they had done you the courtesy to send you a copy or not.

Probably they did. When a letter is open before it gets to me, I always suppose it does not need an answer.

Are they justified in the assertion that industrial conditions are getting worse rather than improving?

No, sir, they are certainly not.

Mr. President, can you say anything about the trade commission? Is it going in this week?

No, sir, it is not going in this week.

Mr. President, have you been advised that the revised estimates of expenditures of appropriations will exceed the estimated revenue by one hundred million dollars, as asserted by Mr. Mann?[9]

No, sir.

What is the situation?

I haven't seen the balance sheet.

You would be informed of that if it were so?

Yes, of course I would; and I haven't seen the estimated balance sheet at all yet. But I am quite confident that there is nothing like that in it.

You rather expect the appropriations to remain within our revenues?

Oh, yes, I confidently expect that.

Mr. President, can you say anything about whether or not the reports are true that there are strained relations between you and the Senate?

No; it is quite the contrary. Strained relations seem to afford more public interest than normal relations; that is the only way I can account for the newspaper accounts. There are no strained relations between me and the Senate.

Mr. President, the story says there is danger of your legislative program not getting through at this session?

You will recall that that has been said about every piece of legislation that has gone through, and it is no more true this time than then.

There was no time limit on the others.

No, but the time limit acts as a spur.

Have you sent any telegram, Mr. President, about the withdrawal of troops from Colorado?

No. Governor Ammons and Governor-elect Carlson were here the other day, and they had a conference with the Secretary of War about that and I suppose laid out a general plan.

They told us that they would begin withdrawing the troops as soon as the Governor got back to Colorado; and he got back Sunday.[10]

Did he? I daresay that they have started to carry out their plan then. Our only object is to keep them there as long as they need them.

Anything new from Mexico, Mr. President?

Nothing at all.

I noticed in one of the morning papers a statement that this government had requested a general amnesty down there.[11]

We did advise it, yes, sir.

Well, does it seem to be pretty well established that there are to be no careless executions?

I haven't noticed any great carelessness. I don't think there has been a large number of executions. Many of the executions are strictly private and so I don't know.

Mr. President, it has been said that the administration is behind the move in the Senate to sidetrack the immigration bill. Is that true?

No, sir, I am not engaged in any Machiavellian schemes. It is true this far: it is well known that there is one provision in the bill which I am opposed to.

Mr. President, will there be any notice of the statement issued by Governor Colquitt?[12]

Has he issued another?

Not since Sunday morning.

I am sorry I did not see it.

[1] On December 26, the State Department forwarded a protest note to Ambassador Page in London that expressed American concern over British seizures of ships and cargoes. See the Secretary of State to the Ambassador in Great Britain, Dec. 26, 1914, in *FR, 1914-WWS*, pp. 372-75, and Link, *Struggle for Neutrality*, pp. 171-75.

[2] The *New York Times*, December 29, 1914, e.g., published the note. See also, the Diary of Colonel House, Dec. 29, 1914, printed in *PWW*, Vol. 31, pp. 549-50.

[3] Twenty Filipino rebels captured on December 29 near Navotas in the Philippines disclosed plans for a large-scale rebellion against American authority in the islands. Later reports indicated that the situation had been exaggerated. See the *New York Times*, Dec. 27-28, 1914.

[4] Venezuela had proposed a meeting in Washington of the Pan American Union and other neutrals to discuss the rights of neutral nations in time of war. See *ibid.*, Dec. 28, 1914, and the Venezuelan Minister [Dr. Santos A. Dominici] to the Secretary of State, Dec. 14, 1914, in *FR, 1914-WWS*, pp. 447-50.

[5] The German government, on December 28, asked the United States and other neutrals to remove their Consuls from those parts of Belgium occupied by German armies. See the *New York Times*, Dec. 29, 1914, and the Ambassador in Germany to the Secretary of State, Dec. 4, 1914, in *FR, 1915-WWS*, p. 916.

[6] On December 26, two duck hunters from Buffalo were fired on by Canadian officials near Fort Erie on the Niagara River. One of them, Walter Smith, was killed. See the *New York Times*, Dec. 27, 1914.

[7] *Ibid.*, Dec. 27, 1914, reported that Secretary Bryan had requested an explanation.

[8] The association, in an open letter dated December 26, asked Wilson to use his influence to bring about repeal of the Underwood tariff, which they said was causing a business depression. See *ibid.*, Dec. 27, 1914.

[9] Representative James Robert Mann, minority leader in the House, was critical of expenditures in the urgent deficiency bill. See *ibid.*, Dec. 22, 1914.

[10] *Ibid.*, Dec. 28, 1914, reported that Ammons had just announced troop withdrawals beginning that week.

[11] According to the report, Wilson had warned President Gutiérrez that reprisals would make recognition more difficult. See *ibid.*, Dec. 29, 1914, and Bryan to Silliman, Dec. 13, 1914, in *FR, 1914*, pp. 628-29.

[12] In a statement published on December 27, Colquitt denounced the "utter incompetence" of the administration and termed its foreign policy "imbecilic." See the *New York Times*, Dec. 27, 1914.

# 1915–1919

Mr. President, I notice there is a little discussion of an extra session?

Not by me.

Predicting some of the problems—the probable failure of the rural-credits bill. Mr. Glass of Virginia—

Nobody is thinking about a special session.

The morning papers are treating it rather seriously.

Well, they can dismiss it from their minds. There is nothing in it.

What is the status of rural credits, Mr. President?

I can't tell you because it is very mixed. I don't know, even after my interview with Mr. Glass, what the likelihood is of an agreement by the committee.[1] There has been considerable disagreement in the committee on certain features of the bill—a natural disagreement. As to whether it will be reported out or not, I don't know.

Mr. President, do you find greater demand for rural-credit legislation at this session than you had expected?

No.

You don't regard it as one of the legislative necessities of the session?

As a matter of fact, an extraordinary amount of relief was afforded in the granting of rural credits by the Federal Reserve Act. Before the recess of Congress, before this short session, a number of men who represented the agricultural interests of the country were very emphatic in their statement that they thought that a great deal had been done and that the situation had been a good deal relieved, the necessity had been a good deal relieved. But that doesn't slacken our desire to go forward. It's wise to go forward only when we can get a thoroughly satisfactory bill.

The failure of rural credits in this session wouldn't be considered a reason for an extra session?

It would be a reason for taking it up very early in the next session.

Would the failure of the ship-purchase bill, would that be regarded in the same way?

That is another matter, because we are in pressing need of shipping facilities, and we must get them. So that that might make a different case. But I don't expect that to be a failure.

Doesn't it seem apparent, Mr. President, that private capital is ready to go into it[2] with confidence?

There is plenty of capital. That is not the difficulty. The difficulty is the subject of adequate security which is recognized as adequate throughout the investing community. That is all the trouble about it. There is capital.

Then there is also the question as to whether or not the government is capitalizing these [rural-credit] banks, or whether private capital is. There is one source of capital, apparently, eager to supply considerable money.

Those, of course, are fundamental questions, and it is because we want to be ready to throw that in the discussion that we found it necessary to go slowly.

Mr. President, is it a fair inference from what you said just now that failure of that bill might make an extra session possible?

I never go on hypotheses. That is a hypothesis I deplore.

Mr. President, in connection with that rural-credits bill, has anything come to your attention to show that there is almost a deliberate effort to conceal the advantages which the Federal Reserve Act provides for rural credit?

Well, I don't like to express an opinion about those things. I try not to be suspicious.

Mr. President, have you decided to hold the hearing on the immigration bill?

No hearing has been proposed, sir.

I thought it had been proposed?

(Mr. Forster[3]) Some time ago.
And I understood that Mr. Hammerling[4] was coming again and urging you—

I simply wasn't informed. I hadn't heard anything of the proposal recently.

Mr. President, I notice in the *Post*[5] this morning a dispatch from London, probably Associated Press, indicating that the United States Government might send a representative to the Vatican to cooperate with other representatives there, with a view to helping the efforts of the Pope to bring about peace?

I took that as one of the many ways in which the *Post* amuses itself, sir. Of course it is ridiculous.

Mr. President, that is an Associated Press dispatch.

I don't know where those things are invented. I think not very far away from Washington.

Mr. President, do you regard the preamble of the Philippines bill as an essential feature of that measure?[6]

Essential in this sense: I think it is straightforward to declare purposes, to declare the point of view, the general line of policy upon which the bill is conceived—essential in that particular. Of course, the bill will work just as well because the substance, the effective substance, will be there. But the preamble is a very important part.

You weren't influenced, Mr. President, by anything Mr. Taft said, were you?[7]

Well, with apologies to Mr. Taft, I must—I mean, I have not read what he said. But Mr. Taft has often very frankly avowed his views on that subject so far as he could, and from the headlines, there was nothing he said that he had not said before.

The point would be, with reference to that preamble, though, that it is representative of American sentiment. There is actual damage done by those promises in the Philippines.

So it is alleged.

Yes, sir.

Of course. But the allegations about the effect in the Philippines have been so many that it is a matter of judgment as to which are well founded.

Mr. President, some time ago, when you told us that you were opposed to the literacy test in the immigration law, you said that it was because it was not a fair test of quality of citizenship. I mentioned that to a couple of Senators after you said that, and one was one of them who helped frame the literacy test. In the first place, he never intended it to be a test of quality but a device to keep out certain kinds of people. He asked if you were just opposed to the method of restriction?

Well, if he will ask me, I will tell him.

Could you tell us about anything—whether you are opposed to restriction?

I am not going to discuss the general policy. That leads chiefly— I feel I would have to hire a hall. It would take an hour.

Mr. President, do you expect to see Colonel Goethals this week? He said yesterday he would not come again unless you wanted him.

There is no special reason why I should see him. I am sorry I missed him. There is nothing special that needs to be discussed.

Have you discussed this matter of the possibility of the warships not being able to go through the canal at the opening on account of slides?[8]

Several times, but nobody has taken it seriously. I don't think it's anything serious.

Isn't it true that Colonel Goethals says that they can't go through?

Not so far as I know, sir.

I thought that was a statement.

He certainly didn't make it to me.

Then the proposition, the plan, will go through on schedule—that has been arranged for?

That's the last I heard, yes, sir.

Mr. President, there was a paragraph in one of the papers to the effect that the President of France is to transmit to the French Academy some letter which he received from you. Could you tell us about that?

Well, it is simply this: Monsieur Brieux[9] was in this country as a representative of the French Academy, a very old body and representative of the chief literary men in France. He came over to bring greetings and make an address to the American Academy of Letters, which is a recent body and has by no means as much prestige as the French Academy. And he brought with him a letter to me from the President of France, a personal letter, simply because the President of France is a member of the French Academy and I am a member of the American Academy. It was—it had nothing in it but conventional salutations. It was not a personal letter. And I have replied, and he will transmit that letter to the French Academy. It is altogether just a matter among literary fellows.[10]

Mr. President, it has been stated, in this matter of the passport fraud,[11] which has been brought personally to your attention, that you have had something to do with setting the procedure to be followed in the investigation?

No, it has merely been brought to my attention, as everything is. It is in the hands of the district attorney in New York.

Any developments, Mr. President, in the controversy with Great Britain?

Not any, sir.

Mr. President, will your Indianapolis speech[12] be of a political character?

Decidedly. It will be political.

Mr. President, are you planning to prepare anything in advance on that?

No. I have suffered all my life under the incapacity of writing a speech. It is just about as dry as sawdust if I write it, so I always speak extemporaneously. But the speech is going to be delivered in the afternoon, so there will be time enough for telegraphic transmission,[13] at any rate.

How about the trade commission, Mr. President?

No further progress.

Mr. President, could you take us enough into confidence on that speech, on your ideas in advance on that speech, to say what topics will be taken up?

[No answer recorded.]

Mr. President, it has been said with a good deal of definiteness that you have decided upon three members of the trade commission?

That is not true, sir, except in this sense—that I have made three lists and torn them up.

[1] The House Banking and Currency Committee.
[2] That is, on rural credit.
[3] Rudolph Forster, Executive Clerk at the White House.
[4] Louis Nicholas Hammerling, president of the American Association of Foreign Language Newspapers.
[5] The *Washington Post*, Jan. 5, 1915.
[6] The preamble to the Jones bill (H.R. 18459) read as follows:
"Whereas it was never the intention of the people of the United States in the incipiency of the War with Spain to make it a war of conquest or for territorial aggrandizement; and
"Whereas it is, as it had always been, the purpose of the people of the United States to withdraw their sovereignty over the Philippine Islands and to recognize their independence as soon as a stable government can be established therein; and
"Whereas for the speedy accomplishment of such purpose it is desirable to place in the hands of the people of the Philippines as large a control of their domestic affairs as can be given them without, in the meantime, impairing the exercise of the rights of sovereignty by the people of the United States, in order that, by the use and exercise of popular franchise and governmental powers, they may be the better prepared to fully assume the responsibilities and enjoy all the privileges of complete independence." See *Cong. Record*, 63d Cong., 2d sess., p. 16027.
[7] The former President gave testimony opposing the Jones bill before the Senate Committee on the Philippines on January 2. Among his remarks were quotations from Wilson's *Constitutional Government in the United States* to support his contention that the Filipinos were unprepared for self-government. See the *New York Times*, Jan. 3. 1915.
[8] At a meeting with Secretary Garrison in Washington on January 4, Goethals suggested that earth slides in the Culebra Cut might prevent the fleet from passing through on its way from Hampton Roads to San Francisco in March. See *ibid.*, Jan. 5-6, 1915.
[9] Eugène Brieux, the French dramatist.
[10] For the letters, see Raymond Poincaré to WW, Oct. 29, 1914, and WW to Poincaré, Dec. 7, 1914, both printed in *PWW*, Vol. 31, pp. 247-48, 410.
[11] Four German reservists had been captured on the liner *Bergenfjord* with false United States passports. It was suggested that American passport officials might be implicated in illegalities. See the *New York Times*, Jan. 3 and 6, 1915.
[12] Wilson was scheduled to deliver a Jackson Day address in Indianapolis on January 8. It is printed in *PWW*, Vol. 32, pp. 29-41.
[13] That is, by reporters to their newspapers.

Jan. 12, 1915

Mr. President, can you tell anything about the visit of Dudley Field Malone and Mr. Davies?[1]

It was just about an appointment out in one of the western states.

Could you tell us something about your conference with the Alaska Railway Commission last night?[2]

With pleasure. It was just a conference to go over the maps and the details and to acquaint them with the questions I understand they should answer in the report they are preparing. It was just a go-over-the-ground interview.

Do you know when they are likely to submit their report?

In a few days now; within a couple of weeks.

Has it been determined whether the road is to be built by army engineers or civil engineers?

That has not been decided.

Has the administration at this time in mind pressing any one of the employment bureau bills now before the House committee?[3]

Well, I haven't in mind, to tell you the truth, any additional legislation at this short session, because it is so obviously too short a session in which to accomplish so crucial a piece of legislation.

Mr. President, in view of what has already been done in the departments about the matter,[4] is legislation on the subject really necessary?

I think it is. We are doing and can do a great deal, and of course we will continue to do so, but I think for the proper coordination of it all, legislation is necessary.

You can accomplish that legislation within the next two years?

Yes, I am confident we can.

If the legislation can be accomplished within the next two years, a platform declaration on the subject[5] will hardly be necessary.

I suppose not. I simply put it the way I did in my speech because I was not authorized to commit anybody but myself. But I have not heard any dissenting opinions.

Mr. President, an effort has been made in some of the papers this morning to show that the British note[6] is unsatisfactory in some respects to the American government?

I saw an article headed "Note Unsatisfactory to Wilson," or something like that. I thought of writing to the editor and asking him how he found out. He didn't ask me, and nobody has asked me, and I have not expressed an opinion, because I haven't studied the note yet. It is merely preliminary, anyway.

You are not likely to send any reply until the full text is received?

No, we couldn't until the full text is here.

Mr. President, there has been some question as to whether or not we in Indianapolis interpreted your speech correctly on the point of your candidacy.[7]

I said at the time I did not intend to start anything. But, honestly, I wasn't thinking about that; I was thinking about the judgment sooner or later that would be expressed by the country upon the party.

Mr. President, despite your desire not to start anything, it seems to have started something.

Yes, sir, so I have noticed.

Mr. A. Mitchell Palmer puts forward the suggestion that if your candidacy is intended it can be done by repealing a section of the Baltimore platform;[8] do you regard that as necessary?

You must permit me, gentlemen, not to talk about myself. I don't know how.

Mr. President, how much of an appropriation would it require, probably, for the purposes of a federal employment bureau?

I haven't gone into that. I do not know.

Could such a bureau be used effectively, Mr. President, to divert a good deal of the immigration to the land instead of to the big industrial centers?

Yes, undoubtedly it could. One of the things that I have had at heart for a great many years has been some means by which we could guide immigrants to the places where they could find the most suitable employment—employment best suited to what they had done at home and what they knew best how to do. That has never been supplied except by private agencies. Certain societies have interested themselves in that, but they have not had the access or the authority that would enable them to guide the immigrant.

There was a report by Mr. Husband about a year ago to the Secretary of Labor,[9] following his investigation in Russia, in which he said that one of the greatest problems was to place the Russian peasant, who had been on the land over there, in the proper environment here.

And a great many of the Portuguese and Italian immigrants are admirably suited for farming; they have been accustomed to truck gardening and intensive cultivation of various sorts.

They pointed out, in that connection, that one of the important deficiencies was the lack of rural-credit facilities for these people who came over here.

You mean to give them credit to buy land and settle?

Yes.

That is being done by private individuals; there is a notable scheme in the Carolinas.[10]

Mr. President, are you willing yet to let us know what action you are going to take with regard to the immigration bill?

No; I am willing that you should form a shrewd guess. But the bill, of course, hasn't come out of conference yet, and the final form of it is not determined.

But the provision which is objectionable to you remains in the bill.

Necessarily, I suppose, because both houses approved it.

Mr. President, you spoke at Indianapolis about a plan for the speeding of justice.[11] Have you any definite plan in mind, any details of that worked out?

I can't say that I have them worked out. It is a matter I have discussed again and again and taken part in discussing with the bar associations, so that there is a very considerable number of very definite items in my mind, but I do not think it would be wise for me to put forth a scheme of any sort.

There has been some controversy in the papers that official recognition has been taken of conditions on the Crow Indian reservation; have you any knowledge of that?[12]

No, sir, I have not.

Is there anything you can tell us about Mexico, Mr. President?

No, sir, except that once again things seem to be quieting there. I suppose you know that certain arrangements have been made at the border.[13] They have been fighting too near the edge.

Mr. President, can you develop a little more the idea of the trade commission taking up the work of a tariff commission?[14]

No, that has to be developed by the commission itself. The powers are there; and the powers had been partly granted, you may remember, only very partially, to the Bureau of Corporations. It is a matter of development. Some of the later reports of the Bureau of Corporations show an admirable method of investigating the conditions of particular lines of business.

Isn't there a bureau of the Commerce Department that has that power?

The Bureau of Foreign and Domestic Commerce has, inferentially, those powers. It handles questions of commerce, upon which it reports, and its reports are naturally the source of a great deal of information with regard to foreign-trade conditions.

Mr. Underwood, when the tariff bill was in process, laid some stress upon the powers which had been granted to these bureaus.

Yes, he did. I don't think that there is any lack of power now. It merely is a question of development.

Would it be the idea, Mr. President, to have all these separate organizations— of course, the Bureau of Corporations goes out of existence—study along the same lines and make independent reports?

Of course, their independence is almost inevitable, because the function of the Bureau of Foreign and Domestic Commerce is to send agents to foreign countries and study the opportunities there for American merchants, and then get American merchants in touch with those opportunities. It is an active sort of business of promotion, which is different in kind from the business of scientific study. What they report will naturally be very serviceable to the men who are making a more scientific study of it on the trade commission.

Is there any progress on the trade commission, Mr. President?

I think I am nearing a solution.

Are you expecting the passage of the Philippines bill this session, Mr. President?

Well, under the rules of the Senate one can never tell what one expects, but I hope for its passage at this session. I haven't heard anything to the contrary.

Mr. President, a suggestion was made by the Secretary of the Treasury calling for a Pan-American business congress to be held in the spring, and the Secretary of State says the invitations are being held up pending an appropriation by Congress to meet the expenses. Have you requested any of the committees concerned to arrange for this appropriation?[15]

Through the departments, yes, but not directly; I have not had any personal conferences.

[1] Joseph Edward Davies.

[2] The commission was studying the best route for construction of a railroad from the Alaskan coast to the coal fields.

[3] H.R. 19015, sponsored by Representative William Josiah MacDonald, Progressive of Michigan, called for the creation of an employment bureau within the Department of Labor.

[4] The Department of Labor, the Department of Agriculture, and the Post Office Department were making nationwide employment information available. See the *New York Times*, Jan. 10, 1915.

[5] In his Jackson Day address at Indianapolis on January 8, Wilson had said of the creation of a national employment bureau that "if I were writing an additional plank for the Democratic platform, I would put that in." See *PWW*, Vol. 32, p. 36.

[6] That is, the preliminary reply to Wilson's note of December 26. See the *New York Times*, Jan. 12, 1915, and the Ambassador in Great Britain to the Secretary of State, Jan. 7, 1915, in *FR, 1915-WWS*, pp. 299-302.

[7] See, for example, the *New York Times*, Jan. 10, 1915, which suggested that the speech was the beginning of Wilson's campaign for reelection.

[8] That is, the section calling for a single presidential term of six years. See *ibid.*, Jan. 10, 1915, and Schlesinger and Israel, *American Presidential Elections*, III, 2170.

[9] "Report of W. W. Husband, Special Immigrant Inspector, Regarding Immigration from Eastern Europe," printed as an appendix to *Annual Report of the Commissioner General of Immigration to the Secretary of Labor, 1914* (Washington, 1915), pp. 391-406.

[10] This scheme was the establishment of several farm communities, composed primarily of immigrants, near Wilmington, N. C., by Hugh MacRae. See Conkin, *Tomorrow a New World*, pp. 277-79.

[11] Wilson said that the United States was lagging behind the rest of the civilized world in its judicial processes and called for steps to remedy the situation because "if you have to be rich to get justice, because of the cost of the process itself, then there is no justice at all." See *PWW*, Vol. 32, p. 36.

[12] Testimony before the joint congressional commission on Indian Affairs suggested that Indians were starving on the reservations. See the *New York Times*, Jan. 11, 1915.

[13] That is, to keep the fighting from endangering American citizens. See *ibid.*, Jan. 12, 1915, and Hill, *Emissaries to a Revolution*, pp. 287, 290.

[14] Wilson had raised this issue in his speech at Indianapolis. See *PWW*, Vol. 32, p. 37.

[15] Secretary McAdoo asked Congress for an appropriation to fund the conference on January 15. See the *New York Times*, Jan. 16, 1915. The Pan American Financial Conference met in Washington, May 24 to 29, 1915; its object was to discuss reciprocal trade relations between the United States and the eighteen Latin American nations represented. See *Proceedings of the First Pan American Financial Conference . . . Washington, May 24 to 29, 1915* (Washington, 1915).

Jan. 19, 1915

Mr. President, I understand that you have sent a letter to Attorney General Gregory in regard to the rise of food prices?[1]

I merely asked him to investigate for the purpose of finding out if there was anything illegal, really, at the bottom of it. Of course, only illegal things are being investigated. The investigation has already begun.

In that connection, Mr. President, will you regard the possibility of an embargo on war materials?[2]

Of course, there is no authority lodged anywhere to place an embargo.

Could not that authority be conferred by legislative action?

It would have to be conferred that way, if at all.

Isn't that contrary to international law?

I can't answer that question. I have never looked into it.

Mr. President, is there anything you can tell us about your recent conference with Mr. Gompers?[3]

Mr. Gompers brought the executive committee of the American Federation of Labor here on Saturday afternoon merely to go over the various things in which they were interested. One of them was the immigration bill. Another was the seamen's bill. I don't recollect any other particular topics. Those are the ones most particularly talked about, and they left me a memorandum.[4]

Any suggestion of additional legislation?

No, except the seamen's bill. Oh, yes—I beg your pardon—they did. They expressed their interest in further legislation on employers' liability and workmen's compensation, but we didn't go into that. That was merely a suggestion.

In a general way, Mr. President, you had already expressed sympathy with this program, except one or two features of the immigration bill.

Yes. They were coming to urge it upon me so much as to keep it fresh in my recollection—their interest in it.

Was the [blank] mentioned in that controversy?

Yes it was. I can't remember just now in what section.

Passed the House and in conference report?

They spoke of that, but my recollection has grown a little dim just what phase of it they spoke of.

One of the Japanese newspapers, Mr. President, seems to express confidence that the government will interest itself in the antialien bill in Idaho.[5] Did you notice that—of Idaho?

No, I did not.

It expresses the hope that the federal government will intervene. Is it true that one of the federal courts, in the first instance, declared the Arizona statute unconstitutional?[6]

Yes, sir. The circuit court of appeals of San Francisco.

It was the circuit court of appeals?

I am not sure that it was a circuit court. It was a court of appeals.

Have you seen the Idaho bill?

No, I have not familiarized myself with it.

Mr. President, do you still regard the passage of the ship-purchase bill as certainly probable?

I think it is extremely probable.

With some amendments?

Oh, I daresay with some amendments, but no amendments going to the essential features of the bill.

Mr. President, did Mr. Underwood say that they would hold night sessions from now on to facilitate the passage of legislation in the House?

No, he did not. He didn't speak of legislation.

Mr. President, do you regard it as essential to the shipping bill that the shipping board be made up of cabinet members, as provided for? Some of the progressive Republicans said it should be nonpolitical and nonpartisan.

I discussed that. I think the arrangement in the bill is much more to be preferred than any other.

Mr. President, does that cover the point of the time of government ownership? They also suggested that the bill ought to read that if the venture was successful, government ownership should be continued.

I don't want to discuss out of court, so to speak, the details of the bill, because I don't know just what is in the minds of the gentlemen up there.

Mr. President, some of your callers have suggested that, because of the European situation, you might not make the Panama Exposition trip?[7]

I see the papers have been talking about that. That is nothing new. I have felt obliged to say all along that, while I confidently expected to go, of course it was possible that a situation might arise that would make it necessary for me to stay here. You see, the plans contemplated the greater part of the Executive branch of the government being at sea for some weeks, literally and figuratively.

Mr. President, in that connection, have you any intimation at all of any likelihood of peace, come this spring?

No. I wish I could say yes. There are no signs as yet.

The morning papers, Mr. President, say that the Democratic caucus last night endorsed the rural-credits legislation as proposed.[8] Does that mean this session?

Not necessarily. That depends on how soon the shipping bill passes.

Mr. President, last summer, when the ship-registry bill passed, there was an expression of desire to encourage the American merchant marine. The question was brought up as to whether the seamen's bill and similar legislation might have a deterrent effect in keeping American capital out of it. Has that been brought up lately?

No, that is a question which has been debated all along. There have been two sides to it.

Mr. President, does the apparent reluctance of the British government to allow the [Dacia] to make the first trip[9] interfere in any way with your resolution on the shipping bill?

No, I don't think it is a parallel instance.

Mr. President, there is much interest in the baby.[10]

He is all right.

Have you any idea as to when you will hear from Great Britain on the note?

No, we have not. I haven't seen anything except the preliminary note.

Mr. President, you made it clear in your Indianapolis speech that certain powers had been granted the trade commission with reference to tariff investigation. Could you tell us what your personal views are as to when and in what way that board could exercise that authority?

No, I think I had better choose it first. Then I will be able to cast its horoscope. I did not go into the matter fully in Indianapolis, as a matter of fact. You know, the Congress turned over the powers of the old board to the Bureau of Foreign and Domestic Commerce in the Department of Commerce, and the other powers that I spoke of at Indianapolis were conferred upon the trade commission.

Have you made some inquiry into the assertion that the paragraph in question was drawn up by Mr. Stevens of Minnesota?[11]

No. I didn't know who it was drawn up by.

It was stated by Mr. Mann on the floor of the House, in order to contravert the assertion that something has been put over, to the effect that Mr. Stevens, a Republican, had drawn up the provision.

Was that the reason he was defeated in the election?

No. He has most recently—

Mr. Stevens is a very fine man, I know that.

[1] WW to Gregory, Jan. 18, 1915, WP, DLC.
[2] See the New York Times, Jan. 16, 1915.
[3] Wilson met with Gompers and the executive council of the American Federation of Labor at 6 p.m. on January 16. See ibid., Jan. 17, 1915.
[4] It is missing.
[5] The Idaho legislature passed a measure on January 20 to prohibit land ownership by aliens until they had taken out first citizenship papers. See ibid., Jan. 21, 1915.
[6] On January 7, a special federal court consisting of two district court judges and one circuit court judge found that the Arizona law violated the right of aliens, under the Fourteenth Amendment, to work. See above, Dec. 15, 1914, and the New York Times, Jan. 8, 1915.
[7] Wilson's plans called for a trip through the Panama Canal at the time of its official opening in March; he would then continue on to the Panama Exposition in San Francisco. See ibid., Jan. 19, 1915.
[8] The Democratic caucus in the Senate voted on January 18 to report the Hollis-Bulkley rural-credits bill out of the Finance Committee. See ibid., Jan. 19, 1915.
[9] Edward Nicklas Breitung, an American citizen of German background, purchased the

steamship *Dacia* from the Hamburg-America Line on about December 28, 1914. On January 4, he transferred the vessel, then at Port Arthur, Texas, to American registry. He planned to use the ship to transport cotton to Europe, and, if he was successful, to purchase other German ships in American ports for the same purpose. By the time of this press conference, the State Department had received protests from the British and French Ambassadors, as well as from Sir Edward Grey. See *ibid.*, Jan. 12, 1915; *FR, 1915-WWS*, pp. 674-90; and Link, *Struggle for Neutrality*, pp. 179-87.

[10] Francis Woodrow Sayre, born to Jessie Wilson Sayre on January 17; his father changed his name to Francis Bowes Sayre, Jr., in 1919.

[11] Representative Frederick Clement Stevens, Republican.

Jan. 26, 1915

Mr. President, there seems to be an organized effort on the part of the Republicans to defeat the shipping bill.[1] I was wondering whether you had anything to say about the responsibility for holding up legislation?

No, sir; I think that will be very obvious.

Mr. President, the treatment which is being accorded the ship-purchase bill endangers the passage of some of the appropriation bills, doesn't it?

No, sir.

At this session?

I did not say at this session.

I was coming to that.

No, I don't honestly think that it imperils their passage at this session.

Do you think, then, that both the appropriation bills and the ship-purchase bill will pass?

Yes, sir, I do.

That would obviate the danger of an extra session?

Yes, sir.

But, if either fails, do you regard an extra session as [possible]?

I don't go on a hypothesis. "Sufficient unto the day is the evil thereof."

Mr. President, do you think there is any effort being made to force you to have an extra session?

None that I am aware of, sir. I have the good fortune to be insensible to pressure.

Mr. President, when the immigration bill goes back to the House, will it be accompanied by a message?

What makes you think it will go back? If I sign it, it will not have to go back. If it goes back, it will be accompanied by a message.

Won't you tell us which way it is going, Mr. President?

No; I have a conference tomorrow with members of the two houses.

Mr. President, the chief opposition to the ship-purchase bill seems based on the belief that we are going to buy ships of some nations and get into trouble. Have you any assurances that we will not?

Of course, that is a matter that is not necessarily involved in the bill at all. They always question the discretion of the administration; so there is nothing new in that.

Is it possible to put into a bill in exact words an exclusion of the right to purchase certain ships; in other words, to differentiate between one ship and another?

No. Of course, literally speaking it would be possible, but it would be a very questionable practice.

The Lodge amendment[2] provides for prohibiting the purchase of belligerent vessels. I wonder whether that would appeal to you.

It appeals to me just exactly as it is going to appeal to the majority in the Senate.

Senator Simmons says that the belligerent ships will be purchased only on assurance that the transfers will be recognized. Is that with authority?

I daresay he has conferred with the Department of State.

Mr. President, there is a group of private bankers in New York who are arranging to finance the neutrals; and, in connection with that, it is said that no systematic scheme of aiding South American trade will be adopted until it is known what will be the policy of the administration in respect of the enforcement of contracts. Do you happen to know about that?

No, I don't know anything about that.

Mr. President, some of the Republican Senators—Senators Root and Borah[3] and others—lately have had a good deal to say in opposition to the method of caucus legislation in the dark, and they say there hasn't been any real discussion on the floor because the Democrats have made up their minds in advance.[4] They are not open to conversion; and they place that alongside your stand in the campaign in favor of open discussion. I wonder if you could let in any light on that?

I could let a great deal, but I am not going to.

Mr. President, as a result of your talk yesterday with Colonel Goethals, do you still think it possible to go through the canal?[5]

Of course, no engineer can be certain of the future, but there will not be any permanent trouble about the canal.

Has any arrangement been made to include the press on that trip, Mr. President, officially?

As a matter of fact, no detailed plans have been made at all. I have taken it for granted that arrangements would be made for the press.

Mr. President, the inquiry that is being made into the number of people out of work in New York City by the Department of Labor—is that to be extended to other cities?[6]

It will be extended to other cities if we can get the facilities. You see, we haven't an appropriation for that purpose, and the investigation is possible only through such agencies as the immigration bureau at certain ports, and wouldn't be possible with the present level of appropriations elsewhere. Wherever it is possible, it will be looked into.

You don't intend to ask for an appropriation to furnish machinery for that purpose?

No, it hardly seems to me necessary in view of the very careful investigation that is being made by municipal authorities. It would be merely in many instances to check their inquiries, to see whether they were correct or not.

As it was explained, the purpose of that was to meet some of the statements that have issued from partisan sources. In order to make the inquiry satisfactory to you, it would have to come through sources of your own.

I don't understand that those statements which are said to be partisan proceeded from municipal authorities. They proceeded from other sources and were largely guesswork. In one statement, with regard to the country as a whole, there were said to be more men out of employment than there are men ever employed in the United States, in the industry spoken of, I mean, which does not seem to be likely. That would mean that all that were ever employed in that industry were out of employment, and some more besides. They don't look up the statistics of employment before they invent the statistics of unemployment. It would be prudent for them to do so.

The ordinary police census would be acceptable?

If conducted in a systematic way, I should feel that we had no right to question it. As a matter of fact, I am told—I don't know this officially—that the municipal lodging houses in New York are not full. Notwithstanding that, we have opened some of the accommodations at Ellis Island to those out of employment to sleep overnight, and they are carried back and forth, you know, on the boat; and there is no great crowd there. From those indications, it wouldn't look as if the distress is as extreme as has been feared.

Are the avenues of employment gradually being opened in New York?

I am told they are. A gentleman was telling me only yesterday that he thought that that, slowly but steadily, was taking place.

Do you see other evidences of a return to more satisfactory business conditions?

A great many, taking the country at large; a great many, and there is no depression west of the Mississippi.

Can you point us to some of these circumstances?

I can't offhand. The newspapers, Mr. Tumulty suggests.

We get letters indicating the same things. Again, by such statements as are made to me by such men as the editor of *System*,[7] for example, who was here the other day, and who spoke in very confident terms.

Anything on Mexico, Mr. President?

No, sir; things are still fermenting down there.

Is there anything with regard to the rural-credits situation?

There is a unanimous desire to pass it, but you see how the ways are blocked. That is all that is standing in the way of it.

There has been no agreement, so far as you are concerned, on the bill, has there?

Not a final agreement, no, sir.

[1] Led by Senators Root and Lodge, Republicans in the Senate were attempting to kill the ship-purchase bill by prolonged debate. See the *New York Times*, Jan. 22, 1915, and Link, *Struggle for Neutrality*, pp. 147-48.
[2] About this amendment, see *ibid.*, pp. 149-51, and *Cong. Record*, 63d Cong., 3d sess., p. 964.
[3] William Edgar Borah, Republican of Idaho.
[4] The Democratic caucus in the Senate voted on January 23 to make the ship-purchase bill a party measure, thus prompting this criticism. See the *New York Times*, Jan. 24, 1915.
[5] Goethals told Wilson on January 25 that mud slides had made it impossible for the fleet to pass through the Panama Canal. See *ibid.*, Jan. 25, 1915.
[6] *Ibid.*, Jan. 24, 1915, reported that the Department of Labor had asked for the results of a police census of the unemployed then being undertaken by Howard Bradstreet of the Mayor's Committee on the Unemployed. See also *ibid.*, Jan. 17, 1915.
[7] Arch Wilkinson Shaw of Chicago, publisher of *System: The Magazine of Business* and other business publications.

Feb. 2, 1915

Mr. President, can you say anything about the ship-purchase bill?[1]

That needn't bother you.

It does.

Well, you must not let it.

It doesn't bother us, Mr. President, we just want to know about it.

It is going through all right.

With some changes, Mr. President?

No changes of any sort that are not consistent with the principle of the bill.

Will these changes be of a character to meet some of the progressive Republican objections?[2]

I hope so, but so far as I can learn, they are not asking anything that is not perfectly consistent with the principle.

They ask a provision in it that will prohibit the purchase of ships from belligerents.

I think you have misunderstood their wish, so far as I can learn it. Their wish is to declare a policy, not to surrender a right. I don't find anybody who wishes to waive the rights that the country may have.

Senators Kenyon and Norris have proposed certain amendments with reference to the purchase of belligerent ships.[3]

So I understand; I did not see the text of them. I don't know just what terms they are in.

Do you feel now, Mr. President, that the progressive Republicans will support the bill?

They have supported it all along, in the sense that they were in favor of the principle of it and merely wanted some modifications in details that, so far as I know, were not inconsistent.

Mr. President, do I gather from what you have said that there will be no objection to saying that German ships shall not be bought as a matter of policy, but reserving the right?

I am not expressing an opinion of what amendments would be acceptable, or unacceptable; that belongs to the other end of the avenue. I am just trying to give the situation so far as I see it.

Mr. President, Senator Norris insists that the ships should not be resold or released at the end of the period when there is no profit. He insists that when the lines become profitable, they should not be put in private hands. That seems to be rather vital.[4]

There is nothing in the bill saying they shall be. It will take an act of Congress, you know.

They insist that there should be something in the bill saying that they shouldn't be.

That, you see, would not bind future Congresses. Future Congresses are at liberty to pursue what policy they please. Nothing that you can put in this bill by way of details can stand in the way of their repeal by future Congresses. One Congress cannot bind another.

Another point that was made, Mr. President, was that they wanted the organization of the government line taken out of the control of the cabinet and put, rather, in a nonpartisan board.

As I understand it, the bill, as it is now framed, provides for a board of five, two of them *ex officio* and three of them appointed outside the cabinet; so that point is already covered. That was the bill as it came out of the Democratic caucus.

Are you advised, Mr. President, as to what the program at the Capitol will be? Will this bill maintain its right of way, or will it be displaced temporarily?

I am not informed, I am sorry to say. I don't think it will be displaced; if so, it will be only temporarily.

If these amendments are made acceptable to the progressive Republicans, still that will not do away with the objection of the other branch of the Republican family, will it?

No, I suppose not.

So that the filibuster will continue until it is broken in some other way?

I suppose so; but I don't know, of course.

Mr. President, have you been advised that the acceptance of the amendments desired by the progressive Republicans might lose some Democratic votes?

No, I have not.

Do you understand that this so-called bolt of the seven Democrats is a permanent position on this bill?[5]

No, I do not understand that.

Mr. President, I was told at the Treasury Department yesterday that the congestion of grain and cotton and other products in American ports, to relieve which the bill was framed, in the first place, it was said, has been very much relieved now, and that the necessity for it had largely passed.

Where did they tell you that?

In the customs division of the Treasury Department.

That is news to me.

They said that the country had passed the emergency point; that the grain situation was nearly normal.

They know more than anybody else knows. I don't mean to be disrespectful to the customs division.

Mr. President, is any legislation under consideration, or is any legislation necessary, to meet the Treasury conditions which were pointed out?[6]

No, sir.

The income tax receipts will be sufficient to meet whatever deficits there will be?

It is believed that they will. Of course, we can't be absolutely certain from the estimates.

There is some suggestion, Mr. President, that the war tax might be extended for a period of six months or a year.

That is not in contemplation now, at any rate. Of course, if the war were to last indefinitely, something might have to be done.

You had some visitors yesterday, Mr. President, who were presumed to have made some suggestions to you about peace.

Did I?

That is what we understood.

I didn't mean to contradict you; I had forgotten who came to see me.

The editor of the *Christian Science Monitor*.[7]

Oh, yes. He didn't make any suggestions about peace. He came for what was to my mind a very welcome purpose: simply to know what was the truth about certain things he had been in doubt about. No, he didn't have any suggestions at all.

There is nothing working now that you can see that is helpful?

I am sorry to say I don't see anything definite working. There is a very strong and growing hope and sentiment, I think, all over the world for peace, but I don't see anything definite.

I don't suppose you gave much consideration to the plans of Representative Bartholdt?[8]

He hasn't presented them to me.

In the first place, Mr. President, on this ship bill, you gave as one of the purposes of the ship line to open up new lines of trade, with South America, and so on. Would it be practicable to build ships for that purpose, or would we need them immediately?

Of course, we shall build ships, and there is no reason to suppose that they can't be built, of the type we wish. You see, people haven't thought very carefully about what sort of ships we will need. We will need ships of what are called the tramp type—ships built entirely for cargo and not necessarily running on fixed routes.

None of those German ships are of that type, are they?

None, so far as I know.

Mr. President, can you say anything about the trade commission this week?

I hope I shall before the end of the week.

Mr. President, have you any information as to the available supply of ships of the tramp type?

I have not. I think they have a partial list at the Treasury Department; I don't know that they have made a systematic census.

Mr. President, do you expect to meet with the Democratic National Committee when it meets here next month?

Well, it hasn't resolved to meet here next month. I got a letter from Mr. McCombs only yesterday saying that that interview that was given out in his name was absolutely a piece of fiction.[9]

Does that refer, Mr. President, to the story with regard to your candidacy or to the plans?

It refers to the whole thing. So his letter stated to me.

Mr. President, I got it directly from him.

I think you must have got it in a different form. Mr. McCombs did discuss with me the propriety or the advisability of having such a meeting, but he did not state it as a plan, and it is not a plan, an adopted plan. That is what I mean, that the statements of facts, not what was being considered, but the statement of facts, was unfounded.

I think he said, Mr. President, when he came out, that the idea was to have a dinner or a banquet of some sort here.

That is what he suggested to me here.

As an anniversary of your administration.

He did state that to me as an idea, but as I said, not as a plan.

Mr. President, have any of the belligerent powers expressed, either directly or indirectly, an opinion with regard to the policy involved in the shipping bill?[10]

I do not think we are apt to get into a tangle about that. No government has made any representations to us on that subject.[11] Of course, it has been a subject of conversation with the representatives of different governments, and I daresay that it is those conversations that have given rise to the idea that something formal was up, some protest. There has been no protest. Of course, we can't meet these gentlemen without discussing what we are all interested in, but they were not authorized to make any protests.

Were they speaking by direction of their government informally, do you know?

I think not, so far as I know.

They couldn't make a protest about anything that has not passed Congress.

No, you can't make a protest about anything that hasn't happened, either. It is, of course, what is usually called academic.

¹ The ship-purchase bill, against which Republican Senators were filibustering, had nearly been recommitted by the Senate on February 1. See the *New York Times*, Feb. 2, 1915.
² Wilson met on February 2 with the progressive Republican Senators, George William Norris of Nebraska, William Squire Kenyon of Iowa, and Moses Edwin Clapp of Minnesota, to discuss the possibility of winning their support for the bill through amendments. Clapp stated his intention to vote against the measure, but Norris and Kenyon indicated that they might vote for the bill with certain amendments. See *ibid.*, Feb. 3, 1915, and Link, *Struggle for Neutrality*, p. 154.

³ Norris' amendment, introduced in the Senate on January 28, said: "No vessel shall be purchased under this act, which sails under the flag of any nation which is at peace with the United States, unless prior to such purchase an understanding or agreement shall have been reached that will avoid any international difficulty or dispute regarding such purchase." *Cong. Record*, 63d Cong., 3d sess., p. 2543. Kenyon's amendment, introduced January 29, called for the creation of an all-civilian shipping board. See the *New York Times*, Jan. 30, 1915, and *Cong. Record*, 63d Cong., 3d sess., p. 2538.

⁴ Norris introduced an amendment to this effect on January 29. See the *New York Times*, Jan. 30, 1915, and *Cong. Record*, 63d Cong., 3d sess., pp. 2538-43.

⁵ On February 1, Senator James Paul Clarke, Democrat of Arkansas, suddenly moved to send the bill back to committee, which would have killed the measure for the current session. The administration spokesman, Senator Stone, attempted to table Clarke's motion, but lost when Democratic Senators Clarke, John Hollis Bankhead of Alabama, Johnson Newlon Camden of Kentucky, Thomas William Hardwick of Georgia, Gilbert Monell Hitchcock of Nebraska, James Aloysius O'Gorman of New York, and James Kimble Vardaman of Mississippi voted with the Republicans. A vote on the motion to recommit was put off, but the status of the bill on February 2 remained very uncertain. The Democratic rebels claimed that their motive was to halt the Republican filibuster, but it later became apparent that they intended to defeat the ship-purchase bill. See the *New York Times*, Feb. 2, 1915, and Link, *Struggle for Neutrality*, pp. 153-55.

⁶ The *New York Times*, January 28, 1915, reported that the Treasury deficit for the first half of the fiscal year was $87,000,000. McAdoo predicted a final deficit of approximately $10,000,000. See *ibid.*, Jan. 29, 1915.

⁷ Frederick Dixon.

⁸ The German-American societies, of which Representative Bartholdt was a leader, met in Washington on January 30 to draw up plans for the promotion of Germany's interests in the United States. These plans included a ban on the sale of munitions to all belligerents and the continued unrestricted sale of noncontraband items. See the *New York Times*, Feb. 2, 1915.

⁹ The interview, which followed Wilson's meeting with McCombs on January 30, concerned plans for the Democratic campaign of 1916. McCombs said that he planned to call a meeting of the Democratic National Committee within two months, to be followed by a dinner celebrating Wilson's two years in the White House. He also said that, whether Wilson decided to run for reelection or not, his record would be the major issue of the campaign of 1916. See *ibid.*, Jan. 31, 1915.

¹⁰ *Ibid.*, reported that the British had given an unofficial warning about the possible difficulties that the ship-purchase bill could create. See also *ibid.*, Feb. 1, 1915, and the Ambassador in Great Britain to the Secretary of State, Jan. 18, 1915, in *FR, 1915-WWS*, pp. 682-83.

¹¹ Although this statement was technically correct, it was not the whole truth. Ambassador Page reported that his discussion of this matter with Sir Edward Grey had produced "the most ominous conversation I have ever had with him," although Grey said that he was not making official representations to the United States Government. *Ibid.*

Feb. 9, 1915

Mr. President, is this situation [the filibuster over the ship-purchase bill] certain to bring on an extra session?

No, I don't think it is.

How do you reason it out?

Why, I reason it out that nothing is certain.

Isn't that the most hopeful view of the situation, Mr. President?

I was at first jesting. I don't see that it is necessary to come to that conclusion, what little I know about it.

Senator Williams[1] told us yesterday that he thought it was "inescapable," to use his word. I wondered whether that was your opinion.

No, it is not. I don't feel the force of that conclusion yet.

Mr. President, you will not consent to the dropping of the shipping bill, will you?

No.

Mr. President, there have been some publications with regard to Mr. House's alleged mission in Europe,[2] the character of the credentials he carries from you. Can you tell us something?

He doesn't carry any credentials, and his mission is a very simple one. In the first place, he often goes abroad just at this time; he is going abroad a little earlier than usual, because there are a great many things we want to keep in touch with—the relief situation and everything of that sort. There is no formal mission of any kind.[3] The papers have been imagining that.

The credentials that he carries are merely letters of introduction?

Letters of introduction; that is all.

Has he any particular itinerary mapped out?

Not that I know of. He didn't when he left.

Mr. President, the same article under a London dateline said that there have been some conferences between the representatives of Russia and Austria and the United States all bearing upon this question of a possible peace. Is that true?

No, sir, it is not.

Has there been any discussion by the representatives of other nations with reference to the prisoner-of-war situation?

There may have been; if so, I don't know.

Mr. President, it is a common practice for belligerents to use neutral flags, as the *Lusitania* used our flag the other day, for the purpose of deception?[4]

It has been very common, yes, sir.

There is no basis for a protest, then, in that sort of practice?

I would rather you gentlemen would not quote me on this subject, but I am perfectly willing to show you my mind about it, on that understanding. There is no rule of international law that prevents it. Of course, it involves manifest risks and embarrassments, but there is no basis, so far as I now know, for anything like a protest by one government to another. Besides, it wasn't a government ship; it was a privately owned ship. My information is that it is not an uncommon practice, though I must admit that I didn't know it until recently.

Does the German declaration of a war zone furnish ground for a protest?[5]

There we are waiting for what Mr. Gerard has promised us—a more extended explanation of just what is intended by the German proclamation, and, not having received that, I don't feel that I know what it is they have in mind. The brief proclamation as published, of course, bristles with things one would like to know more about.

The German Ambassador's explanation of the subject[6] has been somewhat reassuring, hasn't it?

Yes, he intended it to be so.

Do you so regard it?

Well, that is as you look at it. I wouldn't like to express any opinion about that.

Mr. President, the mere fact that there may not be any rule in international law regarding this flag incident, any precedent for protesting it—that does not preclude your right to make it a matter of protest in these circumstances?

Again speaking in the same way, without being quoted, it does not at all prevent our making representations as to the troubles that might arise if the practice were resorted to very often. I don't mean troubles between the two countries, but the embarrassments to neutral commerce.

There is some suggestion of drawing up a law in Congress to meet the situation.[7]

That wouldn't touch the situation; it would have to be an international agreement.

Mr. President, do you attach any significance to England's long delay in answering our note of protest?

No, I think it is entirely the absorption of her Foreign Office in other matters.

We can't answer her preliminary note until her final one?

No, because when she sent the preliminary note, she promised a final one, as if expecting us to wait for it.

Mr. President, aside from this war-zone matter and the flag incident, does the administration find any favor in the suggestion of the Dutch Minister for some common expression by neutral powers as to their rights?[8]

There is no dispute as to the rights of neutrals.

The Dutch Minister, though, proposed some definite—

He did not make any proposal of that sort to our government. He may have expressed that opinion.

Mr. President, does this German blockade lessen the necessity for government ships of ours?

It isn't a blockade.

It amounts to the same thing.

No, it doesn't. That is where you are mistaken. It isn't even a paper blockade. It is a warning. It is interpreted by them as being a warning, as to danger existing in that zone. It is not a blockade.

Mr. President, is there anything about Mexico that you can tell us? The situation down there seems to have been stirred up again by some trouble with the foreign diplomats.[9]

They haven't been having any active troubles. They have just been left high and dry a bit by having no foreign office to deal with in the City of Mexico. There has been no intimation of the slightest danger to them.

Mr. Duval West[10] is in town now, I believe; is he to go back to Mexico on any mission?

He came up to consult with Mr. Bryan about some Mexican affairs. I don't know anything further about that.

Mr. President, one of the arguments which have been advanced against the ship-purchase bill is the condition of congestion in foreign ports, the inability to unload the ships that are going over there now. Have you any information about the situation abroad in that respect?

Such information as I have does not verify that statement.

Will the United States embassy, or what remains of it, remain in the City of Mexico, Mr. President?[11]

Yes, we expect it to—unless all the foreign representatives go.

Wouldn't it be a matter of delicacy to accept Carranza's invitation to go to Veracruz?

It would be a matter of extreme delicacy, yes. Of course, all relations with any of the various Mexican authorities now are private relations, not public, nor formal.

Do you expect to get the trade commission this week?

I hope so, sir; I always hope so at the beginning of the week.

[1] Senator John Sharp Williams, Democrat of Mississippi.

[2] Col. Edward Mandell House arrived in London on February 6, and there were immediate reports that he was in Europe on a peace mission for the President. See the *New York Times*, Feb. 8, 1915.

[3] This is another example of what House once termed Wilson's method of "grazing the truth"—of making a statement that was literally true but gave a false impression. House did not carry official credentials or an official message, but he was touring Europe as Wilson's representative for the purpose of determining a way to bring the war to an end. See Link, *Struggle for Neutrality*, pp. 214-18.

[4] The British liner *Lusitania* had flown the American flag on February 5 to escape German raiders in the Irish Sea. Because of its implications for the safety of American ships, this ruse caused considerable press comment and criticism of British tactics as well as a formal diplomatic protest. See the *New York Times*, Feb. 7-8, 1915, and the Secretary of State to the Ambassador in Great Britain, Feb. 10, 1915, in *FR, 1915-WWS*, pp. 100-101.

[5] On February 4, the German government declared the "waters around Great Britain and Ireland, including the whole English Channel, a war zone from and after February 18." The order warned that neutral vessels exposed themselves to danger from attacks by submarines if they ventured into the war zone, but left a path for neutral commerce outside the "danger zone" to the north. See the *New York Times*, Feb. 5-7, 1915, and the Ambassador in Germany to the Secretary of State, Feb. 4, 1915, in *FR, 1915-WWS*, p. 94.

[6] In a public statement issued on February 6, Ambassador von Bernstorff interpreted the war-zone proclamation, although he made it clear that he had not yet been instructed on the matter. He said that there was nothing new in the proclamation, and that the German government did not "profess to close even the English Channel to neutral commerce and she does not intend to protest or seize American vessels laden with foodstuffs for the civilian population of enemy countries." Bernstorff added, however, that the British use of neutral

flags might endanger neutral shipping in the war zone. See the *New York Times*, Feb. 7, 1915.

[7] The issue had been discussed with Secretary Bryan by Representatives Flood and Cyrus Cline of Indiana and had been raised in the House by Representative Eben Wever Martin, Republican of South Dakota. See *ibid.*, Feb. 9, 1915.

[8] The Dutch Minister, Chevalier Willem L.F.C. van Rappard, visited the State Department on February 6 to discuss the matter of neutral rights. See *ibid.*, Feb. 7, 1915.

[9] Following an incident involving the threatened deportation of the Spanish Minister, the foreign diplomats in Mexico City expressed their displeasure with Carranza's harassment by threatening to leave the country. See *ibid.*, Feb. 5-6, 1915.

[10] A lawyer from San Antonio, Texas, who was being sent to Mexico by Wilson for the purpose of assessing the prospects of a settlement there. See Hill, *Emissaries to a Revolution*, pp. 309-11, and WW to West, Feb. 9, 1915, in *PWW*, Vol. 32, pp. 203-204.

[11] The situation for diplomats in Mexico City had grown difficult after the city was captured on January 28 by the *Carrancista* General, Álvaro Obregón. Soon thereafter, Carranza announced the transfer of the capital to Veracruz and invited the diplomats to move their offices there. See the *New York Times*, Feb. 7, 1915, and Link, *Struggle for Neutrality*, pp. 266, 456-58.

Feb. 16, 1915

Are you in favor of cloture, Mr. President?[1]

I am.

Are you in favor of the Norris amendment to the cloture system which would abolish caucuses also, practically?[2]

I haven't seen it.

It provides that no one shall vote on the cloture rule whose freedom of action is tied by the caucus rule.

I have no comment on that. There are various ways of making one man the Senate of the United States.

Do you favor a general cloture rule, or one to fit this particular case?

I favor a reasonable cloture rule in general. I don't mean one that will cut off reasonable debate, but one that will cut off obstruction.

Mr. President, isn't it a fact, as it is reported in some newspapers, that you are keeping the ship-purchase bill before the Congress in the face of advice to the contrary from leading Democrats who are unnamed?

No, sir.

There is no such advice?

There is such advice from Democrats, but not from those who are unnamed. Everybody knows who they are.

This wouldn't mean the seven gentlemen?

I didn't necessarily mean them, either. There is no such thing as you have evidently in mind.

Mr. President, the *Post* says you favor an extra session?[3]

Who says so?

The *Post*, to revise the tariff?

The *Post* has exclusive information that nobody else has, not even myself.

Mr. President, are there any suggestions of an extra session that might be scheduled on the tariff because of information showing that there are schedules that it would be well to revise?

No, sir.

The tariff is working satisfactorily?

It is working absolutely satisfactorily.

Is there any need for an extra session to devise new revenue legislation?

No, sir.

If the ship-purchase bill and the appropriation bills are passed, there will be absolutely no need of an extra session?

None whatever.

If either fails?

I will cross that bridge when I get to it. I don't expect either to fail. As a matter of fact, that is the reason I don't intend to face that "If" again. Sufficient unto the day is the "If" thereof.

Are you going to be able to break the filibuster, Mr. President, or satisfy the Republicans?

No, sir. I don't think I am, but I think the Senate is.

Any additional evidences that there is need for a shipping bill for filling the orders of different countries and the carrying of congested freight?[4]

There is accumulating evidence. When a case is proven, however, you don't need additional evidence.

Any information bearing on the German note[5] that you can make public?

No. There is none of any kind that I know of.

There has been none since Mr. von Bernstorff's statement yesterday?[6]

None at all that has been brought to my attention, unless it came since I saw the Secretary a few minutes ago.

How about the situation in Mexico, Mr. President?

I haven't heard from Mexico today. One has to hear every day to be sure what the situation is.

Any message confirming the alleged action of Spain with regard to a concert of action?[7]

I haven't seen any confirmation of that at all.

The general inference has been, Mr. President, from this decree of General Carranza—his general order—that the restrictions would apply to confidential agents, particularly with special reference to agents of the United States going down there on special missions.[8]

Yes, that would be the inference. But we are very dull here. We don't draw inferences. Our minds work slowly.

Mr. President, would not the adoption of a cloture rule to prevent a filibuster largely remove the need for the party caucus?

I don't know.

Because the two have been linked together more directly in the Senate, by saying that one is the cause of the other?

Never having been a member of the Senate, I am not qualified to say how far those are connected.

[1] The Senate was considering a cloture rule which would have required a vote on the ship-purchase bill not later than 5 p.m. on February 19. See the *New York Times*, Feb. 16, 1915.
[2] This amendment was actually offered by Senator Cummins of Iowa. Norris' amendment, also proposed on February 15, was to limit debate to three hours per Senator. See *ibid.*, Feb. 17, 1915, and *Cong. Record*, 63d Cong., 3d sess., pp. 3781, 3789.
[3] The *Washington Post*, February 16, 1915, reported that Wilson, fearing a large budget

deficit, wanted a special session of Congress to produce a "thoroughly scientific revision of the tariff."

4 See the *New York Times*, February 14, 1915, for a story reporting a protest about freight congestion made by a Mount Union, Pennsylvania, exporting firm.

5 That is, the German response to Wilson's note of February 10 concerning the war-zone decree. In this note, Wilson demanded protection for American citizens and vessels and said that the United States Government would hold the Imperial German Government to "strict accountability" for the acts of her naval authorities and would "take any steps it might be necessary to take to safeguard American lives and property and to secure to American citizens the full enjoyment of their acknowledged rights on the high seas." He asked the German government to "give assurance that American citizens and their vessels will not be molested by the naval forces of Germany." The response of the German government said that it did not intend "ever to destroy neutral lives and neutral property," but that it had been driven to the declaration of a war zone by British violations of international law. In the circumstances, the German government must "expressly decline all responsibility" for "unfortunate accidents" that might befall neutral shipping entering the war zone. The note suggested the creation of recognizable convoys of American ships carrying legitimate cargoes as the best way to prevent such accidents. See the Secretary of State to the Ambassador in Germany, Feb. 10, 1915, and the Ambassador in Germany to the Secretary of State, Feb. 17, 1915, in *FR, 1915-WWS*, pp. 98-100, 112-15. See also the *New York Times*, Feb. 12-13, 1915, and Link, *Struggle for Neutrality*, pp. 320-31.

6 Ambassador Bernstorff made a statement to the press on February 15 which indicated that the German government would revoke its declaration of a war zone if the British would allow food to reach Germany. See the *New York Times*, Feb. 16, 1915.

7 *Ibid.*, reported that Spain was appealing for joint action to protect foreigners in Mexico. The Spanish Minister, José Caro, had been expelled by Carranza. See also *ibid.*, Feb. 18, 1915.

8 Carranza had decreed that none of the military chieftains should have dealings with the confidential agents of foreign governments. See *ibid.*, Feb. 15, 1915, and the Confidential Agent of the Constitutionalist Government in Mexico [Eliseo Arredondo] to the Secretary of State, Feb. 15, 1915, in *FR, 1915*, pp. 652-53.

Feb. 23, 1915

Anything on the *Evelyn* case,¹ Mr. President?

Why no, there is nothing of public significance. I understand, you see, it wasn't in the North Sea at all. I have been told, on what authority I haven't yet examined, that the captain had disobeyed orders and was out of the course that he had been instructed to take. It seems to have been a sort of tragic accident.

Mr. President, will there by any reply at all to either the note of Great Britain² or of Germany?³

I haven't had time to go into that matter, to know whether that— I mean whether there will be further talk or not.

The demands that are made by Japan upon China under their treaty rights and obligations,⁴ would that become any of our business?

Well, I don't think it would be wise for me to express an opinion about that because I haven't gone over it thoroughly enough to be justified in expressing an opinion.

Any conflict as to the evidence?

Yes, there is a conflict of evidence as to just what demands were made, and in what way they were made.

And we are not yet sufficiently informed to formulate a policy?

Not sufficiently to adopt a policy.

To return to those notes, there is nothing you know of at this time which would alter our position in either matter?

Not in the least. The only question, you see, in my mind, is whether it is necessary to state our position again or not.

Mr. President, at the time the English planted mines in the North Sea, it was reported that they had offered to furnish pilots to American vessels going through that area. Do you know whether that practice is being kept up now?

They did not maintain that. They carefully designated the area so that any captain familiar with his chart could keep out of trouble.

Mr. President, in considering the appointments to the Federal Trade Commission board, there is some refusal in Congress, on the alleged ground that there is no Republican on that board. Was it your belief that you had named a Republican?[5]

Certainly. Mr. Parry is a Republican. The act says that not more than three shall be Democrats. I can appoint a Prohibitionist, I suppose, if I want to. But Mr. Parry, I have every reason to believe, has always been a Republican, and Mr. Rublee too, for that matter.

Can you say anything as to your attitude toward the seamen's bill, Mr. President?

What state is that in? I saw something yesterday in the paper that it is in conference. Is it in conference?

In the House version, with the so-called convention amendment in it.

You say it's in conference, eh?

Apparently with the House bill being preferred in the Senate.

I am not in touch with it.

The story went out last night that you were likely to veto it?

Nobody was authorized to say that. I haven't considered the bill at all.[6]

Mr. President, even though there should be no action on the ship-purchase bill at this session, has the danger of an extra session passed?

I honestly think that there is a possibility of its passing, yes.

Do you anticipate, Mr. President, that that bill will be at all changed in Congress to meet any objections at either end of the Capitol?

No, I do not. It may be changed in Congress to be a little more explicit on some points, but not by way of substantial alteration.

Retaining the Weeks bill?[7]

I understand so.

Mr. President, has it been brought to your attention that certain large electrical concerns in the country are urging a "prosperity week"—a boom in their particular industry, a general boom, and reports went out from New York that conditions were good.

That hadn't reached me. I hope they won't confine it to a week. I hope they will extend it.

One paper states this morning that you have given some consideration to an embargo on foodstuffs and war ammunition, with a view to determining whether or not an embargo is constitutional?

No, sir. That is not true. I also learn that I have a bad attack of influenza, which I am happy to deny.

Mr. President, there is a great deal of attention over this war-zone situation. Can you give any encouragement on that situation now?

I haven't any new light of any kind on it.

Mr. President, has there been any further inquiry into the complaints of the German and Austrian Ambassadors with regard to the manufacture of submarines in this country for shipment abroad?[8]

Oh, yes. When I last met the cabinet, the Secretary of the Navy said he was having a very thorough investigation made. He has not reported to me yet, and I don't know what the result is. But we will follow the matter up very carefully.

Have you got any report, Mr. President, from the Attorney General on the food investigation?[9]

I have got a number of oral informational reports from him. They will follow that matter up just as thoroughly as they can. You see, the only jurisdiction that the federal Department of Justice would have would be over combinations in restraint of trade, and, so far, the investigation has not disclosed anything of that sort.

There have been some reports from the Department of Justice that they are having difficulty in finding out whether sales are actually bona fide or simply speculations.

You see, there is a natural difficulty there. Unless they can get from the grain brokers the names of the persons with whom they are dealing, it is difficult to piece things together and find out whether there is any attempt to form a corner or not. So far, they have been unable to uncover anything of that sort.

Any recent reports with regard to unemployment?

No, sir.

You don't know whether the situation is changing for the better?

No, sir, I don't.

Any change in the situation, Mr. President, with respect to the necessity for a special session?

No, sir. It's just the same.

[1] S.S. *Evelyn*, an American steamship carrying a cargo of cotton, was sunk by mines off Borkum Island in the North Sea on February 20. See the *New York Times*, Feb. 22, 1915, and the Ambassador in Germany to the Secretary of State, Feb. 22, 1915, in *FR, 1915-WWS*, p. 339.
[2] On February 10, Wilson had instructed Ambassador Page in London to call the British government's attention to the risk imposed upon Americans by the use of the American flag by British vessels. The British reply defended the use of a neutral flag by passenger ships such as the *Lusitania* to protect the lives of noncombatants. See the Secretary of State to the Ambassador in Great Britain, Feb. 10, 1915; the Ambassador in Great Britain to the Secretary of State, received Feb. 20, 1915, in *FR, 1915-WWS*, pp. 100-101, 117-18; and the *New York Times*, Feb. 20, 1915.
[3] See above, Feb. 16, 1915.
[4] The so-called twenty-one demands, the full importance of which became known to Washington on February 18. This series of demands and "requests" was made by the Japanese

Minister in Peking, Eki Hioki, to the President of China, Yüan Shi-k'ai, on January 18, 1915. They called for Japanese control of Shantung Province, Japanese economic dominance of Manchuria and Inner Mongolia, and a Japanese sphere of influence in the Province of Fukien. The most sweeping demands were in Group V, which specified that the Chinese should employ Japanese as advisers and as policemen, permit Japanese hospitals, temples, and schools to own land, agree to purchase 50 per cent of their munitions from Japan, grant concessions to Japanese capitalists for the construction of three railroads, agree to consult Japan before borrowing foreign capital to develop Fukien Province, and permit Japanese subjects to carry on missionary work in China. See the *New York Times*, Feb. 19-20, 1915, and Link, *Struggle for Neutrality*, pp. 267-82.

⁵ Wilson sent the nominations to the Senate on February 22: Joseph Edward Davies of Wisconsin, Edward Nash Hurley of Illinois, William Julius Harris of Georgia, William H. Parry of Washington, and George Rublee of New Hampshire. Republicans contended that Parry and Rublee were really Progressives. See the *New York Times*, Feb. 23, 1915.

⁶ The Senate approved the seamen's bill on February 27 and Wilson signed it on March 4. See *ibid.*, March 5, 1915, and Link, *The New Freedom*, pp. 272-73.

⁷ S. 5259, "to establish one or more United States Navy mail lines between the United States and South America," was introduced by Senator Weeks of Massachusetts on April 14, 1914, and passed the Senate on August 3. When it came to the floor of the House on February 16, 1915, it was amended to include a version of the ship-purchase bill (S. 7552), introduced by Senator Thomas Pryor Gore, Democrat of Oklahoma, which was similar to the administration's ship-purchase bill except for the promise that "during the continuance of the present European war no purchases shall be made in a way which will disturb the conditions of neutrality." The Weeks bill, with the Gore amendments, was approved by the House as a compromise bill on February 15. See *Cong. Record*, 63d Cong., 2d sess., pp. 6662-63, 13134-41, 13276; *ibid.*, 63d Cong., 3d sess., pp. 3875-3923; and the *New York Times*, Feb. 16, 1915.

⁸ The Germans and Austrians were complaining that submarines were being built by the Bethlehem Steel Company and the Union Iron Works and shipped in pieces to Europe via Canada. See *New York Times*, Feb. 20, 1915; the German Ambassador to the Secretary of State, Jan. 27, 1915, and Feb. 19, 1915, in *FR, 1915-WWS*, pp. 781-82; and Gaddis Smith, *Britain's Clandestine Submarines, 1914-1915* (New Haven, Conn., 1964).

⁹ See the statement by Attorney General Gregory in the *New York Times*, Feb. 24, 1915.

March 2, 1915

Do you expect to be in the city after the fourth of March, Mr. President?

Yes.

Will you tell us whether you have decided definitely whether you will go to 'Frisco?

Unfortunately, I cannot decide definitely. I am waiting to see if there is rope enough.

Mr. President, the big question this morning is the British note¹ and our attitude toward it. Can you give us any light on it?

I cannot define our attitude toward it yet, because I have not had a chance to digest it—I mean to canvass the whole situation.

As you understand it, does the British note merely declare a blockade or does it go farther than that?

That is just the question I cannot answer. Apparently, it seeks to establish a blockade, but I cannot answer that question with confidence.

If England establishes a blockade, it would be her right, or alleged right, to seize neutral ships in the waters of the blockaded ports, but under this order Great Britain would go a great deal farther than that, wouldn't she? She would arrogate to herself or claim the right, at least, to seize a neutral ship, no matter in what waters it may be.

The precise meaning I have not got at yet. It will need further correspondence to get at it.

Any attempt to send ships in there would involve merely a risk, then, rather than a violation of neutrality?

Oh, yes. That would be true of a strict blockade.

Do you mean, Mr. President, that the note does not define Great Britain's position clearly, or that you have not yet studied it?

Both are true. I have not had time to study it. As I read it, it merely defines in general terms a policy without defining the means by which they intend to enforce that policy—whether that means a definite blockade or not.

Mr. President, submarines seem to have changed the rules of warfare considerably. Has any information come to you that a blockade under modern war conditions is a very different matter from what it has been, and that therefore the lines are made broader?

Yes, sir, but no nation has the right to change the rules of war. I think that it would be more precise to say that the conditions of war have changed radically; the rules of war have not.

Can you say anything with reference to the seamen's bill, Mr. President?

I am in executive session on that.

Can you say whether or not you have heard from the State Department on that?

Yes, I have heard from the State Department concerning the degree to which it affects treaties with foreign nations.

Can you say anything about that?

I would rather not say anything just at present, because I am studying the matter.

You know, Mr. President, there are always some leaks in executive sessions.

But not until after they are over.

Is the rural-credits situation satisfactory to you now?

I don't know what it is this morning. It changes kaleidoscopically.

Mr. President, when the matter was up before, it was understood that you were opposed to any form of federal aid in the rural-credit plan. Is that true still?

Yes, sir.

One Congressman informed me that the Hollis bill was the only one you would sign, Mr. President?

Oh, well, there are a great many people who know my mind better than I do myself.

Mr. President, I thought it was the Hollis-Bulkley bill that was laid aside because it had federal aid in it.[2]

Yes, it was.

Federal aid is out of the bill?

Out of the most recent form.

The House put it back in at 1:30 this morning.

Did it?

Mr. President, could you say anything about this passport investigation?[3] It is reported to have been brought to your attention.

It was, of course, but I merely directed that there should be a full investigation. I haven't had time to follow the testimony.

Do you expect, Mr. President, that an extra session of the Senate will be necessary?

No, sir, I don't expect it.

Mr. President, have you any plan of doing anything further with regard to the southern Ohio coal strike?[4]

Well, the Department of Labor is seeking to do everything that the law permits us to do. I merely said to one of the representatives from Ohio the other day that I would be pleased to play any part in it that I could play. Of course, I am interested in a settlement.

Did he suggest any definite course?

No, he did not.

Didn't he suggest that you might receive the representatives of the miners and the operators? Have you agreed to that?

I haven't been asked to do it. The representatives of both sides were to be in Washington, I think it was, yesterday, to see the Secretary of Labor; they were invited by him, I believe, to a conference.

Mr. President, have you given any consideration to the suggestion—I don't know that it has been made to you personally—of a special session of Congress in the fall?

No.

Mr. President, have you heard that Ambassador Bernstorff from Germany was expected to be recalled by his government?[5]

No, sir.

[1] The British note, delivered at the State Department on March 1, was a declaration of the right of reprisal against the German use of the submarine. It did not use the word blockade but proclaimed a policy which amounted to one by stating that "the British and French Governments will, therefore, hold themselves free to detain and take into port ships carrying goods of presumed enemy destination, ownership, or origin." See the New York Times, March 2, 1915; the British Ambassador to the Secretary of State, March 1, 1915, in FR, 1915-WWS, pp. 127-28; and Link, Struggle for Neutrality, pp. 335-40.
[2] In the spring of 1914, Wilson had opposed the federal credits provision of the Hollis-Bulkley bill because he regarded it as class legislation. The matter was resurrected on February 25, 1915, when the Senate adopted an amendment to the agricultural appropriations bill presented by Senator Porter James McCumber, Republican of North Dakota, which provided for the creation of a federal rural-credits system in the Treasury Department. The House approved the Hollis-Bulkley bill on March 2 after restoring Section 30, which called for federal credits, to the bill. The session expired, however, before the conference committee could take action. See the New York Times, Feb. 26 and March 2, 1915; Cong. Record, 63d Cong., 3d sess., pp. 5008-56; and Link, The New Freedom, pp. 262-64.
[3] The investigation into the use by Germans of false American passports had led to the German Naval Attaché, Capt. Karl Boy-Ed. Wilson directed that the grand jury in New York City conduct a thorough investigation. See the New York Times, March 1-3, 1915.
[4] The coal strike in southern Ohio had begun on April 1, 1914. The Secretary of Labor had

sent in federal conciliators in January, but the situation had not improved. See *ibid.*, Jan. 6, 1915.
      ⁵ *Ibid.*, March 1, 1915, reported that Bernstorff was to be recalled because of embarrassment in Berlin over the Boy-Ed affair. For more on this matter, see the German Ambassador to the Secretary of State, Dec. 1, 1915, in *FR, 1915-WWS*, p. 947.

March 9, 1915

Mr. President, the main thing seems to be Mexico this morning; can you tell us anything of the government's intentions?[1]

The government has no intentions. We have represented our views to them on what appears to be the danger in Mexico City. Of course, you have to discount a great deal that comes from Mexico City, because there are certain persons down there who are determined to have us intervene, even if they have to manufacture the facts on which the intervention takes place.

Mr. President, are our representations in anything like the shape of an ultimatum?

Oh, we don't utter ultimata; we represent our views and act accordingly.

Are any new naval vessels required there?

I don't think there are any required. There are a couple[2] that are going down preparatory to coming home for their annual repairs. I mean a couple going from Guantánamo.

Mr. President, could you tell us something about the views that we have presented to Carranza in this note?

We haven't presented any views. We have simply told him what we have heard of the situation in Mexico City, how serious it seems to be, and have called upon him to take the necessary steps to protect the foreign population of the city. That is all.

Have we been requested by any foreign governments to urge—

The representatives of one or two foreign governments have informally expressed their anxiety to us, but no request of any sort has come.

Mr. President, they are depending upon us, are they not, to handle the situation, and are not figuring on doing anything themselves, so far as you know?

Oh, no; there has been no suggestion about their doing anything themselves. They have depended upon us all along.

Does that apply also to South American countries? There has been some suggestion of Pan-American action—some of the South American countries getting together with the United States in joint representation.[3]

That has not reached me. I had not heard that suggestion. Where did you learn that?

It was printed in the papers the latter part of last week. The story was that the Pan-American countries were considering this proposition of eventual intervention by joining with the United States.

I don't think that can have a substantial foundation. It has not come to me at all.

Mr. President, have any outrages actually been committed in Mexico City, or is it just the fear that there will be?

Just the fear. The fear is that the city will be evacuated and left without protection. For some reason, they all want to get out of it; I don't understand why.

Have you any information of a new movement of Félix Díaz?

Yes, I have had such an intimation about once a month. I don't take Félix Díaz seriously.

Mr. President, what is the situation in Mexico in that territory that is supposed to be controlled by Villa? Has there been any complaint in recent weeks, any outrages?

None at all in recent weeks.

How about the famine conditions?

Well, I have been told that for about seventy-five miles south of the border—the border between the United States and Mexico—there is distress and some fear of famine. That is the only part of the country in which I have heard of that.

Mr. President, have you begun to hear from Mr. West[4] yet?

Oh, yes, but simply of his movements.

Anything as to his conclusions?

No.

With which side has he been conferring?

With all sides. I will not attempt to enumerate them.

Mr. President, do you know where he is right now, whether he is with Carranza or not?

My latest information is that he is on his way to Mexico City.

There was some suggestion some time ago that John Barrett[5] would be able to settle this thing very quickly down there?

Who made the suggestion?

Mr. President, one of the morning papers, through a correspondent whose name appears in black type, states that some individual[6] has been wandering through Wall Street with a document addressed "To whom it may concern" and signed by you, in an effort to secure cooperation of the business interests. Can you say anything about that?

Well, I can't imagine who that is. Does it name him?

No, it seems to be very mysterious. Apparently, he has a blanket commission to smooth over the business interests of New York.

My only comment on that would be "Rats!" That's a fairy tale.

Mr. President, this government has been discussing recently with the belligerents of Europe various issues arising out of the war. Can you tell us anything about the status of those discussions?

All that I know is that the final notes in the matter have not been received.

Mr. President, has this government made any inquiry for a more explicit statement of the last British note?

Yes, sir.

As to the policy aimed at by the British?

No; as to the particulars of the policy.

Have you received any word yet when the Order in Council contemplated by Great Britain will be issued?[7]

No; it was supposed to be yesterday, but apparently it was not issued. Still, I was merely gathering that from what I had heard. I have not had any official news.

Mr. President, there has been a great deal said about the number of treaties which will be violated by the passage of the seamen's bill. Have you heard anything from the State Department as to what the status is?

Yes, I have a detailed statement as to what treaties would be affected by the bill.[8] You notice we are given plenty of time to deal with that matter.

It gives you ninety days in which to give notice, and a year from the time in which the bill goes into effect.

No, it is a year from the time that the notice takes effect. Each treaty, of course, provides a time for notice, how many months or whatever period it is in which notice shall be given, and then a year is allowed after that, so that in most instances it will be about fifteen months after the ninety days.

Great commercial treaties are not affected in every instance, are they?

No, and in many of the most important instances—I mean in cases of countries with which we have the largest commercial dealings—they are not affected at all—the commercial treaties are not affected at all.

Mr. President, is the point with regard to the detention of deserters the only one raised in connection with the treaties?

That is the only one.

Foreign governments, Mr. President, do not object to meeting our lifeboat requirements?

Those requirements are identical with those in the Convention of London, which three governments have ratified—our own, the English, and the German.

Our own conditionally?

Yes, conditionally, on being understood that we have the privilege of exacting further safeguards in our own ports.[9]

As to the manning of the ships, Mr. President, the requirements are not alike?

Not identical in all respects.

Had you heard that some American ship lines, that have recently taken the flag, were to go to foreign registry again because of the seamen's bill?

That would not be very intelligent unless they were going to stop using our ports, because the requirements apply to all users of our ports, under whatever registry.

They could use Chinese crews and fly the Chinese flag;[10] that is the principal objection they have to it.

No, I had not heard that.

Mr. President, you read Secretary Redfield's report on the industrial situation in Montgomery County, Pennsylvania.[11] Can you say anything about it?

No; I think it speaks for itself.

Mr. President, have we made any representations to China or Japan recently with reference to the situation in China?

No.

Mr. President, Senator Lodge came out the other day with a statement on the ship-purchase bill.[12] Have you any comment to make on it?

No, sir.

[1] Wilson, through Bryan, sent a sharp note of protest on March 6 in comment on a statement by General Obregón that he might remove his troops from Mexico City and leave the foreigners there unprotected. It said: "When a factional leader preys on a starving city to compel obedience to his decrees by inciting outlawry and at the same time uses means to prevent the city from being supplied with food a situation is created which it is impossible for the United States to contemplate longer with patience." The administration ordered additional warships to Veracruz on March 8. See the *New York Times*, March 4 and 9, 1915, and *FR, 1915*, pp. 659-61.
[2] The battleship *Georgia* and the armored cruiser *Washington*. See the *New York Times*, March 10, 1915, and Link, *Struggle for Neutrality*, p. 462.
[3] The story was attributed to a statement by Representative James Luther Slayden, Democrat of Texas. See the *New York Times*, March 8, 1915.
[4] That is, Duval West in Mexico.
[5] Director-General of the Pan American Union.
[6] Charles Ferguson of New York, an editorial writer for the Hearst newspapers.
[7] The Order in Council of March 11, 1915, put into operation a new British maritime system which, in effect, blockaded Germany by interdicting *all* trade between the neutrals and Ger-

many, by whatever route. See the Ambassador in Great Britain to the Secretary of State, March 15, 1915, in *FR, 1915-WWS*, pp. 143-45, and Link, *Struggle for Neutrality*, pp. 338-40.

[8] Bryan and Lansing urged Wilson to give the bill a pocket veto because to sign it would mean renegotiating commercial treaties with twenty-two nations and provoke trouble over its provision which abolished the imprisonment of sailors for desertion. See Lansing to Bryan, March 1, 1915, in *PWW*, Vol. 32, pp. 302-303, and Link, *The New Freedom*, p. 272.

[9] See above, Dec. 15, 1914.

[10] This action was threatened by the Robert Dollar Line. See the *New York Times*, March 9, 1915.

[11] The Manufacturers' Association of Montgomery County, Pennsylvania, had issued a statement that a business depression there was being caused by the Underwood tariff. Secretary of Commerce Redfield ordered an investigation by D. M. Barclay, Commercial Agent of the Bureau of Foreign and Domestic Commerce. Released by Redfield on March 7, the report attributed the depressed conditions to faulty business methods. See *ibid.*, March 8, 1915.

[12] Lodge felicitated the country on the defeat of the bill on March 4. See the *New York Times*, March 8, 1915.

March 30, 1915

Mr. President, could you tell us whether the note to Great Britain is in final shape?[1]

I think it is about in final shape and is to go—probably go within the next twenty-four hours. Let me revert just a moment to what I was saying to you gentlemen, and beg that you will assist me to observe the courtesies on correspondence. Of course, soon after the note reaches Great Britain, it will be given out, just as their note was given out by arrangement after it had reached here. And I ask for your cooperation in not speculating as to its contents until it is given out at its destination. Things are very much more effective when they are managed according to etiquette.

Mr. President, what is the status of the note to Germany about the *Prinz Eitel*?[2]

So far as I know, that note is not ready yet, for some reason which I have not had time to inquire about. We are not fully informed as to the questions of ownership. This I get secondhand and merely repeat it to you for what it is worth.

The statements in the paper this morning are that it has been determined that the crew was ordered by the British—

I think that that must be unauthoritative. I don't know. I am not informed. When I can wait for twenty-four hours, there are a good many things I don't know that I find out about.

Mr. President, has any tentative draft of a proposed treaty with Russia been submitted to you?

No, sir.

Mr. President, have you considered the idea of sending General Scott back to the border to try to straighten out this situation at Brownsville?[3]

No. Poor General Scott is very useful, but we are not going to impose that upon him.

Has any arrangement been made to protect American territory there?

Oh, yes. We are taking the usual precautions.

Mr. President, this *Eitel Frederich* down there seems to be exciting a lot of trouble.[4] Have you anything to say at this time?

It is exciting a lot of interest and speculation, but no trouble that I know of.

Yes.

We would know ourselves if there was something in the air.

There is an assumption in the papers that if this ship attempted to go to New York within the three-mile limit,[5] it might draw some—

Of course, no ship of that draft can get to New York within the three-mile limit—so I am informed. The three-mile limit is rather a jagged line between New York and the Capes. I am not a nautical man, but that is what I feel quite sure is true. For example, yesterday, when I went to Annapolis,[6] we found that the *Moreno* was anchored about four miles off Annapolis. Not that that was not in our territorial waters. It was in our bay, but ships of that draft can't run near the shore.

If the German commander announced his intention to be interned, there would be no difficulty in transferring him from Hampton Roads under convoy, as was done in previous—

I don't know. I can't answer that question.

I have in mind the big liner that was brought down from Portland, Maine.

She was brought down under a customs officer. She was lying where it wasn't safe.

Mr. President, going back to Haiti for a moment,[7] has there been any correspondence with other nations about when recognition should be accorded?[8]

No. None at all. Of course, they are perfectly free, legal agents. I hadn't heard of any such thing mentioned.

Is there anything with reference to the situation between Japan and China that you can discuss with us?

No, there is nothing new at all since I saw you last.

Is there anything new in Governor Fort's report on Haiti that would keep us from recognizing the government?[9]

No, he just reported on the conditions that he had found there. He didn't draw any conclusion at all.

Mr. President, in his address the other night,[10] Mr. Taft said that the Harrison administration in the Philippines had substituted incompetency for efficiency, and cited the loss of millions of pesos. Are you familiar with that?

I am, but I hope that, when I get out of office, my successors will not express any opinion with regard to what I say about them. I have no opinion to express about what my predecessors say about me. It is not often that there are two ex-Presidents living, and we are trying to invent an etiquette.

Have you gotten anywhere with your effort on that line?

Well, I am trying to make it up all by myself.

Is it a fact, Mr. President, that the collection of these friar-land monies has fallen back a million and a half pesos?[11]

Without a reexamination of the figures, I wouldn't like to undertake a comment of any kind. I can't, offhand.

Can you say anything, Mr. President, as to Mr. Phelan's report on Santo Domingo?[12]

I haven't seen it. He hasn't made it yet.

Mr. President, is there anything you can say about the Colonel's visits? Have you had any communications from Colonel House?

A great many. There seems to be a lot of notions as to what he is up to. He isn't up to anything. That is the answer to that question. He is on a tour of information entirely.

Is the Recorder of Deeds anywhere near?[13]

No, sir.

You see, I have to keep on writing the same thing over and over again.

Why don't you arrange a stereotype as well?

Mr. President, does your rule on Mr. Taft apply to Mr. Roosevelt's comment the other day?[14]

I suppose the Colonel would be willing to make it only a committee of one on this etiquette business.

[1] That is, the note responding to the British Order in Council of March 11. This note protested against the "practical assertion of unlimited belligerent rights over neutral commerce within the whole European area" embodied in the Order in Council and particularly against Great Britain's attempt to interdict neutral trade in noncontraband items to and from neutral ports. It went to London late in the day on March 30. See Link, *Struggle for Neutrality*, pp. 340-48, and the Secretary of State to the Ambassador in Great Britain, March 30, 1915, in *FR, 1915-WWS*, pp. 152-56.

[2] This note protested against the sinking, on January 28, 1915, of an American schooner, the *William P. Frye*, by the *Prinz Eitel Frederich*, a German auxiliary cruiser. See Link, *Struggle for Neutrality*, p. 454, and the correspondence in *FR, 1915-WWS*, pp. 341, 357, 360-61.

[3] As a result of fighting at Matamoros, two Americans near Brownsville, Texas, had been wounded by stray bullets. Residents of the area also feared that artillery shells might stray on to American territory. See the *New York Times*, March 28-30, 1915.

[4] The *Prinz Eitel Frederich* had put in at Newport News, Virginia, on March 10 for repairs and refueling and had reached the time limit after which it must either leave or be interned. Anticipating this, British warships had gathered outside the three-mile limit to sink the German auxiliary cruiser when it departed American waters. The Wilson administration had expressed its concern over the potential for a breach of neutrality through hostilities in the area by ordering the battleship *Alabama* to Newport News. See *ibid.*, March 27-28, 1915, and the correspondence in *FR, 1915-WWS*, pp. 824-33.

[5] The *New York Times*, March 30, 1915, reported that the cruiser's commander was considering being towed to New York for internment.

[6] Wilson went to Annapolis on March 29 to lunch with the Argentine Ambassador, Rómulo Sebastian Naón, on board the *Moreno*, a new Argentine battleship that had been constructed in the United States. See *ibid.*, March 30, 1915.

[7] This is the first reference to Haiti in Swem's notes of this press conference.

[8] That is, recognition of the government of President Vilbrun Guillame Sam, established on March 4. See Link, *Struggle for Neutrality*, pp. 527-28.

[9] Former New Jersey Governor John Franklin Fort had reported to Bryan on March 13 that the commission to Port-au-Prince, which he headed, had failed to elicit a positive response from President Sam. The other commissioners were Charles Cogswell Smith and Arthur Bailly-Blanchard, the American Minister in Port-au-Prince. See *ibid.*, p. 529, and Fort, Bailly-Blanchard, and Smith to Bryan, March 13, 1915, WP, DLC.

[10] To the National Geographic Society on March 26. See the *New York Times*, March 27, 1915.

[11] Former President Taft had been in Rome negotiating the question of friars' lands in the Philippines. See *ibid.*, March 27, 1915.

[12] Senator-elect James Duval Phelan, Democrat of California, had been appointed by Wilson

to investigate the charges against James Mark Sullivan, Minister to the Dominican Republic. See Link, *The New Freedom*, pp. 109-10.

[13] The issue here was whether or not the custom would be continued of appointing a black man as Recorder of Deeds of the District of Columbia.

[14] Roosevelt had renewed his criticism of the ship-purchase bill and of Wilson's handling of foreign affairs. See the *New York Times*, March 28, 1915.

April 13, 1915

Mr. President, is there anything to be said at this time with reference to the memorandum recently left at the State Department by the German Ambassador?[1]

No, sir. Nothing just now.

Mr. President, can you tell us when it was you received the assurance that the Holy See would cooperate with you in any move you might inaugurate for peace?[2]

That intimation has been conveyed to me a number of times. I can't recollect just what individual is referred to, but the matter referred to can be any one of several.

Could you tell us the form in which it came?

It didn't come in any formal way at all.

Have there been any intimations to you, official or unofficial, which would indicate the basis on which peace negotiations might begin.

No, none whatever, I am sorry to say.

This peace gathering,[3] from the viewpoint of the United States Government, hasn't any official standing or sanction?

No. I don't wish, by saying that, to discountenance it in any way, but it has no official sanction of any kind. Indeed, so far as I know, they didn't ask for any.

It has been intimated in some of the press dispatches I have seen, Mr. President, that the delegation had a preliminary meeting of the peace conference at The Hague and had adopted a program in line with the American idea. Were any inquiries made as to the attitude of this government at that time?

No, sir, none whatever. I daresay they meant by that only the attitude of the American people, for whom there is no executive spokesman among the group.

Mr. President, on the fiftieth anniversary of the death of Lincoln, there is some suggestion from local people that you might close the departments on the day, out of respect, for the day or something.[4] I don't know whether you have given that any consideration, or whether you will do so?

That suggestion hasn't been made to me. Of course, the flags will be at half-mast and all other symbols of respect of that sort will be paid.

Mr. President, Congressman Gardner, at a dinner here, made the assertion that, after having made certain suggestions to you, the Joint Army and Navy Board was dissolved?[5]

I have no comment whatever to make upon anything Mr. Gardner said.

Mr. President, have you anything regarding the plans of General Huerta?[6]

No, sir. I am not in his confidence.

Mr. President, would you care to say whether the German note came from the Ambassador or from the German government?[7]

I don't know. You mean whether the text was sent over?

Whether it was authorized by the German government?

He said it was authorized, at least he said so in the newspapers. I don't know whether he said so to the State Department or not. I haven't conferred with Mr. Bryan about it yet.

Mr. President, have we any, have we received assurances that the Japanese-Chinese negotiations are progressing satisfactorily to the United States?

No, we haven't received any assurances one way or the other. We have simply tried to keep in touch with them.

The announcement from Peking, that the United States has not given assurances, or rather has asserted or has told China that she could not rely upon any representations from the United States, is not correct?[8]

All those are without foundation. We haven't entered into that sort of business at all.

---

[1] Bernstorff's memorandum, which he made public on April 11, criticized the United States Government for its unneutral attitude toward the shipment of war goods to the Allies and of

foodstuffs to Germany. "If the American people desire to observe true neutrality," he wrote, "they will find means to stop the exclusive exportation of arms to one side, or at least to use this export trade as a means to uphold the legitimate trade with Germany, especially the trade in foodstuffs." See the *New York Times*, April 12, 1915, which printed the text of the memorandum; the German Ambassador to the Secretary of State, April 4, 1915, in *FR, 1915-WWS*, pp. 157-58; and Link, *Struggle for Neutrality*, pp. 350-53.

[2] In an exclusive interview granted by Benedict XV to Karl H. Von Wiegand, of the New York *World*, on April 6, the Pope had encouraged the American people to continue their efforts on behalf of peace. According to Von Wiegand, the Pope said, "America, when the favorable moment comes for the initial step for a peace suggestion, may be certain of the utmost support of the Holy See. SO I HAVE ALREADY LET YOUR PRESIDENT KNOW THROUGH ONE OF HIS HIGHEST FRIENDS." The friend was Herman Bernstein, an author from New York. See the New York *World*, April 11, 1915, and Bernstein to WW, May 20, 1916, printed in *PWW*, Vol. 37, pp. 84-88.

[3] A reference to the International Congress of Women, held at The Hague, April 28-May 1, 1915. Jane Addams, who served as president of the conference, led the American delegation of more than forty women who sailed from New York on April 13. See the *New York Times*, April 13, 1915, and Marie Louise Degen, *The History of the Woman's Peace Party* (Baltimore, 1939), pp. 64-91.

[4] Wilson issued a proclamation on April 13 which closed the Executive offices and ordered all flags lowered to half-mast on April 15, the fiftieth anniversary of Abraham Lincoln's death. See the *New York Times*, April 14, 1915.

[5] In a speech following a dinner which he gave on April 10 to members of the "Reserve Army of the United States," Gardner claimed that the board had been dissolved for recommending preparations for war in the Pacific. This incident had occurred in May 1913 when, during a time of tension with Japan, the Joint Board of the Army and Navy had recommended moving warships to Manila and Hawaii to prepare for war. Wilson had rejected this proposal. See *ibid.*, April 11, 1915; the Diary of Josephus Daniels, May 16-17, 1913, printed in *PWW*, Vol. 27, pp. 442-48; and Richard D. Challener, *Admirals, Generals, and American Foreign Policy, 1898-1914* (Princeton, N. J., 1973), pp. 368-79.

[6] Huerta arrived in New York from Spain on April 12. Villa's supporters feared that he might be on his way to Mexico. See the *New York Times*, April 11 and 13, 1915.

[7] Bernstorff reported that he had been instructed to submit the memorandum to the State Department, but this statement was not precisely true. See *ibid.*, April 14, 1915, and Link, *Struggle for Neutrality*, p. 350.

[8] Japanese negotiators in Peking had told the Chinese that they should not count on any support from the United States. See the *New York Times*, April 12 and 14, 1915.

April 27, 1915

Mr. President, is it true that you have endorsed the plan looking to a gathering in the United States of the representatives of the neutral governments for the purpose of inaugurating a project of peace propaganda?[1]

No, sir. That's the first I have heard of it. That is Cain confounded. It hasn't been brought to my attention at all.

Has any reply been made to the cablegram about the method that the United States might use to participate in the Japanese-Chinese negotiations?[2]

No. I understand that the Secretary of State had—has intended, for your information, been preparing a reply, but of course—

Mr. President, would you care to say anything about the Chinese-Japanese negotiations?

No, sir. There is nothing new in that aspect of it.

This morning's dispatches seem to indicate that Japan is pressing very hard.

Yes. But that has been indicated again and again. I don't know what that may turn out to signify.

Mr. President, I would like to ask a question about the Riggs National Bank case,[3] but I don't know exactly how to put it. What I want to know, really, is whether the suit is merely a routine departmental matter or whether you regard it as an administration affair?

Why, it is not an administration affair in any sense touching policy, if that is what you mean.

Exactly.

Of course, we didn't inaugurate the suit. We didn't inaugurate it, so that it doesn't express any policy on our part.

There has been a disposition, of course, on the part of a good many newspapers, to make it a sensational matter, one involving the administration.

I know, but I don't think they can make anything out of that because it doesn't bear any characteristics of that sort.

You don't find yourself called upon to challenge the merits of the proposition at all?

No, sir. That is none of my business. They have brought the suit, and of course we will defend against it, and of course in our view the powers of the Comptroller are perfectly clear and indisputable.

Are you saying anything generally, Mr. President, with regard to your plans for the summer, your personal plans?

Well, my family is going to Cornish. How often I can have a look at them there is a matter of conjecture and of serious doubt.

Mr. President, when you speak of the powers of the Comptroller being perfectly clear, that seems to be one of the questions in dispute. I don't know whether you thought of this particular case or not, but the banks, many of them, apparently, think that the powers of the Comptroller are not that extensive; and that is the main issue, as to whether he can or cannot act. And I didn't know whether you meant that particular use of power.

Well, I meant that particular use. Of course, I am not competent to express an opinion as a lawyer. But as I read the statutes, the

English language seems to bring it out pretty clearly in the statutes. I am not trying to prejudice the case. That is for the Department of Justice.

The bank seems to dispute the fact—to say that it is a very dangerous power for the Comptroller to possess.

Whether it is dangerous or not is one question, and whether it exists or not is an entirely different question. If Congress confers a dangerous power, then it exists, whether it is dangerous or not. I don't want to discuss the case. It really is not proper for me to discuss it.

Mr. President, have you anything definite on your review of the fleet, or your visit to the fleet in New York?[4]

No. I am really at the disposal of the Navy Department in that I am going to fall in with their plans.

Anything from Mexico, Mr. President?

No, sir—nothing unusual.

Mr. President, have you any intimation of any further reply from Great Britain?

None at all. No, sir.

Or from the German government?

No. I haven't heard that they are planning one, even.

Mr. President, you have had a request for help from Armenia from the missionaries over there?[5]

If so, it hasn't come to me personally.

The papers said that it had been sent to you.

It may be on its way. I don't know. Is there some special situation alleged to exist there?

There are supposed to be some more stories about conditions over there.

We have been watching the conditions there rather carefully. I hadn't heard of any new developments.

Mr. President, have you been able to address some interesting views, or studies, on the question of relations between the government and the District of Columbia? I mean the broad question.

Oh, no. I have spent several evenings with committees who hardly did more than acquaint me with just what the questions were. And I have expressed offhand opinions in those conferences, but I haven't had time to give it my undivided attention.

It is a fair inference that, when this question comes before Congress, you would be interested in it, more or less?

I hope so. I hope I would be consulted in the meantime, but I don't know.

Mr. President, there is a good deal of speculation as to what you are doing in seclusion at the White House these days. Can you give us any light?

Well, there's no secrecy about it that I know of, or mystery. I am doing what I was not permitted to do when Congress was in session. I am really reading all the dispatches. I am keeping in touch with everything that is going on and expressing an opinion when I am obliged to, and keeping silent when I am not obliged to.

One of the problems of the District of Columbia is the Recorder of Deeds.[6]

I wish, Price, I could help you out on that.

---

[1] The *New York Times*, April 28, 1915, reported that Fridtjof Nansen, Norwegian explorer, was traveling to New York to organize a committee of neutrals for the purpose of disseminating peace propaganda and to request President Wilson's assistance.

[2] At this time, the administration was attempting to find some way to defend China against Japanese demands without openly participating in the negotiations. The cablegram mentioned was sent from Minister Reinsch in China to the Secretary of State on April 24, 1915; it suggested that the United States might send a circular note to all the powers interested in China calling for a reaffirmation of the Open Door. Wilson and Bryan decided instead to make representations to the Japanese government alone. See Link, *Struggle for Neutrality*, pp. 295-98.

[3] The Riggs National Bank of Washington had brought suit against Secretary of the Treasury McAdoo and Comptroller of the Currency John Skelton Williams for exceeding their authority during an investigation of the bank. Williams had requested a list of large depositors and, when he had not received it by June 15, 1914, levied a fine of one hundred dollars per day until the names were supplied. Eventually, the suit was withdrawn and the bank's directors promised not to violate the law. See the *New York Times*, April 21, 1915.

[4] The Atlantic Fleet was scheduled to spend two weeks in New York harbor in May. Plans called for Wilson to review the fleet on May 18. See *ibid.*, April 25, 1915.

[5] American missionaries in Armenia reported that Christians there were being massacred by Kurdish Mohammedans. See *ibid.*, April 26, 1915, and Arnold J. Toynbee, ed., *The Treatment of Armenians in the Ottoman Empire, 1915-1916* (London, 1916).

[6] See above, March 30, 1915.

May 11, 1915

We all have the same thing in mind this morning, Mr. President.[1]

Yes, sir, I daresay we have, all of us, but I have nothing yet to add to what was said on Saturday.[2]

As far as that goes, it may be regarded as a declaration of our policy, may it not—as far as you went yesterday?[3]

I didn't mean that yesterday; I was not thinking of our policy in any particular matter yesterday. I was thinking wholly of the people I was addressing and of the Cain some people have been trying to raise. I did not mean that as a declaration of policy of any sort.

Mr. President, has anything been done yet in the way of communicating with the German government with regard to recent events?

I have nothing more to say about that until I speak finally.

One of the morning papers has what purports to be a report of Duval West with reference to Mexico.[4]

That must be a fake. None has been received, so far as I know. Is it in the form of an interview?

It isn't clear—yes, I think it is, although he isn't quoted.

I sincerely doubt its authenticity.

It claims to present his ideas and conclusions, Mr. President.

That is pretty certainly not so. He is not the sort of man who would do that.

Have you seen him?[5]

No, he was to arrive on Sunday, I think. Probably he is in town, but I haven't seen him.

He would see you first, naturally?

I shouldn't think he would tell anybody else what he thought before he told me.

Mr. President, now that the Japanese-Chinese situation has adjusted itself,[6] can you say anything about our part in it?

No, I think not. Better let it alone as it stands for the present.

Mr. President, does the Japanese-Chinese situation guarantee our commercial rights as they have existed under the Open Door policy?

Well, I can't answer that in the way I would like to be prepared to answer it, because I haven't studied the effects of what China has granted. I haven't been properly advised as to how far-reaching it would be. Of course, we shall expect that nothing will interfere with our treaty rights, either with China or with Japan.

If it is proper to ask, have you been informed by both governments as to what those demands are?

Yes, sir.

And they agree now, do they?

Yes, sir, they agree now.

Mr. President, going back to the first subject of conversation, I would like to know whether we may expect a decision soon as to our policy.

Just as soon as it is possible to be sure I have all the elements in mind.

Then, Mr. President, your statement in Philadelphia about a man sometimes being too proud to fight had no reference to the policy we might adopt?

I was expressing a personal attitude, that was all. I did not really have in mind any specific thing. I did not regard that as a proper occasion to give any intimation of policy on any special matter.

Mr. President, do you expect to see the German Ambassador?

No, sir, I have no appointment to see him.

---

[1] The sinking of the liner *Lusitania* by a German submarine on May 7 with the loss of 1198 lives. See the *New York Times*, May 8, 1915; Link, *Struggle for Neutrality*, pp. 368-83; and Thomas A. Bailey and Paul B. Ryan, *The Lusitania Disaster: An Episode in Modern Warfare and Diplomacy* (New York, 1975).

[2] Tumulty released a brief statement from Wilson about the *Lusitania* on May 8. It said: "Of course the President feels the distress and the gravity of the situation to the utmost, and is considering very earnestly, but very calmly, the right course of action to pursue. He knows that the people of the country wish and expect him to act with deliberation as well as with firmness." *PWW*, Vol. 33, p. 154.

[3] Wilson spoke on May 10 at Philadelphia's Convention Hall to a crowd of 15,000, including

4,000 newly naturalized citizens. His apparent reference to the sinking of the *Lusitania* was: "The example of America must be a special example. The example of America must be the example, not merely of peace because it will not fight, but of peace because peace is the healing and elevating influence of the world, and strife is not. There is such a thing as a man being too proud to fight. There is such a thing as a nation being so right that it does not need to convince others by force that it is right." The address is printed in *ibid.*, pp. 147-50.

4 West arrived in Washington on May 9 and presented his final report to the State Department on May 11. It said that "a condition of permanent peace and order and the establishment of stable government . . . cannot be brought about by any of the contending parties without the aid or assistance of the United States." See the *New York Times*, May 10, 1915, and Hill, *Emissaries to a Revolution*, pp. 328-29.

5 West did not see Wilson until May 24.

6 The Chinese accepted Japan's demands, following the withdrawal of Group V, on May 9. See the *New York Times*, May 9, 1915, and Link, *Struggle for Neutrality*, p. 301.

May 25, 1915

Mr. President, could you tell us anything about Mr. Duval West's call on you last night?[1]

Yes, it was the first chance I had had to see him since he got back from Mexico. I had read his written reports which had preceded him, but I just wanted to get some personal impressions which you can get only in a conversation. It was entirely for information.

Based upon the information received from Mr. West, have you decided upon any change of policy?

No.

Did Mr. West suggest the advisability of an embargo on arms and ammunition?

No, he did not.

Did he bring to you such reports as have shaken your confidence in the conduct of the representatives of this government in Mexico?

Oh, no.

These questions, Mr. President, are all based on publications this morning.

Yes, I judged that they were.

Mr. President, can you give us any information in your own way as to the relations with England about the so-called blockade?

No; that is what the physicians would call a chronic case.

I did not know but that you had some thought or suggestion that you might care to volunteer.

No, sir, nothing new.

Is there any information or intimation from Gerard as to when the German note[2] may be expected?

No, none at all [except] in this sense, that he has conjectured different times, so that we are left to make our own conjectures.

The delay isn't disadvantageous?

To whom?

I don't mean exactly that. I mean chances for an amicable settlement are increased with delay perhaps—a cooling off.

I should think it was good to think that about anything. But I don't know what the causes for the delay are. Of course, we can all conjecture—the new circumstances in the war, and so on.

Mr. President, Senator Lewis and Mr. Kitchin have suggested the necessity of an extraordinary session of Congress to be called in October; do you share their opinion?[3]

Well, I hadn't brought my mind to that subject yet.

Mr. President, can you add to the statement of your address of yesterday[4] regarding the government undertaking shipping lines and communications?

No; I said that merely to show my interest in a very practical aspect of the relations between the two continents.

Mr. President, if you will permit the question to be asked, can you expect capital to go into foreign shipping with the navigation laws unamended and the seamen's bill in force?

I think I can—if they are "up to snuff." We have the most diffident capital in the world.

Perhaps some of the seven hundred-and-thirty-million-dollar surplus lying in the banks might be available for lines of communication?

I don't know to whom that belongs. I met a banker the other day who had the view that deposits were liabilities, not assets. It is an old-fashioned view.

Mr. President, as to the development of the shipping situation, do your ideas on the subject lead to the need of bringing the matter before Congress again at the next session?

I had already stated what was on my mind at present. In answer to the question, I spoke of it yesterday to show that we comprehend it as one of the chief difficulties and knew that it must be met, but it hadn't taken any new phase in my purpose at all.

Has your mind turned to any of the fiscal arrangements of the United States, such, for instance, as the suggestion of Mr. Lewis for the issue of five hundred million dollars in bonds?[5]

No, sir, it has not.

Or the repeal of the free-sugar provision?

No, sir.

Mr. President, there has been some talk of reciprocity between the United States and the South American countries; have you been giving that any consideration?

Reciprocity in what matter?

Tariff, I think.

No, that hasn't assumed any concrete shape.

Does that idea appeal to you, Mr. President?

It hadn't entered my head before, sir. I have been very much absorbed, to tell the truth. I don't know all the things that are being talked about.

These matters with which you have been absorbed, would they be of interest to us?

Yes, sir, they would be if I could talk about them.

[1] West visited Wilson at the White House on the evening of May 24. See the *New York Times*, May 25, 1915.

[2] That is, the response to Wilson's note regarding the sinking of the *Lusitania*. This note, which was sent to Germany on May 13, described the sinking of the *Lusitania* as the last in a series of events that "the Government of the United States has observed with growing concern, distress, and amazement." After calling attention to the fact that the citizens of the United States acted "within their indisputable rights" when traveling on the high seas, it requested the German government to "disavow" the sinking, "make reparation so far as reparation is possible for injuries which are without measure," and "take immediate steps to

prevent the recurrence" of the incident. See the Secretary of State to the Ambassador in Germany, May 13, 1915, in *FR, 1915-WWS*, pp. 393-96, and Link, *Struggle for Neutrality*, pp. 383-89.

[3] For a discussion of their views on the necessity of a special session, see the *Washington Post*, May 23, 1915.

[4] Wilson, on May 24, addressed the Pan American Financial Conference, a meeting in Washington of bankers and finance ministers of eighteen nations with officials of the Treasury Department, members of the Federal Trade Commission, other officials of the Wilson administration, and bankers and business leaders of the United States. The address is printed in *PWW*, Vol. 33, pp. 245-47.

[5] Senator Lewis visited Wilson at the White House on May 22 and called for the issuance of $500,000,000 in government bonds. The bonds, to be sold in small denominations, would serve three purposes: the obliteration of any deficit caused by the European war; the construction of coastal fortifications; and the employment of American workers. See the *Washington Post*, May 23, 1915.

June 1, 1915

We are waiting for you to begin this morning, Mr. President, because the situation[1] is one which will not permit of very close questions, and we thought you might be willing to give your thoughts on it.

I would tell you anything that I could, gentlemen, but, of course, you are all thinking of the German note. I got the text of that only yesterday and I don't feel that it is wise to discuss it today. I know you appreciate the reasons why. And let me ask again that you refrain from conjecturing what the reply is going to be, because some of the conjectures, as you know, are sent across the water and are accepted there as an authoritative forecast. And it is very embarrassing to the government to have those things take place. I hope that our reply will not be many days delayed and, therefore, there will be the less temptation to conjecture what it will contain.

Are you prepared, Mr. President, to present a draft of your reply to the cabinet today?

No, I am not. I want to have a thorough discussion of it first.

What is the status of the Mexican note,[2] Mr. President? When are you likely to give it out?

I am going to discuss that with the cabinet this morning; and I hope it will be ready tomorrow morning.

For the morning papers?

Probably for the afternoon papers.

Thank you! (Laughter)

Mr. President, Senator Kern was suggesting the other day an extra session of Congress in October, to take up the question of amending the rules—[3]

An extra session of the Senate, you mean. That has been several times suggested, but no conclusion has been arrived at about it. I am going to see Senator Kern this afternoon.

Is it likely, Mr. President, that the matter will be determined shortly?

Probably not shortly, because, you see, there is plenty of time, and in these days, when something turns up every morning, one naturally waits to form conclusions of that sort.

But the matter will be under consideration then?

Yes, sir, necessarily.

Mr. President, can you tell us anything about the future work of Mr. Duval West?

No, sir, I cannot. His errand in Mexico is concluded.

He will not go back, Mr. President?

Not so far as appears now. But please don't state that as a fact, because I haven't asked Mr. West whether there is anything he would like to go back and conclude. I wouldn't like to seem to end the matter, because he has done admirable service there. That is just for your information.

Mr. President, may I ask whether you have heard any considerable expression of opinion from various parts of the country regarding either the German situation or the Mexican situation, and whether those expressions give any indication as to the general tenor of public opinion?

There has been a very general expression of opinion in the newspapers about the German matter; not much has come to my attention about the Mexican matter.

I referred more, Mr. President, to the expressions aside from newspapers.

Not a great many. Of course, my correspondence every morning contains a certain number, but not an unusual number.

Mr. President, is it your intention to move for a repeal of the 5-per-cent differential clause of the Underwood bill?[4]

I hadn't taken that up at all. It has just gone through the edge of my mind.

Necessity for such action has not been suggested to you?

Not in any official way; no, sir.

Have you in mind, perhaps as the outgrowth of the meeting of the Pan American Financial Conference, to renew your recommendation for government purchase of ships?

I haven't had a chance to have a conference with the men who were conducting that conference as to what they conceived to be the right inferences to draw from it; so that I haven't formed a judgment about that.

Have you formed any judgment at all as to the practical results of that conference?

Only this judgment—that there was an extraordinary cordiality and readiness to cooperate with the industries of the United States in developing trade and intercourse between the two continents; and I think I am not wrong in saying that an entirely new spirit has arisen between the two continents, of friendship and mutual confidence.

That is sentimental rather than practical, however, isn't it?

I am speaking merely of the impressions of my mind because I haven't had time to go over the discussions of the conference and get the practical inferences from them.

Our government has no very definite idea of establishing a federal bank for South American business, has it, Mr. President?

That is a perfectly novel ideal, and therefore, necessarily in inchoate form. I haven't discussed it with anyone.

¹ The German government's reply to the first *Lusitania* note had been received at the State Department on May 29 and published in the American press on May 31. The note attempted to evade German responsibility for the sinking by claiming that the *Lusitania* was armed, had orders to ram enemy submarines, and carried explosives and Canadian soldiers to Europe. The note also asked for a careful examination of the case by the American government. See *FR, 1915-WWS*, pp. 419-21, and the *New York Times*, May 31-June 1, 1915.
² The note to Mexico, which went out on June 2, warned that the United States could not stand "indifferently by" while Mexico disintegrated. Wilson wrote that, if the leaders of Mexico could not accommodate their differences and unite "for this great purpose" of redeeming

Mexico within a very short time, "this Government will be constrained to decide what means should be employed by the United States in order to help Mexico to save herself and serve her people." This sterner tone was prompted by the reports from Mexico of David Lawrence and Duval West. See the *New York Times*, June 3, 1915, and Link, *Struggle for Neutrality*, pp. 475-78.

[3] Kern hoped to obtain a cloture rule, the absence of which had defeated the ship-purchase bill. See the *Washington Post*, June 2, 1915.

[4] See above, April 28, 1913.

June 8, 1915

Mr. President, has the government any intimation of a [possibility] of peace between the fighting nations from the governments themselves, as mere individuals connected with it have suggested?[1] Any significance?

None that I know of. Of course, being readers of the newspapers, we know what everybody else knows. I say that so that you won't think that we are secluded and uninformed.

Mr. President, was the much discussed delay in the dispatch of the note to Germany caused by any suggestions that were made after the note had been prepared?[2]

There hasn't been any delay. That is the interesting part of the whole thing. It just happens that we can't write a note as rapidly as the newspapers can, and, having to be careful, we have been careful. There hasn't been any delay. Nobody has held it up. It is going just as soon as it is finished.

Has there been a subsequent suggestion, Mr. President, as is printed in some of the papers this morning, that Mr. Bryan has sought a different solution of the problem than the one which is to be found in the note?

Well, I brought the note, or rather the rough sketch of it, before the cabinet.[3] There were all sorts of suggestions there, but nothing has modified the general character of it.

The note as it stands today meets with the approval of the full cabinet?

I think so, sir.[4]

You really submit, then, Mr. President, that the newspapers have been a little rapid on this proposition?

I do, most decidedly. I mean it. And they have embarrassed me infinitely again on my request and prayers that the government should not be forestalled. They have created an initial impression on the other side of the water that will be permanent.

Isn't it a fact, though, Mr. President, that these speculations have appeared in the papers that, generally speaking, are friendly to the administration?

That may be, sir, but the speculations are not friendly.

Mr. President, have you any information that you can give us regarding the situation in Mexico?[5]

No, sir, none that hasn't appeared in the newspapers. We haven't any additional information.

Mr. President, has the government offered any direct encouragement to this League of Peace meeting that is to be held in Philadelphia on June 17?[6]

No, sir. We haven't had anything to do with it one way or the other. They didn't ask for our [encouragement].

Has any other government offered encouragement, so far as you know?

Well, frankly, I don't know anything about it except what everybody knows from the newspapers.

Can you indicate yet, Mr. President, when the note will go forward?

I think very shortly, indeed. I think it is practically completed.

Will it go before the cabinet today again?

Yes, for the last revisions, last suggestions, I mean.

Do you know whether the Allies have given their guarantee of safety to Mr. Dernburg to go back to Germany?[7]

I hadn't inquired about that. I don't know.

Have you gotten any report, Mr. President, on the *Nebraskan* case?[8]

Only a very partial report. Just a preliminary report.[9] It had nothing in it that was not generally known.

Mr. President, is Mr. Lind in any official capacity in the Mexican matter at this time?

No, sir.

Mr. President, can you say anything about the German reply on the *Gulflight* and *Cushing* cases?[10]

In what manner do you mean?

As to their reply to you? Nothing has been said about that. I wondered if that was covered in the negotiations?

Well, the reply speaks for itself. I don't see anything else to say.

May I ask, is the reply satisfactory to this government in the *Gulflight* and *Cushing* cases?

You will notice that the German government admits liability in the case of the *Gulflight* and asks for further information as to the *Cushing*.

Mr. President, does that mean that the German government admits liability, which means that it will go to its prize court without any [protest] of this government?

I don't know what the formal method of it will be. They don't suggest that it will go to the prize court in their communication.

It would seem to be an impression under their ruling. They say it was necessary just as a matter of routine.

It may be. I don't know.

In that connection, Mr. President, the suggestion was made some time ago by the State Department that the German government had the case of the *Frye* demand adjusted through the embassy here. Do you know whether that has gone any further?[11]

I haven't followed that.

---

[1] The *New York Times*, June 8, 1915, reported two peace initiatives: one by the Vatican and the other by a Dutchman, Francis van Gheel Gildemeester, then visiting the United States.

[2] The press had predicted that the second *Lusitania* note would be sent on June 5. When it was not, there was considerable speculation as to the reason for the delay. The real cause was disagreement over what the note should say, which led to the resignation of Secretary of State Bryan on June 8. The note went out on June 8. See *ibid.*, June 5-9, 1915, and Link, *Struggle for Neutrality*, pp. 410-25.

[3] On June 4. See Link, *Struggle for Neutrality*, pp. 414-16.

[4] Wilson had already received Bryan's resignation, and the Secretary of State did not attend the cabinet meeting later in the day. See *ibid.*, pp. 421-24.

[5] The *New York Times*, June 8, 1915, reported that Villa had been defeated by *Carrancista* troops led by General Obregón.

[6] The organizational meeting of the League to Enforce Peace. See Ruhl J. Bartlett, *The League to Enforce Peace* (Chapel Hill, N. C., 1944), pp. 25-42, and Warren F. Kuehl, *Seeking World Order: The United States and International Organization to 1920* (Nashville, Tenn., 1969), pp. 181-92.

[7] Dr. Bernhard Dernburg, the best-known German propagandist in the United States, had decided to leave the country before he could be expelled because of his remarks on the sinking

of the *Lusitania*. On June 8, he was in London awaiting permission to return to Germany. See the *New York Times*, June 4, 1915, and Link, *Struggle for Neutrality*, pp. 377-79.

[8] *Nebraskan*, an American cargo steamer, had been torpedoed off the south coast of Ireland on May 25. Although the crew abandoned ship, there were no injuries, and the vessel returned to Liverpool under her own power but with several compartments flooded. See the *New York Times*, May 27-31, 1915, and the Ambassador in Great Britain to the Secretary of State, May 26, 1915, in *FR, 1915-WWS*, p. 414.

[9] Gerard reported on June 4 that the German Foreign Secretary, Gottlieb von Jagow, would ask the German Admiralty about the *Nebraskan* incident. Gerard's final report was not completed until July 12. See correspondence in *ibid.*, pp. 432-33, 468-69.

[10] The American tanker *Gulflight* had been torpedoed in the Irish Sea on May 1. The captain died of heart failure, and two sailors were drowned after jumping overboard. The *Cushing*, another American ship, was bombed by a German airplane in the North Sea on April 29. See the *New York Times*, May 3-4, 1915.

The German note of May 29, 1915, promised that the German government would make full amends if its naval and air vessels had been responsible. A further statement of June 4 accepted responsibility for the attack on the *Gulflight* but requested additional information about the *Cushing*. See the Ambassador in Germany to the Secretary of State, May 29, 1915, in *FR, 1915-WWS*, pp. 419-21, and the *New York Times*, June 5, 1915.

[11] See above, March 30, 1915, and the *New York Times*, June 11, 1915.


June 15, 1915

Mr. President, can you tell us anything new with regard to plans for the Mexican situation?

No, I can't. It's too inchoate yet. I think it's taking shape.

You have had both the Carranza and the Villa statements?[1]

Yes. I haven't had time to study them carefully.

Mr. President, would you care to tell us what change, if any, was made in your note to Germany, after Mr. Bryan revised it and before it took effect?

I think it would be wise not to discuss anything connected with the revision. That is my instantaneous feeling about it.

I thought perhaps if we confined our questions to that one point?

I would have no objection to discussing it with the utmost freedom, but I think perhaps it would be better not to, sir.

Is it true, as was stated in some South American paper,[2] that South American diplomats were conferred with and consulted before the note went forward?

No, sir, and I would—I hope that you all will say so. Just among ourselves, that is not true.

Referring to another newspaper publication, Mr. President, has the United States had any opportunity to lead or to encourage a number of neutral nations looking to a conference for peace?[3]

No more than has appeared—what everybody knows.

There is a statement to the effect that we are the only nation that didn't encourage that, which is not based on fact.

No, sir. We have encouraged everything of that sort, so far as we legitimately could—I mean, everything that was for peace and accommodation.

Mr. President, it has been printed that you sent for Colonel House to return to Washington?[4]

No, sir, I didn't. Colonel House is not an errand boy.

Do you know whether he will be in Washington soon?

I hope so, yes. He is at present, I think, with either of his daughters.

Has Mr. West returned from Texas?

No, not that I know of.

He is expected back this week, I understood.

Is he? I didn't know that.

Can you say anything as to the attitude of the administration with regard to trust prosecution suits, in view of the decision of the Supreme Court yesterday in the Cash Register case?[5]

I am afraid I haven't heard of that.

The Supreme Court refused to review the judgment of the circuit court in the case of the officials of the Cash Register Company who were convicted under the antitrust act.

In other words, it confirmed the conviction so far as it was—

It reversed it.

It reversed it?

There will be a great deal of speculation as to whether the administration will push cases of that sort.

This is the first I have heard of it.

Mr. President, have you any information or comment to make upon the economic conditions of the country—the question of our crops, the prospects for large crops of foodstuffs?

No, sir. I understood that the prospects are unusually fine, but, to tell the truth, I haven't been able to study economic questions recently.

Mr. President, does the withdrawal of the Pacific Steamship Mail Line from the ocean trade offer any suggestion as to the end of the seamen's law?[6]

I don't know, for the reason that I don't know whether it was really necessary for them to withdraw or not.

Have you been informed by any other ship company, or have you been informed by any other—

No, sir.

Are you making an inquiry into the Pacific Steamship Company?

The Department of Commerce is doing so, I think. Mr. Redfield is out of town today.

In that same connection, the seamen's bill calls for the abrogation of treaties.[7] Is that being considered by the Department of Commerce as a possible hindrance to our commercial relations abroad?

We haven't had any responses yet from the governments we have sent notice to. I would say that our confident expectation was that we could rearrange the treaty agreements so as to accommodate that alteration. It affects, of course, chiefly commercial treaties.

Mr. President, with the return of Mr. Marye[8] from Petrograd, there was a revival of talk of a new treaty with Russia. Is there anything new along that line?

Nothing new. I think the Russian government knows that we are anxious to enter into a treaty consistent with the understandings now obtaining.

---

[1] Both Carranza and Villa responded to Wilson's warning note of June 2. Carranza's "Declaration to the Nation by the First Chief of the Constitutionalist Government of Mexico and Depository of the Executive Power of the Republic" of June 11, 1915, affirmed the legitimacy of his administration and claimed increasing success against the rebels. His government, he

wrote, controlled "seven eighths of the national territory" and "nine tenths of the total population" of Mexico. He declared himself on the verge of putting down the rebellion and insisted that his government had now met all conditions for recognition, "because the Constitutionalist Government is now in fact in definite possession of the sovereignty of the country; and the legitimate army of sovereignty is the essential condition to be borne in mind when deciding upon the recognition of a government." He repeated his "programme of social reform" of December 1914: protection of foreigners and their interests, civil order, separation of church and state, no confiscation of property to settle the agrarian question, respect for private property, and public education. Confidential Agent of the Constitutionalist Government in Washington to the State Department, June 12, 1915, in *FR, 1915*, pp. 705-707.

Villa's response blamed Carranza for the "anarchy" in Mexico. He then disputed Wilson's description of conditions in the country, citing Duval West and Sir Cecil Spring Rice on the protection afforded foreigners in areas under *Villista* control and emphasizing the civil programs developed even during the war. "We have not," he insisted, "arrived at such a state of misery and despair that we require help from abroad." See Villa and Miguel Díaz Lombardo, memorandum, June 10, 1915, SDR, RG 59, 812.00/15389, DNA, and the *New York Times*, June 13, 1915.

² Buenos Aires *Razón*, June 12, 1915.
³ See the *New York Times*, June 16, 1915.
⁴ House arrived in New York on June 13. See *ibid.*, June 14, 1915.
⁵ In the case of *United States v. Patterson*, the Supreme Court on June 14 denied *certiorari* to the government. In a rare case brought against corporate officials under the criminal clauses of the Sherman Antitrust Act, twenty-seven officers of the National Cash Register Company had been given fines and jail sentences. The convictions had been reversed in March 1915 by the Circuit Court of Appeals, Sixth Circuit, and the Supreme Court was now sustaining the appellate decision. See the *New York Times*, June 15, 1915; 201 *Federal Reporter* 697 (1912); and 222 *Federal Reporter* 599 (1915).
⁶ The Pacific Steamship Mail Line withdrew from the Pacific trade because it claimed that the seamen's law made competition with Japan impossible. See the *New York Times*, June 13, 1915.
⁷ Notice of abrogation was sent to twenty-one governments on June 11. See *ibid.*, June 12-13, 1915.
⁸ George Thomas Marye, Ambassador to Russia.

June 22, 1915

Have you anything about Mexico this morning, Mr. President?

Not a thing that is new.

Have you had any word that General [Angeles] is coming?[1]

No word, other than what the public knows. I have read the rumors, but I don't know anything about it.

Mr. President, have the resolutions that were adopted by the League to Enforce Peace, American Branch, been submitted to you for your approval?[2]

They haven't come to me, no.

Do you know in a general way what they are? Have you given them your approval, or do you approve of them?

I must confess that I suppose they have come to me, and I haven't read them. That is perhaps a mortifying confession, but I have been busy.

Are you making any renewed efforts, Mr. President, to submit offers for the good offices of the United States to the warring peoples?

All the offers of that sort that I have made have been made publicly or semipublicly. You know all I know about it. I think it is generally understood that this government would be more than glad to do anything that was possible.

Mr. President, are you ready to take the country into your confidence on the Secretary of State?[3]

No, sir. I haven't taken myself in yet.

Have you had a chance to consider, Mr. President, the suggestion of sending a delegation to a continuous conference of neutrals to make suggestions for peace? Some businessmen laid a resolution before you.[4]

I haven't had an opportunity to consider that.

Have any Americans protested against the order of Japan, the announcement affecting the teaching of religion in the schools?[5]

No. No protest has reached us yet.

Is it a matter in which we are greatly concerned in any way from the American viewpoint?

I don't believe that it would affect very many Americans, and I daresay from the point of view of international law, it is none of our business. But I haven't looked into it. The order refers, of course, not to private schools but to public schools.

Will the note to Germany on the *Frye* case be ready to go before you leave Washington?[6]

I don't know whether it will or not. Mr. Lansing is temporarily out of town, and I shan't see him until tomorrow afternoon, and I don't know what the state of the proceedings is.

Mr. President, have you had any word about the German note that might be expected?[7]

No, not any at all. I saw a dispatch from Mr. Gerard[8] only yesterday, but he didn't seem able to form any conjecture.

Mr. President, last week I think you said that things in Mexico were shaping up somewhat. Have they taken any more definite form?

They have been, apparently, shaping down since then. There is another interrogation point thrown into the machinery.[9]

Anything new on the seamen's law—the foreign answers?

No. We haven't received any foreign answers that I have heard of yet.

Mr. President, now that the fiscal year is practically over, have you any word about the state of finances of the government?

No, I have not. I meant to ask the Secretary of the Treasury about that yesterday, but it escaped my memory.

In that connection, Mr. President, could you say anything about your conference with the Secretary yesterday?

That was about rural-credits legislation.

Anything new on that line?

Something to do with shaping up the matter for the consideration of Congress. It was just one of the stages of that.

You still feel that the government should not participate?

I am not expressing any final judgment on that.

Has the committee of Congress, which is working on it, put it in any definite shape yet?

I think not in definite shape. They are just engaging in conference.

Mr. President, in reference to the seamen's bill, has Mr. Redfield reported to you as to the effect that the seamen's bill would have on American shipping?

No, sir, he has not. What he has done is to send me the opinion of the Solicitor of the Department with regard to some of the legal aspects of it. I mean, how it can be tied in with other legislation and with the statutory laws that existed before the bill was passed. And that opinion I sent to the Attorney General.

Can that law be operative with respect to foreign nations until those treaties have ended definitely?

No.

Does the period vary?

No. So far as I know, in respect to all the treaties, the period is one year.

So that it would be roughly about a year from now?

A year from the time of their receiving the note. Roughly a year from now.

Well, it would be operative in regard to all other nations except those conflicting with the terms of the treaties? Have you received any report on this Pacific Mail Steamship Company?

No. I haven't received anything further about that.

Mr. President, have you received any notice or intimation that Great Britain may modify its Order in Council?[10]

No. We haven't had any intimation at all.[11]

[1] General Felipe Angeles, Villa's top lieutenant, was reported to be on his way to the United States to present a new plan from Villa. He arrived in Boston on June 23, was in Washington on July 1, and visited Wilson at Cornish. See the *New York Times*, June 21 and 24, 1915, and Memorandum by Franklin K. Lane, July 1, 1915, printed in *PWW*, Vol. 33, pp. 463-64.

[2] At its meeting in Independence Hall in Philadelphia on June 17, the League to Enforce Peace supported American entry into a league of nations which would bind its members to submit disputes to a judicial tribunal and a council of conciliation. It also supported holding regular meetings to settle issues of international law and proposed that members enforce military and economic sanctions against any state making war on a member nation before the question was submitted for adjudication or conciliation. The resolutions were presented to Wilson by Abbott Lawrence Lowell on June 30. See the *New York Times*, June 18, 1915, and Lowell to WW, June 30, 1915, printed in *PWW*, Vol. 33, pp. 458-59.

[3] The *New York Times*, June 22, 1915, reported that Robert Lansing would be appointed. The appointment was announced on June 23.

[4] According to press reports, a group of businessmen was promoting such a conference. See *ibid*.

[5] The Japanese Governor of Korea ordered that all teaching of religion must be halted in Korean schools within ten years. American missionaries feared that this order would have an adverse effect on their schools. See the *Washington Post*, June 20, 1915.

[6] See above, June 8, 1915.

[7] That is, the German response to the second *Lusitania* note. See the Ambassador in Germany to the Secretary of State, July 8, 1915, in *FR, 1915-WWS*, pp. 463-66.

[8] This telegram said that the German reply to the second *Lusitania* note was not yet drafted but would probably place much emphasis on the use of neutral flags and on the instructions to British merchant vessels to try to ram submarines. See the Ambassador in Germany to the Secretary of State, June 20, 1915, in *FR, 1915-WWS*, pp. 442-43.

[9] During the previous week the *Carrancista* General, Pablo Gonzáles, had threatened to invade Mexico City, and four members of Carranza's cabinet had resigned. See the *New York Times*, June 19-20, 1915.

[10] That is, the Order in Council of March 11, 1915.

[11] Insofar as is known, this was Wilson's last press conference until September 29, 1916.

There is one thing I wanted to say. I have been very unserviceable to you men about my speech making, because the real, literal, fact of the matter is that, until the day arrives, I haven't finally determined what I am going to talk about. I think that, in the midst of a campaign, is an inevitable thing. I am constantly thinking of what I want to say, but I never know upon which occasion I am going to say what, and that has made it impossible to do what Tumulty and others have urged me to do—prepare something beforehand by way of synopsis or even copy. It literally isn't possible, and I have tried. I have tried the copy so often that what results is an essay, not a speech. There is nothing in it. Tomorrow—I have this general idea—there is going to be a delegation representing associations of young men.[2] I am going to try to tell them just why young men should throw in their fortunes with the Democratic party. That is a very general theme, and I will have to fill it in tomorrow. But this is the idea I have in my mind. Of course, to invite a man into a party is clearly unlike other invitations. You have to give him a reason why he should come and not merely offer hospitality. I have got to tell him what the bill of fare is going to be and what will be the character of the entertainment. That is what I mean to do. Having dealt with youngsters a great part of my life, I know the kind of questions that are in their heads in a general way and why they should be urged to throw their lot in with any party. Now, the impressions of the forenoon, for example, will have a great deal to do with what I fill into that general vessel. [Omission in Swem's notes.]

Then, generally speaking, Mr. President, there have been lots of reports, as you know, about various kinds of campaigns. I should think it would help so that you could use the day to [work out] your idea of a [proper] kind of campaign.

I happened to hear McCormick[3] talk over the telephone with someone, and his idea and mine are exactly the same as if we had worked it out together. I don't feel inclined to campaign, because I think it is a sort of impropriety for the President to campaign, not because of the dignity of the office, merely, but because, after he has served for four years, the record is there, and he can't change it. And he doesn't want to stand up and commend it. It is merely that there is no method of doing it that doesn't more or less offend good taste. What he is doing is standing up before the jury to be judged after four years, and he better appoint counsel to address the jury. Well, that's the way I feel about it.

Mr. President, as the counsel for the other side, which is represented by Mr. Hughes,⁴ has made many attacks and criticisms and all that, isn't it possible that you will answer those?

I have a perfect indifference to them. He hasn't said anything much yet. You know, an old politician said this, once, to his son. He said, "John, don't bother your head about lies you will hear. Take my own self. If you ever hear me denying anything, you may make up your mind that it is so." That's the way I feel when he gets under my skin. I may squirm, but he hasn't even touched my epidermis yet.

Mr. President, in that connection, would you give us something of your idea of the election prospects as you see them now, as they are reported to you by your campaign managers?

I can't because I don't know, and my private opinion is that nobody knows. My private opinion is that an amount of independent voting is going to be done—an independent choosing of tickets in this election that will be unprecedented in the history of the country. That being the case, nobody can tell what is going to happen. That is my feeling about it. I'll tell you on the eighth of November how the country is going to vote, but—

Will you be here until the eighth, Mr. President?

I think so, yes.

Mr. President, you get many letters and telegrams. Do you feel that the war will becloud the other issues altogether, or do you think they understand them pretty clearly?

I think they feel that they are being led in a circle, and, when they look about them, they are just where they were when they started.

Mr. President, don't you think that your stand is all right for the thinking people that follow these matters, but, to the great mass of people that do not follow [them], don't you think that the Democrats should bring out more of what has been accomplished in comparison?

I think that ought to be brought out. Whether it ought to be brought out by myself or not, I doubt.

You are the only man who can get publicity, Mr. President.

Yes. I can tell all the country what it is all about, and I am doing so; but boasting of the record does not go very well with me. I don't know how to do it.

You did it very well in the acceptance speech,[5] Mr. President.

I don't think that was boasting. I think that was simply an exposition of things, which ends uncertainty. Things like this tell what the things done have meant and what it was intended to accomplish. Take, as I have several times talked very briefly about, the Federal Trade Commission, for example. It was intended to substitute the processes of guidance and conference for the harsher processes of being pulled up by the courts. That is my idea of what the Federal Trade Commission is for. And I think that is what business needed—not to be kept guessing as to what was going to happen to it and be told, "Wait until you do it, and we will or will not do something to you." But to have something to go to beforehand and not have [to wait for] an interpretation—that being the courts' jurisdiction—then that would be a remedy from an impartial source, not from counsel. If you ask your own counsel what you can do, he tries to find out how much you can do and keep out of jail. If you consider the counsel on the other side—the counsel for the government—he will warn you how little you can do and how many dangers there are that you will get into jail. Neither of those processes is illuminative. We want to sit down with somebody, like other citizens like yourself, who wants to know what the policy and idea of the law is and how you can be loyal to the whole principle of it. And that means removing the impression, among other things, that the legislation of the last four years has been aimed at big business. I am sure that businessmen have found that that is not true, that in their consultations with the Federal Trade Commission it has helped business, but in a way which is in accord with the public interest, and that is all.

Doesn't that imply, Mr. President, some cooperation between the Federal Trade Commission and the Department of Justice, for example?

Yes. The peculiarity of our government, I suspect more than most, is that the several branches of it are not sufficiently on speaking terms. I was astonished, when I got to Washington, to find how little consultation and cooperation between the departments there was and how much jealousy there was in the matter of cooperation. It was a shaky, one-sided proposition all the time. And now what I know to be taking place is personal conferences between the

Attorney General or someone in the Department of Justice and members of the Trade Commission, not for the purpose of making up a policy, but for the purpose of matching ideas and seeing if they have the same ideas. That is sensible. Any sensible man would do that, and that is being done.

Mr. President, do you contemplate appointing the several commissions authorized by Congress—the Shipping Board,[6] the Tariff Commission,[7] and so on, before the election?

If I can. That is to say, if I can satisfy myself that I have got the right men. That is the one thing to be satisfied about. There are so many of them. I think I'll have to just extend them for two generations. It is a big job. I want to appoint the commission to observe the operation of the eight-hour day as promptly as possible. I think I can do that in a few days.[8]

Now, the Tariff Commission is a more difficult proposition. What I wanted was a nonpartisan board. What Congress gave me was a bipartisan board, and that is a different proposition. They made it six [members] and said that not more than three, in the usual language, should belong to the same party. Now, what their idea was, I don't know, because I can't understand it. I would like to appoint a commission in regard to something where I was privileged not to ask to what party they belonged. Just among ourselves, I don't care to what party they belong if they will tell us the actual facts of foreign trade and the relations of foreign trade to our industries in this country. That is all I want to know. I don't like the idea of asking what their politics are, any more than I would like the idea of asking what their religion was. It seems to me almost unconstitutional, when you want an absolutely impartial board, to ask which side they are partial to, because, as I have said in public several times, both the theory of free trade and the theory of protection are unscientific, and no serious economist ties his kite to either of them. Because what we are trying to find out is facts and how to deal with them.

Now, in one period of a nation's history, it will be doing one thing and in another, another. My own idea is, at present, that having—whether as a result of the policy of protection or not we need not stop to debate—but having, by hook or by crook, built up a vast body of national industries that have got too big for our borders and the outlet—a free outlet into foreign markets—is absolutely essential to them, they would burst or shrink. Now, you can't have a free access to foreign markets unless you allow a free access to our own markets—I mean, more or less free. Trade is reciprocal. It never was anything else, and it never will be anything else. And you have got to go forward, therefore, on the idea that if you don't take trade you can't get it. That is my idea of what has happened. Now, in such circumstances, if I am right, the policies and theories of the time behind us simply do not apply. We have got to do new things with a new knowledge of what is going on. If we don't, we are going to get ditched, that is all.

McKinley had arrived at about that same conclusion.

He had. One of the last things he said was, "The time for the restriction of our commerce has passed."⁹ Now, it is a long time since he said that, and some gentlemen who would profess to be his followers have forgotten that he said it.

Do you expect to touch on the tariff question in any of your speeches?

Only in a general way, because I have been alluding to it already and to what I have been alluding to just now. I feel this way: the tariff question is not what it used to be, and therefore to discuss the tariff question as Blaine¹⁰ and his contemporaries used to discuss it is simply an anachronism. They discussed it in another age. He would have sense enough, if he were here, to change the whole method of discussing it. The way some men's brains stay put and never grow and work excites my astonishment.

Mr. President, don't you think the period immediately following the war is going to be such an abnormal period that it is going to require a new policy?

No more abnormal at the end of it than it was at the dawn of it, because it is going to be the dawn of a new age. Now, I don't know, and I suspect that nobody knows.

You haven't prejudged the effects of after-the-war conditions at all?

You can't prejudge them because you find the day you do you are very indiscreet. If you try to take a single matter which is not a trade matter—say, immigration—some persons, as qualified to judge as anybody, say there is going to be an increased immigration into the United States—I mean increased as compared with the decades preceding the war. And some of those equally competent to judge say that there will be very little immigration. There is a good theoretical case, a good argumentative case, to be made for each of those opinions.

Now, whether more are coming or not depends upon them, not on us. We have got to wait and see. On the other hand, there is this certainty, after the war, that there will be a shortage in the labor supply in Europe for some time to come because of the enormous carnage and wounding and physical impairment that have been rendered by this war. I should think that was obvious, and I should assume that that would lead to the offering of sufficient consideration to working men to stay on that side of the water. In other words, a bigger opportunity than would be offered them here, where our labor market is reasonably well supplied.

Now, on the other hand, it is said that the debts that have been piled up by the various belligerent governments are so enormous that taxes will be uncommonly burdensome, and that that will mean a great increase in the cost of living, and that that will drive people out. They can't stand the financial situation. Well now, I don't know whether they can or not but, don't you see, nobody can know.

What is your idea, Mr. President? Do you think we will have a larger immigration?

I think we won't, but then it is only a "think." I don't know anything about it.

Then don't you think, Mr. President, in view of this shortage of labor all over the world, there is likely to be a law passed preventing emigration to foreign countries?

I don't know. I doubt that, because new methods have always been created anyhow.

Mr. President, do you think there will be a great influx of manufactured goods into this country after the war?

I understand they are making them, but I do not see who is making them.

I understand they are making them in Germany.

I have been told that, but I don't understand it. I have heard that dyestuffs were piled up there, upsetting the balance.

Mr. President, you don't take much stock, then, in temporary prosperity?

I don't take any.

Mr. President, about the tariff. Is there anything you could say to us as to the people who will be in control of Congress in case the Republicans should be returned to Congress—the people who will make the tariff?

That is too picturesque a story.

The people who will want the chairmanships?

That would need a brush with a great deal of color on it.

Mr. President, what is your idea about the political situation in New York State?

Well, I think it is very much mixed and intensely interesting, and that is the situation. New York State is one of the situations that makes me say what I said awhile ago, about not knowing what is going to happen.

Are you going to speak to the soldiers tomorrow, Mr. President? I understand you are going to review them.[11]

For one thing, I am going to be on horseback. I would have to stand up in the saddle.

Is there any likelihood, Mr. President, that you are going to the coast?

To the Pacific Coast? Oh, no. It is impossible. You see, what escapes so many people's attention is that I have got to be President in the meantime, and there's such a lot of work going on that I have altogether too little time to attend to, with such speech making as I am doing.

Then we can anticipate that you will make no—not more than a dozen—addresses between now and the time of election?

Not that many. I don't see how I can possibly make more than a dozen.

There are five, I believe, scheduled—

Three for the Middle West and two for New York State—those three at the invitation of nonpartisan committees[12] like next week—the semicentennial of Nebraska.[13]

Will you make nonpartisan speeches in all states?

I hope so. There may be complications, you know. Inferences can be drawn, you know.

Well, will your speeches here be more of a political character?

I will let loose more on them.

Can you indicate, Mr. President, some reasons that you will have in your mind why a young man should vote the Democratic ticket this year?

You come around tomorrow.

Well, we have all presumed that it is to be a rip-roarer tomorrow.

I don't know. I don't know whether you unlimber all the cannon or not. You don't want to shoot at flies with a cannon.

You will have to help us out, Mr. President. We have all said you were going to.

We don't want to get into bad habits here.

Mr. President, will you tell us something of the impressions you get about the progress being made by the Mexican commission?[14]

Well, I really don't know anything more about that, Mr. Bryant,[15] than the newspapers contain. I mean, the letters and messages I get are practically what the public knows—nothing in addition. What is happening there, as I make it out, is a thorough and mutual get-acquainted, not with each other, but with the circumstances, on the one hand, in Mexico, conditions under which they are working there, and, on the other hand, the things that are affecting the judgment of our own government and opinion of the people in the United States about it.

Mr. President, because I was so much interested in Mexico and those with whom I am connected in Mexico, I had meant to ask a question, but since you brought it up, I do want [blank].

In spite of appearances in all the surface things that one deplores, there is a profound revolution going on in Mexico, and I am for it.

Mr. President, the revolution in Mexico is in the hands of the unarmed people who want peace.

I don't care in whose hands it is. I am for it.

Mr. President, the State Department feels that there has been a marked improvement in conditions in the past six years. Is that feasible?

It is not only feasible, but it is so. I simply know that the success that Villa was reported to have had at Chihuahua[16] has not panned out upon investigation. I think those who have been very closely in touch with the situation of course understand what happened. It is not Villa in northern Mexico. It is very difficult for the United States to play the part which we ought to play—of impartial friend of both sides. If they don't believe that the President of the United States is an impartial friend of both sides, of course they won't have anything to do with it. They won't have, and, similarly, the kind of thing that is going on makes a right settlement of Mexican matters more and more difficult.

Mr. President, you have indicated in your addresses that we had a stake in the peace conference.[17]

Yes. I was at pains to say not a stake in the terms of the settlements between the belligerents—the territory and indemnity or whatever may come up among them, that is none of our business—but we have a stake in what is going to support peace after the war is over.

Do you think it will be possible for the neutrals to ask admission to the peace conference?

I don't know. You see, if the neutrals are seated also they can dominate by their numbers, and it is a study in psychology. It is a very mixed business.

Mr. President, isn't it possible that matters in Mexico will so shape themselves as Funston[18] is getting—

But he is not.

Isn't it possible that matters will so shape themselves that it will be absolutely imperative to go there? I don't say in a few months—right now.

I don't see anything of the kind. It has been said for four years, to my certain knowledge, that it was going to be necessary tomorrow. It depends upon what you mean by "necessary."

I wonder whether you consider that the hyphenate issue had died out [until that telegram was sent by O'Leary]?[19]

No, but the damn fools that insist upon discussing the thing won't let it die, themselves. They pop up and emphasize it themselves. So if they had any grain of sense, they would lie low. You know that it is one of the fine points of Providence that Providence so often makes damn fools of crooks; they haven't got sense enough to be successful. I praise God for that. A telegram like that is the most silly indiscretion that a man could possibly commit.

Do you think, Mr. President, that there is any real large percentage of American citizens of German descent or parentage who will let anything of that kind sway them, who are not Americans above—

No, I do not. I haven't at any time. Let us discriminate, however. There is a considerable body that have been misled about various things, but there is not a considerable body that would act out of personal motives. I am convinced of that. The only danger, so far as their action is concerned, the only danger is they will be misinformed and misled, by not reading anything but certain papers, for example, which don't contain the real truth about things. If they exclusively read one paper that is constantly misrepresenting things, it may be that they will be honestly misled by believing what they read. So I don't think the number is considerable. I know and honor so many men of German extraction as citizens of this country that I couldn't believe it.

They are Democrats or Republicans, as the case may be.

Exactly. What I regret about the campaign or voting is that so many Germans who are Republicans now, and would vote that way in any case, are going to get the discredit of voting on these motives. That is a sort of moral tragedy. A man of German origin who is going to vote in the next election is put in this quandary: if he follows his genuine convictions, let us say, in voting the Republican ticket, a large part of his fellow citizens will think he voted disloyally to the United States. That, I say, is a moral tragedy.

Don't you think, Mr. President, there are a great many men who feel themselves in that position who are not going to vote at all?

I hadn't heard that suggested.

I have heard that suggested in Wisconsin, that they expected a great—

I hadn't heard that suggested. It is very possible.

Have you any definite indications, Mr. President, that the pro-German hyphenates are secretly inciting you and [seeking an] opening [with] the other party? You remember your Flag Day speech,[20] Mr. President. Can you say there was a conspiracy to debase American politics? We have been wondering, all of us.

But a conspiracy—that was a word loosely used.

I meant a concerted effort. You haven't any word that Mr. Taft is with Mr. Hughes' stand?

No, none whatever. On the contrary, the opposite evidence seems to accumulate.

Colonel Roosevelt says he is going to tear the shirt off of you again, as he did in his Grand Rapids speech.[21]

The funny thing about this campaign is that it doesn't make any difference. That's the happiest family, considering its differences of opinion, that I have ever known.

I heard him speak there. The men who listened to him were apparently, from their faces, three quarters of them were Germans. He pitched into this Germanness, the hyphen-ness, very strongly, and, by the time he got through, they were cheering. That gave me the idea in spite of his talk.

Look at this: Milwaukee is a center of German Americans, and Mr. Nieman,[22] the editor of the *Milwaukee Journal*, started in on a crusade against this thing, in the confident expectation that he was going to lose money, but not that that was going to influence his paper. And his subscriptions have increased 20 per cent. In Milwaukee! You remember the famous saying of Edmund Burke, that you can't bring an indictment against a whole people.[23] It's the fellow who is mocking you you can bring an indictment against. Because it is what you are saying—that you are a part, you are a self-respecting part of the citizens of German origin. I don't like to call them German Americans because I want to leave the hyphen out. The great body of them are just as thoroughly American as we are, more thoroughly than some people born in the United States, because they chose to come here.

It did not happen to all of us. We were born here. They broke up—they broke family ties, local ties, and came here with a definite choice of sovereignty that none of us who were born in this country has made. I used to say, sometimes, you know, how foreigners used to laugh at us for boasting of the size of the United States, suggesting that we hadn't made it. I used to reply to that, that a man was as big as the thing that he successfully took possession of, and that, therefore, we were as big as America.

Now that is what has happened to these people who have chosen this as their place of allegiance. They have chosen this kind of government and this kind of life. And that is what most of us can't say we did. So that it doesn't stand to reason. Of course, this is taking a very unusual case, but take men like Carl Schurz.[24] There wasn't a more intense American in his day than Carl Schurz. There wasn't anybody in America who could explain what American ideals were better than Carl Schurz. He came out of the fires of the Revolution of 1848, when men were thinking fundamentally about government. He knew what he came for. The passion remained in his blood all his life. You would leave out some of the best expressions of what we are fighting for if you left out the men of those origins.

[1] This conference was held at Shadow Lawn, Wilson's summer home in Long Branch, New Jersey. According to the *Washington Post*, September 30, 1916, this conference was to mark the resumption of twice-weekly meetings for the remainder of the presidential campaign, but no other transcripts exist from this immediate period.

[2] Wilson addressed the Young Men's League of Democratic Clubs at Shadow Lawn on September 30. See the *Washington Post*, Oct. 1, 1916, and Arthur S. Link, *Wilson: Campaigns for Progressivism and Peace, 1916-1917* (Princeton, N. J., 1965), pp. 105-106. The address is printed in *PWW*, Vol. 38, pp. 301-12.

[3] Vance Criswell McCormick of Harrisburg, Pennsylvania, the new Democratic national chairman.

[4] Charles Evans Hughes, Republican candidate for President in the campaign of 1916.

[5] On September 2, Wilson received notification of his nomination from Senator Ollie Murray James of Kentucky, the permanent chairman of the Democratic National Convention. Wilson responded with an address which strenuously defended his administration's record in domestic and foreign affairs. See Link, *Campaigns for Progressivism and Peace*, pp. 94-95; the address is printed in *PWW*, Vol. 38, pp. 126-39.

[6] The Shipping Act of 1916, which Wilson signed on September 7, created a five-member United States Shipping Board to regulate and develop the American merchant marine. See Safford, *Wilsonian Maritime Diplomacy, 1913-1921*, pp. 67-93.

[7] The Tariff Commission Act, introduced by Representative Henry Thomas Rainey, Democrat of Illinois, created a six-member Tariff Commission to investigate the effects of tariff rates and report to the President and congressional committees. See Arthur S. Link, *Wilson: Confusions and Crises, 1915-1916* (Princeton, N. J., 1964), pp. 341-44.

[8] The Adamson Act of 1916, which established the eight-hour day for carriers engaged in interstate commerce, created a three-member commission of inquiry into the effects of the eight-hour day on the railroad industry. Wilson appointed the commission on October 5. See Link, *Campaigns for Progressivism and Peace*, pp. 88-91, and the *Washington Post*, Oct. 6, 1916.

[9] In his last speech at Buffalo, New York, President William McKinley said: "The period of exclusiveness is past. The expansion of our trade and commerce is the pressing problem. Commercial wars are unprofitable." The speech is printed in Charles S. Olcott, *The Life of McKinley*, 2 vols. (Boston, 1916), II, 378-84.

[10] Senator James Gillespie Blaine of Maine, Republican presidential nominee in 1884 and Secretary of State under Presidents James Abram Garfield and Benjamin Harrison.

[11] Wilson inspected the New Jersey National Guard at Sea Girt on September 30. See the *Washington Post*, Oct. 1, 1916.

[12] Wilson had announced that he would not be making political speeches but would only discuss public questions. See *ibid.*, Sept. 30, 1916.

[13] Wilson spoke in Omaha on October 5 at a celebration of the fiftieth anniversary of Nebraska's statehood. The address is printed in *PWW*, Vol. 38, pp. 343-49; see also the *Washington Post*, Oct. 6, 1916.

[14] Following Mexican-American hostilities at Carrizal on June 20, in which fourteen Americans were killed and twenty-five captured, the two governments created a joint high commission to look into questions concerning the protection of the international boundary and the withdrawal of the Punitive Expedition which the Wilson administration had sent into Mexico on March 10. The American commissioners were Secretary of the Interior Lane, Judge George Gray of Delaware, and the Y.M.C.A. leader, John R. Mott. See the *New York Times*, Aug. 23, 1916; Link, *Confusions and Crises*, pp. 303-18; and Link, *Campaigns for Progressivism and Peace*, pp. 51-54.

[15] Henry Edward Cowan Bryant, Washington correspondent of the New York *World*.

[16] Reports from Mexico during September indicated that Villa had gained strength in Chihuahua following victories at Chihuahua City and Cusihuiriachic. See the *Washington Post*, Sept. 22, 29-30, and Link, *Campaigns for Progressivism and Peace*, p. 122.

[17] In a series of addresses begun on May 27, 1916, Wilson had attempted to alert the American people to their responsibility for helping to maintain the peace following the European war. See Hilderbrand, *Power and the People*, pp. 136-41.

[18] Gen. Frederick Funston, commander of the Southern Department.

[19] On September 29 Wilson received a telegram from Jeremiah A. O'Leary, president of the pro-German and anti-British American Truth Society, which set forth the issues of the campaign as he perceived them. Wilson's response was: "Your telegram received. I would be deeply mortified to have you or anybody like you vote for me. Since you have access to many disloyal Americans and I have not, I will ask you to convey this message to them." Both telegrams were printed in the *New York Times*, Sept. 30, 1916; they are also printed in *PWW*, Vol. 38, pp.285-86. See also Link, *Campaigns for Progressivism and Peace*, pp. 104-106.

[20] In his Flag Day address at the Washington Monument on June 14, 1916, Wilson assailed certain German-American groups for "disloyalty" and "political blackmail." See the *New York Times*, June 15, 1916; the address is printed in *PWW*, Vol. 37, pp. 221-25.

[21] In his address in that city in early October 1916.

[22] Lucius William Nieman.

[23] Burke said: "I do not know the method of drawing up an indictment against a whole people" in his "Second Speech on Conciliation with America: The Thirteen Resolutions" of March 22, 1775.

[24] An immigrant from Liblar, Germany, Schurz became a leading Liberal Republican and served as Lincoln's Minister to Spain, Senator from Missouri, and Secretary of the Interior in the cabinet of Rutherford Birchard Hayes. Schurz was president of the National Civil Service Reform League from 1892 to 1901.

Dec. 18, 1916[1]

It is understood that nothing that I say shall be quoted outside. And I want to say another thing. There are some things that I ought not to discuss just now, and if I decline to discuss them, I beg that you won't draw the inference that I am trying to hold something back. It won't be for that reason. It will be merely for this, that anything that is said now will lead to speculation, and there ought not to be speculation. That will be my only motive. I won't hold anything back because, sometimes, when a man declines to discuss a thing, the inference is drawn that he would rather not discuss it for some reason that he doesn't want to explain. For example, these peace negotiations.[2] And I judge that it is a source of irritation on the part of the belligerents to have foreign nations discussing whether they will come in and tell them how to settle their own affairs or not, and, therefore, the discussion back and forth—whether they

will or won't—is disadvantageous to the thing that we all ought to
serve with every devotion that is in us, and that is the peace of the
world. It is inconceivable that we should put any slightest grain of
difficulty in the way of arriving at some basis of peace. And, therefore, since the government of the United States is doing nothing,
I think perhaps it is best not to discuss whether it is going to do
anything or not.

Mr. President, to start with a harmless topic, what is the status of this cost-
of-living investigation?[3]

I haven't followed it the last half week, and I daresay you know
about as much as I do. We are pushing it along every channel that
is open to us under federal law. You, of course, understand that,
so far as the Department of Justice is concerned, the difficulty is
that the only thing we can attack men for is combinations affecting
interstate commerce, and it is precious hard to prove that, in many
instances. But the investigation itself, I think, is helping and is
helping clear up a great many of the details.

Mr. President, as a result of the difficulties that exist, is it likely that any
additional legislation will be asked for?

It is possible, but, you see, Congress, in any case, would have to
keep within the limits of its power, and it has no power over any
trade that is not interstate.

There is a bill that has been introduced by Mr. Fitzgerald that limits the
holdings of cold-storage companies by seeking to prohibit the interstate transportation facilities to companies that violate these provisions.[4]

That hasn't been brought to my attention. We tried the regulation
of cold storage in New Jersey by state legislation, and, while we
accomplished something, I must say we didn't accomplish enough
to be very encouraging.

Mr. President, are there any other bills which have been introduced which
have your approval, which you are looking over?

None that I have any knowledge of.

Mr. President, there is a good deal of interest now in this public-buildings bill[5]
in view of Secretary McAdoo's warning regarding the condition of the Treasury,
and attracted particularly to the public-buildings legislation.[6] Has that matter
been brought to your attention, this specific bill, providing for thirty-eight
million or thirty-nine million dollars?

Yes, it has, by the Treasury Department.

Is there anything you could say on it with regard to expressing your opinion?

No, I will have to reserve what I have to say until it gets here.

Mr. President, it is reported that the brotherhood men and the railroad managers are about to come to an understanding with regard to the Adamson Act.[7] Will that in any way affect the need for action at this session on the railroad program which you submitted?[8]

I don't think so.

You think that that program will be carried out at this session of Congress?

Yes, I think it will.

Does the request of the Newlands commission for an extension of time in any way affect that possibility?[9]

Oh, no. That request was made merely because Senator Newlands wanted to release himself and other members of the committees of both houses to give their entire time to this legislation. You see, the Congress had set a limit of time on them, had set a date by which they would report.

Yes. The eighth of January.

And they can't get through their investigation and, at the same time, to release members [blank].

There is no need of Congress waiting for a report of this committee before acting on the program submitted?

Oh, no, because the program submitted has nothing to do with the subject matter of that investigation.

Of course this is a hypothetical-type question, but, if this program should fail, do you think an extra session would be essential?

I don't know. It would depend upon how much it failed. I can't imagine its failing. If it failed, it would be for lack of time.

Mr. President, have you any idea when they are going to pay attention to these—your recommendations to Congress?

They will pay attention to those now in the committees. The bad part is starting at the Senate end, because the pending part was at the Senate end—the bill to increase the Interstate Commerce Commission[10]—and, therefore, that seemed the natural end for it to begin at. That is the only reason why the House committees have not taken it up, I understand.

Have these labor leaders said anything to you in regard to their attitude?

I haven't seen them since I got back except just to shake hands.

I thought you had seen Mr. Gompers?[11]

Oh, I did see Mr. Gompers, but he didn't say anything about that. I thought you meant the brotherhood men.

The American Federation of Labor seems to be just as much interested as the brotherhoods in the matter of compulsory investigations.

Yes, they do seem to be, very naturally, because the principle of it might be adopted in other legislation, though Congress has very little to do with most of the elements that the Federation of Labor deals with, because their activities are local and not interstate. You see, this legislation of Congress is specifically limited to those employees of the railroads that are actually engaged in the running of trains in interstate transportation.

It has been stated, Mr. President, from time to time, that you are in favor of this proposal to federalize more effectively the control of the railroads. Have you expressed any opinion on that subject?

No, I haven't, because I was waiting for the conclusions of that investigation. I don't know enough about it.

The proposition seems to be, as presented by the commission now, that they can't conclude their investigation in a proper way unless they are allowed an extension of time.

Well, I daresay that is true also, but that is not because the subject matter is shifting in any way. I mean that isn't because the field of inquiry is being enlarged or altered. It is merely because of want of time.

Mr. President, has either side brought to your attention this settlement of the Adamson Act out of court—by an agreement among themselves?

No. We can't settle our part of it out of court.

Mr. President, about two or three weeks ago *Sea Power*, which is the organ of the Navy League, said it had reason to believe that you were in favor of universal military training, and we have never been able to find out whether you were or not.

Well, some of the gentlemen who represent the navy, particularly the retired officers of it, know a great deal that is not so. They are very accomplished in that. I haven't expressed any opinion on that at all.

Would you care to say anything at all? I am making a distinction between universal training and universal service.

No, because in that case, as in every similar case, my attitude would be entirely dependent on the plans. The idea is easy enough, and it is attractive enough, but how it is to be done is the essential matter. It is the way I feel about every big public question—I want to see the bill before I form an opinion.

That is implied, in a measure, in the Chamberlain bill.[12]

Yes, in a measure, but it is not thoroughly worked out.

Mr. President, has the immigration bill reached you?[13]

No. Has it passed?

It passed both houses this morning by a two-thirds vote.[14]
Would that influence your action on it?

Better wait and see. I didn't know that it had passed, to tell you the truth.

Mr. President, with regard to this matter of universal military training, have you been urged recently to take some measures with reference to the federalized militia? Have you been told that it was a failure, or asked to take up the question with that in mind?

I have heard a great many men say very loudly that it was a failure, but they are the same men who said it was a failure before it was tried. It hasn't been thoroughly tried out yet by any means.

Mr. President, do the amendments of the Senate, put in the immigration bill, with regard to the literacy test and legal offenders,[15] meet with your approval?

I don't know what they are. What were they?

Yes, sir, the literacy test is amended so as to permit those that are religiously persecuted and political offenders to be exempted from the literacy test.

Let in, whether they could read or write?

Yes, sir.

That is interesting! Well, I have several times pointed out the difficulty about exempting from the literacy test those who have been subject to religious persecution. It throws on the United States Government the very unpleasant and invidious task of determining which governments have been guilty of religious persecution. It is a very delicate thing to undertake.

Mr. President, is it your intention to make any further recommendations to Congress with reference to legislation that may be required to meet conditions that will arise after the war?

No, sir. We have got the instrumentalities created now that are intended to assess those changes as they take place, which is as it should be, and, until they are assessed, I don't see that we know our ground well enough. Had you something special in mind?

Oh, no. Naturally, the tariff and the progress in the Congress on action with regard to the Webb bill.[16]

But I thought that the country, for the time being, had got the tariff off its mind. I am going to urge the passage of the Webb bill. I have already done that. I thought you meant something in addition.

Oh, no.
One thing that is interesting, Mr. President, is Mr. Hurley's suggestion about the cost-accounting system.[17] I wondered whether that had come before you or not?

Suggestion about legislation about it?

He wanted that discussed generally from a larger approach—greater Federal Trade Commission service in the matter.

That is a matter of appropriation, not legislation. There is not any legislation that could oblige the adoption of a cost-accounting system.

Mr. President, in this connection, when may we expect an announcement on the Tariff Commission?

Why, I am pretty nearly ready, but one man has eluded me and I am looking for a man.

Does the same apply to the Shipping Board?

Yes. There, I am one man shy, too.

Mr. President, when you speak of instrumentalities, do you mean the Tariff Commission as one of them?

I mean that, so far as legislation is concerned, we are supplied with instrumentalities.

Mr. President, have the conferees on the water-power bill communicated with you as to any plan as to working out the bill?[18]

I have had one conference with a group of them, and incidental talks with individuals about it. I think they are going to work something out. That is my present impression.

You haven't gotten any impression [blank].

No, I haven't, because the conferees didn't indicate.

Mr. President, have you taken any position on Senator Owen's bill or any other bill with regard to the expenditure of campaign funds?[19]

No, I haven't.

Mr. President, nobody has mentioned Mexico.

No. We wouldn't be at home if they didn't.

Will you tell us something about that situation?

I daresay that you know as much as I do. I merely know that the commissioners[20] will meet again to receive the suggestions, I would call them, with which Mr. Pani[21] has returned, and I haven't yet learned what those suggestions are.

Mr. President, Mr. Fitzgerald on Saturday said there would be a deficit of three hundred million dollars.[22] Have you any views as to revenue measures?

Mr. Fitzgerald didn't just discover that, did he? That had been discovered sometime before. That, of course, is for the fiscal year 1918, not for the present fiscal year.

Mr. President, just about the time that the general revenue law was being passed by the Senate, Mr. Simmons read a statement from the Treasury Department to the effect that it would cost, I think, one hundred and thirty million dollars to pay the expenses of the Mexican trouble that—

You mean of the border patrol?

Yes.

And if that trouble, with the necessity of keeping those troops there, continues after January first, it would cost us another eighty-six million dollars. Now, I said that this new revenue measure wouldn't provide for raising revenue to meet those expenses, as I would call it. The Treasury Department suggested that we would have to issue bonds.

Now that we are getting very near to the first of January, I wonder if anything had been done in connection with meeting those expenses?

We are all right until the end of the present fiscal year.

Until next July?

Oh, yes. There is plenty of margin until then.

Yes, sir. I understood that we were getting sufficient revenues, but it was my impression that we would have to make up those revenues in some way.

I can't answer that as clearly as I would like to. I don't think so. I think the whole difficulty is for the succeeding year, when there will be very much of an increase in the expenditures on the preparedness program, as well as a possibility of continuing this large expense on the border. Of course, in that case, that would have to be met and added as an unusual expense.

Won't it be necessary to meet that at this session, Mr. President?

It will be necessary to provide by legislation as to how it will be met, certainly—how it is to be met by revenue arrangements after the first of July.

You don't mean raising any additional revenues?

It will have to provide for raising additional revenue, yes.

Well, just now we are getting enough revenue to meet current expenses?

Yes, and expenses that are enacted—that are provided by statute—during the present fiscal year.

Hasn't the Secretary of the Treasury reported[23] that June 1917 will show a surplus of one hundred and five million dollars in the present fiscal year?

At the present rate, yes. In the year later, there will be a deficit, according to his figures, of one hundred and thirty-five million dollars, but that has been increased by various measures that have been taken, until some people estimate it at three hundred million dollars.

Will this Congress have to make provision to guard against that deficit?

It will have to make provision to increase the revenues in an arithmetical proportion as they go along.

Mr. President, as I recall, the Secretary of the Treasury has reported—he said that that one hundred and fifteen million dollars did not take into consideration a continuation of the troops on the border after December 31, 1916.

No, it doesn't, but it takes in this calendar year.

Do you not hold that additional taxes will have to be levied at this session of Congress?

I am talking about—I am going on scraps of paper, on what I have heard from the Secretary of the Treasury, and I ought not to consider it because I don't know enough about it. I don't know when the legislation to meet the deficit will have to be enacted. My impression is that part of it, at any rate, will be proposed at this session.

Then there is no comprehensive program as yet, regarding the raising of this revenue?

No. There have been a great many suggestions. That was one of the things we were discussing in cabinet, not because it is our business to suggest it, but because we wanted, if called on, to know just what we thought it was wise to suggest.

Do you think, Mr. President, the Tariff Commission will be able to make any report so as you could take action in that regard? Will they be ready to do that?

I shouldn't think so.

Mr. President, last session you went before Congress and outlined what you thought ought to be done to raise revenue.[24] If you do arrive at the point where you think it is necessary, will you go before Congress to make a similar suggestion?

Whenever I have anything to say, I will go.

Mr. President, it has been suggested that bonds be sold. Could you tell us your attitude on that question?

That depends entirely on the particular circumstances. My general attitude is that it is bad finance to issue bonds for permanent expenses, that the only excuse for bonds are extraordinary and temporary expenses. You see, that was the idea that Congress had in mind when it authorized the Panama bonds—that we were not going to build canals all our life. That was a temporary and extraordinary thing and, therefore, we were providing for the expense of that canal over and above what they could not appropriate, by bonds. That illustrates the principle I have in mind. If it is clearly temporary and something one generation ought not to be made to pay for, I think it is legitimate to issue bonds. But I don't think it is wise to issue bonds for permanent expenses when a nation can pay the bill, as we undoubtedly can.

Will the expenses of the border patrol be considered in that light? Extraordinary and temporary?

I don't know yet whether it is going to be permanent or temporary.

Mr. President, this question of a nitrate plant,[25] is this being held up now until we hear from these experts?

It isn't exactly being held up. We are waiting for the necessary information.

Senator Smith of South Carolina was over to see you, I think, about a place on the Savannah River.[26]

Yes. It would be hard to name a Senator who hasn't been.

Mr. President, some of us are interested in the appointment of a postmaster in New York. Can you tell us anything about that?

I can't.

Anything on the half-holiday,[27] Mr. President?

No, sir. I am looking for one myself. You see, it doesn't seem all the departments [blank].

Mr. President, there is a bill pending in Congress with regard to which there is some difference of opinion in the Democratic party about the District of Columbia—the Sheppard bill I am referring to. Do you think it will be subject to a referendum?[28]

Do I think it ought to be? I really have no opinion on that subject.

Mr. President, there is a lot of talk about the result of the sinking of the *Marina* and *Arabia*.[29] Could you give us anything you know on that?

No, sir, because we haven't yet settled the question of fact.

[1] With this conference, Wilson again resumed his weekly meetings with the press. The resumption seemed important enough to newspaper editors that it was front-page news on December 19 in both the *New York Times* and the *Washington Post*. Both newspapers reported that Wilson seemed in good health and high spirits. For a discussion of the decision to resume the conferences, see Hilderbrand, *Power and the People*, pp. 103-104.

[2] German Chancellor Theobald von Bethmann Hollweg on December 12 initiated a peace démarche through Joseph Clark Grew, American Chargé d'Affaires in Berlin. Bethmann Hollweg's note stated that, although Germany had proved its invincibility on the battlefield and was willing to fight on to victory if necessary, the Imperial German Government was prepared to meet the Allies at the conference table and restore peace. Reports of this démarche disturbed Wilson because he was planning his own peace initiative, which went out to American diplomatic missions on December 18. In his note, Wilson, who hoped to break the diplomatic deadlock and end the war, called upon the belligerents to state the terms on which they might make peace. See the *Washington Post*, Dec. 15-18, 1916; the Secretary of State to Ambassadors and Ministers in belligerent countries, Dec. 18, 1916, in *FR, 1916-WWS,* pp. 97-99; and Link, *Campaigns for Progressivism and Peace*, pp. 210-19.

[3] Wilson, on December 11, approved a cost-of-living investigation conducted by the Department of Justice to be directed by Federal District Attorney George Weston Anderson of Boston. See the *Washington Post*, Dec. 11-12, 1916.

[4] Fitzgerald's bill (H.R. 17816) provided for the regulation of cold-storage food transportation companies engaged in interstate commerce. See *Cong. Record*, 64th Cong., 2d sess., p. 6.

[5] The omnibus public-buildings bill provided $35,000,000 for construction. See *Cong. Record*, 64th Cong., 2d sess., p. 6.

[6] McAdoo, in his annual report of December 6, criticized omnibus public-building laws for constructing unneeded buildings which drained the Treasury. See the *Washington Post*, Dec. 7, 1916.

[7] William Granville Lee of Cleveland, a former brakeman and conductor who was president of the Brotherhood of Trainmen, stated on December 15 that managers and labor leaders were attempting to negotiate a settlement of their differences by January 1, 1917, when the Adamson Act would go into effect. See *ibid.*, Dec. 16, 1916.

[8] Wilson addressed a joint session of Congress on August 29, 1916, about the "very grave

situation" caused by the demand of railroad employees for an eight-hour working day. After expressing his support for the eight-hour day, Wilson recommended six pieces of legislation for (1) an enlargement and reorganization of the Interstate Commerce Commission, (2) the establishment of the eight-hour day for railroad employees, (3) the authorization of a commission to observe and report upon the effects of the eight-hour day on the railroad industry, (4) approval by Congress for the Interstate Commerce Commission to consider increases in railroad freight rates, (5) the amendment of existing statutes to permit a full public investigation of labor disputes in the railroad industry, and (6) the granting to the Executive of power to take control over the railways and to draft train crews and administrative officials in the event of a military necessity. The Adamson Act, which Wilson signed on September 3, provided for items (2) and (3). Wilson's address is printed in *PWW*, Vol. 38, pp. 96-101; see also the *New York Times*, Sept. 4, 1916.

9 The Newlands commission, a joint congressional committee to investigate railroad conditions and problems, requested an extension of its authority until January 1, 1918. See the *Washington Post*, Dec. 16, 1916.

10 S. 6972, introduced by Senator Lewis. See *Cong. Record*, 64th Cong., 1st sess., p. 13417.

11 Gompers was in Washington to address governmental employees at a mass meeting to call for higher wages. See the *Washington Post*, Dec. 19, 1916.

12 Senator George Earle Chamberlain, Democrat of Oregon, on December 13, 1915, introduced a bill (S. 1695) "to provide for the military and naval training of the citizen forces of the United States." The final form of the bill, reported on February 10, 1917, by Chamberlain, chairman of the Committee on Military Affairs, called for six months of training for all ablebodied nineteen-year-old males, followed by membership in a reserve citizen army or navy until the age of twenty-eight. A Senate subcommittee, headed by Chamberlain, was conducting public hearings on the bill. See the *Washington Post*, Dec. 18-19, 1916; 64th Cong., 2d sess., Senate Report No. 1024; John Gary Clifford, *The Citizen Soldiers: The Plattsburg Training Movement, 1913-1920* (Lexington, Ky., 1972), pp. 203-14; and John P. Finnegan, *Against the Specter of a Dragon: The Campaign for American Military Preparedness, 1914-1917* (Westport, Conn., 1974), pp. 112-13, 179-83.

13 A revised version of the Burnett bill, which Wilson had vetoed in 1915.

14 The revised Burnett bill had passed the House by a vote of 307 to eighty-seven on March 30, 1915; a slightly different version was approved by the Senate on December 14, 1916, by a vote of sixty-four to seven. See the *Washington Post*, Dec. 15, 1916, and *Cong. Record*, 64th Cong., 2d sess., p. 316.

15 These amendments exempted from the literacy test those fleeing persecution on account of religious and purely political beliefs. See *Cong. Record*, 64th Cong., 2d sess., pp. 265, 313.

16 This bill, introduced by Representative Edwin Yates Webb, Democrat of North Carolina, provided for an amendment of the antitrust laws to allow American firms to combine to sell goods abroad. The Senate Interstate Commerce Committee was currently holding hearings on the bill. See the *Washington Post*, Dec. 16, 1916.

17 Edward Nash Hurley, chairman of the Federal Trade Commission, was promoting cost-accounting methods in business and government. See the *New York Times*, Nov. 8, 1916.

18 The Ferris bill (H.R. 408) was in conference committee at this time.

19 The Owen bill (H.R. 15842) provided for limiting contributions to political candidates and campaigns. See the *Washington Post*, Dec. 6-7, 1916.

20 In meetings at the Hotel Traymore in Atlantic City since October 2, the Mexican-American Joint High Commission had attempted to resolve the problems arising from the Mexican Revolution and the Pershing expedition. On November 21, the Americans presented what they described as their final proposal, which called for approval of a protocol to permit American pursuit of marauders into Mexico and serious discussion of Mexico's internal difficulties. Carranza did not reply until December 26. See Link, *Campaigns for Progressivism and Peace*, pp. 328-35.

21 Alberto J. Pani, the Mexican commissioner who carried the American proposal to Mexico City.

22 See the *Washington Post*, Dec. 18. 1916.

23 In his annual report of December 6, 1916. See *ibid.*, Dec. 7, 1916.

24 Wilson made suggestions for raising additional revenue in his Annual Message of December 7, 1915. See *Cong. Record*, 64th Cong., 1st sess., p. 98, and *PWW*, Vol. 35, pp. 304-306.

25 That is, consideration of S. 4971, a bill introduced by Senator Ellison DuRant Smith, Democrat of South Carolina, to designate water-power sites for use in the manufacture of nitrates. See *Cong. Record*, 64th Cong., 1st sess., p. 3882, and the *New York Times*, Dec. 18, 1916.

26 In addition to nitrates, Smith discussed a bill (H.R. 14777) introduced by Representative

Benjamin Grubb Humphreys, Democrat of Mississippi, for flood control. See the *Washington Post*, Dec. 18-19, 1916.

[27] Senator Penrose had proposed an amendment to the District of Columbia appropriation bill (H.R. 19119) which provided for a year-round half-holiday on Saturdays for federal employees. See the *Washington Post*, Dec. 13, 1916.

[28] A bill (S. 1082) introduced by Senator Morris Sheppard, Democrat of Texas, provided for prohibition in the District of Columbia. Senator Underwood had proposed an amendment calling for a referendum on the issue. See the *Washington Post*, Dec. 16-18, 1916, and *Cong. Record*, 64th Cong., 2d sess., pp. 153, 369-72, 471.

[29] The British armed merchantman *Marina* was torpedoed without warning by a German U-boat on October 28, 1916, with the loss of six American lives. Another submarine torpedoed the Peninsula and Oriental armed liner *Arabia* on November 6; this time fifty-seven died, none American. The United States Government had requested information on these sinkings from the German government, and the American press speculated that a break in relations was possible. See the *Washington Post*, Dec. 8, 1916; the Secretary of State to the Chargé d'Affaires in Germany, Nov. 18, 1916, in *FR, 1916-WWS*, p. 310; and Link, *Campaigns for Progressivism and Peace*, pp. 186-87.

[Jan. 15, 1917]

Mr. President, is there anything you can tell us about peace today?

No, sir. I think you know as much as I do.

Mr. President, there seem to be different interpretations placed on your idea for a league to enforce peace.[1] Are you free to discuss that at all in any way?

It is not in shape to be discussed. That would entirely depend upon the course of events and the terms of the peace by which the war was concluded.

It has been said that you would not favor a league that would enforce it through the use of the military and naval parts of it.

There are so many people speaking for me that I wouldn't like to be held responsible. I have stated often exactly what I believed. I haven't altered my opinion in the least.

Mr. President, the substance of a letter to Senator Shafroth, written by yourself, on the constitutionality of the thing has been made public. We have been wondering if we can get the text of that letter upon the powers of the Senate in connection with it?[2]

I haven't written any such letter.

Isn't that with reference to this plan of Oscar Crosby,[3] which would deprive the Congress of the power of making war—the Shafroth resolution?

Well, I simply don't remember ever having expressed my opinion about it to anybody. There must be some mistake somewhere. Of course nobody can deprive the Congress of the right to declare war. Since the Constitution confers it, nobody can take it away.

It requires a constitutional amendment?

Yes. I understood that he had submitted such an amendment. I don't remember expressing any opinion about it to anybody. There must be some mistake somewhere.

Mr. President, the resolution now in the Judiciary Committee of the Senate, introduced by Senator Walsh, to have cloture in the Senate—have you any opinion on that resolution?[4]

Well, I stand on the party platform which calls for a reasonable restriction of unlimited debate in the Senate.

Have you any opinion as to Senator Walsh's theory that the Senate shall terminate at the end of the session on March 4 and is not a continuing body?

No, that is a new idea to me. I am not ready to express an opinion about that, even if it were any business of mine.

Mr. President, I just want to ask for some information about the use of the information that comes out here. I was absent the first two conferences. I want to get it clearly in mind. Of course, there are various ways by which it [a presidential statement] can be used, and direct quotation, I understand, has always been barred. And there is the way of a direct attribution that either the President said or the President told correspondents. There is also a way of saying the President's opinion is so and so. I just wonder which of those was the proper way?

I regard all those as quotations and as unjustified. I understand the object of this conference to be for you men to find out what I am thinking about and not make direct use of it. Of course, there are so many things you ask me that I would have to be extremely guarded about if I did not go on that theory. Because I think it is imperative, just at this critical period of our affairs, that I say, myself, anything I have to say and don't say it through another medium. I am frankly astonished at the things I see in the papers every day—what I think and am going to do.

It is pretty important to have a definite understanding on that.

That is my understanding: no direct use is to be made of this. It is for the guidance of your own minds in making up your stories, and it is not legitimate to say that the "President thinks this," or that the "President intimated that," or the "President intends the other." I think that is quite a part of the understanding. These quotations, because of its being known that you see me—it doesn't make any difference if you use my quotations or not, if after seeing me, you say that I think so and so.

Mr. President, take, for example, this matter that you spoke about a moment ago, of your attitude towards the cloture rule in the Senate. Now, in writing a story today on that subject, wouldn't we be permitted to say that the President regards this as a matter that comes within the scope of the party platform?

Well, now, you see, that is an excellent example to take, because it involves things that I have constantly in mind. When a matter comes up in the Senate, for example, like this, that concerns the Senate's own rules and the Senate's own business, Senators rather resent gratuitous opinions from this end of the avenue. What I mean to say is that they are often, they are generally, kind enough to consult me and find out themselves what my attitude is. But until they do, for me to volunteer an opinion sometimes complicates matters and but irritates instead of assisting them. And my wish would be to exercise the most punctilious courtesy towards both the houses and not, for example, condemn anything they were doing and hold back opinion upon what some individual member had proposed until my cooperation had come about in a more regular way.

I think you see the delicate position I am placed in by things of that sort. Now, having said that, I am in favor of the position of the party platform. I think that can be taken for granted, that I feel bound by that. I am always in favor of that, but that does not depend on my initiative; I have no initiative in the matter. I can only support something when my support is asked, or is of any use to anybody.

Mr. President, what I had in mind is different—that from the standpoint of the public or readers, whom we are trying to serve, there are certain matters which come up from time to time where the views of the President are very important. Now, we come to you and get your views. Now, to what extent, if any, can we make use of the information we get in that way?

Well, I admit that that is a difficult question. In ordinary times, when our affairs are domestic affairs, we could exercise a great deal of freedom about that, but just now such—let me say such excessive—importance is attached to the President's opinions that a thing said offhand may have an effect that was not contemplated

beforehand. I speak, of course, offhand here, without any calculation as to the general effects upon the opinion of the country, and
I just don't know what answer to make to that.

I think, to go back to your other question, you could say this,
that it can always be taken for granted that the President will
support what is in the party platform. I think I have proved that
that has been my bulwark in the matter of woman suffrage, because
I have pointed out to the ladies that my personal opinion, and wish
for, is in favor of suffrage soon, and is not a highly harming factor.
Inasmuch as I am considered a party leader, I have got to take
what my party says. I tried to get more than I did get in the St.
Louis convention[5] in the platform, and I have to be satisfied for the
time being with what I got then.

And I pointed out to them that there never has been a Wilson
policy. All the policies I have urged upon Congress have been policies that were contained in the party platform, so that I could show
chapter and verse for it, with one exception. And then I took the
position, which I always take, that a treaty of the United States
takes precedence in importance and authority over the party platform. When the country has given its solemn promise about anything in a treaty, that concludes it until the promise is altered by
a change in the treaty. But that was such plain sailing that I don't
think it constitutes an exception. That was not a Wilson policy.
That was the policy of the country embodied in a treaty which the
Constitution itself says is part of the supreme law of the land. So
there "ain't been no such animal" as a Wilson policy.

Are we to understand, Mr. President, that you don't want us to say that you
said that?

Said what? What I have just said now? I don't care how you wish
to call that general discourse. I have said that before, but don't
apply it to woman suffrage. I am in trouble enough.

Mr. President, several weeks ago, you said that you were opposed to an issue
of bonds except in cases of special emergency. Now, in using that, is it proper
to say that the President is opposed to using the borrowing authority?

Well, that is another case of domestic etiquette, so to speak. The
houses are in some trouble—very deep trouble, I believe—about
making up a revenue bill. I mean, there is a great variety of opinion.
The minute you tax any one thing, you affect one part of the country
more than another, and the representatives of that part of the country aren't very happy about that suggestion. When you suggest

something else, another part of the country may be hit harder, and the representatives of that part aren't very happy about it. So there is general anxiety. I say this with some hesitation, but there is a general disinclination to tax anything. They would rather find things for which it is appropriate to issue bonds and postpone the responsibility of imposing taxes. Now, I have taken the position in private, when consulted by members of both houses, that I thought the only suitable objects for a bond issue were permanent improvements.

One generation shouldn't be asked to pay for an unexpected emergency that rendered insufficient the expenditures asked for of long standing. For example, suppose it is something that calls for large expenditures at this moment and you put taxes on enough to pay for those, then when the emergency is over you have got too many taxes. You have provided for the excess taxes, and the taxes are permanent while the expenses are temporary. Those are legitimate objects of a bond issue. But aside from those general principles, the best thing to do is to wait until you have got a bill and then comment on it. We haven't got a bill yet.

Mr. President, have you noticed anything that was disagreeable to you in the way of inferences? You probably read some of the Washington papers. I think all of us realize you give the authority to do that, but on these local questions, or about the tariff board, if you say it is understood that the President said he is waiting to get—

About those things such as you refer to, there is no trouble, and I haven't found anything by way of direct or indirect quotations of myself that has irritated me. What has irritated or has distressed me, as I have said several times, is this. For example, I read in one of the papers the other day, a very responsible paper too, that the President, it was understood in high quarters—I am sure you know the phrases—that the President was looking around to see what should be his next move in regard to peace, and that he had summoned Colonel House from New York, which I did not. Colonel House came down to take dinner. He was summoned by a gastric summons and not by me. And that I had been consulting with the Secretary of State, and that there was a grand pow-wow as to what would be our next step.[6] All of that was pure fiction. Nothing of the kind was happening. I haven't summoned anybody, and I haven't consulted anybody since I last saw you, for example, as to what our next step should be with regard to a peace move. That does make me a little hot under the collar because it is really interfering with public affairs by making the government seem mindless. You don't simply cater to American audiences. These impressions get to other parts of the water, these impressions get abroad. They are carried by the general press associations, and then the foreigner says, "Well, what in thunder is this man going to do next? Isn't he ever going to mind his own business?" I am stating it from their point of view. "What monkey wrench is he going to throw into the machinery next?" That's the kind of irritation—and, if I were in their places, I would be very much irritated. I would say, "Why doesn't he mind his own business?" Now, I am trying to mind my own business, but I haven't received your cooperation. That is the trouble. There wasn't any quotation from the President in these things. There couldn't be. I hadn't said anything, for the natural reason that there wasn't anything in my mind to say. I try not to be the quicker one. James Russell Lowell[7] said, "If you have anything to say, then say it." It is an admirable example of what not to say in public affairs.

Might it not be a suggestion, then, that at all times about things—that is to say about foreign affairs—we should exercise a great deal of delicacy with reference to the foreign questions?

Yes. And yet, in dealing with the Senate and House, I am dealing with powers just as sensitive as the foreign governments.

Mr. President, here is another concrete case of confusion in the Secretary of State's other statement, that our situation is critical, that we are near the verge of war.[8] Can you inform us as to whether you are initiating any measure for national defense?

No, I am not.

You wouldn't want us to say that you were?

You see, Senator Chamberlain has a bill,[9] for example, which is very much discussed, and I am waiting for that plan to be a discussable plan before forming an opinion about it. But it didn't come on my initiative and, therefore, I am not initiating anything new.

May I ask you, Mr. President, if you had given consideration any time to a suggestion for a referendum in the District of Columbia on matters of great importance here—on local matters? For instance, I don't mean this present prohibition bill, but your idea generally about more important matters.[10]

On that, the matter, of course, applies to that, as you give it, I want to warn you in advance. Even if you have to say that it is understood in high quarters—

As a matter of fact, I had not, Mr. President, given any special consideration to that.

You see, there is no voting machinery in the District of Columbia. It would have to be created. There are some practical difficulties about it. Of course, the District of Columbia is an exceptional community, since so very large a proportion of the people here are governmental employees.

Can you say anything, Mr. President, about Mexico?

No. The joint commission is, I believe, meeting today, or is to meet today.[11] And I thought it was a week ago. And I was expecting to have their recommendations before now, but I will meet them, I understand, as soon as they meet.

Do you know, Mr. President, whether it is a fact that the War Department did instruct General Funston to pay over some money to the Carranza authorities to get the body of that soldier of the Fifth Infantry who was killed on the other side?[12]

I don't know. I doubt very much it is true.

Mr. President, have you selected a Tariff Commission?

I have selected all but one man. I can't find him yet. He is in the woods yet.

You are not prepared to tell?

I would rather tell the commission as a whole. It is always a question of a combination, since I am definitely instructed that not more than three of them are to be of the same party.

Anything on the railroad situation, Mr. President?

Nothing new, sir.

Mr. President, is the so-called compulsory investigation bill[13] an essential part of the railroad program?

Oh, yes.

Is the feature against strikes and lockouts pending investigation an essential feature of that bill?

Yes, of course, but you must understand this—I am always ready to accept anything better. There are imperfect remedies. If there are new railroad remedies, I am amenable to a palliative rather than an entire remedy. But it is the best thing. I say I think I am from Missouri with regard to anything else.

Nothing better has been shown?

Nothing better has been shown. I am perfectly willing to accept anything better.

You expect it to pass substantially in that form at this session?

Yes.

Mr. President, the Federal Reserve Board has sent the Congress a series of proposed amendments to the Federal Reserve Act.[14] The most important of these deal with the supply of gold in the United States. Have you had an opportunity to study those amendments?

No, I have not.

Mr. President, have you formed any opinion about the public-buildings bill or the rivers-and-harbors bill?

No. Those are things that I always wait for, until they get to me.

Is there anything new, Mr. President, on Saturday half-holidays for the government's closing?

No. That is complicated because it does not affect the departments uniformly. The practical arrangements of it in some of the departments seem almost impossible. I hesitate to let it apply to some and not to others. It is a very difficult question practically. It looked simple when I first tackled it. I find that it is not.

To what extent can we quote you?

I think it has been said frequently that that is taboo.

---

[1] Wilson was continuing his campaign for American membership in a league of nations. He was at this time preparing an address to Congress on the subject, which he delivered on January 22, 1917. See Link, *Campaigns for Progressivism and Peace*, pp. 264-68.

[2] Senator John Franklin Shafroth, Democrat of Colorado, had, on May 18, 1916, proposed an amendment to the Constitution (S.J. Res. 131) which authorized the President "to negotiate, and after ratification by two thirds of the members of both Houses of Congress, to sign a treaty for the creation of an international peace-keeping tribunal." The amendment would also commit the United States to supply funds for the tribunal's activities and to recognize its authority to settle disputes. In his letter of January 3, 1917, to Shafroth, Wilson wrote that the treaty-making power of the Constitution was already sufficient for the President and Senate to make the United States a member of a world court of arbitration. See the *New York Times*, Jan. 14, 1917; *Cong. Record*, 64th Cong., 1st sess., p. 8228; and WW to Shafroth, Jan. 3, 1917, in *PWW*, Vol. 40, p. 386.

[3] Oscar Terry Crosby of Virginia, founder in 1910 of the World Federation League and author of a draft constitution for an international court. See David S. Patterson, *Toward a Warless World: The Travail of the American Peace Movement, 1887-1914* (Bloomington, Ind., 1976), p. 166.

[4] Senator Thomas James Walsh, Democrat of Montana, on January 11, 1917, introduced a resolution (S. Res. 313) to consider the Senate dissolved at noon on March 4. Because the Senate was regarded as a continuing body, its rules, including unlimited debate, were held over from one Congress to the next; Walsh's resolution would require new rules for each session, thus allowing for the limitation of debate without recourse to cloture. See *Cong. Record*, 64th Cong., 2d sess., p. 1164.

[5] The Democratic National Convention of 1916.

[6] This is another example of Wilson's "grazing the truth."

[7] American poet and essayist, 1819-1891.

[8] Secretary of State Lansing told reporters on December 21, 1916, that the United States was "drawing near the verge of war." About this statement, which Wilson had not approved, see Link, *Campaigns for Progressivism and Peace*, pp. 221-22; the *New York Times*, Dec. 22, 1916; and especially *PWW*, Vol. 40, pp. 306-11.

[9] See above, Dec. 18, 1916.

[10] Representative William Joseph Cary, Republican of Wisconsin, had also introduced a bill (H.R. 20048) calling for a referendum on prohibition in the District of Columbia. See the *Washington Post*, Jan. 14, 1917.

[11] The Mexican-American Joint Commission met at New York and adjourned *sine die* on January 15. See the *Washington Post*, Jan. 16, 1917.

[12] Corp. John H. Seward, U.S.A., was found dead on the Mexican side of the border. His throat had been cut, and it was believed that he had committed suicide. On January 12, the War Department authorized payment of fifty dollars to Mexican officials for the recovery of the body. See the *Washington Post*, Jan. 13, 1917.

[13] This bill (H.R. 19730), introduced on January 6 by Representative Adamson, would have required arbitration of railroad labor disputes and given the President authority to take over operation of the railroads under emergency conditions. This most important part of Wilson's program for the railroads was defeated in the Senate Interstate Commerce Committee on January 16 by a vote of seven to three. See the *Washington Post*, Jan. 12 and 17, 1917, and *Cong. Record*, 64th Cong., 2d sess., pp. 1763-64.

[14] The Federal Reserve Board on January 13, 1917, proposed a series of amendments to the Federal Reserve Act. Inspired by the financial changes caused by the European war, these amendments were intended primarily to increase the board's control over the nation's gold supply. See the *New York Times*, Jan. 14, 1917.

Jan. 23, 1917

Mr. President, can you tell us just what you are thinking about the Shields bill[1] and the Myers bill[2] and the Walsh bill?[3]

I would detain you too long if I told you what I was thinking about them. But my only relation to them at present is in trying to bring the different views together so as to get some action, and just what progress I am making in that, I don't know. I haven't heard the results yet. There were to be some conferences which I think have not yet taken place. I am sincerely interested in getting water-power legislation. I think it is of the utmost importance.

Mr. President, is the war still barred?

Yes, sir, simply because I don't know anything that is profitable to say.

Mr. President, there seems to be general disagreement as to what you mean by the force guaranteeing peace.[4] Is that moral or economic or also military force? At one time, you spoke of the cooperation of the nations.

Well, I can't discuss that. That is a proper subject for the discussion of the conference and for submission to the league. This is not the time to discuss that.

If there were such a league to enforce peace, would it carry with it the possible abandonment of the Monroe Doctrine?

I expressed my view about that yesterday.[5]

You would be saying it was merely an extension of the Monroe Doctrine?

Yes, sir, it is.

Mr. President, have your conferences in the Capitol evolved any possibility of an agreement with reference to the compulsory investigation bill?[6]

I think so. The thing is not as far advanced in committee action as I should like it to be, and therefore I can't answer that question with any degree of confidence. My impression is that it is possible.

That wouldn't carry with it any abandonment of the no-strike feature of the bill?

Perhaps I didn't understand your first question. You meant whether there was any progress towards an agreement on the process of delaying strikes until there has been an investigation. I think there has been progress in that direction. Because, of course, there is no proposal to prevent strikes.

It is merely to prohibit them while this inquiry is in progress, and, yes, that feature is not in danger?

So far as I can see, it is not. I again have to qualify that by saying I don't know of any.

You said a week ago, Mr. President, that you were of course not opposed to any better plan that may be suggested as a substitute for the present plan.

Yes.

Has there been any substitute considered by you?

No, sir. None has been proposed to me, as a matter of fact.

Mr. President, in the morning papers there are dispatches saying that two of our Ambassadors[7] abroad delivered copies of your statement[8] to the governments. How was that?

Merely for information. It was not official at all.

Any resolution of the oil-leasing question,[9] Mr. President?

I wish I could say "Yes." I don't see it yet. I conferred yesterday with a group of western Senators about it, and I think they were in a very reasonable frame of mind about it, but just what can be generally agreed upon, I don't know.

Mr. President, can you say just when your address was cabled abroad to our Ambassadors?

No, sir. That would be a leak. A sort of reverberatory leak.

Mr. President, can you tell us anything about the immigration bill?[10] I believe it is before you now.

Yes, sir, it is technically before me. As a matter of fact, I haven't had time to tackle it. I have got a week or more on it. I am going to turn my attention to it very soon.

Is it your understanding of it, Mr. President, that it removes your objections on the score on which you vetoed it the last time?

Perhaps I had better say that later.

Is the tariff board ready, Mr. President?

No. The trouble there is that the men I have asked don't want to serve. There isn't any trouble about finding men. It's finding men who will take it when I find them. It is a big job to tackle, and very few men of the sort and size I want are able just to lay down their affairs and turn entirely to this matter. That is the real difficulty. It is not their lack of interest or unwillingness, but it is not feasible in many cases.

Could you say, Mr. President, whether in your conferences at the Capitol you reached any understanding as to the character of the revenue legislation to be [considered]?

I didn't have any conferences about the revenue legislation, because there were conferences about that previously. I think things are going with a very considerable degree of unanimity about that.

Mr. President, do you know whether the plans for the establishment of a nitrate plant contemplate the establishment of one plant or more?[11]

That is an open question. I hope there will be more than one, if it is feasible to build them out of the appropriation. Of course, the site chosen will partly determine the amount of money that has to be spent. And I have appointed a committee from the cabinet to visit the proposed sites, the most feasible sites, in prospect, as an additional precaution to the reports we have had from engineers and others.

Can you say who is on that committee?

I would, if I hadn't forgotten. The Secretary of War and the Secretary of Agriculture—of course, the Secretary of the Interior.

Mr. President, would these all be water-power plants?

That, you see, is part of the determination also. I would rather assume they will, but that is not finally determined. You see, there are four processes of production of nitrates, and three of the four are water-power processes, and the fourth is a steam process.

Mr. President, going back to the oil bill, our understanding is that the Public Lands Committee of the Senate is very anxious to effect a compromise. Do you expect to see Mr. Daniels in the hope of working out an agreement?

I am going to see the Attorney General rather than Mr. Daniels, because of course I don't want to do anything that will prejudice the legal claims of the nation in the settlement effected. And I haven't yet had time, since yesterday, to confer with the Attorney General about that.

Mr. President, we have had intimations that the German government would submit its peace terms to you. Would you be willing to say whether you had any intimation about that?

No, sir, I have not had any.

Any danger of an extra session, Mr. President?

Why do you say "danger?" Why don't you say "promise?" I see no prospect of an extra session. I won't commit myself to the need.

Mr. President, can you tell us whether you are going to make it a regular practice to go up to the Capitol?[12]

I am going there frequently for the present time only because it is a short session, and that is the rapid way to consult with Senators.

Well, are there any specific days that you are going? Is it going to be a regular thing?

Well, I think it will be only when there is a clearance to effect, so that I can see a number of men within the shortest time.

The reason I asked that, Mr. President, is, we heard that you were going to take three days every week.

I haven't anything so disproportionately arranged as that.

Are you going down there today?

No. This is cabinet day.

Mr. President, could anything be said about Mexico now?

A great deal could be said. No, there really isn't anything to say.

There are a lot of reports from the border, Mr. President, that the withdrawal of General Pershing's troops has already been begun.

He is withdrawing his troops from the outposts.

Can you say, Mr. President, whether there is any immediate intention of lifting the embargo on the border?

No, there isn't any immediate intention, but, you know, that is a question that is very difficult to answer competently because it is very complicated, because we are willing to let them have arms any time we can be sure whose hands they are going into.

Mr. President, when you say that General Pershing is withdrawing his outposts, could it be said that he may now exercise his discretion as to further
withdrawals?

He will wait for orders.

No orders have been issued?

I didn't say that. "Further, the deponent sayeth not."

Can you say how soon the Ambassador will go to Mexico?

No, I can't say.

Mr. President, a new code of maritime neutrality has been taken up by the
American Institute of Law.[13] Has that been placed before you?

No, not in recent months. Not for a long time.

I understood it was the result of a letter from Secretary Lansing to Mr. Scott.[14]

I think it was at the time it was first taken up. The Secretary
consulted me about it more recently.

Can you say, as it was in the form recently presented, whether it has the
sanction of this government?

I can't say. I have forgotten all about it, to tell the truth.

Mr. President, about a year or so ago—two years ago, I think it was—we asked
you about the invitations for the next Hague peace conference,[15] and the matter
was dropped just about the time the war began, I think. Has any other step
been taken since then about invoking another Hague conference?

Not that I have heard of.

Could you tell us anything about the high-cost-of-living inquiry, Mr. President?
There has been a drop, apparently, so far as the public press has been concerned—there has been very little written about it.

That is not our fault.

It has been forgotten?

No, certainly not. It has been going on, as far as it can. It is going
on, and thoroughly.

Can you tell us whether you have been considering legislation to bring in or submit before Congress adjourns?

Not before the report. We wouldn't know what to suggest.

You haven't received any report from Mr. Gregory recently?

No. I know he is hard at work on it. I saw him last night for a few minutes, but he hasn't made any report.

Mr. President, there are a number of bills which undertake to solve the high-cost-of-living situation now pending in Congress. Have you had an opportunity to study those?

No, I haven't. I find there isn't room enough in my head for a daily study of all of them.

[1] Senator John Knight Shields, Democrat of Tennessee, introduced a bill (S. 3331) on January 10, 1916, for the improvement and development of waterways.

[2] A bill (S. 1060) introduced by Senator Henry Lee Myers, Democrat of Montana, for water-power development.

[3] A reference to the Ferris bill (H.R. 408), which Walsh was supporting in the Senate. The issue here was the control by power companies over hydroelectric projects to be developed under the bills. The administration supported the Ferris bill, but the Senate passed the more conservative Shields measure, which was in conference committee at this time. See the *Washington Post*, Jan. 19, 1917, and Link, *The New Freedom*, pp. 129-32.

[4] In his "Peace without Victory" speech, delivered before the Senate on January 22, Wilson said: "It will be absolutely necessary that a force be created as a guarantor of the permanency of the settlement." The text is printed in the *Washington Post*, Jan. 23, 1917; in *FR, 1917-WWSI*, 24-29; and in *PWW*, Vol. 40, pp. 533-39.

[5] In his address Wilson said: "I am proposing, as it were, that the nations should with one accord adopt the doctrine of President Monroe as the doctrine of the world: that no nation should seek to extend its polity over any other nation or people, but that every people should be left free to determine its own polity, its own way of development, unhindered, unthreatened, unafraid, the little along with the great and powerful."

[6] See above, Jan. 15, 1917.

[7] Sharp in Paris and Francis in Petrograd. See the *New York Times*, Jan. 23, 1917.

[8] That is, Wilson's address to the Senate.

[9] A bill (H.R. 406) sponsored by Representative Ferris and Senator Phelan for the exploration and disposition of natural resources on public lands. Secretary of the Navy Daniels opposed the bill but western Senators urged its passage. See the *Washington Post*, Jan. 22-23, 1917; Link, *The New Freedom*, pp. 132-35; and J. Leonard Bates, *The Origins of Teapot Dome: Progressives, Parties, and Petroleum, 1909-1921* (Urbana, Ill., 1963), pp. 117-24.

[10] Wilson vetoed the Burnett bill (H.R. 10384) on January 29, citing the literacy tests as an objectionable feature. It was passed over his veto on February 1 and 5. See Link, *The New Freedom*, pp. 274-76, and *Cong. Record*, 64th Cong., 2d sess., pp. 2212-13, 2629.

[11] Congress was at this time debating the construction of a federal nitrate plant. See *Cong. Record*, 64th Cong., 2d sess., Appendix, pp. 581-83.

[12] The *Washington Post*, January 23, 1917, reported that Wilson would visit the Capitol on Mondays, Wednesdays, and Thursdays to press for important legislation.

[13] The American Institute of International Law, meeting in Havana, Cuba, on January 22 began consideration of a code of rules of maritime neutrality prepared at the suggestion of Secretary of State Lansing. See the *New York Times*, Jan. 23, 1917.

[14] For the letter from Lansing to James Brown Scott, president of the American Institute for International Law, see the *Washington Post*, Jan. 23, 1917.

[15] See above, Jan. 15, 1914.

Jan. 30, 1917

Mr. President, have you selected a new successor for Mr. Martin[1] as Vice-Governor of the Philippines?

No, I haven't found a man.

The report is published this morning that Governor Harrison was to resign, and that Governor Glenn[2] was to succeed him?

That is made up. I know nothing of either. I have seen in the papers, and I think a friend of Governor Harrison told me, that he was likely to resign because he felt that he had been there as long as the situation justified. I haven't received any communication from him.

Have you received a communication for a six months' leave from him?

Yes, I believe that has been received. I am not sure of that, but I think that that is true. He is certainly entitled to it by this time.

Have you started on your Inaugural Address yet?

No, I have got to sit up all night soon, some time, to do that.

Mr. President, will it be a short one similar to the one you delivered last time?

I honestly don't know. I haven't thought about it one way or the other.

Mr. President, can you give us a clear insight into the legislative situation?

I wish I could, Mr. Oulahan. I don't know the details of it. So far as one can judge in the interpretation of things, it is going as well as could be expected.

Aren't they rather banking on the supposition up there that you are not disposed to call an extraordinary session of Congress and have taken advantage of that?

I don't think so, because I haven't told anybody I felt that way. The way I feel about an extra session depends entirely upon what is done at this session, so I am suspending judgment.

You wouldn't like to take us more fully into your confidence?

I am not taking you in because I can't make up my mind one way or the other until I see whether the horse is before the cart.

Is the proposed railroad program working out towards a compromise?

I think not. It is working out towards an act.

Towards an act. Towards the lines you want?

Essentially as I suggested.

Mr. President, your world-peace-league plan you unfolded to the Senate seems to give the United States a certain interest in the possible future quarrels of Europe. It occurred to me that if the European nations would be given a reciprocal interest—

My dear boy, do you suppose I am going to tell you an answer? If you want to find out, attend the conference that brings this thing about. I don't know anything about it.

Mr. President, it has been published that we have sent to some Latin American countries a new trade treaty as a result of the financial conference.³ The story was printed yesterday.

That may be so. I don't know of it. That may have been done in a regular diplomatic conference to clear up doubts and points, but I really know nothing about it. If so, it is probably just details that need clarification.

Has any progress been made, Mr. President, in the oil-leasing situation?

I don't see any. I wish I did. Things are tied up on that just about as badly as on anything that has been discussed, because there are wide differences of view—very genuine differences. And I haven't seen any common ground yet myself.

Is it a subject on which you could express a view?

I might express one after I have one that would be serviceable, but I haven't been able to see the way out myself.

The Secretary of the Navy seems to be thoroughly convinced of the vital interests of the navy in the situation.

There is no doubt about that. The navy has the most vital interest.

And he takes the view that there has been found no means by substitution to protect those interests. It must be in California or not at all?

Well, of course, it is only in those fields that we know just what we are dealing with. The other fields are undeveloped, if they exist. And the Secretary of the Navy's feeling is that the navy is not so much interested in getting a royalty in the shape of money on oil as in knowing that there is a reserve of oil in the earth for future development, because our navy has not been equipped to burn oil to any great extent yet.

That necessity has impressed itself upon you?

I think it is very obvious, yes. But that, unfortunately, does not settle this leasing question, because the leasing arrangements ought to go through, and yet the navy's interest ought also to be safe-guarded.

Mr. President, have you found a tariff board yet—all the members?

To tell the truth, I have had several declinations. That is what is holding me up. You see, as I explained once before, it is asking a good deal of the type of man I want to give up his other business connections and come here on seventy-five hundred dollars a year.

Mr. President, has Ambassador Fletcher[4] been ordered to his post yet?

I believe not.

Do you contemplate sending him?

I believe very soon, yes.

Has the Department of Justice reported, Mr. President, on the equities of these various claims?

No, it has not. It has intimated to me that it would take a mi-croscope to find them, but that is only my conclusion. That is not what they have said. They have not reported at all.

Mr. President, there is a story being printed today that there is some kind of negotiation or communication passing between the State Department and the German government with reference to arming merchant vessels.[5]

There are no communications passing about that just now.

Or with the British government?

Or with the British government.

The armed ship question is one which you can't discuss?

No, it is not. It is a very complicated question, to tell the truth.

Could you tell us whether you are contemplating making any pronouncement as to the government's policy in the future on that question?

No, except in the sense that it will, in time, become a practical question.

But no announcement will be made until a definite occasion?

No, I suppose not. I really hadn't answered that question even in my own mind.

Mr. President, have you found a successor for Mr. Baker as a member of the Shipping Board?[6]

No, I haven't. Of course that took me very much by surprise, and I haven't had time to look around yet.

Will you fill the Federal Trade Commission before this Congress adjourns?

Oh yes, after I check.

Mr. President, on the proposals of the brotherhoods, with reference to a commission which will investigate grievances in the railroad program, have you given that act a thought?[7]

Yes, I have given thought to that act and all the other suggestions that have been made. I have just put them all before the two committees of the Senate and House and asked their advice about them, and I haven't received it yet.

Mr. President, Judge Adamson told me that, if a representative of the public were added to such a commission, it would meet with his approval. Would it meet with yours?

I didn't get that impression from my conversation with him. Of course, that wouldn't amount to anything. It would simply mean that they meet here to decide anything. My idea, instead of having representatives of the two sides and then appoint an umpire between them, would be just to appoint an umpire by himself to begin with. That is just a snap, horseback judgment.

Mr. President, will you have occasion to do anything further about the increase of salaries of government employees?[8]

The committee of the employees visited me yesterday at the Capitol and presented a very formidable looking petition. I haven't had time to examine it yet, except the language. All the signatures I haven't examined. And it is largely, I understand—everybody understands—a matter of finance. With the tremendously increased expenditures of the government, it is a very serious matter whether we could finance a general increase.

You would, as I understand, favor an increase for the smaller-salaried men?

That depends on the budget, whether I would or would not. I have to be a housekeeper.

They seem to have reported something of that sort.

No, I told them that, having lived on a salary myself, I understood the situation they were in, and that I would give it, of course, my most friendly consideration.

Some of us would like to get your help along the same line.

I told them that once a committee of a bankers' association asked me to address them on the elasticity of the currency, and I told them I supposed they assumed me an expert, because I knew how elastic it was from personal experience.[9]

Mr. President, we are still very much interested in the New York Post Office.

So am I.

Have you taken the matter up lately?

No, I haven't. I am thinking of hiring another mind besides mine. I haven't got enough.

Senator Lewis is worrying a good deal about the Chicago and New York offices.

Yes. I worried about it so much, perhaps he can take it off my mind.

Will the new government down in Costa Rica be recognized?[10]

I don't know the circumstances there enough to answer that.

Mr. President, is there any information you wish to detail to us that we haven't touched on this morning?

No, I think not.

Mr. President, can you say anything about the cabinet? There was a story yesterday that four members would not be in the cabinet after March fourth.[11]

All that is "guff." I don't know who is interesting himself in that, but it is "guff."

Does that apply also to the diplomatic corps?[12]

In general terms, yes. Somebody is trying very hard to get the Secretary of State out of the cabinet. I don't know who that somebody is, tending to business which is not his own.

[1] Vice-Governor Henderson S. Martin of Marion, Kansas, had just resigned.

[2] Robert Brodnax Glenn, Democrat, Governor of North Carolina, 1905-1909.

[3] The story was about a meeting of the National Foreign Trade Conference in Pittsburgh. See the *Washington Post*, Jan. 29, 1917.

[4] Fletcher presented his credentials to Carranza on March 3, 1917. See Hill, *Emissaries to a Revolution*, p. 372.

[5] Ambassador Gerard in Berlin was discussing the question of armed merchant ships in connection with Americans taken prisoner in the capture by a German cruiser of the British armed merchant ship *Yarrowdale*. The difficulty here, apart from the routine protection of American citizens, was that, if the United States Government permitted the crewmen to be held as prisoners of war, as the Germans were threatening to do, it might be admitting that armed merchantmen were warships and thus were subject to unrestricted submarine attacks. The Americans were released. See the *Washington Post*, Jan. 27 and 30, 1917; the correspondence in *FR, 1917-WWSI*, 208-15; and Link, *Campaigns for Progressivism and Peace*, pp. 281-84.

[6] Bernard Nadal Baker of Baltimore resigned from the United States Shipping Board on January 27 because Secretary of the Treasury McAdoo had designated William Denman of San Francisco as the board's chairman. See the *Washington Post*, Jan. 28, 1917.

[7] This proposal was introduced in Congress as a bill (H.R. 20844) on February 9 by Representative Edward Keating, Democrat of Colorado. See *Cong. Record*, 64th Cong., 2d sess., p. 2974.

[8] At the Capitol on January 29, a delegation of federal employees led by Howard Marion McLarin, president of the Federal Employees' Union, presented Wilson a petition with 50,000 signatures calling for raises for federal workers. See the *Washington Post*, Jan. 30, 1917.

[9] In an address to the New York State Bankers' Association. See *PWW*, Vol. 14, pp. 298-99. See also *ibid.*, Vol. 18, pp. 424-34.

[10] Costa Rican President Alfredo Gonzáles Flores was deposed on January 28. The new government was headed by Minister of War Federico Tinoco Granados. See the *Washington Post*, Jan. 29-30, 1917.

[11] Stories had circulated that Secretaries Lansing, McAdoo, Gregory, Redfield, and Houston might resign. See *ibid.*, Jan. 31, 1917.

[12] *Ibid.*, Jan. 28, 1917, reported that political appointments among the diplomatic corps were to be replaced by more qualified Ambassadors. Page in London was rumored for replacement by House.

July 10, 1919

I am very glad to see you gentlemen. The job, the main part of it, is over, and the rest of it is outlined.[1] Before I left Paris I think we were substantially agreed. We had agreed upon all the lines of the Austrian treaty and we had substantially agreed upon everything else that the United States had any part in—though that latter is hard to determine, what we had a part in and what we hadn't. For this reason: the Covenant of the League of Nations is to go into each treaty. If these treaties are ratified by the United States, that makes the United States a party to the execution then of the treaties with Turkey and Bulgaria, though we were not at war with Turkey and Bulgaria. For that reason, our men, the expert advisers, and so on, who are over there are not only sitting in on the conferences on the Bulgarian and Turkish treaties, but are giving actual advice.

In one sense they have no determining voice, but I am happy to say that the people over there have learned to seek their advice and have found it very valuable. Therefore they are taking part in the framing of them. I thought you would be interested to know where we came in on the rest of the job that remains to be done in Paris. But in working out the German treaty we tackled every tough subject that there was, and found the way around it, and established the main lines that would govern in all the treaties. So that I felt that I was free to come away, inasmuch as the main things were determined.

I am very much interested to learn by the papers this morning that the German Assembly has ratified the treaty.[2] That lifts the blockade, because we told them that we would not wait for the other ratifications to lift the blockade, since there were sure to be enough to put the treaty into effect, but would lift the blockade when they ratified.

I thought you would be interested to see the document. It is a nice little book. One of the things that makes it heavy is that it contains the maps in connection with the territorial settlements. It has elaborate maps and things of that sort in it, and in fact it is only half as big as it looks, because one page is French and the other is English. The two languages were put on an equal footing as an authoritative text of the treaty, so that it is printed in both languages, on the one side French and the other English. I had to bring an unsigned copy, because the only signed copy had to stay in one place and remains in Paris.

If the blockade is lifted, does it follow that the Trading-with-the-Enemy Act is suspended?[3]

No. I cannot answer that with as much confidence as I could if I had recently consulted the act, but as I remember it, the act remains in force if we choose to enforce it, until the proclamation of peace is made by the United States. That is my recollection of it.

Is there any likelihood of its being retained?

I really hadn't thought of that at all. I just assumed that we would not exercise any more restraint than special circumstances demanded.

Is there anything you could say with regard to the resumption of trade relations with Germany?

I have nothing special to say about that. Of course the resumption of trade relations with Germany is a very important part of the carrying out of the treaty, because Germany cannot pay reparations unless her trade is resumed, and it becomes important, therefore, to the whole group of nations, not to ourselves particularly but to the whole group of nations, that her trade should be resumed. By the way, do not quote me on any of these things.

Does lifting the blockade remove all obstacles from trade with Germany?

No. It does not create ships enough and it does not release ships enough. Of course, until we bring all our men home, for example, our ships are tied up in the transport movement.

Does it remove all legal obstacles?

Yes.

She is free to trade with Russia?

Yes.

There is no restraint on the part of the other Allied nations?

They would exercise restraint if they could.

Is the United States free to trade with Germany before the treaty is ratified here? Does the Trading-with-the-Enemy Act remain in force?

Yes. That is literally right, but of course it is left largely to the discretion of the government how far it exercises the restraint. Again I am speaking with a distant recollection of the act.

I understand it is in force unless the President proclaims the act at an end?

The board[4] which exercises that control goes out of existence for lack of breath—otherwise known as lack of money. The instrumentalities for control are largely gone. I do not mean gone altogether, because the things that turned out to be useful in these boards are turned over to the regular departments.

Can you say anything about your trip to the West?[5]

No. I have not been home long enough to more than see that terrible looking table in my study with documents piled on it.

Have you anything to say about when demobilization will be completed?

No. I have not. That depends—well, I should say the chief thing it depends on is the rate at which the various governments ratify the treaty. And then there is another element in it which has been somewhat overlooked, apparently. I mean by general opinion. It has not been overlooked by the army. The treaty provides for a period of from one to four months for the execution of various parts of it that have direct bearing on the military status of Germany. For example, the yielding up of military materials of which they have still a great store. You see, the situation is this. Germany still has several million men, and she has munitions for several million men. Commissions acting under the treaty are going to superintend the delivery of all of that material, except that which she is allowed to retain. Now, while that process is going on, it will be wise to maintain sufficient forces of occupation to keep everybody from being nervous, and so that will be an element in the situation.

Are the men under arms chiefly regulars?

They are being more and more reduced to regulars. There are not many drafted men remaining to come home, as I understand it.

Would you be willing to make a statement about Shantung?[6]

No. That is a long story and a very complicated one. I would not like, offhand, to try to explain it.

Can you say anything about Fiume?

I understand that the street in Rome that they had called "Via Wilson" has been changed to "Via Fiume." That is the latest information I have, which is a practical joke on myself. The Fiume business is very singular. Because, as I daresay you all know, it was expressly provided in the Treaty of London that Fiume should go to the Croatians. Italy signed the document that it was not to go to her but to go to the Croatians. She was indeed to get a number of islands and a big slice of the Dalmatian coast, but Fiume she gave up, and now she seems indifferent to the other parts of the thing and she wants Fiume.

These other things, she has obtained?

No indeed. Things are at a complete standstill. You see, in the Austrian treaty this is an important thing to note. In the Austrian treaty, Austria renounces any political claims she may have had to any of those territories outside of the boundaries fixed by the treaty and assigns to the Principal Allied and Associated Powers the right to make such disposition as they think proper of those territories. So that is the present status of Fiume and those islands. I mean, when the Austrian and Hungarian treaties are signed, they are in the hands of those five powers to determine their political future.

Do you intend to discuss the French alliance?[7]

I am going to ask the Senate's permission to bring it up later, because it is too complicated. I will take it up separately.

Can you say what part America will have in financing reconstruction?

No, sir. I wish I were wise enough to answer. I think we are all agreed that it should not be governmental assistance, but assistance, I was going to say, on the usual bases of credit. But that will not be possible, because it will have to be on a delayed basis of credit, but it will be on a sound basis.

Would you be willing to discuss the criticism of Article X of the League Covenant?[8]

No; only to say that if you leave that out, it is only a debating society, and I would not be interested in a debating society. I have belonged to them and found them far from vital.

Won't this alliance be submitted to the Senate until after the treaty is disposed of?

Yes, but not immediately. As soon as I can write a proper exposition of it. I have not had time to do that yet.

Is the alliance of equal importance with the treaty itself?

No, it is subsidiary to the treaty. But don't call it an alliance, for it is not an alliance with anybody. This is the point. You see, it hangs on the League of Nations, because in its terms it is made dependent upon the approval of the Council of the League. I am assuming, of course, that the League of Nations will be adopted. If it is, the process is this. There is no provision for military action except upon advice of the Council, advice given to the several governments. Of course it follows that the several governments will take the advice or not, as they please, and it will be a matter of honor with them whether they will or not. There is no legal obligation. So that what we assumed in discussing the Covenant was this. If fire broke out in the Balkans, for example, the Council of the League would advise that certain nations mobilize their armies and undertake the military pressure that was necessary, and the others play some other part, and that some natural arrangement for exercising a portion of the forces be devised. But, of course, it might take some time for the advice to materialize in action. One nation would be prompt, another would be slower, and so on. Now all that this treaty contemplates is this: that until a majority of the Council of the League of Nations shall declare that the permanent arrangements are sufficient, the United States agrees, upon any unprovoked aggression by Germany against France, to immediately come to her assistance with military forces. That is to say, she promises not to wait for the advice of the Council. We all agreed that it was necessary that the Council itself should assent to the treaty, so we put in the assent of the Council so as to tie it right in and make it consistent.

In the event the Senate failed to accept the agreement, what would be the attitude of France toward the League of Nations?

I don't think it would affect that. I think the French would be cut to the heart if we didn't do it.

Who is the judge of provocation?

I have to answer that the way I answered the question a year or two ago, when I said, if Germany committed an act of aggression, we would go to war with her. I did not know, but I was sure I would know it when I saw it. Now I feel that way about this. I think you can tell an act of aggression when you see it. In the region of the Rhine there will be a number of persons looking on, and it could not go unnoticed.

Would the determination rest with the Executive?

I should assume that it would be with the legislative. In other words, I suppose the process would be this: the Executive would advise that such an act had occurred and ask for the necessary means of action, but the legislature could refuse it, of course.

It does not rob Congress of its power to declare war?

No. I explained that so often that I got tired—that I had no power to define the causes or to make war. That is really the reason the clause was put in about advice with regard to military action. Not only the United States, but Brazil and other countries, are in the same case. We could not suspend the right of the legislature to make war.

It has been suggested in the Senate that some of the objections raised would be removed by a reservation defining the right of Congress, making that clear just as you have expressed it here. Would that be regarded as an amendment, and would that prevent the ratification of the treaty itself?

Well, I do not think that any explanation of the power of Congress is necessary. Reservations are a complicated problem. I take it for granted that no reservation would be of effect unless it passed by a two-thirds majority, by the same majority that is necessary to ratify the treaty.9 And if it had to be considered as an "If" in the adoption of the treaty, then we would have to go all over the process of the treaty again. All the countries concerned would have to be consulted. For you have to find out just what the reservation meant, and then they would have to decide whether they consented to it. In the meantime we would be at war with Germany for months altogether. That is the most serious side of it.

The suggestion is made that a number of these reservations that are desired are what might be called innocuous. An innocuous reservation, I take it, is one that does not go to the vitals of the treaty.

But who is to certify that it is innocuous? That is the difficulty of that class of reservations. The other countries would have to know just what they meant. If you had been at Paris with us, you would have found that things do not look the same to different nations, and what the United States would consider so and so, probably nobody else would. There were many curious points of view, and so I could not be sure that what we considered innocuous would be so considered by any other country.

I think the Senate is going on the assumption that it can make reservations by majority vote.

That is a very dangerous assumption.

If war should break out in the Balkans, would the nations selected to put it down be governed by proximity?

I am not going to run the League of Nations until it is adopted. I cannot answer questions of that sort. Nobody could.

You said there would be a natural selection. What assurance is there that there would be?

You have to take it for granted that they are going to have horse sense. They would not ask Japan to go into the Balkans when everything was on fire.

We noticed that the order in which the representatives of the various countries signed the treaty was changed at the last moment. Was that because there was some fear that the Germans would back out?[10]

What was changed was the information of the press. It was all along intended that we get them salted down.

In the cable dispatches on the Anglo-French and the American-French agreements, there is a difference of language. It looks as though we were bound to come to the immediate relief of France, but England only assents to come to her assistance.

It means the same thing. There is no difference in the obligation.

In the message on wartime prohibition[11] you said, when the army was demobilized, you would act. Mr. Palmer[12] expressed the view that you were not empowered to act now.

You see, I cannot declare demobilization completed until I declare peace. The peace declaration has to precede that.

Do you expect to ask that the United States act as mandatory for Armenia?[13]

Let us not go too fast. Let's get the treaty [ratified] first.

Do you care to express your attitude toward the Kolchak[14] government or the other governments of Russia?

No, sir. That is an athletic feat, to adjust one's mind to those things.

Do you care to say anything about Mexico?[15]

I am not informed on Mexico as yet.

Do you hold that if the Senate were to adopt reservations to the treaty of peace with Germany, the treaty could not be ratified?

I do not think hypothetical questions should concern us. The Senate is going to ratify the treaty.

---

[1] That is, the job of making the peace treaties to end the World War. Wilson met the reporters for this conference following his address to the Senate presenting the Treaty of Versailles.

[2] The German National Assembly at Weimar passed a resolution ratifying the peace treaty on July 9. See the *New York Times*, July 10, 1919.

[3] The Trading-with-the-Enemy Act (H.R. 4960), signed by Wilson on October 6, 1917, was "to define, regulate, and punish trading with the enemy." See *Cong. Record*, 65th Cong., 1st sess., pp. 7340-53, 7417-28.

[4] The War Trade Board.

[5] The *New York Times*, July 10, 1919, reported that Wilson would make a speaking tour to the West on behalf of the treaty beginning late in July. In fact, the final decision for the trip had not yet been made. See Hilderbrand, *Power and the People*, pp. 193-94.

[6] Under the terms of the treaty, Japan acquired German economic rights and holdings in Shantung. See Thomas A. Bailey, *Woodrow Wilson and the Lost Peace* (New York, 1944), pp. 276-85.

[7] That is, the security treaty whereby the United States and Great Britain pledged to aid France in the event of an "unprovoked movement of aggression." Wilson submitted it on July 29. See Bailey, *Lost Peace*, pp. 231-36, and Thomas A. Bailey, *Woodrow Wilson and the Great Betrayal* (New York, 1945), p. 8.

[8] Article X said: "The Members of the League undertake to respect and preserve as against external aggression the territorial integrity and existing political independence of all Members of the League. In case of any such aggression or in case of any threat or danger of such aggression the Council shall advise upon the means by which this obligation shall be fulfilled."

[9] Several Senators disagreed with this assessment and argued that the rules of the Senate required only a simple majority for reservations. See the *New York Times*, July 11, 1919.

[10] The Germans signed first. See *ibid.*, May 8, 1919.

[11] In an amendment to a bill (H.R. 4961) sponsored by Representative Asbury Francis Lever, Democrat of South Carolina, Congress prohibited the use of grain and other foodstuffs in the making of alcoholic beverages during the war. See *Cong. Record*, 65th Cong., 1st sess., pp. 4158-90.

[12] Attorney General Alexander Mitchell Palmer.

[13] No European nations desired the Armenian mandate, which would require the protection

of Christians there. Wilson proposed on May 24, 1920, that the United States accept the Armenian mandate, but the Senate rejected the request on July 1 by a vote of fifty-two to twenty-three. See Bailey, *Woodrow Wilson and the Great Betrayal*, pp. 295-96, and Edward M. House and Charles Seymour, *What Really Happened at Paris: The Story of the Paris Peace Conference* (New York, 1921), pp. 178-80, 227.

[14] Admiral Aleksandr Vasil'evich Kolchak, commander of the White Army forces in Siberia and leader of the anti-Bolshevik government at Omsk. See John M. Thompson, *Russia, Bolshevism, and the Versailles Peace* (Princeton, N. J., 1967), pp. 268-308.

[15] The *New York Times*, July 10, 1919, reported that Wilson would soon tackle the issue of American claims, especially concerning oil, against the Mexican government.

# INDEX

## NOTE ON THE INDEX

THIS volume of *The Papers of Woodrow Wilson* consists almost entirely of Woodrow Wilson's views, opinions, and ideas. For that reason, this index differs from the indexes of other volumes by usually eliminating the entry "WW on," which is used here only for topics especially pertinent to this volume—press conferences, reporters, use of the news, direct quotation, etc.

The index covers all references to books and articles mentioned in the text or notes. Footnotes are indexed. Page references to footnotes which place a comma between the page number and "n" cite both text and footnote, thus: "624,n3." On the other hand, absence of the comma indicates reference to the footnote only, thus: "55n2"—the page number denoting where the number of the footnote appears. To be more specific, references to newspapers, magazines, authors, and titles are to the footnote numbers in the text of the press conferences.

The index supplies the fullest known form of names and, for the Wilson family, relationships as far down as cousins. Persons referred to by nicknames or shortened forms of names can be identified by reference to entries for these forms of the names.

# INDEX

## WOODROW WILSON

killing load of the presidency, xii; on public opinion and his administration, 3; on genuine public government, 3-4; on importance of press, 4-5; asks reporters for help, 5; plans to address Congress on tariff reform, 6,n5-6, 7; on breaking precedents, 14; criticizes press for breach of his confidence, 119; and war lobby, 186-87; ill with a cold, 322,n1; on difficulties with press over foreign questions, 355-56, 769-70; on changing public opinion, 415; criticizes press for printing stories about his family, 418-20,n1; on being quoted, 430-31, 437n7, 753, 766-70, 772; on development of public opinion by special interests, 486,n2, 490-91; reported to be tired, 527,n8; asks for reporters' cooperation concerning the World War, 535-36; on press during World War,

*Woodrow Wilson (cont.)*
575-76, 634-35, 769-70; candidacy in 1916, 674,n7, 690,n9, 691; and grazing the truth, 693n3, 769n6; on etiquette regarding former Presidents, 715-16; on press reports concerning the first *Lusitania* note, 731-32; on speechmaking, 741; on cooperation in government, 743-44; on speculation by reporters, 753

### PRESS CONFERENCES

first press conference, ix; dislikes "degree of formality" at first conference, ix; promises regular conferences, ix; makes success of conferences, ix-x; criticism of conferences, x; invokes rule against direct quotation, x; anger at correspondents for quoting him, xi; threatens to discontinue conferences, xi; places value on conferences, xi; talents suited for press conferences, xi; humor in press conferences, xi-xii; studies to prepare for conferences, xii; covers a variety of issues in each conference, xii; disappointment with conferences, xiii; sees difficulty in after beginning of European War, xiii; cancels conferences, xiii; 740; restores conferences in September 1916, xiii, 741n1; cancels again because of crisis with Germany, xii; discusses formality of, 3; explains difficulties of, 3; sets goals for, 3

### APPOINTMENTS

9, 12,n26, 47, 347, 417; fourth-class postmasters, 15,n6, 51n5; Governor of Alaska, 15,n7-10; Philadelphia customhouse, 15,n12, 32; federal judgeships, 28; Comptroller of the Currency, 29, 46, 63, 97, 328,n4; Washington, D.C., 30, 65, 78, 136,n1; Director of the Census, 31,n2, 96; collectorship of New York, 33,n9, 46, 47,n16-17; 52n10, 61n6; Commissioner of Pensions, 47,n18; Commissioner of Corporations, 51n8; Ambassador to Russia, 77, 306,n5, 371,n7, 393, 405,n9, 417, 450, 457,n14, 483, 488; Minister to China, 77; Ambassador to France, 77, 371, 483; Governor of Hawaii, 77; Public Printer, 78, 99; Commission on Industrial Relations, 79,n1, 80, 95, 103, 126-27; Civil Service Commission, 80, 96; Boston Collector of Customs, 96,n11, 108,n5, 249; Portland, Maine, Collector, 98,n15; Solicitor General, 99; Governor of Canal Zone, 101,n7, 102; excise commissioners, 140; Philippines commissioner, 235,n11; Minister to Greece, 288,n7; Interstate Commerce Commission, 322,n3, 330, 347; Federal Reserve Board, 327-28, 334, 337-38, 346, 357, 375, 401, 405,n10, 413-14, 416,n6, 432, 479, 482, 484, 486,n1, 537,n5; Counselor, Department of State, 396,n8, 407, 409, 417, 423,n15; District Supreme Court, 423,n13-14; Governor of Federal Reserve Board, 485-86; Postmaster of New Orleans, 495,n5-6, 496; Supreme Court, 519,n16, 530; Am-